Madame du Deffand
and Her World

Madame du Deffand and Her World

Benedetta Craveri

TRANSLATED FROM THE ITALIAN AND THE FRENCH

BY TERESA WAUGH

DAVID R. GODINE, PUBLISHER

BOSTON

For My Mother

First published in the U.S. by

DAVID R. GODINE, PUBLISHER, INC.
Horticultural Hall
300 Massachusetts Avenue
Boston, Massachusetts 02115

FRONTISPIECE: Madame du Deffand, by Carmontelle.

Library of Congress Cataloging-in-Publication Data

Craveri, Benedetta, 1942–
[Madame du Deffand e il suo mondo. English]
Madame Du Deffand and her world / Benedetta Craveri ; translated
from the Italian by Teresa Waugh.
p. cm.
Includes bibliographical references and index.
ISBN 1-56792-001-2
1. Du Deffand, Marie de Vichy Champrond, marquise, 1697–1780.
2. Authors, French—18th century—Biography. 3. France—Social life
and customs—18th century. 4. France—Court and courtiers—
History—18th century. I. Title.
PQ1981.D65C713 1994
848'.509—dc20
[B] 94-34283 CIP

FIRST AMERICAN EDITION

PRINTED AND BOUND IN THE UNITED STATES OF AMERICA

Contents

Madame du Deffand

and Her World

I

Youth

"MADAME LA MARQUISE DU DEFFAND appears to be difficult to define; the great naturalness which forms the basis of her character shows her to be so different from one day to the next, that just as she seems to have been captured in her essence, she reappears a moment later under another guise. Would not all men be so if they revealed themselves as they are; but in order to acquire respect, they take it upon themselves to play, so to speak, certain parts to which they often sacrifice their pleasures and their opinions and which they ever maintain at the expense of the truth.

"Madame du Deffand is the enemy of all falseness and affectation; her words and her face always interpret faithfully the sentiments of her soul; she is neither beautiful nor ugly, her countenance is simple and smooth, she has a good mind; but this would have been more developed and sounder had she found herself among people capable of educating and informing her. She is rational, has good taste and if she is sometimes led astray by her high spirits, she is soon brought back by the truth. She has a lively imagination which needs awakening. She often falls into an ennui such as to extinguish all light from her mind; she finds this condition so unbearable and it makes her so unhappy that to deliver herself from it she blindly embraces whatever may appear; hence the frivolity of her conversation and the imprudence of her behaviour which are hard to reconcile with the idea which she gives of her judgement when she is in a gentler frame of mind. She is generous-hearted, soft and compassionate, her sincerity goes beyond the limits of prudence; it costs her more to make a mistake than to admit to one; she is most enlightened as to her own faults and quick to discern other people's; the severity with which she judges herself leaves her impatient of folly in others. Hence her reputation for mischievousness, a vice from which she is far removed, having neither maliciousness nor jealousy nor any of the base sentiments which give rise to this fault."[1]

This captivating self-portrait which seems to require both indulgence and sympathy is written by a woman of about thirty-two at a crucial point in her existence. In 1728 Madame du Deffand has a questionable reputation and a failed marriage behind her; she suffers from a profound existential malaise and must feel the need to have the past forgotten and to present a completely new picture of herself. The reasons which drive her to change direction are primarily of a social nature: the rules of *bienséance*—perhaps the only criteria which the *marquise*'s corrosive scepticism will always allow her to respect—regained the upper hand in the years following the death of Philippe d'Orléans. Madame du Deffand's youth coincided with the Regency and her dissipation during those years was in keeping with the times. Now, on the threshold of maturity, her preoccupation with her own reputation reflects, if not a revival of morality in the society in which she lived, certainly a greater respect for form.

Marie de Vichy-Champrond, later Marquise du Deffand, was born on 25 September 1696[2]—under the sign of Libra "which preserves us from misunderstanding the sentiments we inspire and those we ought to have"[3]—probably in the family château at Champrond,[4] in the centre of a vast estate on the edge of Burgundy in what is now the Saône-et-Loire, twenty-eight kilometres from the small town of Charolles and thirty from Roanne. She was the third of four children: first came her brothers, Gaspard III and Nicolas, and after her, her sister Anne, the future Marquise d'Aulan. "I do not know whether I have English pride, but I have French nobility and my relatives have no need to blush for me,"[5] she was to write when old, in a combative reply to the Duchesse de Choiseul who was suspected of wishing to teach her a lesson about honour. It is one of Madame du Deffand's rare allusions to her family and indicates that she must have been motivated by a wave of legitimate pride.

The Vichys were one of the most important families in the region.

Their roots went back to the year 1000 AD, and in the centuries which followed many illustrious members brought distinction to the family.[6] In later times the Vichys continued to distinguish themselves as good servants of the king; they followed military careers which brought no glory but did consolidate their honourable reputation; they also established a broad network of family alliances in the Mâconnais. Not least among these was the alliance forged by the marriage of Marie's father to Anne Brûlart, daughter of the first President of the *Parlement de Bourgogne.*

At the beginning of the eighteenth century the family fortunes were no longer in very good shape. Monsieur de Vichy (the self-styled Gaspard II, comte de Champrond) not only gives the impression that his marriage was far from happy, but seems to involve his wife in a share of responsibility for the economic decline: "If my wife had not had a passion for Paris, we would have sold a further six thousand livres of grain each year."[7] But it would be unjust to blame Anne Brûlart's frivolity entirely for the decline in the family fortunes. Such a decline was a common phenomenon for many French aristocrats of the time.

But their financial difficulties were not such as to force the Vichys to too great a sacrifice: a list of servants employed at the château includes "a chaplain, a steward, a major-domo, two cooks, four footmen, a coachman and two postilions, two secretaries and an under-governess,"[8] and this list does not include the housemaids. The children were educated according to their social standing, starting with Marie who was sent to school in Paris, to the elegant convent of the Madeleine du Traisnel, because, as Gaspard said, "That is where young ladies should be educated."[9] The school was run on traditional lines and was very well known, although partly for secular reasons.[10]

So the future Madame du Deffand was destined to the same woman's fate which was to be denounced with such enlightened indignation fifty years later in the *Correspondence littéraire*: "Exiled . . . since birth from the family home, they are raised in religious houses of which the least that can be said is that young women receive a correct idea of neither their condition, nor their duty, nor of honour, nor decency, nor of the world, nor of any of the situations in which they will afterwards find themselves and for which they should be prepared in order to avoid the dangers thereof. The morality of women is based entirely on arbitrary principles, their honour is not true honour; their decency is false decency; and all their worth, all their propriety, consists in the disguise and misrepresentation of natural feelings which a fanciful duty forbids them to overcome and which, for all their efforts, they would be unable to destroy. Imbued with these principles on leaving the convent, they find themselves in the arms of a stranger to whom they discover their destiny is linked by eternal and indissoluble ties. So the gentle and sacred duties of marriage become, through the tyranny of our society, outrages against modesty; and the victim is sacrificed to the desires of the man who, by the rights of marriage, destroys the veil which decency and the delicacy of a respectful, tender love would have drawn back imperceptibly and with timid defiance. So the tumult of desire vies with uncertainty of principle. Whom will a woman obey when thrown into a world whose dangers she ignores, and when left to herself or given over to a man who demands as his right that which the heart can grant only to the submissive lover capable of moving her? How can she distinguish between the essence of honour and the virtue and the precepts of an imaginary virtue learned from the cradle? Swift to recognise the futility of the latter, is she not likely to allow the contempt they deserve to extend to the most essential virtue? By dint of having felt the shackles, she will no longer recognize the limits; and unable to distinguish between real duty and arbitrary practice, or substituting the latter for the former, she will discover herself to be lost before she has been able to formulate her first intelligent thought."[11]

In their excellent book *La Femme au dix-huitième siècle* which enlightens precisely by virtue of its historical bias and a nostalgia for a way of life which a century later and despite a revolution, still feels contemporary, the Goncourts vividly evoke the atmosphere in girls' schools of the time. The bleak drama of forced vocations, the brutality of superstition and the harshness of the rule are all avoided and the convent is acquitted of the widely believed accusation of licence, but is seen to dispense "an education which oscillates between worldliness and self-denial, between retreat and the genius of the time, an education which wavers between God and a doctor of philosophy, between meditation and lessons in curtseying."[12] But this: "gentle and happy convent education, ceaselessly cheerful, free from the day-to-day severity and sadness of the cloister and little by little directed almost entirely towards the world,"[13] leaves us with a final impression of emptiness and of a pleasant yet disturbing shallowness. The brief but numerous references made during her long life by Madame du Deffand to the education she received as a child, give the same impression. "One is sometimes asked if one would like to return to a certain age: Oh, I would not like to be young again, to be brought up as I was, living only with the people with whom I lived and having the kind of mind and character which are mine."[14]

Thus speaks a failed education, a feeling of uselessness and the pain of an intelligence which has not been given the wherewithal to develop. "You know nothing ... of the condition of those who think and are reflective, who have a certain energy, but who are without talent, passion, occupation or distraction."[15] And it was the pain of being deprived of a religious faith which she would eagerly have embraced for the same reasons which caused her to say in old age: "To be devout ... would be for me the happiest condition of my life,"[16] and which would lead her to seek some kind of consolation or at least relief from her ennui in religious observance.[17] "But our disposition is not decided by will; it is not an attachment to the things of this world which turn me away from religion, it is my misfortune."[18]

Very little is known about Madame du Deffand's school years—not even the date of her arrival at the convent—so the only recorded episode—and this from various sources—takes on a particular significance sensed by Chamfort in the following account: "As a little girl in the convent, Madame du Deffand preached irreligion to her small companions. The Abbess summoned Massillon to whom the child explained her reasons. Massillon left, saying 'She is charming.' The Abbess, who attached importance to these things, asked the Bishop what book should be read to the child. He thought for a moment, and replied 'A fivepenny catechism.' He would say no more."[19]

Round about the age of eighteen, Marie left the convent and returned to Champrond, but only for a little while. In the summer of 1718 she went to Paris as the bride of a distant cousin, Jean-Baptiste-Jacques du Deffand, Marquis de la Lande.[20] "As the result of a coincidence which might be described as fate, Mademoiselle de Vichy, young, pretty and clever but not very rich, entered society by way of her marriage, at the height of the Regency—that is to say at the very moment when, liberated from the severe disciplines of the end of the preceding reign and fifteen years of compulsory devotion, morality triumphantly took her revenge and turned society upside down. . . . This universal corruption was to spread and spread ceaselessly in a sea of ignominy and to engulf in a whirlpool of impurity all those ancient virtues without which there can be neither family nor society. It was on 2 August 1718, when debauchery was at its most rife, and while Paris with naked cynicism slept off the effects of supper parties and of John Law's financial boom, when marriage was no more than a formality, when fidelity was folly, that Mademoiselle de Vichy was thrown by the solicitude of a family eager to give her a legal partner, and sustained by a convention which guaranteed everything except happiness, into the arms of a husband whom she did not even know until the day when she belonged to him for ever."[21] In these apocalyptic terms Madame du Deffand's most authoritative biographer, Lescure, sets the scene for the young *marquise* to play the sinister part which, given the circumstances, was inevitably hers. But if we are not put off by the typically nineteenth-century moralistic emphasis, the description is in its way effective, provided we realise that the first victim of the brutal system which we have already seen denounced with such passion in the *Correspondance littéraire,* is on this occasion—although probably quite exceptionally—the man and not the woman, the marquis du Deffand and not Mademoiselle de Vichy.

Marriage—described by Chamfort later as that "mutually agreed indecency"[22]—was a source of many advantages for the young *marquise.* It marked not only her entry into society which was to become her *raison d'être,* but also her escape from the threat of a country existence and freedom from a father whose horrible nature had certainly not improved since he had been widowed a few years earlier. (Madame d'Houdetot's famous words: "I married in order to be able to enter society, to go to the ball, to take walks, to go to the opera and the theatre"[23] speaks for all young married women of the day.) So Marie de Vichy's romantic aspirations were probably not very great. She was to write many years later: "Not to love one's husband is quite a common misfortune"[24] and it seems to have been clear from the start that she had no intention of investing any affection whatsoever in her marriage.

The marquis du Deffand on the other hand definitely had domestic aspirations in keeping with his mild, open temperament and with the education of a provincial gentleman, who wished to divide his time peacefully between Paris and his country property.[25] The life style proposed by his wife and directed entirely towards entertainment and worldly success, could not have been less agreeable to him, but his patience and acquiescent behaviour make him appear to be the first, perhaps chance, victim of the art of seduction in which Madame du Deffand was beginning to try her hand. It was not so much the differences of taste and character which made compatibility impossible, as the difference of temperament and intelligence. The *marquis* could not keep pace with his wife's restlessness nor with her lust for life which, from the beginning, expressed itself in a need to escape her ennui, and neither had he the authority with which to oppose her. Perhaps unknowingly under her sway, he fussed about her with what Madame du Deffand pitilessly described as his *"petits soins pour déplaire."*[26] The differences were impossible to overcome so the only solution was the convenient and widespread practice dictated by the times: a *de facto* separation arranged without fuss and with mutual indifference.[27]

Madame du Deffand's career as a libertine began brilliantly: her first lover was the Regent. It was a love affair, as she told Walpole later,[28] between two people obsessed with ennui, but it was enough to make her forget to take the slightest precautions to protect her reputation. The affair lasted a fortnight. The little we know of her from contemporary chronicles implies, more than lack of scruple, an actual desire for degradation. Madame du Deffand became part of Philippe d'Orléans's circle of favourites and made friends with Madame d'Averne, the Regent's official mistress. So the *marquise* was admitted to a world whose behaviour was even capable of scandalising a profoundly liberated society: "At around supper time he [the Regent] would shut himself up with his mistresses, sometimes girls from the Opera—or others of a similar breed, and ten or twelve intimate men friends whom he called his roués[29] . . . Each supper was an orgy. Unbridled licence reigned; filth and blasphemy formed the basis of, or were the seasoning of all conversation until total drunkenness made the guests incapable of speech or understanding. Those who could still walk retired; the others were carried away."[30] Lescure records more subtly than Duclos and with a passionate attention to detail how that eighteenth-century prince of libertines, the maréchal de Richelieu, initiates us to the ritual of these suppers which he did not fail to attend himself.

"We are received by virtue of our privilege as an historian, which we do not mention as it would give rise to laughter; after six o'clock in the evening the Regent no longer believes in history. We cross halls whose soft carpeting silences the footsteps. So long as we have no papers for the Regent to sign, nor any bad news to bear, his valet, Coche, who is lying in wait with orders to refuse entry to anyone on business, obsequiously allows us in whilst d'Ibaguet, the porter at the Palais-Royal who, most extraordinarily, happens to be an honest man, hurries away with his hands raised to the sky at the sight of this daily spectacle to which he has never been able to become accustomed.

"In the antechamber there are only two of those trusted herculean footmen known as *Mirebalais*. They belong to the duchesse de Berry and they blush at nothing. Never mind; there is pleasure to be had in serving oneself, and while the kitchen boys from the Palais–Royal play faro in the pantry or loll in the stalls at the Opera, the roués amuse themselves by doing their own cooking and supervising silver saucepans on the stove placed at their disposal.

"They laughingly put the finishing touches to their last dish. Madame de Parabère has just spoilt an omelette and the Duc d'Orleans has created a strange dish, the recipe for which he brought back from his Spanish campaigns.

"Noisily the guests sit down. Flowers scent the air, the crystal shines. The first half hour is devoted to eating. As yet there are only a few jibes to be heard interspersed with the frothing of champagne.

"For champagne is the Regent's favourite wine. He never drinks anything else, and of the very best, despite the frequent treachery of this bubbling liquor which sometimes enflames where it should but warm.

"Meanwhile the conversation grows lively and the guests become excited . . .

" . . . many glasses have been emptied. Madame de Sabran begins to rant, Madame d'Averne complains of a pain in the stomach, Madame de Phalaris has a headache and Madame de Parabère feels sick. Perhaps Mademoiselle de Valois is thinking of me. Broglie becomes more and more impudent . . . But the Regent is speaking. He is telling one of those funny stories which he learnt in Spain or Italy and which he recounts so well that one listens to him as if he were not a prince . . .

"All the lights but one are put out. Now is the moment to slip away for La Fare's prattle is unrepeatable and the candle held by his accomplice, Broglie, has nothing to do with history."[31]

In *Nouveaux mémoires du maréchal duc de Richelieu*, Madame du Deffand's name is not among those of the courtesans who attended the Palais-Royal suppers, but according to the *Vie privée du marechal de*

Richelieu she was present at those which were certainly no less compromising, held by Madame de Berry at the Luxembourg.

"I went to the Luxembourg where I found Madame d'Averne, Mesdames de Parabère, de Gesvres, du Deffand. Madame de Berry did the honours very well. We were as many men, the Regent, the marquis de la Fare, Riom, Fargis and myself.

"After cards we sat down to eat and the Regent decided to make the women drunk so as to reveal their characters. Everyone agreed and we all became inebriated. The Regent, who was more befuddled by drink than the others, sang songs which were more than cheerful, and accompanied them with even more expressive gestures directed at the women. Everyone followed his example. La Fare offered to show us a magic lantern he had made. The apartment was prepared and he showed us some of Aretino's engravings on which he had written appropriate rhymes. While we were in the darkness required for this spectacle, everyone took hold of a woman; my hands attempted to wander over one next to me, but wherever I tried to put them, I found others already there. I was less unfortunate when I turned to her neighbour."[32]

But Madame du Deffand's description of her own respectability is better described in Mathieu Marais's *Mémoires* than in the fanciful souvenirs of the famous libertine. On 30 July 1721, the *marquise* defied public opinion by attending a festivity on which even the most unscrupulous women seem to have turned their backs and which was the object of general curiosity. "The Regent gave a magnificent reception for the maréchale d'Estrées in a house in Saint-Cloud which formerly belonged to the Elector of Bavaria. Madame d'Averne shone as did Madame du Deffand and another lady. Several other ladies made their excuses, not wanting to take part in such pleasure. There were many men from the Regent's court. The festivity lasted for part of the night. The gardens at Saint-Cloud were lit by more than twenty thousand candles, which with the waterfalls and the fountains, created an amazing effect. Every carriage in Paris was in the Bois de Boulogne at Passy or at Auteuil and the delights of Caprée were to be seen on all sides."[33]

A year later, in September 1722, Madame du Deffand, according to Marais, took two definitive steps. She confirmed her brief relationship with the Regent by the infamous acceptance of a life annuity, and she became the official mistress of one of the most questionable and corrupt members of the Palais-Royal circle. "By her plotting with Madame d'Averne and the Regent's favourites, Madame du Deffand has obtained a life annuity of six thousand livres from the city of Paris. Now on good terms with them, now on bad, she picked her moment, and captured a six thousand livres annuity which is worth more than all her securities. Her husband has repudiated her, he could no longer tolerate her flirtation with Fargis, otherwise known as Delrieu, and son of the financier Delrieu of whom it was said that he had *tant volé qui'l avait perdu une aile.*[34] These are the people who find favour and profit at court. Fargis is one of the Regent's chief courtiers and one of his debauchees."[35]

The death of the Regent in 1723 put a sudden stop to these increasingly permitted irregularities. The old group of companions dispersed, and as if there were a moral to the tale, Madame du Deffand began to feel the consequences of her licence. "Now she is a lost woman who wants everything but can attach herself to nothing. She takes a new lover like a new dress because she wants one and she abandons him the next day merely for the pleasure of taking another."[36] Her separation from her husband deprived her of any official support and made her economic situation precarious. She could certainly not depend on Fargis; the relationship probably lasted only because each was drawn to the restlessness and infidelity of the other. With her moral reputation in shreds, Madame du Deffand began to value herself for her mind and her intelligence. In 1723 she achieved genuine success with a parody in the popular idiom of Houdar de la Motte's tragedy *Inès de Castro* which had kept the Parisian public in tears for two months. It was also a way of avenging Voltaire with whom she had made friends and whose tragedy, *Artémise,* had been declared a flop by that same public.[37]

Friendships like those she made with the Tencins, the Ferriols and Bolingbroke and to which she was to remain faithful throughout the years, show the direction in which her tastes were heading. The courtesan in her, as Mademoiselle de Lespinasse would say, or perhaps quite simply her realism and necessity, encouraged her meanwhile to cultivate the friendship of Madame de Prie, mistress of the new Prime Minister, Louis-Henri de Bourbon. But a few years later, the young woman, disgraced by Monsieur le Duc, was exiled to her Château de Courbépine, where she died a year later in terrible and mysterious circumstances which suggest suicide by poisoning. "A *lettre de cachet*[38] confined the marquise de Prie to the provinces (June 1726). She was accompanied there by Madame du Deffand, her equal in beauty, intrigue and malice.

Every morning these two friends exchanged satirical verses which they composed at each other's expense. They could think of no better way to ward off the enemy than by this poisonous occupation."[39] This account does not fully explain why Madame du Deffand followed the favourite into exile. Such an act of solidarity was probably based on a proud refusal to recant, a definite taste for defiance (a constant in Madame du Deffand's character) and, perhaps, real friendship with Madame de Prie. But the detail concerning the satirical couplets is accurate, and is a terrible example of the school of insensitivity in which both ladies had been trained.

It is highly probable that Madame de Prie's tragic end gave the *marquise* pause for consideration. If, in addition, her economic problems, her fading youth, and her uncertain future are taken into account, the tone of the following letter to her sister, Madame d'Aulan, is not surprising:

MADAME DU DEFFAND TO MADAME D'AULAN   *{Paris} 15 March 1727*

My dear Sister, I am feeling better at present. My brother[40] has been here for nearly a month; he left two days ago. He is quite taken up with the company of cavalry which he wishes to form; he is looking everywhere for money and is presently in Dijon. My grandmother[41] has been at Lépire for eight or ten days. She feels better than the rest of us. I intend to go to the country soon; Paris is like a dull Lépire for anyone as little well off as I . . . I have a great deal of chagrin and melancholy.[42] You are happy, my dear sister, you have a husband who loves you and whom you love, you know nothing of the misfortunes of life and you rejoice in all its pleasures. Far from envying your happiness, I hope that it will further increase and that it will continue for you for ever; but for myself I neither expect nor hope for happiness. I wish only to be free from sorrow. You see my thoughts are not very gay, but I count sufficiently on your friendship to believe that you are concerned with my situation and that you will temper it by the assurance of your affection. You must count on mine for as long as I live.[43]

The domestic idyll is certainly no usual part of the *marquise*'s repertory, and it is highly likely that these melancholy meanderings express no more than the desire for a quieter, less exposed life. Along these lines, there is, even for her, a partial solution to all her problems. It is simply and readily available and Madame du Deffand finally resorts to it:

MADAME DU DEFFAND TO MADAME D'AULAN

{Paris} Friday 10 September 1728

I reproach myself, my dear Sister, for not having expressed my joy at your happy confinement. I thank you for having sent me your news; you would have had mine earlier if I had not been quite indisposed and greatly occupied with some important business. You know of my reconciliation with Monsieur du Deffand; to bring this about we did not resort to a thousand intermediaries, but explained ourselves to each other and are reunited for ever. I have no doubt that you are overjoyed. I would very much like Monsieur d'Aulan to tell you how much I love you, we speak about you often.[44]

The reconciliation was to take place towards the middle of 1728 and lasted but a short while. Necessity had done nothing to improve Madame du Deffand's temper, nor had her husband's available resources increased with time. But the letter written towards the end of 1728 in which the *marquise* finally terminates the marriage, reveals not the unscrupulous heedlessness of early youth, but rather a selfish determination capable of imposing itself by quibbling hypocrisy: "My letter, Monsieur, must not have surprised you and will seem quite suitable when you remember the reproaches you made me in our last conversations, the complaints you have made about me and the extraordinary way in which you left. I can only believe that you deeply regret having seen me again and that you are only inconvenienced as to how to find an honest way of withdrawing; with this in mind, I tell everyone that you are in the country and that we have not yet decided to live together; that the state of our affairs requires some further delay and that we need much greater means than we have in order to establish a household. This reasoning is all the better for being truthful and for the fact that I am actually greatly inconvenienced and out of sorts at having to move soon. With regard to your father, he was so shocked by our reunion that I don't doubt but that he will be delighted to find you an honourable reason for separation. Besides, on close reflection I think that you find that my disposition does suit you so little that even my pastimes displease you. But if I were to limit my circle, I would remain alone and you would find no pleasure in my company which constrains and bores you. With regard to certain duties, my health is an unsurmountable obstacle. . . . You know, Monsieur, how great is my esteem for you, I have given you most convincing proof of it, I am persuaded that you do not wish to make me unhappy and that you would not like to put us in the position of making scenes in public. It is very easy to avoid doing so at present, perhaps later it will no longer be possible. I speak to you in all sang-froid and I wish you would listen likewise. You will certainly judge that your interests are as dear to me as my own. Consider the matter and know that the worst of all solutions would be to cause eternal misery. I know my duty and do not intend to fail in it; perhaps that is all you ask in which case you can count on it as you can on the respect with which I have the honour to remain . . ."[45]

But a letter from Madame du Deffand's friend, Mademoiselle Aïssé, probably gives a fairly impartial account of this attempted reconciliation in which, once again, the victim seems to have been Monsieur du Deffand: ". . . For a long time Madame du Deffand had a violent longing to be reconciled to her husband. Being intelligent she supported this desire with excellent reasoning. On several occasions she behaved in such a way as to make the reconciliation both desirable and honourable. Her grandmother died and left her an income of four thousand livres.[46] In possession of this greater fortune she could offer her husband happier circumstances than had she been poor. She claimed that his desire for heirs made her husband's wish for a reconciliation less ridiculous. As we expected she succeeded. Everyone congratulated her. I would have liked her to be less insistent, a further noviciate of six months was needed, with her husband remaining with his father. I had my reasons for advising her thus; but as this good lady followed her spirit, or rather her imagination, instead of depending on reason and stability, she wrapped the whole thing up in such a way that the husband, who was in love with her, interrupted his journey and came and settled with her. That is to say he came to dinner and supper since she would not hear of his living with her for three months in order to avoid speculation which might be harmful either to her or to her husband. It was the most beautiful friendship in the world for six weeks; but at the end of that time she revived an exaggerated aversion for her husband, and without showing him any discourtesy, she adopted such a desperate and sad air that he decided to go to his father.

"She takes every imaginable precaution to prevent him ever returning . . .

"This miserable behaviour ended with her being unable to live with anyone. A lover[47] she had had before the reconciliation, having had enough of her, left, but when he learned how well she was getting on with Monsieur du Deffand, sent her letters full of reproach; then the barely extinguished flame of his passion was fanned by pride and he returned. The good lady simply followed her whim and, without reflection, she imagined a lover to be better than a husband and forced the latter to cede his place. He had barely gone when the lover left her, too. She remains the laughing stock, blamed by everyone, despised by her lover, abandoned by her friends; she no longer knows how to untangle it all . . ."[48] Such a realistic assessment was not likely to divert Madame du Deffand from what she had to do when the adventure was over. How was she to climb up again? She had to put order into her life, to forget the past and have it forgotten, to regain social credibility and to insinuate herself into a circle with some prestige. And all this she had to do alone, with no family to support her and with only modest means. Help came from a man who embodied the social ideal of the time and who was one of the most accomplished and brilliant of society men, the Président Hénault.

Madame du Deffand probably knew Hénault during the Regency when as a young and rich magistrate, faithful to the dictates of fashion but against his natural inclination, he did his best to adapt to the debauchery which ruled the day. Marais, with his usual pitilessness, tells how the Regent, when praised for his conquests, replied with a sneer, "Why should I not have conquests? The Président Hénault and little Pallu have enough! . . . (They both have wit, but they are not cut out to be lovers.)"[49]

Years later the marquis d'Argenson gave a more articulate and convincing explanation for Hénault's success with women: "His character, especially when he was young, seemed designed to appeal to the ladies; for he had wit, charm, a certain delicacy and finesse. He successfully wrote music, poetry and light-hearted literature. His music was not of a learned nature, but it was agreeable. His poetry was not sublime but he nevertheless attempted to write a tragedy: it is weak but neither ridiculous nor boring. Besides, his verses are in the style of Fontenelle, they are gentle and witty; his prose is fluent and simple; his eloquence is neither virile nor is it in the grand style, despite the fact that he won prizes at the *Académie Française* more than thirty years ago. He is neither intense nor elevated, nor insipid, nor flat ... He is rich enough to need no one else and in this happy condition he affects no pretension; he places himself wisely between insolence and servility. There are great ladies who have forgiven him his birth, his lack of beauty and even of vigour. He has always behaved on these occasions with modesty, claiming only what he had a right to claim. Nothing has ever been demanded of him but that which he could easily accomplish."[50]

The Président Hénault has left a detailed account of himself in his *Mémoires*[51] which are an invaluable mine of information. Charles-Jean-François Hénault was born in Paris in 1685 into a rich and cultivated bourgeois family; he attended the Jesuits' school and, probably influenced by that great preacher and personality, Massillon, he then spent two years as a novice at the Oratoire. Abandoning his plans for a career in the church, he studied law, became a magistrate and alternated between professional and literary success. The two disciplines have a long tradition of running hand in hand. In 1714 he married Mademoiselle Lebas de Montargis who bore him no children and who left him a widower in 1728. She was a meek, discreet woman who did not prevent him from being part of the Regent's dissipated circle nor from being, for a moment, the lover of the celebrated Maréchale d'Estrées.[52] But he gradually became more and more interested in the study of history and in 1744 the first edition of his *Nouvel Abrégé Chronologique de l'histoire de France*[53] appeared. Hénault owes his fame to this work which became his main and constant source of interest. He was to return to it, developing and perfecting it, for most of his life. "These short histories are always very useful and very convenient and Président Hénault deserves that praise above all others; but when the author, flattered by his vanity and by the exaggerated compliments of his friends, wants me to see his work as a masterpiece of the human spirit, I would willingly tell this Président who was famous for his supper parties first and then for his *Chronologie*, that it does not take a magician to write a short history."[54] This acid comment which reflects the critical position of the Encyclopaedists, is surely indicative of the Président's psychological attitude towards his own work. But Grimm's verdict is prejudiced and belittling. In addition to qualities of accuracy and conciseness, the *Abrégé* is a history of France seen through its institutions and its legal system, and precisely because of this "parliamentary" perspective it remains an essential text for students of eighteenth-century historiography.

When his relationship with Madame du Deffand began, Hénault was about forty-three years old, recently widowed, rich, cultivated and brilliant. For him, desire to please was a real passion to which he systematically dedicated himself. Madame du Deffand has left us a description of him written at around that time.

"All Monsieur le P... H's qualities and even his faults are to his advantage in society; his vanity makes him extremely desirous to please, his manner gains him the favour of all different people and his weakness seems to make him deficient only in that which in others is savage and coarse.

"His feelings are refined and delicate but his intelligence too often comes to their aid, to explain and unravel them, and since the heart rarely requires an interpreter, one might sometimes be tempted to believe that he only thinks what he imagines he feels. He seems to give the lie to Monsieur de la Rochefoucauld whom he would perhaps have say that the heart is often the mind's fool.

"Everything conspires to make him the most agreeable man in society; he pleases some by his good qualities and many others by his failings.

"He is impetuous in all he does, in argument and in approbation; he appears to be acutely affected by what he sees and by discussion, but he changes so swiftly from extreme vehemence to the utmost indifference that it is easy to infer that if his soul is so easily moved, it can very rarely be touched. This impetuousness which would be a failing in another, is almost a virtue in him, it lends to all his actions a sense of feeling and passion which is infinitely pleasing to people in general. Everyone imagines himself to be of tremendous interest to him, thus he has gained the many friends he has by virtue of his genuinely likeable and admirable qualities. He could be reproached with being too susceptible to this kind of success and one would prefer his eagerness to please to be less universal and more discerning.

"He is free from the passions which most trouble the soul; ambition, self-interest and envy are unknown to him; gentle passions stir him, his mood is naturally gay and equable and if it is disturbed, it is so for reasons outside himself and not within . . .

"He has every talent and can deal equally well with all kinds of subjects, both serious and pleasant. Everything is within his competence. Finally Monsieur le p. . . H. . . is one of the men in society who united the greatest number of different groups and whose charm and wit are most widely recognized."[55]

Madame du Deffand's and the Président Hénault's relationship was fundamentally a social one between two people who had a basic absolute need of society. Above all the *marquise* found in Hénault what was necessary to prevent her from being excluded from the only scene in which it was possible for her to play her part. So by this wise choice and through this stable relationship her former mistakes and instability would be forgiven. Prestige was not the only card held by Hénault. He was an extremely agreeable man who knew the art of pleasant living which was not something to be overlooked by a restless woman obsessed by ennui.

Hénault, in his turn, must have been fascinated by Madame du Deffand's instinctive assurance of her worldly vocation. One observation, one witty remark, was enough to create a magnetic circle of attraction around her. Besides, who better, versed as he was in the art of pleasing, to appreciate her immediacy, or what Walpole called her "prodigious quickness,"[56] the authority with which she imposed her tastes and her intelligence? Together Hénault and Madame du Deffand could form a truly formidable worldly partnership.

II

Friendship without romance:
the Président Hénault

IN THE SUMMER OF 1742 a suspected tumour on the breast obliged Madame du Deffand to go to Forges for the thermal waters, leaving Hénault in Paris. The letters which the two lovers exchanged during the course of this month's separation, the only private papers we have concerning their relationship, reveal a great deal about the nature of their liaison and about their characters. Ten years into the relationship it is Madame du Deffand who seems to call the tune, inspiring Hénault with an admiration which verges on awe. The Président replies to the *marquise*'s irony and aggression with courteous bonhomie and to her attempted provocation with brilliantly elusive tactics. The dialectic is obvious: it is not so much a confrontation of two different temperaments as of two types of egoism. United by the strong bond of a convenient friendship, Madame du Deffand and Hénault experience the imperfection which this also involves. Thus these papers give the impression that, for an instant, the rules of the game are set aside so that each correspondent seems to demand of the other that passion of which they both sense the lack, but which neither of them can feel.

From an abundance of news, comment and gossip in the twenty-seven letters exchanged between the Président and the *marquise* over a period of less than twenty days, only those passages which refer specifically to their states of mind and to the sentimental attachment between them have been extracted. The arbitrary nature of the choice is unquestionably two-sided, since a passion for news and gossip was a fundamental of the relationship between the two lovers. However, an exception has been made of Madame du Deffand's first letter from Farges which is reproduced in its entirety.

The waters at Forges, a small spa on the way to Dieppe, not more than a hundred kilometres from Paris, were discovered in 1553 and became famous after the visit of Louis XIII who went there with Richelieu and Anne of Austria to undergo a cure for sterility.[1] Forges enjoyed greater popularity than other French spas, mainly because of its proximity to Paris, but its reputation for curing all ills went hand in hand with a certain scepticism concerning the efficacy of spas in general: places, wrote Voltaire, "invented for women who are bored at home."[2]

In fact, a hundred years before Madame du Deffand went there, a high born lady—Mademoiselle de Montpensier—observed that "life at Forges is very pleasant and quite unlike what life ordinarily is ... It is the one place on earth where one most easily meets people."[3]

Although Madame du Deffand did not think so, by the eighteenth century Forges as a resort was still as agreeable,[4] if not more so, but the journey there was tiring. Despite the proximity of Paris (today it would be no more than two hours by car), both Mademoiselle de Montpensier in 1656 and Madame du Deffand in 1742 took nearly three days to reach the small town by coach. The condition of the French roads was, in fact, frightful until Turgo's intervention in the last quarter of the eighteenth century.

Madame du Deffand shared the exhausting journey and her lodgings in Forges with Anne-Josèphe Bonnier de la Mosson, wife of the duc de Pecquigny (later duc de Chaulnes). It was not a happy association, at least not according to the *marquise*'s letters. Gradually, as the days passed, Madame du Deffand's impatience with her travelling companion grew more and more acute and Hénault was treated to some picturesque descriptions. Since the *marquise* did not abide by her intention: "Our present association will have no continuation in the future,"[5] but continued to see and to quarrel with Madame de Pecquigny for a long time, it is worth saying something more about this curious character. The first spiteful information naturally comes from Madame du Deffand herself: "The Pecquigny creature has no resources, and her mind is like space: there is breadth, depth and perhaps all those other dimensions which I am unable to describe because I know nothing of them; but it is all emptiness. She has felt everything, judged everything, experienced everything, chosen everything and rejected everything."[6] The *marquise* cannot have been totally mistaken. There was something extravagant about this grand lady, and something odd. The wife of a *maréchal* of France, she was cultured, blessed with a lively intellect, vital and impulsive, and provocatively indifferent to the rules of the society to which she belonged. Even Sénac de Meilhan who came to know her later and who appears to have been susceptible to her charms, dwells on her restlessness: "Her thoughts never had either a past or a future: she saw things now from one angle, now from another. Her life has been one long youth which never enlightened her mind. Her mind seemed like the chariot of the sun abandoned to Phaeton."[7] Memoirs of the time tell some disgraceful anecdotes about her, but they also record some memorable witticisms. As a widow she managed once more to astound and scandalise society by marrying, as a somewhat unorthodox debt of gratitude,[8] Monsieur de Giac, an obscure magistrate some years younger than she. But "For a bourgeois, a duchess is never more than thirty years old."[9] Naturally the marriage proved a failure, but nothing could curb the prodigious vitality of the *duchesse* who ironically described herself as *"la femma à Giac".* Irony was probably her strong suit. "Wit was everything to her, and she could not have failed to notice the lack of it in the man who saved her life."[10] She proved as much even on her death-bed when, on hearing that her husband was in the next room, wishing to see her, she replied with a final sally, "Let him wait. He will come in with the sacrament."[11]

MADAME DU DEFFAND TO THE PRÉSIDENT HÉNAULT

I have just arrived in Forges without incident and even without excessive weariness: not that I slept last night, nor that we have not been thoroughly jolted about since eight o'clock this morning when we left Gisors, until this moment of our arrival. There are no more than fifteen hours of road between Paris and Forges. Yesterday we travelled seventeen leagues in nine hours and today eleven in six and a half. Nowhere are the roads dangerous at this time of year, but it is easy to imagine that they are impassable in winter. Yesterday I ate for the first time at eleven o'clock at night; fortunately I had brought some fowls for we found nothing at Gisors but a few bad eggs and a little piece of veal which was as tough as iron. I was very hungry but

I ate only a little, and digested no better than I slept. What I dreaded has not yet happened and so my journey passed very happily. But let us turn to a far more interesting subject, my companion. O my God! How she displeases me! She is completely mad: she has no set hours for her meals and breakfasted at Gisors at eight o'clock in the morning on cold veal. At Gournay she ate enough bread soaked in broth to satisfy a bricklayer, then she ate a piece of brioche followed by three quite large biscuits. We arrive at only half past two and she wants rice and some meat stew. She eats like a monkey, her hands are like monkeys' paws and she never stops talking. Her claim is to have imagination and to see everything in a singular light; she makes up for her lack of original thought by a bizarre form of expression which she excuses as being natural. She tells me her every whim and assures me that she wants only my convenience; but I fear I am obliged to be complacent although I certainly hope that this will not interfere with whatever concerns my régime. She is mean and narrow, and seems to me conceited, in fact I could not dislike her more. Just now she thought she was going to settle in my room to take her meals, but I told her that I was going to write. I begged her to tell Madame La Roche at what times she wanted to eat and what she would like to eat; and that I was counting on the same liberty for myself: consequently I shall have some rice and a chicken at eight o'clock in the evening.

Our house is pretty, my bedroom is beautiful and my bed and my armchair will console me for many things. That is all that I can tell you today. Near Forges we met two gentlemen who were returning, having taken the waters.

It is said that there is a Monsieur de Sommery here and another man whose name I don't know. This Monsieur de Sommery could well be a friend of Monsieur du Deffand's (he knows someone of that name), and it could be that the other man is Monsieur du Deffand: that would be amusing. I will let you know by the first post. I greatly need you to remember me and to give me proof of it by writing me long letters full of details about your health; I will forgive you for being slightly less precise about your amusements: a distance of twenty-eight leagues forms too thick a curtain to be seen through. Besides I have put my head in a bag, like a carriage horse and think of nothing but taking the waters. Adieu, I shall be a long time without seeing you, and it vexes me more than I would like to admit to myself.

THE PRÉSIDENT HÉNAULT TO MADAME DU DEFFAND

{Paris} Saturday 7 July {1742}

. . . So then you have at last arrived at Forges safe and sound; you made the only wise decision [not to sleep at Pontoise]. Your house is agreeable to you, you have your bed and your armchair; and if you add to that a bolt, you will have no more need to fear the intrusion of a cultivated gentleman than any conjugal enterprise. Take care for the waters at Forges are specific;[12] and it would be devilish to have gone to Forges for a growth and to come back with two . . .

Monsieur de Céreste laughed a good deal about Monsieur du Deffand. I am dying of impatience to know more; but I daren't guess; and then to say that theatrical coincidences are thought unrealistic! If it were he, however, what would you do? I suppose that he would make up his mind to flee for the third time. But what an amusing fate to have a husband and a lover both of whom turn up at any given moment and both of whom one leaves in the same way! . . .

It turned out that the unknown gentleman was not in fact Monsieur du Deffand who, besides, would probably not have been amused by the joke. He was permanently marked by his matrimonial misfortune: the *marquis* loved his wife, he never remarried and spent the rest of his life gloomy and alone in the country.[13] On his death-bed he sent for Madame du Deffand who did not excuse herself from a duty imposed by convention. But we know nothing of this last conversation.[14]

MADAME DU DEFFAND TO THE PRÉSIDENT HÉNAULT

{Forges} Wednesday, {4} July {1742}, 11 a.m.

. . . I believe you are enduring my absence with patience; but what I absolutely do not wish to believe is that you do not desire my return; on this point I will not heed sad thoughts; that which is in front of my eyes is much too disagreeable for me to wish to add unpleasantness which may turn out to be imaginary. Tell me, to reassure me, everything which needs to be said and I will allow myself to be convinced. Good-day. I wish you as much pleasure as I have ennui.

{Forges} Thursday, 5 July {1742}

. . . I became painfully aware that I was as susceptible to ennui as I was hitherto; only I have understood that the life which I lead in Paris is even more agreeable than I believed it to be and I would be infinitely unhappy if I had to give it up. From that conclude that you are as necessary to me as my own existence since every day I would rather be with you than with anyone else I know: I do not claim to flatter you, but to give you geometric proof . . .

Here we find the second specific allusion to one of the two dominating themes—if not the dominating theme—of Madame du Deffand's correspondence: ennui, once called *tedium vitae* but which might today be known as existential *Angst*.

There is already a reference to it in the self-portrait of 1728—"she often falls into an ennui which extinguishes all light from her mind"— where such an emphatic denunciation may be suspected as serving to excuse the irregularity of her behaviour during those years. But the way in which she returns to the subject with Hénault who doesn't seem, however, to attach too much importance to it, suggests the re-emergence of an old threat from which she thought she had distanced herself, rather than a chronic ill. Now the *marquise* has something to fight for or at least to distract her. For several years to come her financial problems, plans for a house of her own and her social standing would be distraction enough to delay the inevitable process of withdrawal. But when in 1751 Montesquieu wrote to her: "but I forget that I am boring you to death and that that which causes you most suffering in the world is ennui!"[15] the phenomenon had already taken hold of her.

THE PRÉSIDENT HÉNAULT TO MADAME DU DEFFAND

{Paris} 8 July {1742}

. . . Farewell; your ennui grieves me. Yet it reminds me of the tale about the thunder which afforded a husband an embrace which he had long been denied. All the same I understand: at the moment you believe you miss me; but you would not be able to prevent yourself from thinking that you must tell me your troubles because you think that not many people are so sensitive, or to tell the truth, you are certain of it . . .

MADAME DU DEFFAND TO PRÉSIDENT HÉNAULT

{Forges} Friday, 6 July {1742}

. . . I wrote you a long letter yesterday, so today you will have but a few words. Your feelings for me are all the finer for the fact that every one of them is spontaneous. I believe what you tell me, that the pleasure of being with me is always spoilt by regret or by the constraint which you believe prevents you from being elsewhere. It would indeed be difficult to please someone for whom happiness can only be supernatural. I can only advise you to take full advantage of my absence, to enjoy yourself with your lady friends, and to keep your regrets to exchange them for real and simple pleasures when next you see me. For my part, I am vexed at not seeing you; but I suffer this misfortune with a kind of courage because I do not think that you greatly share it, and that you are quite indifferent to everything; and then I imagine that I will not tyrannise you for at least two months . . .

THE PRÉSIDENT HÉNAULT TO MADAME DU DEFFAND

{Paris} 9 July {1742}

. . . You say that you do not read me as a novel: that is, in fact, as it should be and I admire your prudence in that; but it seems to me that from the style of my letters you should not exhort me to continue them as pious works: I do not think they give that impression. I could even tell you that I have transformed my evenings into mornings and that the time when I write to you is the best time of my day. I would further add, that you should see me in my letters just as you used to see me in person because nothing offends me and because I leave you with only a favourable idea of me . . .

MADAME DU DEFFAND TO THE PRÉSIDENT HÉNAULT

{Forges} 9 July {1742}

. . . Your letters afford me infinite pleasure and I would say of you what Madame d'Autray said of Monsieur de Céreste: "Your absence is delicious . . ."

Know that there is no change and that at Forges as in Paris and everywhere else, I have recourse only to you and I count on you alone; I would have said "need you" but you do not like the ring of these words . . .

A minimalisation of feeling seems chiefly to inform these letters in which mistrust prevails over trust and irony over tenderness. The correspondents confront each other affectionately but guardedly. By nature diffident, as she herself often admitted, Madame du Deffand seems to protect herself from possible disappointment with a kind of defensive aggression, neither giving nor demanding, whilst Hénault has no difficulty in adapting himself to the rules of the game and, knowing his dangerous correspondent as he does, he carefully avoids exposing himself. The exchange is one of minimum sentiment based on egoism and controlled by a respect for form. And when, as in the last letter, Madame du Deffand dwells too much on her disenchantment, the Président reacts firmly in the name of offended decorum rather than of hurt feelings.

THE PRÉSIDENT HÉNAULT TO MADAME DU DEFFAND

{Paris} 14 July {1742}

. . . I turn to your letter of yesterday—it is dated Monday 9th July at five o'clock and Tuesday at one o'clock. I am re-reading it in order to reason with you as to its contents, because I do not think as you do, that it is unnecessary to follow a letter which one has received in order to reply to it. That at least proves that one has paid attention to it. Every man to his own manner of feeling, or rather, some feel whilst others amuse themselves.

I can only take as a jest the tone in which you say to me: "Why! Can you not give me half an hour a day?" So much the better that I do not bore you by virtue of regularity and length; that is all that the abbé de Sade and I can ask. However, if you had answered the points in my letters, you would have seen that in one I tell you that my evenings have turned into mornings because that is the time when I concern myself with you, which is clear; but sweetness is not your style with me, and you surely believed it was an obscenity when you wrote today, as if in an excess of passion, that I am the only one on whom you count. Your truthfulness permits of no further excess, and I am glad that I perceived all that long ago . . .

I find that you never said anything truer than that my absence is delicious; but it is not good to tell all the truth. I think in fact that if you had to arrange your life, you would divide it into two parts, and absence would be my part. Absence is like the Elysian fields: everyone in it is equal, or I would rather say, I think I would be at some advantage there and it is the right position from which to pour one's love out in song.

I do not know why I should dislike the ring of the word "need": there is none sweeter when it springs from trust; but you are trusting, and then you are not according to your convenience. I continue to follow your letter . . .

You do not tell me that you take pleasure in writing to me, but that if you did not occupy yourself by writing to me, you would bore yourself to death. That is exactly like Caylus who engraves so as not to hang himself. However, I truthfully recognise that I must be very flattered that you should believe me capable of feeling everything that you write and I gladly accept such praise . . .

Ah! What the devil, do you need an excuse to claim yourself free of all sentiment? You have too elevated a soul to have recourse to that. Say everything frankly. I feel, or rather I see, that you have been doing your best for ten years to make me love you; but I declare that I will have none of it. That is called talking, and instead of that you pay me my dues with a mistrustful air. It is time (as the *Faux Sincere* says)[16] that that is at least something. But it would be better to allow me to serve after my own style. I only concern myself about things for which I care and am not at all like Madame du Maine.[17] It is certain that I miss you a great deal, and just as certain, as you must have noticed if you had read my letters that I have not made more fuss of my other women friends since your departure. I would do better to tell you nothing of all this, but to tell the truth, if you read your letters in Paris, I think you would lose patience with them a little . . .

With regard to your ugliness, I console myself for that so long as you lose nothing of your sweetness or of your feelings for me. I laugh at this point. What a consolation I offer you in saying that it doesn't matter to me! But to tell the truth, I am persuaded on the contrary, that you will be much better after you have taken the waters, for if I did not believe it, I would not have replied to this point, it being no concern of mine.

Farewell; there is an end to your letter and to mine also. I have my fits of truth just like anyone else and I lack the courage to send you my regards which would be the regards of your most humble and obedient servant.

MADAME DU DEFFAND TO THE PRÉSIDENT HÉNAULT   {*undated*}

. . . Believe me that you are more important to me than you think; and when you are natural, and you let yourself go artlessly and without care, then I could not find you more to my liking. For instance your letter today is charming; it gives me inexplicable pleasure and I wish to reply to it at once . . . Do you speak in good faith when you say that in appearing to doubt your feelings, I wish to be free from gratitude? Do you sincerely believe that such a motive is mine? Oh, but no: it is as clear as daylight to you that when I notice a grain of sentiment in you, it has the miraculous power of the grain of mustard in the Gospel, to remove mountains. But you rarely allow me to rejoice in such illusion or such truth: but let us discuss the matter no further and not disturb my depths . . .

Hénault's resentment seems to have had a vitalising effect and for a moment the two correspondents flirted with sincerity. Reassured by the authenticity of the feelings which provoked the Président's indignation, Madame du Deffand abandons—for an instant—her weapons of aggression and irony; and it is this very act of confidence which helps us to understand how, contrary to appearances, these weapons were necessary for her to be able to confront her lover.

Hénault already emerges from the *marquise*'s description of him many years earlier, as an exquisitely artificial and profoundly unreachable man, all of which is confirmed by this correspondence. The Président so perfectly assumed the mask of a man of the world that his true face became elusive, and his tremendous availability must have reflected indifference. Although Madame du Deffand rejoiced for a moment in establishing the miracle of the grain of mustard seed, in reality the relationship between the two lovers had been petrified too long for it to be in any way revived. Hénault proved that to his cost when he took the *marquise*'s sermon too literally.

THE PRÉSIDENT HÉNAULT TO MADAME DU DEFFAND

{Paris} 12 July {1742}

. . . I went yesterday to *Brutus*;[18] there was quite a crowd. I was confirmed in what I have always thought, that it is Voltaire's finest play. La Nove played with that intelligence which you dislike because it presupposes a lack of fire: so one may say of a girl about to be married that she plays the clavichord well, meaning that she is not at all pretty. But I found that he did have fire. It is not that which he lacks, but strength; on the whole I was pleased. Gaussin's performance was as usual; but it was Sarrasin who enchanted me, he invested in the part of Brutus all the nobility, all the compassion and all the tragedy which you could wish for. I then returned home to await my guests who were not numerous as we were only seven, the *maréchale*,[19] her daughter,[20] her son,[21] Madame de Maurepas, Céreste, Pont-de-Veyle and myself. Our supper was excellent, and you will be surprised to hear that we enjoyed ourselves. I swear that on leaving there, had I known where to find you, I would have come to fetch you. It was the loveliest evening imaginable, the moon was beautiful and my garden seemed to request you. But, as Polyeucte says, what is the use of speaking of such things to hearts untouched by God? In fact I missed you all the more for being able to lend you feelings which your presence alone has the power to destroy . . .

MADAME DU DEFFAND TO THE PRÉSIDENT HÉNAULT

{Forges} 14 July {1742}

. . . It is the moonlight, there are certain circumstances which make you desire my presence; I am missed and longed for depending on how the fine weather has affected the disposition of your soul; I desire you everywhere and I know of no circumstance which could render your presence less agreeable. It is that I have neither temperament nor romanticism.

15 July {1742}

Do you know that I am beginning to fear that my letters bore you? I do not know from what this springs, but I feel that I am becoming mistrustful: I think it is as a result of ennui. However, I think I am wrong and I admit that your letters are such as should reassure me. They could not please me more and I feel that they alone sustain me here. I do not know what you will say about the one I wrote yesterday. I was not in a bad humour, neither was I cross with you, but I was overcome by a moment of frankness and had to say what I think. One thing is certain and that is that I love you and that my feelings are unconditional. All that my reason can do, is to prevent me from succumbing to the misery that my mistrust could cause, but it can in no way diminish my fondness . . .

THE PRÉSIDENT HÉNAULT TO MADAME DU DEFFAND
                                                        {Paris} 18 July { 1742}

You have "neither temperament nor romanticism"! I pity you greatly, and you know as well as another the price of this loss, for I think I have heard you speak of it. What you call romanticism in your letters are memories; the moonlight, the thought of a place where one has seen a loved one, a state of mind which induces one to think more lovingly, a reception, a fine day etc., in fact everything that poets have said on the subject; that did not seem at all ridiculous to me. But perhaps it is for my own good that you don't like me to fill my head with all this nonsense. So let it be! I beg forgiveness for all rivulets past, present and to come, and for their brothers, the birds, and their cousins the young elms and for all the feelings from which they result. I stand corrected and my letters will not only be agreeable to you by virtue of all the news of the town which I can pick up and which I imagine might amuse you. I revert to the historical style and will only speak of myself where matters of fact are concerned . . .

MADAME DU DEFFAND TO THE PRÉSIDENT HÉNAULT
                                                        {Forges} 21 July { 1742}

I wrote to you yesterday begging you not to alter the style of your letters in any way. If I am displeased, it is not by feelings, I only quarrel with contradiction; and when I appear to make fun of everything to do with *daydreaming,* it is because it seems petty to me, and is no substitute for the essential, and it doesn't dazzle me enough to make me lose sight of the *important points.* So, be assured that I have no natural repugnance for this kind of thing; but the circumstances of daydreaming, its correlation and accompaniment determine its worth . . .

You have a veneration for Madame de Rochefort which amuses me . . . What matter? You love me after your fashion, I neither should nor am able to wish you to do otherwise. I have always thought that in thirty years you will begin to believe that I love you and that you will no longer mistrust my frivolity . . .

But thirty years later it was to be Madame du Deffand herself who made a discovery about Hénault's feelings towards her. Walpole recounts with slightly sinister humour, the final exchanges of a relationship which was so burnt out that to break it off would have been superfluous: "The Président Hénault . . . had been the lover of Madame du Deffand and of Madame de Castelmoron, and preferred the latter. The last time I was at Paris, a little before the Président's death,[22] and when he was grown superannuated, I one evening found him alone with Madame du Deffand, who could scarce stifle her laughter till he was gone, at what had been passing. She had perceived that he did not know where he was, nor with whom, though he had not entirely lost his memory. From question to question, she led him to talk of Madame de Castelmoron, and said, *'À propos, Président, avait-elle de l'esprit?' 'Oui, oui, elle en avait.' 'En avait-elle autant que Mme du Deffand?' 'Eh! mon Dieu! non, il s'en fallait beaucoup.' 'Mais laquelle aimiez-vous mieux?' 'Hah! j'aimais mieux Madame de Castelmoron.'**

"As soon as he was gone, she repeated this conversation to me, and was infinitely diverted with it, and it was a strong proof of her quickness and wit, as she herself was then seventy-eight."[23]

This cunningly extracted confession had already been made freely by Hénault years earlier in his *Mémoires*. "Everything is over for me, it only remains for me to die," he wrote on hearing of the death of Madame de Castelmoron,[24] and he did not hesitate to add: "For forty years she has been the principal object of my existence."[25] Yet the description the Président left of her arouses the suspicion that this sweet, comforting,

---

*"By the way, Président, did she have wit?' 'Yes, yes, she did.' 'Had she as much as Madame du Deffand?' 'Oh, my God! No, not nearly!' 'But which did you love more?' 'Oh, I loved Madame de Castelmoron more.'

modest, humble, pious woman played not an alternative part to Madame du Deffand, but a complimentary one. Madame de Castelmoron probably offered Hénault a safe refuge where, removed from scepticism and irony, he could express outbursts of affection which, if not sublime, were at least sincere. The Président had learnt to know the *marquise* to his cost and never to expose himself defencelessly to her judgement; and the Forges letters show in fact how Madame du Deffand's mistrust made it impossible for her correspondent to place any real confidence in her. But fear[26] kept the admiration intact and Hénault was never able to escape the fascination the *marquise* held for him, or to remove himself from her power. Madame de Castelmoron certainly became "the principal object of his existence," but Madame du Deffand remained "the person who had made him most happy and most unhappy, because it was she whom he had most loved."[27]

III

Sceaux

THE FAMOUS COURT AT SCEAUX was the principal setting for the first years of Madame du Deffand's relationship with Hénault. He was already at home there by the time she, with great speed, managed to make herself indispensable to the duchesse du Maine, the capricious *châtelaine* of Sceaux whose misfortune it was "not to be able to do without things which she didn't care for."[1]

In his *Mémoires* Hénault describes those years at Sceaux and traces the strengthening of Madame du Deffand's worldly position. But in order fully to understand this little court, it is necessary to go back not to Hénault, but to the *Mémoires* of Madame de Staal. Madame de Staal lived at Sceaux for nearly thirty years and devoted her exceptional intelligence to inventing situations and plots for the most sumptuous and demanding theatre in the whole of eighteenth-century France.

When, in about 1710, Marguerite-Jeanne Cordier Delaunay, the future baronne de Staal, entered the service of Anne-Louise-Bénédicte de Bourbon, grand-daughter of the Grand Condé and wife of the duc du Maine, himself the bastard son of Louis XIV and Madame de Montespan, Sceaux was just becoming, in the words of Saint-Simon, "more than ever the theatre of the duchesse du Maine's folly; of her husband's shame and embarrassment, and by virtue of expense, his ruin; as well as the spectacle of the court and the town from whence crowds came to mock. Several times a week she herself acted in *Athalie* and other plays with a company of actors and actresses. Whole nights were spent gambling, feasting, with illuminations and fireworks; in a word there was entertainment and extravagance of all kinds every day."[2]

Incapable of forgiving her husband for his illegitimate birth, and unable to take precedence at court, the duchesse du Maine in fact created her own private court at Sceaux, a few kilometres outside Paris. The château was built by Colbert at the height of his glorious ministry and was a perfect example of the architectural aesthetic of the *Grand Siècle.* It was built according to the architect Perrault's plans,[3] and decorated by the painter, Le Brun. It stood in extensive and beautiful parkland laid out by Le Nôtre, with large pools, innumerable fountains, and where statues by Puget and Girardon adorned the woods. It was in this grandiose and noble setting that the duchesse du Maine held her court, despite changing circumstances, for fifty years. Although, as Saint-Simon suggests, this court may have resulted from wildly frustrated ambition, it was the intellectual and social centre of the day in contrast to the gloomy conformism of the aging Louis XIV's Versailles.

"With the appearance of a little monster, vivacious, ambitious, witty and with whatever judgement might remain to an overgrown child spoiled by adulation,"[4] this "doll of the blood royal," according to an envious sister-in-law,[5] was above all, concerned with weaving a web of ambition.[6] In Madame de Staal's words, "the elevation of her family had reached the highest point to which she could take it. Since her marriage to Monsieur le duc du Maine she had been ceaselessly occupied in procuring for him and her children a rank to equal her own, by degrees they had acquired all the privileges of princes of the blood; and, owing to circumstances, they obtained the remarkable edict whereby they and their descendants were called in line to the succession. . . . This actual prosperity which allowed no glimpse of the collapse for which it was preparing, filled the court with joy."[7]

The duchesse du Maine's longing for power vied in her with an equally potent longing to escape reality. How else can her frantic need for entertainment be explained—the frenzy with which she incessantly planned a complicated network of amusements, making life at Sceaux a permanent celebration?

"In the life of a social group which devotes itself entirely to the pursuit of pleasure, the fête with its artifice and expense, seems like a moment of truth in which creatures can abandon themselves without a thought and almost without hindrance to their 'ruling passion.' It is spending *par excellence* in a life of spending. But it is also *the* moment *par excellence* in a life made up of an anxious succession of moments; the fête brings together in a short space of time a chain of closely associated moments, of pleasures almost linked together, in such a way that the delighted conscience rests not for a second. There is a perpetual rekindling of a continuous present which overwhelms these fickle creatures for whom the thing of the moment is ever paramount. The fête brings about this 'rapid continuity of pleasure' (La Morlière, *Angola*) through the profusion of people and chance. Swiftly exhausted and easily wearied, desire wants only to savour more moments through more objects, and it finds them; it wants to repeat itself through diversity and it finds diversity; for the fête arranges a cumulus of variety, a perpetual triumph of surprise, a pretence at inexhaustibility (with, at heart, a premonition of exhaustion and ennui)."[8] Nothing captures the essence of Sceaux better than the above description by Starobinski of eighteenth-century celebrations. But fact and fiction were closely interwoven in the life of the little kingdom. Banished from Versailles, the theatre took its revenge here. A singular mixture of masterpiece and mediocrity combined to provide the tragedies, comedies, *opéra bouffe,* puppet shows, ballets and allegories which succeeded one another on the stage at Sceaux and in the *duchesse*'s other domains.[9] Professional companies alternated with groups of *habitués* from the small court, and often, with a total disregard for etiquette, amateurs and professionals united, for as Saint-Simon remarked, the duchesse du Maine "had already shaken off the yoke of the court and had given herself entirely to pleasure, to remaining at Sceaux and to living for herself."[10]

The organiser of entertainment at Sceaux was the poet and academician Nicolas de Malézieu who with the help of the abbé Genest, wrote and commissioned plays and compositions in verse and in prose, and organised every kind of spectacle. The demand seemed to be inexhaustable so that even Madame de Staal was called upon to make a contribution: "The princess's taste for pleasure was in full flight and the only thought was for new spices to render it ever more piquant. Plays were performed or rehearsed every day. Consideration was given as to how to put the nights to good use, with suitable entertainments. Nights which came to be called *grandes nuits.* Like everything else, they began very simply. Madame la duchesse du Maine who liked staying up, often spent all night playing different games. The abbé de Vaubrun who was one of the courtiers most eager to please, imagined that during a night devoted to pleasure someone should be made to appear in the guise of Night, enveloped in black crêpe, to thank the *princesse* for her preference of Night over Day; the goddess should have an attendant who would sing a fine song on the same subject. The abbé confided his secret to me and asked me to write and recite the part of the nocturnal deity . . . The idea was applauded, and so magnificent celebrations came to be given at night by different people for Madame la duchesse du Maine."[11]

Watteau is said to have been thinking of Sceaux[12] when he painted his second *Embarquement pour Cythère* which now hangs in the Louvre.[13] It is no accident that the picture which Rodin interpreted as a "psychological journey" through the three phases of love: persuasion, consent and full accord,[14] is imbued with theatrical action.[15] The mythical island of Cythera, "the island for which one departs, not where one arrives,"[16] and for which the *bâteau-lit* is about to set sail with its cargo of lovers, is far more real despite its absence than the mysterious-looking garden which the little group of travelers is preparing to leave. Venus's isle, evoked only by the title of the picture, assumes the reassuring form of conventional Arcadia whilst the wood behind the travelers waiting in the "expectancy or remembrance of pleasure"[17] is inhabited by an invisible enemy—ennui—making escape improbable. The real protagonists of the *Embarquement* are the same as those at Sceaux: restlessness and the desire to escape; and whatever the outcome of their continual journeying, the boat and the river evoke lacustrine waters and funereal expeditions.

Day and night Sceaux was the implacable stage on which the curtain never seemed to fall. But fêtes and theatricals were not the only entertainments. There was the order of the "Honeybee" whose motto was taken from Tasso's *L'Aminta*: "Small is the bee yet his little sting great and gaping wounds doth bring,"[18] and which provided the *duchesse* with thirty-nine knights who swore obedience to her and who undertook to dance at any given moment, even during the dog days of summer, and never to squash the bee. There were literary competitions for which pieces had to be written in a genre which depended on the random selection of a letter. When, in 1715, Voltaire was a guest at Sceaux, he wrote the novella *Un petit mal pour un grand bien* for a lady who had drawn the letter "N."

The ludicrous Cellamore Plot put an end to the *duchesse*'s political ambitions and for a while suspended the hard labour of those whom Malézieu called *'les galères du bel esprit.'** When the shutters at Sceaux

*The galley slaves of wit.

were once again opened in 1720, Hénault wrote: "The court was quite unlike what it had been under the late king ... Times had changed considerably; I had the honour of being presented to Madame la duchesse du Maine only after her return from prison. But even if the court was less brilliant, it was no less agreeable. It was composed of people of distinction and wit: Madame de Charost, subsequently duchesse de Luynes, Madame la marquise de Lambert, Monsieur le cardinal de Polignac, Monsieur le premier président de Mesmes, Madame de Staal, Monsieur de Staal, Monsieur de Sainte-Aulaire, Madame la marquise du Deffand. It was she who answered the cardinal de Polignac so amusingly when he was talking to the duchesse du Maine about the martyrdom of Saint Denis. "Can one imagine, Madame, that the martyred saint carried his own head in his hands for leagues ... Two leagues!"

"Oh Monsieur," Madame du Deffand replied, "it is only the first step which counts!"[19]

Sceaux was no longer the meeting place for aristocrats who turned their backs on Versailles—the Cellamare Plot had compromised it—it now became more a centre for literary society. The *duchesse* resigned herself—in so far as she was able—to being less egocentric ("I adore life in society: everyone listens to me and I listen to no one"[20]), and apparently less tyrannical. In Paris the marquise de Lambert and Madame de Tencin's *Salons* provided fearful competition for the old monopoly at Sceaux. But the *duchesse's* objective remained the same: constant entertainment, occasionally pursued with real ferocity. "One evening when we supped at the Arsenal in the pretty pavilion that Madame la duchesse du Maine had built there by the river, she asked Madame Dreuillet who was over seventy and very ill, to sing, which was usual; but on that evening when Madame Dreuillet was even more ill, she was made to sing from the moment the soup was served. I pointed out to the *princesse* that if we were to remain at table for four or five hours, she would not be able to sing until the end. 'You are quite right, Président, but don't you see that there is no time to be lost, and that that woman could die before the joint is served!' "[21]

The list of writers who came to Sceaux during this second period of its history is long and distinguished. Voltaire, Piron, Fontenelle, Marmontel, Montesquieu, Diderot, Voisenon, Crébillon, Raynal, Prévost, Houdar de la Motte, d'Alembert all came to make their contribution to the uninterrupted flow of conversation, theatricals and poetic banter. The most exquisite figure in this Arcadia was the celebrated and extremely old Fontenelle who was the link between the two Sceaux periods and more especially between the cultural lives of the two centuries. His contemporaries, like the marquis d'Argenson noticed how exceptional he was: "One looks at him as one looks at an artistic masterpiece worked with care and delicacy and which one must be careful not to destroy because they are no longer made that way. He reminds us not only of Louis XIV's beautiful century, so noble and so great which some of us saw ending, but also of the spirit of Benserade, of the Saint-Evremonds and the Scudérys, and of the habitual style at Rambouillet, whose air we can be sure he breathed. He has that style, but it is gentler in him, more refined, and adapted to our times ... His conversation is infinitely agreeable, more delicate in manner than striking and interspersed with anecdotes which are sharp but never malicious since they concern either the literary or the gallant, or society's minor tribulations."[22]

The other literary centenarian was the marquis de Sainte-Aulaire whom the duchesse du Maine called "shepherd"[23] and whom she forced until he was practically on his deathbed to improvise verse—verse to "infuriate" Boileau.[24] The old poet remained faithful to his inspiration:

> *En vain vous me prêchez sans cesse*
> *Pour me faire aller à confesse.*
> *Ma bergère, j'ai beau chercher*
> *Je n'ai rien sur la conscience*
> *De grâce, faites-moi pécher,*
> *Après, je ferai pénitence.*[25]

And the *duchesse* replied with remarkable promptitude:

> *Si je cédais à ton insistance,*
> *On te verrait bien empêché,*
> *Mais plus encore du péché*
> *Que de la pénitence.*[26]

In such a theatre there must be a perpetual search for new actors, and Madame du Deffand, introduced by so distinguished an *habitué* as Hénault, was soon to play a leading part. Madame de Staal's *Mémoires* faithfully record the rise of the *Marquise*'s star, around 1730. "At that time we had Madame du Deffand at Sceaux. Her irresistible charms predisposed me in her favour. No one is wittier nor more naturally so. The sparkling fire which animates her, penetrates and reveals everything, showing up the simplest of features. She is supremely talented in the depiction of different characters and from her descriptions which are more alive than the originals one comes to know people better than one does from the most intimate exchange with them."[27]

For many years Madame du Deffand's dedication to the duchesse du Maine's entertainment was apparently total. "She had no other home but Sceaux where she stayed for most of the year,"[28] Hénault wrote. And this is apparently confirmed by the *marquise*'s own correspondence with her friends: "I lead a somewhat itinerant life, sometimes at Sceaux, sometimes at Clagny or in Paris, but always with Madame la duchesse du Maine which lends certain irregularity to my relationships," she wrote to her brother-in-law on 18 September 1731.[29] And three years later to her sister: "The life I lead is very healthy. I do not sit up at night, I eat and sleep well, I have neither sorrow nor anxiety and I could not wish a sweeter condition for those I most love."[30] A message of rare serenity from Madame du Deffand which, moreover, reflects a totally negative conception of happiness defined only by exclusion and absence. Such a notion was shared by many of Madame du Deffand's contemporaries: "Happiness is a shy flowering whose frailty needs preserving. It is only a matter of determining the minimum meaning of the word and somehow taking the reality it evokes at base level. More often such definitions are accompanied by latent pessimism and a somewhat nervous smile: happiness is that fragile measure wrenched from universal nothingness and universal suffering."[31]

But Sceaux was not the Elysian fields. It had its price. "It is not possible for me on this occasion, to take advantage of your visit [to Champrond]. Monsieur le duc du Maine's condition worsens every day; he cannot go far and under these circumstances I must stay with Madame la duchesse du Maine," Madame du Deffand wrote to her sister on 1 April 1736.[32] The duc du Maine's appalling agony, resulting from cancer of the face, was long drawn out.[33] With a truly theatrical change of disguise, the *duchesse,* in an exemplary fashion, stayed until the end with her husband, this "prince subjugated by an invincible ascendancy to her every wish and from whom she gained great advantages without losing that of complete freedom."[34] Then, little by little, her old passions regained the upper hand. "Every time I write to you, I tell myself that I will write often, but as I am nearly always at Sceaux or one other of Madame la duchesse du Maine's properties, frequently I do not have a single free half hour during the day. The society of princesses is not like the society of others. It is impossible to be their friend and to retain one's freedom, the loss of which I often regret but one must sustain the decisions one has made when, by the way, they bring stability and comfort."[35] (To her brother-in-law, 28 November 1740.)

For more than fifteen years Madame du Deffand's behaviour conformed to this "decision." In collaboration with Madame de Staal, the *marquise* devoted all her talent to the laborious theatricals at Sceaux which grew to resemble the expensive and intricate toy of an old, spoilt child. She played a dual role: that of entertaining the duchesse du Maine who had developed a real passion for her; and as an attraction for other visitors who were less well disposed to suffer the *duchesse*'s misplaced bullying. By 1732, we find her seeking help from Voltaire, who, however, replied, "You suggested, Madame, buying the office of equerry to Madame de la duchesse du Maine, but not feeling myself to be sufficiently energetic for the post, I have been obliged to await other occasions to pay you my court . . ."[36]

For her part, Madame du Deffand made use of Sceaux as the arena where she could effect a definitive metamorphosis. There she buried the embarrassing memory of her libertine youth and entrusted her new image to the seductions of the mind. But even in her metamorphosis, the *marquise* remained true to her nature. From her unscrupulous behaviour, an intellectual lack of prejudice developed; her restlessness and intolerance only enhanced the cutting edge of her conversation.

At Sceaux Madame du Deffand mastered every kind of resourcefulness as well as the endless refinements of polite society. Her great natural talent could not have found a better field of action than this small court which for fifty years, and with ever-increasing indifference, continued in a purely artificial existence whose only criteria were respect of its social code.

In her correspondence Madame du Deffand describes life at Sceaux at that moment in which she was beginning to reap the benefits of her slavery and when she was no longer prepared to sacrifice the freedom which she had so knowingly bartered in exchange for "security and advantage." It was the summer of 1747 and the duchesse du Maine's empire was in its last years. The *marquise* had already spent the months of May and June at Sceaux and on 22 June she wrote to Maupertuis: "As for me, I lead a flat, ordinary existence which suits me very well. I have been at Sceaux since early in May. I am not staying in the château but in a house in the park where I am alone as much as I please and where I see the people I like. At 8 o'clock I go to the château where I play games and sup with Madame du Maine and Madame de Staal; after which I again play games before returning here to retire."[37] Despite the unquestionable privilege which she now seemed to enjoy of still being called upon to entertain the *duchesse,* Madame du Deffand managed to withdraw behind a clever method of refusal. For three months, while the little court moved from place to place, she excused herself from the ever more pressing invitations.

Since childhood Madame du Maine, who had been accustomed to being obeyed and praised and whose "*amour propre* has advanced only along the path laid out for it"[38] sent her a request in which the apparent amiability in no way disguised the authoritarian tone of one used to giving orders and to being obeyed. On 7 June she wrote: "I received only today, Madame, the letter which you took the trouble to write to me on Friday. I received it with great pleasure, but it would have pleased me more if it had not told me of your delay in returning to Sceaux. I had hoped to see you back here today, and I avow that I am very displeased at having to wait until Wednesday. I understand that Madame de Luynes finds your company so agreeable that she would wish to keep you with her longer, but I flatter myself that you have not forgotten your word, which you gave me, that you would not stay away for more than eight days, and that the two which you have been unable to refuse Madame de Luynes will not be followed by any further delay." The suspicious Madame du Maine had acute antennae, for Madame de Luynes was a rival to be feared and was made so particularly by Madame du Deffand's opportunism. By a second marriage, the *marquise*'s maternal aunt, Madame de Luynes, became a person of considerable standing and first lady-in-waiting to the Queen, Maria Leszczynska. The *marquise* would never lose sight of the advantages she might gain from this connection and, as we shall see later, she always paid especial attention and was particularly deferential to her influential aunt. Madame du Maine's irritation must have been considerably aggravated by the fact of Madame de Luynes' official position with the Queen. A reminder however indirect, of Versailles, had to be intolerable to one who only wanted to forget it. The duchesse du Maine was not really able to keep a hold over Madame du Deffand; she might as well have tried to capture her own reflection—the marquise and she were too alike. They were both overbearing, egoistical, mistrustful, indifferent to others, and incapable of being otherwise. They could stand up to one another, but they could never love each other: for that they would have had to examine their darker sides and question their consciences.

It was Madame de Staal, Madame du Maine's companion, who really communicated with Madame du Deffand at Sceaux. The two women were bound by reciprocal admiration and by the solidarity which comes when two people find themselves, albeit under different circumstances, fighting the same battles. They were both obliged to make a profession of using their intelligence in the service of others: Madame du Deffand in order to regain standing which she once spent in the art of seduction, Madame de Staal simply to guarantee her survival. Without name, family or fortune, the duchesse du Maine's lady companion had only her wit and intelligence to thank for her standard of living and her dignity. In her *Mémoires,* Madame de Staal pinpoints the moment when, by sheer chance, Madame du Maine, after years of total indifference, allowed her inattention to give way to curiosity and directly acknowledged the housemaid's existence: "The Serene Highness lowered herself to talk to me; she then became accustomed to doing so. She was pleased with my replies and noticed my approval. I noticed that she sought it directly and that often, when speaking, she would turn to me to see if I was paying attention."[39]

"The indelible attribution of housemaid,"[40] Madame de Staal stated bitterly, was, however, to cling to her for the rest of her life. Nothing succeeded in inwardly freeing her from her dependence on the duchesse du Maine. Neither loyalty, nor the courage with which she faced the Bastille after the Cellamare plot, nor the marriage arranged for her by Madame du Maine,[41] nor the personal prestige which she gained were enough to buy her her liberty. But Madame de Staal's real autonomy consisted in the dignified acceptance of her fate. According to Sainte-Beuve, "that perfect and often cruel precision of observation, that inexorable sense of reality" arose from her resignation and caused her to say, "Truth establishes itself as best it can and its only merit lies in being what it is."[42] Besides, this resignation nourished the drive and bitterness which lent vigour to her work without ever turning it to invective.

Madame de Staal's letters written to Madame du Deffand during that summer of 1747 constitute an "unofficial" memoir, and paint a picture of life at Sceaux as seen from behind the scenes. Unshackled by the considerations which presided over her *Mémoires*—"I only gave a half-length portrait of myself"[43]—Madame de Staal speaks freely to her friend who knew from experience about the frenzy, the hard work and the humiliation necessary to ensure that uninterrupted flow of amusement, that unending *Embarquement pour Cythère*. Unfortunately we do not have Madame du Deffand's replies, but the rhythm of Madame de Staal's correspondence (twenty letters in less than three months), the subjects discussed, the expression of trust and understanding, and frequent references to her friend's replies, give not only an extraordinary account of life at the small court, but are also an illumination of the *marquise*'s personality and feelings.

MADAME DE STAAL TO MADAME DU DEFFAND

Sorel[44] Saturday 20 July, 1747

Yesterday, my Queen, I read your letter to Her Highness. She was suffering an attack of fear of thunder so did not appreciate your pretty speeches. I will take care another time, not to expose you to the storm. For the last few days we have been swimming in joy, but now we are swimming in the rain. Our thoughts which had become gentle and agreeable are about to become quite black again. On top of that, our princess has been visited for the last two days by a cold and a fever: despite this and in spite of the diabolical weather, outings go on just the same. It would seem that Providence takes care to suit the bodies of princes to their fancy, or they would not reach man's estate. As you can see, my Queen, I am reduced to telling you about the rain and the sunshine; but what is to be done with all we have here? One Ribérac, three Castellanes, two Caderousses, two Malézieux, one Villeneuve and his wife and the household. You may gain something from all that: for my part, my arms are by my side, I can find nothing to pick up. I did, however, during the last few days, take a walk with Gruchet who said some quite delicate things to me in a vulgar way:

which made me notice the degree to which the least discerning can penetrate the characters of their masters . . .

Despite a third thunder storm, more violent than the first two, we have just returned from hunting. The worst of the storm caught us in the middle of the forest. As usual I hoped to avoid this outing; but the reasons which I presented to excuse myself were cleverly twisted, making it impossible for me to withdraw. It is a shame that such an ingenious art should be used to make people unhappy.

"Wit and ironic gaiety survived in a pleasureless existence overflowing with boredom,"[45] and the two friends practised both as part of the indispensable discipline of professional society ladies, but in this private exchange, the wit becomes genuine. Voltaire and especially Madame du Châtelet who came to Sceaux for a theatrical performance were to reap the benefit.

MADAME DE STAAL TO MADAME DU DEFFAND

Anet,[46] Tuesday 15 August 1747

Your letter, my Queen, which I received today, should have reached me on Sunday. I would have written had there been anything to answer; for myself, I have nothing to tell: the heat is overpowering and the monotony which does nothing to arouse one, leave me stupefied . . .

Madame de Châtelet and Voltaire who announced their arrival for today and of whom we had lost sight, appeared yesterday at midnight, like two ghosts with a smell of embalmed corpses which they seemed to have brought with them from their tombs. We had just left the table. The ghosts, however, were famished. They needed supper, and not only that, beds which were not prepared. The caretaker who had already gone to bed, arose hurriedly. Gaya who had offered to give up his room if it were urgently needed, was obliged to give it up on this occasion and he moved out with the speed and displeasure of an army surprised in its camp, leaving part of his baggage in enemy hands. Voltaire was pleased with the lodging which was no consolation to Gaya. As for the lady, her bed turned out to be badly made. She had to change rooms today. Note that she had made this bed herself for lack of servants and had found the wrong number of mattresses which I think offended her precise mind rather than her not very delicate body. For the moment she has an apartment which is reserved for someone else and which she will exchange on Saturday for that of the maréchal de Maillebois who is leaving one of these days. He came here at the same time as us with his daughter and his daughter-in-law. One is pretty, the other ugly and sad. With his own hounds he chased a roebuck, but caught a young hind. That is all that can be said of them. Our new guests will have more to provide. They are going to produce their comedy:[47] Vanture is to play Boursouffle. One would hardly say that he looks the part, nor does Madame de Châtelet look the part of Mademoiselle de la Cochonnière who ought to be short and fat. That is enough of them for today. Let us turn to you, my Queen. I strongly approve of your decision to write to the du Châtels. Their reply will make you finally decide about your journey. I am horrified by all the Président's journeys. Were he to consult him, Monsieur de Pourceaugnac's[48] doctor would advise that so much displacement augurs ill.

I am very vexed that you are not well. The habit of accumulated indigestion seems pernicious to me, and I think, my Queen, that you would do much better to reserve your strength rather than to adorn your armchair. You wrote a letter to our princess which greatly pleased her. I think you will have her box at the theatre for the holidays, but I have not yet been commissioned to tell you. I have been enjoined to beg you, if you decide to come, to warn us in advance so that you may be well housed; your presence is much looked for and your comfort is desired . . .

Our phantoms do not show their faces during the day. Last night they appeared at 10 o'clock. I do not think we will see them any earlier today. One is occupied in describing great things, the other in commentating on Newton. They wish neither to play nor to walk. They add nothing to a society where their learned writings have no place. What is worse, this evening's apparition made a violent protestation against your cards at *cavagnole*;[49] all this in a tone quite unheard of here and maintained with equally surprising moderation. But my Queen, my excessive chatter is not to be tolerated. I will spare you my metaphysics. To reply on that matter, I would have to know more precisely what you mean by "nature" and "proof." It would seem to me that whatever serves as principle or as a rule of conduct is not on a par with the proven, but is none the less customary. Farewell, my Queen, that is enough for now.

Voltaire was one of Madame du Maine's long standing visitors,[50] but from 1746 to 1749 he was particularly pressing in his visits to the little court. Between the end of October and the beginning of November 1747, shortly after this correspondence between Madame de Staal and Madame du Deffand, and after the regrettable episode at Fontainebleau in which he and Madame du Châtelet were the protagonists, he immediately went into hiding at Anet. In the palace where Louis XV and his court had taken up residence on 14 October, Voltaire quietly suggested in English to *la belle Emilie* who was losing nearly a thousand louis at gambling, that she abandon the game since she was playing with cardsharpers. The advice did not pass unnoticed and Voltaire, concerned for the consequences of his indiscretion, and mindful of the wrath of the great, ordered his carriage in the middle of the night and fled to Anet. He remained in his apartment with the blinds drawn during the day and came out only at dead of night to sup in the duchesse du Maine's apartments.

"Every night, at about two o'clock, as soon as Madame du Maine had retired and sent everyone away, he went down to her bedroom. A footman set up a little table in the space between the bed and the wall and brought Voltaire's supper. These delicious hours passed equally swiftly for both. Madame du Maine . . . told Louis XV's future historian of a thousand intrigues at court which she had seen from close to, but in which she had not been involved . . . After supper Voltaire read a chapter of a story or a novel which he had written to entertain the princess."[51]

So, almost as a joke, *La vision de Babouc, Scarmentado, Memnon* — later to become *Zadig* — and *Micromégas* saw the light of day. Voltaire and Madame du Châtelet's unexpected arrival at Anet — shortly before the flight from Versailles — provided a delicious subject for conversation of which Madame de Staal immediately took advantage.

As practised in self-control as she was in irony, Madame de Staal could not but smile at the lack of moderation which characterised *la belle Emilie,* and above all, she who was obliged to employ her intelligence merely to survive, could not help being irritated by so emphatic an announcement of an intellectual vocation. Madame de Staal entirely trusted her friend's reactions — and not on this point alone. She echoed Madame du Deffand;[52] "When the body is free from pain and the mind is at peace, one must consider oneself happy."[53] How then could two people entrenched in the negative belief of happiness as an absence of ill, sympathise with Madame du Châtelet's existential triumphalism? It is enough to consider the aggressive formula in the opening passages of her *Discours sur le bonheur,* written by Madame du Châtelet around 1747, in which traditional, personal elements become part of her philosophical creed: "To be happy one must be free from prejudice, virtuous, in good health, one must have leanings and passions and one must be susceptible to illusion . . ."[54]

Madame du Deffand's ferocity only echoed Madame de Staal's denigrating irony. The *marquise's* dislike of Voltaire's companion inspired one of her most extraordinary portraits.

"Imagine a tall, dry woman with a highly-coloured complexion, a narrow face and pointed nose, that is *la belle Emilie.* She is so pleased with her appearance that she overlooks nothing in an attempt to make the most of it. Curls, pompoms, jewels, paste, there is a profusion of everything. But as she wishes, despite nature, to be beautiful, and despite poverty, to be magnificent, in order to have the luxuries, she is obliged to go without necessities, like chemises and other such trifles.

"She was born with a certain intelligence; the desire to appear cleverer than she is caused her to prefer the study of the most abstract science to more agreeable subjects. She thinks by such unusualness to gain a great reputation and a definite superiority over all other women.

"She did not limit herself to this ambition, she wanted to become a princess and she became one—not by the grace of God, nor by the King's grace, but by her own. This idiocy passed like the rest and it has become so normal to think of her as a princess of the theatre, that the fact that she is a lady of birth has almost been forgotten.

"Madame works so hard at seeming to be what she is not, that it is no longer possible to know what she really is. Perhaps even her failings are unnatural; they may depend on her pretensions. Her lack of consideration on her princely condition; her dryness on her scholarship; and her thoughtlessness on her beauty.

"However famous she were, Madame du Ch. . . would not be satisfied unless she were fêted; and she has even achieved this by becoming Voltaire's official lady-friend. He lends lustre to her life and it is to him that she will owe immortality."[55]

But we may suspect that the widespread dislike which Madame du Châtelet seemed to provoke among her contemporaries could not be attributed to her pretension and whimsicality alone. Her association with Voltaire may well have caused bewilderment and irritation and provoked someone as different from the *marquise* as Madame Geoffrin to write: "... Voltaire and the du Châtelet woman ... are both more ridiculous than words can say, and are hated and despised as they deserve. I predict that in ten years time they will have nowhere to lay their heads."[56] Quite indifferent to ridicule, the two old lovers flaunted a picturesque and unusual relationship in which they appeared to pay no attention to others. Their normal behaviour seems to have been more or less as the abbé Le Blanc described it to his friend La Chaussée. "The philosophers and lunatics behaved as usual and did not for an instant concern themselves with the others."[57]

This perhaps shocked a society which whilst morally totally unscrupulous, remained conformist in its obsession with style. Even the profound nature of their liaison failed to conform to contemporary fashion, pre-dating rather the modern literary couple. By this time the love affair was over, and Voltaire and *la belle Emilie* seemed, with single-minded egocentricity, to make use of the advantages of their relationship. Although both were driven by obsessive personal ambition, they were each ready to support the other with unreserved admiration, and together they presented a front of total solidarity.

But this woman whom Madame du Deffand and Madame de Staal describe as so sure of herself, so arid, and so entirely preoccupied with her own prestige, unlike the two friends "knew complete happiness and the ravages of passion,"[58] and died, two years later, a victim to her feelings. At the tragic and farcical end of her life—she died giving birth to the daughter of a much younger man who did not love her—Madame du Châtelet for ever indifferent to ridicule, came courageously face to face with the female destiny which Madame du Staal and Madame du Deffand had rejected.

Even if Madame du Deffand was not responsible for some anonymous verses[59] written on the death of *la belle Emilie,* Voltaire's letter to her, written to express his misery and in ignorance of such malice, has an added terrible slant in the light of her merciless portrait.

VOLTAIRE TO MADAME DU DEFFAND   *10 September 1749*

Madame, I have just watched a woman die who was my friend for twenty years and who really loved you. Two days before that woeful death, she spoke to me of the pleasure she would have in seeing you in Paris on her next journey. I begged Monsieur le Président Hénault to tell you of a confinement which seemed so curious and so happy. There was a long paragraph dedicated to you in his letter. She asked me to write to you and I felt I had carried out my duty in writing to Monsieur le Président Hénault. That unfortunate little girl of whom she was delivered and who caused her death did not interest me greatly. Alas, Madame, we turned the event into a joke and it was in such a disastrous vein that I wrote on her instructions to her friends. If anything could add to the horrible situation in which I find myself, it would be to have taken so light-heartedly an adventure, the outcome of which will poison the rest of my miserable life. I did not write to tell you of her confinement and I write to announce her death. I turn to the tenderness of your heart in my despair. I am being dragged to Cirey with Monsieur du Châtelet. From there I will return to Paris, not knowing what will become of me, and hoping soon to join her. Allow me on arrival, the painful consolation of speaking to you about her and of weeping at your feet for a woman who, for all her weaknesses, had a respectable soul.

During the summer of 1747 Madame de Staal had kept Madame du Deffand in touch with the daily life of the little court of Sceaux with a wealth of correspondence. Unlike *la belle Emilie* the two friends could not allow themselves the luxury of overlooking what happened around them or of disregarding the code of *bienséances,* for they could only hope to defend their fragile position as single, penniless women by a perfect knowledge of the rules and a subtle interpretation of events.

MADAME DE STAAL TO MADAME DU DEFFAND   *Anet, 20 August 1747*

You are not well and you lead a sad life. That vexed me, my Queen. I would like you to make your journey to Montmorency;[60] although it may not be very cheerful, at least it is a diversion; here that only adds to our ennui: the ebb and flow of the tide, taking some of our company away and bringing back others . . .

    Yesterday Madame du Châtelet moved to a third lodging. She could no longer bear the one she had chosen; it was noisy and there was smoke but no fire (I think that could be her emblem). The noise does not inconvenience her at night, so she says, but during the day when she is hard at work it disturbs her ideas. She is at present working on an examination of her principles: an exercise which she repeats every year and without which they might escape and perhaps go so far away that she would be unable to recapture a single one. I truly believe that her head is a prison for them rather than their birthplace. It's a case of watching carefully over them. She prefers the healthy air of such an occupation to all other entertainment and persists in appearing only at nightfall. Voltaire has composed some pretty verse which to some extent makes up for their unusual behaviour.

I am delighted that you are happier about your apartment; I would like it even more should you be so about your health. It is too kind of you to have worried about mine. Rest assured, my Queen, that I am as strong as an ox.

Her Serene Highness, whom you did not want to write to you in person, charges me to send you sweet messages on her behalf, and to say especially how much she would like to see you. How anxious I am, my Queen, that this woman[61] should be happily confined and that Lassay may bring you that we might have you here for a few days at least.

I have partly distributed your greetings and will complete the task; they were gratefully and graciously received. You may not be pleased with all your friends, but I am very pleased, my Queen, that there are at least some who are all right. As for those who can only be caught in full flight, it is just as well to console oneself in their absence and not get too upset.

More fortunate than Madame du Châtelet, Voltaire was given what had been Sainte-Aulaire's room which provided an excuse for a delightful madrigal:

> *J'ai la chambre de Sainte-Aulaire*
> *Sans en avoir les agréments*
> *Peut-être à quatre-vingt-dix ans*
> *J'aurais le coeur de sa bergère;*

Il faut tout attendre du temps,
Et surtout du désir de plaire.[62]

Irony was not merely a social weapon for Madame de Staal, it was above all one of the few means of self-expression available to her, and the only way in which she could, at least internally, distance herself from a life of servitude. Her friendship with Madame du Deffand was probably helpful too as a means of escape. Through the sympathy with which she followed and encouraged her more fortunate friend's progress towards emancipation, she may have experienced indirectly the independence which she had had to renounce herself. Not long before, Madame du Deffand had decided to rent rooms in the convent of Saint-Joseph. For years, as we shall see, she had to put up with makeshift accommodation—the small apartment in Rue du Beaune and then sharing with her brother, the abbé at the Sainte-Chapelle, but the desire for a degree of permanency and the hope of creating in her turn, a social centre, pushed her towards this important decision. A decision which was not to be taken lightly. One of the most urgent problems was the somewhat delicate one of how, with a good grace, to refuse the duchesse du Maine's demands without giving the impression of a betrayal and without risking a disagreeable breach. The *marquise*'s health troubled her at this time and provided a valid excuse for delaying her visit to Anet.

MADAME DE STAAL TO MADAME DU DEFFAND

Anet, Sunday 27 August 1747

I have just received your letter of 23rd, my Queen. I am extremely vexed that your indisposition has returned. I always want to tell myself that you are rid of it, but I see with sorrow that I am wrong; but I am very glad that you did not suffer.

An interruption called me down. I have just thanked her Serene Highness on your behalf for the box. She showed me a letter from the Président with which she is very pleased, at the same time she was very cross to hear that you have been ill. Like me, she thinks that with the indisposition over, you should be safe for a while and that you should take the opportunity to come and see us. But Lassay— Madame de La Guiche's confinement! You may as well try to drink the sea. Could you not persuade the Président who moves around so willingly, to make a little trip to see us and to bring you with him? That would be delightful. Do your very best: no one could be more wanted than you.

I wrote to you on Thursday that our du Châtelets were leaving the following day and that the play would be performed that evening. All that happened. I can only describe Boursouffle vaguely. Mademoiselle de La Cochonnière played her extravagant role so perfectly that I really enjoyed it. But Vanture only invested his own complacency in Boursouffle who demanded so much more. He acted naturally in a play in which everything needs to be as far-fetched as the subject. Pâris played the part of Maraudin as a gentleman, when the name alone expresses the character. Motel played the baron de La Cochonnière well; d'Etissac was a knight, and Duplessis a valet. It was all quite good and one can say that the farce was well performed. The author adorned it with a prologue, a part which he recited himself and excellently, with our friend du Four, who, without this brilliant performance, could not come to terms with being Madame Barbe: she was unable to tolerate the simple dress which her part demanded, just like the principal actress[63] who showed a greater concern for her appearance than for the play and who came on to the stage with all the glitter and in all the elegant attire of a court lady. Voltaire had a bone to pick with her on this point; but she is the sovereign and he the slave. I am most displeased by their departure, although worn out by the various demands made on me by Madame du Châtelet.

So on 24 August 1747 Madame du Maine's long theatrical season was enriched by a new performance in which exceptional actors played a part. *Le Comte de Bursouffle*, an old farce by Voltaire, but whose authorship he continued to deny, was performed for the first time in 1734 in Madame du Châtelet's little theatre at Cirey.

Driven by the insatiable demands of the small court and perhaps, not least, by the desire to give his companion an opportunity to shine, Voltaire revived the play and added a short prologue, the last lines of which reflect the spirit of the undertaking.

> *Allons, soumettons-nous: la résistance est vaine,*
> *Il faut bien s'immoler pour les plaisirs d'Anet.*

Vous n'êtes dans cex lieux, Messieurs, qu'une centaine:
Vous me garderez le secret.[64]

Meanwhile Madame du Maine's impatience for Madame du Deffand's company increased daily and it became more and more difficult for the *marquise* to refuse. Even the endlessly agreeable Président with years of loyalty to Sceaux behind him, had become less attentive, although he certainly still played a part in society. To judge from the honest assessment of life at Sceaux which Hénault was preparing for his *Mémoires,* he too must have found the last years of the little court very melancholy: "... I have spent nearly twenty years there and depending on my good fortune, I have suffered there from highs and lows, contradictions and constraints. I hope that God will forgive me all the compliments I have paid in mediocre verse. Were I so unfortunate as to be survived by these miserable offerings, this *princesse* would be thought of as beauty personified: Venus floating on water, and what was meant for the charm of her conversation would be applied to her face. Madame la duchesse du Maine was the oracle of the little court. No one could be more intelligent, more eloquent, more waggish, nor more genuinely courteous: but at the same time, no one could be more unjust, more haughty or more tyrannical."[65] The Président's lack of solicitude could not even be excused on grounds of his excessive devotion to Madame du Deffand who in her turn used the difficulty of finding travelling companions as a pretext. The duchesse du Maine was in danger of putting her finger on the disagreeable truth.

MADAME DE STAAL TO MADAME DU DEFFAND

Anet, Wednesday, 30 August 1747

I had hoped to receive news from you yesterday, my Queen. If I hear nothing tomorrow, I will be quite anxious for you. Our *princesse* has written to the Président to invite him to come here and to bring you with him, of which you are doubtless aware? I did what I could to dissuade her from such action which may be fruitless and the failure of which will anger her. If your health is favourable and the Président so inclined, it would be delightful. In any case we are reserving a good apartment for you: it is the one which Madame du Châtelet claimed after a thorough examination of the house. There will be rather fewer pieces of furniture than she had there, since she robbed all the apartments through which she passed to furnish that one. Six or seven tables were found there: she needs them in all sizes. Large ones on which to spread her papers; solid ones to support her personal effects; more delicate ones for pompoms and jewels. And all this fine arrangement did not guarantee her against an accident like the one which happened to Philippe II when, after a night spent writing, a bottle of ink was spilt on his dispatches. The lady did not attempt to imitate that Prince's moderation, because he had been writing only on affairs of state; whereas for her it was algebra which had been spoiled and which was far more difficult to copy out.

That is enough on this subject now, there is no more to say; but I will add just one more word and then it will be finished. The day after their departure I received a four page letter with a note in the same envelope announcing an appalling confusion. Monsieur Voltaire has mislaid his play, forgotten to collect the parts and lost the prologue: I am charged with finding everything, with sending the prologue as soon as possible, but not by post because "it would be copied," with keeping the parts for fear of the same misadventure, and with placing the play "behind a hundred locks." I would have thought a simple latch enough to protect that treasure! I duly carried out my orders properly . . .

Voltaire was only too justified in fearing the tricks and manipulations of people, libraries or actors who were interested in procuring the play at whatever the cost, to publish or produce it abroad; for all the precautions which Madame de Staal claimed as exaggerated were useless in preventing the manuscript of *le Comte de Boursouffle* from being stolen from Voltaire . . . As soon as he heard that the *Comédie-Italienne* was about to present his *Comte de Boursouffle,* Voltaire fell into a passion and felt—or simulated the greatest indignation . . . On the very day of the first performance, he wrote to d'Argental from Ferney: "Is it true that at the *Comédie-Italienne* they are acting a charade called *le Comte de Boursouffle* under my name? Justice! Justice! Heavenly powers prevent this profanity, do not allow a name that you have always deigned to love to be prostituted in a bill at the *Comédie-Italienne.* I imagine that it is easy to forbid them in Paris from publicly imputing to a poor author a play for which he is not guilty."[66]

A man of a thousand truths; Voltaire was able by means of his dramatic temperament to reconcile his numerous contradictions. With the persuasiveness and adaptability of a great actor, he donned in turn masks to alter his personality. So Madame de Staal's entertaining and subtle attempt in her letters to Madame du Deffand to capture Voltaire in the part of a courtier poet and tyrannised lover, amounts merely to an affectation. The two friends would doubtless have been disconcerted had they been able to read Madame du Châtelet's "slave's" hurried dismissal of the expedition, and had they known what really mattered most to him at that moment. The note is amorous and written in Italian, the language of Arcadia.

VOLTAIRE TO MADAME DENIS   {ca 25 August 1747}

I was ill at Anet, my dearest, but I hope to recover my health with you. As soon as I returned I ran to your house to regain my strength. Today I will see you, today I will find the only consolation that can sweeten the bitterness of my life. Nature, which gave me the softest heart, forgot to give me a stomach. I cannot digest but I can love. I love you, I will love you till I die. I kiss you a thousand times, my virtuous love. You write Italian better than I do. You deserve to be a fellow of the Academy of "La Crusca." My heart and my cock salute you most tenderly. This evening I will certainly see you.

Once Madame du Châtelet and Voltaire had left and Madame de Staal had recorded the last eccentricities of that extraordinary couple, there was nothing left to distract her from the permanent monotony of life around her. Although no longer capable of real surprise, she wondered ceaselessly at the weariness and repetition of a life whose principal object was entertainment. Necessity had long since forced her to take refuge in renunciation and in closing in on herself as the only means of preserving her integrity. To this extent, she took the opposite path to Madame du Maine who obstinately sought what she did not value, but she also took quite a different path to Madame du Deffand. For Madame de Staal, indifference was something to be achieved, gained by detachment and renunciation; for Madame du Deffand it was already there as a void which needed filling, and as a lack of interest in others which, however, did not prevent her from needing their presence.

Even ennui, the great scourge of Sceaux which obsessed Madame du Maine as much as it did Madame du Deffand, was not a real threat for Madame de Staal. If ennui is born of unfulfilled expectation and absence of pleasure, how can it attack where there are no expectations and where pleasure has wisely been dispensed with?

MADAME DE STAAL TO MADAME DU DEFFAND

Anet, Sunday 17 September 1747

... the desire for company increases every day and I foresee that if an apartment is always kept empty, the absent guest, whoever he might be, will be missed. The powerful, by dint of spreading themselves, grow so thin that you can see the daylight through them: the contemplation of them is an interesting study. I know of nothing which leads more to philosophy. I accept yours of not wishing to be without one's habitual comforts; but I disapprove of anguishing over consideration for one's own comfort, which I often see. I see too, that delicacy increases with use, and that the desire to be comfortable produces discomfort. Since I no longer want anything, I am happier than if I had had everything I have ever desired: but who knows if I will persist in this happy condition? Not I, but I won't concern myself about it in advance ...

Anet, Thursday 21 September 1747

Your said disgrace, my Queen, is none other than the sorrow that you are not here. You could not come: but perhaps it will be thought that you did not much want to, and not all your sweetness will make up for this failing. I also suspect that the fear of having one fewer guest by allowing you an extra apartment, may interfere with the affection in which you are held, for our ruling passion is for a crowd. Perhaps this passion grows and strengthens as one finds fewer resources within oneself ...

I have not been bored here at all: it is the intervals of pleasure which give rise to ennui; but one no longer feels it once one has grown accustomed to it. You are proof of that. ... Let us not spread

ourselves but rather close in on ourselves: you lose nothing from the
point of view of the spirit; by allowing it less room you give it greater
strength: the fire and charm of yours will never abandon you . . .

In her delaying tactics Madame du Deffand had underestimated the
duchesse's character, and had forgotten that she "passionately wants what
she desires; no excuse appears to satisfy her when one is not obedient
to her will."[67] For her part, Madame de Staal overestimated her ability
to remain detached and her resistance to bullying. She was once more
overwhelmed and humiliated by Madame du Maine's violence and once
again she brought flattery to her defence.

MADAME DE STAAL TO MADAME DU DEFFAND

Friday, 13 October 1747

Nothing can equal the state of surprise and sorrow, my Queen, into
which we have fallen here on learning that you have been to stay
with Madame la duchesse de Modena. A passionate and jealous lover
would have been able to suffer the most suspicious behaviour more
calmly than yours is tolerated here. "You are going to dedicate
yourself to another, abandon the rest; that is what awaited us, therefore are we the picture of misery, the pain of which we had hoped to
be rid will be revived because of you, and ever the same stumbling
block: it is a truly cruel destiny, etc." I said what was necessary to
restore calm; we wished to hear nothing. Although I should no longer
be surprised, this scene managed to astound me. Come, I beseech
you, my Queen, and reassure us against such alarm. Do not praise
the person in question and, above all, do not speak of her grief for
that would be taken as a reproach. I understand that you may be
tempted to abandon so rough a path; but consider that if you do,
everything will fall back on me whom you will have deserted. We are
already very ill-disposed with regard to me, and I entreat you, under
the present circumstances, to lend yourself to what is necessary to
improve the state of affairs. If then, you cannot endure it (for I feel
how difficult it is), you will release yourself gently without a quarrel.
I do not demand of your friendship that you make your life disagreeable and prickly: suffice it that mine is. In sharing my troubles, far
from relieving them, you will make them twofold. We are leaving

tomorrow morning and will arrive as I told you. I passionately desire to find you on our arrival. I never needed you so much, my Queen.

The correspondence with Madame de Staal ends on this dramatic note. We do not know whether Madame du Deffand rallied to her friend's appeal, but her relations with the court at Sceaux were certainly steadily maintained until Madame du Maine's death in 1752. Madame de Staal, whose sight was soon to be afflicted by a serious disease, died two years before her patroness, and so her miseries came to an end. It must indeed have been a liberation for one who had long since relinquished any hold on life and who could write to a friend: "I am deteriorating in every way but my judgement is still clear enough for me to realise it, and I do so without sorrow. I am quite pleased to be stupid; I no longer feel very much, except for bodily needs; it is true that they increase as the spiritual ones diminish, but they are not very many, and when all is said and done, I find that there are advantages."[68]

Not surprisingly Madame de Staal's demise in no way affected Madame du Maine's usual attitude. "She is seen to learn with indifference of the death of people who made her weep if they were a quarter of an hour late for the gambling tables or for a walk."[69] Still more terrible is the suspicion that Madame de Staal's life was unnecessarily sacrificed to the demands of Madame du Maine's egoism. To judge by the following extract from a letter of Montesquieu's, dated 6 November 1751, the death of her lady companion did not seem to have affected the *duchesse*'s way of life very much. "I wanted to spend three days at Anet to show Madame la duchesse du Maine that a six months' absence did not prevent me from remembering the honour she had accorded me by inviting me on my return. The three days passed, and eight days passed without my being master of my own movements; there is a streak of authority in this royal blood, requiring obedience without which there can be no mercy. So here I am for several more days at the bedside of a becolded, feverish princess, and fawning upon two or three antique objects whose wrinkles date them."[70]

IV

Madame du Deffand's "Salon"

MADAME DU MAINE'S TYRANNY seemed almost able to conquer time so that the life of the little court seemed petrified by some sinister spell into an unchanging backdrop. But she nevertheless realised that outside her small domain, time did move on and the scene was indeed radically changing. When the Grand Condé's grand-daughter asked to be admitted to the Tuesday suppers, given in Paris by the Marquise de Lambert, it was with an exaggerated humility which amounted to more than a sovereign's coquetry. It indicated that she recognised the strength of a new reality: the literary *"salon."*[1]

The list of those who frequented the Tuesdays at the Hôtel de Nevers includes many who were at Sceaux: Fontenelle, Sainte-Aulaire, La Motte; Montesquieu, Hénault, Madame du Deffand, Madame de Staal and so forth. Yet in such different surroundings these same people found they had quite other parts to play. An entirely new social code replaced the etiquette which ruled Sceaux and other princely palaces and which subordinated the crowd of guests to the whim and the glory of their royal hosts. The *salon* was devoted not to worldly power, but to communication. The host's prestige came not from dominating the guests, but from allowing them equal rights and free expression. Men of letters were no longer there as subordinate entertainers; society instead provided them with the weft and woof necessary to develop and diffuse their ideas. Madame de Lambert's *salon* was the first where writers as such met aristocrats in an alliance whose importance was captured by d'Alembert: "Some bring knowledge and understanding, others bring that elegance of manner and that urbanity which even a man of worth

... needs to acquire ... Society people came away more enlightened and men of letters more agreeable."[2]

This association was to continue outside the drawing-rooms of the Hôtel de Nevers and was to be perpetuated throughout the century. In the chapter dedicated to men of letters and society, Duclos in his *Considérations sur les moeurs de ce siècle* (1751) roughly outlines d'Alembert's observations in the meeting of intellectuals and society. "Both sides have profited from this liaison. Society people have cultivated their minds, formed their taste and acquired new pleasures. The men of letters have gained no less advantage. They have found consideration; they have perfected their taste, polished their minds, softened their manners and on several matters acquired enlightenment such as they would not have found in books."[3]

By the mid-eighteenth century the process of integration between the two worlds seemed irreversible. Duclos again observed: "Manners are to Paris what the spirit of government is to London. They blend and level conditions of men which the State would subordinate. In London all orders live side by side because all the citizens need each other; common interest draws them together. Pleasure has the same effect in Paris; those who are interested in pleasure come together, but with this difference, that equality which is good when it springs from a principle of government, is a great evil when it is derived only from manners, because that is the result of corruption."[4]

The intellectuals used the *salons* to communicate their ideas; for society they provided conversation. In a country where the press is controlled but where freedom of speech is more or less absolute, the intellectuals need society to disseminate their ideas, to support their writings, to mediate with the authorities, to sound and guide public opinion which has only too often been described as a century's real protagonist. In his introductory speech to the *Académie Française* in 1775, Malsherbes remarked: "The public displays an avid curiosity about things to which it was formerly totally indifferent. A tribunal has been set up which is independent of, but respected by all the authorities, which evaluates talent and pronounces on merit in all spheres; and in an enlightened century, a century in which every citizen may speak to the entire nation through the press, those who have the talent to instruct, or the gift of moving men's hearts, men of letters in a word, are to a scattered public what the orators of Rome or Athens were to an assembly."[5]

So society, in the grips of a crisis of traditional values, needed the intellectuals to find new points of reference, and above all to prevent boredom. Thanks to a reciprocal commitment, intellectuals and society alike were drawn to the same topics. Writers couched science and philosophy, ethics and economics in conversation and anecdote. Society proved to be miraculously omnivorous so that even Rousseau was impressed. But conversation was primarily an art so that eventually the content came to be of secondary importance. "The type of well-being provoked by animated conversation does not depend precisely on the subject of that conversation,"[6] Madame de Stael writes of the Parisian *salons* in her youth; and she tells how after the Revolution Volney met some French *émigrés* in America who travelled great distances simply for the pleasure of meeting each other, to talk and preserve that most typical part of their national culture, for in the eighteenth century "there [was] more conversation in France than in any other country in the world."[7] And it is "a kind of conversation" d'Alembert wrote from Potsdam in 1763 "known only in France and which, once known, becomes a necessity."[8]

Conversation has the complexity and the uniqueness of art. It evaporates—or becomes dull—in the abbé Delille's attempts to celebrate it in verse[9] and often loses its fragile grace in the letters and *Mémoires* which provide a continuation of it and a written record. To come to life on the page, it needs to be re-interpreted through the art of a true writer. In his *Essais sur la nécessité et sur les moyens de plaire* of 1738, Paradis de Moncrif takes all this into account: "But how to define in all its facets, that type of genius which depends less on genre and on the breadth of knowledge a man possesses than on the more or less delicate feeling with which he uses both? A man who uses his wit never better than when he appears to ignore it or not to notice that he possesses it, who being constantly transported hither and thither, has but an almost imperceptible instant in which to grasp his rightful treasure, the choice of which is sometimes as happy as it is sudden? This talent, so rich in ways of pleasing, almost entirely conceals its own make up. It can be sensed, but it is almost impossible to say precisely what it is."[10]

But Morellet attempts a list of what to avoid in the interests of a good conversation[11] and stresses the necessity for a master of ceremonies: "I will say frankly that I have only known consistently good conversation where the lady of the house was ... at least a kind of central figure in the gathering."[12] Voltaire suggested that these gatherings were always "presided over by a woman who in her declining beauty shines by her awakening wit."[13] But women's search for a cultural role was not a mere aside, but central to both life in society and the relationship to the family. "We are going to visit Madame . . . ; to dine with Madame . . . ," and so forth. These were all significant new formulas in the language of the time[14]—women were also at the centre of intellectual life. The Goncourts' description is famous: "Women in the eighteenth century were the patrons of literature. By the attention they accorded it, by their interest in it, by the entertainment they ask of it, by the protection they grant it, they attach it to their person, attract it to their sex, direct and govern it. Women are the writers' muses and their advisors, women are the judges and the sovereign public of literature . . . Thought will find no expression, intelligence will take no shape, wit will conceive of no tone, ennui itself will find no disguise if not as homage to this all powerful mistress who decides on the value of a work and on the standing of writers. See how they rule the theatre: their whim decides the fate of a first production. They decide on an author's triumph or failure. They, more than La Morlière, dominate an audience. Their applause can save a struggling tragedy and with one yawn they can destroy a successful comedy. It is they who see that plays are performed, who produce them from the writers, who improve them, annotate them, set them before committees, ministers and even the King. It is they who cause *Les Philosophes* and *Figaro* to be staged. Without their patronage, their recommendation, their passion a writer is neither performed, nor applauded, nor even read. Every literary genre, every kind of writer, every pamphlet, every volume, even a masterpiece needs a woman to sign its passport, to begin the publicity . . . Allowances, newspaper privileges, shares in the *Mercure,* every sou and every favour the Minister lets drop, are collected by women for the benefit of their clients."[15]

Salons were the mainstay of cultural life in the eighteenth century but it is hard to make a coherent plan of them. The result would produce some sort of peculiar family tree whereby different autonomous groups came together and dissolved at different moments, but often developed along the same lines for various lengths of time. Between each of these groups or families there might be sympathy, hatred, rivalry or collaboration, or one might be the heir to another, but none could count on the exclusivity of their members who, for the most part, circulated freely between them.

Regular guests, rather than the ensemble of visitors gave a social circle its tone. Every *salon* was typified by a nucleus of *habitués*. Of course these *habitués* might sometimes visit other *salons* where they would meet a greater or smaller number of permanent guests with whom they would combine to form an original group. So every *salon* had its own unmistakable character, and in every one each *habitué* presented himself a little differently. Thus the same elements regrouped produced something new and inimitable. Under Madame Geoffrin's roof the *philosophes* were ever ready to obey her "voilà qui est bien" ["that is enough: stop"],[16] whilst passionately discussing grand cultural themes in Julie de Lespinasse's apartment, and proclaiming atheism and materialism with the baron d'Holbach. But with Madame du Deffand rigorous frivolity was the order of the day.

Usually a *salon* was held regularly on the same days once or twice a week, but visiting also took place outside these regular hours. A tight and permanently interacting social network was made possible by the lady of the house's almost professional self-sacrifice and by the stability of social life under the *ancien régime*. Dinner and supper[17] provided the two central points of *salon* life. They might be refined and sumptuous meals with, for instance, Hénault or the baron d'Holbach or systematically austere like Madame Geoffrin's famous spinach omelette, whereas Grimod de la Reynière provided extravaganzas of gastronomic and intellectual delight. A whole gamut of nuances which partly escape us influenced the choice between dinner and supper.

"No house in Paris is rich enough to offer dinner and supper. The law dines and high finance sups. Noblemen do not dine until half past three," wrote Mercier,[18] but his explanation is too general as the same house often adopted both practices alternately.[19] Dinners were perhaps more intimate and more private but sometimes, as on the marquise de Lambert's Tuesdays, or with Madame Geoffrin, they were followed by an afternoon of readings or of literary discussion.

In a study of the subject, Jean-Claude Bonnet writes: "It seems that there was no uniformity of practise in eighteenth-century Paris, comparable to that of the nineteenth century. A meal without precise rules has not yet become society's sovereign and exclusive formality . . . This is the era of the *salon* when one supped with intimates and gave pride of place to the exchange of ideas and friendly communication; it is not yet the era of the dining-room ruled over by the mistress of the house who imposes a strict system of meals as well as a rigid guest list."[20] Jean-

Paul Aron confirms that although already established architecturally by the middle of the eighteenth century, the private house dining-room was an invention of the post Revolution bourgeoisie. It is discussed in the *Encyclopédie*, and mentioned, for instance, in the inventory of Madame du Deffand's house, to be found in her Will. But at the time dining-rooms had no special furniture.[21] The tables off which people ate were used for various purposes, they were laid at the last moment and varied in size and quantity according to the number of guests. On reception days, and a little before meal times, the duc de Choiseul's steward would come into the drawing-room where all the guests were gathered, sum up the number present at a glance and then have the right number of the tables prepared within a few minutes.[22]

Bonnet tends to see the meal as being part of the continuum of social life, but without the precise characteristics which by the nineteenth century had made of it an occasion in its own right. Walpole rather confirms this. During a journey to France in 1765 he entertained his English correspondents with what were for him the most exotic and picturesque aspects of Parisian life. His letters speak of tremendous filth in the French capital and of the monotony of French interiors with their small rooms, white and gold paint, inevitable looking-glasses, and of meal times which by the standards of the English aristocracy, were rather early. Dinner was at half past two instead of four o'clock—for late risers it risked coinciding with breakfast—and supper was at ten instead of at midnight. In a letter to Lady Suffolk, Walpole emphasised how naturally supper fitted in with card playing, conversation and handwork, which all combined to constitute life in society: "They constantly tap a rubber before supper, get up in the middle of the game, finish it after a meal of three courses and a dessert, add another rubber to it and then take their knotting bags,[23] draw together into a circle and start some topic of literature or irreligion and chat till it is time to go to bed—that is till you would think it time to get up again."[24]

The *habitués* of the various *salons* had no need of invitation, but a small postal service instituted in 1753 made it possible, with three deliveries in one day, for Parisians to send and receive messages.[25]

In about 1747 Madame du Deffand was ready to experiment on her own with the formula for a *salon* which she had patiently devised throughout the nomadic years whilst devoting her talents to the prestige of others. Both in the small apartment in the rue de Beaune, and with her brother, the abbé at the Sainte Chapelle as well as in stolen hours at Sceaux, Madame du Deffand had made many encouraging experiments.

Madame de Lambert had been dead for over fifteen years and those who attended the famous literary Tuesdays at the Hôtel de Nevers had migrated to Madame de Tencin in the rue St. Honoré. Thus the *habitués* of an aristocratic lady imbued with the culture of the *Grand Siècle* and concerned with her personal glory and honesty—in Racine's sense of both words—had now gathered round an ex-canoness who, having cast off the veil, had distinguished herself as a libertine and given herself to political intrigue, gambling and blackmail. She had abandoned an illegitimate son on the steps of the Church of Saint-Jean le Rond (this son was christened Jean le Rond and later changed his name to d'Alembert); and her last lover committed suicide in her house hoping to blame her for his death. Subtle Marivaux, proud Montesquieu, precious Fontenelle, La Motte, the abbé de Saint-Pierre, the abbé Prevost and many others allowed themselves to become "beasts" in her "seraglio," to be treated with simplicity, good-humour and generosity, but above all to be stimulated by the open intelligence of the lady of the house. Voltaire alone remained permanently hostile. In a famous passage from his *Mémoires,* Marmontel describes these reunions which are more reminiscent of a men's club with the members gathered round a billiard table than of a *salon* presided over by a woman. Among those present were some who a few years later would come to be known as *philosophes.* "One arrived ready to play one's part but the desire to be on stage did not always allow the conversation the freedom to follow its easy and natural course. He who could most readily take advantage of the fleeting moment, said his word, told his story or his anecdote, pronounced his maxim or his biting witticism; the talk involved in bringing up a subject was sometimes a little far-fetched. Marivaux's impatience to prove his wit and wisdom was obvious. Montesquieu with greater calm, waited for the ball to be in his court; but he was waiting for it. Mairan watched for an opportunity. Astruc did not deign to wait. Fontenelle alone let it come to him without seeking it, and he used the attention accorded him so soberly that his wit and pretty tales never took more than a moment. Helvétius, attentive and discreet, gathered seeds to sow them again another day."[26]

During its last years Madame de Tencin's *salon* was assiduously frequented by a neighbour—an obscure but rich *bourgeoise*—for whom the ex-canoness had long shown great sympathy. She was a reserved and composed woman, aged about fifty, still with a certain beauty, about whom Madame de Tencin used to say to her close friends: "Do you know what she comes here for? She comes to see what she can garner from my estate."[27] The lady in question was Madame Geoffrin and the succession was to take place in 1749; it was with her that Madame du Deffand would have to cross swords.

Madame du Deffand did attend Madame de Lambert's *salon* where the Président was a regular visitor;[28] but she ignored Madame de Tencin to whom she refers only once in her correspondence, and that, somewhat uncharitably on the occasion of her death. "Madame de Tencin has just died as she lived: she leaves nothing to those whom honour, friendship and humanity would have her benefit."[29] Yet Madame du Deffand had known the Tencins since the far off days of "La Source"—Lord Bolingbroke's country house. She had been friends with Mademoiselle Aïssé, the Circassian slave brought up by Madame Tencin's sister, Madame de Ferriol. She was also linked by time and habit to Madame de Ferriol's two sons, Pont-de-Veyle and Ferriol d'Argental. The omission was certainly not accidental, but was dictated by dislike and stemmed from an old rivalry dating back to the sins of the Regency[30] when both were the mistresses of Philippe d'Orléans. Then, in Saint-Simon's words Madame de Tencin was "passed from the master to the valet."[31] By "valet" he meant the prime minister and later cardinal, Dubois. Did Madame du Deffand remember Madame de Tencin's dislike of Aïssé which amounted almost to persecution? Aïssé herself had never taken part in the dissolute way of life in those far off days, but she had witnessed it. Or was her dislike influenced by Voltaire who despised Madame de Tencin by whom he had never been appreciated? Or again, perhaps the great friendship with d'Alembert which Madame du Deffand nurtured during those years caused her to keep her distance from his unnatural mother. Above all, however, there was a difference of style between the two women: the *salon* which Madame du Deffand was about to hold at Saint-Joseph resembled, if anything, Madame de Lambert's.

For several years Madame du Deffand had been looking for a house. At the outset of her relationship with Hénault, she had installed herself in a modest apartment on the rue de Beaune and then, in about 1740, she went to live with her brother, the abbé and treasurer at the Sainte

Chapelle. Both were temporary measures and compatible with the *marquise*'s nomadic existence, in which she was almost always away, following the duchesse du Maine. But lack of funds and personal freedom did not prevent her from building up an elaborate network of connections: "The number increased and little by little, as she became better known, her house could no longer accommodate them. Supper was served there every evening, and she came to live in St. Joseph's convent."[32]

So, on 22 April 1746, Madame du Deffand could write to Madame d'Aulan: "I send you the news, my dear sister, that I have from St John's Day next, just rented a very pretty apartment at Saint-Joseph. I am very impatient to live there but cannot do so until my furnishings are ready. So I beseech you to do everything you can to see that my stuffs are made and that I receive forthwith my hundred *aunes* of white serge, my seventy of yellow taffeta and my thirty of crimson taffeta. You would make me happy since you would make it possible for me to leave lodgings which I find extremely disagreeable, and it is essential to move during the fine season when the days are long. I am using an upholsterer of Madame la duchesse du Maine's whom she is bringing with her to Anet at the end of July. I am on excellent terms with the abbé; we are separating gladly, but as friends. I think he will be pleased to be alone in his own home and I will be delighted to be in a different neighbourhood and to be obliged to no one. That is all I have to tell you of my situation. I await for you, of your friendship, to do your best to please me."[33]

The community of the *Filles orphelines de Saint-Joseph dites de la Providence*[34] was situated in the rue Saint-Dominique in Saint-Germain-des-Prés, on the site of the present Ministry of Defence. Plate VII of Turgot's *Plan de Paris* drawn seven years before Madame du Deffand moved to the convent shows a vast building constructed around two great courtyards. The one dominated by the chapel with its high cupola and four large windows, was overlooked by that part of the convent used for secular purposes. It had independent access to a small courtyard which opened on to the rue Saint-Dominique, and was separate from the area lived in by the nuns. In it a series of apartments were let, in conformity with widespread practice, to single women — whether widows, separated or unmarried. The advantages of such an arrangement were various: whilst being economical it guaranteed respectability and decorum and provided the possibility of taking part in the life of the community whilst remaining entirely independent. During the course of the century Saint-Joseph welcomed among its distinguished lodgers, the princesse de Talmont, Madame de Genlis, the Pretender to the throne of England, the last of the Stuarts who for three years divided his time between Madame de Vassé's and Mademoiselle de Ferraud's apartments. Madame du Deffand's lodgings were especially fine, having been built for the convent's patroness, Madame de Montespan. Louis XIV's discarded mistress and mother of the duc du Maine retired to the convent, there to forget Versailles and Madame du Maintenon's victory.

The agreement drawn up on 24 April 1747,[35] stipulates a rent of eight hundred livres[36] per annum. The *marquise*'s financial situation, although modest, was no longer so precarious.[37] But Hénault was called on to help with the considerable expense of furnishing the new apartment— a sort of farewell present, it has been said, at the end of a relationship which had lasted for twenty years. But it has to be admitted that where money was concerned, Madame du Deffand was quite unscrupulous.

A rare enthusiasm seems to have possessed the *marquise*: for an instant, this sceptical lady of fifty, after years of a hard, nomadic existence, gave herself over to the feminine pleasure of decorating her own home, perhaps the first real home of her life. The long sought-after apartment in Saint-Joseph was also the crowning achievement of many aspirations—of a repeatedly stifled need for independence, a desire for a personal stage, a yearning for a quieter and more comfortable life, and as a sign of a respectability regained at last.

With great efficiency, the *marquise* supervised the minutest details of the furnishings. The furniture was arranged even before the agreement had been signed and the upholstery materials ordered from Avignon, renowned for its looms. Whilst researching into the Vichy family among the archives of the department of the Drôme, Segur claims to have held in his hand, pinned to a letter, a swatch of the famous buttercup yellow watered silk decorated with flame coloured bows which was to adorn the walls of Madame du Deffand's drawing room,[38] and to be admired by visitors from all over Europe.[39]

After preparation lasting for eighteen months, Madame du Deffand finally moved into Saint-Joseph.

MADAME DU DEFFAND TO MADAME D'AULAN   *30 October 1747*

I must inform you, my dear sister, that I am in my new establishment, and that I have the prettiest lodgings imaginable . . .[40]

MADAME DU DEFFAND TO MADAME D'AULAN   *9 November 1747*

. . . I have been here a fortnight yesterday and am still not free of
workmen. Nothing is as pretty as my apartment and nothing is more
agreeable than my furniture . . .[41]

MADAME DU DEFFAND TO MAUPERTIUS   *21 November 1747*

I have managed (to my great amazement) to leave the Sainte-
Chapelle and to find lodgings at Saint-Joseph. I spent four months
arranging my apartment: I thought I would never see the end of it.
At last it is done and I am perfectly housed with perfect furnishings . . .[42]

The inventory of Madame du Deffand's household made on her death
at the request of her heirs[43] gives us an excellent picture of what it was
like. She occupied rooms on the first floor in a wing adjoining the chapel
with which the apartment communicated directly. The servants' quarters
were on the mezzanine and the ground floor along with the cellar, the
kitchen, the servants' bedrooms, a stable for two horses[44] and the coach-
house for the "berline with three windows, its panels and bodywork
painted grey and lined inside with crimson velvet from Utrecht."[45] On
the fourth floor, in the attics, there were several rooms for dependents
of a higher order, like the secretary Wiart and his wife.

On the first floor, a huge drawing-room lit by two large windows
overlooked the external garden of the convent, on the opposite side of
the building to the rue Saint-Dominique. Over the fireplace, which still
bore the arms of the last resident, Madame de Montespan, hung a large
looking-glass made of two glasses—one superimposed on the other. A
second identical looking-glass hung opposite the fireplace and another,
rather smaller one, decorated the third wall. The predominant colours
were yellow and red and the walls were entirely covered with yellow
watered silk dotted with flame coloured bows. The curtains framing the
windows and covering the doors were made of the same material; there
were six walnut armchairs[46] stuffed with horsehair and upholstered in
red and yellow striped Utrecht velvet, whilst four other armchairs and
four chairs made of dark beechwood were covered in hand-embroidered
cloth with little red flowers on a yellow background. Gone was the

rigidity of Louis XIV's style: the chairs were adapted to a more informal way of life inviting relaxation and confidentiality. They were spread about the room according to the demands of conversation, reading out loud and cards. Although the inventory describes this as the "dining-room," the absence of a suitable table confirms the eighteenth-century usage of the term. Instead there were two little card tables covered in green cloth: one for piquet and the other for écarté. Two chests with brass fittings added the final touches to this elegant, sober decoration.

The guests were not limited to the drawing-room, however, but were welcomed across the threshold of the *marquise*'s adjoining bedroom. Throughout the eighteenth century, the bedroom retained its old function as a reception room and was complementary to the *salon*.

An engraving by Cochin, *Les chats angoras de la marquise du Deffand* gives us a faithful picture[47] of the old bedroom in the rue de Beaune, but the one in Saint-Joseph can only be imagined from the inventory. The furnishings were more varied and richer than in the *salon*. The wall hangings were the same, but were embellished by a framework of gilded rods. Over the fireplace hung an ogival looking-glass even larger and more expensive than the others. Lit by a five-branched crystal chandelier mounted in gilded bronze, and by four candelabra each with three branches, this room which also looked out over the garden, was furnished according to the "fleeting" and impermanent tastes of the age.[48] There were twelve cabriole armchairs, five *à la reine*, an ottoman, some shelves and numerous small tables for various purposes: ingeniously worked little pieces to be used for cards or for reading, or as dressing tables, and which could be transformed into writing tables, or three legged stands with shelves for books or ornaments. There were *guéridons* and little tables of every kind, objects with which the great cabinet makers of Louis XV's and Louis XVI's reigns crowned the decorative arts of the century. The bed—in the Polish fashion—was draped in the same material as the walls. Here, as in the *salon*, apart from a touch of green on one or two armchairs, red and yellow triumphed.

This elegant stage was rarely empty. Madame du Deffand herself has left a definitive description of some of those who crowded on to it at dinner time, in the afternoon, for supper and in the long evenings after the Opéra or the theatre.[49] The literary portrait or character sketch which had already enjoyed a great vogue in the seventeenth century was based on the classical belief in the immutability of character. In the first half of the eighteenth century it became a parlour game—an exercise in psychological virtuosity, a means of flattery or defamation, and an amusing puzzle to solve.[50] The character sketch is essentially a psychological one wherein physical characteristics are used only "to suggest the psychological diagnosis."

The *marquise* was a recognised adept at the game which was fashionable not only at Sceaux, but also in the Parisian circle in which she moved.[51] To be able to write and to improvise verse was, as we have seen, a social necessity which presented no problem for Madame du Deffand; but the "portrait" was a much more personal means of expression for her, to which she was suited not only by her intuition and the confidence with which she "unmasked"[52] people but because of her vast experience of human nature. The most direct route into Madame du Deffand's *salon* and to a reconstruction of its nucleus, is undoubtedly through her gallery of portraits, particularly since a love of social life was typical of all the people described.

Although he himself received in his elegant residence in the rue Saint-Honoré,[53] and although he was often absorbed by his duties at Versailles,[54] the Président Hénault remained a constant in Madame du Deffand's life and society. Besides him, the *salon* in Saint-Joseph was presided over by two faithful *habitués,* Antoine de Ferriol, comte de Pont-de-Veyle and Jean-Baptiste-Nicolas Formont, both of whom were distinguished by one particular characteristic which made them past-masters in the art of worldliness. They were both prepared to sacrifice their own individuality to the demands of the society in which they moved. In fact the *nécessité de plaire* which governed society forbade anything which might discomfort. Moncrif is convinced of his theory: "Among the most useful principles of everyday exchange, there is one which we cannot recognise too soon, because we must make a habit of adopting it. In fact how many desirable advantages does it bring? It prevents reason from becoming too fierce; and removes the element from *amour propre*; in some way it complements the advantages of intelligence and prevents the jealousy intelligence can provoke; finally it affects our happiness and the happiness of those with whom we live: it consists in ruling our behaviour by the necessity by which we are bound to please."[55]

The dangers of this concept are obvious: such concern for others may make a man untrue to himself and such self-control may stifle his personality. Sometimes the finest exponents of the art, like Madame de Choiseul, were aware of the sacrifices it demanded: "But we wish to please and we must be agreeable; we want respect and must needs appear worthy of it; hence the rules by which we model our characters which are then no more distinct from each other than is our dress."[56] But the moralist could not resign himself with so good a grace to such sacrifice, even though society was a treasure which was unwilling to forgo.[57] For Duclos, the solution to the problem lay in the distinction between *l'homme sociable* and *l'homme aimable,* which demonstrates subtlety of the demarcation line between a positive and a negative interpretation of the necessity to please. The first describes "the qualities required by society: politeness, candour without rudeness; attentiveness without baseness; compliance without flattery; respect without constraint; and above all a heart inclined towards seemliness; thus the *homme sociable* is the citizen *par excellence.* The *homme aimable,* at least the man who is so described today, is quite indifferent to the public good: eager to please in whatever society he finds himself, by choice or by chance and prepared to sacrifice any individual; he loves no one, is loved by no one, pleases everyone and is frequently despised and sought after by the same people. By a strange paradox, he is always concerned with others, but only pleased with himself and finds his happiness in the opinion of others, without exactly considering their esteem which he presumes apparent, or the nature of which he does not understand."[58]

Homme sociable, but with a touch of the *homme aimable,* Jean-Baptiste-Nicolas Formont descended from a rich family of merchants and bankers from Rouen and was the dearest friend of Madame du Deffand with whom he lodged on his frequent visits to Paris. He wrote some literary works which he never bothered to have printed and led an amiable and elegantly epicurean life. A picture of him is preserved in his correspondence with Madame du Deffand and Voltaire both of whom were seduced by the quality of his friendship.

A profoundly indifferent man, lacking in passion, Formont, more than anyone else, could fulfill the requirements of supreme availability where warmth was replaced by courtesy. Madame du Deffand dedicated an elegant character sketch to the man described by Voltaire as "the most indifferent of sages." "Monsieur de Formont's looks do not prepare you for the man within. His face is cold and his bearing lazy, but he has an easy, ready wit and a gay and vivid imagination.

"Such a contrast between appearance and character is rarely seen, which does not make it any more difficult to explain. Wit alone, without passion does not have enough warmth to break through and leave its mark on the outward features. Like Monsieur de Formont, Monsieur de Fontenelle can be taken as an example. The faults in the appearance of both seem to spring from the same cause. Both lack passion, but Monsieur de Formont has a fundamental goodness which recompenses his friends for what he lacks in feeling. He needs no one, but if he believes himself to be needed, he fulfills all the duties of friendship for which at the time he has the necessary concern and sentiment. When no longer needed, he relapses into an indifference in which he will long remain unless a decision is made to take him out of it. But his goodness is always at hand and is manifest in every desirable form. I think one could say that it even comes in the form of love. If something moves him, his emotions are gentle and peaceful; he desires but without importunity or ardour; fear and jealousy are alien to his tastes which are subordinate to liking of others for him. If he notices that he no longer pleases, he makes no further claims. Without vanity, without ambition, without love, I could almost say without friendship, he allows his days to trickle by in idleness and leisure which make him indifferent to the opinions of men and to fortune.

"He sees, examines and judges the human race with the same impartiality with which we judge an opera or a play. Kings and princes, the great and the humble, perhaps even honest men and rascals all seem to him like actors playing their parts more or less well. For him the world is merely an entertainment in which he imagines he has no personal interest. Hence his lack of shyness with more important people than himself and with new acquaintances. He does not think of himself as being on stage, but sees himself in the stalls or a box; it is not, however, that he fails to participate in the play, he warms up and becomes animated when the conversation pleases him and contributes pertinently to it with a gaiety and a light-heartedness which make him the best of companions. And as soon as the moment has passed, he again becomes a spectator and lies back in his armchair with a dreamy, abstracted air, he does not notice that by this lack of attention, he sometimes offends those whom he has just pleased by the attributes of his mind.

"No one is more virtuous, nor could have simpler manners; he excuses everything, forgives everything and his gentleness and quietness are unalterable. Finally, Monsieur Formont is the model of a perfect philosopher and the image of a true friend."[59]

Formont's detachment following a brilliant contribution to the conversation is reminiscent of the behaviour of a more illustrious member of Parisian society who, ten years later, adorned the rival *salons* of Saint-Joseph—the abbé Galiani. "I do not exaggerate in the least when I say that everything was forgotten for the pleasure of listening to him, sometimes for hours on end: but once he had played his part, he was no longer of any account in the gathering; sad and silent in a corner he appeared to be impatiently awaiting his cue to return to the scene."[60]

Formont may have been the *marquise*'s dearest friend, but Pont-de-Veyle was, without doubt, the one she had known longest. He was the son of Madame de Tencin's sister, Madame de Ferriol to whose lot it had fallen to bring up Aïssé, and the brother of Voltaire's great friend, d'Argental. Pont-de-Veyle, Grimm wrote in 1754, "is known in Paris as a man of great wit who has always lived in high society and in the very best company. His songs and parodies are widely celebrated."[61] Pont-de-Veyle's literary ambitions were limited to society to which he contributed indefatigably,[62] by writing, acting and producing theatricals. But when his plays were performed at the *Comédie-Française*, faithful to the aristocratic idea of a dilettante man of letters, Pont-de-Veyle preferred anonymity.[63] Madame du Deffand and Pont-de-Veyle first met in around 1720 at Lord Bolingbroke's property, *La Source* and from that time they sustained a close friendship built on habit and indifference. Grimm and La Harpe both record a conversation which cannot be attributed to malice alone.

"'Pont-de-Veyle, since we have been friends there has never been a cloud on the horizon?' 'No, Madame.' 'Is it not because we are quite indifferent to each other?' 'That may well be, Madame.'"[64]

Apropos of this exchange, Stendhal remarked that sometimes "habit or despair of finding anything better, produces a kind of friendship, the least likeable of all kinds, which boasts its own security."[65] Stendhal was strongly prejudiced against Madame du Deffand whom he judged guilty of arrogantly negating sentiment and he thought her to be the ringleader of the *bon ton* which disguises impotence.[66] But reliable friendship was essential for a pathologically mistrustful woman who throughout her life rejected those she loved for fear of being herself rejected. The exchange recorded by La Harpe can well be countered by the passionate affirmation: "I love him very much, that Pont-de-Veyle. He has always been loyal to me."[67]

"Pont-de-Veyle's intelligence and talents deserve the recognition which is the ambition of all men of letters; but because of his modesty and love of independence he preferred the comforts of society to honour and fame. He avoided anything which might excite envy.

"It was discovered in spite of him, that he had written three plays which were well received. The fear of displeasing made him most circumspect in conversation.

"Those who did not know him well might have found him insensitive to the ridiculous, whereas he perceived it more acutely than anyone ... It might also have been thought that where taste and wit were concerned, he was no judge of literature. He seemed to approve everything and never allowed himself to form a criticism, yet no one was more capable of doing so since all the works he left behind him are in the very best taste.

"Outwardly he was cold; his manner displayed no eagerness: he could quite mistakenly have been suspected of great indifference. He was capable of the sincerest and most constant attachment. None of his friends ever had the slightest occasion to complain about him and nothing could dull his warmth towards them. He recognized his friends' faults and tried to help correct them by pointing out their inconvenience. He never allowed unpleasant comment about his friends. Finally, it can be said of M. Pont-de-Veyle that his wit, his talents, his virtues and his extreme goodness of heart all made him worthy of respect."[68]

This homage of her friend written by Madame du Deffand after his death is an expression of the desire to capture a memory of the ephemeral art of worldly grace.

Like Formont, Pont-de-Veyle was entirely dedicated to social life, but without ever depending on it. "He makes fun of everything, and loves nothing"[69] "sought after by everyone, he is everywhere at ease."[70] His success was due precisely to this obvious contradiction because, as Moncrif suggests, "the desire to please ... is inspired by reason and stands halfway between indifference and friendship."[71]

But society life was mainly shaped by women, and some of the most distinguished women of the Parisian aristocracy were regular visitors to Madame du Deffand's *salon*. First among these was Madeleine-Angélique de Neufville-Villeroy, widow of the duc de Boufflers, who in

1750 was to marry her old lover, Charles-François-Frédéric de Montmorency-Luxembourg, duc de Luxembourg, maréchal de France who
was himself a widower. Madame de Luxembourg had a possibly even
more scandalous past than Madame du Deffand, which it was difficult
to forget and which Besenval records in his *Mémoires* with malevolent
precision. Tressan's lines on the arrival of the beautiful young bride at
court during the Regency will suffice.

> *Quand Boufflers parut à la cour,*
> *On crut voir la mère d'Amour:*
> *Chacun s'empressait à lui plaire,*
> *Et chacun l'avait a son tour.*[72]

She soon became "a woman whom every successful man ought to
have on his list,"[73] and for her part she "satisfied her fancy with a
prodigious number of men."[74] Madame de Boufflers "sensing the advantage of a rich and stupid lover, set her sights on Monsieur de Luxembourg without any sacrifice on her part. She succeeded all the more
easily because of her natural superiority combined with the habit, commonplace among women, of holding sway. Around her she gathered a
circle which included her lover's wife, Madame de Luxembourg, the
duchesse de la Vallière and all the elegant men of the day. Supper was
served five or six times a week in Monsieur de Luxembourg's *petite
maison* in the rue Cadet, where the ultimate in good living was coupled
with extreme licence. As soon as the wine had gone to the guests' heads,
and particularly to Madame de Boufflers's who, wherever she supped,
rarely left the table sober, what was known as 'English' began to be
spoken which meant the most open conversation wherein nothing went
unnamed. And more often than not the guests did not disperse without
certain mutual exchanges between men and women which even
stretched to the ultimate in favours. Madame de Boufflers always prevailed over her companions and Monsieur de Luxembourg noticed
nothing or believed what Madame de Boufflers wanted him to believe
about it all. To stupid blindness he added the indecency of witnessing
his wife's dissolute behaviour."[75]

Not content with being first among the dissolute at a time when such
a prize was hard to come by, Madame de Boufflers was also famous for
her malice: a lucid, knowing malice, artfully cultivated. Bonseval records
a particularly cruel example aimed at Madame de Robecq, Monsieur de

Luxembourg's daughter from his first marriage, who became Madame de Boufflers' stepdaughter when she married the *duc*. No love was lost between the two women and "they barely saw each other any longer when her weak chest caused Madame de Robecq repeatedly to cough up blood, so that she was soon beyond remedy. Custom demands that whatever inner feelings there may be, a close relation must attend a deathbed and weary the poor invalid with his presence, adding to his suffering the displeasure of seeing someone he hates and by whom he knows he is hated. Madame de Luxembourg fulfilled this duty towards Madame de Robecq; but far from being moved by the touching sight of a pretty creature descending to her tomb in the springtime of life, and attempting to distract her from the terror she had of dying, she not only thwarted her stepdaughter's wishes, but she even tried by roundabout means, to tell her of her condition thus making it all the more frightful. She reached the peak of barbarity two days before her death when Madame de Robecq could no longer speak. On entering the bedroom, she said loudly enough for the unfortunate dying woman to hear that it was impossible to stay there because the smell of the corpse was suffocating."[76]

However, like her friend Madame du Deffand, with time and maturity, Madame de Luxembourg underwent a radical change and became the perfect champion of aristocratic civilisation in eighteenth-century France. Even the cynical maréchal de Richelieu who had been her lover, had to admire her theatrical change. "The maréchale de Luxembourg gives a rare example of a pretty woman's victory over time, of an immoral woman's victory over opinion, and of that of a friendless woman over friendship itself. When it pleased her, she acted as she wished because she knew how to want something and how to want it to the point. Some feared her for her character whilst others respected her for her reputation. Despite all this . . . , she had suitors, servants, champions and even admirers. Having exhausted its contempt, she ruled over her world; and having pushed scandal to the very limits, she set the fashion for a whole society."[77]

So, "this infamous woman disposed of reputations, and, without honour, she conferred honour,"[78] and in old age, according to the duc de Lévis who only knew her then, "she held absolute sway over young people of both sexes; she restrained the thoughtlessness of young women, requiring them to be generally coquettish, whilst obliging young men to act with moderation and respect. Finally she carried the sacred flame of French manners. The traditional noble manners which all Europe came to Paris to admire, and tried in vain to imitate, were kept intact with her."[79]

Madame de Luxembourg can boast another accolade, all the more remarkable coming as it does from a writer with a particular horror of worldly manners. In 1759 her protégé Rousseau portrayed her with an analytical precision which could not merely be attributed to obligatory flattery. On close inspection the *duchesse*'s charm seems to have depended on a delicate series of subtleties which lent naturalness to an otherwise entirely artificial creature.

"I had seen her at the theatre and at Madame Dupin's house several times ten or twelve years ago when as the duchesse de Boufflers she still glowed in her first beauty. But she was considered wicked, which reputation in such a grand lady made me tremble. As soon as I saw her I was captivated. I found her charming, with that time-tested charm most calculated to affect my heart. I expected to find her conversation biting and full of epigrams. But it was not like that; it was much better. Madame de Luxembourg's conversation does not sparkle with wit. It does not consist of sallies nor even exactly finesse: but there is an exquisite delicacy which is never striking but always pleasing. Her compliments are all the more intoxicating for their simplicity; they seem to escape without her noticing, and pour straight from her heart only because it is overflowing."[80]

It was Rousseau who was responsible for the only hiccough which occurred in the long relationship between Madame de Luxembourg and Madame du Deffand. The mutual dislike nourished by Jean-Jacques and the *marquise* was inflamed by her friendship with Voltaire. When open hostility developed between the two writers, Madame du Deffand automatically sided with Voltaire, thus showing lack of respect for the Luxembourgs whose protégé Rousseau was. But in the long run, Jean-Jacques's outlandish behaviour proved her right and the friendship between the two ladies which probably dated from the Regency, was renewed with increased intensity. Towards the end of her life, Madame du Deffand briefly summed up her relationship with the *duchesse* who was eventually to be at her deathbed. "If I believed in friendship, I would say that she was my friend. Not a day goes by without her coming to see me."[81]

Rousseau's description concerns the nature of Madame de Luxembourg's attraction, whereas Madame du Deffand's concentrates on her authority.

"... Wherever she is, she commands attention, and always makes the impression she wishes to make, she takes advantage of this in an almost God-like way, by allowing us to believe that we have free-will whilst herself determining our path. Like Him, from the height of her omnipotence, she marks out the chosen and the damned, so that those she punishes for not loving her could say: 'You could have been loved, had you wanted to be.'

"She is so discerning as to make one tremble; the smallest pretension, the slightest affectation, intonation or gesture which is not completely natural is most rigorously judged; her delicacy of taste and refinement of mind allow nothing to escape her notice. These qualities which are so rare and which ought to be so agreeable are, however, very dangerous if not accompanied by some indulgence or considerable prudence ... Generally speaking, Madame de Boufflers is more feared than loved, she knows it and she does not deign to disarm her enemies by manipulation which would deny both truth and her natural impetuosity. She is consoled by the respect for her judgement of those who know her best and by the feeling she inspires in them.

"She is very witty and gay, steadfast, loyal to her friends, truthful, discreet, obliging, generous; in short, if she were less clear-sighted and men were less ridiculous, they would find her perfect."[82]

Towards the end of the 1750s, Madame de Luxembourg founded what, for the second half of the century, was to be the most important society *salon* in Paris. But her *salon* was never in competition with the apartment in Saint-Joseph. The two establishments often exchanged guests and co-operated with each other so that the two weekly suppers which both gave fell on alternate days. They took care not to inconvenience each other, rather preferring to offer mutual support. Madame de Luxembourg and Madame du Deffand shared dominion over the society of their day. "The one has, for forty years, invested wit with nobility; the other has established the ranks of good company."[83]

"Whilst the duchesse de Luxembourg ruled society by terror, Madame de Mirepoix's rule was far gentler and whereas the sarcasms of the one were dreaded, the displeasure of the other was far more greatly feared."[84] Madame de Mirepoix was born Craon, she was the sister of the prince de Beauvau and widow of the prince de Lixen who was killed in a duel by the maréchal de Richelieu. She was married for the second time in 1739 to Pierre-Louis de Lévis de Lomagne, duc de Mirepoix and later maréchal de France. It was a happy marriage in an age when such a thing was an oddity. Madame de Mirepoix was anxious for her husband's success and followed him when he went as ambassador to Vienna and London. Although she was in waiting to the Queen, and despite her natural aristocratic pride, she did not hesitate to befriend Madame de Pompadour in order to further her husband's career, and, according to Hénault, to her own disadvantage. "She had made many other sacrifices for him which he deserved for his nobility of soul, his military talents and his tender respect for her."[85]

Madame de Mirepoix appears as a vague, absent-minded person whose grace was born of detachment. "She had warmth without enthusiasm, and was calm and kind without being insipid,"[86] but she was capable of inspiring strong feelings. Montesquieu professed a real reverence for her and Louis XV expressed both affection and friendship for her. Even Madame du Deffand produces a clear picture devoid of her usual insinuation: "Madame de Mirepoix is so modest, her self-regard is so little in evidence, she is so little concerned with herself that it is difficult to describe her.

"Vanity is the surest key to character: by wishing to boast of qualities they lack, men nearly always reveal their faults which might otherwise remain for ever hidden.

"This method is lacking with Madame de Mirepoix who never speaks of herself, determines nothing, rarely argues; to see her is to find her interesting and agreeable, but to know her real value, one must live with her. Only by chance does she reveal the extent of her wit, judgement and taste; a fundamental noble simplicity informs her character, making all ostentation and pretension alien and keeps her, so to speak, hidden.

"She is shy without ever either appearing embarrassed, losing her presence of mind or what is called the *à propos*.

"Her face is charming, her complexion blooming, her features without being perfect are so well arranged that no one looks younger or prettier than she.

"Her desire to please is more like politeness than coquetry, so women regard her without jealousy and men dare not fall in love with her: her demeanour is so quiet, and there is something so peaceful and regulated about her person that she imposes a kind of respect and prevents unwanted expectation, far more readily than she would with a severe and imposing air.

"Her conversation is easy and natural, she does not attempt to shine, she allows others to take over as they will, without haste, disdain, vehemence or coldness. Her countenance and her expression reflect the fairness of her mind and the nobility of her sentiments."[87] This serenity, however, existed alongside a violent and destructive passion for gambling. Since the earliest years of the Regency there had been a "universal eruption of gambling."[88] In 1739 d'Argenson announced, "Paris is inundated with public gambling, with houses where games of chance can be played and a bad supper is served; the bankers give the mistress of the house three louis a day ... There are more than three hundred such houses in Paris where lotto[89] and faro are played. All the young people ruin themselves there."[90]

From the middle of the century onwards, an ever increasing reiteration of the same repressive decrees only highlighted the law's inadequacy with regard to this scourge of society. Whole families were ruined, usury was encouraged and conflict created. At Versailles, as in the great Parisian houses, gamblers escaped the law, but not the driving passion. We have seen Madame du Châtelet lose nearly a thousand louis in one evening in the Queen's apartments at Fontainebleau. Maria Leszczynska herself was a compulsive gambler, and, as Mercier wrote in the *Tableau de Paris*, "women of the highest rank sometimes cheat with quiet daring: they have the effrontery to say to the person whose money they have placed on a winning card, that they have not done so. Since this happens at the tables of princes, there is no revenge other than to spread the news throughout Paris the next day. They pretend to know nothing of the rumour in question."[91] And in the *Correspondance secrète, politique et littéraire*: "Sometimes it is a lady of quality who robs the banker of three louis by placing a finger on the middle of one of the cards, thus transforming a twenty-two into a triumphant twenty-one; or sometimes an abbot, when playing piquet in one of the best houses in Paris, picks a card to suit him from his card pile, thanks to which convenient procedure he manages to win enormous sums."[92]

Madame de Mirepoix merely lost astronomical sums, often without knowing how to pay them. At the time of his death in 1757, her husband was a maréchal de France. But *la petite maréchale*, as Madame du Deffand called her, became increasingly a slave to her passion. Although Louis XV out of genuine, disinterested friendship, paid her debts several times, the time came under Madame du Barry's empire, when Madame de Mirepoix was obliged to sacrifice her legendary reputation to her gratitude. Whilst the flower of the French aristocracy defied the old King by refusing to pay their respects to the new favourite, Madame de Mirepoix could not refuse Louis XV's request for her to continue to frequent the *petits appartements.* "Poor Madame de Mirepoix plays a pitiful part . . . No one is more worthy of compassion. A great lady, fine behaviour, much wit, much charm; all these things united to make her slave to a strumpet."[93]

Another Madame de Boufflers who frequented Saint-Joseph dominated the Temple. The *salon* of Madame de Luxembourg, formerly Madame de Boufflers, was one of the great aristocratic centres of the second half of the century. Marie-Charlotte-Hyppolyte Camps de Saujon was separated from her husband, Edouard, comte de Boufflers and was the official mistress of Louis-François de Bourbon, prince de Conti. Madame de Boufflers had her own apartment in the Temple over which the Prince de Conti, as Grand Prior of the Order of Malta, had jurisdiction. She came to be regarded by everyone as the lady of the house. Madame du Deffand was obliged to recognise her standing and, for tactical purposes, be on apparently good terms, although she had no very kind feelings towards her. The irony of the nickname "the Temple Idol" turns to caustic wit in a truly merciless portrait.

"Madame de . . . , without being beautiful, or fresh or even pretty (for her somewhat faded features do not bear close examination) and without a good figure, has a considerable amount of charm in her face and person. Her charms which make her approach most agreeable to those she wishes to please, prevent the same approach from seeming disdainful and harsh to those she dislikes . . .

"Her heart, or rather her soul, for I do not know if she has a heart, is as artificial as her mind. It cannot be said that she has neither vices nor virtues, nor even faults or failings; but in so far as one studies her, one finds neither feeling, nor passion, nor affectation, nor preference, nor hatred.

"Her good qualities, for she has several, depend on the nothingness of her character and on the little impression made on her by everything around her; she is neither envious, nor back-biting, nor dangerous, nor interfering for the good reason that she is only concerned with herself, not at all with others . . .

"Her morality is of the strictest. For ever standing on the highest principles which she pronounces in the firmest and most decided tone and in the softest voice, she is like a flute dictating the law or speaking as an oracle. The pleasing, if somewhat troublesome, aspect is that all this high morality is not quite in keeping with her behaviour; even more pleasing is the fact that this contrast does not frighten her; she is quite ready to recognise it. She will tell you coldly that it is contrary to good form for a woman not to live with her husband and that the mistress of a prince of the blood royal is a fallen woman; but says all this so simply, with such conviction and so gently in such a pretty voice that one is not even tempted to find her ridiculous; she is merely funny, the word seems to have been invented purposely to describe her.

"Such is Mme de . . . , agreeable to meet, little suited to making friends, deserving neither affection nor hatred since she neither knows how to love, nor does she wish to hurt; neither would one know how to be angry with her; she is made to please and is unusual enough to be amusing, dry enough to provoke no interest, yet gentle enough for her company to be sought after, but cold enough and indifferent enough for the lack of it not to cause the smallest sense of loss or the least regret."[94]

Remorseless as ever, Madame du Deffand puts her finger on the sore point—Madame de Boufflers's irregular relationship with the prince de Conti. Had she been asked, the *comtesse* would have explained the remarks quoted by Madame du Deffand: "I wish my words to repay what my actions have robbed from virtue."[95] But even the kind maréchale de Mirepoix was irritated by Madame de Boufflers's moralistic tone. When reprimanded for associating with Madame de Pompadour "who in the end is only the first whore in the kingdom," Madame de Mirepoix replied dryly, "Don't force me to count to three," the implication being that the duc d'Orléans's mistress was the second, and that Madame de Boufflers herself was the third.[96]

Despite Madame du Deffand's malice, and thanks above all to Sainte-Beueve who wrote at length about her, Madame de Boufflers lives on as one of the most original and fascinating women of the time. She was curious, cultivated and a passionate traveller. She spoke three languages and was the first person in Paris to open her *salon* to foreign visitors. Her journey to London in 1763 which "was the first for two hundred years to be undertaken by a French woman of rank as a simple traveller,"[97] was memorable and contributed to the widespread fashion for English culture. Her friendship with Rousseau whom she met with the Luxembourgs, and her correspondence with Hume reveal her understanding of intellectual quality. After the Paris *Parlement* condemned *Emile* in 1762, it was she who put the two writers in touch with each other with a view to Jean-Jacques fleeing across the Channel. There was nothing special about her friendship with Rousseau which inevitably ended in a quarrel, but her friendship with Hume developed into a strong and complicated relationship. She could hardly have been paid a greater compliment than she was by Hume during his stay in France: "Despite the anxieties of the most unhappy passion, you have saved me from a total indifference towards life."[98]

Far from being fanciful in her literary and political tastes, the comtesse de Boufflers stood out as "a woman of great sensibility destined to be at the meeting place of *philosophes* and *parlementaires,* of Rousseauist hopes and the constitutional aspirations of the sovereign French courts."[99] On the death of Conti who never made up his mind to marry her, Madame de Boufflers moved to Auteuil where she held a literary *salon* whose *habitués* included Beaumarchais, the poet J.-A. Roucher and the prince de Ligne. Her final triumph was a friendship with the heir to the throne of Sweden, later Gustavus III with whom she corresponded assiduously.[100]

A painting by Barthélemy Ollivier which hangs in the Louvre, *Le Thé à l'Anglaise dans le salon des quatre glaces au Temple* takes us into the prince de Conti and Madame de Boufflers's world. The date[101] is that of the little Mozart's second visit to Paris. The high room with its pale panelling and four huge looking-glasses is lit by two big windows hung with pink curtains and overlooking a garden. The sober elegance of the decoration heralds Louis XVI's style; and the English tea,[102] being served with ostentatious simplicity whereby, in the absence of servants, some of the grandest French ladies wait on the guests, reflects not only the recent anglomania—Madame de Boufflers had been in London only three years before—but the longing for a more private life which would have its apogee with Marie-Antoinette in the Petit Trianon. The child, Mozart, is playing the harpsicord whilst Jélyotte, the greatest French singer of the day, accompanies him on the guitar. The guests, quite unaware of the exceptional nature of the concert, gather in small groups to talk, read, play cards and drink tea.[103] Several *habitués* of Madame du Deffand's *salon* are recognisable: the prince de Beauvau, the maréchal de Luxembourg, the maréchal de Mirepoix, the Président Hénault, Pont-de-Vayle, and the *marquise*'s nephew the archbishop of Toulouse. Although the prince de Conti and Madame de Boufflers were patrons of the arts there are no men of letters and there are no financiers. Wearing a white tulle apron over her vivid pink dress, "the Idol to whom all Paris offered sacrifices"[104] waits on her guests, and we are made to think of the ten commandments written by the *comtesse* and which hang on her bedroom wall: "Courage and pride in adversity," but "modesty and moderation in prosperity."[105]

Amidst so much studied elegance, Anne-Charlotte de Crussol de Florensac seems remarkably out of place. "Madame la d. . . d'A. . . has a sunken mouth, a crooked nose, and a mad, bold look but despite it all she is beautiful. The bloom of her complexion compensates for her irregularity of feature. Her waist is thick, her breasts and arms are enormous and yet she appears neither heavy nor solid: in her, strength takes the place of delicacy. Her mind is much like her face; it is, so to speak, as badly designed as her face and just as striking. Richness, vitality and impetuosity are its outstanding qualities. Without taste, charm or accuracy she astounds and surprises but she is neither pleasing nor interesting. She has no expression on her face and everything she says springs from a disordered imagination. At times she is like a prophet inspired by a demon, who can neither foretell nor choose what he is about to say; at others, she is as several loud musical instruments incapable of harmony; like an over-contrived, over-elaborate theatrical performance in which some marvellous details appear without sense or order to be admired in the pit and booed in the boxes.

"Madame la d. . . d'A. . . could be compared to those statues made to be placed high up and which appear monstrous on the ground. Neither her face nor her mind bears too close examination; her beauty requires a certain distance. Only unenlightened judges, lacking in delicacy can admire her intelligence.

"Like the trumpet of Judgment Day, she is made to awaken the dead, for the impotent to love and for the deaf to hear."[106]

Everything, even joy, was exaggerated in Madame d'Aiguillon. It was said[107] that when, in 1731, her husband was made a duke, which gave her the right to sit[108] in the King's presence, she was so happy that she developed smallpox. But the most remarkable thing about Madame d'Arguillon was her intellectual curiosity. She knew four languages, translated Pope and Ossian[109] and, like her husband, was fascinated by science. Her interest in culture had little to do with the worldly dilettantism of the day. She sheltered the abbé de Prades when he was about to be arrested, made propaganda for Voltaire's *Lettres philosophiques*[110] and was a friend of Montesquieu's in whose life she played "an important part"[111] and whom she defended from the Jesuits on his deathbed.[112] Hence, no doubt, Bachaumont's[113] certainly exaggerated assessment of her atheism and materialism but which, nevertheless, reflects her freethinking. Madame du Deffand leaves us in no doubt that Madame d'Aiguillon lacked the diplomacy and patience needed to hold a *salon,* but her Saturday suppers were frequented by foreigners, statesmen, philosophers and men of letters like Maupertuis, Duclos, Prévost, Bernis and Hénault.

In around 1740 the Président managed to introduce Madame du Deffand to the Brancas's exclusive circle. The Brancas's surrounded themselves in Paris and in their beautiful château in Meudon with a refined group of aristocrats whose passion was the theatre.[114] Duclos, a protégé of the family, described this society which was transposed to Saint-Joseph a few years later in *Considerations sur les moeurs de ce siècle.* Of the old maréchal de Brancas's numerous children, Madame du Deffand and Hénault were particularly friendly with Louis-Bufile, comte de Forcalquier and Marie-Thérèse, comtesse de Rochefort. The Président was also friendly with the maréchal's younger brother, the comte de Céreste. Cheerful, witty and brilliant, Forcalquier with his "delightful banter"[115] "illuminated any room he entered"[116] although "he too easily indulged his desire to shine."[117] In 1742 Forcalquier married the marquis d'Antin's widow, born Carbonnel de Canisy. The duc de Luynes describes her sitting at court as the wife of a Spanish grandee: "No one could be prettier than Madame de Forcalquier; she is small but perfectly made. She has a beautiful complexion, a round face, big eyes, a frank look, and all her facial expressions add to her beauty."[118]

Madame du Deffand's worldly relationship with Madame de Forcalquier never really developed into friendship. The two women knew each other for more than forty years and professed great intimacy whilst remaining fundamentally strangers. Madame du Deffand was sometimes amused by Madame de Forcalquier's volubility, coquetry and frivolity, all of which went to make up her essential femininity. But she was more often annoyed. *"Minet," "Chat," "Bellissima"* are sweet little names which recur ironically in Madame du Deffand's letters. The long, unlikely relationship between the two women can be explained by the fact that their spheres of competence in the *salons* were complementary rather than contradictory. Madame de Forcalquier was totally absorbed in playing the part of a beautiful woman whilst Madame du Deffand concentrated on intellectual prestige.

Madame du Deffand's friendship with Madame de Forcalquier's sister-in-law, Madame de Rochefort, was considerably more complicated. In a letter to Walpole written in old age, she claims to have loved her "passionately"[119] and to have been betrayed by her. Unfortunately little is known about a relationship which provoked such unusual feelings in Madame du Deffand. Both Hénault and Walpole describe Madame de Rochefort as cultivated, intelligent, witty and, despite financial problems and a "cook who differed from [the famous poisoner] Brinvilliers in intention only,"[120] able to attract a select circle of *habitués* to her *salon.* As a widow she became the "decent friend"[121] of the duc de Nivernais, a great aristocrat and a writer of elegant fables, to whom she devoted herself and whose "high priestess"[122] she was. Referring to this relationship, Walpole remarked that in Paris lack of moral prejudice did not bring with it a disregard for form. "It requires the greatest curiosity or the greatest habitude to discover the smallest connection between the sexes here. No familiarity but under the veil of friendship is permitted, and love's dictionary is much prohibited—as at first sight one would think his ritual was."[123]

Quite unembarrassed by their new dukedom, Monsieur and Madame du Châtel, already intimate friends of the Brancas's—moved at ease amongst the old aristocracy. Monsieur de Châtel's father, the banker Crozat, was one of the richest men in France, whose daughter the impoverished comte d'Evreux married for her millions though the marriage was never consummated.[124] In fact the values of the son were radically different from those of the father. Du Châtel turned his back on business, preferring to cultivate the aristocratic ideal of an *"honnête homme"* and to refine his mind, "to analyse his ideas and to go always to the root of things."[125] Indifferent to economic and social standing, Crozat's son wanted only to be a man of culture and an intellectual, even at the risk of seeming "a little too metaphysical."[126] A full awareness of this is expressed in his self-portrait: "He seems to owe neither his tastes, nor his ideas, nor his feelings to [nature] but has earned them through cultivation and work; his heart and mind are like strange guests residing within him, whom he has welcomed in order to complete and perfect his soul; he has learned to think as others learn to play musical instruments or dance; he is a true craftsman."[127]

How, for decade after decade, did the Saint-Joseph apartment come to be included in the frantic worldly round of these aristocrats whose houses were already social centres of tremendous standing?[128] No doubt the attraction lay, as it did in other *salons,* in the variety and quality of the guests and the balance between *habitués* and occasional visitors. Madame du Deffand's was a *salon* for aristocrats united by habit, but who liked a more relaxed atmosphere than was to be found in their own grand house. Saint-Joseph held a double attraction for its aristocratic *habitués.* Whilst remaining familiar territory, it provided novelty with guests from other social circles, intellectuals and foreigners. There was the possibility of excitement within a social framework where people spoke a recognisable language. But the character of a *salon* depended not so much on its guests, as on the tone lent by the particular personality of the lady of the house. The tone at Saint-Joseph was ironic and light-hearted. Intelligence was the only quality required, provided it was accompanied by wit. There was no room for pedantry or preaching; moralising and pomposity were banished and understatement was the order of the day. Besides lending inimitable tone, Madame du Deffand presided over her *salon* in a way that was quite unlike anyone else. The competence of a *salonnière* manifested itself in two essential ways. Firstly, as we have seen with Madame du Deffand, in the ability to form a stable group of chosen guests, and secondly but no less importantly, in the ability to administer this society with equal attention to the whole and to the individuals. The *salonnière's* supreme talent lay in knowing how to create a harmonious gathering of people who differed not only in temperament and intelligence but in their social background, whilst allowing them all to express their own personalities and to show themselves at their best. These women needed the prestige of brilliant guests, but in return they provided these guests with a platform for their talents. In the intellectual *salons* the lady of the house did not merely accommodate her guests' worldly vanity, but rather played the part of "animator." Thus she required patience, tact and self-sacrifice. She acted almost from behind the scenes, renouncing any aspiration to shine in favour of others.

Madame du Deffand was not given to such self-denial. She had no illusions about others, was impatient and egocentric. Above all at this time she had no desire to be over-concerned with her guests. She wished to play her own part and not merely to manipulate their vanity. Visitors came above all for the pleasure of admiring and listening to her. Two successive generations bear this out with enthusiasm. In a letter of 1742 Monsieur du Châtel wrote: "You are made to capture nature at a bound; as suited as she to creation, you cannot comprehend imitation. If it were necessary to write comedies spontaneously you would be the person to turn to. I have often had this pleasure by your fireside, where you are admirable. What variety and what paradox in your sentiments, in your character and in your way of thinking! What naturalness, what strength and what soundness of judgement even when your passions are inflamed! Nothing lacks, it is enough to make one mad with pleasure, impatience and admiration. You are invaluable to a watching philosopher."[129]

Twenty-five years later, Monsieur du Châtel's daughter, the duchesse de Choiseul wrote to Madame du Deffand: ". . . I think it is impossible to have more wit than you do. For it to be more fluent, more easy, more at hand; nor is it possible to have more imagination, more fire, more strength, more charm than you have. Who says strength and charm, says one and the same thing, for with strength comes ease and with ease comes aptness, precision and proportion."[130]

Such an admired performer had her own repertoire and her own style of which she was perfectly aware and which was sure to enchant a public trained in the school of artifice. Truth, simplicity and spontaneity are all terms which recur in contemporary descriptions of Madame du Deffand and which recur with insistence in her own letters, in contrast to falsity, pretension and artifice. But this was no pre-Romantic conception of naturalness seen as rebellion against convention and trust in instinct, or as an Enlightenment adherence to reality. We have only to consider the *marquise*'s indignation at Diderot's realistic innovations,[131] which were beginning to appear at the *Comédie-Française* at the end of the sixties. Monsieur de Forcalquier, husband of the *"Bellissima"* has left a portrait of Madame du Deffand on the threshold of maturity and just as her career as a hostess was about to begin. "Madame du Deffand's

face is lively and sprightly, her laugh is agreeable, her eyes are delightful; every movement of her soul is expressed on her face; pleasure,
boredom, humour, the whole gamut of her feelings. A man could read
her judgement of him on her face before he heard it, due to her extreme
sincerity which constitutes the charm and perhaps the weakness of her
character.

"It would be impossible to be wittier than she; so difficult is it to be
as witty, that I would put her above everyone I know in this respect,
were she never to see this portrait.

"She has a sensitive, gentle soul; today friendship profits from the
charms that nature intended for love. She is forty years old and all her
qualities should be seen from one point of view: her passion is reason,
her sin is idleness. She has taken to reason as ordinary women take to
religion. Madame de Flamarens[132] is the most renowned and the most
sought after leader of this extraordinary sect. At her feet Madame du
Deffand renounces the errors of imagination. Such is her hatred for the
false that there is no fault which she will not pardon before preciousness.
The narrowest of minds, provided it were simple would be preferred by
her to the most extensive and dazzling intelligence by which nearly all
the smart people are blinded.

". . . These are all Madame du Deffand's failings: an extreme sincerity
concerning anything which presents itself to her judgement, be it men
or their works; too scrupulous a sincerity which puts her on her guard
against solicitude and praise, the common currency of men which must
in turn be accorded them; a reason too certain and too opposed to
illusion which overvalues sentiment; too much vehemence in argument
which discredits her reasoning provoking the desire to escape its light;
too much inflexibility. I would name many others; if I knew them or if
they existed she would have shown me them. But I cannot help noticing
that she has none which do not come from her virtues and thus her
failings are of the century, not her own."[133]

Madame du Deffand's cry for simplicity in contrast to the pretentious
fatuity around her expresses a nostalgia for the past. With her tastes
formed in the classical school, she had a conception of purely intellectual, rational values. For her and for her contemporaries, naturalness
was merely a question of style and artificiality a failure of execution.
Her favourite style was sober, concise, swift, cutting and hard. Simulated
naturalness was so general and sometimes reached such perfection as to

fool and disconcert Chamfort himself: "A cruel truth, but one which we must recognise is that in society and especially in good society, everything, even apparent simplicity and the most agreeable ease, is art, science and calculation. I have seen men in whom a seemingly elegant movement was a contrivance, genuinely prompt, but refined and clever. I have seen them cloak the most studied calculation in the apparent *naïveté* of the dizziest abandon."[134]

Madame du Deffand was aware of this loathsome falseness and was tormented by mistrust which with the passing years became almost pathological. Sometimes she deluded herself into finding a negative certainty which forced the rules of the game. Then, according to Forcalquier, she displayed an "extreme sincerity concerning anything which presents itself to her judgement, be it men or their works." Duclos noticed this reaction which naturally led to a different kind of response in several people. Falseness of manner was sometimes so obvious and so repugnant "that one sets out to seek individuality; in wishing to appear brusque, one becomes ferocious, and in wishing to appear lively one is only petulant and thoughtless."[135]

Impatience with banality and a mistrust of pretence cannot have been the only reasons which twice drove Madame du Deffand to put her trust in men who were both difficult and bad-tempered and who displayed a sincerity which was sometimes brutal.

The first of these men was d'Alembert. In 1747 Jean le Rond was thirty years old, twenty years younger than Madame du Deffand, and he had already published his most important scientific works which established him as one of the greatest mathematicians of all time. Nevertheless, his name was as yet unknown to society, except for a small circle of scholars. "Besides in the early 1740s Diderot and Rousseau were quite unknown. They belonged to a new generation and to an entirely different social circle to Fontenelle, Montesquieu or Voltaire, to name but those who dominated the French intellectual scene. It was a strangely lively world of bohemians, translators, those who lived by their pen and for their ideas . . . A group of people who were extraordinarily free among themselves and with others. Diderot who was the moving spirit, d'Alembert who followed him reluctantly, Rousseau who interpreted the group's ideas and enthusiasms in his own particular way, declining any form of protection for the *Encyclopaedia* in its early stages, like every strict inside organisation. Neither a State nor an academy, but a group of free-thinking philosophers."[136]

In the unpublished diary of police inspector, d'Hémery, there is a memorandum on d'Alembert, dating from 1753. This brutally frank memorandum provides some precise details about the writer and his appearance which it would be impossible to find in the literary portraits dedicated to him. "It has been said that d'Alembert was Madame de Tencin's son, and many people believe it still; but it is by no means certain. What is certain is that he is the son of a Monsieur Destouches, lieutenant-general in the Artillery who was known as Handsome Destouches. His father, on his death, left him a life annuity of two hundred *livres*. This Destouches was chased by women and it is true that he had Madame de Tencin; but he had a lot of others too. What proves that d'Alembert is not Madame de Tencin's son is that she has done nothing for him, and surely a woman like her who was above being prejudiced and who did not believe in God would have taken pleasure in seeing her son bring her so much honour. According to his friends, d'Alembert is Europe's greatest geometer. He has a smooth, ruddy face, almost red; is small and of average girth. He has a great deal of vanity and presumption and is closely associated with Diderot and Rousseau from Geneva. They are all three lovers of Italian music, and are three somewhat fanatical beings."[137] D'Hémery is mistaken about Madame de Tencin. The former canoness really was d'Alembert's mother, but pride in a famous son came too late to expunge the shame of his birth. Jean le Rond was not tempted to turn his back on his adoptive mother, the wife of the glazier, Rousseau,[138] with whom he continued to live in a humble apartment on the outskirts of Paris, dedicating himself to "work and solitude."[139]

"He only went into society much later (after the age of twenty-five) and never liked it very much; he could not adapt himself to learning the tricks and the language, and perhaps he even took a little pride in despising them."[140]

Madame du Deffand met d'Alembert at Sceaux on one of his excursions into society, and was dazzled by him. The young genius seemed wonderfully rebellious and reassuringly genuine: "When he pays compliments, it is only because he means them and because he likes the people to whom he is speaking."[141] To tame him and to gain his friendship presented her with a challenge which took her back to the days when she depended entirely on her powers of persuasion and seduction. Once again she proved herself and was able to write to Maupertius in 1746: "D'Alembert comes to see me almost every day, I love him with all my heart, he is the most honest of men, the best boy in the world, and no one could have more wit. We often speak of you; he is very attached to you and if there is anything you can do to help him, I hope you will do so with pleasure. His circumstances are miserable and you know that merit is not the best path nor the safest way to obtain goodwill or benefit."[142] And so this moody, uncouth outsider became the star of the most refined *salon* in Paris. He was an arrogant intellectual, fully aware of not belonging, and as such delighted the flower of the French aristocracy with his comic verve. But d'Alembert's role at Saint-Joseph was not that of an entertainer; he was much too proud to lend himself to that, but with Madame du Deffand's friendship to vouch for him, he was true to himself and indifferent to the public around him: "He is, besides, so gay as sometimes to be childlike and the contrast between this schoolboy gaiety and the reputation he has earned, justly or not, in the sciences means that, although he is rarely concerned with pleasing, he is quite generally liked. He only wants to be amused and to entertain those he likes; the rest are amused from a distance without him thinking or caring about them."[143]

But d'Alembert never really felt a part of Saint-Joseph. Despite his intellectual reputation, despite Madame du Deffand and despite the changing times, he continued to be and to feel like an outsider among the other guests in the buttercup yellow, watered-silk *salon*. An anecdote of Chamfort reveals just how little things had in fact changed: "D'Alembert, who already rejoiced in a great reputation, happened to be at Madame du Deffand's with Monsieur le Président Hénault and Monsieur de Pont-de-Veyle. A doctor called Fournier arrived and said to Madame du Deffand on entering, 'Madame, I have the honour of presenting my humble respects.' To Madame le Président Hénault he said, 'Monsieur, I have the honour . . .'; to Monsieur de Pont-de-Veyle, 'Monsieur, I am your humble servant'; and to d'Alembert, 'Good-day, Monsieur.'"[144]

If love means understanding another, then Madame du Deffand's portrait of d'Alembert written in about 1754 eloquently expresses her feelings for him. She did not allow his differing social background, intellectual formation, tastes and values, nor his attitude to life, to blind her to the complexities of his personality. She sensed the challenge which allowed him to turn an initial setback into a life force. She was even able to accept the negative effect this constant support for d'Alembert had on her relationship with others—to wit an independence of mind not far removed from indifference.

"D'Alembert was born without parents, without support, without fortune; his only education was the communal education given to all children; no one in his youth took care to form his mind or his character. The first thing he learned on beginning to think, was that nothing mattered to him. The independence which resulted from this abandonment was his consolation; but as his intelligence developed, he discovered the inconvenience of his situation. He sought within himself the means to counteract his misfortune. He considered himself to be a child of nature and thought that he had to consult and obey only her (a principle to which he remained faithful); his rank and titles in the universe were summed up for him in his condition as a man; nothing was beneath him nor above him; virtue and vice, talent and folly alone deserve respect or contempt; for him freedom was the wise man's prized possession and man was always master of the ability to acquire it and to profit from it by avoiding the passions and all occasions which might give rise to them.

"The surest way to subject them was, he believed, through study, and his active mind could not limit itself to one subject: all kinds of science, all kinds of knowledge occupied him in turn; he formed his taste by reading the Ancients and was soon able to imitate them. Finally his genius developed and when he appeared in society it was as a prodigy. At first his simplicity of manner and the purity of his morality, his youthful appearance and a sincerity of character combined with all his other talents, astounded those who met him; but everyone did not judge him so kindly; some saw him as a young man lacking in social graces. To them his simplicity and sincerity were merely coarse ingenuousness. The only quality they could recognise in him was his singular talent for mimicry; they were amused by him but did not judge him to be worthy of any greater consideration.

"Such a debut in society was quite enough to disgust him, so he promptly withdrew and devoted himself more than ever to study and to philosophy. It was then that he published his *Essai sur les gens de lettres, les grands et les mécènes.* This work did not have the success which might have been expected; the great aristocrats thought that to advise against seeking their patronage was to deprive them of their titles. Men of letters were not pleased to be given advice which was so contrary to their self-interest; patrons and protégés alike were against him. He was now only referred to as a proud man. Everything he had said in favour of freedom seemed to favour licence. His love of truth was equally badly interpreted; but his disinterestedness, his contempt for such criticism, the silence he kept, the wisdom of his conduct, in fact the merit which sooner or later will triumph over envy, forced his enemies to concede or at least to keep quiet; they no longer dared to stand out against public opinion.

"D'Alembert rejoices in a reputation owed to the most distinguished talents and to the constant and punctilious exercise of the greatest virtues. Disinterest and truth are the basis of his character; generous and compassionate, he has all the essential qualities without having all those demanded by society; he lacks a certain gentleness and the charm that should attend it. He does not seem so tender-hearted which leads one to believe that he has more virtue in him than sentiment. Neither does one have the pleasure of feeling with him that one is necessary. He demands nothing of his friends; he prefers to be of service to them than the other way round. Gratitude too closely resembles duty and would restrict his freedom. To him all constriction, all constraint, whatsoever its nature, is unbearable. He has been perfectly described as freedom's slave."[145]

Madame du Deffand's *salon* became an integral part of the civilisation and way of life which made France, regardless of her political reality, the ideal country for all the brilliant and cultivated of Europe. Her house was a cosmopolitan centre which changed and developed over the years and where distinguished foreigners gathered. These were often diplomats who were in Paris for a few years and for whom return to their native land felt like exile.

Thus the ambassador Caracciolo, an *habitué* of Saint-Joseph, replied when Louis XV congratulated him on his nomination as viceroy of Sicily, "nowhere . . . is worth the *place* Vendôme."[146] And Johan Bernstorff, the envoy extraordinary from the Court of Denmark when recalled to Copenhagen to take up the post of Foreign Minister, wrote a letter to Madame du Deffand in which his nostalgia for Paris is made all the more acute for missing her.

COUNT BERNSTORFF TO MADAME DU DEFFAND   *Friedemberg, 11 May 1751*

You can never be forgotten, Madame, by anyone who has had the honour of knowing you. I beseech you to believe me, and I know full well that the hours which I have spent with you, listening to you, are permanently in my memory and will be permanently missed.

It would, however, be a happy thing for me were the memory less vivid! The hopes which I had preserved until now of revisiting the charming country in which you live, have vanished, or at least retreated. My fate is decided, I remain here; I have just been nominated Minister of State and I must take my seat in the Counsel the day after tomorrow. From this moment it will no longer be possible for me to make plans other than for a time and events which I must believe to be far off, however close they may perhaps be. Many people will envy me, who would pity me often if they could see into my heart.

Count Carl Fredrik Scheffer, the Swedish Plenipotentiary to France since 1744 and also a close friend of Madame du Deffand, reacted similarly when recalled to Stockholm in 1752 to take up the post of Senator. He later became preceptor to the future Gustav III. Letter writing was for him and for many other exiles, the only relief from this "pain,"[147] and the only straw to grasp at in the hope of not being totally excluded from the civilised world. Scheffer was terrified lest postal delays might discourage Madame du Deffand from writing: "In God's name do not give way to this disgust; you would deprive me of a pleasure which truthfully constitutes an essential part of my happiness in life."[148] To be allowed to correspond with the *marquise* was recognition indeed.

COUNT SCHEFFER TO MADAME DU DEFFAND   *Stockholm 24 August 1753*

Your goodness, Madame, in consenting to, and even praising, my letters, brings me, I have to admit, infinite pleasure. I have always wished to please you, I have aspired to your approval which I have always seen as dictated by the surest of taste and the most exquisite judgement; nothing then could flatter me more than the assurance of it by your very self . . . Your public affairs touch me greatly. I love the glory of France, my love for the nation often leads me to think that I am French . . ."

Lord Bath, too, vividly recalls the charm of Madame du Deffand's *salon*. He spent six months in Paris between 1749 and 1750 and dispatched great parcels of tea from England.

LORD BATH TO MADAME DU DEFFAND   *25 April 1751*

... I often recall the agreeable suppers with you in the most amiable
society whose conversation was always as engaging as it was profit-
able. I particularly remember one evening when it turned by chance
to the history of England. I was at once surprised and confused to
realise that the people of that company all knew it better than I did
myself!"

For the absent, letters provided a method of participating indirectly
in the life of the *salons*. But it was not a one way traffic, for as a distant
echo of that life, they in turn, enriched it. The letters were read aloud,
admired and commented on; they were both informative and entertaining. Their contents were rarely exclusively private and they were intended for more than one recipient, the correspondent and his circle of
friends and acquaintances. Madame du Deffand's correspondence with
the French Ambassador to Constantinople, the comte des Alleurs, is just
such an example. His letters describing among other things the ceremony at the Grand Sultan's court, Turkish life and the use of opium
were certainly a welcome distraction in the *salon* at Saint-Joseph.

V

Illness

TWENTY YEARS HAD PASSED since the time when it could have been written of Madame du Deffand that she was "the laughing stock, blamed by everybody, despised by her lover, abandoned by her friends."[1] Now her star shone brightly in the firmament over Paris. No longer driven by necessity and ambition, however, she found she was indifferent to the ends she had achieved. The extraordinary energy which had driven her forward turned in on her and transformed itself into the unbearable pain of ennui. "Ennui" was to become the catchword of her existence.

This change coincided with and partly resulted from a very real threat to her way of life. Madame du Deffand was just over fifty when her sight began to fail. A slow and unstoppable decline into the anguish of darkness began.

Like a traveller suddenly engulfed in a blanket of fog, the *marquise* never despaired of coming out into the light and "for five years she kept alive the hope of regaining her sight," by consulting "all the charlatans in the world."[2] But little by little the fog grew denser, the light that filtered through grew dimmer until finally there was total darkness.

With nothing left to strive for and threatened by a condition which must enormously affect her independence, Madame du Deffand, who had reached a time for stock-taking rather than planning, was finally forced to confront herself. Until this time, her life seems to have been a continual flight from an implacable enemy which with the passage of time grew ever more powerful and ever more invasive until it threatened to overthrow her entirely. She never hesitated to identify the enemy who lay in wait as ennui.

Ennui appears in Madame du Deffand's first self-portrait, written in 1728, and is immediately recognised as a force to be reckoned with. It was to be glimpsed behind her youthful restlessness; it fed her insatiable need for society and expressed itself in impatience and intolerance. It was like an underground river which surfaced briefly but violently at times, but which never really marked the surface. Madame du Deffand seemed able to live with the threat, to analyse it and discuss it with her friends without allowing it to overwhelm her. During her stay at Forges in 1742, ennui reappeared like an old, almost forgotten demon, but it was not until about 1750 that it became a permanent problem to such an extent that Madame du Deffand can now be seen as "the most distinguished and perfect incarnation" of this "sickness of the soul."[3]

Towards the end of the eighteenth century Paradis de Raymondis, a contemporary of Madame du Deffand's, attempted to define this sickness which was becoming so common: "Ennui is that langour which takes possession of us when both the mind and the body cease to be moved. It is an illness of the mind, just as fever is an illness in the blood."[4]

"Ennui" according to Robert Mauzi, "is not simply a tone of inner life. It always provokes a sickness of the soul which poisons the natural happiness of existence."[5] Madame du Deffand herself wrote, "What prevents my happiness is an ennui resembling a solitary worm which consumes everything that could make me happy."[6] Yet she knew that she was not alone in suffering. Ennui seemed to her to be like a motivating force.[7] "Everybody is bored; no one is sufficient unto himself and it is this hateful ennui which haunts each one of us and which we all wish to avoid, that puts everything into action." But as the phenomenon took an increasing hold of her she found herself unable to react, and allowed herself to sink into some sort of artificial lethargy, a kind of painful suspension of life.

William Klerks has recently outlined, in so far as is possible, the genesis, character and mechanics of Madame du Deffand's illness. He starts by recognising that there is a distinction to be made between the passing ennui which affects everyone and the pathological, chronic variety from which Madame du Deffand suffered, and which he confines himself to discussing. "The man who suffers from ennui will be he who, oblivious to his human condition, has heard the call of freedom and refused to accept it or to call himself to question. He will have increased his inner chaos. He is no longer able to be alone in his room, but flees the misery which eats away at him in a search for diversion and distraction. With him any confrontation of the self will remain sterile and be transformed into idleness and despair. He needs people, an absorbing occupation and, above all, he needs noise. A man who suffers from ennui is a man afraid of silence. He has deserted himself."[8] Klerks sees the chronic sufferer not as someone who has sated all his desires, but as a permanently insatiable person whose desire is burnt out before being realised and who perpetuates permanently unsatisfied expectation.

We know that with Madame du Deffand ennui was a condition of long-standing but we are unable to ascertain its date of birth. She who was so willing to talk about herself rarely looked to the past, did not treasure her memories. She had no hope for the future, but neither did she console herself with the past. However, suspended as she was between two equally uninviting voids, she was even unable to live in the present: "I waste all my time in regrets or desires. I live only in the past or the future. I make nothing of the present . . . I am ashamed of the use to which I put my life . . ."[9]

"This inability to live in the present is," according to Mauzi, "both the sign and the cause of a dispossessed self. Not only was Madame du Deffand disgusted by herself . . . , but she experienced her own life as something opaque, alien and anarchic which her conscience could neither reduce nor take upon itself . . . Ennui reflects a discordance between conscience and existence."[10] Klerks suggests an adolescent trauma which may have halted her emotional development at an early stage whilst her intellectual growth continued. This would produce a profound internal imbalance, an incapacity to accept life and a paralysis of feeling. From the beginning Madame du Deffand chose to escape, but her flight was shortlived and always led back to the point of departure. "We would be happy indeed if we could abandon ourselves as we abandon others."[11] The self-loathing which drove her to escape from herself was certainly not transformed into solidarity with others whom she saw as no more than a reflection of her own psychological deformity. Besides which to use others as mere instruments for her own distraction would remove any element of surprise and would in no way enrich her existence. Madame du Deffand was "a solitary woman who [feared] solitude."[12]

As she herself said, "Solitude is not the cause of my ennui, I see enough people, I am rarely alone; but everything leaves me indifferent."[13]

Egocentricity and suspicion prevented Madame du Deffand from making emotional ties; her ennui resulted from an inability to take up the
challenge, from her initial refusal to live. She preferred to deny her
feelings rather than to run the risk of being betrayed, to destroy her
values rather than to be disappointed by them. The *marquise* continuously expressed her inability to make an objective choice, which, in its
turn, reflected the subjective indifference typically resulting from ennui.
She trusted in a permanent levelling down of values as a means of
survival, if not of salvation: "To govern a state or to play with a top are
all the same to me."[14] "I would like to be an automaton or a saint, they
are equivalent."[15] Before turning on others with her usual implacable
clarity, she said of herself, "No greater disgust for anything can exist
than that which I have for myself."[16] As Klerks quite rightly points out,
"This lucidity is of no use to her at all because she delights in a certain
determinism which justifies her behaviour. It is a form of self-knowledge
which is worth no more than a complete ignorance of the self. She
denies responsibility by laying it at the door of her own nature, thus
providing herself with an alibi. It could be said that by seeing man's
nature as inescapably dominating his destiny, she was a victim of
herself."[17] "We bring our vices and our virtues with us at birth," she
wrote, "and consequently our happiness and our unhappiness. We can
alter nothing."[18]

For a self-declared enemy of contemporary philosophy, Madame du
Deffand revealed a determinist materialism as rigorous as any philosophy of Holbach or Helvétius, bereft though it was of any delight in
speculation or of any intellectual challenge to prejudice. Her inability to
change could only be observed. For her knowledge meant resignation,
never acceptance; the principle was always passive, never active: "She
judges herself, but never takes her destiny in hand for she considers
herself as acted upon, never active."[19] Thought could only be a source
of suffering; "Whoever is by himself, given over solely to thought, must
be the most unhappy of men."[20] Yet intelligence was the only quality
which she felt disposed to value. The feeling that her own intellectual
faculties were useless must have been as painful as her emotional
indifference. On its own, intelligence can only underline the awareness
of an existential defeat, for it to be active it needs to be accompanied by
creativity or at least to have learned how to organise resources.

On the rare occasions that Madame du Deffand looks back, she expresses only one regret: that of not having been properly educated. This lack, for which the Vichy's cannot really be blamed, deprived her of knowledge, interests, passion, and rendered her intelligence fruitless. When Voltaire suggested that in order to combat a particularly violent attack of ennui she should try to put her thoughts on paper and to make use of her own intellectual resources, the *marquise* replied with a negative assessment of her talent, "You can never know what unhappiness is and, as I have already told you, a man with a great deal of wit and talent can find vast resources within himself. One must be Voltaire, or vegetate. What pleasure could I find in writing down my thoughts? They only serve to torment me and that would hardly satisfy my vanity."[21]

It was no accident that the only literary form attempted by Madame du Deffand was letter writing. Letter writing, being of an occasional nature and requiring, as it does, a dialogue, is not specifically creative. It is not an exacting exercise in the abstract, nor does it require isolation. On the contrary, its primary intention is to negate isolation by contact with the outside world and fill the intervals between conversations. Such extempore communication entirely suited Madame du Deffand who, having been educated entirely by society, always needed an interlocutor before being able to express herself. She refused to take the initiative, preferring to react to questions from others. She was frightened, and therefore irritated by philosophical speculation and abstract ideas, and was interested only in man's immanence, the only—when all is considered—incentive for communication. In old age, having read a great deal, she was to describe precisely what interested her: "All universal stories and research into the cause of things bore me. I have exhausted all novels, stories and plays; only letters, lives and memoires written by those who recount their own history amuse me and arouse my curiosity. Ethics and metaphysics bore me intensely. What can I say? I have lived too long."[22]

Insistence on the non-literary aspect of Madame du Deffand's letters by no means implies that their writing was spontaneous. In the introduction to his *Recueil de Lettres du XVIII siècle,* Lanson claims that the letter is not a literary genre since it has no aesthetics and its function is practical: "One writes what one cannot say."[23] It is above all improbable that an artificial society whose every action and every word is studied should suddenly become relaxed on paper. Besides, as Duisit stresses in his study, *Madame du Deffand epistolière,* "the letter in the eighteenth century was all the more skilful, for the fact that the basis of what there was to say hardly varied, and a considerable amount of time was spent in saying it. No century has ever pushed the cult of fine manners and delicacy of expression and sentiment further."[24] Madame du Deffand was no exception. Her obsession with naturalness, combined with her critical sense, made her supremely aware of the problem of transposing her legendary conversational talent into writing.

According to Mauzi, "Madame du Deffand's whole inner life can be reduced to two elementary conditions both of which she was quite incapable of controlling. She knows only these two ways of existing. The secret of her over-simple soul lay in an incredible longing for the absolute: "I am not happy enough to make do with what I have when I have not what I lack."[25] So what was she lacking? The security of exclusive friendship, a totally committed relationship? These were unlikely aims since Madame du Deffand preferred an exaggerated image, for a measured participation in life might lead to disillusion. She was not lacking in true friends, but rather than put her trust in them, she protected herself by a reserve which they in turn reflected back; and thus she was sure to have no illusions. The *marquise* rationalised her mistrust as a defensive mechanism, as born in her and as an intuitive faculty. She claimed to be able "to feel and perfectly understand everything that is thought about me; and to receive so strong an impression of it that I have not the ability to temper my displeasure or my satisfaction."[26] In an undated letter, surely written at one of those moments of not infrequent tension between them, Hénault reacts violently against such perversity which destroys a relationship and claims Madame du Deffand herself as its first victim. "Oh my God! My God! What pleasure you take in tormenting yourself and others! ... What! Did it please Nature to make two creatures destined to tear each other's hearts out! For we do nothing else when we ought to love and respect each other. There is no more noble sentiment than trust which wins all, subjects all and calms all. Everything smiles on you, everything should amuse you and yours is a safe haven; but no, you will chase despair."[27]

The crisis which struck Madame du Deffand half way through the century is fundamental to her life story, not because of any real change it provoked so much as for the subsequent burst of egocentricity, fear and suspicion. All of these had hitherto been disguised by the existence of very real problems and by youthful ambition. It was a crisis for which there could be no solution and which had no outlet other than its own expression.

From this time forward the unchanging landscape of Madame du Deffand's inner life was without incident. She imposed her will on details only. The light and the colours changed, contrasts were accentuated, but basically the landscape remained the same. Only Madame du Deffand's vision changed; with the passage of time "a reason too sure, too opposed to illusion which over-values sentiment"[28] gave way to feeling. "It is the heart which teaches us everything, which reveals everything: everything depends on it."[29] But the suspicion remains that reason and heart merely express differently the same negative search. The tests to which Madame du Deffand put her friends, her bitterness at often imaginary wrongs, and her conventionally sentimental scolding of Hénault, all spring from her demand in whatever name, of the absolute.

Her threatened blindness must have triggered an inevitable existential crisis, the symptoms of which had been mounting. In a portrait of the *marquise* written at about this time,[30] Monsieur du Châtel describes the characteristics of her depression. "She has moments of darkness: suddenly all light is eclipsed. Sometimes Madame du Deffand appears to be stunned. At times her soul is, so to speak, abandoned in her body as if in a deserted, empty house where only phantoms return to frighten her and to fill her with bitterness and sorrow: she complains and feels herself to be in a state of misery and despondency all the more painful for the remembrance of strength and of mental resources which she feels will be useless from now onwards."[31] A very eighteenth-century conceit is expressed in the image of the deserted house. "Consciousness is seen as a simple container, like a vessel gaping and greedy. Paradoxically images of the inner life have often to do with space, not time. Besides, a weary consciousness is not fundamentally distinct from an ordinary consciousness; and presupposes no particular, aberrant understanding of existence. It is no more than a healthy consciousness, but poorly furnished, ill-decorated and badly filled."[32]

The "moments of darkness" intensified and became a continuous malaise. Then inevitably the "vapours" developed. This term which was as general as it is suggestive was used to describe all mental illness in the eighteenth century. The *Nouveau dictionnaire universel et raisonné de medecine etc.* of 1771 has this to say: "Hypochondriac and hysterical

maladies are so described since it has long been believed that they are
caused by vapours which escape from the intestines and the uterus and
give rise to all the symptoms to be seen in these maladies. See *passion
hysterique* and *passion hypocondriaque.*"[33]

Vapours, ennui, melancholy—they were all part of an existential
malaise which from the middle of the eighteenth century onwards
claimed an ever increasing number of victims[34] and which imposed itself
as a new way of life. Ennui expressed the most complex sensibility and
informed a large part of pre-Romantic literature on which it also fed.
Although hers was one of the first and most advertised cases, Madame
du Deffand, unlike her contemporaries, did not delight in narcissistic
suffering, nor did she rejoice in her own sensibility and the feeling of an
exceptional destiny. Madame du Deffand referred to her symptoms with
classic moderation and a scientist's impersonal precision. Her notes are
brief, effective and without a trace of self-pity: "When I am overcome
by the vapours and a profound ennui, I try to escape from them; I am
no longer natural. I search for my soul and I find only the reminder of
it."[35]

The insomnia which perhaps tormented Madame du Deffand more
than anything else, probably dates back to this time. She wrote to
Walpole: "It lengthens my days and shortens my life."[36]

At night, when to her chagrin the last visitors had left, the conversation had died down and the servants had retired, she reflected, "Like
Zaïre, I am left to myself, and I cannot be in worse hands."[37] There was
soon a regular ritual to her sleepless nights. For her at eighty, as at fifty,
the night constituted a long, agonising wait to go on living which she
claimed to hate. "I go to bed at one or two, I do not sleep at all. I await
seven o'clock with impatience; my *invalide*[38] arrives, I want to sleep.
Sometimes he reads to me for four hours before I fall asleep. . . . I go to
sleep at eleven o'clock or midday or often even later and I do not get up
until five or six o'clock."[39]

Madame du Deffand was doubly tormented. Crowds, entertainment
and activity had provided a means of escape from herself, but now this
only means of escape was threatened by blindness which would deprive
her of her independence. She felt her restless spirit which so needed
freedom to be doubly enclosed by walls. Just as she began to recognise
her need for others, she suddenly noticed in a typically self-destructive
way the frailty of the relationships on which her everyday life was

based, and so projected her own insecurity and fear of abandonment on others. Paris suddenly seemed hostile to her. "When all passion is spent, there is a terrible void, you depend on everything and hold to nothing, and seek friendship and society only to find coldness, indifference and vexation etc. You believe yourself to be alone in the universe. Of all the places in the world, Paris is the most likely to produce this attitude; there people are drunk with pride, self-interest and ambition, not to mention affectation and persiflage."[40]

In 1751 she began to think about retiring for a while to the country. But it took a long time for her to reach a decision as gradually her eyesight deteriorated and as her sense of estrangement from the life she had so carefully built up increased. Her longing to leave Paris and her disgust for it finds an echo in a letter from a Genevan friend, Jean-Louis Saladin, who had recently returned home from twenty-five years in the French capital. "I do not know what I would not give for you to have good reason to prefer Champrond to Paris; but do not suppose yourself to be right in thinking that to be bored in a place full of amusement is a hundred times worse than to be bored in seclusion."[41]

The country was not merely a quiet place of retirement, but was thought to provide the best cure for the vapours. Many doctors at the time, including the famous Genevan, Tronchin, prescribed as an antidote a healthy life away from the feverish, suffocating night-life of the urban aristocracy. The open air, exercise, less spicy food and less restricting corsets were primarily recommended. So Champrond was the obvious choice, but it was also a flight which questioned a whole way of life, a position assiduously sought after and a solid social network. Rather than risk losing control of an obviously uncertain situation, Madame du Deffand did a characteristic about-turn and abandoned Paris before it could abandon her.

Few letters date from these years of crisis, but one from Montesquieu, dated 12 October 1753, reveals that the *marquise*'s ambitions and youthful energy had run their course. Madame du Deffand had reached the depths of pessimism and found a formula with which to express it. Montesquieu quotes her typically eighteenth-century allusion to the sublime and the ridiculous, one to which she would continue to refer for the rest of her life: "No one from the angel to the oyster is happy."[42]

VI

The Return to Champrond

ON 1 MAY 1752, Madame du Deffand set out for Champrond accompanied by her personal maid, her secretary and probably a few other domestic servants. She had left her paternal home more than thirty years earlier when, in 1718, she went to Paris to be married. On 22 May she wrote to Madame d'Aulan from Champrond, "I put off writing to you, my dear sister, until arriving here as I wanted to give you an account of my journey. I left Paris on 1 May, I reached Roanne on the 4th, stayed there on the 5th and on Saturday the 6th I reached Champrond. I found the château and the park greatly improved and would not have recognised either. I bore the tiring journey quite stoutly and my health is not bad. I delight in being here; I would be very glad to see you here which, I flatter myself, would be soon, if it were my home."[1]

A detailed description written in 1735 and a drawing of 1784[2] show how her childhood home must have appeared to the *marquise*'s already failing sight. The château which was more like a fortress than a private house, consisted of a large square tower flanked by two wings; it was approached by a drawbridge over a deep surrounding moat. Its severity, however, was softened by two large terraces, by flowerbeds and by a big aviary. The park was divided by a stream and two hornbeam avenues, one of which led to an old chapel. Inside, the château must have been decorated with a degree of opulence as when it was sold by auction in 1793 during the Revolution, the furniture fetched 48,000 livres.[3] The new comtesse de Vichy's initiative, and more particularly her dowry, were responsible for these improvements. Madame du Deffand's sister-in-law, although attractive and not without character, was nevertheless completely subservient to her husband. Gaspard de Vichy had retired from the army with the rank of maréchal du Champ and returned to his estate to rule his family with a rod of iron, whilst still pursuing a career as a ladykiller. Madame de Vichy could not but be aware of the pitiless egoism of the family into which she had married: "It must be said that they are quite unusual . . . ; the poor abbé has basically a good heart; but as for the others, I doubt if they really know that they have a heart."[4]

By nature cheerful and accommodating, she consoled herself with a truly Rabelaisian greed. She tempted her sister-in-law to Champrond, with a menu: "We have an excellent cook; let me describe one of our daily meals: a good rice soup, some figs, small turnips, sausages, fillet of lamb *à la provençal* to make your mouth water. For the first course there is a pullet *fricassée,* a leg of lamb with spinach; then there are the boiled meats, a piece of beef and a loin of mutton; for the roast we have excellent red partridges, and after that the desserts . . . I have eaten like a horse and now we are going to have supper."[5]

It would be hard to imagine a greater change than that which Madame du Deffand chose to undergo in a supreme attempt to ward off the horrors of blindness. Here she was shut up in an old château in a tightly-knit family circle, surrounded by relations who were totally alien to her. Around her the natural world to which she had always been perfectly indifferent, stretched endlessly away. Madame du Deffand was entirely uninterested in contemporary discovery of nature and the new rapport between the natural world and science and literature, albeit mythical, progressive or philanthropic. This is reflected in her quip about Buffon: "He only concerns himself with animals; he must be something of one himself to be so devoted to such an occupation."[6]

On the other hand, little by little, as the great themes of the day were defined and gathered momentum, the *marquise* became more and more estranged from her contemporaries and gradually the conservative nature of her way of thinking became more evident. Only the closed circle of the *salon* was congenial to her and only human beings interested her.

The move from the artificiality of Paris to the harsh realities and monotony of country life must have been all the more difficult for one with absolutely no feeling for nature. Later, thinking back perhaps on this painful period, she wrote that she was not insensible to the beauties of the countryside, but that she needed peace and serenity to appreciate them. Now, rather than serenity, she seemed to seek only physical and emotional numbness.

MADAME DU DEFFAND TO COUNT SCHEFFER   *Champrond, 23 July 1752*

. . . I have forbidden myself to think. Thought only provokes the feelings and now my system is to extinguish them. The place where I am and the life that I lead are admirably suited to my success; such was the hope that led me here and I will stay so long as I believe it necessary for my plan.[7]

So ennui, chosen not suffered, became a means of therapy.

I find that it is not worth changing one form of ennui for another. In the provinces it is duller, but in Paris it is more unbearable. Here one expects nothing, one has no pretensions, no desires and one is consequently without disgust or disappointment. Laziness takes the place of everything else."[8] (to Scheffer, 8 November 1752)

The way for Madame du Deffand to regain strength and to begin the steady climb out of her depression could not be, as she sometimes seemed to delude herself, through familiar surroundings, silence, the countryside and a regular healthy life. These all provided a haunting echo to her existential malaise, not a remedy. She should have sought relief in attempting to forget herself rather than in solitude, and Champrond was the worst possible choice. But surprisingly it was while exiled here that a flame of genuine interest in the affairs of men was rekindled.

The magic was worked by an unhappy humble young woman of twenty. Julie de Lespinasse lived with the Vichys in the ambiguous position of an inferior friend. Her youth can best be understood from what she herself confided in her lover twenty years later: "Eliza told me several times about her early years: everything you hear in the theatre, everything you read in a novel is without interest once you have heard this tale! Great scenes of passion and human calamity can be found only by penetrating to the heart of family life. In imagining them, writers contort them and they can be described only by those who have experienced them or by their victims. Eliza was born under the auspices of love and misfortune. Her mother had a great name but lived separately from her husband. She brought Eliza up publicly as if she had the right to admit she was her daughter, but kept from her the secret of her birth. She often bathed her secretly in tears. By redoubled tenderness, she seemed to want to console her for having presented her with the melancholy gift of life. She showered her with affection and kindness. Firstly she herself gave her daughter an excellent education: soon that was all that would be left. She died suddenly, just when she was about to try everything to give her daughter such status as the law might allow. Eliza was abandoned to relations who soon became no more than persecutors. They taught her what she was: from eldest daughter, cherished daughter, she suddenly became an orphan and a stranger in the same house. Cruel condescending pity claimed this unfortunate child who until then had been so tenderly cared for by nature and remorse. She survived because she was at an age when misfortune is not fatal, or rather at which there is no misfortune."[9] The key to the mystery is to be found in a fine work on Julie, written by Ségur, a hundred years later. Even without Guibert's pathos, the truth is just as terrible.

Julie de Lespinasse was born in Lyons in 1732, the illegitimate daughter of Julie d'Albon, last in the line of a great aristocratic family from the Dauphine, the Saint-Forgeux. Madame d'Albon, who was separated from her husband, had already given birth to an illegitimate child the year before. Unlike her brother who was brought up secretly in a convent in Lyons and of whose fate we know nothing, Julie was given a family surname, welcomed into her mother's house and openly recognised as her daughter. Her unknown father did not completely disappear but turned up seven years later in a remarkable new guise; he came not as Madame d'Albon's lover, but as her son-in-law, not as Julie's father but as her legitimate half-sister's husband. We know nothing of the circumstances of the marriage[10] nor of Madame d'Alban's attitude to it, but such incidents were not unusual at the time. We only know that from that time onwards, all the mother's attention was concentrated on her illegitimate child. Not only did she love her with a passion in which pity and guilt played a part because of the horror of the situation she had created, but she tried to have the child legitimised, to provide for her future.

Such maternal passion was disastrous for Julie. It was responsible for her over-sensitivity and emotional instability, and was probably the root cause of an existential obsessiveness which made her seem both vulnerable and remorseless. Instead of preparing her daughter for the trials which lay ahead, Madame d'Albon's love deprived her daughter of any means of self-defence: "By an unheard of peculiarity my childhood was disturbed by the very care which went to increasing my sensibilities; I knew terror and fear before I was able to think or to pass judgement!"[11]

Madame d'Albon's very desire to legitimise her daughter and to provide her with a future helped to prevent the family conflict thus created from being resolved. By marrying Marie-Camille-Diane d'Albon, Julie's father was no longer an absent parent, but a hostile brother-in-law defending the legitimate interests of his wife and children against a bastard's illegitimate claims. The fact that this bastard was also his daughter can only have added to the inconvenience and annoyance. The father of whom we treat so disparagingly was one of the "heartless" clan of the Vichys, and none other than Madame du Deffand's oldest brother, Gaspard.

When the *marquise* arrived at Champrond in 1752, Madame d'Albon had been dead for four years. She had died without being able to have her daughter legally recognised. For reasons of loyalty and pride Julie refused a large sum of money wished to her by her mother on her deathbed. Thus she renounced her independence and was forced to accept hospitality from her father and her sister. At Champrond she was informed of the "horror"[12] of her birth and employed as nursemaid to the two youngest Vichy children. Her little nephews provided her only source of affection, but the talent she proved in educating them contributed to making her position in her paternal home unbearable. Julie's presence in the house became indispensable but it was also a permanent threat to the Vichy's patrimony and their reputation. Soon the hospitality offered her was no more than a form of humiliating segregation. Self-interest and mistrust were translated into "an affected reserve, wounding supervision, and the incessant reminder, not spoken but implied, of the disgrace of her birth from which her youthful pride suffered so cruelly. Her nature was refined and she was impressionable. She was swift to catch any nuance and for her impetuous self, judgement was synonymous with feeling; thus it is easy to imagine the silent, soon to become exasperated irritation that swelled the heart of this twenty-year-old girl ... After two years of this lamentable existence, her patience was at the end and her mind was made up. She would no longer eat the bitter bread of pity without kindness. She would abandon this refuge where she had found nothing but sorrow and humiliation, and suppressing the hopes of a trembling soul which was attracted to the unknown as to a mirage, she would obey her mother's wish and bury her youth behind the veil in a cloister."[13]

By the time Madame du Deffand arrived at Champrond the quarrel between Julie and the Vichys was already insoluble. To begin with it seemed that the *marquise* might be a mediator but her intervention soon provoked the final break. The coming together of an indifferent woman of fifty and a passionate twenty-year-old who lived for her "plan," was bound to affect them both profoundly. Not only was Madame du Deffand brutally realistic, but she strongly mistrusted the current vogue for sentimentalism and the pathetic which she saw above all as inspiring romantic trivia, so she was not likely to be particularly moved by Julie's story. Julie's fate did not seem much worse to her than the fate of so many others for generations; her sister's daughter, for instance, was given no other choice but to take the veil: "A nun's condition is perhaps preferable to many others; the regularity of life saves her from much distress."[14] Neither was Madame du Deffand mainly interested in Julie's lively intelligence and discreet education which must have been an unexpected source of comfort in the isolation of Champrond. She was attracted by the very nature of her niece's intellectual passion. For Julie, understanding did not mean distancing yourself from the world, as it did for her aunt, but going out to conquer it. She had an avid, curious, lively and imaginative intelligence. Her contagious vitality—"I have seen apathetic hearts electrified by her,"[15]—could hardly change Madame du Deffand, but such indirect vitality might allow her to confront her own paralysing ennui. Probably for the first time, the *marquise* felt an inclination to trust; Julie may have been unable to break down her aunt's wall of mistrust, but at least she breached it.

Considering Madame du Deffand's strong aversion to the artificial, it is hardly surprising that Julie's most powerful weapon was her naturalness. This aversion did not arise from any enlightened belief in spontaneity, but from the *marquise*'s mistrustful nature combined with aesthetic awareness and the belief that naturalness is often the touchstone of worldly wisdom. "Naturalness, above all naturalness," was one of the Prince de Ligne's favourite sayings—artificiality being primarily a failure of style. Julie's transparent grace was quite free from affectation; brought up alone, she had only her natural inclinations to follow.

For six months Madame du Deffand and the orphaned girl lived together in the old château, isolated from the rest of the world, part of a monotonous family life in which, for different reasons, neither could fully participate. The two women were bound to be drawn together by the awareness of themselves as outsiders. It is easy to imagine them during those six long months walking side by side under the hornbeams and facing together the long dull evenings, the monotony of Champrond with visits from neighbours, rare social outings, the comtesse de Vichy's greed and the *comte*'s cold authority. Little by little Madame du Deffand's interest in Julie developed into a plan to take her over.

Madame du Deffand sensed in Julie's nature, a sunny version of her own. She recognised in her a vocation for society not yet put to the test but strikingly evident, an eagerness to communicate and a concern for others which was all the more attractive for being disinterested and genuinely lacking in affectation. Why not make use of this newly discovered energy which might revitalise, however indirectly, the only form of existence she knew? Why not derive warmth from this disinterested enthusiasm, and benefit from this innocence? It was not a free association which she planned so much as a takeover bid in which her liking for Julie was not entirely divorced from a realistic assessment of her position.

In fact the measure of Madame du Deffand's trust depended on objective certainties: the young woman had no status, no money and no future other than a choice between two equally mortifying alternatives. She could continue to accept the family hospitality which was already unbearable to her pride, or she could retire to a convent, a choice repugnant to her nature. There was, it is true, a third possibility but one which the poor girl did not seem to welcome: the support of her mother's eldest son, Camille-Alexis-Eléonor-Marie, comte d'Albon. Julie was very attached to this older half-brother with whom she grew up and to whom she had shown great loyalty by refusing the large sum of money her mother had wished for her. No doubt Monsieur d'Albon was fond of his sister, but that would not have been enough to touch the remorseless self-interest which dominated family relations under the *ancien régime*. An illegitimate girl's life must be sacrificed in the interests of the family, to the safeguarding of its patrimony and to its reputation. If all this escaped Julie's innocence, it certainly did not escape Madame du Deffand's consummate realism. So the *marquise* preferred to wait patiently for the young girl to reach the point of despair when her surrender would be unconditional and she would know that there was nothing but what Madame du Deffand had to offer and that the rules of the game had already been established.

It is not known how long it took Madame du Deffand to elaborate her plan, nor how soon she judged it opportune to inform Julie. She certainly said nothing whatsoever to her relations and the girl is never even mentioned in letters of the period. On the other hand, the *marquise* was equally reticent about her future plans, the real state of her health and the nature of her ills. Perhaps she had not entirely given up hope of an unexpected recovery and so remarked only occasionally on her fluctuations of health and adapted her plans accordingly. However, on 3 September 1752 she wrote to Madame d'Aulan from Champrond: "I am very far from being decided to pass the winter in the country. I have no fixed opinion about this, but it is, however, possible that I may be in Paris around Saint Martin's day. I will inform you of my journey. My health has not been good for some days, and I very much fear that it may become as bad as it was before."[16]

Madame du Deffand was not in Paris by Saint Martin's Day, but neither did she spend the winter with the Vichys. Towards the end of October Julie left the château to retire to the des Chazeaux convent at Lyons and Champrond lost any attraction it may have had for the *marquise*. So she too left her brother's and sister-in-law's home at the beginning of December and moved to Mâcon. The Président Hénault wrote to Scheffer on 16 December: "Mme du Deffand is in Mâcon. Who would have looked for her there ten years ago? She is planning to make a trip to Lyons to see the Cardinal de Tencin. She means to return in the spring. I very much hope she will, but who can tell, unless the same tide which bore her away brings her back to us."[17]

At Mâcon Madame du Deffand stayed with the bishop, Henri-Constance de Lort de Sérignan de Valras: "There is no friend on earth like him, I love him passionately. I would be ungrateful indeed if I thought otherwise. Not that he does not get very angry with me at every moment; but far from being vexed, I am delighted to see him follow his inclinations, it gives me proof of the frankness of his character and of the sincerity of his friendship."[18] Judging from a letter dated 15 September 1752 from Count Scheffer in Stockholm, her stay in the provinces did not seem likely to end soon: "When I consider, Madame, the vast space which at present separates us, I am surprised that your letters can reach me; however I have received the one which you were gracious enough to write on the 8th of last month. Your perseverance in doing without Paris confirms me in the opinion which I always had of your character. A truly enlightened mind perceives the value of things, whether good or bad, with such evident clarity that it seeks or flees them far more determinedly than does a mediocre intelligence. You have known grand society better than anyone, I am not surprised that you have become disgusted by it, and more so than anyone else."

But Madame du Deffand knew that provincial life did not provide a possible alternative for her. Hénault, too, was convinced and wrote to tell her so a few months later (5 April 1753): "I do not think that one can be happy in the country when one has spent one's life in Paris; but happy is he who has never known Paris, and who does not feel the necessity of adding to this life imaginary ills which are the worst! One can console a nobleman who complains about a storm by proving that he is mistaken and showing him the plentiful grapes on his vine; but metaphysical storms can not be overcome. Neither Nature nor Providence is as unjust as one might like to think; the less we add of our own, the less we will need to be pitied: and let us look at the approaching end, the hammer which strikes the hour and think that it will all disappear."

All that was needed was an antidote, or at least a partial antidote, to Scheffer's "disgust," and Madame du Deffand certainly found one in Julie. Having decided to return to Paris, the *marquise* postponed her departure in the hope of overcoming the obstacles to her removal of the young woman.

Meanwhile, after months of profound apathy, Madame du Deffand's interest in Paris was once again stirring. Her intellectual curiosity was rekindled by a correspondence with d'Alembert who had inspired her admiration and indulgence more than anyone else. Unfortunately, with the exception of one from Madame du Deffand, only d'Alembert's letters remain. Despite their obsessive egocentricity, these reflect and indirectly record the *marquise*'s existential suffering and above all, they are the first documents to establish her as a *femme de lettres*. Before her correspondence with Voltaire reveal true brilliance, Madame du Deffand's intellectual authority is clearly seen reflected in the letters of one of the most influential and disdainful of the *philosophes*.

1752 was a year of battles for d'Alembert. In February, following the

Sorbonne's condemnation of the abbé de Prades article *Certitude,* the *Conseil d'Etat* pronounced judgement against the *Encyclopédie,* now in its second volume. D'Alembert, who with Diderot was co-editor, threw himself into the polemic in quite a different way to his friend. He did not grasp the political and religious sides of the quarrel, but limited himself to formalities. An offence had been perpetrated against freedom of expression and the dignity of letters; firstly the newspapers which attacked the *Encyclopédie* should make amends and then a guarantee should be obtained from the authorities to protect the work in continuation.

This intransigent attitude, unlike Diderot's flexibility, sprang from a conviction that the monarchy should provide a support for religious and philosophic polemic and that "Philosophy remains, and must remain . . . autonomous and dignified, but parallel to the monarchy."[19] So it was necessary to fight rigorously. Diderot, on the other hand, neither hoped for, nor expected official protection. He avoided confrontation and contented himself with fighting for the *Encylopédie*'s continued appearance. Until then, as can be seen from the article *"Encyclopédie"* Diderot expressed one of the essential characteristics of the philosophy of French enlightenment come to maturity. At a time when Voltaire was still torn between the courts of princes and independence, the *Encyclopédie* was laying the foundations for a free and autonomous movement. If eighteenth-century France was not a land of enlightened despotism, but was instead ruled by the government most hostile to philosophy in enlightened Europe, this was partly because an attempt had already been made in France to establish a cultural class around the monarch. The experiment could not be repeated in the middle of the eighteenth century. The encylopaedists themselves reveal their awareness of the situation. There was no misunderstanding, as has too often been thought, between the enlightened *philosophes* and the monarchy, but a natural separation of forces whose aims from that time were separate.[20] This basic difference of position was destined to explode in 1758 when the second judgement against the *Encyclopédie* was proclaimed; for the time being it was resolved by the fortunate coexistence of ideas which seemed to support d'Alembert.

He derived ample personal satisfaction from the *Journal des Savants* and in the preface to the third volume of the *Encyclopédie* which appeared at the beginning of 1753 under conditions not entirely to his liking, he stresses that the work had been resumed not so much as a result of government action, but in deference to the readers who "by opposing our withdrawal . . . seemed to approve our reasons."[21] Thus, "whereas Diderot's strength and determination had made the continuation of the *Encyclopédie* possible, it was the precision, not to say the arrogance of d'Alembert's stand which effectively assured the *Encyclopédie* of a greater freedom for a few years. Above all his attitude contributed to the atmosphere of respect and dignity which surrounded the *Encyclopédie* and to its prestige during its most fruitful period, the period between the first and second crisis."[22]

Towards the end of 1752, at the time of his correspondence with Madame du Deffand, d'Alembert was just emerging from this hard battle. The victor's insolence of tone does not imply a lack of awareness of the cost of victory, so much as a sensation of having been besieged in his solitary stand.

D'ALEMBERT TO MADAME DU DEFFAND   *Paris 4 December 1752*

I would be most vexed, Madame, were you to believe you had lost me; but despite my great desire to write to you frequently, for two months it has been impossible for me to satisfy this wish as often as I would have liked. I have been very occupied with different pieces of work: I have completed the devil's own piece of geometry on the systematics of the world, which now lacks only a preface. I have written lengthy, reasoned articles on mathematics for the *Encyclopédie*. I have replied to a man who attacked my *Eléments de Musique* and my reply is at the printers: it would bore you. What might perhaps bore you less, but about which I beg you most urgently to speak to no one, are two volumes of *Mélanges de littérature, d'histoire et de philosophie* which I am having printed and which will appear at the end of this month. I would like you to let me know how I may convey them to you immediately. At the beginning of these *Mélanges* there is a philosophical enough *Avertissement*; there follows the *Discours préliminaire* from the *Encyclopédie* and then the *Eloge de l'abbé Terrasson*; Bernouilli's discourse is greatly augmented by details which everyone will be able to read. The second volume is entirely new, it contains some *Réflexions et Anecdotes sur la reine Christine* and *Essai sur les gens de lettres, les grands et les mécènes* and the translation of a dozen of the finest pieces of

Tacitus which will encourage me to translate the rest, if this translation is liked. I have just sent the rest of my manuscript to the printers,
and no longer think about it. I beg you once more to keep this work
a great secret, and above all to write nothing about it to Paris: very
few people are in my confidence here and I am hastening the printing
as much as I am able.

But that is more than enough about myself. I can see from your
last letter that Champrond has not cured you. Your soul seems sad
unto death; and wherefore Madame? Why do you fear to be back in
your own house? With your wit and your income, would you lack
acquaintances there? I do not speak of friends for I know how rare
that commodity is, but I speak of agreeable acquaintances. With a
good supper you can invite whom you please and if you deem it
suitable you can even make fun of your guests. I would almost say
about your sadness what Maupertius said about Madame de La Ferté-
Imbault's gaiety, that it is based on nothing. And as for Maupertius,
he will not be with us this winter; he is sick at the moment and
overwhelmed by pamphlets against him in Holland and Germany
about a certain Koenig with whom he has just had, without much
cause, dealings which were disagreeable to both. It would bore you
and would not amuse me to tell you about it. The King of Prussia is
very busy finding a successor to him as Président, which is another
secret that I must ask you not to repeat and which I would not tell
you if I were not allowed today to tell my friends. More than three
months ago the King of Prussia wrote to me through the Marquis
d'Argens, to offer me the position in the most gracious manner. I
answered, thanking the King for his kindness and the offer. I wanted
you to read my answer which touched the King and only increased
his desire to have me. Monsieur d'Argens wrote to me again, answering my objections more or less well. I answered and once again sent
my thanks. Voltaire has written about it again to Madame Denis, but
I persist, and will persist in my resolve. It is not that I am very pleased
with the ministry or more particularly with the friend—with the so-
called friend—of your Président.[23] Far from it. I know beyond any
question of doubt, that he is very ill disposed towards me, for what
reason I am completely ignorant. But what does it matter? I will
remain in Paris where I will eat bread and walnuts and I will die there
a pauper, but I will be free. I lead a daily more reclusive life; I dine

and sup at home, I go to see my abbé at the *Opéra,* I go to bed at nine
o'clock and work with pleasure, albeit without hope.

I beg you urgently to write nothing about my offers from Berlin to
the Président or to anyone else, although Monsieur d'Argens writes
that secrecy is now useless. I am too grateful for the King's kindness
to wish to parade this little vanity . . .

The *Essai sur la société des gens de lettres et des grands, sur la réputation, sur
les mécènes, et sur les récompenses littéraires* represented d'Alembert's theoretical elaboration of his practical attitude. There is an occasional fastid-
iousness which is also apparent in his correspondence with Madame du
Deffand.

The chief enemies of philosophical progress were the nobility, the
powerful and the patrons of art. Their influence could only corrupt for
their worldliness removed any depth or seriousness from the philosophical movement. The *philosophes* had to resist the temptations of an extra-
neous world. "Dragged from their solitude, men of letters see
themselves carried away by a new whirlwind in which they frequently
find themselves quite displaced. It is an experience which I have had and
which can be useful so long as it does not last."[24] They had to learn to
defend their own integrity: "They must cease paying homage to people
who think they honour them with a look and who seem to announce
that their very politeness is an act of condescension rather than justice;
they must cease seeking the society of the great."[25] In the light of such
considerations, both the events of d'Alembert's life and his temperament
seem somehow exemplary. At first rejected and then courted by society,
on the second occasion he chose autonomy and proud isolation.

It was this concept of independence and dignity which dictated
d'Alembert's refusal of Frederick II's invitation to preside over the
Prussian Academy of Science: a kind of indirect manifesto of an intellectual's duty. Besides, he had affirmed in his *Essai sur la société des gens de
lettres* that an exile could feed only on real persecution, a principle to
which he remained faithful throughout his life.

Nevertheless, the King's proposal filled him with pride. And not only
with pride. The invitation meant far more to him than personal gratifi-
cation, it proved that a collaboration between authority and culture such
as d'Alembert dreamed of in vain for France, was possible. Frederick's

enlightened protection in fact made the French authorities' ambiguous attitude seem all the more cruel.

One may wonder what common ground there was at this stage between Madame du Deffand and d'Alembert. What was it about the monologue of a philosopher bent on changing the world that so fascinated such a disappointed onlooker? How was it that d'Alembert chose to confide his plans to a typical representative of the very society whose undermining frivolity threatened the path of true philosophy? Mistrustful an individual herself, Madame du Deffand loved d'Alembert's moody independence and preferred to ignore his commitment and ideological solidarity with the other *philosophes*. She was fascinated by d'Alembert's work as an intellectual exercise, not for its reforming zeal. It was the cut and style of the *Essai sur la société des gens de lettres* which interested her, rather than the problems it discussed and with which she could only disagree. For his part d'Alembert knew that in Madame du Deffand he had an absolute judge of style, an infallible touchstone against which to measure his own intelligence and at the same time a highly sensitive intermediary who could test public opinion. But whereas the marquise's admiration for the *philosophe*'s intellect was tempered with affection and an almost maternal tolerance, d'Alembert seems bereft of any real feeling for her as a person. He rather sticks to the official image of herself as a *femme d'esprit* which she both presented and imposed, and her intelligence reflected and stimulated his own. The relationship was entirely intellectual and served as a training ground for d'Alembert's intelligence. Questions concerning his friend's personal crisis merely bear witness to offensive indifference on his part and the remedies he suggests crudely over-simplify Madame du Deffand's complex and dramatic personality.

D'ALEMBERT TO MADAME DU DEFFAND *Paris, 22 December 1752*

Herewith, Madame, a large packet which will not compensate you for the cost of delivery;[26] but since you want to have my letters and Monsieur d'Argens' about the King of Prussia's offer, here they are. I beg you to return them when you have finished with them. The rumor is beginning to spread here that I have refused the presidency in question. A person I hardly know told me yesterday that she had heard the news in a letter from Berlin. I replied that I did not know what she was talking about. After all, that it should or should not be known neither vexes nor pleases me. I will keep the King of Prussia's secret even when he no longer asks me to, and you will easily see that my letters were not written for the eyes of the French Minister; I am determined to ask no greater favour than I would ask from the ministers of the King of the Congo and I will content myself with knowing that posterity will read on my tomb: *He was respected by honest men and he died poor because he so wished it.* That, Madame, is how I think. I wish neither to provoke nor to flatter people who have treated me badly or who are disposed so to do; but I will behave in such a way so that the worst they can do is not to help me. In the work I am sending you you will find some truths both bold and wise. I have above all avoided offending anyone, but I have described frankly our folly and our mores, especially those of the patrons of the arts: *D'un soldat qui sait mal farder la vérité.*[27]

You will probably receive my treatises around the 15th of next month; I estimate the printing will be finished in two weeks and I will lose no time in sending them to you by the means you indicate.

Your letter pleased me all the more for making me think that you are better. You must have been truly ill not to have been bored by the life you have been leading for nine months, and I am beginning to think that you are better since this life is beginning to displease you. You speak of your past condition with a fear that amuses me; I flatter myself that this fear will serve to prevent a relapse. Besides you do very well not to boast of it, although in fact you have done nothing unreasonable. You were discontented in Paris; you thought you would feel better at Champrond: you went there. That is only natural. You were bored at Champrond, you tried Mâcon; you felt no better there; you yearn to return to Paris: that is only natural. (This is Mademoiselle de Clermont's confession). To tell the truth, it is very easy for you, even by giving dinners, to lead an agreeable life in Paris. I will see you there as often as I can, but I will only dine with you when you do not fear that I will bore you in a tête-à-tête, for I have become a hundred times fonder of retreat and solitude than I was when you left Paris. I dine and sup at home every day, or nearly every day, and I am very comfortable with this way of life. I will see you then when you have no one and I will hope to find you alone; at other times I would meet your Président which would embarrass me since he would think he had reason to reproach me. I do not think I deserve this and neither do I wish to offend him by self-justification. It is impossible to grant what you ask on his behalf and I can assure you that it must be impossible since I will not do it for you. In the first place *Discourse préliminaire* was printed more than six weeks ago; so I would not be able to add to it even if I wanted to. Secondly, do you honestly think, Madame, that in a work designed to celebrate the nation's geniuses and the works which have genuinely contributed to literary and scientific progress, I ought to discuss the *Abrégé chronologique?* It is a useful work, I admit, and convenient; but in truth that is all. That is what literary people think and what will be said when the Président is no more. And I am concerned that when I myself am no longer, I shall not be reproached for having praised anyone excessively. If you take the trouble to re-read my *Discours préliminaire,* you will see that I praised Fontenelle only for the method, the clarity and the precision with which he was able to deal with difficult subjects: therein lay his real talent. Buffon I praised for his noble and exalted style in inviting philosophical truths: that is just; Maupertius for the advantage he had in being Newton's first follower in France; and that is just; Voltaire only for his pre-eminent talent for writing; and that is just; the Président de Montesquieu only for the attention paid quite rightly throughout Europe to the *Esprit des lois*; and that is just; Rameau only for his symphonies and his books: that is just. In a word, Madame, I can assure you that in writing that work, I had posterity in view on every line and I tried only to make judgement which she would ratify.

"Whoever writes about *"Chronologie"* for the *Encyclopédie* is at liberty to say what he wants about the Président; but that does not concern me, and I will not even undertake to speak about it because I could say no more than that his book is useful, convenient and that it has sold well. I doubt that such praise would satisfy him. Besides I was extremely shocked by the resentment he bore me on that occasion. I sent him my book on fluids for which he did not even deign to thank me. It is to you, much more than to him that I owe my free entries to the *Opéra* which is nothing to me since they were granted with a bad grace and since I have certainly been made to pay since by attitudes to the *Encyclopédie* affair and by conversations about me which do not worry me in the least.

I did not collaborate in the *Apologie de M. l'abbé de Prades* which does not prevent it from being good: I doubt however that it would amuse you. The end of the *Réponse a l'évêque d'Auxerre* and several other passages in this *réponse* are masterpieces of eloquence and reasoning. The propositions are very well justified in the second part, and the first part is a true and well written account of his affair and all the atrocities done him . . ."

The egocentric tone of d'Alembert's letters did not seem to discourage Madame du Deffand from an unusual inclination to confide. But, in the light of her future relationship with Walpole, it may be surmised that it was precisely d'Alembert's brutality that she liked and which inspired her trust. Her suspicious nature, ever ready to interpret kindness as hypocrisy could also entertain another over-simplification: that lack of kindness is a proof of sincerity. When obliged to take account of the *marquise*'s references to her inner suffering, d'Alembert replies with crude rationalisation. He seems to be entrenched behind a principled refutation of existential problems. His deafness to his friend's irrational malaise is such as to make him appear obtuse. Her "terror" amuses him, her "ennui" becomes a symptom of ill-health, her dramatic flight is seen in terms of common sense. Madame du Deffand takes note and proceeds with her usual restraint.

D'Alembert immediately turns his attention back to himself. The insistence with which he stresses his need for solitude and his unworld-liness cannot but be reminiscent of Jean-Jacques Rousseau despite the great difference between the two men. D'Alembert's anti-establishment polemic, like Rousseau's, is strongly rooted in his background with overtones of a persecution complex and it was the Président Hénault who bore the brunt of it this time. This was prompted by Madame du Deffand's appeal for her old lover to be included in the illustrious list of names mentioned by d'Alembert in his *Discours préliminaire* for the third volume of the *Encyclopédie*. His blunt, well-reasoned and final refusal sprang from more than a critical evaluation of Hénault's historiography. In d'Alembert's eyes, the Président had many other faults. He enjoyed a large exaggerated intellectual reputation due to privilege, wealth and connections rather than to the originality of his work. What influence he had depended on his association with the most reactionary and bigoted people at court. And, more generally, just as the professionalism of the intellectual was coming to be defined in the modern sense, the Président was emerging as a dilettante—of which he was indeed a perfect example. Noble disinterest gave way to negative forces.

Bursts of acrimony against Hénault reappear in later letters. The dislike was no doubt mutual, but in d'Alembert's case it was nourished by a feeling of personal resentment and social exclusion making it more suspect than reasonable. Whatever Hénault felt about d'Alembert, he did not turn a deaf ear to Madame du Deffand's requests and resigned himself at least to not blocking d'Alembert's candidature to the *Académie Française.*

Despite his all too frequent—and therefore suspect—declarations of independence and detachment in later letters, d'Alembert reveals a constant preoccupation with his own reputation, and an exasperated mistrust pointing to manipulation, calumny and intrigue on all sides.

D'ALEMBERT TO MADAME DU DEFFAND   *Paris, 27 January 1753*

I appreciate your approbation, Madame, all the more for the fact that I truly desired it. Your approval is infinitely flattering for I know you to be just and your taste to be sure: I did not have to write books and to hear that they were good to tell you that. You do me justice by finding neither malice nor satire in my work. Here everyone is not of the same opinion. I am told that the Bissy–Brancas, etc. etc., are crying out against me. They would do me greater honour by thinking no more of me than I did of them. But what does it matter since I have nothing with which to reproach myself.

I do not know if the *Essai sur les gens de lettres* should have been in the form of portraits and maxims as you would like. Apart from the fact that we already have a considerable number of books of the genre, likenesses to real people would have been all the more readily made. Besides this form would have suited neither the tone which I wanted for the work, nor the continuity of ideas which I sought; and it seems to me, if I am to believe what people say, that this tone and this continuity make the piece even more interesting on a second reading. Pedants are speaking as ill as possible of my translation of Tacitus; but I can tell you that I am not frightened of their criticism, and I would gladly see them at the same task. I do not think that the original loses much by my translation, and I admit in good faith that

I believe it to be at least as beautiful. What I think about Tacitus is exactly what I said in my *Avertissement* which I beg you to read if you haven't already done so. What a man, Tacitus! Ask Formont. As for him, I would be glad to know what he thinks of my two volumes. If you re-read the first volume, you will find some additions to the *Eloge de Bernouilli* which I think interesting.

I have just had my entrée to the *Comédie-Française*; it was through Mademoiselle Clairon's kindness on having read my book; I had only met her to speak to once in her box. La Tour wanted absolutely to paint me[28] and I will hang in the *salon* this year with La Chaussée whom he is also painting, and one of the Italian jesters. There I shall be in the company of the gay and the sad.

I have already had the honour to tell you that you may keep my letters and read them to Formont, but to him alone. Very few people have seen them and only you have a copy. Of everything I have done in my life, they are the only thing which I would like to last when I am no more.

I saw Monsieur de la Croix recently at the *Opéra*. He gave me news of your health and I spoke to him at length about you. He says that you go to bed very late. That is not how to live when you come to Paris. Besides, I believe that you would feel better, whatever your way of life, if you were to watch what you ate; for, as Vernage says, one must not eat too much.

And what condolence should one offer you on the death of the duchesse du Maine? Now is the moment to print Madame de Staal's *Mémoires*. Farewell, Madame, be assured of the tender attachment which I have sworn to you for life.

Madame du Deffand's reading of the *Essai* seems to have been essentially a literary one. Her regret that d'Alembert did not resort to the medium of the literary portrait or the maxim sprang from a classical education and a loyalty to the great models of the preceding century. D'Alembert on the other hand, was entirely concerned with the political and innovatory significance of his work. His exalted intellectualism and taste for provocation were part of an enormous egocentricity which expressed itself in somewhat contradictory attitudes. His need for solidarity and for unreserved agreement was interwoven with a taste for martyrdom and an undoubted sense of persecution. The justly proud awareness of belonging to an intellectual élite in opposition—to what Voltaire called a "persecuted party"[29]—was married in d'Alembert to an ambition to be seen as an exemplary person, a lonely, unassailable Titan.

D'ALEMBERT TO MADAME DU DEFFAND   *Paris, 16 February 1753*

I await with great impatience, Madame, the comments which you promise: I believe them in advance to be most just and I reply in all humility. The outburst against me and my work is prodigious. The interest you take in the matter would be sufficient to console me if I were not philosopher enough to support patiently and listen indifferently to all the ill I hear spoken. But you will be surprised to know that it is not so much my criticism of the great as my praise for Italian music which has made me such a bunch of enemies. I thought one could love everything including puppets without hurting anyone; but I was mistaken. A powerful and formidable group led by Monsieur Jélyotte and the Président Hénault goes from house to house baying for my blood. You can imagine the effect that has had on me and how much I would need my stoicism at this time if I did not deem it necessary to preserve it for even more important occasions. Monsieur de Forcalquier, they say, was also very exercised against me. I do not know why. As for him, he is dead, thank God and we will no longer hear everyone saying, "How is Monsieur de Forcalquier?" as if they were speaking of Turenne or Newton! As for Bissy and company, I think that it is as grandees and patrons of the arts that they bear me ill-will although as you rightly say, one may question their right to such titles. It is said that the Comte de Brissy took the beginning of page 157 of the second volume as a personal attack. It refers no more to him than to anyone else; but it is true that it applies to him. You see, Madame, there is but chance and mischance. You are grateful to me for having avoided satire in my work, but here I am regarded as the most satirical of writers. I have nothing with which to reproach myself; and living in retreat as I do, without seeing anyone, what can their discussions matter to me? My work is public, it has sold quite well, the printing costs have been recovered; praise, criticism and money will come when they will. I have made a fairly ordinary agreement with my booksellers: that they should pay the costs and we will share the profits. I have not yet received anything. I will tell you what I earn. There is no indication that it will be very much; there is no indication either that I will continue to work in this vein. *I will apply myself to geometry and I will read Tacitus.* It seems that there is a great desire for me to keep quiet, and in truth I ask for nothing better. When my little fortune no longer suffices to support me, I will retire to some place where I can live and die cheaply. Farewell, Madame. Like me, judge men for what they are and nothing will spoil your happiness. They say that Voltaire has made it up with the King of Prussia[30] and that Maupertius is out of favour. Upon my word! All men are mad, starting with the wise.

Justified or not, d'Alembert's mistrust did not spare Madame du Deffand's friends. Jélyotte and Hénault whom he sees as united in persecuting him are depicted together in the house of a great Maecenas[31] and in social surroundings, which d'Alembert is accustomed to thinking hostile. The *marquise* seems to ignore or rather not to want to take in this mistrust of her circle. In the only available letter of hers belonging to this correspondence, Madame du Deffand appears affectionately indulgent and concerned only lest the polemic distract her protégé from his vocation as a writer. The nature of their friendship reveals itself here as a personal and private one, capable of flourishing away from society, nurtured in solitude by an intellectual understanding.

MADAME DU DEFFAND TO D'ALEMBERT   *Mâcon, 22 March 1753*

If you have ever heard of the Vaugirard Registrar,[32] tell me about it. You have decided to tell me that you have shown some of my letters to the abbé de Canaye and that they pleased him. How do you suppose that I can continue to write to you? It is beyond imagination. But as you will not show him my letter, if you do not think it worth it, I say to myself that he will not see this one, and that puts me at my ease. I would be delighted if you could persuade this abbé to make my acquaintance, but you will not succeed. It would be at best like Diderot, for whom one visit was enough: I have no means of attracting him.

I have written to Formont telling him to send you his opinions on your work. He thinks more or less as I do: he finds your *Essai sur les grands, les mécènes* ... lengthy but he is enchanted by the style. He claims that La Bruyère's genre would have been better suited, but he agrees that you were right not to adopt it as too many people have tried it. He would despair, as I would, were you to shut yourself up with your geometry: that is all the self-styled fine minds and minor authors want, and it is what they are aiming at by inveighing against you. Be enough of a philosopher not to care about seeming one, that your scorn for men be so sincere as to enable you to deprive them of the means and the hope of offending you.

I propose to see you soon, that is sooner than I had expected unless some accident occurs which I am unable to foresee. I shall be in Paris during the month of June; I will be exceedingly vexed if on arrival I learn that you are in the country. I am truly impatient to see you and to talk to you. The life I lead will suit you, I hope. We will often dine together alone and we will each confirm our resolve to allow our happiness to depend only on ourselves. I will teach you perhaps to be able to bear mankind and you will teach me how to do without it. Find me some secret cure for ennui and I will owe you more than if you gave me the secret to the philosopher's stone. My health is not entirely bad but I am going blind. I intend to go next week to Lyons where I will see the Cardinal.[33]

I doubt that his purple makes him any happier than the barrel makes a certain nephew of his.[34] Do not let this journey of which I speak prevent you from writing; it will be very short and I will still receive your letters. Farewell. Do your very best to persuade the abbé de Canaye to make my acquaintance: I do not know why his niece and he have always put me in mind of *Thérèse philosophe*.[35] Perhaps you do not know that book. Should you make enquiries, do not say that it is because I told you about it.

Madame du Deffand's allusion to the impossibility of establishing any kind of rapport with Diderot refers to the writer's noticeable absence from her *salon* at Saint-Joseph.[36] There was reason enough for antipathy. The bruises he dealt Catherine the Great's legs while conversing with her are proof enough of his legendary coarseness and intractable character.[37] But Madame du Deffand must have put up with considerable rudeness from d'Alembert. The insuperable reasons for her dislike of Diderot were not merely personal and they help to throw some light on her attitude to d'Alembert. She probably sensed a far more dangerous radicalism in Diderot than in her protégé. Whereas d'Alembert wanted to reform the world within the context of the established order, Diderot sought to change it radically. D'Alembert's rigid theorising combined with a contempt for compromise rendered him harmless whereas Diderot's passionate contradictory views constituted a threat to Madame du Deffand's unyielding conservatism. Without fearing it, she allowed herself the luxury of at least partially ignoring d'Alembert's ideology and concentrated on his literary and humanistic talents instead. He may only have been striking attitudes, but d'Alembert's threats to take refuge from polemic in the study of science alarmed her. She encouraged him, not without irony, to be both more detached and truer to his professed position as a *philosophe* and not to become childishly involved in the game of provocation which ought not to touch him.

She spoke with authority: the simplicity with which Madame du Deffand confronted her own destiny was nothing if not "philosophical." The only letter to d'Alembert dating from these years suddenly gives the impression that the *marquise* has decided to turn the page, to abandon her hopes and fears and to take account of reality. It is a rare moment in the whole correspondence, in which Madame du Deffand accepts not only infirmity and sickness which she faces with her usual dignified stoicism, but also—and above all—her difficulties in coming to terms with herself.

A letter to her friend Scheffer predating the one to d'Alembert by a few weeks, reflects a determination to obliterate the past and to discourage any embarrassing, moralistic or existential understanding of her crisis.

MADAME DU DEFFAND TO COUNT SCHEFFER   *Mâcon, 7 February 1753*

Your letter gave me infinite pleasure. It is charming and greatly increases my displeasure at our separation. I am more than ever persuaded of your friendship; you do not forget me despite the distance and among the things which you regret, you have the goodness to preserve a little place for me. I had no right to expect such favours. My departure from Paris and the condition I was in before leaving were enough for me to be forgotten by those who loved me only moderately. You, Monsieur, are luckily for me not of this number. Your goodness goes so far as to imagine excuses to justify my conduct and I would be flattered if I did not know myself to be the less and if I wanted to deceive others. But I do not have any illusions and I wish to deceive no one. I was very ill when I left Paris. Physical weakness brought with it weakness of the mind and had produced in me what are called the "vapours." It is a condition which I hope you will never know and to which death is preferable.

My health is now greatly improved; the life I lead here, where I have been for two months, has almost entirely cured me; I propose to return to Paris during the summer. . . ."[38]

Scheffer did not conceal his surprise at Madame du Deffand's explanation of her illness as entirely physiological, but he obediently accepted her word.

Count Scheffer to Madame du Deffand   *Stockholm, 9 March 1753*

. . . the news which you have graciously given me of your health and of your plan to return to Paris is as good as any I could hope to hear. Was it absolutely a matter of the "vapours" only? I admit that I believed the physical sickness to be accompanied by a moral sickness far more difficult to cure, by a disgust of the world which fed your vapours and made them the bitterer. It is with great satisfaction that I acknowledge my mistake. God grant that you never again succumb to such a condition!

Madame du Deffand left Champrond and spent the winter at Mâcon in the hope of resolving the problem of Julie and of being able to take her niece with her to Paris. Mâcon is closer to Lyons where the girl had retired to a convent and Madame du Deffand could go to see her and correspond with her regularly away from the supervision of the Vichys. True enough Julie was by now of age and so no longer under the guardianship of her brother, d'Albon and theoretically free to do as she pleased. The Vichys never had any authority over her other than that of their terrible bounty. Julie's freedom was, in fact, only theoretical. The tiny annuity left by her mother did not provide financial independence and despite the "horrors" of the situation, the bastard orphan could not and did not want entirely to renounce her family. It was the only real affection that remained to her—for the remainder of her life she kept determinedly in touch with her nephews and nieces—and, however confused and embarrassing, it was the only means of identification available to her. Besides, pride forbade her to deny her origins. So Julie hesitated to make a decision which whilst allowing her to escape from an unbearable situation, ran the risk of causing an irreversible break with the past whereby her independence would not be guaranteed and her conditions of slavery would only change.

For her part, Madame du Deffand wanted to avoid quarrelling with the Vichys. Although her feelings for them were only luke-warm, bordering on indifference, the *marquise* always wished to remain on good terms with her family and to show social solidarity. With the passage of time she became increasingly attentive to form and at the same time more definitely realistic. The family remained a force within the social structure of the *ancien régime*. Scandal and internal quarrels were best avoided and could only constitute a threat to the prestige and interests of all concerned. Madame du Deffand feared above all that an echo of a quarrel with the Vichys might reach Madame de Luynes's ear. Because of her position as lady-in-waiting and friend of the Queen, this maternal aunt had become the family matriarch and no one wished to run the risk of her disapproval or of losing her authoritative support and the hopes of an eventual legacy.

With this in mind Madame du Deffand devised an elaborate plan to persuade the Vichys by indirect means that her annexation of Julie was the safest possible course of action.

The Vichys and d'Albon all of whom were probably indifferent to Julie's fate, were obliged to take care of her as a potential risk. Julie could in fact, at any given moment, and with a possible chance of success, claim her birthright and so she represented a permanent threat of scandal. This risk was in inverse proportion to the family's control over her. At Champrond where Julie was more or less a prisoner, the risk was non-existent, but at Lyons where she was born and where her history was known, it became a definite possibility. It would, of course, have been possible to arrange a marriage for her but no one was rich enough or generous enough to provide her with a dowry. Madame du Deffand hoped that her offer of taking Julie with her would provide the Vichys with the same guaranteed control as imprisonment at Champrond (with the additional advantage of the absolute anonymity in which the girl would arrive in Paris), and that they would see it as a reasonable solution to their problem. But in order to achieve her ends, Madame du Deffand had carefully to prepare the ground and at the same time to be quite sure of having her niece in her grasp. Her correspondence with Julie bears witness to this two-fold anxiety and to an impressive hardness.

MADAME DU DEFFAND TO MADEMOISELLE DE LESPINASSE
Mâcon, 16 January 1753

If I told you that your letters resemble Madame de Vauban's, I take it back. The one I received yesterday bears no resemblance to hers. She did not set an example of four pages of fear and anxiety without the slightest foundation. You cannot convince me that you took literally what I told you about the *Filles de Sainte Marie*. To tell the truth I do not think you know what to tell me, which is not surprising if you do not wish to speak with trust. A little while ago I would have forgiven you for behaving like this, but now you have no good reason for not speaking naturally to me or for not naming things by their names. It would have pleased me had you told me all you know about Madame de L'Argentière and of the visit which Monsieur and Madame d'Albon intend to make before going to Roanne etc. One should either not write to one's friends, or the letters should be part of a conversation: assurances of attachment and friendship are so commonplace and so frequently used by those who do not love each other at all, that those who do love each other should avoid them. I have scolded you enough. Now I will answer the three points in your letter which deserve attention.

The first concerns Madame de la Motte. I had been discussing her at length with Monsieur de Mâcon two hours before your letter arrived, and I had decided how to behave towards her which was to show infinite friendship for you. I would speak of the regret which I had witnessed at your departure, of the reasons which caused you to go into retreat and of the incongruity of your choice of a convent in Lyons, which could only displease those to whom you are connected. I would explain that both their interests and yours would best be served by your moving to another part of the country and perhaps even changing your name. Thus I would lead her by such considerations, step by step, to think of the plan in question herself, and would allow her merely to suspect that my friendship for you and my need for agreeable and constant companionship would make it easy for me to undertake to have you with me. I have decided that if she puts the suggestion to me I will create some difficulties which I will, however, make it easy to overcome. When I have yielded I will suggest a convent in Paris to begin with: firstly so that we cannot be thought to have come to any understanding between us and secondly because that suits me better with regard to the respect I have for my friends. I wish them to see you established by degrees in my house.

One of the motives which I will use to explain my yielding is that I shall be able to guarantee your relatives of your safety.

The second point in your letter concerns the desire you may have to learn something. If that is what you want, I can see nothing to prevent it; the question of expense does not seem important to me. It is only right that you should amuse yourself and therefore you must choose to learn what would most please you. Since I have learned nothing in my life, I would not know where to tell you to begin.

The third point is Monsieur d'Alban's letter. It seems neither good nor bad to me. When I come to Lyons we will discuss the matter further.

Farewell. I think this letter will be a greater proof of my friendship than if it were filled with assurances of attachment and affection which are but commonplace and not to be used, as I have told you, by those who love each other.

MADAME DU DEFFAND TO MADEMOISELLE DE LESPINASSE

Mâcon, 3 February 1753

This time, my Queen, I am very pleased with your letter and I reply with great pleasure. For days I have reproached myself for not writing to you, but, I don't know why, I do not have a single minute to myself. I write only during my *toilette* in the morning and the evening . . .

It will be a critical moment for you, my Queen, when I am at Lyons. You must arm yourself with courage and make a great many decisions, but whatever your success, it will never be said that you are abashed. I promise that if you back me, I will arrange things well. I hope to be able to contribute to your happiness if you decide to be the source of mine, but I want your unreserved trust in every way; the slightest reserve would mortally wound my friendship.

Having decided to return to Paris by the beginning of the summer at the latest, Madame du Deffand meant to take Julie with her. She travelled to Lyons around Easter with the intention of obtaining Julie's definite consent. Madame du Deffand interrogated her niece for ten days, subjecting her to a kind of general examination, sounding her feelings and her intentions, scrutinising all the possibilities and to the last detail laying down the rules for their future life together. Julie's indecision gave way under pressure from her aunt. The carping egoism and humiliating mistrust hidden behind the seductive front must both have chipped away at Julie's courage. Any illusions as to her brother's loyalty were gradually fading and Julie had learned how hard is the path of lonely, poverty-stricken independence. The only privileges to alleviate the harshness of convent life were a room to herself and a certain freedom of movement which she owed to the protection of an old friend of her aunt's — Cardinal de Tencin, the Archbishop of Lyons whose support the *marquise* had guaranteed.

As soon as she had extracted Julie's promise, Madame du Deffand returned to Mâcon, but before she was able to confront her family she received a letter from Vichy who had heard of his sister's maneuvers.

THE COMTE DE CHAMPRON TO MADAME DU DEFFAND

Champrond, 14 April 1753

If, my dear sister, Deschamps had left only this morning instead of Thursday, the letter which I sent you by him would also have concerned some news which I received yesterday from our châteaux messenger. That is, one of my friends has written to me from Lyons. As I put no faith in tittle-tattle and since I am convinced that, as in the comedy *Le Méchant*,[39] the best hearsay is worth nothing, I could give no credence to the contents of this letter. I even think that you have not followed me so far. Here then is the news: you are taking Mademoiselle de Lespinasse with you to Paris. What a suggestion is this, that you could have thought of such a thing without having told me about it first or that I might imagine that you could wish in sang-froid to shock me so deeply! No, my dear sister, I believe nothing of it. This young lady did not leave my house in a sufficiently agreeable manner for my sister to play a trick such as a total stranger would not play on me. So, I repeat that far from giving credence to this news, I am sending my friend a sharp answer. I am, however, glad to inform you of this rumour although I believe it to be senseless, so that you can tell me what you think gave rise to it.

Since I wrote the day before yesterday, I have nothing further to tell you, except that Madame de Vichy sends her compliments and that I embrace you with all my heart. We are about to get into the coach to go to Roanne where we will stay until the Monday after Low Sunday, so I will have more than enough time to receive your answer if you mark the address "at Roanne, by Lyons."

MADAME DU DEFFAND TO THE COMTE DE CHAMPROND

Saturday 21 April 1753

A simple detail, true and precise, with regard to my behaviour to-wards Mademoiselle de Lespinasse will serve as an answer to your letter of 14 April which I received yesterday, my dear brother.

I was at Champrond when Mademoiselle de Lespinasse resolved to go to the convent. She told me that there was nothing new about her decision, that she had informed Madame de Vichy of it the winter before, and had declared that in deference to her wishes she could postpone her departure for several months, but that she would never change her mind. I did everything possible to make her change her mind. She was unshakeable. We spoke about it to Madame de Vichy; I witnessed the regret which she felt at losing her, and even under-took, on her behalf, to try again to persuade Mademoiselle de Lespi-nasse to stay with you. Such attempts were again useless. I was then informed of Madame de Vichy's offer to take her back were she subsequently disgusted by convent life, and of the invitation you gave her to come and spend some time with you at least once a year. All these things which you know to be true convinced me (and I am convinced) that Mademoiselle de Lespinasse did not leave you in a disagreeable way.

I started from that premise when I conceived of the idea of

befriending Mademoiselle de Lespinasse. I am old, increasingly infirm and I am losing my sight, this makes me wish to have someone with me who will do little things for me, keep me company and be my friend. Mademoiselle de Lespinasse is the one person in the world who seemed best to suit me. I have spent six months with her; I know her mind; I have studied her character and I am quite satisfied with both. Once I had considered the matter, I dreamed of a suitable way in which to carry out the plan I had formed. I realised that success depended on three people, or rather I wanted to execute my plan only with the approval of three people: yourself, my dear brother, Monsieur d'Albon and Mademoiselle de Lespinasse. I began with the last. Had she refused me, that would have been the end of it. I spoke to her. She did not show me the door, but neither did she wish to promise me anything. Finally, as my sight grew worse every day, I realised sadly that I needed a companion as soon as possible and that I should consider attaching myself to someone quite else since I could not have Mademoiselle de Lespinasse. So I spoke to her at length about it during my visit to Lyons and demanded a decisive answer. I even offered to give her an annuity of 400 *livres* as soon as she came to live with me. She replied that she would be glad to come but that such was her attachment to Monsieur d'Albon that she could make no decision without his consent and approval. On Thursday, the 19th of this month, I received a letter from Mademoiselle de Lespinasse saying that she had written to Monsieur d'Albon and that she will tell me his answer as soon as she receives it.

Now is the moment when I can and must speak to you, my dear brother, and that is what I am doing. Does my proposal suit you, or does it not? Your opinion will decide me. This is what I decided yesterday to write to you today. I wanted to write to Monsieur d'Albon at the same time, to enclose my letter and to beg you to give it to him and to urge him to grant me Mademoiselle de Lespinasse. Your letter of 14th which I received yesterday prevents me from writing to Monsieur d'Albon until I have received your answer to this. It is with pain that I see from your letter of 14th that you do not approve of my ideas, but I would like to think that when you have further considered the matter, you will either consent to it (in which case I will send you my letter for Monsieur d'Albon) or, whilst refusing, you will agree at least inwardly, that my request was reasonable and that I need not have expected it to displease you, but rather than your friendship for me and your consideration for my condition would be enough not to deprive me of the assistance I need.

Madame du Deffand's answer is a clever mixture of justification and clarification leading to a final act of submission. She probably thought that these were the best tactics with which to confuse Vichy, to oblige him to be generous, make it impossible for him to say no. There is no trace of such placid reasonableness in the letter which Madame du Deffand wrote to Julie three days later on 24 April. "Indignation," "anger" and "fear" overcome the *marquise* who borders on a nervous collapse. The violence of her reaction which was far more "natural" than she would have expected, goes to show what an important part Julie played in her plans and hopes. But Madame du Deffand's realism soon got the better of her emotions, and disappointment and anger gave way to reason and determination. She sent Julie with cold authority, the draft of a letter for d'Albon and dictated the new line of tactics. An attempt must be made to move Vichy by meekness and to reassure and convince him that Julie's hope of going to live with Madame du Deffand was the best possible solution to this prickly family problem.

THE COMTE DE CHAMPROND TO MADAME DU DEFFAND

Roanne, 26 April 1753

. . . It is true that you rectify everything perfectly and that there is nothing more to say once you have said that my opinion will decide you. I recognise my sister in these words, and by taking advantage of the opportunity she gives me to explain myself to her, I once again beg her to abandon her plan all the more because I see it as misplaced. I beg even more urgently that this matter be kept between ourselves. We have no need of a third—what good would that do? I will certainly not change my mind over this matter. I believe it is even useless to speak further about it because I have had all the time I need to think carefully about it.

As for the assistance which you claim you will be able to get from this girl, I can reply with all the sincerity demanded of the most loving friendship, that you will have no difficulty in finding it elsewhere. If, by chance, you tire of one another, imagine the embarrassment in which you would find yourself! Believe me, my dear sister, enough trouble comes to us naturally in this life without our going out to look for more.

As you may imagine, I have shown your letter to my brother-in-law. He had already expressed considerable surprise on reading the first two which I received from Lyons. He told me on reading yours that he had answered the request made him concerning this matter to the effect that he did not approve. So his way of thinking happened to be the same as mine. Monsieur d'Albon is in a position to help this young lady; he has already given her unequivocable proof of this. His friendship for her which she cannot doubt, should leave her with no fear for the future. So, my dear sister, I beseech you to leave it at that. Nothing can come of it but nonsense which would do no honour to anyone; you could give me greater pleasure . . .

Although Madame du Deffand may have deluded herself that she could assuage her brother by diplomacy and humility and that her infirmity might move him to change his mind, this second letter from Vichy made it clear that no further discussion of any kind was possible. To take Julie away with her would unquestionably mean a break with the Vichys and the d'Albons. Neither woman was prepared for such definitive action and at the end of May Madame du Deffand set out for Paris alone.

VII

Paris Again

MADAME DU DEFFAND TO COUNT SCHEFFER   *Paris, 12 July 1753*

... I have been back for six weeks. There are a lot of people whom I have been glad to see, and who have welcomed me kindly but I have felt no great joy and no swelling of the heart: I did not find provincial dullness unbearable, I expected nothing else; more is expected of Paris and so one suffers more from the privations. Besides, monotony is a gentle condition to which the soul easily becomes accustomed. However, I do not at all despair at being in Paris, I have decided to take things as they come and people as they are. I neither claim nor demand anything of the objects around me, I try to appreciate everything according to its own value and to enjoy all the indifference which I inspire; it would be a very happy state without the attendant disadvantage which is ennui. Of all the soul's sicknesses, it is the most horrible, it is the forerunner of annihilation and can alone suggest the torture of the after-life. In a word it is an appalling ill and one which is inevitable for anyone who, having been racked by passion, suffers from its absence. Only continuous, excessive dissipation or forced activity can serve as a palliative. There might be one better thing; that one thing would be religion, but I fear it would only be useful were it to become a passion in itself and one has no greater command over this passion than over any other. My usual refrain is to say that there is only one misfortune in life, which is to be born ...

You will suppose from this letter that I am very sad and very gloomy, but you would be wrong. I do not at the moment feel any sorrow, everything I write is the result of years of reflection. No particular circumstance provokes me at present. I have found my friends solicitous and I see them again with pleasure. I am touched by their pleasantness, but rather, I admit, as one is moved at the theatre. I have seen behind the scenes and I am waiting for the curtain to fall.[1]

In the late spring of 1753, after a year away, Madame du Deffand returned to Paris, by now almost completely blind. She was not so much cured as inured to suffering. Unable to enjoy life, she thought she could protect herself from it by detachment. Strengthened by her indifference, she returned to her usual way of life; she re-opened her *salon,* exchanged visits, supped out and was accompanied to the *Opéra* and the theatre. This required an enormous effort on her part which was all the greater for her determination to prevent her blindness from changing her old habits whenever possible.

To prevent over-exhaustion, she decided, among other things, to receive her guests for dinner rather than supper. An expert on Parisian life such as Scheffer was aware that the importance of such a decision should not be overlooked and was indeed worthy of comment: "It is time to say that the decision you have taken to dine, can be equally recommended from the point of view of society and from the point of view of your health; the hour is more agreeable and those who dine willingly acquire a quietness of manner which is most agreeable for those with whom they live. To tell the truth I have attended more gay dinners than suppers." (From Stockholm, 2 November 1753.) The choice of dinner was not, however, definitive, since in December of the same year Bulkeley wrote to Scheffer: "Madame du Deffand's Wednesday suppers have begun again."[2]

Once again Madame du Deffand's friends gathered round her; not least among them Montesquieu whenever he was in Paris. On 16 November 1753, in a reply to an invitation from d'Alembert to collaborate in the *Encyclopédie,* the author of the *Esprit des lois* wrote, "I beg you to tell Madame du Deffand that I continue to write about philosophy, she will be my *marquise*[3] ... As for my participating in the *Encyclopédie,* it is a fine palace in which I would be interested to tread; but as for the two articles, 'Democracy' and 'Despotism'[4] I would not like to do them.

I have dragged from my brain all that I can on these subjects. My mind is like a mould which always produces the same thing; so I would only say what I have said and would perhaps say it less well than I have already done. So, if you want something from me, leave the choice of subject to me; and if you like, it can be made at Madame du Deffand's with a glass of maraschino."[5]

The select mixture of guests at the Saint-Joseph *salon* provoked a certain nostalgia in one erstwhile member of society. The chevalier d'Aydie—Aïssé's one time lover—who had long since retired to the country, wrote: "I congratulate you Madame, on the pleasure you have in seeing Monsieur Formont and Monsieur de Montesquieu again: you certainly have a great deal to do with their return. I know how attached the former is to you, and the latter has often told me with his usual sincerity and naïveté: 'I love that woman with all my heart; she pleases me and amuses me; it is impossible to be bored with her for a moment.' ... So when I think, firstly of you Madame, and then of those you gather around you, Mesdames de Mirepoix, du Châtel, the Président Hénault, Messieures de Bulkeley, d'Alembert etc., I am enraged to be a hundred leagues away, but I have neither the ambition nor the vanity of Caesar. I prefer to be least and barely tolerated in the best of company, rather than first and the most highly considered in the worst or ordinary company." (From Mayac, 28 January 1754.)

But the strategy of indifference she developed during her months of illness was not enough to prevent Madame du Deffand from needing others. Without needing personal relationships, she required the presence of people around her, and thus adopted the duchesse du Maine's famous motto for herself, frequently quoting it in her correspondence: "I cannot do without things which are unimportant to me." Her plans for a quiet life surrounded by a few friends soon gave way to the old need for continuous distraction and permanent excitement, made all the more essential by her blindness. On 21 February 1754 she wrote to Scheffer: "I do not believe that I have been alone for one hour during the last three weeks; and company is so essential to me because of the condition of my sight, thus I put off writing what pleases me most until I am alone and I do not have the courage to seek that solitude. I ingenuously offer you this excuse and this confession. The new acquaintances of whom I spoke are men of letters, philosophers of great intelligence whose names you do not know, but whose worth you would be swift to recognise and who for their part would be struck by yours."[6]

To the outside world this dependence made Madame du Deffand seem remarkably courageous and heroically true to herself, whereas her fear of solitude was interpreted as spirited light-heartedness. The Président confided in Scheffer: "Madame du Deffand bears her unfortunate condition with great courage. Her blindness, which is total, has not detracted from her gaiety, she always sees the best and the grandest people."[7]

But she could not always avoid reality and on occasions it was a relief to face up to it. It was no coincidence that she chose Montesquieu as her confidant. He, too, was going blind, and in a reply which has often been judged superficial and cynical, he delicately and ironically finds a way of belittling their shared drama:

"I begin with your footnote. You say that you are blind! Do you not see that you and I were once little rebellious spirits who were condemned to darkness? We should be consoled by the fact that those who see clearly are, for all that, not luminous. I am glad that you are accommodating yourself to the learned magistrate:[8] if you manage not to amuse him too much, you will be all right; and when it has gone too far, you can send him to Chaulnes.[9]

About the Academy post, I will do what Madame de Mirepoix, d'Alembert and you wish; but I cannot speak for Monsieur de Saint-Maur, for no man has ever been so private as he. I am glad that my *Defense* pleased Monsieur Lemonnier. I feel that what pleases him is to see the venerable theologians not so much knocked down, as left to sink slowly.

It is remarkable that a lady with a Wednesday *salon* should have no news. I will let that pass. Here I am overwhelmed with business; my brother is dead; I read no books, I walk a lot, I often think of you, I love you.

With my greatest respects . . .[10]

D'Alembert alone could shake Madame du Deffand out of her indifference. She became passionately involved in his career as an Academician, thereby giving reign to a double ambition: her intense maternal feelings towards her protégé which led her to seek ever greater recognition for him, and the far more direct need to establish her own prestige. She at first cherished a plan for d'Alembert to become Secretary of the *Académie des Sciences* of which, in recognition of his precocious genius, he had been made a member at the age of twenty-three.

D'ALEMBERT TO MADAME DU DEFFAND   *Blanc-Menil, 3 September {1753}*

However much I wanted to, it was impossible for me to see you in Paris, Madame, for I left on Wednesday morning for Blanc-Mesnil where I am at present. I am more than aware of all your kindness and of all that you have said on my behalf to Monsieur d'Arg . . . ;[11] but I beg you not to consider the position of secretary to the *Académie*. When that post is as easily obtainable as it is at present difficult, I will be no more disposed to make any move to obtain it. I am much less suited to it than you imagine. It requires considerable servitude and precision and you know me well enough to be aware that my freedom is what I most love. It also requires a great knowledge of chemistry, anatomy, botany etc: which I do not have and which I am in no hurry to acquire. It demands frequent praise of very mediocre people and things, and I do not know how one can resolve to praise where no praise is deserved, nor how one continues to do so; this task is too difficult for me. Besides, since Monsieur de Fontenelle, the public is used to seeing the task done in a certain way which would not be mine at all, and to ask him to change his style once he had adopted it, for good or ill, would involve too great a risk. So I beseech you, Madame, to forget any ideas inspired in you by Monsieur de Saint-Marc and which I deeply regret, of my filling that post. If I have any talent for writing, I will easily be able to exercise it without being Secretary to the *Académie* and will have more time for geometry which I would be extremely loath to give up; it is a reliable resource: with it one is never bored; one makes no noise, and few enemies. My position in the world is not great and I work every day to make it smaller. To find oneself in nobody's way is a sure path to happiness. I am none the less aware of everything you want to do for me, but Monsieur de Maur . . .[12] and Madame de Ten . . .[13] have taught me to do without position, fortune and esteem.

I will return to Paris around the 12th. If you are there I will have the honour of seeing you.

Madame du Deffand allowed neither the failure of her plan for the *Académie des Sciences* nor her protégé's contentious nature to discourage her, but concentrated instead on a new and more ambitious project. Ever since d'Alembert's *Discours Préliminaire* to the *Encyclopédie* had won him a reputation as a writer, Madame du Deffand had aspired to see him installed in the *Académie Française*. The prestige of the women who held *salons* depended not only on their ability for original social organisation, but on their ability to influence both opinion and the great institutions of which the *Académie Française*, founded by Cardinal Richelieu, was the greatest challenge to their authority. The marquise de Lambert's influence over elections to the *Académie* had been even more remarkable than the duchesse du Maine's: "It was impossible to be received into the *Académie* without being presented at her house," d'Argenson[14] wrote of Madame de Lambert. However, neither of these ladies presented candidates arbitrarily. They spoke, rather, for the tastes and attitudes of those who surrounded them. "But between 1735 and 1755, an infinite multiplicity of influences developed; nothing remained of the erstwhile literary coterie, the *Académie* was ruled by intrigue and vanity."[15] In 1732, in his famous letter to Lefèvre about the inconveniences of being a professional man of letters, Voltaire describes the frantic atmosphere which surrounded every election: "Barely has one of the forty breathed his last before ten candidates present themselves; . . . they hurry to Versailles; they have all the ladies talking; every intriguer begins to plot and every resource is tapped."[16]

Amidst such anarchy, where there was more competition for the protector's prestige than the applicant's, and where grandees backed a candidate whose main qualification was his dependence, Madame du Deffand had not only to deal with the usual cabal of intriguers, but to face enormous hostility to d'Alembert, not only from court circles and high society, but from most of the academicians themselves. The *Académie* was a conservative stronghold, faithful to the cult of Louis XIV, linked to the Jesuits, hostile to innovation, and impervious to the cultural renewal which was then rife in France. As the years went by, some of the "new" men were grudgingly and with difficulty elected to it: Montesquieu (1727), Voltaire after three attempts (1746), Duclos (1747), Buffon (1753). D'Alembert was bound to seem like an enemy and a conscious and aggressive one at that: "The *Encyclopédie* came out yesterday," he wrote to Madame du Deffand in October 1753, "pray to God for us; we are going to cause a deal of shouting perhaps, but we do not care";[17] and a few days later about the Jesuits' reaction, "We tiptoed around them in the first volume; but in case they are not grateful there are six or seven hundred articles pertaining to them in the other volumes."[18] And as if that were not enough, the "Sublime Geometer,"[19] in his *Essai sur la société des gens de lettres,* denounced the decadence of the *Académie* itself: "That rare man [Richelieu], who recognised the value of talent, wanted intelligence in the *Académie Française* to be placed on a level with rank and nobility, and for all the men of letters to take precedence there over all titles. He wanted this academy to be almost entirely composed of the nation's good writers that the wise might recognise its distinction, and a small number of grandees to impress the people; but the latter should fill only the places left empty by the great writers. Thus in the *Académie Française* prejudice should honour talent, rather than talent flattering prejudice."[20] By making this distinction between professional and non-professional writers, d'Alembert sowed the seeds of discord in the *Académie* itself and by urging men of letters "to recognise at last that the surest way to be respected, was to be united ... and almost enclosed among themselves,"[21] he alienated, "most of his natural protectors, those grandees who were happy to have literary protégés whose useless homage they repaid with concrete favours."[22]

Under the circumstances, d'Alembert's candidacy for the *Académie* came as an exciting challenge and a wonderful tonic for Madame du Deffand. The first major obstacle was created by d'Alembert himself: although he was not at all without vanity and clearly understood the political importance of eventual success, the *philosophe* persistently displayed his cult of integrity. "We are not of the *Académie,* but we are Quakers," he wrote to Madame du Deffand, "and we pass in front of the *Académie* and in front of those who belong to it with our hats on our heads."[23] The *marquise* wove her web patiently. Inside the *Académie,* d'Alembert could count on Montesquieu's authoritative support. "You defend yourself against the *Académie* in vain," the author of the *Esprit des Lois* wrote in a humorous mood, "we too have some materialists."[24] He could also depend on Duclos's devoted propaganda. Outside, Madame d'Aiguillon and Madame de Mirepoix were loyal and powerful allies. The Président Hénault, on the other hand, constituted a delicate problem. His support was of fundamental importance and although his obedience to the *marquise* was almost absolute, d'Alembert's scorn had put his patience and good nature to the test. Besides, Hénault whose *Chronologie* had been so badly treated, was the *Académie* spokesman for the Queen's God-fearing, conservative opinions.

D'ALEMBERT TO MADAME DU DEFFAND   *Paris, 19 October 1753*

The arrival of your letter, Madame, was most well-timed for I was concerned about you and would even have written to you had I not received yours. The letter you wrote to Monsieur de Mâcon was blacker than Tartarus and sadder than the Elysian Fields. I imagine the secretary Wiart is better since you do not mention him. Do not be too alarmed by what I wrote to you about the article *"Chronologie."* I feel sure that the Président Hénault will not thank me for it. He ought to however, as I say that we have several good works of this kind in our language, his own, one by a certain Macquer (which is better although I do not say so), and the one by the two Benedictines (which is better than either of the first two), and which I merely cite. He will do whatever he pleases about the *Académie*; my behaviour proves that I have no desire to be part of it, and to tell the truth, even if I did, I would have no need of him; but the pleasure of speaking the truth freely without shocking or attacking anyone is worth all the academies in the world, from the *Académie Française* to Dugast's . . .

Do not worry about my Quakerism; it will never be for you: on the contrary, the more of a Quaker one is with people one despises, the more sensible one becomes to the friendship of those one loves and respects . . ."

The friendship between Madame du Deffand and d'Alembert had reached its height. Through the *philosophe,* Madame du Deffand participated in the intense intellectualism of the 1750s—years in which the enlightenment became established. Her passionate friendship for d'Alembert and her curiosity concerning him, drove her to take an interest in the new developments and to stand back from them critically without withdrawing completely or taking refuge in the past. For his part, d'Alembert repaid so much interest with total confidence. The *marquise* became the repository for his plans, his moods, his hopes. The tone of the letters written during a brief visit to the country by Madame du Deffand, denotes a close friendship and a boorish but affectionate intimacy. In the following letter d'Alembert resents being compared to a cat, but he cannot ignore the fact that the *marquise* has a passion for cats and they are even depicted stamped on the binding of the books in her library. He jokingly threatens his possessive and jealous old friend with the daughter of Madame Rousseau, the humble woman who brought him up and with whom he still lodges.

D'ALEMBERT TO MADAME DU DEFFAND   *Paris, 21 October 1753*

First of all, Madame, you are wrong to be angry with me; I was mislead by the postal list which says that the courier leaves Nemours at midnight on Fridays and I wrote to you on Friday morning. I would gladly have left on Friday morning but business has kept Duché in Paris; so we will leave on Thursday and be at "Boulay"[25] on Sunday or Monday next for a whole week.

I have arranged for my printers to do without me for eight days and the four holidays give me a further four days. I must want to see you as much as I do if I am to abandon the solitude in which I live and in which I am the happiest man in the world. Convalescence of the soul is like that of the body: one feels the value of it more than one feels the value of health. I do not know what the cats are like with whom you do me the honour of classing me; but I pity them greatly if they have suffered as much as I have. I am glad to tell you, incidentally, that every time you call me a moral cat, you increase the rights of Mademoiselle Rousseau to whom you have taken such an aversion; frankly I love you madly, you can ask Duché: I am dying to see you again and this winter I will see no one but you and the abbé de Canaye. It's a shame that your wretched Saint-Joseph is so far away, but we will do what we can. I hope to see Quesnay at Fontainebleau and I will tell you of our conversation.

What the devil did you write to the Président about me? Is it still about the *Académie?* What! In the name of God! let it rest; I will be there if they put me there. That is all. Since I am already a member of one academy it is but a small additional pleasure to belong to others. Farewell, Madame, be assured for all eternity of my tender and respectful attachment. On leaving for Fontainebleau, I will send you news of the exact date of our arrival at "Boulay."

Madame du Deffand was still concentrating on the *Académie.* Having planned her campaign carefully and at length, she eventually came, after a few initial skirmishes, to the final confrontation at the end of 1753 and 1754. Three seats became vacant in less than a year and three times her candidate was defeated. D'Alembert saw himself beaten by the aristocrat Clermont who had never published a line and who did not even deign to make his maiden speech; and by Bougainville, a mediocre and bigoted historian whose ill-health seemed to be the strongest point in his favour. ("It is not the *Académie*'s business to administer the Last Sacrament," protested Duclos.[26]) Finally d'Alembert was beaten by Boissy, a colourless playwright. Madame du Deffand's friends offered their condolences. Aydie wrote from the heart of the country: "Would it not have been more decent and more honourable for the *Académie* . . . to have followed the spirit of its foundation and firmly to have preferred d'Alembert to all the others, for he is without comparison, the most worthy, and the one designated by public opinion?"[27] But suddenly in August of the same year the Bishop of Vence (Father Surian) also surrendered his soul to God, leaving not only his see but a seat in the *Académie*. This time the *marquise* was backed by popular indignation at the outcome of the earlier elections and by the Président Hénault who wished to make amends for having supported the Queen's protégé, Bougainville. Nevertheless, Madame du Deffand had to face a bitter campaign against her in favour of the abbé de Boismont, led by Madame de Chaulnes, her old travelling companion on the road to Forges. The candidate was harmless enough in himself, and to be feared only because of the fanaticism of his protectress who displayed a "scandalous"[28] ardour for him. The battle was memorable, no holds were barred and endless epigrams were composed. The difference between the two candidates was enormous but d'Alembert's qualities were not so likely to decide the outcome as were Madame de Chaulnes's arrogance and exaggeration.

On 29 November 1754, the duc de Luynes noted: "There was yesterday an election at the *Académie Française* to fill the place vacated on the death of the Bishop of Vence. The ladies are usually given to much canvassing in these elections; there were several candidates: Monsieur l'évêque de Troyes (Poncet de la Rivière), the abbé Troublet, the abbé de Boismont, d'Alembert and perhaps a few others whom I do not know. Madame de Chaulnes was rooting most vivaciously for the abbé de Boismont. She had written to all the academicians, or been to see them. Madame la duchesse d'Aiguillon (Crussol) and Madame du Deffand strongly supported Monsieur d'Alembert; the greatest number of votes was cast for the last one."[29] The decisive part played in the outcome by Madame du Deffand was obvious to everyone and her friends congratulated her as if on a personal triumph. "I am delighted by d'Alembert's election; it seems that he had only to show himself for the matter to be decided. However, you needed all the talents at your disposal to negotiate this affair, which is hardly surprising considering that you had to do with the illustrious and skilful duchesse de Chaulnes . . ."[30]

A new academician was officially installed at a public ceremony which was a social occasion of the greatest importance. It can hardly be doubted that Madame du Deffand was present at the ceremony for d'Alembert. On hearing her protégé's "haughty and rebellious"[31] speech, she must have felt a great surge of pride and a moment of true happiness. Like a Roman tribune "facing the public and the court, he preached tolerance and exhorted respect for unbelievers; he spoke against the meanness and the base intrigue of men of letters."[32]

The implications of d'Alembert's election went far beyond Madame du Deffand's indirect success and recognition of him; it signified a turning point in the spread of enlightenment. With inevitable bitterness, the *marquise* must have come to realise this years later: "First among the new generation of *philosophes* to be elected to the *Académie,* d'Alembert found there a territory in which to rally, just as he had wished, all men of letters to the new ideas, by turning them against the society of the great and the powerful. The *Académie* . . . was to become the natural centre for the new class of intellectual, precisely aware of its rights and duties, which had gradually developed."[33]

Although once again immersed in Parisian life, Madame du Deffand had not forgotten Julie. Since last seeing her in Lyons, she had never abandoned the hope of being able to take the girl to live with her. It was a question of patience. It meant waiting for time to prove definitively that Julie's autonomy was illusory, thus leading her to overcome her reluctance to break with her family, especially with her brother, d'Albon. Time showed Madame due Deffand to be right: after waiting a year Julie failed to acquire a small subsidy[34] from her brother which would have made her life slightly less wretched. It was she who returned to the Paris plan but her bargaining powers were almost negligible: she was obliged to submit to whatever conditions Madame du Deffand deemed suitable.

Time and the ways of the world had made the *marquise* something of a tactician. Her long and lonely path in which, with no support other than her own intelligence, she had relied on expediency, had taught her to foresee the pitfalls and to arm herself against them in good time. She knew that the precious reputation required for safe-conduct in society was based on the interpretation put on a person's actions, rather than on the actions themselves. It was therefore essential to influence public reaction carefully.

Two last letters devoted to this episode reveal a horrifying network of seduction, harshness, persuasiveness, calculation, deceit and brutal sincerity. Madame du Deffand waited determinedly and patiently to catch Julie in her web.

MADAME DU DEFFAND TO CARDINAL DE TENCIN

Tuesday, 12 February 1754

I have received a letter from Mademoiselle de Lespinasse which is quite unlike those she was writing to me two months ago. The impatience and determination she shows in her desire to come to me are as great as her former uncertainty and coldness. What I cannot quite understand, is that she asks my forgiveness and begs me to forget her offence. What does that mean? How can she expect me to forget that she told me she feared the boredom of the quiet life she would lead with me, that this boredom could throw her into such a state of discouragement as to make her company unbearable and so cause me to regret having taken her? Where did she get those ideas? What has made her change them now? My conditions have not altered; I have not changed on a single point. I hope therefore that she will consider and reflect very carefully on her decision. I do not want to be responsible for her regrets; she must be quite certain of not repining, and quite determined to be satisfied with the life I have described to her and which she will lead with me. It will involve great friendship, great consideration, and considerable attention; but at the same time I will not be subject to any kind of constraint and I will live as freely as I would if she were not with me; I will dine and sup out, spend time in the country without being obliged to take her with me, especially during the early days of her being with me. It is highly likely that she may often be bored. These rules will certainly be relaxed eventually, but I think it would be advisable to produce her only little by little and to wait for a spontaneous desire for her acquaintanceship to be born. We will have plenty of time to discuss this affair, but meanwhile, I beg you to read her what I have the honour of writing to you.

The following day Madame du Deffand wrote to Julie. Here the same concerns mentioned to the Cardinal are expressed more affectionately and present an opportunity for the *marquise* to specify a line of action.

MADAME DU DEFFAND TO MADEMOISELLE DE LESPINASSE

13 February 1754

I am very glad, my Queen, that you are pleased with my letters and that you have decided to explain yourself clearly to Monsieur d'Albon; I am not of your opinion concerning a successful outcome. I am certain that he will decide to assure you of a pension; the whole world would throw stones at him were he to do otherwise. So I see the prospect for my plans growing fainter, but should he refuse, you will be entirely free to do as you choose, and I hope that will still be to live with me; but, my Queen, you must consider carefully and be quite certain that you will not regret your decision. In your last letter you write the most affectionate and flattering things, but do you remember that you thought differently only two or three months ago, and that you admitted that you were frightened of the boredom I led you to expect? And that accustomed as you might become to it, it would be more intolerable in society than it would be in your retreat, and that you would become so discouraged as to be unbearable and to disgust me and cause me to repine. Those were your words and it is apparently this offence which you ask me to forgive and beg me to forget; but, my Queen, it is not wrong to say what one thinks and to explain one's attitude; it is, on the contrary, the best thing to do, so, far from reproaching you, I wrote that I was grateful for your sincerity and that although it caused me to abandon my plans, I would not love you less fondly for it. I repeat the same thing today. Reflect on the decision you will make. I have told you what your life will be like with me; I will tell you again so that you cannot be in the slightest degree mistaken.

I will tell no one of your arrival, I will tell those who see you at first that you are a young lady from my part of the country who wishes to enter a convent and that I have offered you lodgings until you find what suits you. I will treat you not only politely but with respect in public to establish the consideration which is your due. I will confide my true intentions to a very small number of friends, and after a period of three, four or five months, we will both know how well we suit each other and will be able to behave less reservedly. I will at no time appear to wish to introduce you. I propose to make you sought after and if you know me well, you should not be concerned about my treatment of your self-respect; but you must trust to my knowledge of the world. If it was initially thought that you were established with me, no one would know (even if I were a far grander lady) how to treat you. Some might suppose that you were my own daughter, others my subordinate etc: about which they might comment impertinently. Your worth and your charms must therefore be recognised before anything else. This you will easily achieve with my help and the help of my friends; but you must be prepared to bear the boredom of the early days. There is a second matter about which I must be clear with you which is that I will not be able to tolerate the slightest artifice, even the smallest affectation in your behaviour towards me. I am naturally mistrustful and anyone in whom I detect guile becomes so suspect that I can no longer have any confidence in them. I have two intimate friends, they are Formont and d'Alembert; I love them passionately, less for their charm and their friendship for me than for their absolute sincerity. I could add Devreux since true worth makes everything equal and for this reason she is more important to me than all the potentates in the world. So, my Queen, you must resolve to live with me in the greatest truth and sincerity; never resort to insinuation, nor exaggeration; in a word, do not stray and never lose one of youth's greatest attractions which is *naïveté*. You are very intelligent, you have gaiety and are capable of feeling. With all these qualities you will be charming so long as you behave naturally and are without pretension or deviousness.

I have no doubt whatsoever of your disinterestedness which is all the more reason why I should do everything in my power for you.

Please tell me the result of your conversation when you have seen M.D.[35] Until I have this information I shall have no more to tell you.

Devreux showed me the letter you wrote her; it is full of friendship but the number of "mademoiselles" which you have used cancel each other out. You will find me very critical, but I swear that I am not so, excepting where sincerity is threatened; but where that is concerned I am merciless. Goodbye, my Queen; you may show this letter to our friend.[36] I hide none of my thoughts from him.

MADAME DU DEFFAND TO MADEMOISELLE DE LESPINASSE

Paris, 29 March 1754

I have just received your letter of 26th in reply to mine of 20th. It was the day after writing this last letter that I was informed of my brother's intention of writing to Madame de Luynes, as I let you know. I was quite vexed to have sent you my letter; I felt it was cruel to have given you such immediate hope when the affair was not yet finally decided at all. I have not yet written to Madame de Luynes: I am waiting for the Président Hénault to be at Versailles before I do that. I will write him a letter for all to see which will serve as a supplement to the one to Madame de Luynes. I strongly insist on demanding impartiality; I cannot believe that she will refuse me; but should we suffer this inconvenience, I will have recourse to M. le cardinal de Tencin that he might persuade her. I advise you, my Queen, to allow no one to know of your plans. It is absolutely essential that we are not stopped. I have one other favour to ask you (and it is the most important of all), it is not even to think of coming to me unless you have perfectly forgotten who you are, and unless you are firmly decided never to think of changing your situation. It would be perfidious to make use of my friendship only to shame me, to expose me to the reproaches of respectable people and to alienate me irreconcilably from my whole family; the slightest attempt you might make to this effect whilst with me, would be an unpardonable crime. I hope, my Queen, that you will have no further need to think this over. A long time ago you promised me everything I could hope for on this matter. I am perfectly certain that anything you undertook in that direction would be in vain, but none the less dreadful for me were you to make an attempt, and I repeat, I would never forgive you. Write me a letter about this which I could show to Madame de Luynes if it were necessary...

Farewell, my Queen, do not lose heart. I hope that in the month of May we will be happy, both of us, and happy with each other.

There is a second version of this letter which until the publication of W. Hunting Smith's exemplary work was thought to be the original text. Since both letters are copies, we do not know which of the two was in fact sent to Julie. The two letters are essentially the same but comparison of them reveals the concern and minute attention to detail with which the *marquise* weighed every word of her delicate transaction. The second version is perhaps tougher; in it she demands assurance in an explicitly threatening reference to "powerful enemies"[37] who would make Julie regret having failed to keep her promises. These threats are repeated in detail, even in the letter in which Madame du Deffand announces her "joy" that all the problems have been overcome and that she and Julie can live together.

The letter in quite another style directed to Madame de Luynes at Versailles expresses, however, a radically different attitude. Conditions and threats give way to deferential begging. Madame du Deffand displays dignified humility, obliged, despite herself, to remember the misfortune which has struck her. The ingratiating diplomacy of the letter is disguised by apparent objectivity.

Madame du Deffand caught her family on the hop and achieved her desired end. In fact Madame de Luynes wrote back to her: "Monsieur and Madame de Vichy have told me nothing although I had news of them in the last few days; so I imagine that they do not have the matter at heart." Flattered by her niece's deference and convinced by her version of the facts, Madame de Luynes the matriarch, agreed not to stand in the way of the plan; but long experience of the world prevented her from overlooking the inherent dangers of the situation which she listed one by one in replying to Madame de Deffand. First of all there was the possibility that the two women might tire of each other for which reason it would be wise to avoid living too closely together by sending the girl to a convent and allowing her to visit Saint-Joseph. But above all Madame du Deffand should not delude herself: were the bastard girl to decide to claim her birthright—perhaps even with the help of new connections in Paris—the *marquise* wold not be in any position to dissuade her. However, Madame du Deffand's need amply justified the risks and Madame de Luynes's letter ends in the most agreeable manner possible: "wishing only for whatever might sweeten your situation and make you happy; these are the hopes of a heart which is warmly attached to you."[38]

In thanking Madame du Luynes for her affectionate kindness, the *marquise* uses reasonable, if somewhat sinister arguments, to justify her decision to keep Julie with her, despite her aunt's express advice to the contrary. "The most important aspect is the girl's situation; I admit that it is worrying but it is an added reason for me to decide to keep her with me, rather than putting her in a convent, because I could not know what she might do in the convent, whereas with me, out of propriety and consideration for herself I would only allow her out with people I trusted, or accompanied by one of my servants."[39]

The reasons why Julie would never think of claiming her birthright entirely escaped her relations who would have been somewhat surprised to read Julie's declaration twenty years later: "What praise I have received for my moderation, my nobility of soul, my disinterestedness, the sacrifices I am supposed to have made to a respectable and cherished memory and to the house of d'Alb. . . ! So the world judges me, so the world sees it. Ah! Good God! What fools you are, I do not deserve your praise: my soul was not made for the petty intrigue which concerns you; entirely possessed by the happiness of loving and being loved, I needed neither strength nor honour to bear poverty and to scorn the advantages of vanity."[40]

At last, after a year of negotiations, the *marquise* could go ahead with her plan, the Vichys and the d'Albons were in no position to interfere and Julie was caught in the spider's web.

MADAME DU DEFFAND TO MADEMOISELLE DE LESPINASSE

Monday, 8 April 1754

I have just received, my Queen, Madame de Luynes's reply which is exactly as I had hoped. It is full of gratitude for my trust in her, full of reflections on the difficulties to which I am exposing myself and expresses an interest and friendship which lead her to wish for anything which suits me. I hope, my Queen, that I will never have to regret what I am doing for you and that you would not decide to come to me unless you were determined never to make any attempt to alter your situation. You know only too well how useless that would be, but to attempt it now with me, would be quite fatal for you. The sorrow it would cause me would make powerful enemies for you and you would find yourself abandoned quite without help.

That said, it only remains for me to tell you of the joy that living with you and your presence will bring me. I will write presently to Monsieur le Cardinal to beg him to send you as soon as possible. Let it be known that you are leaving on the day of your departure only. Let me know the date when it is settled, and when you set out send me a letter from Chalons so that I know you are on your way and so that I may know the date of your arrival . . .

Farewell, my Queen, pack your baggage and come and be my happiness and my consolation; that this should be reciprocal depends not on me."

VIII

Madame du Deffand and Julie
de Lespinasse at Saint-Joseph

HENCEFORTH, WHEN AT ABOUT 6 o'clock most evenings the doors of the buttercup-yellow moiré drawing room were opened, Madame du Deffand no longer received her guests alone. The *marquise* waited in her armchair—the famous *tonneau*—whose high-back curved forward, framing her in a niche, whilst Julie greeted the guests and acted as hostess. The *habitués* of Saint-Joseph soon became accustomed to the curious friendship between the elderly and infirm *femme d'esprit* and the unknown girl from the country.

Madame du Deffand looked not unlike a waxwork. Pale and tiny, she dressed with refinement and monastic simplicity. Her large, once beautiful eyes were always wide open. But the first impression of immobility was belied by the nervous, restless hands busy with fashionable pastimes,[1] or stroking the angora cats and fearful little dogs that ran about the house; hands which with time learned to recognise the faces of the guests by gently running a finger over them.[2]

Julie, on the other hand, was all warmth and colour and animation. She was tall and slender with an elegant bearing and a mass of dark hair that framed her irregular features. According to her contemporaries, the secret of her charm lay in an extraordinary intensity and transparency whereby her face faithfully registered every one of a vast gamut of expressions. "I have seen faces animated by intelligence, by passion, pleasure, pain, but such nuances were unknown before I met her!"[3] Guibert wrote.

The contrast between the two women was not limited to appearance and age, but was an essential part of their whole way of being and it was to prove wonderfully fruitful. Together Madame Du Deffand and Julie created the most extraordinary alliance of the time between polite society and the intelligentsia. Under the auspices of two such different personalities Saint-Joseph went through a golden period and was the embodiment of the most perfect eighteenth-century, Parisian *salon*.

Julie's presence did not in any way detract from Madame du Deffand's prestige. The part she played was complementary to the *marquise*'s, adding breadth and variety, like a shadow which gives greater relief to the figure in the forefront. Conflict arises only when the main figure is overshadowed. The two women were not entirely unalike, but were two different versions of one type. It was their fundamental affinity which made them so complementary to one another. Primarily what they had in common was passion. In Madame du Deffand it had been crushed and continuously denied, for Julie it took on the importance of a vocation; for both it was at once destructive and a determining factor. Whilst the *marquise* continued to repeat her refrain, "There is only one misfortune in life, which is to be born," Julie announced, "I, on the contrary, inspired by a burning desire to live, am grateful to nature for my birth."[4]

Aunt and niece were situated on either side of what in those years constituted a revolution of sentiment which cause Sainte-Beuve[5] to speak of two different categories of woman: the pre-Rousseau woman and the post-Rousseau woman. Despite Jean-Jacques, and like Madame du Deffand, Julie knew nothing of the natural world. The two women were united by a single interest, a single field of enquiry, which was the study of mankind, of his soul and his passions as revealed in the closed world of one room. Social life was essential to them both for their existence. Madame du Deffand and Mademoiselle de Lespinasse also shared a language and a style. Julie was certainly under the *marquise*'s influence—"Look at the education I received: Madame du Deffand, for her intelligence must be quoted . . . ,"[6] but must herself have been receptive. Like her aunt, Julie developed a cult for the truth, and, like her, she had the gift of naturalness and a preference for simplicity. This she felt, when reflecting on her life years later, was the secret of her success. "She always adhered to the truth in everything and herself chose to be true in every way."[7]

Visitors continued to come to Saint-Joseph to see Madame du Deffand, to admire her intelligence, to hear her expounding, to listen to her judgements, and to be entertained by her inexhaustible wit. But besides a brilliant conversationalist, the *salon* now had a wonderful listener. Unlike the *marquise,* Julie preferred to remain in the shadows and allow others to shine. "I can say," wrote La Harpe, "that I have never known a woman with so much natural intelligence and less desire to show it off, nor who had so great a talent for bringing out others. Neither was anyone a better hostess. She gave everyone a part and everyone was pleased with the one he was allotted."[8] Madame du Deffand's part in the salon was that of a star whilst Julie was the stage manager. Grimm compared her at her peak to a conductor concerned both for the general harmony and for the individual members of the orchestra. Even her conversation gave way to concern for others, for as Guibert says: "it was never above or beneath those to whom she was speaking; she seemed to hold the secret to everyone's character, to have their measure and understand their subtleties"[9]; "she was the soul of the conversation without ever making herself the object."[10]

The greatest difference between the two women lay, perhaps, in their behaviour towards others. Too proud to charm, too suspicious to be trusting, too frail to risk a rebuff, Madame du Deffand's friendships were based entirely on expediency, and yet she was the first to suffer from the lack of any sentimental involvement. But conquest and seduction were for Julie "a necessity of nature."[11] Moncrif's "need to please" in her became a condition of existence. "The indifference of anyone who approached her caused her, almost without her realising it, an indefinable malaise, a kind of physical suffering; she could not rest until she felt the ice melt in her radiant charm."[12]

Years later d'Alembert wrote with a certain bitterness: "I know no one, I will repeat no one, who is generally so pleasing as you are, and few who are more aware of it. You do not even refuse to take the first step if you are not approached and on this point you sacrifice your pride to your vanity: quite sure of keeping those you have acquired, you are mainly concerned with acquiring others."[13]

Just as Madame du Deffand was inaccessible, arrogant and caustic, so was her companion approachable, sweet, passionate, forever seeking approval. So in differing ways they both expressed the same pathological need for attention. The altruistic, anxious Julie proved to be no less egocentric than the sceptical, indifferent *marquise.*

It is not known if Mademoiselle de Lespinasse settled into Saint-Joseph exactly as her aunt had planned, but according to d'Alembert who witnessed her début in society, it happened surprisingly naturally: "From the first day you were as easy and as little out of place in the most brilliant and difficult company as if you had spent your life in it; you sensed the conventions before you had learned them which implies a most unusual precision and finesse and an exquisite knowledge of propriety. In a word, you divined the language of what is called "good society.""[14]

The *habitués* of the *salon* were soon enchanted by the new arrival; instead of inhibiting relations between them and the lady of the house, as the *marquise* might initially have feared, she brought them closer together and Madame du Deffand was the first to rejoice.

MADAME DU DEFFAND TO THE CHEVALIER D'AYDIE
Monday, 14 July 1755

. . . Mlle de Lespinasse is deeply touched by the charming things you said about her; when you know her better you will see how she deserves them: I grow more pleased with her every day.

THE CHEVALIER D'AYDIE TO MADAME DU DEFFAND
Mayac, 29 July 1755

. . . Through Mlle de Lespinasse you regain your sight and what is even more necessary, Madame, she expresses your goodness and sensitivity of heart. I am pleased with the first opinion I formed of her and I beg you to continue to spare me some of her goodwill . . .

Always available and "sure of moving from conquest to conquest" and with his talent for "adapting to everything and pleasing everyone,"[15] the Président Hénault was the first victim of Julie's charms. "There is a piquancy about you: it would take some determination to turn your head and one would bear the cost. One must wait for you, for you cannot be forced to move, your coquetry is imperious . . . But you have two things which do not go together: you are gentle and strong; gaiety enhances your beauty and relaxes your nerves which are too tense. Your opinion is your own and you allow others to have theirs. You see everything from a bird's eye view. You are extremely polite;

you have divined society and to uproot you would be vain for you could take root anywhere: in Madrid you would look out from behind a blind; in London you would wear your neckerchief at an angle; in Constantinople you would tell the Grand Vizier that you had no dust on your feet; as for Italy, I do not really advise you to go there unless you wish to catch some Father of the Church. All in all, you are a person like none other. And to finish, like Harlequin, with a whiplash, you please me greatly."[16] In spite of this somewhat ridiculous gallantry, Hénault developed a genuinely paternal feeling for Julie who became the means by which the *marquise* brought the all too available Président back to Saint-Joseph. Madame du Deffand always needed Hénault as a point of reference, if only so as not to deny the past. Even the friends they had in common noticed this so that Aydie felt bound to reassure the *marquise* in that respect: "I am sure, Madame, that he always returns eagerly to you."[17]

It was not only men who became infatuated with Julie. The formidable maréchale de Luxembourg immediately took a great liking to her and adopted her as an intimate. Madame du Deffand's anxiety to remain free to accept invitations to go alone to the country did not last long. Barely a year after her arrival at Saint-Joseph, Julie accompanied her to Montmorency to which she later returned alone. As she wrote to Abel de Vichy: "Such a displacement is no small thing for your aunt, but they invited her so persistently that in the end she had to give way. Besides she will find everything she needs there, just as if she were at home. Monsieur and Madame de Luxembourg take great care of us there and we will be with all the people we see most often: Monsieur le Président, Mesdames Mirepoix and Boufflers, Monsieur de Pont-de-Veyle etc."

D'Alembert was one of the first people Julie met on her arrival in Paris. She must have been prepared for this introduction since Madame du Deffand had told her that with Formont, the *philosophe* was one of the people she most loved and she must have talked about him at length during the months at Champrond.[18] The *marquise* had probably also told d'Alembert something about Julie; and it would not be long before Julie would fill in the missing parts of the story.

However, according to d'Alembert, the meeting was inevitable: "Parentless, and without family, abandoned from the moment of birth and having suffered from misfortune and injustice, nature seemed to have put us both in the world to find each other that we might each be everything to the other, to support each other mutually like two storm battered reeds which cling together for support."[19] In 1771 d'Alembert wrote that his "feeling" for Julie had lasted for seventeen years.[20] It was love at first sight which had all the violence of novelty although, as he said himself, it was long awaited. "The sentiment slept in the heart of his being but the awakening was terrible. Having spent his early years in meditation and work, he saw, like a sage, the emptiness of human knowledge; he felt that it could not satisfy his heart and like Tasso's Aminta he cried out, "wasted is all the time not spent in loving."[21]

Why this feeling lay so long dormant and the nature of its sudden awakening in d'Alembert are matters for conjecture. Until the age of thirty-seven d'Alembert had apparently never been interested in any woman, with the exception of a brief and probably platonic infatuation for his foster mother's daughter.[22] His presumed impotence was the subject of many jokes and was also stated openly in the *Journal de l'inspecteur Hémery*: "You must know that d'Alembert is almost impotent. He is very cold towards women and cannot conceive of the pleasure to be had with them."[23] Madame de Chaulnes did not hesitate to make use of this to discredit d'Alembert in his candidacy for the *Académie*. On 4 December 1754 Formont tactlessly repeated the somewhat explicit allusions to the *philosophe*: "The duchesse de Chaulnes thinks that you lack certain talents which she regards as indispensable to a great man. She said that you were only a child; the meaning is clear. She thinks that even in a seraglio you would retain eternal childhood. I at least do not believe it and I am sure that you will always succeed very well in anything you undertake including the speech you have to make at the *Académie* which is more difficult than satisfying a duchess." The rumours about d'Alembert's doubtful virility may merely have been suggested by his austere way of life, his great shyness with women and his high, rather shrill voice. Questions about the exact nature of his relationship to Julie de Lespinasse are premature and the matter is anyway of secondary importance.

For years d'Alembert did not even dare to declare his love for Julie, but this did not prevent them from establishing a close understanding. The two "children of love," as Marmontel called them, were drawn together by the similarity of their backgrounds, by their youthfulness and by the fact of their fringe existence in a society of older people to which they belonged by birth and culture and which accepted and even courted them, whilst refusing them the prerequisite of legitimacy. There was also an undoubted natural affinity of mind between them. Julie and d'Alembert shared a strong visionary sense and both sought perfection. Madame du Deffand's friendship with the *philosophe* was inevitably altered by his deep understanding with Julie. Nothing can yet diminish Madame du Deffand's intellectual prestige, but in d'Alembert's eyes every comparison between her and Julie will favour Julie, so that eventually his opinion of his old friend must be affected. Madame du Deffand is sceptical, negative, disillusioned, hostile to the times and backward looking, whereas Julie, despite her personal experience, is trusting, positive, hopeful and forward looking. The present times annoy Madame du Deffand because they are flat, graceless and lacking in elegance, Mademoiselle de Lespinasse is shocked by their injustice, corruption and immorality.

Because of Julie, one corner of the *salon* is devoted to discussions of philosophy, reform, constitutionalism and republican liberties. Besides the old *habitués* of the high aristocracy, the delettanti literati and distinguished foreign visitors to Paris, Madame du Deffand's *salon* began to welcome newcomers attracted initially by the presence of d'Alembert. They were men of the new enlightenment like Turgot, Marmontel, Chastellux, La Harpe, Grimm and Condorcet. Together in the midst of such company Madame du Deffand's and Julie's personalities alternately harmonised with each other and restrained each other. A jealous awareness of aristocratic tradition was combined with the reforming zeal of modern opinion, frivolity went hand in hand with passion and authority with kindness. Saint-Joseph had reached its apogee and for ten years was to hold unrivalled sway over all other Parisian salons, beginning with Madame Geoffrin's, its chief bourgeois-intellectual rival.

The crisis which suddenly upset the equilibrium of this state of affairs is well-known as one of the colourful tales of Parisian culture in the second half of the eighteenth century. Marmontel has left us the fullest account of it.

"There was in Paris a marquise du Deffand, an intelligent woman full of caprice and malice. In her youth she was a coquette and beautiful enough, but by the time I am about to speak of, she was old, nearly blind, tormented by the vapours and had retired with modest means to a convent, but nevertheless she still saw the high society amongst which she had lived. She had met d'Alembert with her old lover, the Président Hénault, whom she still tyrannised, and who, being naturally timid had remained a slave to fear long after ceasing to be a slave to love. Madame du Deffand, delighted by d'Alembert's intelligence and gaiety enticed him to her house and so captivated him that they became inseparable. He lived a long way away but not a day passed without his going to see her.

"Meanwhile to fill her empty solitude, Madame du Deffand looked for a young, well-brought-up person with no fortune who would like to be her companion and who would as a friend, that is to say a subordinate, live with her in her convent. She found such a person and was, you may well believe, delighted. D'Alembert was no less delighted to find a third no less interesting person in his old friend's house.

"Between this young person and himself misfortune had placed a link which was bound to draw them together. They were both what are called love children. I witnessed their burgeoning friendship when Madame du Deffand brought them to supper with her friend Madame Harenc; my acquaintanceship with them dates from that time. No less a friend than d'Alembert was needed to sweeten and render the sorrow and harshness of Mademoiselle de Lespinasse's situation bearable, for to be obliged to attend perpetually on a vapourous blind woman was not the end of it. To live with her meant, like her, making the day into night and the night into day, sitting by her bed and reading her to sleep, work which the naturally delicate young girl found deathly and from which her weak chest has never recovered. She resisted however until the incident occurred which broke her chains.

"Having sat up all night at home or with Madame de Luxembourg who did the same, Madame du Deffand spent all day asleep and could only be seen at about six o'clock in the evening. Mademoiselle de Lespinasse retired to her little room overlooking the courtyard of the same convent and rose only an hour before her lady, but in this precious hour snatched from hours of slavery, she received her personal friends, d'Alembert, Chastellux, Turgot and occasionally myself. Now these men were also habitually guests of Madame du Deffand, but sometimes they lingered with Mademoiselle de Lespinasse and these were stolen moments; besides such meetings were hidden from Madame du Deffand as it was rightly thought that she would be jealous. All was discovered and, to hear her speak, it was nothing less than a betrayal. She shouted loudly and accused the poor girl of taking away her friends and declared that she no longer wished to nourish this serpent in her breast.

"Their separation was sudden, but Mademoiselle de Lespinasse was not abandoned. All Madame du Deffand's friends had become hers. It was easy for her to persuade them that the anger of this woman was unjust. Even the Président Hénault declared himself for her. The duchesse de Luxembourg found her old friend to be in the wrong and gave Mademoiselle de Lespinasse a complete set of furniture for her new apartments. Finally, the duc de Choiseul obtained an annuity for her from the King which put an end to her need and the most distinguished society in Paris fought over the pleasure of owning her.

"D'Alembert to whom Madame du Deffand imperiously presented the alternative of choosing between herself and Mademoiselle de Lespinasse, did not hesitate and dedicated himself entirely to his young friend."[24]

Marmontel's fairy-tale style account is both partisan and over-simplified. The conflict between the two women developed gradually and the outcome of it was complex. Above all it could not be reduced to a simple tale of oppression. To begin with there was genuine understanding between the aunt and the niece. Madame du Deffand knew how much she needed Julie's help; she was fond of her niece, appreciated her qualities and in so far as she could, she put her trust in her and it is difficult to imagine that she could have been jealous. The *marquise* was old and infirm and it would be ridiculous to imagine sexual competition. An intellectual rivalry developed later. In their early years together Madame du Deffand must have taken a Pygmalion-like delight in forming the tastes and style of such an extraordinarily talented and receptive pupil.

For her part Julie was undoubtedly deeply attached to the *marquise*: Madame du Deffand was the first person of importance in her life who had given her the chance to turn her back on the past; she presided over her début in society which turned out to be entirely congenial. Julie was enthralled by her intelligence, her wit and her culture and must in addition have felt tremendous compassion for her protectress. The role of helpmeet would have perfectly suited someone of her feeling nature and she dedicated herself with enthusiasm to the improbable task of alleviating her aunt's unhappiness. But Julie needed warmth, life, passion and her relationship with Madame du Deffand and all her worldly success could not appease her "voracious need for affection."[25]

Surprising though it may seem, Julie's first choice was not d'Alembert but a visiting foreigner, John Taaffe. Of Irish origin but resident in

London, Taaffe was one of that vast company of foreigners who were fascinated by French culture, who thought of Paris as their adopted home and to whom the Goncourts referred when speaking of the "*esprit français des etrangers.*"[26] In 1756 John Taaffe together with his older brother, Theobald, was tasting the delights of an intensely social Parisian season. Although Theobald, who was a dedicated and unscrupulous gambler, had in the past run afoul of the French law, he was still introduced to court circles. "He came yesterday and supped with me," wrote the duc de Luynes, "and he had the honour of playing *cavagnole* with the Queen."[27] John, on the other hand, had friends among the *philosophes* and so did not fail to visit the salon at Saint-Joseph. "A man of sense and good company,"[28] Taaffe found the ideal conversationalist in Mademoiselle de Lespinasse, and with her full consent soon stepped beyond the bounds of simple courtesy. The affair did not escape the notice of the *marquise* who demanded and obtained an explanation from her niece.

To judge from her correspondence with Taaffe, Madame du Deffand's behaviour under the circumstances was exemplary. She took a firm but eminently tactful line. She seems to have been concerned only with Julie's reputation and happiness. It is tempting to believe that what Madame du Deffand felt for Julie was disinterested, maternal affection.

MADAME DU DEFFAND TO MR TAAFFE   *19 June 1756*

You know by what chance, or rather under what circumstances it was thought necessary to make me a confession which I was far from expecting. I would find it difficult to express my surprise to you. All my feelings were suspended by the violence of the condition and the most important thing for me was to calm the agitation, and so I showed friendship, compassion and interest. I even allowed myself to say that I preferred it to be you than another because apparently, in my confusion, I could only call to mind my customary opinion of your probity and discretion. After the first few moments, I saw everything there was to be seen, your behaviour towards me, your behaviour towards her. I told her everything I thought which could not be done without causing her great anxiety of soul and wounding her self-respect. She was sensible of all her imprudence and, despite the trouble I took to console her, I could not prevent the most violent access of the vapours I have ever seen in her. Since Thursday she has not been able to swallow a drop of water without falling into a fearful fit and then fainting. An enema produces the same result. The friendship I have for her is so tender and so sincere, the fear of losing her is so great that there is nothing that I would not do to keep her. Here then, Monsieur, is what I propose; it is that you profit from your absence to examine your feelings carefully and to decide what you will do in consequence. If your passion for her is stronger than you, make haste to reassure both her and me that your intentions are both honest and legitimate. If they are not so, do all you can to detach her from you. You owe it to her happiness and to the consideration which I have a right to demand of you.

If your intentions are as I desire and hope, I promise complete oblivion of the past and the tenderest and most sincere friendship such as I have had until this moment for you.

She has read this letter; I excuse her for not having demanded of you the same proof of respect and attachment which I demand. Her unfortunate situation was the reason. I am sure that had she had a fortune to offer you, she would not have hesitated. I bear her the love of a mother; you should not be surprised if I also have the language, the behaviour and the firmness of a mother.

Madame du Deffand's doubts about Taaffe's intentions were well founded. Reminded of his responsibilities as a gentleman, Taaffe withdrew with humiliating haste.

MR TAAFFE TO MADAME DU DEFFAND   *Tuesday, 1 July 1756*

I am not ignorant of the circumstances which appeared to force Mademoiselle to tell you what she could have continued to keep secret had she wished to, so it would be unfair to take away all merit from the confidence she made you. Her condition and her state of health have prevented me from thinking of anything else since reading your letter of 19 June. I wanted to write to her immediately. Fortunately I had a day in which to think. I have carefully weighed the alternatives which you gave me and consequently I have torn up the letter which I have just written her and since nothing has happened to prevent me from attempting to disengage myself from her,

I wished to begin by doing myself this first violence. With regard to what concerns you personally, Madame, I hope that you will allow me to call upon your goodness, not knowing what else I can say at the moment; it would be difficult at all times to express my attachment to you.

For Madame du Deffand, the real surprise was not—as she was obliged to claim in her letter to Taaffe—the discovery of a love affair, so much as the revelation of an unknown side to Julie. Wounded to the heart, the sweet, mild, reasonable girl she knew had turned into a violent and rebellious young woman. Although Madame du Deffand's behaviour was unexceptional from the point of view of form, her intervention seemed offensive to Julie. Mademoiselle de Lespinasse was naturally driven by her heart, not her head. She wanted to love and be loved and she found the brutal return to reality unbearable. To sacrifice a love affair that occupied her heart and mind to a code of behaviour which turned against her at every opportunity without ever protecting her, must have been the ultimate injustice. Her reaction was one of violent hysteria. Besides Madame du Deffand's letter to Taaffe, we have La Harpe's description of Julie's condition at the time. Although La Harpe does not relate Julie's crisis specifically to the episode with Taaffe, of which, in any case, he appears to be ignorant, his description is very effective.

"Her already lively mind became so excited that she wished to poison herself. She took sixty grains of opium[29] which did not bring about the death she desired, but gave her appalling convulsions which left a permanent mark on her nerves. Madame du Deffand dissolved into bitter tears at her bedside: 'It is too late now, Madame,' said Mademoiselle de Lespinasse who thought she would not recover."[30]

Madame Geoffrin's daughter, Madame de la Ferté-Imbault, also talks of suicide: "In her fury, the young lady took such a dose of opium that it affected her for the rest of her life."[31] But, as Ségur suggests, rather than a suicide attempt, it was "a violent *crise de nerfs* which she sought to calm by repeated doses of opium in keeping with the fatal habit which she developed then and in which she persisted for the rest of her life."[32]

Once the crisis was over, the episode was apparently forgotten and life at Saint-Joseph went on as usual. But something fundamental had changed, as much for the aunt as for the niece. Madame du Deffand had

discovered that Julie was indomitable and Julie had discovered resentment and the need for subterfuge. From henceforth their relationship
was outwardly harmonious and the conflict which was developing beneath the surface was only expressed indirectly through a third party,
indeed through the very person who would eventually cause the final
rupture.

Madame du Deffand was probably aware of d'Alembert's feelings for
her niece before Julie was herself and for some time she must have
decided to consider only the positive aspects of the matter. The attachment was an added reason for her favourite to continue visiting Saint-
Joseph. It was not d'Alembert's interest in Julie which hurt her, so much
as his gradual loss of interest in herself. She was offended, and to avenge
herself Madame du Deffand resorted to the only possible means
whereby she could be sure of wounding d'Alembert. She distanced
herself with ever increasing polemic from the passionate political and
intellectual battle which d'Alembert was fighting from the front line of
the philosophers' party. The weapons available to her—enormous
social prestige and terrible irony—were a very real threat to a battle
whose principal aim was to win over public opinion. The *marquise*'s
authority was reinforced by Voltaire with whom she corresponded
frequently, and her friendship with the patriarche de Ferney constituted
a permanent risk of misunderstanding within the philosophers' party.

Madame du Deffand had every right to resent d'Alembert's behaviour. His passion for Julie extinguished any interest he might have had
in his old friend. He was entirely absorbed by the complete understanding between himself and the new arrival and so was gradually alienated
from the *marquise*. Without the complicity and indulgence essential to
the friendship, the fundamental intellectual, moral and cultural disagreement which had been a vital part of the relationship, came to the fore.
Admiration was replaced by indifference and then increasing ideological
intolerance. The polemic was indirect—never openly declared. His love
for Julie obliged d'Alembert to be careful: besides he saw Julie more and
more as the victim of injustice and this aggravated his irritation with the
marquise. For her part, Madame du Deffand hesitated between polemic,
the desire for the *philosophe*'s presence and the hope of regaining his
friendship.

As we shall see, the correspondence of both d'Alembert and Madame
du Deffand with Voltaire record the main incidents of this cold war in

which the *marquise* displays far more style and elegance than the *philosophe*. At the beginning of May 1760, d'Alembert wrote to Ferney, whether or not in good faith we do not know, accusing the *marquise* of supporting Palissot's comedy, *Les Philosophes*[33] which cruelly satirised the Encyclopaedists and which had opened to great acclaim in Paris three days earlier. The wording of his denunciation is far from elegant: "The declared female protectors of this play are Mesdames de Villeroy, de Robecq et du Deffand, your friend and formerly mine. So the play has on its side acting whores and honorary strumpets."[34] Twenty days later d'Alembert made matters worse: the *marquise*'s age and infirmity do not seem to have caused him to restrain his verbal violence. Voltaire had urged him not to concern himself: "the only reasonable attitude in a ridiculous century, is to laugh at everything,"[35] but this advice only enraged d'Alembert more: "I know that that old whore du Deffand has written to you, and is perhaps still writing to you about my friends and me, but one must laugh at everything and fuck old whores since that is all they are good for."[36] Voltaire tried in vain to calm the situation by maintaining a humorous tone, "I did not say that Madame du Deffand should be fucked"[37]—and above all by denying that his correspondent was to blame: "I swear that Madame du Deffand has not written me one word which could displease you."[38] D'Alembert, on the other hand, in order to win Voltaire over, had disloyally referred to an old incident, the memory of which must have provoked Voltaire: "It is not surprising that you no longer remember the impertinences Madame du Deffand wrote to you about me; such folly is meant to be forgotten, just like the satire which she circulated about Madame du Châtelet after her death; but as she is as hare-brained as she is malicious, she showed me what she was writing to you about me (about fifteen months ago), since which time I no longer visit her and I despise her as she deserves."[39]

The incriminating documents—if they ever existed—are not available and it is even uncertain to what d'Alembert refers. Ségur has used Madame de La Ferté-Imbault's evidence to reconstruct this critical incident:

"In a letter to Voltaire Madame du Deffand allowed herself to make some 'very biting' jokes about their friend d'Alembert; and Voltaire in replying referred to these stinging strokes of the pen. A few days later, 'in order to amuse the company' the malicious blind *marquise* brought the conversation round to these two letters and asked someone to read

them aloud. She did not know that d'Alembert had just come into the
salon without being announced, which was his custom. He did not say a
word, listened to the reading and only made himself known afterwards
and affected to laugh about the matter. But he was deeply hurt and the
mathematician, Fontaine, who had witnessed the scene and who 'could
read characters as well as he could numbers and lives,' told the story in
Madame Geoffrin's *salon* the same evening, and predicted that without
doubt 'd'Alembert would take revenge on Madame du Deffand in the
most biting manner and that he would make use of Mademoiselle de
Lespinasse for that purpose.' "[40]

In fact there is no mention of the episode in Voltaire's and Madame
du Deffand's letters, but the incriminating documents may have been
lost or destroyed although nothing appears to be missing from the
correspondence after that date. Besterman thinks that Madame du Deffand simply wanted to tease d'Alembert, but it would have been a
dangerous joke in a tense and difficult situation. In any case d'Alembert
did not stand by his decision to desert Saint-Joseph and, probably thanks
to Julie, there was a formal reconciliation about which Voltaire was
promptly informed in mid-October: "I forgot to tell you that, for what
it is worth, I have made it up with Madame du Deffand. She claims
never to have protected Palissot or Fréron . . . just as she claims not to
know that I wrote to you to complain about her. That would cause me
more trouble which I would like to avoid."[41]

Julie had the difficult and delicate task of mediating between the two
of them. To judge from some letters written by her to Madame du
Deffand in July 1761 when the *marquise* was staying with the duchesse
de Luxembourg at Montmorency, the relationship between aunt and
niece was perfect—perhaps too perfect. Within the space of four days,
Julie, who had remained in Paris mildly indisposed, wrote as many
letters to her aunt, full of concern and declarations of affection and
recounting the details of her day. The two women were used to being
together and had developed a remarkable understanding. The *salon* was
a shared enterprise for them and a fascinating and inexhaustible fount
of news and comment. But whilst an element of formality might be
expected, these letters seem somewhat artificial, and even servile. Julie
continually stresses her devotion and affection for the *marquise*. In two
of these four letters she speaks of d'Alembert, but tactfully sees her role
as that of a simple intermediary and spokesperson for sentiments which

d'Alembert was far from feeling.[42] She seems to have to allay Madame du Deffand's suspicions with continuous assurances which hide an awareness of a tension that can no longer be put down entirely to the *marquise*'s pathologically suspicious nature. "No, Madame, I will not forget what you have ordered for Monday, and I will do my best to bring you Monsieur d'Alembert: I am seeing him today and even spending part of the evening with him at Madame de Boufflers; which is why I have the honour of writing at this hour so as not to upset the established order of going to the hôtel de Luxembourg every morning. I will no doubt surprise you by telling you that Monsieur d'Alembert is leaving tomorrow for Saint-Martin, to return only on Thursday. He was not asked if he wanted to make this journey; he was told he had to and so consequently Madame de Boufflers says that she is taking him away tomorrow. He made me promise to tell you that he much regrets Montmorency and is distressed to be so long without seeing you." (4 July 1761.)

In the spring of 1763 d'Alembert left Paris on a much longer and more exacting journey, but separation from Madame du Deffand was the least of his worries. Following the peace treaty which for the French put a somewhat inglorious end to the Seven Years War, d'Alembert solicited an invitation to Potsdam from Frederick of Prussia. Throughout the war the *philosophes* never disguised the fact that they were more concerned for the forces of their colleague "the philosopher king"[43] than for those of Louis XV. The journey was of ideological and political significance and d'Alembert undertook it as a genuine philosophical pilgrimage to the sanctuary of enlightened despotism. As he wrote to Frederick II before leaving Paris, "Philosophy will come to learn and to be enlightened at your side; she will bring your Majesty (without fear of being reproached for flattery) the good wishes, the love and respect of all those who cultivate literature and who have the good fortune to see their leader and their model in the hero of Europe."[44]

While he was away (from May to September 1763), the "marquis de Brandebourg" as padré Paciaudi[45] dubbed him, did not let a single courier leave for Paris without a letter to Julie. The ensemble of this correspondence constitutes a detailed diary of his journey, but unfortunately it only comes to us partially transcribed by Julie who cut out almost everything personal, leading us to suppose that there must have been considerable intimacy. But, despite the censorship, the intimacy and shared interests which unite the couple are evident. This long separation probably proved to d'Alembert the strength of his attachment to Julie. One teasing allusion escaped the censor: "I know that the king is greatly distressed at my departure . . . but apart from a thousand reasons, *not one of which you would have the intelligence to divine,* I think that the climate in this country would eventually be fatal to me."[46]

Madame du Deffand is only mentioned once in these letters and in such a way as to infer that she was unaware of the correspondence, unless Julie—ignoble thought—taking advantage of her blindness, read them to her only in part. Considering Madame du Deffand's pride and suspicious nature, the few lines which refer to her are cruel indeed. They imply exclusion, detachment, irony and complicity between the two people in whom she most trusted and on whom she most depended: "I will write by this courier if possible to Madame du Deffand. . . The King asked me if she was still alive. Obviously Voltaire and Maupertius spoke to him about her. You can well believe that I will make use of this question to pay her court; I will add two or three words from the King which I think will greatly dispose her in his favour . . ."[47]

The letter d'Alembert wrote to Madame du Deffand was courteous and correct: a formal duty to be done and forgotten.

D'ALEMBERT TO MADAME DU DEFFAND   *Sans-Souci, 25 June 1763*

You have allowed me, Madame, to send you my news and to ask yours. I am eager to take advantage of this permission. I arrived here on 22nd after a very happy and very pleasant journey. This journey was not even as tiring as I might have feared although I often travelled day and night, but my desire to see the King and the order to follow him here from Gelderland where I found him, gave me strength and courage. I will not sing the praises of this prince to you; from my mouth they would be suspect. I will merely tell you of two things which will allow you to judge his way of thinking and feeling. When I spoke of the glory he had won, he replied with the greatest simplicity, that glory should be greatly denied, that it was almost entirely due to chance and that he would have preferred to have written *Athalie*[48] than to have gone to war. *Athalie* is in fact the work which he likes best and re-reads most often. I think you would approve his taste in that as in all our literary works about which I would like you to hear his judgements. The other thing I want to tell you about this prince is that when on the day his peace was so gloriously concluded, someone remarked that it was the finest day of his life, he replied: 'The finest day of one's life is the day on which one leaves it.' That, Madame, is tantamount to what you so often say to me, "the greatest misfortune is to be born."

I will not speak, Madame, of the infinite kindness with which this prince honours me, you would not be able to believe it and my vanity spares you the boredom. Neither will I speak of the welcome which Madame la duchesse de Brunswick, the King's sister and the whole house of Brunswick have seen fit to give me; I will satisfy myself with assuring you that in the midst of the whirlwind I do not forget the goodness and friendship with which you so kindly honour me. I flatter myself that I deserve it a little by my respectful attachment to yourself. As I know that nothing bores you more than to write letters, I dare not ask for your news directly, but I hope that Mademoiselle de Lespinasse would care to send me some. I forgot to tell you that the King spoke to me of you, of your intelligence and your wit and he asked me your news. I have not yet been to Berlin but Potsdam is a very beautiful town and the château where I am staying is of the greatest magnificence and in the best taste. Farewell, Madame, take care of your health; mine is always good. Dare I beg you to remember me to Monsieur le maréchal and Madame la maréchale de Luxembourg?

Madame du Deffand replied with a howl of passion. Her feelings for d'Alembert which had been humiliated, disappointed and stifled, only needed a spark to rekindle them. Her hankering for the former relationship was so strong as to make her—suspicious and cunning as she was—reply to the icy politeness of this letter with an offer of peace and renewed friendship.

A painful misunderstanding left her, unarmed and trusting in the hands of her now merciless friend.

MADAME DU DEFFAND TO D'ALEMBERT   *7 July 1763*

No, no, Monsieur, I will allow no one to give you my news, and even less to answer the most charming letter that I have received from you.

On reading it, I thought I was twenty years younger and that I was at "La Sainte-Chapelle,"⁴⁹ and that you were as pleased to be with me as I was with you. In fact this letter reminded me of the golden age of our friendship, it awoke my affection and made me happy. Let us go on from there, believe me, and let us love each other as we once loved. I do not believe we could do better; believe it too if you can.

You are in a sea of delight where no pleasure, no satisfaction is lacking; all your feelings and all your tastes are gratified; you will no longer be accused of vanity when your head has been turned. And whose would not be? You have done enough to turn mine by telling me that the King with whom you are, mentioned my name; how did he know it? He knows then of my misfortune and apparently of my quip about Saint-Denis. I dare not formulate the wish that he might know of my admiration. His esteem for you and for *Athalie* conform entirely to what I thought. I could not agree that the finest moment in life is when one leaves it although I am quite convinced that the most unhappy moment is when one begins it. But can the King of Prussia fail to find life delightful? Should one not wish to be eternal when one unites so many great advantages with so much good fortune, *o altitudo?*

You do not mention your return, but you have an Academician to elect.

I have been told of a catechism which has been attributed to Voltaire; might it not be yours? Have I not heard you say that you were writing something of the kind? You could confide that secret in me as well as many others, but, but, but . . . well, it will come again, we are made to love each other, we will love each other all our lives.

My health is not good and I have no hope that it will ever be so.

Madame de Luynes is in Paris, she is much better. I am glad that she will be here during your absence as I will see her between seven and nine, the exact time of your visits.

Farewell my dear d'Alembert; I am and will always be the same for you, do not doubt it, and love me in your turn.

Since writing my letter I have read the catechism of which I spoke; I do not suspect you of being the author, it is not at all in the style in which you planned to write.⁵⁰

Madame du Deffand's happiness was short lived. With d'Alembert's return to Paris the enormity of her mistake became evident. When he reappeared at Saint-Joseph, his behaviour towards her was as cold and distant as it had been for some time, all his attention was turned on Julie. The friendly hand held out so warmly with the generous offer of forgetting a painful misunderstanding might have been the hand of a beggar, to be thrown a little something and glanced at distractedly. The precious gifts of d'Alembert's friendship, trust and intellectual understanding were lost forever to Madame du Deffand. In a flash she comprehended the serious and irreversible revolution that had taken place in her little kingdom without her knowing and despite numerous warnings. Her lady companion had taken her place and robbed her of that which she held most dear. Not content with being kindly treated and courted for her charm and youth, she had taken advantage of the trust placed in her to usurp the crown. Julie had become for d'Alembert— and not only for him—the real and vital centre of the *salon* at Saint-Joseph whereas the *marquise* was by now an old institution to be looked at with curiosity, admired perhaps, but who had outlived herself and who belonged irretrievably to the past.

Madame du Deffand felt a terrible sense of injustice and the presence of her niece became unbearable to her. Resentment destroyed the delicate and complicated balance which controlled their relationship. Julie began to be treated as a subordinate whose master in a moment of weakness had placed too much trust in her and who needed to be put back in her place. The young woman's pride was crushed with haughtiness, insinuation and harshness; deprived of respect and attention, her life of dependence became unbearable. Guilty only of existing, Julie found herself in a situation not unlike that which had made her leave Champrond twelve years earlier.

Within six months of d'Alembert's return from Prussia, the quarrel was over. The episode recounted by Marmontel was the last act in the drama. Life at Saint-Joseph began late in the afternoon; the *marquise* who suffered from insomnia, slept long into the day and did not settle in her *"tonneau"* ready to welcome her visitors until around six in the evening. In the little apartment with its independent entrance which had been especially rented for her in 1754,[51] Julie had evidently taken to receiving a little before the statutory hour, those of the *marquise*'s guests who had especially become her friends. This was not so much an infringement of rights on Julie's part, as a brief moment of autonomy when she could be herself and speak freely to her friends. When Madame du Deffand discovered this innocent habit she saw it as proof of betrayal by her niece and a much awaited opportunity for her anger to explode.

Julie was dismissed from the house without mercy. Ten years earlier the *marquise* had warned her niece that any improper conduct on her part would bring her "powerful enemies." But by now not one of Madame du Deffand's friends was prepared to side against the supposedly guilty party. The *marquise* soon realized that to ask the *habitués* of Saint-Joseph to choose between her and Julie would be tantamount to suicide. From Hénault to Madame de Luxembourg they all vied to provide Julie with lodgings, furniture and a respectable income.

So Julie moved into an apartment which was no more than a hundred metres away from Saint-Joseph, in the very same rue Saint-Dominique. But before finally deciding that all the bridges were burned, and moved no doubt by a generous feeling of *pietas,* Julie humbly held out an olive branch in the hope of placating her aunt's anger.

MADEMOISELLE DE LESPINASSE TO MADAME DU DEFFAND

Tuesday, 8 May 1764

You have fixed a time, Madame, before which I cannot have the honour of seeing you. This time seems long indeed to me and I would be very happy were you to consider shortening it. I desire nothing so much as to deserve your kindness; deign then to grant me that, and give me precious proof of it by allowing me to come and renew the assurance of my respect and attachment which will only end with my life and with which I have the honour of remaining, Madame, your very humble and obedient servant.

MADAME DU DEFFAND TO MADEMOISELLE DE LESPINASSE

Wednesday, 9 May 1764

I cannot consent to see you again so soon, Mademoiselle; the conversation which I had with you and which decided our separation is at present still too much with me.

I cannot believe that feelings of friendship cause you to wish to see me. It is impossible to love those by whom one knows one is detested, abhorred etc. etc. and who ceaselessly humiliate and crush one's self respect etc. etc. These are your expressions and they result from the impressions you have long received from those whom you claim to be your true friends; in fact they may well be and I hope with my whole heart that they will procure you all the advantages you expect: comfort, fortune, regard, etc. etc. What would you do with me today, of what use can I be to you: My presence would not be agreeable and would only remind you of the early days of our acquaintanceship, the years which followed and all that are best forgotten. However, if you later come to remember them with pleasure, and should this memory produce some kind of remorse in you, or regret, I do not pride myself in an austere or brutal determination, I am not insensitive and I can easily distinguish the truth. A sincere return might touch me and reawaken the liking and the affection which I had for you; but meanwhile, Mademoiselle, let us remain as we are, and be content with my wishes for your happiness.

Not content with sending her niece away, and never ever receiving her again, Madame du Deffand also tried to expunge everything about Julie from her memory. But it was not easy—particularly to someone like herself who thrived on social life—to avoid hearing at least an echo of Julie's success. Her own mistress at last, "without fortune and without birth,"[52] the young woman presided over a *salon* which for about ten years was the real centre of intellectual Paris. Although to begin with it was mainly d'Alembert who attracted visitors to the rue Saint-Dominique, according to Grimm,[53] it was not long before Julie's charm alone detained them. La Harpe wrote, "The choicest society and the most agreeable people from every field were gathered in Mademoiselle de Lespinasse's house. From five in the evening until ten o'clock the élite from every walk of life were sure to be found there, courtiers, writers, ambassadors, foreign grandees, ladies of quality; to be received in this society was almost a mark of success. Mademoiselle de Lespinasse was the principal allurement."[54] Guibert claimed that all these people with nothing in common often found themselves "united by a kind of interest of which she was both the driving force and the point, and went on to add, "We felt that we were all friends at her house because we were gathered there by the same feelings, the desire to please her and the need to love her."⁵⁵ But what Caracciolo called the *"avant-soirée du coin de la rue Saint-Dominique"* was reserved for the closest friends: d'Alembert, Condorcet, Suard, Chastellux, Morellet, Marmontel, Turgot, Malesherbes. Then Julie's *salon* became a centre for the initiated and the lady of the house revealed her intellectual passion, her moral strength and her *"âme citoyenne"*⁵⁶ hungry for reforms and freedom. Where Madame Geoffrin's house continued to be the headquarters of enlightenment, it could be said that Julie's became the heart.

Many of these visitors were old *habitués* of the *salon* at Saint-Joseph only a few hundred metres away, and had either come from there or would soon be going back there. The *marquise* was therefore reminded daily, albeit indirectly, of her niece's existence as much by the absence of those who had deserted her and by the presence of those who attended her *salon*.

Among visiting foreigners at least it may have been possible to sustain the quarrel between the two *salons*. Ten years after Julie left Saint-Joseph Horace Walpole wrote to General Conway, who was going to spend the winter in Paris and who had an introduction to Madame du Deffand: "I must give you another piece of advice without which everything would be useless. There is at Paris a Mademoiselle de Lespinasse, a pretended *bel esprit,* who was formerly an humble companion of Madame du Deffand, and betrayed her and used her very ill. I beg you not to let anybody carry you thither. It would disoblige my friend of all things in the world, and she would never tell you a syllable."⁵⁷ Although her friends were careful to avoid mentioning anything to do with Julie, the *marquise* sometimes heard news which must have been particularly disagreeable to her.

Madame Geoffrin's tremendous liking for and genuine interest in Mademoiselle de Lespinasse—who was the only woman admitted to the gatherings at the rue Saint-Honoré—must have annoyed Madame du Deffand considerably and have seemed like intentional provocation even though the *marquise* had always treated her rival with aristocratic disdain and called her names, like *"omelette au lard."*⁵⁸ But it must have wounded her to the heart to learn that about a year after the rift between aunt and niece, d'Alembert had gone to live in the same house as Julie. She probably knew them both too well to wonder about the nature of their cohabitation. Marmontel praised its platonic nature which Rousseau maliciously claimed was a necessity since "it could not be other than a platonic relationship"[59] and Galiani wrote to Tanucci, "In Naples one would say that they had been secretly married. Here such superfluous words are not considered, the customs of the country do not require them."[60] For the Neapolitan diplomat, Julie existed *"velut ens a se."*[61] For Madame du Deffand the news that d'Alembert had moved to the rue Saint-Dominique was no more nor less than a death knell for a lost loved one whom to the last she fondly imagined would reappear. Now for her the game was over. When she heard in 1776 that her niece had died at the age of only forty-four, the *marquise* merely commented, "She would have done well to die fifteen years earlier; I would not have lost d'Alembert."[62]

Nor, in the course of her remaining fifteen feverish years, did Julie forgive Madame du Deffand the humiliation she had suffered. "You hate no one," d'Alembert wrote in a description of Mademoiselle de Lespinasse, "except perhaps for one woman who, to tell the truth, certainly did everything necessary for you to hate her, and yet your hatred for her is not active although hers for you is to a ridiculous degree and so excessive is it as to make this woman very unhappy."[63] Mademoiselle de Lespinasse has left us an implacable account of this "passive" hatred of Madame du Deffand, in which she explicitly accuses the *marquise* whilst implicitly defending herself against the judgement of posterity.

PORTRAIT OF MADAME DU DEFFAND
BY MADEMOISELLE DE LESPINASSE

"Madame du Deffand is at an age and in a condition which forbid further comment being made about her appearance. Those who knew her when she was young, and even when she was no longer young, remember that she had the most beautiful complexion in the world, quite a noble appearance, all her expressions were extremely agreeable, her physiognomy was very animated and spritely, her look was charming, her eagle-eyes were lively, piercing and perfectly beautiful. Voltaire used to write to her that since going blind she 'had been punished whereby she had made others sin.' The thinness of her bust and hands did not detract from these attractions, and the charm of her intelligence almost prevented the failing she had of talking through her nose from being noticed: a failing which she accepted in good faith and which provoked the quite pleasant remark that 'her nose was what she most loved in the world because she was always talking about it.'

"Among her several agreeable qualities she has one which is quite rare although essential to the art of pleasing: she has an easy naturalness of manner. She cannot tolerate affectation of any kind whatsoever; so she has an acute awareness of the ridiculous whom she seizes upon and describes most amusingly. This same taste for the unaffected make whatever is called eloquence, grand style and high-flown sentiment odious to her; and it cannot be denied that she is often justified; but it is true that her aversion to such things is often pushed too far so that she deems affected whatever feelings she does not have and whatever thoughts she has not had. Although of uneven temper, she is, or rather was, naturally gay and agreeable. Some of her witticisms have become proverbs and there are still some sharp flashes of wit in her conversation. I say that she was agreeable and gay for she is no longer, except at very infrequent intervals. Her bad health, the loss of her sight, the real or imagined ills which she believes it necessary to complain about to her friends, have given her a fundamental sadness and moodiness which often make her boring and displeased with everything she sees, everything she reads and almost everything she hears. To this failing which is so disagreeable for others is added that of always believing herself to be just, and she especially prides herself on two virtues: taste and fairness. In fact these are quite marked when she makes a judgement in cold blood, but unfortunately this is a rare thing in her. Passion rules most of her decisions. She becomes at first infatuated and then excessively disgusted with the same work and the same people; she vilifies what she has praised only a few days earlier and praises what she has vilified, and all this without any falseness but merely to satisfy the feelings which sway her at the moment and to which she gives way in all good faith and which she firmly believes to have always been the same, since only the present counts with her. She barely remembers the past and never thinks of the future.

"She has taken an aversion to what she calls modern philosophy, which springs from various causes. Some of those who advance this philosophy have displayed an affectedness in their work which has some reason to shock her. Perhaps they preach too ostentatiously the virtue which she never knew and a contempt for grandees whom she adores whilst believing herself to be indifferent to them. Besides, some of those who see her have displeased her by not wishing to submit themselves entirely to her will and her opinions. Finally, this philosophy and those who have distinguished themselves in it have the misfortune of being highly regarded by a woman whom Madame du Deffand considers and at least treats as her rival in intelligence and reputation and for whom, for this reason alone, she has vowed an implacable hatred and whom she takes pleasure in denigrating on every occasion.

"If Madame du Deffand shows any justice, it is only with regard to her servants whom she does not treat entirely ill. This justice towards them depends on another quality of hers: she is noble and generous albeit careful, for there is no real generosity without husbandry. But in her a good quality seems incapable of depending on a good principle, so her generosity springs not from the nobility of her spirit which is naturally greedy and mean, but from the need she has of those around her. She tries to make herself liked by her servants only because she cannot make them her slaves, for she has often been heard to regret the abolition of slavery; so she is a great enemy of natural equality which is another reason for resenting philosophy. Besides she is hard towards those of whom she has no need, without humanity, without charity, without compassion, having no idea of these virtues and always ridiculing them in others. As a result of her prejudice and aversion to equality, she flattens herself in front of any of the so-called court people, especially if they are in favour; she often debases herself to them in the most humiliating fashion without getting anything in return. She is quite surprised that almost no one expresses any friendship or trust for her, for in her folly she believes that she deserves friends, although she has precisely what is required to alienate them. Inconsiderate, indiscreet, egoist and jealous; these four words sum up her character.

"Inconsiderate: she is brusque and disdainful in her conversation; she makes little effort to hide how little she regards those she despises; she answers them with a shrug of the shoulders; in front of them, in a loud voice to her neighbour (whilst believing that she speaks quietly) she describes everything about their person and their conversation which rightly or wrongly displeases her. What surprises her after all that, is not to see everyone at her command and at her feet. Convinced that her lack of consideration for others is no more than estimable frankness, for frankness is yet another virtue on which she prides herself, she is frank only with those of whom she believes she has nothing to fear. Noble, disinterested frankness is a virtue of which she knows nothing and which she calls impertinence in others.

"Indiscreet. To the last degree: she is absolutely incapable of saying nothing about what interests her and about what essentially interests others. Everything she knows, everything she guesses, everything she suspects, even everything she thinks, she repeats to the first comer, without regard for those she might wrong and without meaning to wrong them for she is far more superficial than malicious. She has neither friendship for, nor trust in those to whom she tells her secret— or rather other people's secrets—but does so only out of a need to talk, unless it is for reasons of vengeance; then she pushes indiscretion to the point of baseness and perfidy by abusing the trust which has been placed in her in order, if she can, to damage the honour and reputation of those who have been weak enough to speak to her about matters which touch them.

"Egoist. Lacking all consideration and modesty, she does not mind showing herself as she really is on that point, unlike most men who, whilst being very concerned with themselves, wish to appear a little concerned with others. Madame du Deffand is ignorant of this social nicety; she demands all and gives nothing in return and at the same time she persuades herself that she is not demanding because she does not have the power to command and because she has not been obeyed, or because people have been obliging. Since she brings everything back to herself, she cannot bear anything to be done for others especially if it inconveniences her in any way. She is not jealous of attraction or intelligence in others, but only of preference and of attentions for which she forgives neither the giver nor the receiver. To everyone she knows she seems to say, like Jesus Christ to his disciples, 'Go and sell that thou hast and come and follow me!' It is harder to be at peace with her than with God; a venal sin destroys in an instant the merit gained from several years of diligence. She pays for the preference accorded her with praises which the slightest displeasure causes her to retract the next day, which turn to satire or are changed into libellous songs whilst the displeasure lasts. Having the character I have just described, it is hardly surprising that she is excessively curious and mistrustful—curious about what concerns others, but only in order to know what has been said and done, and above all what has been thought and said about her.

Mistrustful because she judges others by herself, and because being entirely concerned with herself, she always suspects that traps are being laid for her, even when no one is thinking about her at all.

"Such is Madame du Deffand. She is sought after for her intelligence, which makes her curious and which is alone responsible for the kind of reputation she enjoys. Understanding of her character causes one to withdraw from her and prevents attachment. She is ignoble with her superiors, quite just with her inferiors, insupportable and tyrannical with her equals. She cannot claim to have one true friend among her vast number of acquaintances. She is full of wit, prejudice, caprice and injustice. In fact she is like a wicked child, one who has not been spoilt, however, but whose character has been his misfortune."[64]

IX

Friendʃhip with Voltaire

WITH THE DEPARTURE OF JULIE, the aristocratic tendencies of the Saint-Joseph *salon* became accentuated. So, during the 1760s when French foreign policy was in crisis and internal policy was becoming gradually more complicated, the *salon* maintained a disdainful, almost hostile distance from the cultural scene which was developing in an atmosphere of polemic, recrimination and hope.

In the fevered, crowded world of Paris, Madame du Deffand's *salon* seemed to isolate itself increasingly from the mainstream and to become a precious, *recherché* meeting place for the true connoisseurs of a gradually disappearing way of life. It was a refuge for great aristocrats who were not prepared to sacrifice taste and *"bon ton"* for the pleasures of intellectual curiosity; and together with the *salons* of Madame de Luxembourg, the Prince de Conti and a few others, it was an unprofaned sanctuary where the real French *esprit* was still celebrated. A dilettante attitude towards politics, literature and philosophy was rigorously maintained.

As the *marquise* aged with the century, so she lost none of her vivacity or theatrical talent. The pessimistic conservatism which increasingly dominated her decisions and caused her to reject more and more, did not dampen her voracious worldliness nor did it affect the incomparable verve of her conversation or her lucid wit. Her intelligence continued to blazen forth like a firework display arousing both amazement and awe. She owed her reputation for malice, referred to by Rousseau in his *Confessions,* to both the provocative freedom of her incisive, unfashionable judgement and to the campaign of more or less explicit denigration conducted against her by d'Alembert, Madame Geoffrin and Julie. It is not surprising that Rousseau and Madame du Deffand were incompatible, but is rather a credit to the integrity of both.

"I at first began by being very interested in Madame du Deffand, the loss of whose sight made her an object of pity in mine; but her way of life, so unlike mine that one of us rose almost as the other retired, her unlimited passion for the trivialities of the '*bel esprit,*' the importance she attached, good or bad, to the least scribblings which appeared, the despotism and passion of her judgements, her exaggerated infatuation with things or hatred of them which caused her to speak of everything convulsively with unbelievable prejudice, her invincible stubbornness, the unreasoning enthusiasm into which she was thrown by the obstinacy of her passionate opinions; all that soon discouraged me from giving her the attention I had wished. I neglected her and she noticed it. That was enough to put her into a rage and although I sense how much a woman of her character was to be feared, I preferred to expose myself to the scourge of her hatred than that of her friendship."[1]

But as the *bête noire* of the *philosophes,* she could still boast of her friendship with Voltaire as the one irrefutable testimony to her intellectual quality. The fact that the most famous writer of the century corresponded with her over the years was a trump card against which her detractors had no power: it proved that hers was not a blind refusal of new ideas but of sectarian fanaticism only, not of real genius, but of its flunky. It was Madame du Deffand's great revenge against d'Alembert and all those who sided with Julie.

Voltaire, who had left the French capital in 1750, still ruled the Parisian scene. From his much visited refuge on the banks of Lake Geneva, Voltaire cultivated his image by his writings, his opinions and by polemic and various other undertakings. His constant influence depended on a deluge of brochures, letters, novels, poems, stories, tragedies and occasional verses printed in Geneva, Berne, Amsterdam and London and smuggled into France by bold travellers and salesmen, to be read immediately by the whole nation including its rulers. But his constant participation in the cultural debate and his enormous influence were also due to his inexhaustible letter writing.

His correspondence with Madame du Deffand had a particular part to play. To be in touch with the *marquise* meant remaining in contact with the old aristocracy to which Voltaire continued to be exceedingly sensitive: most particularly with the Luxembourgs, the Beauvaus, the Mirepoix and the d'Aiguillons to whom his letters would be read aloud before being discussed and commented upon. Madame du Deffand was able to act not only as mediator in purely social circles, but thanks to her relationship to Madame de Luynes and her old liaison with Hénault, she had some influence on the most conservative and hostile factions at court, on the Dauphin and Marie Leszczynska who on her deathbed begged the king to punish the writer for impiety. During the 1760s the *marquise* became, above all, a much valued intermediary with Louis XV's all-powerful Minister, the duc de Choiseul.

The main reason for these letters was not desire for prestige, vanity and calculation, but disinterested pleasure and long-standing habit. Madame du Deffand and Voltaire were almost the same age and had met in the long distant past[2] when both were driven by ambition and neither could yet think of using the other. On the same summer evening in 1721 when Madame du Deffand risked her reputation in the company of Madame d'Averne, Voltaire gladly made himself available as poet to the Regent's mistress. During the celebrations at Saint-Cloud, the favourite had offered Philippe d'Orléans an embroidered belt and some verses written for the occasion by the young author of *Oedipe*.

The writer's letters trace the beginnings of this relationship which perhaps never developed into an unrestrained friendship but which depended rather on intellectual admiration. Behind Voltaire's conventional gallantry can be perceived an equal relationship between two people who value each other realistically, who judge each other and who respect each other's brilliance. On 20 August 1725, in a letter to the Présidente de Bernières, Voltaire speaks of "Madame du Deffand's lively and fertile imagination." It was at around this time that, after dining with the *marquise,* Voltaire dedicated the following chivalrous verse to his hostess:

> *Qui vous voit et qui vous entend*
> *Perd bientôt sa philosophie*
> *Et tout sage avec du Deffand*
> *Voudrait en fou passer sa vie.*[3]

Their friendship was consolidated at Sceaux; the *marquise* and Voltaire both went there frequently and often for long periods. The pleasure of being together and their intellectual affinity must have been strengthened by a feeling of solidarity—which would have included Madame de Staal—at having to entertain so demanding and capricious a patron.

In 1732 Voltaire[4] had refused the office of equerry to the duchesse du Maine, but two years later, on 23 May 1734 he appealed to the *marquise* that she might intervene both at Sceaux and in Paris to help appease the scandal of the *Lettres philosophiques*:[5] "Truly, Madame, when I had the honour of writing to you and of begging you to prevail upon your friends to speak to Monsieur de Maurepas, it was not out of fear that he might harm me, it was in order that he might do me good. I prayed to him as to my good angel, but unfortunately my wicked angel is far more powerful than he. Do you not admire, Madame, all the fine speeches which are made about these scandalous letters? Is Madame la duchesse du Maine really vexed that I put Newton before Descartes? And what does Madame la duchesse de Villars who is so fond of innate ideas, think of the boldness with which I treat her innate ideas of chimera?"

This letter bears witness to the fact that with her libertine past behind her, Madame du Deffand's prestige in society was growing. Voltaire at first turned to the *marquise* for help, but a letter written two years later leaves no doubt about his disinterested admiration for her and the nature of their relationship. Madame du Deffand was someone whose approval was to be sought, whose judgement was requested, someone with whom to share the most serious of thoughts; someone with whom Voltaire could discuss his own work on equal terms.

VOLTAIRE TO MADAME DU DEFFAND   *Civey, par Vassy-en-Champagne*
                                  18 March 1736

Quite a long illness, Madame, prevented me from answering sooner the charming letter with which you honoured me. You should be interested in this illness. It was caused by too much work; and what purpose do I have in all my work, but the desire to please you and to deserve your approbation? Your approval of my Americans[6] and particularly of Alzire's tender, simple virtue quite consoles me for all the criticism from the little town four leagues away from Paris and five hundred from good taste which they call the court. I will as-suredly do what I can to make Gusman more bearable. I do not want to justify myself about a character who displeases you, but did

Grandval not do me an injustice? Did he not exaggerate the character and make ferocious what I wanted only to paint as severe? You thought, you say, from the opening lines, that this Gusman would have his father hung. Well, Madame, his first line is this: *Quand vous priez un fils, seigneur, vous commandez.*

Does he not have the authority of all the viceroys of Peru and is it not possible for such inflexibility to go hand in hand with filial sentiment? Silla and Marius loved their father. Finally, the play is based on his change of heart and if this heart was soft, tender and compassionate in the first act, what would one do at the end?

Allow me to speak to you more positively about Pope. You tell me that social love means that "whatever is is right."[7] Firstly, what he calls quite unsuitably "social love" is not for him the foundation and proof of the order of the universe. Whatever *is* is right, because it is the work of an infinitely wise being, and this is the subject of the first epistle. Then in the last epistle he describes as *social love* that benign providence whereby animals subsist by serving each other. Milord Shaftesbury[8] who initially established part of this system, claimed with reason that God gave man both self-love to induce him to preserve his existence, and *social love* which is a benevolent instinct towards the species and quite subordinate to self-love and which in becoming part of the great momentum is the basis of society.[9] But it is quite strange to impute to I know not what social love in God, the irresistible fury which drives all species of animals to devour others. It may be part of a design, I agree, but a design which certainly cannot be called love. All Pope's work is swarming with such obscurity. There are a hundred admirable flashes of lightning which break through this darkness all the time, and with your brilliant imagination you must love them. All that is beautiful and luminous is of your element. Do not be afraid of discussion. Do not be ashamed to add the strength of your intelligence to the charms of your person. Make your *noeuds* with the other women, but speak reason to me. I beg you, Madame, to procure Monsieur de Président Hénault's goodwill on my behalf. His is the most upright and amiable intelligence I have ever known. A thousand respects and my eternal attachment.

Here was a real tribute. Thus Voltaire incited his friend to take cognisance of her intellectual potential, not to deny it nor to sacrifice it to a social code which demanded understatement, charm, frivolity, and which was horrified by bombast and pomposity. In this sense Madame du Deffand's and Madame de Staal's ironic perception of Madame de Châtelet was exemplary: the label of *"femme savante"* was loaded with negative implications for a society lady. Here Voltaire seizes on one of the central problems of Madame du Deffand's existential malaise, her profoundly negative attitude to her exceptional intellectual ability. Intelligence was the only absolute quality the *marquise* recognised. She used her intelligence with disinterested passion and as an aggressive weapon. It clarified, revealed, mocked, conferred prestige, but was never in her case used creatively, or as a constructive force. From a certain moment it brought her only frustration and sorrow.

The first letter in our possession from Voltaire to the *marquise* is dated May 1732. In all there are sixteen letters in his own handwriting, covering the succeeding twenty-five years of their friendship, until 1758. Sainte-Aulaire[10] sees the long silence which coincides more or less with Voltaire's relationship with Madame du Châtelet as indicating a possible old love affair between him and the *marquise*. Voltaire would have taken care to avoid any possibility of friction with *la belle Emilie*. This is somewhat implausible. Even if there really had been a romantic interlude, it is hard to imagine that, given the times and the people involved, it would have given rise to embarrassment. Madame du Châtelet might have interfered with the relationship between Voltaire and Madame du Deffand, not out of sexual jealousy, but because she wished to have a monopoly of intellectual prestige: the cult of *la belle Emilie* left little room for admiration of a serious rival's intelligence.

The gaps in the correspondence, however, can be explained above all by the frequent meetings of the two during those years. Despite his wanderings throughout Europe and long visits to Cirey and Lunéville, Voltaire was often in Paris from whence he frequented both Sceaux and the *salons*, visiting in particular Hénault and Madame du Deffand. Besides, Madame du Deffand's name recurs regularly during the 1730s and 1740s in Voltaire's letters to Formont and then with Hénault, two shared friends to whom the *marquise* appears to have entrusted power of attorney over her correspondence with Voltaire. The result is a kind of conversation through a third party and evidence of a continued relationship can be inferred from extracts from Voltaire's letters to Formont and Hénault between 1738 and 1744.

VOLTAIRE TO FORMONT   *Cirey, 11 November {1738}*

. . . No doubt you often see Madame du Deffand; she forgets me which is reasonable, but I remember her always; I will make of her an ungrateful woman, I will always be attached to her . . .

Brussels, 1 April {1740}

> *Vous voilà dans l'heureux pays*
> *Des belles et des beaux esprits,*
> *Des bagatelles renaissantes,*
> *Des bons et des mauvais ecrits.*
> *Vous entendez les vendredis*
> *Ces clameurs longues et touchantes*
> *Dont le Maure enchante Paris.*
> *Des soupers avec des gens choisis*
> *De vos jours filés par les ris*
> *Finissent les heures charmantes.*
> *Mais ce qui vaut assurément*
> *Bien mieux qu'une pièce nouvelle*
> *Et que le souper le plus grand,*
> *Vous vivez avec du Deffand;*
> *Le reste est un amusement,*
> *Le vrai boneur est auprès d'elle* . . .[11]

VOLTAIRE TO HÉNAULT   *Brussels, 20 August {1740}*

. . . If Madame du Deffand and the people with whom you live deigned to remember that I exist, I would beg you to give them my respects. . .

The Hague, 31 October {1740}

. . . Madame du Deffand must never think that the desire to please her and to meet with her approbation ever leaves my heart. Is Monsieur Formont in Paris? He is, as you know, one of the small number of the chosen . . . Give my respects to *quelli pochissimi signori*[12] . . .

VOLTAIRE TO FORMONT   *Brussels, 3 March {1741}*

> *Formont, vous et les du Deffand,*
> *C'est à dire les agréments,*
> *L'esprit, les bons mots, l'éloquence.*

. . . one of your conversations with Madame du Deffand is worth more than everything in the storehouse of the booksellers' corporation. Madame du Châtelet sends you many compliments. She knows your worth, just like Madame du Deffand. Those are two very agreeable women! . . .

VOLTAIRE TO HÉNAULT   *Cirey-en-Champagne, 1 June 1744*

. . . I ask you of your favour to remember me to Madame du Deffand. Do not forget your goodwill towards me, nor hers. She writes most agreeable letters to Madame du Châtelet. *Tentat eam,* sometimes, *in aenigmatibus.*[13] One guesses them immediately . . .

Voltaire had resumed his correspondence with Madame du Deffand on the death of Madame du Châtelet with a heart-rending letter. Five years later genuine feeling once again moved him to answer a letter, now unfortunately lost, in which his old friend informed him of her permanent blindness.

VOLTAIRE TO MADAME DU DEFFAND   *Colmar, 3 March {1754}*

Your letter, Madame, moved me more than you think; and I assure that my eyes were a little damp as I read what had happened to yours. I judged from Monsieur Formont's letter that you were in the twilight, not entirely in the dark. I thought that you were more or less in the same condition as Madame de Staal having, unlike her, the inestimable good fortune of being free, of living in your own house and not in a princess's house and subjected there to embarrassing behaviour tinged with hypocrisy, having in fact friends with whom you can think and speak freely. I only regretted, Madame, the loss of beauty in your eyes and I knew you to be philosophical enough to console yourself for that. But if you have lost your sight, I pity you infinitely. I do not propose that you follow Monsieur de Senneterre's example.

He was blind at twenty and always merry, too merry even. I agree with you that life is not good for much; we only bear it by virtue of the power of an almost invincible instinct given us by nature: to this instinct has been added, at the bottom of Pandora's box, hope. It is when this hope deserts us absolutely or when an insupportable melancholy takes hold of us that we overcome the instinct which makes us love life's chains, and then have the courage to leave an ill-built house which we despair of repairing. This decision was taken recently by two people in the village where I live. One of these two philosophers was a girl of eighteen whose head had been turned by the Jesuits, and who, to be rid of them, went to the other world. It is a decision that I will never make, at least not soon, for the good reason that I have an annuity for life from two sovereigns and I would be inconsolable were my death to enrich two crowned heads. If you have a life annuity from the King, Madame, look after yourself well, eat little, retire early and live for a hundred years . . .

Who, then, Madame, can have told you that I am marrying? I would be an agreeable man to marry. For six months I have not left my room and out of twelve hours every day I spend ten in suffering. If there were some apothecary's daughter with a pretty figure who knew how to give a clyster, how to fatten poultry and read aloud, I admit that I would be tempted. But my truest and my dearest wish would be to spend with you the evening of this stormy day which we call life. I saw you in your brilliant morning, and it would be a great sweetness for me were I able to help console you and converse with you freely in those short moments which remain to us and which will be followed by nothing. I do not really know what will happen to me, and I hardly mind. But consider, Madame, that you are the one person in the world for whom I have a tender respect and unalterable friendship. Allow me to send a thousand compliments to Monsieur Formont. Does the Président Hénault still give preference to the Queen over you? It is true that the Queen is very intelligent.

Farewell, Madame. Know that I feel your sad condition acutely, and that from the edge of my grave, I would like to be able to contribute to the sweetness of your life. Do you remain in Paris? Will you spend the summer in the country? Are men and places indifferent to you? Your fate will never be to me.

It could be said that the real correspondence between Madame du Deffand and Voltaire began in January 1759, to be interrupted again by his return to Paris and his death there in 1778. It encompasses twenty years and despite moments of lassitude comprises a hundred letters from the *marquise* and a hundred and sixty-four from Voltaire, not including the sixteen written by him between 1732 and 1758. It is not surprising that the death of Formont who had acted as an intermediary between them for so many years, provoked Madame du Deffand to renew her friendship with Voltaire.

MADAME DU DEFFAND TO VOLTAIRE   {*ca. 5 January 1759*}

I thought that you had forgotten me, Monsieur; I was wounded without complaining, but the greatest loss which I could experience, and which completes the measure of my misfortune, reminded me of you.[14] No one but you has spoken so perfectly of friendship; understanding it so well, you can judge my sorrow. The friends[15] whom I will mourn all my life made me feel the truth of the lines in your discourse on *la Modération*.

O divine amitié! Félicité parfaite! etc.[16]

I used to say it ceaselessly with delight; now I will say it with bitterness and sorrow! But, Monsieur, why do you refuse my friend a word of praise? Surely you found him worthy of it: you valued his intelligence, his taste, his judgement, his heart and his character. He was not one of those folio philosophers who teaches contempt of the public, hatred of the great, who refuses to recognise greatness in any field and who takes pleasure in confusing people with sophistry and tiring, boring paradox; he was far removed from such folly. He was the sincerest of your admirers and, I believe, one of the most enlightened. But, Monsieur, why should he be praised by me alone? Four lines from you in either verse or prose would honour his memory and be a real consolation for me.

If you are dead, as you say you are, there can no longer be any doubt about the immortality of the soul: never has anyone on earth had as much soul as you do in your tomb! I believe you to be very happy. Am I mistaken? The country you are in seems made for you: the people who live there are the real descendants of Ishmael, serving neither Baal nor the God of Israel.[17] They respect and admire your talents without hating or persecuting you. You also enjoy a tremendous advantage: great opulence, which makes you independent and able to satisfy your tastes and your fantasies. I think no one has played the game more cleverly than you: chance has not always been on your side, but you have known how to correct misfortune and you have profited properly from good fortune.

Finally, Monsieur, if your health is good and if you enjoy the sweets of friendship, the King of Prussia[18] is right: you are a thousand times happier than he, despite the glory which surrounds him, and the shame of his enemies.

The *Président* is all my life's consolation; but he also causes all my suffering because of the fear I have of losing him. We speak of you very often. It is cruel of you to tell us that you will never see us again! Never! That is more or less the language of a dead man; but, thank God, you are well and alive and I do not give up hope of seeing you again.

I remember perhaps a little too late that you were tired of entering into a correspondence with me: the length of this letter exposes me to the same dangers.

Farewell, Monsieur; no one has a greater liking for you, more respect nor greater friendship: I have thought the same way for forty years.

Madame du Deffand's appeal did not go unheard. Voltaire's reply is solicitous, affectionate and unusually melancholy. His sorrow at Formont's death is transformed into a more or less general feeling of nostalgia for the long ago days of shared youth. But Voltaire's sense of reality, his confidence in past decisions and future aims, and above all his extraordinary energy soon gain the upper hand.

VOLTAIRE TO MADAME DU DEFFAND   *Les Délices, 12 January {1759}*

> *Libre d'ambition, de soins et d'Esclavage,*
> *Des sottises du monde éclairé spectateur,*
> *Il se garda bien d'être acteur,*
> *Et fut heureux autant que sage.*
> *Il fuyait le vain nom d'auteur;*
> *Il dedaigna de vivre au Temple de mémoire,*

Mais il vivra dan notre coeur:
C'est sans doute asseʒ pour sa gloire.[19]

The flowers which I throw, Madame, on the grave of our friend Formont are dry and faded like me. Talent abandons me, age destroys everything. What can you expect from a country bumpkin who knows no more than how to plant and sow in the right season? I have retained some sensibility: it is all that I have left and it is for you; but I only write when the opportunity arises.

What shall I tell you from the depths of my retreat? You can send me no news of the wheel of fortune on which our ministers are turned upside down, nor of public or private folly. Letters which once painted the landscape of the heart and were a consolation for absence and the language of truth, are now no more than the sad, empty expressions of constraint and of the fear of saying too much. One trembles lest a word escape which might be misinterpreted: one can no longer think by letter.[20]

I do not write to the Président Hénault, but I wish him, as I do you, a long and healthy life. I owe mine to the decision I made. If I dared I would think myself wise because I am so happy. I only began to live on the day I chose my retreat. I would find any other way of life unbearable. You need Paris; it would be fatal for me: everyone must needs remain in his own element. I am very vexed that mine should be incompatible with yours, that is indeed my only trouble.

You also wanted to try the country; but, Madame, it does not suit you. Just as Rameau needed the company of connoisseurs of music,[21] so you require the society of amiable people. Besides a liking for property and work is an essential in the countryside. I have great possessions which I cultivate. I prefer your apartment to my cornfields and my pastures, but it has always been my destiny to end up between a seed-bag, a herd of cows and the Genevans. These Genevans have all cultivated their reason and are so reasonable that they come to my house and are satisfied that I should never go to theirs. Only Madame de Pompadour could live more conveniently.

So that is my life-style, Madame, just as you imagined it; quiet and busy, opulent and philosophical and above all entirely free. From the bottom of my heart it is entirely devoted to you with the most tender respect and the most inviolable attachment.

In his famous assessment of Madame du Deffand as being "with Voltaire, the purest writer of prose of the time,"[22] Sainte-Beuve was certainly thinking of the proof she gave of her talent in direct comparison with the great writer. In Madame du Deffand's correspondence with Voltaire, two virtuosi, impatient to shine, vie with each other whilst realising that each other's skill is essential for the full development of their own. They send the ball backwards and forwards, like two players who are not concerned with the score, but rather with the spectacular effect of the encounter as a whole, in a game where the public is never forgotten, but one which is, nevertheless, an exclusive game for the initiated, full of subtle allusion. The mainspring of a correspondence which also deals with the most serious subjects whilst subsisting on almost nothing, changes from adulation to irony to conciseness and eloquence, complicity and polemic. It may lapse for long periods, but a mere spark will be enough to reawaken the interest and renew the energy of the two correspondents. Voltaire abandoned himself to the game for the pure pleasure of writing whilst Madame du Deffand grasped at it as a means of avoiding ennui for a few moments. It was made possible by a shared code of values which guaranteed its development.

As "contemporaries"[23] Madame du Deffand's and Voltaire's minds were formed by art, literature and the tastes of the *Grand Siècle*; during their turbulent youth, they knew and loved the elegant, unscrupulous Regency society, they retained an aristocratic worldly style which was linked to life at court and in the houses of great princes. The theme of the good old days and of loyalty to their own tastes and education runs through the whole correspondence but is expressed by both writers with very different tone and depth. The *marquise*'s regret for the past is total and recalls a culture and a way of life which both seem lost for ever. For her literature, life-style, aesthetics and morals were, in accordance with the classic ideal of the *honnête homme*, closely connected. Taste was the criterion by which she judged both people and art. An infallible instinct, almost a privilege of birth, led her, sceptical and independent as she was, to absolve and to condemn with impunity. And yet she knew the dangers inherent in the rule of taste. When the miraculous balance between intelligence, lightness of touch, the natural and the artificial is unsupported by talent, then taste is reduced to an easily repeated formula, a boring mannerism which can damage both literature and life.

Madame du Deffand knew this from experience. For the great seven-teenth-century writers, taste was the corollary of genius. With Fonte-nelle and his contemporaries it helped to develop a literary civilisation and a way of life the last bastions of which were Sceaux and Madame de Lambert's *salon*. In the second half of the century, it survived only among a few isolated supporters. But the enlightenment campaign with its preaching and didactics, its bourgeois influence on the theatre, its *sensiblerie larmoyante,* and its enjoyment of realism disgusted and an-noyed her no less than mediocrity in the traditional literary forms— from poetry to tragedy—whose humiliating banality betrayed the very taste it sought to serve. The *marquise* was rarely insensible to greatness in literature, even when it ran counter to her own aesthetic criteria: so we see her both defending—with Voltaire in fact—Corneille's[24] occa-sional splendour, and "resuscitated"[25] by reading *Othello* and *Henry VI.* In old age she re-read the *Iliad* and the *Odyssey* and was affected by their power. "I think that your Shakespeare bears some resemblance to Homer. You will find that this makes little sense, but there is a certain boldness and a certain strength in the style which defies all caution and decorum; I like the way that in Homer the gods have all the defects and vices of men just as in Shakespeare the kings and great lords have the same tone and the same rude manners as the people."[26]

English writers are baroque, "now harsh, now tender, now wild, now tame," but they are always "true" and unlike the French, they never have "a formula of compliments and banal civility which produces a most revolting tedium."[27] Her dislike of Rousseau, of his morality and his ideas did not prevent her from recognising the quality of his writing and being able to distinguish him from the other writers of his genera-tion. As Sainte-Beuve[28] remarked, Madame du Deffand's assessment of the writers of the time was as "alive" and as "accurate" as any to be found. The *marquise* rallied her resistance to and launched her attacks against the new culture in the name of taste, trusting in Voltaire's total support. Naturally this was not always possible. First of all Voltaire himself did not entirely escape Madame du Deffand's criticism. She loved Voltaire the story-teller, the historian, the essayist, the author of *La Henriade,* but she disapproved of the polemicist, had no respect for the philosopher and despised the vulgarity of works like *La Pucelle.* And then in Voltaire, admiration for the past and loyalty to his own training did not at all involve distancing himself from contemporary culture:

200 }   MADAME DU DEFFAND AND HER WORLD

Voltaire lived in the present and was inspired to fight to make it more acceptable. Madame du Deffand warned him in vain when a statue was raised to him in Paris: "Never forget, my dear contemporary, that you belong to Louis XIV's century."[29] Voltaire belonged to the century in which he lived and Madame du Deffand's criteria would have prevented him from giving his full measure: "It is not enough to hate bad taste, you must detest hypocrites and oppressors."[30]

So the theme of taste runs through the whole correspondence, providing it with a premise and a necessary condition. On this point the *marquise* demands complete equality with her correspondent and abandons any pretence of modesty. But, as Duisit[31] points out, this great symphony of sensibility, style, language and humour constitutes only the most superficial level of the correspondence, a brilliant cloak to disguise two contrasting conceptions of existence. The *marquise*'s pessimism caused apathy and a mistrust of her kind, whereas in the author of *Candide* it inspired action and solidarity with the human race. For Madame du Deffand, intelligence meant an awareness of suffering and of the pointlessness of existence, for Voltaire it was man's redeeming weapon. The *marquise* replied to Voltaire's systematic attempt to provide answers, to accept contradictions, to overcome superstition, in fact to fight man's self-degradation, with mistrust and the denial of any system. For Madame du Deffand the only possible mentor was Montaigne "in whom one finds everything one has ever thought and no one has a more energetic style than he: he teaches nothing because he decides on nothing; it is the opposite of dogmatism: he is vain, and are not all men so? And are not those who seemed modest, doubly vain? The 'I' and the 'me' reappear on every line, but what knowledge can one have if not through the 'I' and the 'me'? Fie . . . he is the only good philosopher and the only good metaphysician there has ever been. It is all rhapsody; perpetual contradictions if you like; but he establishes no system; he seeks, he observes and he remains in doubt: he is useful for nothing, I agree, but he is detached from all opinion and destroys the presumption of knowledge."[32]

Despite the satirical verve of Madame du Deffand's and Voltaire's exchanges concerning contemporary political events, their attitudes towards public life were naturally quite different. The *marquise* could unravel a single thread from the web of politics, but she could not discern the design as a whole, which was a nonsense that left her entirely indifferent except when it constituted a threat to her friends or her own particular interests. Politics for Voltaire were an absorbing passion involving calculation and vanity but with a moral slant as well, which no distance could dampen. Despite his ostensible separation from France, his detachment and cosmopolitanism, he had a strong sense of nationality. At the slightest provocation his sarcasm turned to action.

From 1757 France, like the rest of Europe to a greater or lesser degree, was involved in the complexities of the Seven Years War. Initially at least, Louis the *Bien-Aimé*'s subjects followed the events of the struggle they were asked to support against Prussia and England with very different feelings. England was France's natural enemy and where she was concerned there were many great interests at stake including France's very prestige. But Frederick II was an ex-ally who had only been driven into the enemy camp by reason of the balance of power. It was not long before the war began to go very badly for the French. Within a few years, under the iron hand of Pitt and as a result of immense economic sacrifice, England had gained complete control of the seas and subjected the French colonial empire, from India to North America and Canada, to an exhausting war. In Europe, after an unremarkable start and against all expectations, Frederick II inflicted two memorable defeats on the allied troops at Rossbach and Leuthen, which underlined the tremendous decadence of the French army, the folly of its commanders and the fecklessness of the government. Neither was France's internal situation very reassuring. Although with Choiseul's appointment as foreign minister in 1758, France regained a certain political stability, and by his diplomatic ability avoided a further succession of military defeats, the decline in production and trade, the abandoned state of the land, the scarcity of grain and the need for new taxes combined to present a demoralising picture.

In the face of this social and economic crisis, the financial and economic measures adopted in 1759 by Silhouette, the new finance minister, turned out to be derisory despite the hopes to which they at first gave rise. Besides, well thought out or not, Silhouette's reforms immediately encountered the usual opposition on principle that the "fundamental laws" of the French monarchy were henceforth to invoke when faced with any attempt at innovation. The Parliament of Paris refused to register the reforms and with further remonstrance brought about a *lit de justice* during the course of which the edicts were partially registered (three out of seven on 20 September 1759). Surrounded by such difficulties and with such opposition, the finance minister's policies which were probably worked out in a rash and superficial way, resulted in a kind of bankruptcy of State securities which was aggravated by a ridiculous measure for the recovery of precious metals. Silhouette was finally dismissed.[33]

The finance minister who was to gain much wider recognition in the field of fashion—his name which became synonymous with parsimony was used to describe *"culottes sans gousset,"*[34] *"surtouts sans plis"*[35] as well as the well-known outline drawings[36]—had tried to impose a policy of austerity by reducing court spending and taxing the private incomes of the nobility. This gave rise to the hostility of the aristocracy whose privileges were threatened and to Madame du Deffand's indignation in the following letters.

MADAME DU DEFFAND TO VOLTAIRE   *Paris, 1 October 1759*

I was complaining to you, Monsieur, because I did not know what to read; well the government has made provision: ten or twelve edicts which require a good three quarters of an hour's reading.[37] I will not give you the details; they are not yet taxing the air which we breathe; apart from that I know of nothing which they spare. Despite the immense emoluments accorded to those who will advance these sums, it is feared that they will not be able to find the monies. The vicissitudes of this world give rise to some mistrust; so in order to reassure the public and to show pleasure at the finance minister's[38] talents, he has just been given a life annuity of sixty thousand livres, twenty of which are in his wife's name.

What advice do you give me? Read the Old Testament! Is it because one will then not have the means of making one's own? No, Monsieur, this I will not read. I will abide by the respect it deserves and to which there is nothing to be added; I am surprised that anyone should dare consider it. Do you know that I find you very young still, for you nothing has lost its flavour; but, very well, forget the fools and their opinions and give yourself up to your talent, treat of interesting and agreeable subjects, your travels, your visits, your observations, your reflections on manners, customs, portraits of people you have seen, that would give me great great pleasure. Your opinion of literary works above all would please me infinitely because I feel and think just as you do.

A few years ago I had a frightful attack of the vapours, the remembrance of which still terrifies me; nothing could drag me from the void into which my soul had plunged but the reading of your works. I read a great many histories, but I have exhausted them. I did not read the de Thous[39] and the Daniels[40] and the Griffets,[41] I find all that tedious. I do not at all like to feel that the author I am reading is thinking about making a book, I wish to imagine that he is talking to me. Any work without ease of style tires me to death. Our writers of today are made of iron, not in terms of health, but in terms of style.

Monsieur, you have not read English novels. You would not despise them if you knew them. They are too long, I admit, and you make a better use of your time. There morality is seen in action and never has it been treated in a more interested manner. With such reading one dies of impatience to be perfect, and one believes that nothing can be easier. But I perceive that I am very impertinent in telling you all that I think. It would be a way of swiftly disgusting you with a correspondence for which my heart longs and which would be a great amusement for me and to which you must lend yourself if you have any kindness and humanity.

The Président does quite well, but he is becoming deaf which combined with advancing years often makes him sad. He is meanwhile still sometimes cheerful, and then he is a hundred times better company than what passes for good company today. There is no more gaiety, Monsieur, no more grace. Fools are flat and cold, they are no longer absurd and extravagant as they used to be. The clever are pedantic, correct and sententious. Neither is there any more taste. In fact there is nothing, heads are empty and now they wish our purses to be so too ... Oh! how fortunate you are to be Voltaire! You have every blessing; talents which give you an occupation and a reputation, riches which give you independence.

I can understand the liking you have for domestic cares; there is a pleasure to be had in watching cabbages grow. Are you not concerned with the poultry yard? I would like it; but in truth, that is enough, I must not try your patience to the end.

Send me, Monsieur, some trivia, but nothing about the prophets, I maintain that everything they predicted has happened.

Monsieur le duc de Broglie has just been declared General of the army.[42]

VOLTAIRE TO MADAME DU DEFFAND   *Les Délices 13 October {1759}*

It is very sad, Madame, for a man who lives with you, to be a little deaf;[43] I pity you less for being blind. So the dispute between the blind and the deaf is decided: certainly the one who cannot hear you at all is the most unhappy.

I write only to you in Paris, Madame, because your imagination has always accorded with my heart; but I will not allow you to wish to make me read English novels when you do not want to read the Old Testament. Tell me then, if you please, where will you find a more interesting story than that of Joseph becoming Controller General of Egypt and recognising his brothers? And Daniel who so subtly confuses the two old men, do you count him for nothing? Although Tobias is not so good, it seems better to me than *Tom Jones*[44] in which there is nothing of any quality apart from the character of a barber.

You ask me what you should read, as the sick ask what they should eat; but they must be hungry and you have little appetite but considerable taste. Happy is he who is hungry enough to devour the Old Testament! Do not mock it. This book is a hundred times more enlightening about the customs of Ancient Asia than Homer. Of all ancient monuments, it is the most precious. Is there anything more worthy of attention than a whole people situated between Babylon, Tyre and Egypt who for six hundred years were unaware of the dogma of the immortality of the soul which was accepted in Memphis, Babylon and Tyre? When one reads to learn, one sees all that one has overlooked by reading with one's eyes alone.

But what pleasure could you, who did not concern yourself with the history of your country, take in that of the Jews of Egypt and Babylon? I like the customs of the patriarchs, not because they all lay with their maidservants, but because they cultivated the land as I do. Allow me to read the Holy Writ and let us speak no more about it.

But you, Madame, do you claim to read as one converses? To take a book as one asks for news, to read it, to leave it there, to take another which has nothing to do with the first and to abandon it for a third? In that case, you do not have much pleasure.

To have pleasure, a little passion is needed. A great object of interest is required, a determined desire for instruction which occupies the soul continuously: it is difficult to find and cannot be given. You are disgusted with life, you want only to be amused, I see it clearly, and even amusements are quite rare.

If you were fortunate enough to know Italian, you would be sure of a good month of pleasure with Ariosto: you would be transported by joy; you would see the most elegant and the simplest poetry which effortlessly adorns the most fertile imagination with which nature has ever blessed any man. All novels become insipid beside Ariosto, everything is flat compared to him, above all the translation by our Mirabaud.[45]

If you are an honest person, Madame, as I have always believed you to be, I would have the honour of sending you a canto or two from *La Pucelle,*[46] which are known to no one and in which the author has tried to imitate, however feebly, the naive style and the simple brush strokes of the great man. I do not come near to it at all, but I have given at least a faint idea of this school of painting. Your friend[47] must read it to you, it will provide a quarter of an hour's amusement for you both, which is considerable. You will read it when you have nothing at all to do, when your soul is in need of trifles; for there is no pleasure without need.

If you like a very faithful portrait of this wicked world, you will find one one day in the general history of the follies of the human species which I have finished with great impartiality. Out of vexation, I presented a draught of this history because some fragments from it had already been printed; but since then I have become bolder than I was; I have painted men as they are.

The semi-freedom with which one begins to be able to write in France still manacles us shamefully. All your great histories of France are diabolical, not only because the content is horribly dry and petty, but because the Daniels of this world are even pettier. It is trite prejudice indeed to claim that France has been anything in the world: from Raoul[48] and Eudes[49] until the time of Henri IV and the *Grand Siècle* of Louis XIV we have, compared to the Italians, been foolish barbarians in all the arts.

We have not even, until the last thirty years, learned a little good philosophy from the English. No invention comes from us. The

Spanish have conquered a new world; the Portuguese have found the path to India across African seas; the Arabs and the Turks have founded the most powerful empires; my friend, Tsar Peter has, in the space of twenty years, created an empire of two thousand leagues; my Empress Elizabeth's Scythians have just beaten my King of Prussia whilst our armies have been routed by the peasants of Zell and Wolfenbüttel.[50]

We had the wit to settle in the snows of Canada, surrounded by bears and beavers after the English had established their flourishing colonies in four hundred leagues of the most beautiful land on earth; and now we are being chased out of our Canada. From time to time we still build a few ships for the English; but we build them badly; and when they deign to take them, they complain that we give them only bad sailors.

Judge from that if the history of France is a fine thing to treat widely and to read about. France's great merit, her only merit, her only superiority, lies in a small number of sublime or amiable geniuses who cause French to be spoken in Vienna, in Stockholm and in Moscow. Your ministers, your inspectors and your functionaries have no part in that glory.

What then will you read, Madame? The duc d'Orléans when Regent, deigned to speak to me one day at the *Opéra* ball. He praised Rabelais highly to me. I have taken it up again since, and as I have made a closer study of all the things which he mocks, I admit that except for the baseness of which there is too much, a good part of his book gave me great pleasure. If you would like to make a serious study of it, that will depend only on you, but I fear that you are not sufficiently learned and that you are too delicate.

I would that someone had cut in French, the philosophical works of the late Milord Bolingbroke: he was a verbose person and without any method; but a work could be compiled which would be truly damaging to prejudice and very useful to reason. There is another Englishman who is worth much more than he is: that is Hume, something of whose work has been translated with too much reserve. We translate the English as badly as we fight them on the seas.

Please God, Madame, for the good that I wish you, that at least Dean Swift's *Tale of a Tub*[51] is faithfully reproduced. It is an unimaginable treasury of jest. Pascal amuses me only at the expense of the

Jesuits. Swift amuses and instructs at the expense of the human race. How I love the English boldness! How I like people who say what they think! To dare to half-think only, is only to half-live.

Have you ever read, Madame, the feeble translation of the Cardinal de Polignac's *Anti-Lucrèce?*[52] He once read me twenty lines of it which seemed very beautiful. The abbé de Rothelin assured me that the rest was considerably superior. I took the Cardinal de Polignac for an ancient Roman, a superior man to Virgil, but when his poem was printed, I took it for what it is: a poem without poetry, philosophy without reason.

Apart from the admirable descriptions to be found in Lucretius which will ensure that the book passes into posterity, there is a third canto the reasoning of which has never been clarified by the translators and which well deserves to be exposed to the light of day. We have only a bad translation of it by a baron des Coutures.[53] If I live I will put this third canto into verse[54] if I am able to.

Meanwhile, would you be bold enough to have merely forty or fifty pages of this Coutures read to you? For example book *III,* page 281, volume I, beginning with the words: "One does not notice,"[55] in the margin is written: "twelfth argument." Examine this twelfth argument up to the twenty-seventh with some attention, if it appears to be worthwhile.

Nature has us all on trial, a process that will shortly be ended, and practically no one examines the papers concerning this trial. I ask you only to read fifty pages of this last book, it is the finest protection against the foolish ideas of the vulgar; it is the strongest bastion against miserable superstition. And when one thinks that three quarters of the Roman senate, starting with Caesar, thought like Lucretius, it must be admitted that we are great blackguards, beginning with Joly de Fleury.

You ask me what I think, Madame? I think that we are quite despicable and that there is only a small number of men around the world who dare to have common sense. I think that you are of this small number; but of what use is that? None at all. Read the parable of the Brahmin[56] which I had the honour of sending you; and I urge you to enjoy life as much as you can, it is but a little thing, without fearing death which is nothing.

Since you have only life annuities, the tedious work[57] of which you speak affects you less than another. Every man for himself! Ask your friend if it was not a hundred times worse in 1708 and 1709: such memories are a consolation.

The first scene of Silhouette's play was well applauded, the rest was hissed. But it is quite impossible that the audience was mistaken. It is clear that money is needed for defence since the English are ruining themselves in order to attack us.

My letter has become a book, and a bad one. Throw it in the fire and live as happily as the poor human machine will allow.

In December 1754, Voltaire had settled in Switzerland with Madame Denis who became his companion after Madame du Châtelet's death, and there he must have felt something approaching happiness. After so much restless wandering around Europe, after trusting to the whims of the great and experimenting with the contradictions of his own dual nature as courtier and political agitator, he discovered "a republic to whose leaders one could say, come and dine with me tomorrow."[58] Not satisfied with one house, Voltaire divided his time between *Monriond* near Lausanne and the villa in Les Délices near Geneva. In 1758 he acquired the property of Ferney in French territory near the Swiss frontier and was granted the feudal rights by Choiseul. There he built a château which was to become his final residence. Thus with his independence ensured in either France or Switzerland, he could justifiably write: "I hear a great deal of talk about liberty, but I do not believe that anyone in France has created his own liberty as I have mine. Let he who would, or can, follow my example."[59] Both an ideological and an entrepreneurial challenge. In fact, to a feeling of greater political safety was added a very strong sense of economic independence without which there is no freedom since "poverty saps courage and every philosopher at court becomes as enslaved as the first officer of the crown."[60] Voltaire was a rich man who had, over the years, by his intelligence and far-sightedness, accumulated a considerable fortune the fruits of which he gathered in old age. Like a solid, hard-working bourgeois, he delighted in his property and the land which gave him wheat, wine and timber, and like a great aristocrat he enjoyed comfort, leisure, entertaining, the theatre and the arts. Ferney was in the end a reproduction in miniature of the life at princely courts which Voltaire had never ceased to admire. It was a château peopled by relations, protégés and acolytes, a place of pilgrimage for princes, aristocrats, scholars and even strangers from all over Europe, whose owner put in an appearance according to his mood or his health whilst leaving his regular visitors to entertain the guests. Next to the château was a village entirely created by Voltaire, the inhabitants of which he protected and helped like subjects and where he set up industries—a silk factory and a clock factory—and directed the commerce.

This serene, protected existence allowed Voltaire to develop the most intensely creative period of his writing career, but did not prevent him from maintaining a rich network of relationships nor from vigilantly and anxiously following the dramatic events as they unfolded in Europe. As usual Voltaire took an elusive, histrionic position, not devoid of opportunism. But a hidden coherence of thought lay behind the continual contradictions, and behind the vacillation lay the intelligence of historical relativism. Although he often claimed French citizenship, Voltaire felt no loyalty to those who had banished him from Paris and on more than one occasion. His attitude to France was that of a foreigner judging another country with disdainful detachment. But his was a passionate denial, as passionate as the suffering for a rediscovered homeland. "You do not know, Madame, what it is to be French in a foreign land."[61] So, during the Seven Years War, his ideological sympathies were with the English whose success reflected their great institutions, and with the King of Prussia whose courage and intelligence filled him with admiration. But on the other hand, with the memory of Frederick's humiliating offensive and a horror of the evils of war, he had a very real concern for France's destiny. His readiness on more than one occasion to act as unofficial mediator between Versailles and Potsdam was naturally encouraged by a realisation of the importance of the diplomatic role and by continuous anxiety to maintain good relations with both sides. "This indecision which is his, expresses the political embarrassment of the *philosophes* who are divided between loyalty, for reasons of both principle and tactical expediency, to the reforming absolutism of the enlightened sovereigns and the still vague and confused requirement to translate their ideas of tolerance and freedom of thought into liberal, political claims along English lines."[62] In the end, Voltaire's attitude to the *philosophes* who looked on him as their doyen, was not without ambiguity; the intellectual fellowship, his belief in the necessity of an *esprit de corps* did not prevent him from continually distancing himself from his companions in arms and keeping in touch with old aristocratic acquaintances and influential friends who regarded the *Lumières* unfavourably. In fact he never lost hope of a reconciliation with Versailles.

MADAME DU DEFFAND TO VOLTAIRE   *Paris, 28 October 1759*

Your last letter, Monsieur, is divine. If you wrote me such letters often, I would be the happiest woman in the world and I would not complain of lack of reading matter. Do you know what it made me want to do, as did your parable of the Brahmin? It made me want to throw all the immense volumes of philosophy on the fire, except for Montaigne's, who is the father of them all; but in my opinion he begat some silly and tedious children.

I read history because one must know the facts up to a point and because it teaches you to understand men. The understanding of men is the only science which excites my curiosity because one could not live without them.

Your parable of the Brahmin is charming, it is the fruit of all philosophy. I do not know which I would prefer to be, the Brahmin or the old Indian woman. Do you believe the Capuchin friars and nuns have no sorrows? They are not troubled, if you like, by what the soul is, but their souls torment them. All conditions and all circumstances seem equally unfortunate to me, from the angel to the oyster. The grievous thing is to be born. One can however say about that misfortune that the remedy is worse than the condition.

I will read what you note about the translation of Lucretius, but I will not let you know my thoughts, that would be to take advantage of your patience and to give myself airs, *à la Prasline* (an expression of Madame de Luxembourg's).[63] I must limit myself to telling you only what will provoke you to talk to me. But, Monsieur, if you were as good as I would like, you would have a notebook on your desk where in your moments of leisure you would write down everything that goes through your head. It would be a collection of thoughts, ideas and reflections which you would not yet have put in order. It is entirely true that your mind alone satisfies me for only in you is one quality not dependent on another. But I do not wish to praise you too much.

I will certainly not read Rabelais; as for Ariosto, I like him very much and have always preferred him to Tasso who seems to me to have a languid rather than a touching beauty, more restrained than majestic, and then I hate devils to death. I cannot tell you what pleasure I had in finding in *Candide* all your criticism of Milton.[64] I believed that I had thought of it all myself because I have a horror of him. In fact when I read your judgement of whatever it might be, my good opinion of myself increases because I am always in agreement. I will say no more about English novels; you would certainly find them too long. Perhaps one should have nothing to do in order to enjoy reading them, but I find they are moral treatises in action, very interesting and they can be exceedingly useful. They are *Pamela, Clarissa* and *Grandison*; the author is Richardson[65] and he has, it seems to me, considerable intelligence.

Do you know, Monsieur, what to me most proves your superiority and why I think you are a great philosopher? It is that you have grown rich. People who say that one can be free and happy in poverty are liars, madmen and fools.

Do not, I beg you, support our financial plans; not only will they lead us to the poor house, but they will diminish the King's revenue. Everyone has been made sensible of the increased cost of tobacco and of sending letters, and everyone is retrenching. New decrees have just been published ordering that all funds for the reimbursement of the Farmers General lottery tickets etc. be taken to the Royal Treasury. In fact nothing at all which could destroy credit absolutely has been overlooked, so that today one would be quite unable to find one *écu* to borrow. We will see what the *parlement* does when it reconvenes.

Canada has been taken; Monsieur de Montcalm[66] has been killed, in fact France has become Job's wife.[67] Have you any news from your King of Prussia?[68] I would be very curious to see the letters you receive from him; I promise you to be entirely trustworthy. I am counting on the cantos from *La Pucelle* which you promised me. Take care to amuse me, I beseech you, no one can do it so well as you.

Did you not wish, Monsieur, to buy an estate in Lorraine, and was this estate not Craon? Was Menou's father not your negotiator and is Menou's father not an ass? If you still have such a fantasy, entrust me with the business; I am an intimate friend of Madame la maréchale de Mirepoix and of Monsieur le prince de Beauvau: I would like you to have an establishment in that province. Who knows what would become of it? In fact I would then hope not to die without having the honour of seeing you again, either because you would come to see us, or I would go and find you.

Farewell, Monsieur, it is not for me to write long letters and to pay for the pleasure yours give me with the tedium mine will bring you. The Président sends you a thousand tender compliments. He has great pleasure in reading what you write to me.

VOLTAIRE TO MADAME DU DEFFAND   *3 December {1759}*

I have not sent you, Madame, the old canto from *La Pucelle* which the King of Prussia sent back to me;[69] the only restitution he has ever made in his life. The letters and verses should arrive at a suitable time at least. I am persuaded that you would not receive them well immediately after reading some decree removing half of your property and I always fear that this may be the situation. Neither can I imagine how they dare to present new plays in Paris. Only I can be forgiven for that, surrounded as I am by the Alps and the Jura mountains. It is permissible for me to build a little theatre, to act with my friends and for my friends; but I would not care to brave Paris with its ill-humoured people. I would like the audience to be composed of happier and calmer souls. Besides, you tell me that people of taste hardly ever go to the theatre any more, and I do not know if, like everything else, taste has changed in those that do go. I no longer recognise France, on land, on sea, in verse or in prose.

You ask me what you can read which is interesting. Madame, read the newspapers where everything is as surprising as it is in a novel: there you will find ships laden with Jesuits,[70] and one never ceases to wonder that they have been expelled from only one kingdom; you will find the French beaten in all the four corners of the earth; the marquis of Brandenburg[71] alone facing four great kingdoms armed against him; our ministers collapsing one after another like figures in a magic lantern, our boats, our defeat in Vilaine.[72] A resumé of all that might make a volume that, without being cheerful, would occupy the imagination.

I thought they would make Resnel finance minister because he translated Pope's "whatever is is right"[73] into verse. He must know more than Silhouette who can only translate into prose. Not that this

Monsieur de Silhouette is devoid of wit or even genius, nor that he is not learned; but it appears that he knew nothing about the nation, about finance or about the court, and that he wanted to govern in wartime as could hardly be done in peacetime, that he destroyed the credit which he needed and imagined that with money which he did not have he could supply the state with her needs. His ideas seemed very fine to me but unsuitable in practice. I imagined them to be formed along English principles, but he does everything quite contrary to how it is done in London where he lived for a year with my banker, Benezet. England supports herself on credit and this credit is so big that the government only borrows at a maximum of four per cent. We have not yet learned how to imitate the English in economics, or seamanship, or philosophy or agriculture. It only remains for my dear country to fight over *billets de confession*,[74] for a place in the poor house, and to throw around the china off which we eat, having sold the silver.[75] You spoke to me, Madame, about Lorraine and the estate at Craon. You make me regret it since you claim that you might go one day to Lorraine. I would have willingly settled at Craon, and congratulated myself on having the honour of receiving you there with Madame la maréchale de Mirepoix. But those are beautiful dreams.

It is not the Jesuit, Menou's, fault, that I do not have Craon; I think that the real reason is that Madame le maréchale de Mirepoix was unable to settle the affair. The Jesuit Menou is not as you suspect, a fool. On the contrary. He extorted a million from King Stanislas on the pretext of setting up missions in the villages of Lorraine where they are not wanted; he built himself a palace in Nancy. He made that joke Pope, Benedict XIII,[76] author of three tedious folios, believe that he would translate all three. He showed him two pages, thereby robbing the Benedictines of a good benefit and making a fool of Benedict XIII and of Saint Benedict.

Besides he is a great schemer, a great intriguer, alert, obliging, a dangerous enemy and a great converter. I consider myself cleverer than he because, without being a Jesuit, I have made myself a little retreat of two leagues of my own land.[77] I am obliged to Monsieur le duc de Choiseul, the most generous of men. Free and independent, I would not change places with the General of the Jesuits.

Enjoy, Madame, the sweets of quite a different life. Converse with your friends and nourish your soul. The ploughs which turn the sod, the stock which fertilises the land, the granaries, the wine presses, the fields which border the forests are not worth one moment of your conversation.

When it freezes really hard and when we are no longer able to fight in Canada or in Germany; when two weeks have gone by without a new minister, or a new edict; when conversation no longer turns on public misfortune; when you have nothing to do, give me your orders, Madame, and I will send you the wherewithal to amuse you and something to blame me for.

I would like to be able to bring you these trifles myself and enjoy the consolation of seeing you again, but I like neither Paris nor the life one leads there, nor even the figure I would cut there, nor even the way one behaves there.

I must love retirement and you, Madame. I present my most humble respects.

In the late 1750s, in a climate of general economic and political malaise brought about by the Seven Years War, the attitude of the authorities towards the *Lumières* gradually hardened. Whilst still indirectly taking advantage of the *philosophes'* stand against feudal privileges, the monarchy felt the need to distance itself increasingly from a movement which might from one moment to the next, question the legitimacy of absolute power. "The conflict which set France against both the England of the House of Commons and against the Solomon of the North, gave the court and all the conservatives an excellent opportunity to carry out an important internal operation. The country's enemies were precisely those States with whom the *philosophes* had sympathised in turn for twenty years."[78] But the *philosophes* were not prepared to be intimidated by reactionary, convenient patriotism—Voltaire's article *Patrie* in his *Dictionnaire philosophique* had not yet appeared—and they behaved with dignified detachment. The fact that the most enlightened and liberal thinkers of the time, beginning with Montesquieu and Voltaire, had studied and admired English philosophy, English institutions and English liberty and that they had looked hopefully towards a prince who before ascending the throne of Prussia had written the *Anti-Machiavel,* did not mean that they were traitors to their country.

But the *philosophes* were slow to realise the gravity of the attack which was taking place against them. Diderot and d'Alembert were grappling with the *Encyclopédie*, Holbach and Helvétius were busy composing their own theoretical works, Rousseau was immersed in creative isolation at L'Ermitage in Montmorency, Voltaire was absorbed in the completion of his *Histoire Générale*, all occupied with their own learning and so, during the first years of the war, the coterie was incapable of organising a defence, let alone a counter-attack. The campaign against "philosophy" was truly imposing, united as it did, the usually opposing forces of the court and the *parlement*, the Society of Jesus and the Jansenists, and supported by Freron's influential and widely distributed *Année Littéraire*, the Jesuit's *Journal de Trevoux* and the Jansenist *Nouvelles ecclésiastiques*. At the beginning of 1759 criticism and polemic gave way to tribunals and theory to fact. Between the end of January and the beginning of February, the Paris *parlement* began simultaneous proceedings against eight "impious" books, among them Helvétius's *De l'esprit* and the *Encyclopédie* which was now in its seventh volume. Helvétius's book was condemned and the *Encyclopédie* was subject to a second *arrêt*.

This blow provoked an acute internal crisis within the philosophical movement which was divided over whether to insist on remaining within the law as d'Alembert wanted, or to go underground as Diderot intended. From Switzerland Voltaire took stock of the situation.

"Several men of letters worthy of esteem for their learning and their conduct, joined together to compile an immense dictionary of everything that might enlighten the human mind; it was a great commercial affair for French booksellers: the chancellor and the ministers encouraged such a fine enterprise. Seven volumes had already appeared; they had been translated into Italian, English, German and Dutch and this treasury made available to all nations by the French could have been regarded as the one thing which brought us most honour since the excellent articles in the *Dictionnaire encyclopédique* greatly outnumbered the bad ones which were, nevertheless, quite numerous.

"But then Omer Joly de Fleury on 23rd February 1759 accuses these poor people of being atheists, deists, corruptors of youth, rebels against the king etc. Omer, to prove his accusations, quotes Saint Paul, Théophile's trial and Abraham Chaumeix. All he had failed to do was to read the book against which he was speaking, or if he had read it, he was a strange imbecile. He asked the court to pass judgement against the article on the 'Soul' which, according to him, was pure materialism. You will note that this article, one of the worst in the book, is the work of a poor doctor at the Sorbonne who takes abundant pains, turning himself inside out, to inveigh against materialism. Omer Joly de Fleury's whole speech was a tissue of similar blunders. So he submitted to the court a book which he had not read, or which he had not understood, and at Omer's request the whole *parlement* condemned a work, not only without examining it, but without having read a single page of it . . .

"One might believe this event to have taken place in Garasse's day when decrees were pronounced against emetics, whereas it happened during the only enlightened century France has known, so it is true that one fool is enough to dishonour a nation. It can easily be admitted that under such circumstances, Paris should not be the home of a philosopher, and that Aristotle was very wise to retire to Calcis while fanaticism ruled Athens. Besides the position of a man of letters in Paris is only just above that of a juggler. The position of Ordinary Gentleman to His Majesty which the king reserved for me is not much. Men are very foolish and I think it better to build a fine château as I have done, to perform theatricals and to feast there, than to remain in Paris like Helvétius, subject to those who hold court in the *parlement* and in the menagerie of the Sorbonne. Since I could certainly not make men more reasonable, nor the *parlement* less pedantic, nor theologians less ridiculous, I will continue to be happy far away from them."[79]

Distance was not enough to protect Voltaire, had he ever wanted such protection, from the Parisian polemic. When, the following year, the *Académie* became the centre of the offensive against the *philosophes*, the attack was turned directly on the patriarch. On 10 March 1760 the new academician, J.-G. Lefranc de Pompignan, made his inaugural speech, but instead of an exercise in humanist rhetoric, he made a violent attack on Voltaire, enemy of religion, corruptor of morals, who was responsible for "that infinite series of scandalous libels, insolent verses and frivolous, licentious writing."[80] It was an extremely serious matter. Not only had the censureship commission which consisted of academicians "allowed an inaugural speech to be a satire,"[81] and not only did the academician, Dupré de Saint-Maur reply, comparing Pompignan and his brother, the Bishop of Puy, to Moses and Aaron, but it was obvious that the speech was meant to be heard by a much wider audience than the *Académie*: to wit, the court where the author and his brother enjoyed the royal favour and held official positions. It was, in fact, a plot to weaken and discredit the *philosophes* within the *Académie* and, despite the presence of the faithful Duclos, it was not entirely without success.

Voltaire's answer was not long in coming. On 14 April[82] a pamphlet arrived from Geneva, the first edition of which was entitled, *Les Quand, notes utiles sur un discours prononcé devant l'Académie française, le 10 Mai 1760, par M. de Voltaire,* in which Pompignan was accused of being an informer who wished to prove that "the philosophy of today undermines the foundations of the throne and the Church," and "dare[d] suggest that hatred of authority is the chief characteristic of our literary work ... nothing is more criminal than to wish to give princes and ministers unjust ideas about loyal subjects whose learning is an honour to the nation."[83] The crushing pamphlet seemed to silence Pompignan, but the war against the *Lumières* could by now no longer be stemmed,[84] and on 2 May in the same year, a new comedy by Palissot, *Les Philosophes* was put on at the *Théâtre Français* with a play by Voltaire. As d'Alembert wrote to Voltaire, "They say ... that it is not badly written, especially in the first act, but that it is disconnected and lacking imagination. Neither of us is attacked *personally,* the only ones to be badly treated are Helvétius, Diderot, Rousseau, Duclos, Madame Geoffrin and Mademoiselle Clairon who has decried the infamy ... The aim of the play is to present the *philosophes,* not as ridiculous, but as scoundrels without principles or morals; and it is Monsieur Palissot, his own wife's pimp and a bankrupt who teaches this lesson."[85]

This time, probably because the attack was less direct, Voltaire underplayed the provocation: "The play which is being performed in Paris is a despicable nonsense which will soon be forgotten."[86] But contrary to his expectations, Palissot's play was a great success with the public and the *philosophes'* demands to forbid such an openly defamatory work were ignored. The play was protected from on high, it had found a champion in the maréchale de Luxembourg's young and beautiful daughter, Madame de Robecq, who, approaching the terrible death described by Besenval,[87] was trying to gain favour in heaven by organising a crusade against the enemies of faith. Among her sins needing forgiveness was that of having been the duc de Choiseul's mistress. As a minister he was usually tolerant of the *philosophes,* but on this occasion, by no accident, he turned a deaf ear to their protests. It was a very bad time for supporters of the *Lumières* and Lefranc de Pompignan took the opportunity to present the King who had been quite favourable to his speech in the *Académie*, with a *Memoire justificatif*. Printed on 24 May, the memoir's explicit purpose was the expulsion from the *Académie* of Voltaire and subsequently of the remaining *philosophes*.

The first to strike back was Morellet with the *Vision*,[88] a highly successful satirical pamphlet attacking Palissot and his supporters and Pompignan. Allusions to Madame de Robecq who was dying enraged the right-minded. The *Vision* appeared anonymously but, nevertheless, Morellet was sent to the Bastille. Meanwhile Voltaire was replying to d'Alembert's letters urging action, "One must laugh, and laugh frequently at little persecutors and their little emissaries."[89] All the same he withdrew his play from the *Théâtre Français*. "I did not want the actors to perform anything of mine immediately after having dishonoured the nation."[90] That was what was expected of him and d'Alembert rejoiced, "My dear and illustrious philosopher, I have just received your letter of 26 May, and I hasten to thank you in the name of philosophy for the decision you have just made. All men of letters regard you as their worthy leader which you well prove yourself to be on this occasion."[91] The designation was highly symbolic; d'Alembert sensed that Voltaire was radically changing his attitude, and preparing wholeheartedly to adopt his new role. "It has already been shown how in the delicate twist of the struggle between the *philosophes* and their enemies, Voltaire finally took up an avant-garde position, becoming the leader of his fellows, and attempting to disregard opportunistic or personal considerations. He noticed with remarkable decisiveness that confronted as they were by an orchestrated campaign of enemies, encouraged in high places, all supporters of the *Lumières* needed to pledge themselves to an active solidarity. Equally remarkable was the firmness with which, in corresponding with Palissot, who wanted to justify himself and dissociate himself from the ridiculed *philosophes,* he reaffirmed his loyalty to the ideas of the "sect" and the need for uncompromising joint action to defend these ideas against every form of obscurantism: piety, patriotism or offended good taste. But what counted most was the link which the "solitary Swiss" constantly revealed between apparently unimportant literary happenings—Pompignan's speech or Palissot's play—and the general march of events, that is the worsening war and the increasingly reactionary offensive."[92]

The most immediate aim to which Voltaire dedicated the whole of

June in that turbulent year of 1760, was the annihilation of Pompignan. Three extraordinary satires, *Le Pauvre diable*,[93] *Le Russe à Paris*[94] and *La Vanité*,[95] cruelly mocked the imprudent enemy and acted as a threatening lesson to possible future polemicists. "Lefranc did not recover. His faithful, like the marquis de Mirabeau, could only offer their condolences. And society (including Versailles) only remembered one Pompignan—Voltaire's."[96]

From her *tonneau* in Saint-Joseph, Madame du Deffand followed the crossfire of these polemics with a mixture of curiosity and annoyance. Any news, any event provided a diversion, an idle subject of conversation for anyone faced as she was with an endless number of empty hours to fill. The war being waged against the *philosophes* was much more than a simple curiosity or a series of skirmishes between men of letters, but Madame du Deffand seemed determined to attach to it an anecdotal value only. Polemic was alien to her, she was not uninterested in it although her reaction to it was negative. She did not see herself in either of the two camps. She was on officially cordial terms with d'Alembert, but her relationship had already been compromised and her reservations concerning the *philosophes* were clear; the vulgarity and stupidity of the opposition prevented her from taking a stand. Conducted as it was, the polemic could only advantage the encyclopaedists, so it must be discredited, its importance minimised and its value negated.

The *marquise* hoped to persuade Voltaire to follow her example. His abstention from the discussion would alone imply a partial failure for the *philosophes*. Madame du Deffand's objective, which she intended to pursue by means of indirect persuasion, was a far from easy one. Adulation was her primary weapon, and it was Voltaire's actual greatness which naturally isolated him and prevented equality and therefore solidarity with the other philosophers. Throughout their correspondence, she reminded Voltaire constantly of the responsibility of his own glory, and of the obligation not to diminish himself. So insinuation was mixed with praise: association with the *philosophes* was frankly undermining and should be denied. Praise was laughingly turned to threat: "I will no longer rebel, as I have done until this moment, against all our sophistical philosophers who claim to make common cause with you. These poor people are dead before their time, whilst you on the contrary live, and you will live for ever after your death."[97]

To counterbalance the dogged polemics Madame du Deffand launched a far more important and difficult crusade in defence of taste. It was a campaign for the survival of the most distinctive elements of French culture, and only Voltaire in the dual role of an upholder of tradition and as master of the literary scene—both classical and contemporary—had the authority needed to lead it. The campaign would mean a change of alliances and would naturally bring Madame du Deffand in line with Voltaire: the *philosophes* would be condemned in the only field where, in her opinion, they seemed truly vulnerable. This theme runs through the entire correspondence, and Madame du Deffand besieges Voltaire, begging him to take a stand, and provokes him repeatedly and more or less directly, with anything from despairing declarations about the decadence of the times, to praise for his work and explicit requests to intervene.

But Madame du Deffand could not always claim to be ignorant of Voltaire's polemics and she dealt with them with elegant ambiguity. She had already written to him in February of that year, "I will tell you that I am quite convinced that *la Mort et l'Apparition du père Berthier*[98] is not by Monsieur Grimm nor by another on whom it has been blamed."[99] The Pompignan affair and the resulting unavoidable polemic drove the *marquise* to adopt her usual minimising tactics. She did not intend to read Pompignan's speech because it was certainly boring which was always the worst accusation. Pompignan was so mediocre that he could not be interesting in any way, he was no more than a creation of Voltaire's satiric genius. More is demanded of a friend in war than a simple denial of the danger of the enemy. Voltaire knew Madame du Deffand would probably not have noticed her lack of interest in the polemics—the political significance of which certainly escaped her—if her evasiveness over the *philosophes* scandal, which broke out in May, had not been swiftly succeeded by d'Alembert's denunciation of her.

Voltaire behaved like a true friend over the matter. He could not have been indifferent to the accusations, but he appeared to ignore them and warmly defended Madame du Deffand against d'Alembert's vehemence. He only allowed his doubts to surface with his trusted friend, d'Argental, a brother of the *marquise*'s close friend, Pont-de-Veyle: "Is it true that Madame du Deffand is siding against philosophy and unworthily abandoning me?"[100] To be sure, during the two most heated months of the polemic, the *marquise* was dissatisfied with the letters she received from Ferney and so interrupted the correspondence. When it began again in

July at Voltaire's instigation, the worst was over and the two friends could face an explanation.

In the preceding months' letters, as if to make up for her reticence, the *marquise* seems to want continually to confirm the length and solidarity of her friendship with Voltaire, and to underline their great affinity of interests and feeling. She needs Voltaire's letters. Only they can wake her from her "lethargy"; but hers too have a particular function and are intended to remind him of the increasing lack of intelligence, imagination and taste in France. Their correspondence is supposed to bear witness to this crisis and to challenge it with a king of Pascalian *pari*. So the *marquise* continually asks Voltaire to return to literature and criticism.

Voltaire meets evasion with evasion. He has other far more pressing concerns, he mistrusts the *marquise* and is not prepared to expose himself to her in any way in arguments which might be equivocal. He merely joked, dispensed a few of his exquisite gems or displayed a gallantry as of times past.

Confronted with this stalemate, Madame du Deffand suddenly changed her style. Her letter of 16 April was as sudden as a *coup de théâtre,* full of compliment, surprise and paradox, Voltaire's gallantry is countered with vehement, cheerful irony. Voltaire was obliged to adapt himself to the rules of her game, without, however, granting one of the concessions expected of him. He replies to the *marquise*'s theatrical homage with equally theatrical emotion: his correspondent's approval has strengthened his will to live. The ironic tone remains general. There is not a word to clarify his part in the current polemics, there is no allusion to the *philosophes,* no admission or denial of authorship concerning the pamphlets in circulation. Wounded, irritated and beaten at her own game of "*bon ton,*" Madame du Deffand interrupted the correspondence.

MADAME DU DEFFAND TO VOLTAIRE   *Paris, 16 April 1760*

Do you not know, Monsieur, why I have the honour of writing to you today? It is to tell you that I am transported by the joy of knowing you to be alive. Never has anyone been so grieved as I was last Saturday on opening a letter which informed me that you had suddenly died; I gave a cry and had a seizure both of which are certain proof of all that I feel for you. I was at that moment as touched and as wounded as one can be by the loss of the most intimate friend with whom one spends one's life. A thousand other feelings followed this one; it seemed to me that everything was lost for our nation; it seemed that all would return to chaos and I was edified to see that this news had the same effect on everybody. I do not know if you have any enemies, people who envy you etc; but I do know that at the news of your death there were only admirers; everyone spoke at that moment according to his conscience.

But do you know what would have happened to you if you had been dead? You would have been succeeded by the Bishop of Limoges.[101] He would have been very embarrassed to make you a saint. Do you know what will happen to you if you do not write to me? I will suppose you to be dead and I will have masses said for the repose of your soul in all the Jesuit houses; I will have you praised, celebrated and canonised by all the Pompignans; I will attribute to you all the scribblings which circulate around the houses under your name and I will no longer rebel as I have done until this moment against all our sophistical philosophers who claim to make common cause with you. Those poor people are dead before their time whilst you, on the contrary, live and you will live for ever after your death.

You are the most ungrateful and the most unworthy of men if you do not reply to the friendship I have for you, and if you do not make it an obligation and a pleasure to have charge of my amusement.

Tancrède[102] *Zulime,*[103] the life of the Tsar,[104] your collected ideas,[105] am I to see nothing of all that?

VOLTAIRE TO MADAME DU DEFFAND   *25 April* {*1760*}

I am so touched by your letter, Madame, that I have the insolence to send you two small manuscripts which are quite unworthy of you. I so count on your goodness. Read the verse in one of those moments of leisure when you would be amused by a story by Boccaccio or La Fontaine, read the prose when you are a little cross with the miserable prejudice which rules this world, and with the fanatics; and then throw the bundle on the fire. I found these trifles to hand. They were written a long time ago and are no more worthy for that.

I have never been less dead than I am at present. I do not have a free moment. The oxen, the cows, the sheep, the fields, the buildings and the gardens occupy me in the morning. All the afternoon is given to studying and at supper time the plays which are performed in my small theatre are rehearsed. This existence makes one wish to live, but I have a greater desire than ever for life since you deigned so kindly to take an interest in me. You are right, since at bottom I am a good man. My parish priests, my tenants and my neighbours are very pleased with me, and there is no one, even the farmers general, who I cannot persuade to see reason when I have a quarrel with them about frontier rights. I know that the Queen always says that I am ungodly; the Queen is wrong. The King of Prussia is even more mistaken in saying in his *Epître au Maréchal de Keith:*

Allez, laches chrétiens etc., etc., etc.

One should insult no one, but the greatest wrong lies with those who have discovered the secret of how to ruin France in two years by a war of alliance. This morning I received a *lettre de change*[106] from a German banker on behalf of Monsieur de Montmartel. These bills of exchange are numbered, and you will note that my number is the thousandth and fortieth since the month of January. It is a fine thing for the French thus to enrich the Germans. I am sometimes visited by Englishmen or Russians, they all agree in mocking us. You do not know, Madame, what it is to be French in a foreign land. One carries the burden of one's nation and continually hears it abused.

It is disagreeable, and one is like a man who would like to tell his wife she is a whore but who would not like to hear it said by others. Try, Madame, to be rewarded for your merits and to take pity on all the misery which you see about you. Accustom yourself to the dearth of every kind of talent, to intelligence grown ordinary, and to genius grown rare, to an inundation of books about war—then to be beaten—and about finances—then to have not a penny—about the population then to have no recruits and no husbandmen, and above all about the arts—then to succeed in none. Your fine imagination, Madame, and the good company you have at home will console you for all that. All the rest is vanity of vanities as the other one said.[107]. Receive my tender respects.

After a month without news from Saint-Joseph, Voltaire took the opportunity in replying to Hénault, to clarify his position with regard to the current polemic and to soothe his old friend's irritation.

VOLTAIRE TO THE PRÉSIDENT HÉNAULT   *Délices, by Geneva, 20 June 1760*

Illustrious and venerable brother, your letters can help to make me quick witted; but despite Tronchin the flesh is weak. Allow me to dictate. I will say, I will dictate, I will always print that you are the most amiable man of the century; but there would have to be a great many people like you for all the folly of our times to be forgotten. A Homer is needed to celebrate the battle between the rats and the frogs.[108] Is it possible that we are reduced to spreading satire against men of letters in the very sanctuary of letters! To putting on plays where the most honest men in the world are shown teaching how to pick pockets! We must raise our hands to heaven that it please God to give back our money, our ships and our silver,[109] but we must shrug our shoulders about the rest; I make a point of mocking everything, laughing at everything; this regime is excellent for the health and I hope that it will cure me. I imagine that Madame du Deffand uses my recipe. You do not mention her in the letter with which you honoured me. I see clearly that for all her reasoning she is still a woman; she was coquettish with me, she provoked me, she turned my head and when she was quite sure that she had inspired me with a serious passion, she left me there . . .

Voltaire's was an irresistible voice which Madame du Deffand recognised loyally. The letter to the Président presented an opportunity for a long delayed explanation and rang with implicit reproach. The *marquise* had no intention of entering into the merits of a polemic which was devoid of interest to her. Only one thing mattered to her, that Voltaire should not involve himself in an affair which was to all intents and purposes insignificant, nor with the factions of the mediocre.

MADAME DU DEFFAND TO VOLTAIRE   *Saturday, 5 July 1760*

The Président who is staying at *Les Ormes* with Monsieur d'Argenson[110] writes that he has just received a charming letter from you in which you speak of me and in which you complain that I no longer write to you. I am very glad that you noticed it, that was my intention. I was being sullen with you, but this little provocation has made me change my mind. I prefer to tell you all the grievances I have against you. You never reply to what I write nor answer the questions I put to you; you appear mistrustful or disdainful. Here we are inundated with little pamphlets, all of which are attributed to you on the pretext that in fact some of them must be by you. If you treated me as you should, that is like a real friend, ought I not to receive from you what you are certainly sending to others? I decided to deny that any of these words were yours; not that I did not think I recognised you in some of them, but I disapprove so strongly of your being in favour of anything in the war between the rats and the frogs (as you call it so cleverly), not that I cannot consent to flatter the vanity of one or other side, or of both in believing you to be the friend of the one and the other's enemy. I would, however, have been very glad had you sent me *le Pauvre Diable*; I am unable to acquire it. Now Madame de Robecq is dead, but she delayed too long; six months earlier we would have been spared an immense amount of bad writing; but I would have been vexed had we not had *la Vision*. Besides, Monsieur, be assured that there is nothing more tedious nor more irksome than all these writings and all these writers; cynics and pedants, such are the fine minds of today. Your name should never be found among their quarrels. I also find that you have honoured Monsieur de Pompignan far too much. If you were to return here, Monsieur, I would be most surprised if you were to find any one of those people amiable or worthy of your protection. I admit there are some honest people, and even some with taste and intelligence, but none with any worldly sense, any manners, any gaiety or any charm.

I despair at not having been able to foretell the misfortunes that have befallen me and at not having understood the circumstances of old age with only a modest fortune. I would have left Paris, I would have settled in the provinces; there I would have enjoyed greater comfort and I would not have noticed any great differences between society and company.

I no longer know what to read. You could send me plenty of things but you find me unworthy. I will judge from your answer whether you really wish to keep up our correspondence; it must be based on friendship and trust. Without that it is not worth it. I will love you and always admire you; but I will forbid myself to tell you so.

Allow me to end with some advice. Read the fable of the rat, the frog and the eagle.[111]

Now that they had entered into discussion, Voltaire pointed out that polemic was less futile and casual than it might seem, and lightly accused her of having been silent for two months. The tone is that of an old friend who has been slightly offended but whose usual affection remains unaltered. A passing reference is made to the *marquise*'s lesson in aristocratic superiority. By reading Fréron, Madame du Deffand shows that she tolerates vulgarity and in some way participates in "the war of the rats and the frogs." So a careful clarification of both their positions begins. It was to continue from letter to letter throughout the summer.

VOLTAIRE TO MADAME DU DEFFAND   *14 July {1760}*

If you had wanted, Madame, to have *le Pauvre Diable, le Russe à Paris* and other stuff, you should have given me your orders; you could at least have acknowledged my packets. You did not reply to me and you pity yourself. I wrote to your friend to the effect that you are quite like those of your sex who provoke and who then abandon those they have seduced.

You must be put in the picture a little about the war of the rats and the frogs; it is more violent than you think. Lefranc de Pompignan wanted to succeed Monsieur le Président Hénault in his position as the Queen's *surintendent* and to become under-preceptor or preceptor to the Children of France, or to place his brother, the Bishop, in that position. In order to make themselves more worthy of favours at court, this Moses and this Aaron[112] made this fine speech in the *Académie* which resulted in the whole of Paris hissing them. Their plan was to arm the government against all those whom they accused of being philosophers, to have me excluded from the *Académie* and then have the Bishop of Le Puy[113] elected in my place and so to purify the profaned sanctuary. I only laughed about it because, thank God, I laugh about everything. I spoke but one word and that word hatched out twenty pamphlets, some of which are good and some of which are bad.

During that time the scandal of *Les Philosophes* broke out. Madame de Robecq had the misfortune to protect the play and to have it performed. This unfortunate step poisoned her last days. I was told that you had united with her; this news wounded me deeply. If you are guilty, admit it and I will give you absolution.

If you wish to be amused read *le Pauvre Diable,* and *le Russe à Paris.* I think you will prefer *le Russe* because it has a nobler tone.

You read Fréron's[114] filthy stuff which is proof that you like reading; but it also proves that you do not hate the battle of the rats and the frogs.

You say that most men of letters are not agreeable and you are right. One must be a man of the world before being a man of letters. That is the Président Hénault's virtue. No one would guess that he has worked like a Benedictine.

You ask me what you should do to amuse yourself. You must come to my house, Madame, where we perform new plays, laugh at the follies of Paris, and Tronchin cures people when they have eaten too much. But you would beware of coming to the shores of my lake: you are not yet enough of a philosopher, detached enough or disabused enough. However, you have great courage since you suffer your condition; but I fear that you do not have the courage to suffer people or things which weary you.

I pity you, I love you, I respect you and I laugh at the universe to which Pompignan speaks.[115]

Madame du Deffand's first reply was cheerful, joking and designed to make friends with Voltaire and to minimise any eventual disappointment. She denied taking sides with the likes of Fréron and Palissot, and, as a master of hyperbole, resorted to that for her defence: how could she be accused of not having publicly supported the *philosophes?* Did she perhaps enjoy the authority to allow her such a position? "Friendship alone can lead to involvement in such quarrels. I admit that a few years ago friendship might have led me to great acts of imprudence." It is hard to believe that Madame du Deffand had forgotten how, at the time of d'Alembert's candidacy eight years earlier, the *Académie* had been at the centre of a passionate battle for her too.

After such a detailed diplomatic explanation, in her next letter (5 September), the *marquise* could not resist distancing herself again by judging the protagonists of the affair: "I cannot venerate certain things which you so approve." Finally (12 September), Voltaire was obliged to tell her the truth of which she pretended to be ignorant and which she did not wish to hear: "I belong to a party and to a persecuted party." This time she did not hesitate, her disapproval was explicit and absolute, but, as if to lessen her disappointment and Voltaire's very declaration, she added: "If that amuses you, you are right, let us say no more about it." At least the last word on this disagreeable affair was frivolous.

But a delicate problem concerning their shared friend who was at the root of the accusation, remained unresolved. Only when he had explained himself directly to the *marquise*[116] and heard from d'Alembert of his reconciliation with her, did Voltaire introduce the subject indirectly and slip in a conciliatory remark about the *philosophe* (27 October). Madame du Deffand then felt it necessary to go over the whole affair again (1 November). With great dignity she once again reaffirmed her position with regard to the *philosophes* as a coterie. She confined herself finally to establishing their lack of talent and taste. She was perfectly aware of the tell-tale part played by d'Alembert—fortunately she was ignorant of the language he used—but because of his blind gregariousness and because she appreciated his finer qualities which were precisely those that his companions lacked, she forgave him.

MADAME DU DEFFAND TO VOLTAIRE   *Paris, 23 July 1760*

I could tell you that (vanity apart) I am not perfectly pleased with you. Wherefore have you not sent me *La Vanité?* I found it charming. I do not doubt that it is by you, and Pompignan is drawn even better there than in the other two pieces. That poor man owes all his fame to you. Without you one would only have yawned when speaking about him or reading his work; he has deserved the treatment he gets. It is enough to call him a coxcomb, but hypocrite and wicked is going too far. There he is crushed under the mountains of ridicule which you pile upon him. Neither his birth nor his piety will make him attempt to scale the heights of heaven or of the court. God bless him. He is a fool and a cold character.

I do not know which I prefer, your *Russe* and your *Pauvre Diable*: the latter is more comical, the first is nobler. I am very pleased with both of them.

Let us turn to your trial of me. I was angry with you, and instead of thanking you, I would only have blamed you, because I learned that you were sending all sorts of novelties to all sorts of people: so my friendship was wounded; I found you guilty of the sin of Ananias and Sapphira.[117] You were lying to the Holy Ghost and as I could not punish you with immediate death, I resolved to write to you no longer. That cost me a great deal, and you can be the judge of that since at the first provocation I have come running back to you.

I love you very much, Monsieur, because in truth no one pleases me as much as you do, and I am quite sure that you please no one so much as you please me.

So, you have been told a great deal of ill of me? In your mind, then, I am an admirer of Fréron, Palissot and their kind, and I am the declared enemy of the encyclopaedists? I deserve neither such excessive honour, nor such indignity. You ask for my confession and promise your absolution. Know then that I was never allied with Madame de Robecq, that I hardly knew her and that I never wished to know her better. I greatly condemned her vengeance and her choice of avengers. I was well pleased by her comedy's lack of success and its author's lack of skill; he did not know how to ridicule the people he wished to describe; he failed in his aim. By attacking their honour and probity, he did not even graze their skin. I attended a performance of this play, I read it once; I said quite naturally that it did not please me, and that I would have far greater disdain for and indignation against such a work than I would have for the *philosophes*. If that does not seem enough and if I should have raised an outcry against their enemies, I admit that I did not do that but that I felt myself to be ridiculous raising my voice for or against either side; friendship alone can lead to involvement in such quarrels. I admit that a few years ago friendship might have led me to great acts of imprudence; but as for today, I would watch the war between the gods and the giants with indifference, all the more so that between the rats and the frogs; I read what is written for and against it. Some of Fréron's articles have quite amused me; the "Encyclopédie"[118] for example which is, I think, in its fifteenth edition, seemed quite amusing to me. I prefer his style to the abbé Desfontaines's. This is the confession of all my crimes, I await your *ego te absolvo*. I will end this long letter by telling you that I am quite sure that if I were with you, I would always agree with you, but not merely because of the submission and deference due to your intelligence and enlightenment.

Oh, my God, Monsieur, how glad I would be to spend my life at Les Délices! If it is philosophy which breeds disgust, then I am a great philosopher. Nothing keeps me here and I have no better reason for staying than a nanny-goat where she is tethered, she must browse. But if I were not blind, I would certainly go to your house. Nothing in the world can give me so much pleasure as to be with you. I would have a great need of Monsieur Tronchin if I valued life more; but it would be folly in me to seek to prolong it. Oh, my God, what for? To experience new misfortunes? It is enough for me to make the present bearable. I live with a few agreeable people who have humanity and compassion; the result passes for friendship; I am satisfied with that; and I avoid sadness as much as I can; I give way to whatever dissipation which offers itself; finally, when all is considered, I am a great deal less unhappy than I ought to be. You would not be displeased with me, if I explained my way of thinking to you, and it would give me great pleasure. But will we never find ourselves together, Monsieur? This eternal absence and with the loss of my friend[119] are two irreparable misfortunes for which I will never console myself. Write to me often, and send me everything you do. What is "Pot's sister" about which everyone speaks and which no one has seen?[120]

VOLTAIRE TO MADAME DU DEFFAND   *6 August 1760*

If the war with the English drives us to despair, Madame, that of the rats and the frogs is very amusing; I like to see the coxcombs ridiculed and the wicked confounded: it is quite amusing to send rockets from the foothills of the Alps to Paris, to land on the heads of fools. It is true that the most ridiculous and the most shocking have not been attacked specifically, but patience, everyone will have a turn; some good soul will avenge the universe,[121] and the Président Lefranc de Pompignan is not the only one who deserves to be kicked by the universe. I have been told that the illustrious Palissot has had my letters printed, but I strongly suspect him of having adulterated the purity of the text; he is as apt to tamper with his quotations as is Maître Joly de Fleury.

It is good that Paris thrives on this nonsense since it has nothing besides to live off. Alcibiades cut the tail off his dog to distract the Athenians' attention from his foolery at war; without Palissot, Pompignan and Fréron, the talk would all be of warnings. I will admit to you that I do not like that at the moment, and I find the wish to prevent the government from defending itself against the English who are ruining themselves thrashing us is very unreasonable, very cowardly and very absurd. The country has often been more unhappy than it is now, but it has rarely been so dull. Try, Madame, to laugh like I do at such mediocrity in every field. It is true that in your condition one hardly laughs, but you bear this condition and have grown accustomed to it, for you it is a new kind of existence. Through it your soul may have become more contemplative and stronger and your ideas more brilliant. You no doubt have an excellent reader beside you which is a perpetual consolation. You must be surrounded by resources. Here in Geneva, less than a quarter of a league from where I live, there is a woman[122] of two hundred who has three deaf-mute children; they converse with their mother from morning to night, sometimes in writing, sometimes by moving their fingers, they play all games very well, they know everything that happens in the town and mock their neighbours as well as the greatest prattlers do. They understand everything that is said by watching the lips. In a word they are excellent company. Is Monsieur le Président Hénault still so deaf? At least he is deaf to my wishes, but I forgive him for forgetting everyone since he is with Monsieur d'Argenson.

By the way, Madame, do you digest well? I have noticed after considerable reflection on the best of all possible worlds, and on the small number of chosen, that one is only really unhappy when one cannot digest. If you can digest, you are saved in this world, you will live long and pleasantly, provided above all that neither prince Ferdinand's[123] cannon balls nor the English fleet[124] destroys the hand which pays your income.

I have no scraps to send you, and neither do I any longer have an address for countersigned letters, such is the zeal for reform; besides I am more occupied with the Tsar Peter, sailor, carpenter, legislator, called the Great. Having renounced Paris, I have fled to the borders of China, my soul has travelled further than La Condamine's body.[125] They say that this deaf man would like to be a member of the *Académie Française* apparently so as not to be able to hear us. Happy are they who hear you, Madame. I feel the loss of such good fortune acutely. I love you despite your taste for Fréron's pamphlets. They say that *L'Ecossaise*[126] will cause the leaves to fall in the autumn.[127]

A thousand tender and sincere respects.

MADAME DU DEFFAND TO VOLTAIRE   *Paris, 5 September 1760*

I was angry with you; your last letter displeased me; in it you announced that you would send me nothing more; you reproached me for liking Fréron; you treated me as the friend or ally of the Pompignans and the Palissots; I was very indignant as anyone would be with much less reason; but let us make friends; come and let me embrace you.

Yesterday I attended the first performance of *Tancrède*.[128] I wept hot tears at it; a few weeks earlier I had been to *L'Ecossaise* which pleased me greatly. You have swept the theatre clean of all the grotesque authors who have been degrading and defiling it for two or three years. I am mad about you and were you to have a thousand more faults than I, I would always admire you and would admire only you, I decare frankly; I cannot revere some things which you so approve, I am like Mardochée:

> *Je n'ai devant Aman pu fléchir les genoux,*
> *Ni lui rendre un honneur que l'on ne doit qu'à vous.*[129]

By Aman I understand numerous authors whom you honour with your protection and whom I find very tiresome and very proud. Mademoiselle Clairon plays wonderfully well. There is one, *"Eh bien, mon père"*[130] which racks one from the sole of the feet to the top of the head.

Préville is delightful in the part of Freeport;[131] in fact you made me laugh and cry which had not happened to me for a long time and which I no longer hoped for. I thank you a thousand, thousand times. Yesterday I supped with Marmontel, I spoke about you to him endlessly and ceaselessly; he says that you are wonderfully well and that you have not changed at all. The same cannot be said for me, but if I were with you I would have patience. Are you so cruel as to send me nothing? I am not convinced by your reasons, they are only excuses.

VOLTAIRE TO MADAME DU DEFFAND   *Aux Délices, 12 September 1760*

You are a big, amiable child, Madame, how did you not sense that I think like you? But consider that I am on one side, and it is a persecuted side which, persecuted as it is, has finally managed to gain the greatest possible advantage over its enemies by making them ridiculous and odious.

So you understand what one owes to people on one's own side; M. le duc d'Orléans used to say that it was necessary to have the faith of Bohemians.

I do not know if you have seen a letter from me to King Stanislas of Poland.[132] It is going the rounds. It is to thank him for a book which he wrote with dear Brother Menou, entitled *l'Incrédulité combattue par le simple . . . bon sens.*

If you do not have it, I will send it to you and besides, Madame, I will look for anything that might amuse you, for one must always come back to amusement. Without that existence would be a burden. That is why cards occupy the leisure of so-called good society from one end of Europe to the other. One cannot remain serious with oneself. If nature had not made us a little frivolous we would be very unhappy; it is because we are frivolous that most people do not hang themselves.

In a while I will send you a copy of *l'Histoire de toutes les Russies.* There is a preface to make you die of laughter which will console you for the tedium of the book. Farewell, Madame; I am ill, keep well, be as cheerful as your condition allows and do not be gruff with your old friend who is tied to you tenderly and for ever.

MADAME DU DEFFAND TO VOLTAIRE   *Paris, 20 September 1760*

No, no, Monsieur, I am not a big child; I am a little old woman with all the attributes of age except for ill humour. I blame Monsieur Voltaire when he associates himself with, or rather makes himself the leader of a party which has nothing in common with him except one thing; for where ethics and taste are concerned, there is no resemblance or conformity: but if it pleases you, then you are right and let us say no more about it.

Tell me, I beg you, why you never answer what I write? I talk about your tragedy, your comedy and you do not deign to say a word about them. I have reason to believe that my letters tire you; if so I would be vexed because yours give me great pleasure. I await your history of the Tsar with impatience; I have a great need of reading matter to amuse me; I read for six or seven hours by day or by night and I have exhausted everything. I was greatly pleased by the history of the Stuarts;[133] it is a little tiring but there are some sublime passages.

If you had any friendship for me as you would flatter me you do, you could send me a great many things, I am sure, but you treat me rather like a silly gossip.

A messenger arrived yesterday bringing news of the small advantage Monsieur de Stainville[134] has gained over the hereditary prince; as though he had removed a pawn.[135]

Your letter to the King of Poland has been printed; I do not think this was on the instructions of Brother Menou. Farewell, Monsieur, I love you a great deal and I believe that you love me only a little.

The Président wants me to tell you that he infinitely disapproves of your publishing the first volume of your history of the Tsar before the second; I think in fact that he is right, but if the second would make us await the first too long, do not follow his advice, I yearn to come alive.

VOLTAIRE TO MADAME DU DEFFAND   *Aux Délices, 27 {October 1760}*

This is not a letter, Madame, it is only to ask you if you have received two volumes of the tedious *Histoire de Russie,* one for you and the other for Monsieur le Président Hénault. Monsieur Bourret or Monsieur Le Normand should have had the parcel delivered to you. I am equally ignorant of whether Monsieur d'Alembert received his. Would you be so kind, Madame, as to enquire if it has reached him? He sometimes pays you court and I congratulate you both; you will certainly find no one with more wit, more imagination or greater knowledge than he.

I told you, Madame, that I would not write to you, but I want to write to you. I have, however, a good deal of business to attend to; a labourer who is building a church and a theatre, who creates plays and produces actors, and who visits his fields is not an idle man. Never mind, I must tell you that I have just shouted, "Long live the King" on hearing that the French have killed four thousand English at bayonet point.[136] That is inhuman, but it was highly necessary.

I do not know if the King of Prussia will be vain enough to pay Monsieur d'Alembert's pension regularly; the Russians should pay it out of the eight million they have just taken from Berlin.[137] Thank

God not a week has gone by without great adventures since I left the poet of Sans-Soucie,[138] I fear that I brought him bad luck. I wish he would end his life as wisely and as peacefully as I do; but he will do nothing of the sort.

I have no news of Brother Menou, nor of Brother Malagrida,[139] nor Brother Berthier, nor Omer or Fleury, nor Fréron. I will have the honour of sending you a few saucy pieces as soon as I am able.

Always take life patiently, Madame, and if there are a few good moments, enjoy them cheerfully. I complain to everybody about Mademoiselle Clairon,[140] who has a fantasy that we should put a scaffold hung with black on the stage for her because she is suspected of infidelity to her fiancé. Such abominable imagination is only good for the English theatre. If the scaffold were for Fréron, perhaps; but for Clairon, I cannot tolerate it.

What fine idea is it to want to change the French scene to the Place de Grève?[141] I know that most of our tragedies are no more than insipid conversation pieces and that until now we have lacked action and theatrical devices, but what a device for a polished nation, a gallows and the hangman's lackeys!

I address my complaints to you, Madame, because you have taste, and I beg you to shout at the top of your voice against this barbarity. That is the end of my letter; I am going to see my granaries and my barns.

I present my tender respect and I love you even more than my corn and my wine: I have however made some quite good wine, and a great deal of it. I bet, Madame, that you hardly care about that; that is how people are in Paris.

MADAME DU DEFFAND TO VOLTAIRE　　　　　*1 November 1760*

Yes, Monsieur, I received your fine present; Monsieur Le Normand sent it to me. I gave the Président his copy on the same day. You must have already received his thanks. D'Alembert only received your book in the last few days. Do not believe, I beg you, that I am in the wrong if you have not received news of me. My first concern was to read your preface and two or three chapters. Immediately wrote you an eight page letter in my own hand; I spent a night of insomnia at this task. When my secretary awoke, I gave it to him to read; he could decipher almost nothing. I no longer remembered what I had written. I was so vexed that I decided to wait and write to you when I had entirely finished your book. What is agreeable, is that yesterday as I was finishing the last page, I received your last letter. If you are not pleased with your *Histoire* you have neither taste nor judgement. The preface is charming; you treat gentlemen researchers as they deserve; there are so many ways of being tedious that to seek torturously for new ones truthfully cries out for vengeance. I do not think exactly as you do about the portraits and anecdotes, but on explanation perhaps it would turn out that we think the same. Imagined portraits and false or falsified anecdotes make unworthy novels out of history.

I find your descriptions of the Russian Empire, of the institutions, reforms and the Tsar's journeys all admirable. What concerns war did not give me so much pleasure; but that is because you had said everything about that in your *Vie de Charles XII.*[142] I received it with the Tsar. I will not tolerate it being said that there is the least contradiction.

I see, Monsieur, that you are fully apprised of all that I do; I would that you were so of all that I think. You would find nothing to find fault with and you would agree that I am not at all unjust in my judgements or unreasonable in my behaviour. I have been quite impartial in the war of the *philosophes*. I cannot adore their *Encyclopédie* which is perhaps adorable, but some articles from it which I have read have wearied me to death. I could not recognise as legislators people who have wit only, little talent and no taste; who although they are very honest people, write questionably about morality; and all of whose reasoning is sophistry and paradox. It is obvious that they have only one aim which is to chase a fame they will never achieve; they will not even enjoy such notoriety as the Fontenelles and La Mottes who have been forgotten since their death. They will be forgotten during their lifetimes. I make an exception for all sorts of reasons of Monsieur d'Alembert, although he informed on me to you; but I forgive that aberration the cause of which deserves some indulgence. He is the most honest man in the world, with a good heart, an excellent wit, great judgement and taste on many subjects; but there are certain things which have become party affairs for him and about which I find he has no common sense: for example Mademoiselle Clairon's scaffold about which I was transported with rage before receiving your orders. I said word for word what you said to me, and Monsieur d'Alembert will be very surprised when I give him your letter to read; it will be a great triumph. But, Monsieur, know that there is nothing more to be done; all is lost in this country, it is all anarchy; everyone believes himself to be the first in his genre and everyone believes himself to be master of all genres, and I will quote the refrain of a song about the Prime Minister of Mersia on his return from exile:

Lui à l'écart, tous les hommes sont égaux.[143]

You have with you at present a man of my acquaintanceship, Monsieur Turgot; he is a man of wit but not exactly your type.

What is the name of the man who travelled a hundred and fifty leagues to come and see you and who has been with you for six months? I respect him and love him so much for it that I am almost tempted to congratulate him.

Do not forget that you promise me some saucy pieces. In the name of . . . all that you do not like, take care of my entertainment, and rest well assured that apart from you, everything seems to me languid, dull and wearisome. I fear that this letter may have all those faults.

From this moment until 1764 there is a gap of three years in the correspondence between Madame du Deffand and Voltaire. Only one letter from the *marquise* survives (30 September 1763) compared with fourteen of Voltaire's. But the prolific correspondence of 1764 greatly helps towards the understanding of both correspondents, with fifteen letters from Voltaire and eleven from Madame du Deffand.

The rift with Mademoiselle de Lespinasse and d'Alembert was about to take place, and everything in these letters seems to foreshadow it, from the *marquise*'s feeling of isolation and her increasing pessimism to her need to rely on Voltaire's support. Voltaire, for his part, was unsuspicious and took no sides; he gladly gave way to the pleasure of speaking openly to someone with whom he felt a profound affinity. During a period of intense philosophical and civil activity these letters were an intellectual distraction. Voltaire had begun his great struggle against *"l'infâme."* The Calas, Sirven, La Barre, Etallonde-Morival and Lally-Tollendal affairs were all stages in the offensive against superstition.

Thanks to the first and most brilliant journalistic campaign of modern times, the fragile seventy-year-old in exile who had never forgotten the Bastille, shook Europe with his "cry of innocent blood." In 1763 his *Traité sur la tolérance à l'occasion de la mort de Jean Calas*, the *J'accuse* of the eighteenth century, appeared, and the campaign of rehabilitation for the unfortunate family's survivors absorbed him for four years from 1763 to 1766. In 1764 the *Dictionnaire philosophique portatif* about which Voltaire had spoken to the *marquise* four years earlier came out and shocked Geneva where it was burnt in public by the executioner. So it was hardly surprising that despite their usual lightness of tone, both correspondents became inclined to gloomy reflection.

The themes of good times past, of lack of taste and regret for the grace and former elegance of society recur with real feeling on both sides and without polemical undertones. A true and safe consolation lies in literature, the only passion to resist the *marquise*'s inherent pessimism.

Voltaire was seventy years old and had trouble with his eyesight. There was of course an enormous difference between his condition and Madame du Deffand's total blindness, but that did not prevent him from jokingly drawing a comparison. Hence the frequent references to the *Quinze-Vingts*, the Parisian hospice for the blind, so named for its capacity to house three hundred inmates.

VOLTAIRE TO MADAME DU DEFFAND   *Aux Délices, 27 January 1764*

> Oui, je perds les deux yeux; vous les avez perdus.
> Ô sage du Deffant est-ce une grande perte?
>   Du moins nous ne reverrons plus
>   Les sots dont la terre est converte.
> Et puis tout est aveugle en cet humain séjour,
> On ne va qu'à tâtons sur la machine ronde.
> On a les yeux bouchés à la ville, à la cour.
>   Plutus, la fortune et l'amour
> Sont trois aveugles nés qui gouvernent le monde.
> Si d'un de nos cinq sens nous sommes dégarnis,
> Nous en possédons quatre; et c'est un avantage
> Que la nature laisse à peu de ses amis,
>   Lorsqu'ils parviennent à notre âge.
> Nous avons vu mourir les Papes et les Rois.

Nous vivons, nous pensons et notre âme nous reste.
Epicure et les siens prétendaient autrefois
Que ce sixième sens était un don céleste
  Qui les valait tous à la fois.
Mais quand notre âme aurait des lumières parfaites,
Peut-être il serait encoure mieux
Que nous eussions gardé nos yeux,
Dussions-nous porter des lunettes.[144]

You see Madame, that I am a colleague and quite concerned with the affairs of our little republic of *Quinze-Vingts*. You assure me that people are no longer as agreeable as they used to be; yet partridges and pullets have quite as much flavour as they did in your youth, flowers are the same colour. It is not the same with men. The fundamentals remain the same, but talent is not for all time and the talent for amiability which has always been rare, degenerates like the others. It is not you who have changed. It is the court and the town according to what the connoisseurs tell me. It comes perhaps from the fact that people do not read Moncrif's *Moyens de Plaire*[145] as much as they should. The only concern is for the enormous folly perpetuated on every side.

Le raisonner tristement s'accrédit[146]

How can you expect society to be agreeable with so much pedantic rubbish?

You really deserve the homage of a *Pucelle*. One of your witticisms is quoted in the notes[147] to this theological work. There is no way of sending it to you, as you suggest, by way of the Queen; one would not have dared to send it even to Queen Berthe.[148] But know that nowadays it is impossible to send any printed book to Paris from a foreign country, even the New Testament. Even the minister[149] of whom you speak wishes me to send nothing, either by him or to him. They are afraid and I do not know why.

Make your decision. If I do not send you *Jeanne* within fifteen days by some honest traveller, tell Monsieur le Président Hénault to have some hawker find you a copy. It should cost thirty or forty sous; there is no cheaper work of theology.

I am sorry that your friend should be so sought after; so that you enjoy less of his company which is a great loss for you both. I am ending my life pleasantly in the retreat and surrounded by the family which I have made for myself.

Farewell, Madame, take courage. "Make necessity a virtue." Did you know that that was a proverb of Cicero's?

MADAME DU DEFFAND TO VOLTAIRE   *Wednesday, 7 March { 1764}*

I reproach myself every day, Monsieur, for not having the honour to write to you. Do you know what prevents me? It is that I find myself unworthy. Your last letter delighted me but took away my courage to reply. Happy is he who is born with great intelligence and great talents! And how much to be pitied is he who has just enough to prevent him from vegetating. I find myself in that class and am among many. The only difference between me and my fellows is that they are pleased with themselves and that I am far from being pleased with them and even further from being pleased with myself. Your letter is a delight; everyone is asking me for a copy. You almost console me for being blind, but Monsieur, you are not one of our confraternity. I have questioned Monsieur le duc de Villars at length. You enjoy all your five senses just as you did at thirty, and above all you enjoy the sixth one which you mention and which makes your happiness, but makes so many other people's unhappiness.

I have read four stories of which you sent me only the first. *L'Education d'une jeune fille*[150] and *Macare*[151] have been printed and so I have them! But I have not been able to obtain *Les Trois Manières.*[152] It is very bad of you, Monsieur, to grant only half of your favours. I love Théone madly, he is a gem; Eglée is very agreeable; as for Apamisse,[153] I find her a little serious. I have read this last story only once and I was unable to obtain a copy; they say that it will not be printed until you have written enough stories to make a volume. Will you not distinguish between me and the public?

Here we are in a great state of alarm. Madame de Pompadour is very ill:[154] I will not close this letter until I have had news of her.

I would much prefer to be at Les Délices than at Choisy.[155] Macare lives at Les Délices and if it were possible, I would willingly go there to find him. Your letters give me a glimpse of him and I see him only in what you write; so send him me often by post that I might sometimes catch sight of him. Farewell, Monsieur, I beg you to believe that I adore only you, all the rest are false gods.

8 March

The news of Madame de Pompadour is very good, but she is not yet out of trouble; I would be very vexed by any resulting misfortune which could be much greater than anyone thinks.[156]

VOLTAIRE TO MADAME DU DEFFAND   *Les Délices, 7 March 1764*

What you say is witty, Madame, and my texts are bad; but your imagination must indulge mine, since the great must protect the small.

You expressly ordered me sometimes to send you a few scraps; I obey but I warn you that to enjoy these trifles you need to love verse passionately. If poor Formont were still alive, he would bring me into favour with you; he would remind you of your old indulgence for me and would tell you that half a *Quinze-Vingts* had a right to your kindness.

I feel sure that I still count a little, since I dare to send you such nonsense. I even dare to flatter myself that you will speak ill of them only to me. That is the height of virtue for a woman of wit.

You will reply that that would be a very difficult thing and that society would be lost if one did not make a little fun of those who are most attached to us.

It is the way of the world, but it is not yours and in the condition in which we find ourselves, you and I have no greater need than to console one another.

I would like to amuse you more, but think that you are in the whirlwind of Paris and that I am in the middle of four ranges of mountains covered with snow. The Jesuits, protests, petitions and the news of the day all serve to distract you, whereas I am in Siberia.

But you wanted it to be me who sometimes took care of your amusement. So forgive me when I do not succeed in the task you have given me; it is to you that I preach tolerance, one of your oldest servants, and certainly one of the most attached deserves a little.

MADAME DU DEFFAND TO VOLTAIRE   *Paris, 14 March 1764*

I send you a thousand thousand thanks for your *Manières*. Your manners with me are always good except when you ask for my approbation. But you must be forgiven a little mockery. You have all my admiration, Monsieur, and you do not owe it at all to preconception; I owe the little taste I have to you; you are my touchstone; everything which diverges from your "manner" seems bad to me. Judge from what appears good to me nowadays when all is cynicism or pedantry; there is no grace, no ease, no imagination, everything is frozen; boldness has no strength and licence no gaiety; there is no talent and a great deal of presumption. That is the picture of the present moment.

You are delightful in all genres! Why do you abandon the fable? Allow me to give you a subject.

There was a lion in Chantilly to which all the curs that should have been thrown in the river were thrown. He strangled them all. Only one little bitch who happened to be in pup found grace in his eyes. He licked her, caressed her, shared his food with her, he delivered her. He did no harm to her little family and I do not know what became of her, but one day some mastiffs came to bark at the lion's gate. The little bitch joined them and barked and pulled his ears: punishment was immediate. He strangled her but repentance followed fast. He did not eat her: he lay down beside her and seemed overcome by the greatest sorrow. It was hoped that a change of mind might save him, but no. He mercilessly strangled all the dogs he was given.

Does it not seem to you that there is a great moral to be drawn from this story (which is profoundly true) about ingratitude, the need we have to love or at least to have company? The lion's regret at having punished his friend, however ungrateful, must surely furnish you with many ideas.

If I were offered my sight back today, or to have a thousandth part of your talents, I do not know which I would choose. The dependence caused by blindness is no more unbearable than being insufficient to oneself and needing company which is neither agreeable nor pleasurable, in fact where nothing satisfies. It may well be that bad temper which is inseparable from age, makes things worse for me than they are. I often say so to myself and I ceaselessly repeat what you said to me in one of your letters, that one must despise men and tolerate them. It is both singular and fortunate that they are content with tolerance and do not notice the contempt, so one would be quite wrong not to behave thus.

Nothing which happens these days provides any distraction for me, Monsieur. I have a horror of everything which is written, the mandates, the protests, the petitions etc. etc. arouse not the slightest curiosity in me; I am profoundly indifferent to the matters of which they treat and besides they are couched in such paltry verbiage and in such false fine thought as to make one sick to death.

Madame de Pompadour is much better, but her illness is not yet nearly over, and I do not dare to have much hope. I think that her loss would be a very great misfortune: personally I would be greatly afflicted by it not for any direct reason but for the sake of some people I love a great deal, and besides what would happen then?

Ah! I was forgetting to tell you that I am furious about what has just happened: the letter before last that you wrote me has been printed without my consent and without my knowing.[157] Fortunately the Queen's name has been removed; but Moncrif is all there. This incident will make me wise and I promise you faithfully that anything you write or send me will never be allowed out of my hands, and I will make quite sure that nothing can ever be copied nor learned by heart because I will not read it to those who have that particular talent.

Farewell, Monsieur; love me a little; it is just and grateful for I love you, I swear, very tenderly.

VOLTAIRE TO MADAME DU DEFFAND   *21 March 1764*

I will not tell you, Madame, that we are happier than we are wise—You tremble lest some ill-intentioned person may have taken the little word about my fellow, Moncrif, as a bad joke. I have received a letter from him full of the tenderest thanks. If he is not the most dissembling of all men, he is the most self-satisfied. He is a great courtier, I admit, but is it not a waste of politics to thank me so cordially for something which angers him? For my part, like him, I take it literally and I suppose him to be as naïve as I was when I wrote you that unfortunate letter which some pirates have published.

Seriously, I would be very sorry if one of my fellows, and particularly one who talks to the Queen, were displeased with me; I would be ruined at court and would lose the important positions which I might attain with time, for after all, I am only ten years younger than Moncrif and the example given by Cardinal de Fleury who started at seventy-four, gives me great hope.

You would do very well, Madame, no longer to confide your secrets to those who have them printed and who thereby violate people's rights. I knew your story about the lion, it is quite singular but it is not as good as the story of Androcles and the lion. Besides my taste for stories has absolutely faded: long winter evenings inspired me with such fantasy. I think differently at the equinox. The spirit blows where it will, as someone said.[158]

I have often noticed that one is master of nothing: never do we choose our tastes, any more than we choose our size or our face. Have you never considered what poor machines we are? I felt this truth as the result of continuous experience: feelings, passions, tastes, talent, way of thinking, of speaking, of walking, I do not know where they all come from, they are like the ideas we have in a dream; they arrive without our having anything to do with it. Think about that, for we who have weak sight are made for meditation more than others who are distracted by objects.

You should dictate what you think when you are alone and send it to me; I am certain that there would be more true philosophy in that than in all the systems with which we are nurtured. It would be natural philosophy; you would find your ideas in yourself alone and you would not try to deceive yourself. Whoever, like you, has imagination and fairness of mind, can without any other help find in himself alone, knowledge of human nature; for all men are alike at heart and differences of nuance alter nothing of the original colour.

I assure you, Madame, that I would be very glad to see a small outline of your way of thinking. Dictate something, I beg you, when you have nothing to do: how better could you use your time than in thinking? You can neither play nor run nor have company all day long. It would be no mean satisfaction for me to see the superiority of a naïve, honest soul over so many proud and obscure philosophers; besides, I promise secrecy.

You know well, Madame, that the fine place which you accord me in our century is not for me; I, without difficulty give the first place to the person to whom you accord the second. But, allow me to ask for a place in your heart; for, I assure you, you are in mine.

I close, Madame, because I am quite ill, and I fear I will tire you. Accept my tender respects and do not allow M. le Président Hénault to forget me.

The break with Mademoiselle de Lespinasse had just taken place and Madame du Deffand was experiencing one of the darkest moments of her life. From a practical point of view, the "domestic inconveniences" to which she referred in a letter to Voltaire on 2 May, were resolved with customary efficiency. Madame du Deffand was now looked after by her sister, Madame d'Aulan who had, in anticipation of the storm, arrived from Avignon in April. She was to remain in a small independent apartment at Saint-Joseph for three years. The *marquise* had also cancelled the will she had made ten years earlier in which she left Julie fifteen thousand livres and a complete set of furniture. But the double betrayal of d'Alembert and her niece combined with the disloyalty of her old *habitués* irreparably wounded the only passionate feelings which Madame du Deffand had allowed to flourish—her feelings of friendship. And as if this were not enough, Madame de Pompadour's death threatened the political position of Choiseul to whose wife the *marquise* was gradually becoming closer. Had he been alive, Madame du Deffand would certainly have confided in Formont who would have given her sound advice: "Sicknesses of the soul are often cured by a feat of the imagination and always by time and habit . . . You do not make enough use of the strength and light of your reason; you only consider your losses without thinking of the resources at your disposal."[159] But now Voltaire was assaulted by the violence of the *marquise*'s pessimism which he met with not dissimilar arguments.

So absolute was Madame du Deffand's negativism that it caused the patriarch de Ferney to make some of the most precise pronouncements in all his writings on the subject of man's existential destiny. "The most intimate expression of Voltaire's philosophy is to be found in Madame du Deffand's letters; his way of accepting life and confronting death, his metaphysical ideas, his scepticism, his passionate struggles in the name of humanity and his attacks of mystical resignation.[160] The thoughts which obsessed Madame du Deffand when she began to go blind, returned to trouble her with equal violence. It came down to one self-evident truth: "There is, rightly speaking, only one misfortune in life which is to be born." No individual destiny escapes this rule. The repulsive shadow of death with its attendant anguish mars even an exceptionally happy existence like Voltaire's. The idea that life was not worth living did not in fact prevent the *marquise* from fearing the end, but if anything, drove her to "the moral suicide of one who, for fear of risk taking, consents to a form of existence in which all avenues are blocked."[161] She suffered life as inevitable and excused monotony as the ultimate defence against pain. When her correspondent urged her to react with intelligence, the *marquise* renounced all possibility of reason because: "What pleasure could I find in writing my thoughts down? They only torment me." Such an affirmation was blasphemy to Voltaire. Until that moment Voltaire's and Madame du Deffand's different attitudes could be attributed mainly to difference of temperament. It was Voltaire's wonderful vitality (certainly not his convinced theories) which led him to contradict his friend's existential pessimism. But when man's true purpose was denied, the power which enabled him to challenge daily the inscrutable will of a universe which determined and transcended him, then Voltaire revolted with painful indignation.

MADAME DU DEFFAND TO VOLTAIRE   *2 May 1764*

I do not flatter myself, Monsieur, that you have noticed how long it is since I had the honour of writing to you; but if, by chance, you have noticed it, then you must know the reason. Firstly, the Président has been ill, and caused me considerable anxiety; then the sickness and death of Madame de Pompadour which occupied me and interested me as much as it did many others to whom it meant nothing, and then domestic embarrassment and trouble[162] which disturbed my feeble genius.

Your last letter (which you can certainly not remember) is charming. You say that you would like me to tell you my thoughts. Ah! Monsieur, what are you asking me? They are limited to one only: a very sad one; that there is, rightly speaking, only one misfortune in life which is to be born. There is no condition whatsoever which seems to be preferable to nothingness and you, yourself, who are Monsieur Voltaire, whose name encompasses every kind of happiness, reputation, honour, fame, everything to preserve you from ennui, you who find in yourself every kind of resource, and a wide philosophy which made you foresee that wealth was necessary in age; well, Monsieur, despite all these advantages it would have been better not to have been born for the very reason that you must die, of that we are certain and nature revolts so strongly against it that all men are like the woodcutter.[163]

See how sad my soul is; and how ill I choose my time to write to you; but, Monsieur, console me, disperse the black clouds which surround me.

I have just read a history of Scotland which is, so to speak, only Mary Stuart's life; it was the culmination of my sorrow; I hope your Corneille[164] will take me out of this condition. As yet I have only read the *Apître à l'Académie* and the preface. On reading what you write we are all surprised that everyone does not write well: it seems as if there is nothing so easy as to write like you and yet no one in the world comes anywhere near it. There is only Cicero who, after you, is all that I like best.

Farewell, Monsieur; I feel unworthy of taking up any more of your time. I would like to be at Geneva, that is to say with you. I love you with all my heart and you would console me for being born, at least for a moment.

VOLTAIRE TO MADAME DU DEFFAND *Les Délices, 9 May 1764*

It is I, Madame, who ask your forgiveness for not having had the honour of writing to you; it is not for you, if you please, to tell me that you have not had the honour of writing to me. A pleasant honour, indeed; between us more serious things are concerned, given our condition, our age and our way of thinking. I have heard it said only of Judas that it would have been better for him not to be born,[165] and besides, it is the Gospel which says it. Mécène[166] and La Fontaine said quite the opposite:

> *Mieux vaut souffrir que mourir*
> *C'est la devise des hommes*[167]

I agree with you that life is very short and quite unhappy; but I must tell you that I have at my house a relation of twenty-three, he is handsome, well-built and vigorous; and this is what happened to him: he falls from his horse out hunting one day and bruises his thigh a little, they make a small incision and he is paralysed for the rest of his days, not paralysed in one part of his body, but paralysed so that he can not use any one of his limbs nor lift his head and with the absolute certainty of never having the least relief. He has become accustomed to his condition and he loves life like a madman.

It is not that there is no good in nothingness; but I believe it is impossible really to love nothingness despite its good qualities.

As to death, let us be a little reasonable, I beg you: it is almost certain that one does not feel it at all; it is not a painful moment at all but it resembles sleep just as two drops of water resemble one another; it is only the idea that you will never wake up again which is painful; it is the apparatus of death which is horrible, the barbarity of extreme unction, the cruelty with which we are warned that everything is over for us.

What good does it do to come pronouncing sentence over us? It will be perfection well carried out without the interference of lawyers and priests. One should make one's depositions in good time and then think no more about it.

It is sometimes said of a man that he died like a dog, but really a dog is happy to die without all the baggage with which we are persecuted in our last moments. With a little bit of charity we would be left to die without anything being said about it. What is still worse is that you are surrounded at the time by hypocrites who importune you to make you think as they do not at all think, or by imbeciles who want you to be as foolish as they are. All that is quite disgusting. The only pleasure of life at Geneva is that one can die there as one likes. Many honest people summon no priests. You can kill yourself if you want without anyone finding it amiss, or await the moment without anyone importuning you.

Madame de Pompadour had all the horror of the apparatus and of the certainty of seeing herself condemned to leave the most agreeable situation in which any woman could find herself. I did not know, Madame, that you were intimate[168] with her; but I guess that Madame de Mirepoix[169] played a part in making her your friend. So you have suffered a very great loss, for she liked to be of service. I believe that she will be missed except by those whom she was obliged to harm,[170] since they wished to harm her; she was a philosopher.

I flatter myself that your friend[171] who was ill, is a philosopher too; he has too much wit and too much reason not to despise what is very despicable. If he believes me, he will live for you and for himself, without giving himself so much trouble for others. I would like him to advance his career as far as Fontenelle's, and in his agreeable life to be always occupied with the consolations of yours.

You are entertaining yourself then, with the *Commentaires sur Corneille?* You no doubt have the text read to you, without which the notes would weary you considerably. I am reproached with having been too severe; but I wanted to be useful and I was often very discreet. The number of astonishing affronts to language, to the clarity of ideas and expressions, to decency, and finally to interest, so frightened me that I did not say half what I should have said. This work is very thankless and very disagreeable, but it served to marry two young women. This has never happened to any other commentator and it will not happen again.[172]

Farewell, Madame, let us bear life which is no great thing and let us not fear death, which is nothing at all; believe that my only sorrow is not to be able to converse with you, and be assured, in your convent, of my tender and very sincere respect and of my inviolable attachment.

MADAME DU DEFFAND TO VOLTAIRE   *Paris, 16 May 1764*

I am delighted, Monsieur, that honour displeases you: it has shocked me for a long time; it cools and damages familiarity and removes an air of truth. A little while ago I proposed to one of my friends that it be banned from our correspondence; she replied: "Let us do more than François I, let us lose even honour."[173]

You read my last letter very badly for you understood that I was intimate with Madame de Pompadour. I said: "that I had been very concerned by her sickness and death, and that I was as interested in it as many others to whom it meant nothing."

I had never seen her nor met her; but I was, however, obliged to her, and for my friends' sakes I feared her loss. There is as yet no sign that it has altered their situation. So now Monsieur d'Alby[174] is archbishop of Cambrai, and now some ladies are accompanying the King on his first voyage of Saint-Hubert, and they are Mesdames de Mirepoix, de Gramont and d'Ecquevilly.[175] I would willingly undertake to send you this kind of news if I thought it gave you any pleasure and if you did not have better correspondents than I.

Another point in my letter which you have also misunderstood, was that I said that the greatest of all misfortunes was to be born. I am persuaded of this truth and that it does not relate only to Judas, Job and myself; but to you, to the late Madame de Pompadour, to all who have been, all who are and all who will be. To live without loving life does not make the end desirable, and does not even lessen the fear of losing it. Those whose life is happy have a truly sad perspective. They are sure that it will end. These are all quite idle reflections, but it is certain that if we had no pleasure a hundred years ago, neither did we have pain or sorrow; and of the twenty-four hours in the day, those when I am asleep seem the happiest to me. You do not know and you cannot know from personal experience, the condition of those who think, who reflect, who have some activity, and who are at the same time without talent, without passion, without occupation, without diversion; who have had friends but who have lost them without being able to replace them; add to that a delicacy of taste, a little discernment, a great love of truth; put out those people's eyes, and place them in the middle of Paris, of Peking, in fact of anywhere you like and I maintain that it would be happier for them not to have been born. The example you give me of your young man is singular; but all physical ills, however great (except for pain), sadden and depress the soul less than human converse and society. Your young man is with you; no doubt he loves you; you take care of him, you show an interest in him, he is not left to himself, I understand how he can be happy. I would surprise you if I were to admit that blindness and old age are the least of all my troubles. You will perhaps conclude from that that my head is no good, but do not say that it is my fault unless you wish to contradict yourself. You wrote in one of your last letters that we are no more masters of our affections, our feelings, our actions, our behaviour and our way of walking than we are of our dreams. You are quite right and nothing is as true. What can be concluded from all that? Nothing, and a thousand times nothing; we must end one's term vegetating as much as possible.

Only one thing would please me: to read what you write. If I were with you I would be so bold as to remonstrate about one or two of your criticisms of Corneille. I find them nearly all very sound; but there is one about the *Horaces* to which I could not subscribe; but you would mock me, if I were to undertake a dissertation.

Take good care of your health; you alleviate my misfortune by the assurance you give me of your friendship and the pleasure your letters bring me.

VOLTAIRE TO MADAME DU DEFFAND[176]   *Délices, 22 May 1764*

You give me great pain, Madame; for your sad ideas result not only from reasoning: they come from the feelings. I agree with you that nothingness is, generally speaking, preferable to life; there is some value in nothingness. Let us console ourselves; clever people claim that we will have a taste of it: it is quite obvious they say with Seneca and Lucretius, that after death we will be what we were before we were born; but what will we do with the two or three minutes of our existence? We are, so they claim, small wheels in a big machine, little animals with two feet and two hands like monkeys, but less agile than they, just as comical and with a larger measure of ideas. We are carried along by the general tide stamped on nature by the Master: we give nothing, we receive everything, we are no more masters of our ideas than of the circulation of blood in our veins: every being, every manner of being depends of necessity on universal law. It is ridiculous, they say, and impossible for man to give himself anything when the multitude of stars gives itself nothing. It is fine for us to be absolute masters of our actions and our wills when the universe is a slave!

What a dog's condition! You will say: I suffer, I struggle with my existence which I curse and which I love, I hate life and death: who will console me? Who will support me? The whole of nature is powerless to relieve me.

Here perhaps, Madame, is what I would imagine for a remedy. Neither you nor I were responsible for the loss of our sight,[177] for being deprived of our friends nor for being in the situations in which we find ourselves. All your privations, all your feelings, all your ideas are absolutely necessary. You could not prevent yourself from writing the very philosophical and sad letter which I received from you; and I must of necessity write that courage, resignation to the laws of nature, a profound contempt for all superstition, the noble pleasure of feeling oneself to be of a different nature to fools, and the exercise of the faculty of thought are true consolations. This idea that I was destined to represent you must remind you of your philosophy. I become an instrument to strengthen another by which, in my turn, I am strengthened; happy the machines which can be of mutual assistance to each other!

Your machine is one of the best in this world. Is it not true that if you had to choose between light and thought, you would not hesitate, and you would prefer the eyes of the soul to those of the body? I have always wanted you to dictate the way in which you see things and that you would allow me to read it; for you see very well and paint likewise.

Send me, I beg you, Madame, your criticism of my criticism of part of the *Horaces,* it would amuse you and enlighten me. It is a consolation to put one's mind on paper; confide in me everything that passes through your head.

I write infrequently because I am a husbandman. You know nothing of that business; it is, though, that of our first fathers. I have always been overwhelmed by frivolous occupations which swallowed my every moment; but the happiest are those in which I receive news from you and in which I can tell you how your soul delights mine and how much I miss you. Everyone is not like Fontenelle. Come along, Madame, let us drag our chains to the very end.

Be persuaded of the true interest which my heart takes in you and of my very tender respect.

I am very glad that nothing has changed for the people who concern you. So now a counsellor of the *parlement* is *intendant de finances.*[178] That is unprecedented. The finances will be properly controlled. The State, which has been as sick as you and me, will recover its health.

MADAME DU DEFFAND TO VOLTAIRE   *Paris, Monday 29 May 1764*

No, Monsieur, I would not prefer thought to light, the eyes of the soul to those of the body. I would consent far more willingly to total blindness. All my observations lead me to find that the less one thinks, the less one reflects, the happier one is; I know it even from experience. When you have been very ill and suffered great pain, the state of convalescence is a very happy state; you desire nothing, do nothing, and only rest is required. I found myself in this situation, I felt all its value and I would have liked to remain in it all my life. All your reasoning is excellent, every word is of the greatest truth. We must resign ourselves to following our appointed purpose in the general order and to thinking, as you say, that the part we play only lasts for a few minutes. If we only had to defend ourselves against superstition to be on top of everything, we would be happy indeed. But we have to live among men; we want them to value us; we desire them to have good sense, justice, goodwill, sincerity and we find only the opposite faults and vices. You can never know the misfortune, for, as I have already told you, when you have a great deal of intelligence and talent, you must find great resources within yourself. One must be Voltaire or vegetate. What pleasure could I have in putting my thoughts in writing? They serve only to torment me and that would hardly satisfy my vanity.

So, Monsieur, believe me, I am abandoned by God and by the doctors, do not you abandon me however. Your letters give me infinite pleasure, you have a sensitive soul, you say nothing vague; the moments in which I receive your letters and those when I reply console me, occupy me and even encourage me. If I were younger, I would perhaps try to move nearer to you; nothing ties me to this country and the society of which I find myself part might make me say what Monsieur de la Rochefoucauld said of the court. "It does not make you happy, but it prevents you from being so elsewhere."[179]

I do not attribute my troubles and my sorrows to everything around me, I know that our character nearly always contributes most to our happiness; but as you know, we were given that by nature. What can we conclude from that? Only that we must submit. There could be only one cure which would be to have a friend to whom one could say, *"Change en bien tous les maux ou le ciel m'a soumis."*

I have not reached that point, but certainly say without ceasing, *Sans toi tout homme est seul.*[180]

Let us, Monsieur, end this sad elegy which is a hundred times sadder and more tedious than Ovid's.

You want me to tell you what I feel about your Corneille, that would certainly mean mocking me. If I were to see you, I might

· perhaps dare to obey, but how would I have the temerity to criticise you in writing? You must repeat that order if I am to consent. I will only say that you have caused me to re-read all Corneille's plays. I am still only at *Héraclius*. I am enchanted by his sublime genius, and most greatly surprised that at the same time he can be so lacking in taste. I am not surprised and shocked by the banal and the familiar things, I attribute them to his little knowledge of the world and its ways; but rather by the way he turns the same thought over and over, which is quite contrary to genius and nearly always the sign of a small mind. You ought to send me everything you write, I never have it until after everyone else.

You know all our news. I was greatly occupied by Monsieur de Luxembourg's death, Madame de Luxembourg is very afflicted. I would be glad to be able to show her a line from you expressing the concern you have for her situation and saying that you share my grief; be persuaded that you are destined to give me some consideration, to show me friendship and to alleviate my pain. For my part, Monsieur, I feel that since all eternity I must have been born to revere and to love you.

Monsieur le Cardinal de Bernis has the archbishopric of Alby.[181] The curé of Saint-Sulpice[182] has resigned, helped by an annuity of fifteen thousand *livres*; he is replaced by Monsieur Nogent, his curate.

VOLTAIRE TO MADAME DU DEFFAND   *Les Délices, 4 June {1764}*

I write with great pleasure, Madame, when I have a subject. To write vaguely and with nothing to say is like chewing on nothing, or speaking for the sake of speaking; it is equally tedious for both correspondents who soon stop writing to each other.

We have a big subject to deal with; it concerns happiness or at least, how to be as little unhappy as you can in this world. I could not tolerate your saying that the more one thinks, the more unhappy one is. That is true for those who think ill, I am not speaking of those who think ill of their neighbour, that is sometimes very amusing; I am speaking of those who think awry; those who are to be pitied no doubt because they have a sickness of the soul and sickness is always a sad condition.

But you, whose soul is the healthiest in the world, listen, if you

Madame du Deffand, probably
when she was in her early 70s.
Courtesy of The Lewis Walpole
Library, Yale University.

Madame du Deffand,
painted by Carmontelle
around 1767, for Horace
Walpole. Courtesy of The
Lewis Walpole Library, Yale
University.

Président Hénault.

D'Alembert, by La Tour.

Mademoiselle de Lespinasse, by Carmontelle.

Horace Walpole, by Allan Ramsay.

portrait de M.ʳ de Walpole par
Mad. La marquise du deffand fait
au mois de novembre 1766.

Non, non je ne peux pas faire votre portrait, —
personne ne vous connoit moins que moi; —
vous me paroissez tantot tel que je voudrois que
vous fussiez, tantot tel que je crains que vous
ne soyez, et peut etre jamais tel que vous etes.

Je scay bien que vous avez beaucoup
d'esprit, vous en avez de tous les genres, de toutes
les sortes, tout le monde scait cela aussi bien
que moi, et vous devez le scavoir mieux que personne.
C'est votre caractere qu'il faudroit
peindre et voila pourquoy je ne puis pas etre bon
juge; il faudroit de l'indifference ou du moins
de l'impartialité; cependant je peux vous dire
que vous etes un fort honnete homme, que vous
avez des principes, que vous etes courageux, que
vous vous piquez de fermeté; que lorsque vous avez

Madame du Deffand's description of Horace Walpole, November 1766. Courtesy
of The Lewis Walpole Library, Yale University.

Horace Walpole's description of Madame du Deffand, in his hand. Courtesy of The Lewis Walpole Library, Yale University.

The Duchesse de Choiseul and
Madame du Deffand, by Carmontelle.

please to what you owe to nature. Is it nothing then to be cured of the unfortunate prejudices which enslave most men and, above all women? Not to put one's soul in the hands of a charlatan? Not to dishonour your being by terrors and superstitions unworthy of all thinking beings? To be of an independence which delivers you from the necessity of hypocrisy? To have to pay court to no one and to open your soul freely to your friends?

That, however, is your situation. You deceive yourself when you say that you would like to limit yourself to vegetating: it is as if you were to say that you wished for tedium. Ennui is the worst of all conditions. You have certainly nothing else to do, no other decision to make, but to continue to gather your friends around you; you have some who are quite worthy of you.

The sweetness and safety of conversation are as real a pleasure as is an assignation in youth. Eat well, take care of your health, some-times amuse yourself by dictating your ideas so as to compare what you thought yesterday with what you think today. You will have two very great pleasures, that of living amongst the best company in Paris and that of living with yourself. I defy you to imagine anything better.

I must console you even more by telling you that I believe your situation to be considerably superior to mine. I find myself in a country just situated in the middle of Europe. Every passer-by visits me. I have to cope with Germans, Englishmen, Italians and even some Frenchmen who I will never see again; and you only speak to people you like.

You seek consolation; I am convinced that you provide it for Madame la maréchale de Luxembourg.[183] I knew her to have a brilliant imagination and the most amiable wit in the world; I even thought I glimpsed in her some bright shafts of philosophy; she must give herself over entirely to philosophy, that is the only way for fine souls. Look at the miserable life Madame le maréchale de Villars led during her last years; the poor woman went to benediction, and yawned as she read the *Méditations* of Father Croiset.[184]

You who are re-reading Corneille, tell me, I beg you, what you think of my remarks and then I will tell you my secret. Deign always to love your instructor for whom it would be a great honour to be instructed by you.

MADAME DU DEFFAND TO VOLTAIRE   *Paris, 17 June 1764*

My secretary has regained his sight so I will lose not a moment, but continue our correspondence. Let us speak no more of happiness. It is the philosopher's stone which destroys all who seek it. There is no system to make us happy and there are no good receipts for finding it except one of my great-aunts' which is to take the time as it comes and people as they are. I would add one further thing which seems even more necessary to me: to be at ease with yourself.

Ah! if you were here, I would indeed willingly take you for my instructor; but you would not agree to it, I would tire you too much. Somewhere you said that all genres could be good except the tedious which is the one to which I devote myself; I flatter myself that you believe that it is not through choice . . .

VOLTAIRE TO MADAME DU DEFFAND   *Ferney, 31 August 1764*

I hear, Madame, that you have lost Monsieur d'Argenson. If this news is true, I grieve with you. We are all like prisoners condemned to death amusing ourselves for a moment in the prison yard until they come for us to be expedited.[185] This idea is truer than it is comforting. The first lesson which I think ought to be given to men is to inspire their souls with courage; and since we are born to suffer and to die we must familiarise ourselves with this harsh destiny.

I would very much like to know whether Monsieur d'Argenson died like a philosopher or like a wet chicken. In part of Europe your last minutes are accompanied by such disgusting and ridiculous circumstances that it is very difficult to know what the dying think. The same ceremonies attend them all. Some Jesuits have been so impudent as to say that Montesquieu died as an imbecile, and they took it upon themselves to urge others to die the same way.

It must be admitted that the Ancients, who are our masters in everything, had a great advantage over us: they did not disturb life and death with obligations to make both sinister. In the days of the Scipios and the Caesars one lived and thought and died as one wished; but as for us, we are treated like puppets.

I believe you to be enough of a philosopher, Madame, to be of my opinion. If you are not, burn my letter, but always preserve a little friendship for the short time which remains for me to crawl over this pile of mud on which nature has placed us.

Freedom from "prejudice" did not exempt Voltaire from that of seeing a way of death as a necessary confirmation of a way of life. Death is the real touchstone of a freethinker's theories, proof of his most secret convictions. But to die outside the Church in the eighteenth century was not just a personal decision and a statement of laicism, it brought with it serious civil consequences, starting with the impossibility of burial in consecrated ground. Hence the morbid curiosity concerning the minutest details of the deaths of those professed freethinkers who, in their last hours, had to suffer pressure from their relations, the onslaught of priests and fear of a communal grave.

News of comte d'Argenson's death revived these questions. Horror of ideology made Madame du Deffand more prudent than Voltaire. It would not be long before the great writer would scandalise and enlighten the whole of Europe with a series of confessions dictated by fear.

MADAME DU DEFFAND TO VOLTAIRE   *Paris, 10 September 1764*

You have not heard from me, Monsieur, because for six weeks or two months I have been as black as ink, taking no part in anything, wearied by everything, without desires or feelings and always grieving over the misfortune of having been born, for, whatever you may say, it is the only real misfortune since it is the principle and the cause of all the others; but it is as useless to grieve over it as it is ridiculous to pity oneself for it.

Monsieur d'Argenson arrived here half dead on 12 July, with a mild fever and an infected chest. His condition worsened every day, but only slightly. On the 22nd of last month it became clear that he had reached the end. The priest was sent for, who stayed with him until five o'clock in the evening when he died. There was no question of any of the usual practices except for extreme unction. It was impossible to know what he thought since he did not speak. So one can make whatever judgement one likes. The Président de Montesquieu did everything which is usually done. I do not think that the way of death proves very much, and has no authority one way or another; a trick of the imagination is decisive, and foolish indeed is he who restrains himself in his last moments. Do you not write to the Président? Monsieur d'Argenson left him a manuscript of Henri IV's letters; he has been complimented by everyone . . .

MADAME DU DEFFAND TO VOLTAIRE   *28 December 1765*

The letter I am sending you[186] astonished me; I imagine that it will have the same effect on you. Do not the style, the judgement, the taste all lead one to suspect an octogenarian? Would a man of thirty not write with greater strength, elegance and delicacy? The first part in particular charmed me. The end betrays a greater air of maturity, I admit. But, Monsieur Voltaire, declared lover of truth, tell me in good faith if you have found it? You fight against and destroy all error, but what do you put in their place? Is there anything real? Is not everything illusion? Fontenelle said: "There are toys for every age." It seems to me that I have the most beautiful thoughts in the world about that; but I would become so ridiculous as to be pointed at, if I began to philosophise with you; it would be too easy for you to confuse me and leave me without an answer. I remember that when as a child I was in a convent, Madame de Luynes sent Father Massillon to see me. My genius trembled in front of his.[187] I did not submit to the strength of his reasoning but to the importance of the reasoner. All discussion on certain matters seems useless to me. The people do not understand it at all, youth does not care, intelligent people have no need of it, and are we to worry about enlightening fools? Let everyone think and live as he will and let everyone see through his own glasses. Never flatter ourselves that we establish tolerance; the persecuted will always preach it, and if they ceased to be tolerant, they could no longer exercise it. Whatever opinion men hold, they wish to subject everyone to it . . .

Everything you write has a seductive, beguiling charm, but I always regret to see you occupied by certain subjects which I would like to be so respected as never to be spoken of and never even thought of.

Do you know that Jean-Jacques is here? Monsieur Hume has procured an establishment for him in England and will take him there within the next few days. Several people are eager to pay court to him and to honour him in the hope of sharing a little of his fame. For my part, I have no ambition, and limit myself to having a few of his books on my shelves, some I have not read and others I will never re-read. I am sending you a joke of one of my friends;[188] I will name him if he allows me to; I will ask his permission before sealing this letter.

Farewell, Monsieur, your friendship and your correspondence are what most attach me to life: it is the only pleasure which remains to me.

The *marquise*'s emphatic closing lines are certainly sincere. Madame du Deffand had probably not yet realised that her life had reached its last definitive turning point and that within a few months her correspondence with Voltaire would no longer occupy the place of honour. By a curious coincidence, the newcomer to whom the *marquise* would give absolute precedence, and who had nothing in common with the patriarch of Ferney, was the only letter-writer whose correspondence can compare with Voltaire's for vastness and historical importance. Yet if, as Lytton Strachey says: "Voltaire, however, threw off his letters in the intervals of a multifarious literary activity—they were little more than incidents in the great work of his life," the other "did not snatch moments from life to write letters in: he snatched moments from letter-writing in which to live."[189] The newcomer was called Horace Walpole and he was the author of the joke to which Madame du Deffand referred.

X

The Romance: Horace Walpole

WHEN THE *parlement de Paris* condemned Jean-Jacques Rousseau for the publication of *Emile* in 1762, he fled to Switzerland and, when hounded from there, to Strasbourg. This new wave of persecution finally persuaded Rousseau to accept David Hume's longstanding suggestion that he should take refuge in England. So, armed with a special royal passport acquired for him by friends, Jean-Jacques arrived in Paris on his way to London on the evening of 16 December 1765, temporarily taken in by the bookseller, Madame Duchesne, before moving to the Temple and the protection offered there by the Grand Prior, the prince de Conti. During his three weeks in Paris, by one of those remarkable occurrences typical of the whole century of enlightenment, this anti-social, a-social, moody victim of persecution became the object of enormous curiosity and was immensely popular. "It is impossible to express or imagine the Enthusiasm of this Nation in his favour..." Hume wrote to a friend in London, "I am persuaded that, were I to open here a subscription with consent, I should receive 50,000 Pounds in a fortnight ... Voltaire and everybody else are quite eclipsed by him!"[1]

Jean-Jacques, less enthusiastic, complained to J.J. de Luze who was to accompany him to England with Hume, "I do not know for how much longer I will be able to suffer these public scenes. Could you, for the love of God, hasten your departure a little?"[2]

The fugitive writer's brief stay in the capital was an exciting event for high Parisian society. Madame du Deffand did not participate for reasons of personal dislike and probably not out of loyalty to Voltaire who had openly split with Rousseau. The *marquise* was naturally not the only one to have some reservations; Rousseau's extravagances were an inexhaustible source of humour and presented a perfect opportunity for wit, a temptation which Horace Walpole, after only three months in Paris but having been introduced to the heart of society, could not resist. During an evening at Madame Geoffrin's when Jean-Jacques was the sole topic of conversation, Walpole conceived the idea of writing to Rousseau, pretending to be Frederick of Prussia and with the excuse of offering him hospitality, mocking him for his hypocrisy and his persecution mania. The plan was put into action the following day with the help of Hénault, Helvétius and the duc de Nivernais. The letter read as follows: "My dear Jean-Jacques, you have renounced Geneva, your fatherland; you have been chased out of Switzerland, a country much praised in your writings; France has passed decrees against you: come to me. I admire your talents, I am amused by your *rêveries* which (let it be said in passing) occupy you too much and for too long. In the end it is necessary to be wise and happy; you have caused yourself to be talked about enough because of your eccentricities which are hardly fitting to a truly great man; show your enemies that you are sometimes capable of commonsense; it will anger them without harming you. I wish you well and would, if you like, help you; but if you insist on refusing my help, be sure that I will tell no one. If you persist in racking your brains in search of new misfortunes, choose whichever ones you want; I am a king, I can obtain for you what you wish; and as will certainly not be the case with your enemies, I will stop persecuting you when you stop glorifying in persecution. Your good friend Frederick."

It was not a very clever joke and it worried Rousseau hugely, but it succeeded as a *jeu d'esprit*, went the rounds of Paris and Madame du Deffand immediately reported it to Voltaire. When Jean-Jacques had left France, an aftermath of polemic in the English papers only increased his suspicions of the *philosophes*. Walpole had certainly not wanted his joke to cause such a furor, nor foreseen that it would. In a letter to Madame Boufflers, Hume precisely describes Walpole's intentions. The *Idole* was indignant at the joke played on her protégé, and Hume wrote to her from London: "I suppose, that by this time you have learned it was Horace Walpole who wrote the Prussian letter you mentioned to me. It is a strange inclination we have to be wits in preference to anything else. He is a very worthy man; he esteems and even admires

Rousseau; yet he could not forbear, for the sake of a very indifferent joke, the turning him into ridicule, and saying harsh things against him. I am a little angry with him; and I hear you are a great deal: but the matter ought to be treated only as a piece of levity."[3]

This little joke implies a certain fatuity in its author, but also shows how quickly Horace Walpole had made himself at home in Paris and with what ease he trod the uneven path of the capital's coteries and *salons,* after only three months.

Walpole had spent two months in Paris twenty-six years earlier. Then the twenty-two-year-old British aristocrat had seen it only as the first stop on his Grand Tour, a journey which he undertook with his friend Thomas Gray and whose real objective was Italy, Renaissance Florence and the monuments and ancient splendour of Rome. At that time English residents in Paris were a colony unto themselves, it was "not easy to disengage oneself from them so that one sees but little of the French themselves."[4] But the situation had changed a great deal since then. The end of the Seven Years War had opened up the frontiers between the two countries and after a period of forced isolation, London was invaded by French travellers ready to cultivate the most passionate anglomania. On the other hand the splendours of Parisian civilisation attracted a large number of British visitors who were enthusiastically welcomed. One such was David Hume, the first official envoy to be sent across the Channel after the war. The Scottish philosopher came to Paris to take up the post of secretary to the new ambassador and met with tremendous success. His popularity spread well beyond the confines of the philosophical coteries: *"Et verbum caro factum est!"* d'Alembert exclaimed.[5] "He is fashion itself, although his French is almost as unintelligible as his English,"[6] Walpole remarked with surprise as he prepared for a busy social season.

Bearing a distinguished name, armed with letters of introduction and already acquainted with such French aristocrats as the comtesse de Boufflers and the duc de Nivernais lately returned from England, Walpole was welcomed with open arms by both Parisian high society and by his many compatriots already in the capital.

On 17 September, four days after his arrival, he wrote in his diary: "After dinner to visit Madame de Bouzols; to the opera; to Madame du Deffand, a blind old lady of wit. Suppered there, with the Duchesse de la Vallière, still very handsome, Madame de Forcalquier, very handsome and pleasing, who reads English, the Président Hénault, very old, deaf and almost gone, Lord Ossory, Sir James Macdonald, Elliot, Craufurd, and other French. They played at whisk after supper two tables: left several there at past one. This morning in the middle of the town saw a horse-chestnut tree in blossom. At Madame du Deffand's they proposed to me to translate to her a scene in Rowe's *Ambitious Stepmother*: of which Madame de Forcalquier, who understands English, is fond; but I took care not to expose myself."[7] Walpole was introduced to the *marquise* by George Selwyn, a fashionable English eccentric, renowned for his re-partee, his humor and his extravagant crazes, not least of which was to attend executions. To judge from a satirical letter of 2 October to his friend Conway, Walpole does not seem to have been very favourably impressed by his first visits to Saint-Joseph: "Every woman has one or two [writers] planted in her house, and God knows how they water them. The old Président Hénault is the pagod at Madame du Deffand's, an old blind débauchée of wit, where I supped last night. The Président is very near deaf, and much nearer superannuated. His sits by the table: the mistress of the house, who formerly was his, inquires after every dish on the table, is told who has eaten of which, and then bawls the bill of fare of every individual into the Président's ears. In short, every mouthful is proclaimed, and so is every blunder I make against gram-mar. Some that I make on purpose, succeed; and one of them is to be reported to the Queen today by Hénault, who is her great favourite."[8]

In October Walpole's social life was interrupted by an attack of gout; but in November, judging from a letter to Lady Hervey,[9] his opinion of Madame du Deffand had had reason to improve: "All I can send your Ladyship is a very pretty *logogriphe*, made by the old blind Madame du Deffand whom perhaps you know—certainly must have heard of. I sup there very often; and she gave me this last night—you must guess it.

> *Quoique je forme un corps, je ne suis qu'une idée;*
> *Plus ma beauté vieillit, plus elle est décidée:*
> *Il faut, pour me trouver, ignorer d'ou je viens:*
> *Je tiens tout de lui, qui réduit tout à rien.*"[10]

Saint-Joseph was one of many points of interest in Walpole's first few months in Paris. His social calendar was full. One of the first people he visited was Madame Geoffrin who was in close touch with his friend Lady Hervey. Walpole was immediately captivated by Madame du

Deffand's rival hostess. "He discovers a new quality in her every day: 'one of the most remarkable intelligences I have ever known'; a knowledge of the world, 'incredible' common sense; 'a gift for analysing character with remarkable promptitude'; the ability to go to the bottom of things; in short 'a marvellous woman'."[11] The *salon* in the rue Saint-Honoré was to be a permanent centre for Walpole throughout the winter. His curiosity must have been particularly aroused by the famous Monday dinners dedicated to artists and patrons of the arts where he could meet Soufflot, Cochin, Vernet, Mariette, the duc de Marigny. How delighted he was "to totter into vogue"[12] and be able to write to England: "It would sound vain to tell you the honours and distinctions I receive, and how much I am in fashion; yet when they come from the handsomest women in France, and the most respectable in point of character, can one help being a little proud?"[13]

However, towards the beginning of 1766, Walpole became aware of the du Deffand "phenomenon" and described it accurately to Thomas Gray: "Her [Madame Geoffrin's] great enemy, Madame du Deffand, was for a short time mistress of the Regent, is now very old and stone blind, but retains all vivacity, wit, memory, judgement, passions and agreeableness. She goes to operas, plays, suppers, and Versailles; gives suppers twice a week; has everything new read to her; makes new songs and epigrams, ay, admirably, and remembers every one that has been made these fourscore years. She corresponds with Voltaire, dictates charming letters to him, contradicts him, is no bigot to him or anybody, laughs both at the clergy and the philosophers. In a dispute, into which she easily falls, she is very warm, and yet scarce ever in the wrong: her judgement on every subject is as just as possible; in every point of conduct as wrong as possible: for she is all love and hatred, passionate for her friends to enthusiasm, still anxious to be loved, I don't mean by lovers, and a vehement enemy, but openly."[14]

Walpole's diary, in which day after day he punctiliously noted the names of the people he met in Paris, makes it possible to outline precisely the beginnings and the development of his friendship with Madame du Deffand. After a few intermittent visits to the *salon* Saint-Joseph in September, October and November, the diary reveals a certain regularity in December. Walpole and Madame du Deffand met fourteen times and on Christmas Eve they attended Midnight Mass together in the *marquise*'s private pew in the convent chapel. On the 29th Walpole supped at Saint-Joseph, bringing a New Year's gift. In the New Year they became even more intimately friendly. In January, February and March they met on average every other day. In April, as the date of Walpole's departure approached, they met daily. Not only was Walpole a frequent guest at the *salon*, but he had become part of the *marquise*'s circle of friends. They supped together in Hénault's beautiful house where the old Président's two nieces, Madame de Jonzac and Madame d'Aubeterre did the honours. Together they visited the grand establishments of the maréchale de Luxembourg, Madame de Boufflers—the *Idole*—and Madame de Forcalquier.

On 6 March 1766 Walpole wrote to his friend Craufurd, to whom Madame du Deffand was greatly attached: "Your good old woman wept like a child, with her poor no eyes, as I read your letter to her. I did not wonder; it is kind, friendly, delicate and just—so just that it vexes me to be forced to continually combat the goodness of her heart, and destroy her fond visions of friendship ... You will forgive these details about a person you love, and have so much reason to love; nor am I ashamed of interesting myself exceedingly about her. To say nothing of her extraordinary parts, she is certainly the most generous friendly being upon earth."

Walpole was probably beginning to realise that the *marquise*'s anxiety to be loved and her vain illusions were becoming dangerously concentrated on him. A note which can be dated somewhere around April, leaves no doubt that a feeling of expectation had been created which must have alarmed the English visitor.

MADAME DU DEFFAND TO WALPOLE

This Wednesday at 7 o'clock in the morning

If you still intend to see me today, come early, that is to say at around two or three o'clock. I have a hundred thousand things to tell you, I would not be able to talk easily if I thought you were in a hurry to leave.

You are right to love Madame de Choiseul (*love*, forgive me the word, we are agreed on its meaning), she thinks as I do—and speaks about it as I would speak had you not forbidden me. You are wrong to leave us, I am sure you will find great pleasure here in the future.

Your note wrung my heart, and increased in me that word which you have forbidden me. I will not be able to follow your advice or your example, nor even I could add, my own experience. What will happen will happen, but I will be your friend in spite of you and in spite of commonsense.

Any attempt to explain Walpole's personality or to try to understand what it was that inspired Madame du Deffand's fantasy, can only be helped by T.B. Macaulay's famous portrait—or rather indictment: "He was . . . the most eccentric, the most artificial, the most fastidious, the most capricious of men. His mind was a bundle of inconsistent whims and affectations. His features were covered by mask within mask. When outer disguise of obvious affectation was removed, you were still as far as ever from seeing the real man. He played innumerable parts and over-acted them all. When he talked misanthropy, he out-Timoned Timon. When he talked philanthropy, he left Howard at an immeasurable distance. He scoffed at courts, and kept a chronicle of their most trifling scandal; at society, and was blown about by its slightest veerings of opinion; at literary fame, and left fair copies of his private letters, with copious notes, to be published after his decease; at rank, and never for a moment forgot that he was an Honorable; at the practice of entail, and tasked the ingenuity of conveyances to tie up his villa in the strictest settlement."[15]

It could be said in mitigation of such a merciless portrait that nowadays Walpole would be seen as a real "dilettante" in the accepted eighteenth-century meaning of the word: an aristocrat who would regard as degrading any form of professionalism, however erudite, concerning his many, sometimes madcap interests which encompassed literature, gardening, art, history, poetry, the theatre, publishing. In this respect both the creations to which he dedicated nearly half a century of loving care are revealing: his immense correspondence[16] and the museum-house of Strawberry Hill.[17] Both were perfectly compatible with the profession of a gentleman. As far as public life was concerned, Walpole's attitude was that of a man who was used to politics without having a passion for them and who, as the son of a man who had governed the country for over twenty years, sat in Parliament as though by right, preferring not to play a leading part but rather to exercise an indirect influence on the party in the tradition of his father. He gives the impression in politics as in life of not intending to compete in any way with his father, a virile, sanguine man of vitality and interested in women. This did not prevent him from admiring his father and venerating his memory, nor, even though he was the younger son, of having a strong sense of family, and a feeling for its propriety and traditions. He always did his best for his family. The only real passion of his life was for his mother. When Lady Walpole died in 1737, Horace was twenty and he experienced "the first and greatest sorrow"[18] of his entire existence, so that his emotional life was damaged definitively.

Walpole's emotional life was sublimated in social intercourse, habit and great self-indulgence. His interests, tastes and fantasies never developed into passions although they were punctiliously satisfied. Erudition, the delights of society, the cataloguing of antiques, the pleasures of the table, a British love of dogs, the contemplation of a painting, the writing of a letter—these were all equally essential parts of his elaborate daily existence. Yet, according to Lytton Strachey whose portrait of Walpole directly contradicts Macaulay's, it would be wrong to describe the owner of Strawberry Hill as superficial: "He was capable both of sincere attachments and of strong dislikes ... he was sensitive to an extraordinary degree; and the defects—for defects they certainly were—which showed in social intercourse, were caused by an excess of this quality of sensitiveness rather than by lack of genuine feeling. His angry, cutting sentences, his constant mockery of his enemies, his constant quarrels with his friends, all these things were certainly not the result of a coldness of heart. And there was another element in his character which must never be forgotten in any estimate of Walpole's relations with other people—his pride. At heart he was a complete aristocrat; it was almost impossible for him to be unreserved. The masks he wore were imposed upon him by his caste, by his breeding, by his own intimate sense of the decencies and proprieties of life; so that his hatreds and his loves, so easily aroused and so intensely cherished, were forced to express themselves in spiteful little taunts and in artificial compliments."[19]

But Walpole needed the masks not only to present an image of himself which accorded with the code of behavior Strachey describes, but also to prevent others, and perhaps himself, from an awareness of a certain vulnerability which filled him with insecurity. This feeling of discomfort was betrayed by a constant, unrelenting fear of ridicule which sometimes poisoned even the simplest facts of existence. "I took care not to expose myself," is the revealing sentence from this Parisian journal concerning an innocent request.[20] Social life which was so necessary to him was also a dangerous game full of pitfalls and risks, taking place under the supervision of malevolent eyes ready to notice the slightest weakness or the least alteration of tone.

It is strange that someone so suspicious of pretence and so obsessed with the problem of naturalness as was Madame du Deffand should not have been irritated by Walpole's affected behaviour. She may have been distracted by the difference of language, education and culture, or deceived by the brusque, cutting, even disagreeable manner which Walpole occasionally loved to display; or perhaps she simply sensed that he was a fundamentally insecure and vulnerable man.

It would be useless to study all the different portraits of this English writer in order to discover the secret of his physical attraction. Madame du Deffand must have had to reconstruct a picture of this loose-limbed Englishman from other people's descriptions: his gait made hesitant by gout, his elongated oval face, large, black, wide-open eyes, regular nose, strong, rounded chin and delicate mouth on which a faint smile played; a smile which hardened from portrait to portrait until it was transformed into the bitter little grimace of Reynolds's portrait in 1754. The only sensory perception—probably a strong one—which the *marquise* could have had of Walpole must have come from his voice. We know from a compatriot of his, that "it was not loud, but had an extremely agreeable tone and was supremely gentlemanly,"[21] and perhaps all the more seductive to Madame du Deffand by virtue of the particular charm which foreigners sometimes have when speaking one's language.

That voice carried Madame du Deffand back in time, far from the polemics of the *philosophes* and ideological argument, back to the dilettante, aristocratic society of her youth. Walpole had a horror of philosophical discussion. He treated the *Lumières* with complacency[22] and looked down socially on professional writers. For him, as for the *marquise,* culture was a pleasure, a curiosity, a distraction. It may be supposed that he displayed the same qualities as an entertainer as he did in his correspondence; a lightness, swiftness and sharpness of tone and the art of never boring. Even Macaulay at the end of his indictment was obliged to recognise that Walpole "never convinces the reason, or fills the imagination, or touches the heart; but he keeps the mind of the reader constantly attentive and constantly entertained."[23] And again:

"His style is one of those peculiar styles by which everybody is attracted, and which nobody can safely venture to imitate. He is a mannerist whose manner has become perfectly easy to him."[24]

As a stone thrown into a pond is the epicentre of the violent and sudden ripples which spread around it, so the arrival of the Englishman at Saint-Joseph disturbed Madame du Deffand's calm indifference and gave rise to a real change in her life. The *marquise*'s vague and always disappointed expectations that something might happen to catch her attention, to drag her, even for a moment, out of the painful immobility of her ennui, unexpectedly found a new centre.

Prudence, diffidence, reason were all suddenly wiped out and Walpole became the object of her exclusive, violent and passionate attention. Any definition of this sentiment might be questionable, if it were not for the ambiguity of the word forbidden the *marquise* by Walpole.[25] Madame du Deffand, now aged sixty-eight, was old and infirm and had been blind for more than ten years, yet she spoke of "love" to a foreigner who was more than twenty years younger than she, whose appearance she could only guess at and who lived far away in another country. Doubtless the word has many meanings and is weakened by fashionable language, abused by widespread sentimentality, and carelessly used not only to describe emotions, including friendship, but to indicate tastes and passing fancies. Aware of all these nuances, Madame du Deffand thought she could use the word "love" with impunity, but Walpole was not yet well enough acquainted with French usage not to be worried by a term which came dangerously near to describing the real situation.

After an understandable initial hesitation even Madame du Deffand's biographers have to stop juggling with words and confront the nature of her relationship with Walpole. "What name would describe a sentiment which having all the ardour, all the anxiety, all the jealousies, the transports, the exaltations and the tears of love, if not it?"[26] Sainte-Beuve spoke of a "revenge of nature, one of those summers which only decided to blossom after the season had truly begun,"[27] of the late and violent passion of a heart which had hitherto denied sentiment. However attractive this picture may appear, it would seem to be only partly true. Madame du Deffand, who continually denied her passionate nature, had simply reached a stage of life when she no longer had the energy or the will to control herself. At least once before, at the time of her friendship with d'Alembert, the *marquise* experienced similar feelings to those which she now cherished for Walpole. It is impossible to tell how the libertine experience may have affected her and exhausted her emotional expectations, if ever she had any. It is clear that from the time of her relationship with Hénault, the *marquise* seemed to have abandoned all interest of that kind. Friendship with d'Alembert re-awakened her feelings: the passion was transferred on to the level of intellectual understanding, but was none the less violent for that. Her relationship with the *philosophe* was also marked by exclusivity, possessiveness and jealousy; but at the time Madame du Deffand was more than twenty years younger, confident in her personal freedom, her vitality and her success, and in full control of her life. But the two stories are alike in more ways than one. Both friendships were based on intellectual affinity for much younger single men with difficult, suspicious natures and of doubtful virility. Besides neither d'Alembert nor Walpole conformed to the tedious conventions of prevailing fashion which both irritated the *marquise* and aroused her suspicions. They must both have seemed reassuringly un-French to her. According to Galiani, d'Alembert "was not like any Frenchman, and he had Italian rather than French defects and qualities. For instance he was never dressed well nor in good taste ... In conversation he had an Italian openness and wit, not the pedantic affectation of the French *petits-maîtres*."[28] As for the English traveller, everything about him bespoke his origins, and his boorish "Englishness" was Madame du Deffand's delight and torment.

In fact these coincidences count only where Madame du Deffand is concerned: d'Alembert and Walpole could not have been less alike. The first was a nameless intellectual without social position, intent on rigorously and relentlessly following his vocation as a reformer. The second was an aristocrat determined to extract the maximum hedonistic pleasure from the exercise of his intelligence, who mistrusted philosophy and, for all his scepticism, meticulously respected social convention. They were the antithesis to each other and represented the two extremes of the *marquise*'s attitudes over the years. We have seen how her break with d'Alembert drove Madame du Deffand to take up more and more conservative positions and move towards a hostility on principle to anything concerning the enlightenment movement. This negative attitude was unexpectedly confirmed by her meeting with Walpole. She saw the English writer as the perfect incarnation of the aristocratic idea of being, which she thought had been jeopardised for ever, and as the positive champion of a campaign led up to date under a negative banner. Madame du Deffand had finally rid herself of d'Alembert's ghost and no longer suffered from "privation of feeling; with the pain of being unable to go without."[29] She had met someone of equal rank who shared her tastes: a new man to love.

The elation of an infirm old woman with no emotional ties, no resources, tortured by ennui and insomnia who finally finds something to hold on to and a way of feeling alive again may be surprising, but it hardly requires justification. But what led Walpole to become involved in a relationship the ambiguity and embarrassment of which he soon sensed?[30] The author of *The Castle of Otranto* may not have involved himself in love affairs with women, but he frequently chose to make friends of older women with a turbulent past—Catherine Clive, Lady Hervey and Lady Suffolk among others. It was almost as though he participated indirectly in experiences which he did not care to risk personally. Besides Walpole was fascinated by old age itself; he took a fanatical interest in it as though delving into the past were preferable to the present: a delightful, varied picturesque past evoked by a direct witness, but with no dangers for the listener and without the compromising threats of the present. Slices of life seen through glass and ready to be turned into history, the kind of history consisting of personalities and anecdotes and incidents which interested Walpole. Madame du Deffand must have seemed almost mythological to him: "an old sibyl retired in the corner of a convent";[31] she could describe half a century of French history and through her he could participate as a privileged guest in the last act of a long uninterrupted charade now mostly populated by ghosts. "I played at cavagnole there two nights ago with the survivors of the last century; the youngest was Madame de Ségur, a natural daughter of the Regent, who can be no chicken, and I did not once wish myself at a debate on the Stamp Act. An old woman that cheats at brelan, is to me as respectable a personage as a patriot that cheats at eloquence; and if Livy had been a matron and writ the memoirs of the Roman dowagers that played at par and impar, as well as he has done the history of consuls and tributes, I had as lief read them."[32]

But Madame du Deffand was not merely a source of history, she was still considered to be one of the wittiest and most intelligent women in Paris and her house was an exceptional place in which to meet the flower of the French aristocracy. It is hardly surprising if Walpole was flattered by the attentions of the old hostess nor that he thought of her—her correspondence with Voltaire was already famous—as an ideal correspondent for himself. With Madame du Deffand, the vast tableau of contemporary society on which Walpole had been working obsessively for years, would extend even to France. At a time when princes from all over Europe united to hire correspondents to keep them in touch with Parisian life, Walpole saw the possibility of an exclusive source of information. No one could inform him better than the *marquise* of the latest, most secret and most enticing gossip exchanged between Paris and Versailles. But Madame du Deffand's first letter was enough to make him change his mind. They both had quite different expectations from their letter-writing and Walpole soon realised that corresponding with the *marquise* was a dangerous activity to be undertaken with the maximum caution.

During Walpole's last months in Paris, his friendship with Madame du Deffand grew more and more intense and the *marquise* did everything in her power to entertain and amuse him: there were plays, grand society dinners, intimate supper parties with the most distinguished guests, enquiries after antiques and curios to enrich the Strawberry Hill collections. Then there were long conversations interwoven with anecdotes, repartee, literary talk, gossip, and intimate tête-a-têtes between two people with many shared likes and dislikes and who had above all the same taste and the same social attitude.

Walpole was fascinated by the *marquise*, flattered by her attention, attracted to and reassured by her venerable age which precluded any question of gallantry, so he forgot his discomfort and his affectations and gave himself up to the pleasures of confiding in a woman old enough to be his mother. Their conversations gradually took on a more personal tone. Madame du Deffand told him about her life and her youthful love affairs, about d'Alembert, her association with Julie and her sudden betrayal, she confided in him her real feelings about the Saint-Joseph *habitués*, her likes, her reservations and her resentments. For his part Walpole admitted his weaknesses, his private preferences, and he confessed to his terrible fear of appearing ridiculous. It was probably because of her distance from the London scene that he confided in Madame du Deffand with unusual frankness, perhaps more than he had ever confided in anyone else.

At four o'clock in the afternoon of 17 April, after a seven month stay,

Walpole left Paris to return to England. That evening he reached Chantilly where he spent the first night of his journey and immediately wrote to the *marquise,* requesting as he always did that she should either destroy it or return it to him. Madame du Deffand remembered this letter, together with one also sent at a moment of departure on 5 October, with more emotion than all the others she received during the fifteen years of her correspondence with Walpole. The letter which would provide an essential key to their relationship can, alas, only be guessed at from the *marquise*'s reply.

MADAME DU DEFFAND TO WALPOLE   *Saturday, 19 April 1766*

I was very surprised on receiving your letter; I did not expect it; but I see that anything can be expected of you.

I begin by assuring you of my prudence; I do not suspect any disagreeable motive for the advice you give me. No one will know of our correspondence and I will do exactly what you stipulate. I have already begun by disguising my sorrow, and, except to the Président and Madame de Jonzac to whom I have had to speak of you, I have not mentioned your name. I would feel a kind of repugnance at making such a declaration to anyone else but you; but you are the best of men and full of such good intentions that I can never suspect one word or action of yours. Had you admitted earlier what you thought of me, I would have been calmer and consequently more reserved. The desire to conquer and, having conquered, to advance, makes for imprudence: that is my history where you are concerned: remember too, that my age and my confidence in not appearing mad must naturally add to the certainty of being safe from ridicule. Everything has been said on this subject, and as no one can hear us, I want to be at my ease and to say that it is impossible to love more tenderly than I love you; that I believe that one is rewarded sooner or later according to one's deserts and since I believe that I have a tender and sincere heart, I am gathering the fruits at the end of my life. I do not want to allow myself to tell you everything I think, despite the joy you give me: this happiness is tinged with sadness because your absence must be a long one. So I would like to avoid anything which would make this letter into an elegy; I only beg that you keep your word and write to me in the greatest confidence, and be persuaded that I am more yours than mine. For my part I will tell you everything that concerns me and I will talk to you as if we were alone by the fireside.

The evening before last I gave the uncle[33] and the niece[34] your letter to Jean-Jacques;[35] with the exception of three or four names which were changed, it is perfect. The uncle sent me ten or twelve lines which he thought could be added, but I think they would spoil it; I am sure that you would think likewise. I send it you all the same because you might make use of it on another occasion.

My excuses for not going to Montmorency were well received, and perhaps I will go there on Monday. My cold did not develop. I supped at the Président's yesterday with Madame de Mirepoix, Monsieur and Madame de Caraman, *your good friend,*[36] Madame de Valentinois and Monsieur Shuvalov; your name was not mentioned. I sup tonight with Madame Dupin, with Madame de Forcalquier, but tomorrow I will not sup with you.[37] I looked at my post book and saw that you may very possibly be in London early on Sunday: in the same book I saw that the *post-chaise* from Paris to Calais leaves only on Sundays, but that the one from Calais to Paris arrives on Tuesdays and Saturdays.

I do not beg you to write often. Saint Augustin said: "Love and do as you please."[38] It is certainly the best thing he said.

I did not sleep at all last night and I wrote the first four lines of this letter with an inkstand[39] which I do not think I showed you. If they are not indecipherable, I could use it sometimes.

Yesterday I saw Vernage who had arrived from Versailles and who is not due to return there until Monday. The Queen is better, and she improves a little every day. She is spitting up less, and has a light fever, but both must cease if there is to be no need for concern. At the moment there is some hope, but if the quaking returns all will be lost, it would mean a further suppuration.[40]

Last evening I received a letter from Monsieur de Beauvau. He is very friendly towards me, he reproaches me for not having written to him and invites me to sup with him. I could easily go there on Sunday in eight or fifteen days time, but it would not be with you. Why am I not English? I could not say; why are you not French? I would not like you to have the French character.

Remember that you are my tutor, my director; do not abandon my education; I will always be very obedient, but above all never allow me to be ignorant of anything I can do or say which might contribute to facilitating or hastening your return.

Write and tell me when you have seen Monsieur Craufurd. I submit all my judgement to yours, but I am very much mistaken if the two of you are not both made to love each other very much.

To return to your letter to Jean-Jacques. It is perfectly good and in the best possible tone. I wager that now I would recognise your style without being mistaken. I would not be displeased if a little war broke out between you and Jean-Jacques; you could be quite sure that the laugh would be on your side as would all the wits and people of taste. What is the Peasant of the Danube[41] doing and saying? Will we see him again soon? How is Mr Conway?

Farewell, Monsieur, do not forget to tell me about your health. I will number my letters. Do number yours. It is a way of knowing if any of them are lost.

I thought that Wiart had begun this letter after what I had written; he could not have done so according to him, so I sent it you separately.

It is impossible to tell whether the letter from Chantilly was a sudden revelation of an unsusupected truth or if it quite simply gave rise to an enormous, unintended and embarrassing misunderstanding. It was probably a mixture of the two. Alone in his inn room, after an intense Parisian season, about to return to his old habits and in the no man's land of travel, Walpole may have momentarily forgotten his self-image and been moved by the thought of the friend he had just left. He may have questioned the significance of their friendship and allowed himself the liberty of confiding what he felt for her, only to repent it bitterly a few hours later. The exalted tone of Madame du Deffand's reply is not enough to indicate precisely the nature of her friend's feelings. If it were not for Walpole's circumspection and his later anxiety to deny the episode, it would be unreasonable to suppose that the letter from Chantilly contained anything more than a declaration of devotion for an old, infirm lady on the part of a usually hesitant and reserved man. The idea that Walpole may have made a compromising admission is reinforced not only by the determination with which Madame du Deffand clung to the meaning of the letter, but by Walpole's fear of suffering the most appalling fate of being made to appear ridiculous by it. "It was a long time before the date of our acquaintanceship, that this fear of ridicule took root in my soul, and you must certainly remember the point to which it obsessed me and how little I spoke to you about it. Do not seek a recent cause for it. From the moment when I ceased to be young, I have had a horrible fear of becoming a ridiculous old man."[42] But ridiculous for what reason? Because something which is not quite clear and which probably never happened outside the imagination of the one who longed for it and the one who feared it.

The letter from Chantilly was the first of a correspondence which lasted for nearly fifteen years and incorporated almost 1700 letters, of which 955 still exist. Of these, 840 are from Madame du Deffand and 100—mostly fragments—from Walpole. Fourteen are from the *marquise*'s secretary and companion, Wiart, and one from her lady-in-waiting. Seven hundred of Walpole's letters were destroyed on his instructions. From this time onwards the correspondence constituted Madame du Deffand's *raison d'être*, the joy and torment of her existence. Neither anxiety, mortification nor rejection could destroy the miracle of having something to think about, a centre for her emotions and her imagination.

But all these letters that were written with such driving passion neither tell a story nor reveal a developing emotional relationship; they merely display the whole gamut of an obsession. Madame du Deffand wants Walpole's attention, his confidence and his affection, she dreams of a perfect understanding with him and longs to be free to use the language of love. Walpole's refusal pained her, made her indignant and offended her but it did not change her, nor cause her to give up hope. Lewis points out that the *marquise*'s letters covered the same ground in 1780 as they did in 1766, and took the same form: "(1) affectionate statement, mingled with self-analysis, (2) bewildered and angry defence of herself, (3) impersonal recital of 'proper names' demanded by Walpole, followed by (1).[43] The pattern is the same in 1780 as in 1766, one does not feel that the principals have progressed at all in their relationship, but they have seasoned, they have settled down into a routine of affection and exasperation."[44]

One wonders what induced Walpole to maintain a tie which he saw as a constant threat to his reputation and peace of mind, and why he continued year after year to humiliate a poor old lady instead of cutting once and for all the fine thread of the correspondence which united them. Not only did he keep up the correspondence, however, but made on four occasions a long and tiring journey to see his friend. All Walpole's ambiguity was encapsulated in this contradiction, and to it is owed the survival of Madame du Deffand's letters.

We know that Walpole's life's work was his correspondence. He always devoted passionate attention to his letters, often demanding that they be returned to him for final corrections: he wrote them with future readers in mind, always careful to safeguard the self-image he wished to project, that of an ironical, capricious, blasé aristocrat of impeccable honour, impenetrable in his private life. From this point of view, the letters from Saint-Joseph must have been a real nightmare for him. The *marquise* was uncontrollable and uncorrectable, and the reproofs which Walpole was obliged to repeat in letter after letter are no less ridiculous than the old sibyl's effusions. Besides, nothing guaranteed the secrecy of the correspondence; it could have been divulged by the *marquise* herself. In order to avoid this eventuality, Walpole was lavish with his threats: the letters could be intercepted by the *Cabinet noir* and their unusualness could provide the King with a quarter of an hour's amusement—in fact copies of eleven letters from Walpole and seven from the *marquise* ultimately came to light in the archives of the Foreign Ministry—finally, after the death of the *marquise* they might fall into indiscreet hands. So, in the spring of 1769, Walpole asked Madame du Deffand to send him back all the letters he had written her until that date, and demanded the return at regular intervals and by trusted messengers, of any he wrote from that time onwards.

Having regained possession of his correspondence, he wrote to Conway (28 September 1774) justifying his anxiety with the "very bad French" in which the letters are written and the fear of offending people mentioned in them. Walpole bequeathed the duty of destroying his correspondence after his death to his literary executrix, Miss Berry. Walpole, however, never decided to destroy the most exciting documents of the whole affair which were the *marquise*'s letters. He merely excised several passages with scissors whilst conserving them all and leaving Miss Berry with the task of publishing them.

Why did a man so obsessed with his reputation keep such undeniable proof of his own weakness? Proof which was all the more irrefutable for the fact that it twisted his answers which probably represented the voice of reason. "Was it vanity at having over eight hundred love letters from the most brilliant woman of her time? Was it because he saw that these letters were an invaluable historical record essential to his scheme to transmit the eighteenth century to posterity? Or was it that he felt that these letters were works of art, fit to rank with Madame de Sévigné's, and so entitled to exist in their own right? Doubtless it was a combination of all these things, but we may be certain of one thing, that he saw how badly he appeared in them. He must have been tempted to burn the lot, but he didn't, and this should be counted for him."[45]

This assessment of Walpole's enthusiastic editor is excellent, but there may be a fourth hypothesis which need not contradict the others and which concerns Walpole's overall behaviour throughout the whole affair with the *marquise*. Walpole loved Madame du Deffand; he had entirely placed his trust in her like a son finally rediscovering his lost mother. Elsewhere, in literary metaphor, he expressed the obsessive fantasy which was the flip side of his Anglo-Saxon nature: in *The Castle of Otranto*, conceived and written as an hallucination,[46] and in the twisted totalism of his drama of incest.[47] But this placing of trust inspired fear in Walpole; it authorised the *marquise* to make emotional demands which terrified him and made her a permanent witness to a truth which he wished to hide primarily from himself. Hence the necessity for such a lengthy correspondence, the writer's desire to forget whilst finding it impossible to deny his own nature. By destroying his own letters whilst preserving Madame du Deffand's, Walpole did justice not only to the *marquise* and her future readers, but to himself.

MADAME DU DEFFAND TO WALPOLE   *Monday, 21 April 1766 in answer*
                                        to your letter from Amiens

If you were French I would not hesitate in thinking you a great coxcomb; you are English, so you are only a great madman. From what do you deduce, pray, that *I am given to indiscretions and romantic transports?* Let the *indiscretions* pass; that might just be said; but as for *romantic transports,* they make me furious, and I would willingly tear out your eyes which are said to be so beautiful but which you can certainly not suspect of having turned my head. I wonder what insult I could pay you, but none come to me; it must be that I am not yet at ease in writing to you. You are so fond of that saint from Livry[48] that my imagination is bridled. Not that I claim to be comparable to her but I am convinced that your passion for her makes everything which does not resemble her seem silly and flat. Let us return to the romantic transports: I who am the declared enemy of anything with the slightest hint of such things, I who have always declared war on them, I who have made enemies of all those who indulged in such nonsense today stand accused myself! And by whom am I accused? By Horace Walpole and by a certain little Craufurd who dares not explain himself so clearly, but who tacitly gives his agreement. Ah, fie, fie, Gentlemen, that is very wicked. I will say, like my dear compatriots when they hear of something particularly hard and ferocious: "That is very English." But know and keep it in mind, that I do not love you more than I should and not I believe beyond your desserts. Come back, come back to Paris and you will see how I will behave. I am, I admit, very impatient for you to see for yourself the success of your lessons and the effects of my indignation. From this moment I am beginning a new pattern of behaviour; I no longer mention your name; that vexes me a little I admit; it would give me great pleasure to be able to read your letters with someone who recognised their quality and with whom I could laugh about them; but to tell the truth if I were to abandon myself and give full rein to my natural imprudence, I would find no one worthy of such a confidence. Since your departure, everything around me seems to have become even sillier; I fear I may fall into an unbearable ennui. When we were in the same place I divined what you thought, you knew what I thought and it did not take us long to tell each other. This time has passed, and God knows when it will come again. Be Abelard, if you will, but do not count on my ever being Héloise. Have I never told you of the dislike I have for those letters?[49] I have been persecuted by all the translations made of them and which I have been forced to hear; the mixture, or rather the jumble of piety, metaphysics and natural philosophy seemed to me false, erroneous and disgusting. Choose to be anyone but Abelard for me; be, if you like, Saint François de Sales; I like him enough and I would willingly be your Philothée.[50] But let us leave all that.

Do you know that I am hoping for a letter from you from Calais? But the one I await with the greatest impatience is the one which will be dated from London.

My Sunday, yesterday, was pitiful; I was counting on three

Broglies[51] who did not come because their old uncle,[52] the *abbé* was on his deathbed, and he died at six o'clock this morning. Madame d'Aiguillon did not come. I replaced them all with the duc de Villars and Monsieur Shuvalov. I want it to be said of the latter that he has turned my head and that I have quite forgotten the English for the Russians. Madame d'Aiguillon leaves on Friday for Rueil[53] and will only come again in passing. I was to go to Montmorency today but I used my cold as a pretext to excuse myself. I will spend the evening with the Président in deplorable company; but I will recall a refrain from a song which Chardin quotes in his *Voyages* and which was composed for the return of a minister from exile:

Lui à l'écart tous les hommes étaient egaux.[54]

But I am letting this silly prattling run away with me and I am forgetting Jean-Jacques. I like your reflections, but the kindness of your letter[55] and a little drop of malice stifled in me the inner feeling that it was not good to torment a poor creature who had done you no harm. His letter[56] is extremely impertinent, his protectors and protectresses deserve to be reviled, but you want peace. You have excessive sensibility, you wish to return here (do you not?), you do not wish to find the slightest thorn here. Sacrifice this letter then; it will cost me more than it will cost you. If Madame de Forcalquier were worthy, I would ask your permission to show it to her; but she understands nothing about anything, and I see with great sorrow that Mr Craufurd's first judgement of her was absolutely right. Last Saturday when I supped with her at the house of her good friend, Madame Dupin, she read me a little something written by her in the form of a letter which is an apologia for old age in which she demonstrated that one could be in love with someone of a hundred. It disgusted me so much that I was about to try to prove that one could not be in love with someone of forty. This fine work was addressed to me; I begged her to give it me, but she pretended to throw it on the fire and I pretended to believe it had burned; that saves you the trouble of reading it, for I was counting on sending it to you.

For the last five or six days the Queen has been getting better and better; but there is still some pus and she still has a fever and as I have already told you, all is lost if there is any quaking. The children[57] are well; it was indigestion brought on by a stuffed pullet which they had been given to eat. Madame la Dauphine[58] is not well; she was bled on Saturday evening because of a high fever and she was spitting blood. The spitting has stopped but her condition is very worrying.

All Montmorency returns tomorrow after supper. I know that that gives me no pleasure; I will tell you in a few days time whether it will have pained me.

Farewell, my tutor, I do not hold to that name, it is temporary, until another comes to my mind.

I quite like being your dear little one.[59]

Give me some instructions as to the days I should post your letters.

Twenty-four years before receiving Walpole's reprimand from Amiens, Madame du Deffand wrote to Hénault from Forges that she had "neither temperament nor romance." The Président replied, "I pity you greatly and you know as well as another the price of your loss." Now with the repetition of that statement the *marquise* must have felt the irony of seeing the situation turned to her disadvantage. The denial of romanticism was no longer born of arrogant aggression, but of self-defence. So a few years later she was to repeat, "Your reproach that I love the romantic makes everyone laugh who knows me, no one has ever been less suspected of it, I find it quite singular that you should know me so little."[60] Madame du Deffand meant it and was probably unaware that she was concealing the reality of her feelings behind an aesthetic. She supported with conviction the true classic, aristocratic style of her education against the invasion of a modern, bourgeois, *sensiblerie* which was revolutionising taste in all its manifestations, from art to literature and dress. It was an uncompromising and exclusive decision which required considerable sacrifice. "I have a natural antipathy for the crusades, and have had since my childhood. I hate Don Quixote and stories of madmen, I do not like chivalresque novels or metaphysical ones,"[61] probably beginning with *The Castle of Otranto* were it not by Walpole. But Robert Mauzi remarks that "such a vivacious defence seems suspect. The persistent denial of all life of the imagination which is an ideal compensation, must without doubt be the real reason for Madame du Deffand's ennui. And this refusal itself is no more than an inverted form of the need for love and for nearly absolute happiness. Madame du Deffand was permanently paralysed by the fear of suffering, by her hatred of compromise and by a mythical frustration designed to anticipate the risk of real frustration, and so she denied herself the retreat and refuge where she could have unburdened her soul of crude reality and finally lived that life which belongs to the consciousness alone. Does the 'insult' paid her in believing her to be romantic not consist in the discovery of her secret?"[62]

So the woman who a few months later was to write, "I would like to send you my soul in place of a letter" reacted against the accusation of romantic outbursts with a firmness that was untypical of her subjection to Walpole. Now that she needed to, she could no longer rid herself of the ambiguous style, of what Mauzi calls "mythical frustration," which had become indispensable to her defence against the recriminations of her "tutor."

From the start of her correspondence with Walpole, Madame du Deffand was totally submissive, not so much for rational reasons—the letters from England were necessary to her and she was without any bargaining power whatsoever—but because she trusted in her friend's feelings. For a long time the memory of Walpole's presence and of intimate tête-à-têtes unthreatened by the indiscretion of others combined with the "warm, alive" impression given by the Chantilly letter, made Madame du Deffand suffer Walpole's ill-treatment and explain it as the manifestation of a peculiar, unpredictable character, obsessed by suspicion and ridicule. But is anyone more persevering than a submissive person? From the earliest letters, Madame du Deffand entrenched herself behind a line of resistance which consisted in absorbing Walpole's aggression blow by blow, fielding it occasionally with commonsense or irony, sometimes appealing to his compassion. Always convinced there was misunderstanding, she confidently continued the dialogue, initially careful to avoid new disagreements, eventually carried away by the necessity of speaking about the only thing which mattered to her, her feelings. The aim of her letters was to maintain a continuous relationship with Walpole and to prevent distance, a different life-style and different surroundings from alienating her from him. So the *marquise* swamped Walpole with accounts of her daily life and her thoughts and with scrupulously detailed descriptions of events and people in the social circle which they had shared for several months and which had cemented their friendship.

The joy of Madame du Deffand's first letter, its freedom of expression and her hope of intimacy must have annoyed and frightened Walpole and driven him once and for all with a clearly expressed reply, to correct his correspondent's tone and expectations. It was a brutal blow but the *marquise* in the first page of her reply, showed that she absorbed it surprisingly easily. Only two days later she took up the thread again and, in a letter which can be seen as a perfect example of her correspondence with Walpole; one by one she confronted the forbidden subjects. It is a long diary, put down and picked up again six times in five days, from Wednesday 23 to Sunday 27 April. The faithful account of events, encounters and conversations does not hide the fact that the centre of the *marquise*'s existence now lies in this dialogue–monologue. She lived her life daily through a series of incidents which may be of greater interest to her correspondent than to herself. So begins again her old detachment from the world around her, but this time the causes are twofold: the primary importance of her passion for Walpole and her desire to sacrifice anything that might distract her from it. She veers between memories, illusions, fears and hopes, all of which vary according to the mood of the moment, sometimes fired by the power of the past, sometimes by anxiety for the future.

This permanent concentration on the same idea, albeit disguised by the chronicling of events, and the great liberty with which it is continuously and unexpectedly reintroduced, is all the more surprising for the fact that an outside agent was required to do the writing. Except on very rare occasions the *marquise* was obliged to dictate her letters. In the daytime she nearly always dictated to the faithful Wiart, but in the small hours when she was unable to sleep and her anguished mind could find no peace, she turned to the valet, Colmant.

Madame du Deffand's consummate conversational skills must have helped her dictate these monologues. Quickness, conciseness, concentration and an ability to grasp the fleeting, all combined in her to produce a great talent for improvisation which perfectly suited her individual, impatient intelligence. But the obligation to satisfy Walpole with long accounts of society and the literary world created difficulties for her. According to Duisit in his *Madame du Deffand épistolière*, recounting bored the *marquise*. ("What I most hate is recounting"):[63] "Madame du Deffand remembers events and people in so far as they please her taste or aggravate her mood. In both cases it seems that instead of welcoming the real, she rather projects her personality on the real and tends to reshape it whilst judging it, interpreting it (comic spirit), or deforming it (satire)."[64] In any case, despite Walpole's threats, Madame du Deffand continued to speak of herself, of her thoughts, her feelings, and the need to surprise her correspondent, to avoid his anger and to gain his favour drove her to endless efforts of style and of imagination.

MADAME DU DEFFAND TO WALPOLE   *This Wednesday 23 April 1766*
                                      at nine o'clock in the morning

I will not wait until I have received a letter from London to write to you; we agreed that I would do so as soon as I felt the wish. I must tell you that I greatly regret that your pretty letter to Jean-Jacques should be a pure loss, it was certainly the wisest decision; but here is what I think. I should show it to my grandmama,[65] and give her a copy asking her to keep it as a great secret, and allowing her to show it only to her husband if she esteems that it would please him, but that he should not speak about it. That would make you agreeable to each other, and I am certain that the grandmama would not speak about it, even to her husband, if after my remonstrations and the considerations which I would point out to her, she judged it the least inconvenient for you or me. She called yesterday but found me out. I have just written to her and told her that on leaving you charged me with the duty of paying court to her on your behalf, and that I will fill four pages with everything you think about her and feel for her, that I would be obliged only to her for your return, that she alone can draw you here. Do not scold me, it is the first time that I speak of you, I will mention you to no one except my grandmama, and to tell the truth I would have no merit in doing so for there is no one worthy. Since your departure the evenings I spend with the Président are detestable; the Jonzac niece holds court for Charlemagne,[66] the other niece for King Guillemot;[67] on the right there is the greatest dignity and on the left, the greatest triviality, and the greatest tediousness in the centre, I swear! However, it is you who sustain me; when one loves and is loved one is above everything else.

Of all the inhabitants of Montmorency, I have as yet seen only Pont-de-Veyle; he assured me that the *maréchale* [68] is perfectly pleased with me and that the little *comtesse*[69] deigned to mention me. Her Wednesday and Thursday suppers are beginning again; suppers are to take place on Fridays at the Président's house and mine alternately; it will be the most marvellous company, let it not be the most tedious.

I have a fine plan in mind. A beautiful apartment is becoming vacant in Saint-Joseph: I want to have it let to the bishop of Tréguier and to dispose of it at my will when he is in residence in his diocese; imagine what use I mean to put it to; this idea is not at all absurd and it will depend on you for it not to be a dream.[70] I am very impatient to have news of your arrival; I am anxious about the crossing; I would give the two letters I have received for the ones I await. I am counting on your forgetting no detail of everything you will see, say and do; make it so that I can always be with you, that I may follow you to Milady Hervey, to Mr Conway, that I may see you kissing your sovereigns' four paws,[71] but above all that I may be the third between you and my little Craufurd. As for him, he is very careful of the errands he is given: he gave my letter to Mr Taaffe on 15th or 16th of this month, but I noticed with pleasure that letters from London to here could take only four days. Yesterday, the 22nd, I received a letter from Mr Taaffe dated the 18th which reassured me that I would have one from you next Saturday.

I plan to go and visit Milady George today; I desired Monsieur Shuvalov to take me there.

We have here your Hereditary Prince;[72] he arrived on Sunday. I supped with a very few at Madame de Nieukirchen's; then, on Monday, with Monsieur de Soubise where there was Madame de Mirepoix who lost sixty louis. I visited the same *maréchale* yesterday on leaving the Président's house. She had invited me to supper; she was alone with the chevalier de Boufflers; he was quite reasonable. He has in truth a great deal of wit, but his success, which is not always deserved, will harm his advancement: he could well acquire no knowledge, no discernment, no taste and, in growing old, be of very little consequence.

As for me, I am very tedious, admit it; farewell, I leave you, but I will return.

I will only show the grandmama your letter from Jean-Jacques after you have given me your permission.

Two o'clock in the afternoon

You are going to be furious with me and to cry out, "My dear little one is incorrigible, she has relapsed into her former errors; she has written all kinds of silly things to her grandmama," and from her reply which I am sending you, you would be justified in believing it. Ah well! You are wrong; I only said what was purely necessary— but, saving your respect, would you not do well to reply to the sweet things she entrusts me to tell you with a pretty little note?

Thursday 24th, in reply to letter from
Boulogne and from Calais

When you told me not to love, I was angry, I was uneasy, I wanted to make you change your mode of thinking; since you speak to me in a different language I am sometimes happy, sometimes afraid. Your last letter alarms me; you prepare me for lacunae in your correspondence; I see you surrounded by all sorts of distractions; you will give me no more lessons, you will lose sight of me; I should have expected it, but I find myself quite unprepared. What use then is reflection and experience? None, none at all, Monsieur. They belong only to those who are born without feelings. Now I have fallen back into my usual condition; you took me out of it for a moment, but how could I have flattered myself that I had inspired an attachment that would withstand absence? What can I hope from the gratitude which you claim to owe me? Is it based on anything and do you not see that I was seeking my own pleasure in everything that I thought and did for you? Oh no! One must have no illusions; I can, without flattering myself, claim to be preferred by a man such as yourself to such ridiculous, foolish, impertinent people as those you viewed here: but does that mean that you must love me? No, the goodness of your heart can lead you to pity me—but that is all. That is not enough for my happiness, but I would be wrong were I not to admit that it is a diversion from my sorrow. When, for instance, I spend the evenings between the Charlemagne's court and King Guillemot's, I collect my thoughts and I say to myself: "Whilst here I am an object of disdain or envy, there is in the world a man who does not think thus of me; he knows all my faults, but they do not displease him; I could see him again, and perhaps it is not impossible that I might rediscover in him the friendship and indulgence which he has shown me; perhaps my very faults provoked his kindness; they allowed him to understand his influence, the little daily progressions in his lessons flattered his self-respect, besides one is sensible of being loved if only by Tulipe."[73]

These are my thoughts, but they are my agreeable thoughts; I will deny you the sad ones, they would only serve to hasten the misfortune that I fear; so I will finish this matter, treat it as a romance if you dare.

I am sending you the original of Madame de Choiseul's letter; I have kept only the copy. You may show this letter if you wish to those you deem suitable; it shows what Madame de Choiseul makes of your nation and of you in particular; and you, Monsieur, pray agree now that I am authorised to think as I do. I always labour to find rivals for myself (I know it well), and I am all the more mistaken for the fact that I am very susceptible to jealousy—but without charms powerful enough to attract what one loves, one uses whatever means one can find without being prevented by the inconveniences which may result. Romance again; it was left to you to produce this new genre in me.

I will, you say, be without letters from you for three or four posts. I do not know why, but I cannot believe it; however, I remember that I often saw you very troubled in your mind and that then you no longer knew what was on your mind. In those troubled moments I felt myself to be lost like a needle in a haystack: the comparison is not a noble one but I do not pride myself on good form; I leave that advantage to the gods; the Temple goddess[74] has received a letter from her mountebank;[75] he is settled in a magnificent mansion[76] near London: it belongs to a milord whose name they could not tell me. Her protector and guide is to return, or so they say, at the end of next month; he will be reinstated as high priest or porter by his charming goddess. I will invite this goddess to sup with me on Friday, 2 May; the maréchale de Luxembourg decided it. If the grandmama comes with her husband, they will not be very glad to find her, but I have consulted you and I think you said that having been invited by her throughout Lent, I cannot be excused from inviting her in my turn. You will tell me if I have understood you rightly.

I require news of Mr Conway, Mr Pitt, in fact of all that interests you; I would write to you about Spain if I knew what to write, but I do not hear a word about it. Here all the talk is of the Hereditary Prince. Everyone will see him, people desire passionately to see him—a tediousness which we will have to endure for two months, the length of his stay here.

You say that you will entrust Wiart with finding you an apartment this summer. I believe that this is your intention at the moment, for I have faith in you and this faith is not made to remove mountains, but it should be able to bring you here; in the end we will see what happens.

I am very troubled in my mind and I will only be at peace when I have received a letter from London; I infinitely dislike that crossing just at the moment with the wind blowing; if you had had an accident, if I were to learn that you were ill, if several posts arrive without my having news of you—I will not be able to bear it all.

Except for Sundays, I do not know which day our post leaves: I dare ask no one. I wanted to go to Milady George but I cannot decide to go there alone. M. Shuvalov had promised to come and fetch me to take me there yesterday: he forgot. Finally, I am in the depths of all possible darkness, but I regret far more the torch which illuminated my spirit than those which illuminated my sight.

Farewell, dear Tutor; do not call me "Madame," I find it unbearable.

I do not know if this letter, or rather this volume is finished; I will close it only on Saturday so as to send it on Sunday.

I will tell you nothing about Mr Craufurd: you are at liberty to do as you please.

I thought I had finished, but I must tell you that I went to see the maréchale de Luxembourg yesterday. I went with my friend Le Monnier who judged her to be eighty years old; she was sad and languishing, she reproached me very gently for not having been to see her, and she asked if you had left in very pathetic tones which would have suggested to Marivaux: "I pity you, I share your sorrow."

This Saturday, 26th at midday

I feel a profound sadness; if I do not soon receive a letter, if they only deliver the post tomorrow, or if you have not written to me, beware a return of the vapours. My journey yesterday was frightful; everything displeased me. I went to pay a visit on Milady George who had been to see me twice since your departure. I wanted to reassure myself about the workings of the post and to beg her to warn me when the carriers were leaving. I found her alone with Madame de Caraman, I was delighted; that Madame de Caraman has something natural and easy about her—however, I believe there could well be no merit in it; it seemed to me that she was a little mocking about the questions I put to Milady, and at my suggestion that she sup with me three Sundays hence. Next Sunday, I would have no one she knew, the following one I will be at Versailles, the Sunday after which will be 11 May, I will have Madame de La Vallière whom Milady knows and that Caraman. I left with her and we went together to Madame de la Vallière. I cannot tell you exactly what she said, but it seemed that she was not far from finding the supper I had proposed ridiculous. You will have the time to write to the Milady that I told you I had visited her, that I had invited her to supper, but that conveniently in this country, one can easily, under the slightest pretext, excuse oneself from engagements one has made and that, if it is troublesome or embarrassing, you advise her not to refrain from sending her excuses. On the way I talked to Madame de Caraman and Madame de Bussy about her reconciliation with her husband, I asked if she was allowed to see Madame de Boufflers; she told me yes, and started on a eulogy of that goddess which lasted from *L'hôtel de Brancas*[77] until we reached the Carrousel:[78] that displeased me and put me in an ill-humour. I forgot to tell you that the Milady asked me if I had had any news from you; I replied quite naturally that that would be impossible, that you could only have arrived in London on the Sunday so I would not be able to have any news before Saturday. She told me that you might not have arrived before the Monday and that she had received a letter from you dated Sunday when you had only just reached Calais and were not due to embark until the evening. I appeared not to know these details and to take no more interest in them than did Madame de Caraman.

On leaving Madame de Vallières I went to the Président's house to await the high society. The first to arrive were the comtesse de Broglie and her brother-in-law the *abbé*[79] who asked me in a very stupid, jeering tone if you would be coming. I said that I did not think so. "Eh! Why so?" said he. "Because he is in London." "Ah! My God! I feel for your sorrow." "You are very kind monseigneur." "And Mr Craufurd will you see him again?" "I do not know at all." "And," asked the *comtesse* "why will he not return?" "I do not know at all,

Madame," then I turn my back and talk to other people. The *maré-chales* arrived and the rest of the company; games were arranged. The maréchale de Luxembourg played a thousand times worse than usual. She and the maréchale de Mirepoix detest each other at the moment; it is an infernal partnership. Besides all that, the Président is perfectly indifferent to me, he is not even attached to me from habit; far from being grateful for my attentions, I feel that he thinks he is doing me a favour by allowing me to choose to come and see him when I please—what in fact can I tell you? I am overflowing with disgust and ennui. I took the maréchale de Mirepoix back to her house; I stopped there and talked to her for an hour; I was not displeased. She hates the little *Idole,* she hates the maréchale de Luxembourg; in the end her hatred for all these people who displease me made me forgive her her indifference and perhaps the hatred she has for me. Admit what a pretty society it is, what delightful dealings—but my prudence which I believe to be excessive will set me above it all.

My plans concerning Monsieur de Tréguier are in rack and ruin; the flat which I wished him to have has been let to Madame de la Galissonnière.

The day before yesterday I saw Madame d'Aiguillon who left yesterday for the whole summer, but she will return to Paris nearly every Saturday and sup with me on Sundays. She invited me warmly to go often to Rueil. It is a very long time since I saw Madame de Forcalquier; I shall see her today or tomorrow at the latest.

I sup tonight with the Montignys. What can I tell you about myself which is more certain? Nothing if not that I am wearied to death and if you change towards me, there will be nothing left for me but to hang myself.

I am sending you an account of what happened at Saragossa;[80] perhaps you are better informed than we are here.

Farewell until the arrival of your letter. My reply will add to this volume.

This Sunday, 27th, at midday

No letters yesterday; I sent to *l'hôtel de Brancas* but none had arrived. If I have none today, I will be most uneasy; your crossing, your arrival, your health are what concerns and worry me: romance comes a long way behind. I had such vapours yesterday, they were almost as black as those that sent me to the provinces fourteen years ago. At every moment my eyes fill with tears, everything around me seems tiresome. But the condition is not accompanied by insomnia; I slept well last night; it would be a relief if I did not have terrible dreams. I do not know if I have told you of this weakness: they affect me; I have never told you the story of what caused them. However, I had some bad dreams last night; you were there for some reason which seems to augur great misfortune. You will mock me which is what I want.

I remember everything you have said and all the horror you denote for friendship; I die of fear that you may be right. I no longer know where I am, I find that I am not old enough; I wish I were a hundred years old—better still, I would like to be dead. My supper this evening displeases me horribly. I will be alone with Madame de Forcalquier; I will have nothing to say to her unless I have received a letter that can be shown. I saw her yesterday, she found me so sad, so overwhelmed, that she thought I was ill. If, in the end, she, like many others, has often tired me, I will do the same to them in the future. The Président paid me a visit yesterday; he stayed here for two hours; I cannot tell you the effect he had. I would abuse your patience if I were to tell you all my thoughts; to write a letter which becomes a volume requires some folly, some indiscretion and a lack of consideration, however I will only close this one at five o'clock. I will add nothing if I have no news of you.

This Sunday at three o'clock

The postman has just been by, no letter, no news from you. I cannot help being anxious and fearing that some accident has befallen you. How could you not have written: "I have arrived, I am well"? That would have been enough and would have saved me from all the sorrow and all the anxiety. I will say no more; I will close this letter and I propose to write no more until I have heard news from you.

MADAME DU DEFFAND TO WALPOLE

Paris, Monday 5 May 1766 at midday

I have a million things to tell you, and I have lost my voice and have, perhaps, a slight fever. My trip to Versailles went wonderfully well; I did not see the Queen; she is very well, but as yet sees no one. I spent more than a good hour alone with the grandmama; she was charming:

conclude from that that she talked to me a lot about you and in a way that suited me; her husband has been told that you are very amiable. Madame de Beauvau with whom I supped loves you as much as my late friend, Formont, which is to say madly. Pont-de-Veyle praises you ceaselessly; in fact everyone around me misses you, longs for you, and is charmed by you. Imagine my dear Tutor, how happy that makes me! Settle all your business and come back to me; you will have a thousand thousand pleasures in this country, I assure you. One more thing should persuade you; you are the best man in the world; it must be a great pleasure for you to cause the happiness of someone who has never really known any in her life. You will cause me to become devout, you will make me recognise a Providence, you will redeem all the injustices I have suffered, you will dissipate all my sorrow, all my tedium, I will no longer fear my enemies, their weapons will be as pins, we will mock the false gods and perhaps overturn their altars.

... I want never to do anything without your advice, I want always to be your dear little one, and to allow myself to be led like a child: I forget that I have lived, I am only thirteen years old. If you do not change and if you come and see me, it will turn out that my life will have been very happy; you will obliterate all the past and I will date only from the day when I met you.

If I were to receive an icy letter from you, I would be very sorry and very ashamed. I do not yet know what effect absence may have upon you; perhaps your friendship was but a spurt of flame: but no, I do not think so; whatever you may have said to me, I have never been able to think that you were unfeeling; without friendship you are neither happy nor agreeable, and I am positively suitable for you to love. Do not start telling me that there is romance in my head; I am a thousand leagues removed from it, I hate it; everything which resembles love is odious to me and I am almost glad to be old and hideous so as not to mistake the feelings people have for me, and quite glad to be blind so as to be quite sure that I can have no feelings other than of the purest and most honest friendship; but I love friendship madly; my heart has only ever been made for that.

This Tuesday, at half past three o'clock

... You have too much wit and are far too superior to your pupil, you trouble me and make me uneasy, I no longer know where I am.

You are becoming a new acquaintance for me, you are no longer the same as you were by the fireside, you flit about, you are a sylph, an illusion. I will have to stick to my dreams; I often dream of you which is unusual for me for I am not accustomed to dreaming at night about what concerns me by day, but in fact I have dreamt of you three or four times since you left, most noticeably last night. I was beside you, you did not say a word to me and you seemed to be grateful that I was not talking to you. You were serious, severe and I did not think you unfeeling; you have left me, and that is all and this in fact is how I believe you are. What I wrote to you yesterday leaves no question as to how I think about you; look at it again, I wish to say no more about it . . .

I must tell you something which it goes against the grain for me to tell you; I keep your letters and would not be sorry were you to keep mine; I flatter myself that I have no need to assure you that it is not because I think they are worth it, but to prepare for the amusement of seeing later what we have said to one another. I have just acquired a little chest in which to lock yours: romance again, you will say; come, come, my Tutor, you are insupportable.

Walpole had decided to leave England and spend the winter in Paris as the result of enormous disappointment. For two years he had devoted himself to the political career of a cousin on his mother's side, Henry Seymour Conway. In July 1765 Walpole's "political frenzy"[81] met with a double success: a new administration was formed consisting mostly of members of his party—the Whigs—with Conway appointed as Secretary of State. From his new exalted position Conway did not bother to show his cousin any kind of gratitude for his valuable and disinterested support behind the scenes. Walpole had no political ambitions and always said that he would never have accepted an official position, but the absence of any recognition whatsoever, albeit of a merely formal nature, offended him deeply. The disappointment was all the more painful coming as it did from a man for whom Walpole had always cherished an admiration bordering on hero-worship; but having decided not to allow his disappointment to show, he acted instead with great dignity and made up his mind to leave England for a while.

Now, eight months later, Walpole returned to his country quite appeased. The Parisian visit had been a success: personal success had restored his self-confidence, the pleasures of an idle life had put politics in perspective. Conway himself had, meanwhile, partly made up for his oversight by helping the career of a great friend and correspondent of Walpole's, Horace Mann, the English minister to the Tuscan Court.

On returning to London on 22 April, Walpole, having learned from his experience, was prepared to resume his usual way of life. He took up again "with joy his role as political mentor to his cousin"[82] and once more devoted himself to public life until Conway's resignation in January 1768 which coincided with Walpole's final retirement from politics. He was not only swamped by political and social engagements in London, but his beloved Strawberry Hill, which alone gave rise to a note of nostalgia in his letters from Paris, absorbed him with every sort of novelty. It was both a marvellous plaything and a save haven where he could feel voluptuously at home.

The fears expressed in Madame du Deffand's letter of 5 May were well founded. The Walpole who divided his time between Strawberry Hill and Arlington Street, who flitted about like a sylph was indeed a stranger to her, a thousand miles away from the fire burning in the hearth of her Saint-Joseph apartment. From now on the months spent in Paris were no more than an agreeable memory of a good holiday which the *marquise*'s unreasonableness threatened to change into a troublesome persecution. The "icy" letter was not long in coming. On 13 May Walpole subjected Madame du Deffand to an "insolent correction." The *marquise* accepted it with good-natured resignation, giving the impression on the whole that she cannot really take Walpole's irritation seriously, that she judges it to concern form not feelings. And she reassures him with promises as if he were a naughty child.

MADAME DU DEFFAND TO WALPOLE   *Paris, Sunday 18 May 1766*

Oh! how right you are, I deserved the most insolent correction which you sent me, but you must have seen from my last letter that I was disposed to correct myself.[83] I had already made some very judicious resolutions and made decisions which I have obeyed. Note, if it please your severity, that I did not write you one thought on Thursday, Friday or Saturday. I was determined to allow this post to go without writing to you if I had no news from you today. Your letter is original and I am sorry not to behave better. I will answer it suitably, but you are killing me . . .

Rest assured for the future; no more friendship, no more sweetness. I swear it, and will take an oath; no more questions on what you will do, no more curiosity about what you are doing, and even less about what you think. I will expect you in February, or I will not expect you at all if you prefer. Are you satisfied? Is that how it is to be? . . .

The reasonable intentions to which Madame du Deffand refers here were naturally short lived. Barely four days later, on 14 May the *marquise* suffered from one of those sudden attacks to which she was prone and which manifested themselves in complete mental paralysis whilst producing violent self-hatred. This crisis was probably caused by the discovery that before leaving, Walpole had confided in a mutual acquaintance his intention of not returning to Paris before the following February. From the moment her friend left, Madame du Deffand lived in the expectation of his return. It was a hope to which she clung from the very first letter—and Walpole was still on French soil—and on this hope she built her castles in the air. On this return depended the solution to the endless chain of misunderstanding which made his absence all the more painful.

On leaving, Walpole had promised to return during the summer; now, on hearing of a more distant date from an outside person, Madame du Deffand was bowled over and haunted by the suspicion that she had been intentionally deceived by her friend. On the other hand, the *marquise* knew that she could claim no rights, but only oscillate between hope and despair and it was despair which now held sway.

MADAME DU DEFFAND TO WALPOLE   *Paris, this Wednesday, 14 May 1766*

I have lost my head, my dear Tutor; it is not that I am going mad, but that I am becoming totally imbecilic; it is perhaps as a result of the discretion which you so strongly advised and which I observe scrupulously. By dint of forbidding myself to say what I think, I manage to think no more; I seek myself, but I no longer find myself, I am quite dejected and so despondent that you would pity me. To escape this miserable condition I think of you and then I fall even deeper into the abyss: I see only our separation which appears to have to be eternal. All the reasons for which I counted on your friendship disappear. How could I have pleased you? What can attach you to me?

My friendship for you? A fine reason, do you not inspire it in everyone you know? Staying here does not please you at all, what could make you return? Disgust of everything around you? But this disgust does not cast you into an ennui and inertia, neither does it arrest the movement of your soul; you have company you like and talents and occupations of every kind. No, my Tutor, I will not see you again; it was not worth your coming to resuscitate me, to set me in motion that I might die a second time. You see how sad I am, it is a kind of despair. I wanted to write to you yesterday and the day before yesterday; I tore up my letter. Yesterday I waited for your news; there was no post from England. It will come today perhaps, but can I hope that it will bring me a letter? No, I do not count on it, and it is in all truth that I assure you that I will not be vexed with you. It would be absurd, unjust and mad were I to expect to have news of you by every post; I even beg you as a favour not to give in to your excessive goodness; I would like you to write only when you have nothing to do and when it might amuse you to do so. When you will have been absent for several months, I greatly fear that you will discover your friendship for me was no more than a preference you gave me over those you found unbearable or to whom you were perfectly indifferent; however that may be, our friendship at present lacks its most important aspect which is habit. These are all the thoughts which plough through my head.

A few days ago I spent an evening divided between the uncle[84] and the niece.[85] The uncle fell asleep and the niece read me an extract from a London paper where there was an allegorical tale about Jean-Jacques. Madame de Chabot had sent it to her, they both thought that it might have been by you: I denied that it was so. This niece claims to love you a great deal, she praised you, she hopes to see you again, you promised her two days before you left to come back in February. "In February!" I exclaimed and I was concerned. I have not at all recovered and since that moment I no longer exist, I blame myself for everything I have thought, felt or believed; I have lost my way in a labyrinth from which I will never again emerge—but let us forget all that—I am tedious enough without trying to add to it. . . . Farewell, I await the arrival of the postman before closing my letter.

The postman came; he said there were no letters from England so I will say adieu until Saturday or Sunday. Tell me, when you write, if Mr Craufurd will be in London at the beginning of next month. I am not at all enquiring if he plans to take a turn here; there is no sign of it.

Walpole replied immediately, probably in a postscript to his letter of 20 May: "On my return from Strawberry Hill, I find your letter which causes me, could not cause me, greater chagrin ... must your complaints, Madame, be unending? You make me greatly regret my candour; I should have restricted myself to simple acquaintanceship: why did I avow you my friendship? It was to please you and not to add to your troubles. Perpetual suspicion and anxiety! Really, if friendship has all the inconveniences of love and none of the pleasures, I can see no temptation to try it. Instead of showing me its best side, you present only the darker aspect. I will have none of friendship if it breeds only bitterness. You mock Héloïse's letters and your correspondence is becoming a hundred times more tearful. *Reprends ton Paris; je n'aime pas ma mie au gué;** yes I would quite like her gay, but, sad, I would like her very little.[86] Yes, yes, my friend, if you want our correspondence to last, put it on a less tragic note; do not be like the comtesse de La Suze[87] who launched into elegies over the most ridiculous object. Am I made for the hero of an epistolary novel? And how is it possible, Madame, that with your intelligence, you give way to a style which revolts your Pylade, for you do not want me to mistake myself for Oroondate? Speak to me as a reasonable woman or I will copy my replies from *Lettres portugaises.*"[88]

This passage like all the others salvaged by Miss Berry was not chosen by chance. Before burning his letters, Walpole's literary executrix wanted, with a few carefully chosen extracts, to protect his image which must otherwise be compromised by the *marquise*'s agonising monologue. The passages preserved by her tend to show how, over the years, a situation developed in which each correspondent played his allotted part: Walpole was a tormented man, besieged by an obsessive, egocentric, dissatisfied woman. So on 16 March 1770: "You measure friendship, probity, wit, everything in fact, according to the homage paid you. That is what decides your approbation and your judgement, which vary from one post to the next. Rid yourself, or at least pretend to rid yourself of

*Take back your Paris; I do not love my darling *au gué.*

this personal yardstick; and believe that one can have a good heart without having to be in your drawing-room. I have often told you that you are demanding beyond belief; you would like people to exist only for you; you poison your days with suspicion and mistrust and you rebuff your friends by making them feel the impossibility of pleasing you." And on 18 November 1773: "With all the wit and every possible advantage, you allow nothing to please you. You want to hunt a creature which is nowhere to be found, and your knowledge of the world must tell you that such a creature does not exist. I mean a someone who would be uniquely and totally attached to you . . ."

Despite any prejudice in favour of Madame du Deffand, such words inevitably recall similar judgements: Julie de Lespinasse's unquestionably partial opinion: "Egoist . . . , she demands everything and gives nothing in return . . . ; to everyone she knows she seems to say, like Jesus Christ to his disciples, 'Go and sell that thou hast and come and follow me!' It is harder to be at peace with her than with God."[89] Then there is Hénault's more objective view, "age . . . had made her jealous and mistrustful, a little too *bel esprit*, her armchair was a judgement-seat from which she made decisions rather than conversation, her opinions of men depended greatly on the attention they paid her."[90]

With Walpole Madame du Deffand abandoned the tactics of mistrust which had paralysed her emotional life whilst being a sure means of defence, but she continued to suffer from the old poisons of anxiety, suspicion and possessiveness against which she no longer had an antidote. Walpole must have felt himself under unbearable attack, so Miss Berry wanted to preserve a few examples of his justified irritation.

Walpole's reply of 20 May no doubt struck the *marquise* intentionally on the raw over the one matter on which she had no intention of being lectured: style.

MADAME DU DEFFAND TO WALPOLE   *Paris, Sunday 25 May 1766*

I do not know if the English are hard and cruel, but I know they are presumptuous and insolent. They see expressions of friendship and warmth, ennui and sorrow, regret at separation and the desire to meet again as unbridled passion; it all tires them and they announce it with so little tact that one has the impression of being caught *in flagrante delicto*; one blushes and is ashamed and confused, and would fire a hundred cannons at anyone so insolent. This is how well disposed I feel towards you, and you are forgiven only because of the excess of your folly. What offends me is that you find me very ridiculous. I do not know what you will have thought of my last letter. It was an examination of conscience; perhaps it tired you to death, but it amused me a great deal to write. I have become so secretive since your departure that when I write to you I allow myself to say whatever comes into my head: if I have still to restrain myself, even with you, then I will be very sad. You always want to laugh; your element is extravagance, but I am sad and melancholic. Besides I am not well, I wrote and told you so, but it is of no concern to you; you do not even ask my news. You are an original and I do not understand you; sometimes I believe that you have friendship for me, and then I immediately think the opposite: I do not care for such pirouetting; however, when all is said and done, you amuse me. You will not *[reprendre] Paris a cause de vos mies,*[91] be they gay or sad. Tonight I will see your dear gay d'Aiguillon and your dear sad Forcalquier, and your dear gloomy du Deffand will have fourteen people to supper because Madame de Mirepoix like Madame de Montrevel sent to invite herself. There is the small change; I would rather have you, the coin, although there may be doubt as to the alloy.

Write me no more impertinences; there is a moment at which they would pain me greatly. Speak to me no longer of your return, there are five months between now and November, and seven until February, I do not wish to think about that any more than I wish to think about eternity.

I beg you to be infinitely convinced that you have not turned my head and that I claim to care no more for you than you care for me: adieu.

Walpole had struck home and the insult—or the fear of being un-masked—continued to torment Madame du Deffand and to cause her to seek imaginary relief in words.

MADAME DU DEFFAND TO WALPOLE   *Monday, 26 May 1766*

You have irritated and troubled me, and what is worse, frozen me: you compare me to Madame de La Suze! And threaten to send me a "Portuguese" in reply! Those are the two things which I hate most in the world; one for her disgusting and monotonous insipidness and the other for its indecent passion. I am sad, sick, I have the vapours, I am tired and I have no one to talk to: I believe I have a friend, I console myself by confiding my troubles in him, I take pleasure in speaking to him of my friendship, of the need I might have of him, of my impatience to see him again, and he, far from responding to my trust, far from being grateful to me for it, is shocked, he treats me haughtily, ridicules me and affronts me in every way! Ah! fie, fie! it is horrible; if there were not as much extravagance as there is harshness in your letters, they would be unbearable; but in truth they are so made that I alternate between the greatest rage and bursting into laughter: however I will avoid giving you the opportunity to write others of the kind.

For Madame du Deffand style was not merely a means of defence, she used it also as an aggressive tactic, to conceal and surprise. Duisit points out that just as she used irony with Voltaire, so, with Walpole parody serves to protect as well as to amuse: "The imaginary storms intentionally unleashed are the easiest ones to calm: laughter neutralises them. The writer's irresistible verve and her talent for improvisation help her to deal with a delicate situation. On the other hand, when obliged by circumstance, or at other times even, she is able to plead guilty gracefully and ingenuously; then she is all submission and the crime's unimportance is inferred from a lightness of tone so that everything prompts the offended person's indulgence."[92] So in a letter of 30 October 1766, Madame du Deffand has recourse to a "comedy of diversion" whereas in the letter below of 8 June, she exorcises Walpole's fear by means of the "preventative exaggeration" of a series of "reserves of optimism." ("Are you in a good humour? Are you not troubled in your mind?") There follows a "double parody"—a parody of Walpole and a parody of herself ("The sun is not purer than her heart")—and above all the simplistic and intentionally disquieting conclusion, which the writer produces ("I will in future risk everything which passes through my head"), all of this is designed to discountenance Walpole whilst forbidding him to take anything seriously."[93]

MADAME DU DEFFAND TO WALPOLE   *Sunday 8 June*

Are you in a good humour? Are you not troubled in your mind? Are you well disposed towards me? May I write you a volume? How can

I know? I will do what the mystics do and consult my inner self. Ah well! I can hear your voice saying "Dare all; write as much as you please, nothing will vex me, I will not answer with hurtful, humiliating things, I will allow you to say them to yourself, I want my little one to be happy, to love me, to tell me so since it makes her happy; I am persuaded that she will never ridicule me in any way; she is sufficiently tactful to know what causes ridicule, no one will know what she thinks of me, no one will ever know what I told her I thought of her, she is not vain, she is not presumptuous, she has no feeling which is not honest, the sun is not purer than her heart, I no longer wish to hurt her; when she has the vapours I will consent to her writing *Tristia*[94] because I would rather allow her to tire me for a moment than risk sending her mad by forcing her to bite back everything she would like to tell me; I only beg her not to abuse my complacence. She is intelligent enough to understand that there is more kindness than sentiment in my feelings for her, it should not vex her, it depends on character and is unalterable, anything else is subject to change. Besides I told her that friendship had caused me much misfortune, she must be convinced because I always tell the truth and to judge from the last letters she wrote me, I deduce that she has some personal understanding of the matter—where did she gain it? I do not know, but it is enough for her to know it, she will certainly tell me about it if I wish; finally I believe that my little one loves me perfectly and that there is no inconvenience for me in allowing her to do so."

You see, Monsieur, you have said a great deal to me; I have not repeated it all however, but this is enough to put me at my ease. Remember, pray, that it is at your command that I will in future risk everything which passes through my head . . .

MADAME DU DEFFAND TO WALPOLE   *This Wednesday 11 June*

I have re-read all your letters and have concluded from them that I can count on your friendship, that you desire my happiness, that you wish to give me some and that you fear the opposite will happen because of your idea that I am too lively and too easily affected; banish this idea, it is a great blessing for me to have a friend whom I esteem and love. Do not fear that I am too impatient to see you again; I do not wish you were here at present; if you arrive in a month, I would suffer the inconvenience patiently, but I would prefer you to come later: I have my systems like anyone else and provided that I can count on your never changing for me, you can do whatever you please and be sure that I will be happy . . .

MADAME DU DEFFAND TO WALPOLE   *This Sunday 15th*

. . . Do you think you please me by ceaselessly repeating that you do not want any friends, that you do not want any ties? It is hard and sad to hear that. Suffer my expressions of tenderness as I suffer your severity; let us each speak our own language and live in peace . . .

Day after day the tempo of the *marquise*'s life was governed by what were now the fundamental events of her existence, the arrival of the post, her hours of dictation and the re-reading of old letters. But these rituals did not exorcise the thought of Walpole, which was with her at every moment of the day, among the babble of worldly talk or in the long silences of her sleepless nights. There were not many people with whom she could speak of her far-off friend; Walpole's threats caused her to behave with mortifying circumspection. She could vaguely exchange a little news and a few comments with the Président and his niece, Madame de Jonzac, for whom she felt alternate outbursts of warmth and moments of irritation. The imperturbable Pont-de-Veyle occasionally enquired courteously after Walpole, but above all there was the affectionate attention of Madame de Choiseul, the young wife of Louis XV's influential minister. A few casual remarks may have been made in society, but these were the only people with whom she could for a moment dwell on her absent friend. On the other hand, through her attachment to Walpole, the *marquise* was learning to lead a life to which she had long been indifferent: the weft of social life, the events, intrigues and the gossip all went to feed the curiosity of her correspondent and to strengthen the fragile thread that held him to her.

Intransigent though he was in defence of his independence, Walpole was nevertheless prepared to confide his interests and tastes in Madame du Deffand. Such a concession by such a man was remarkable and the *marquise* lost no opportunity to cultivate it. Thus Madame du Deffand memorised many daily incidents of her life for the sole purpose of recounting them to her correspondent, and so she cultivated many acquaintances and abandoned others according to his whim. With tireless imagination, she constantly sought genealogical detail, literary anecdotes, historical curiosities, particulars of society and novelties, like the *Mémoires* of Saint-Simon of which Choiseul had a copy made during his ministry. She overlooked nothing that might amuse her friend.

Before leaving Paris on 2 April 1766, Walpole went to Livry to pay homage to Madame de Sévigné who had lived there for a long time, and with a not untypical carelessness he noted in his diary on 14 December of the preceding year that he had visited what he identified as her Parisian convent. Nevertheless Walpole knew the life of Louis XIV's contemporary down to the last detail and truly hero-worshipped her.

It is not surprising that Madame de Sévigné's letters were Walpole's most loved and most read work of literature. Apart from their dazzling style, these letters were a perfect model for Walpole's own correspondence, presenting as they did, a lively, colourful, fascinating picture of society seen from a personal, aristocratic point of view. It is remarkable, but hardly a coincidence that Madame de Sévigné's letters helped draw Walpole to Madame du Deffand of whom Hénault wrote in his *Mémoires*: "It is to be sincerely wished that what she has written should not be lost: Madame de Sévigné would not be the only one to be quoted."[95]

Sometimes, during the throes of her passion the *marquise* was playfully angry—"You are so extremely fond of that saint of Livry that my imagination is bridled,"[96] or she takes cover behind Madame de Sévigné's example: "Read and re-read her letters, and see if friendship can make one feel and say things which are a thousand times more tender than all the romance in the world."[97] Even before Walpole left Paris she had begun to make complicated plans for a joke which would provoke a reaction quite opposite to the delicate care and affectionate humour with which it was intended.

On returning to London from Strawberry Hill at the beginning of June, Walpole found something which he had never seen before on the desk in his office. It was a round, gold and white enamel snuffbox with a miniature of Madame de Sévigné on the lid and the initials R.S. (Rabutin de Sévigné) on the other side. The box contained a letter written in a woman's hand-writing:

From the Elysian Fields in timelessness with no date

I know of your mad passion for me, your enthusiasm for my letters, your veneration for the places where I have lived; I have heard that you worshipped me there, and am so touched that I have asked and been granted permission by my sovereigns to come and find you, never to leave you again; it is without regret that I abandon these happy places, I prefer you to all their inhabitants; rejoice in the pleasure of seeing me, do not complain that it is merely in paint, that is the only possible existence for the shades. I was empowered to choose the age at which I wanted to return; I chose twenty-five years old so as to be sure of always being agreeable to you; fear no change; the shades have a singular advantage: whilst being insubstantial, they remain immutable.

I came in the smallest possible form so as never to be separated from you, I want to accompany you everywhere, on land, on sea, in the town, in the fields, but I demand that you take me ceaselessly to France that I may see my country again and the city of Paris, and that you choose when there to stay in the Faubourg Saint-Germain. That is where my best friends lived, and it is where yours stay. You will introduce me to them and I will happily judge if they are worthy of you and of being the rivals of RABUTIN DE SÉVIGNÉ.

The letter could only have been written by Madame du Deffand, but surprisingly enough, Walpole did not even suspect it. Yet who could have been more aware than he of the ambiguity and artifice with which the letter was written?

Throughout the eighteenth century letters played many, occasionally contradictory, roles; they might merely serve a practical purpose but sometimes they were intended to mystify. They were a means of contact between people whom distance separated, but they also lent themselves, more than any other formula, to metaphor and fantasy. Real letters may provide an irreplaceable source of information about the eighteenth century, but imaginary ones—from the *Lettres persanes* to the *Liaisons dangereuses*—lie at its heart. Letters added to the complexities of social life. They might be signed or anonymous, addressed to one person or many, true or apocryphal, they might denigrate or praise, amuse or offend, but their function was to entertain and to communicate indirectly.

As we have seen, Walpole himself, who lives in terms of a correspondence aimed at relaying the truth of an age, asserted himself in unfamiliar surroundings, by writing a pretend letter under a false name with the

intention of deceiving a great writer of imaginary letters and so unleashed a reaction which eventually went beyond his control.

By writing a letter signed Madame de Sévigné, Madame du Deffand
thought to enrich her everyday correspondence with fantasy and, by her
elegant jest, to disguise the anxious love which she was forbidden to
express in her real letters. But the device prepared so carefully for
months, played her false. Walpole's unforeseeable lack of intuition in
not immediately recognising her as the author, fired a relentless chain
of doubt which the *marquise,* aware of all the dangers, could not control.

On 10 June Walpole wrote to Madame du Deffand telling her of the
discovery of the box and probably hazarding a few guesses as to the
identity of its sender; he did not suspect the *marquise* for even a moment.
Madame du Deffand was amused but also disappointed by her friend's
lack of intuition. She was worried lest his vanity might lead him to
embarrassing speculation. She could not, however, resist the temptation
of seeing how Walpole would wriggle out of the situation. Thus, to
satisfy herself she sent him, via their friend Craufurd, an indirect exhor-
tation to prudence: "Keep as the most inviolable secret what I am about
to confide in you; the box and the letter came from me. Madame de
Choiseul took charge of having it delivered. She wrote to Monsieur de
Guerchy and gave him instructions. They were followed to perfection;
it is unspeakable that Mr Walpole should suspect anyone other than me;
but I insist that you do not inform him, only prevent him from letting it
be seen that he suspects others. He has written that you are tempted to
hit him when he expresses his doubts. I have no time to tell you more
because I want this letter to leave tomorrow (15 June 1766).

But two days later, when another letter arrived from England containing further speculation, Madame du Deffand felt that the joke was
threatening to become dangerous, and she decided to tell Walpole the
whole story. At the same time she wrote to Madame de Choiseul—who
had meanwhile moved to her country estate—to inform her of the
wonderful results of their plot and of Walpole's reaction.

MADAME DU DEFFAND TO WALPOLE   *Paris, Tuesday 17 June, 1766*
                                               at 3 o'clock

We have both made fools of ourselves: you by not having guessed,
and I by not being suspected; I would like to know who you could
have suspected: forget your mistake, I forgive it you.

I am convinced that you are very glad to discern that it was I, and that friendship prevails over vanity. If the success of this folly was not what I hoped, at least it amused me a good deal at one time: I planned it more than a month before your departure. You remember going to see a Monsieur Doumenil,[98] and being displeased by the portrait you saw there. Madame de Turenne to whom I mentioned the matter, offered to lend me a box of Monsieur de Bouillon's; I accepted; I gave it to Madame de Forcalquier; she showed it to you in my little blue study; you recognised Madame de Sévigné and seemed pleased. The next day I gave this portrait to Madame de Jonzac who undertook to copy it; she is said to be good. She ordered the box, she transcribed the letter; in fact she did everything; you owe her a word of thanks. Write and tell her that I have told you of all the trouble she took, she has great respect and liking for you. All this business done, the box had to reach you and I wanted it to do so mysteriously. I planned to address myself to Mr Craufurd; I begged you to tell me if he was in London, and then I thought that I would cause him considerable embarrassment; I turned to the grandmama for help; and she entered into my plans with her usual goodness, she perfected them and took charge of my parcel, addressed it to Monsieur de Guerchy, wrote instructions to him and asked him to tell her when they were carried out. To judge from your account, he is a very able minister and he obeyed his orders precisely . . .

That is the whole story. If you had guessed it was I, which I did not doubt you would, my pleasure would have been complete; but my Tutor did not recognise his pupil. That is the most useful lesson he has ever given me.

MADAME DU DEFFAND TO THE DUCHESSE DE CHOISEUL

Wednesday, 18 June 1766

Monsieur de Guerchy is a great minister; he followed your instructions so punctiliously that Mr Walpole is nearly going mad; I have received two letters from him since he found the little parcel on his desk; his account of it was enough to make you die of laughter; he made the sign of the cross; he called for help; he thought that there was something magic. I will show you his letters. He tells me in the latest one that he went to dine with Monsieur de Guerchy with all the ministers; he was begged to bring the box and the letter. Since that day he suspects Madame de Guerchy of knowing something about the mystery; that takes his mind away from me because he knows that I do not know her; but he thinks that I am at least in the secret; he is like a soul in anguish. He asks me on his knees to tell him everything I know; after having turned him this way and that and named five or six people, I told him that my secretary says that it may be Madame de Valentinois; and that I think he is right, that it must be she. But I advise him not to be too hasty in thanking her. I am writing to him by this post to tell him the truth . . .

Madame du Deffand decided on the truth too late; ignorant of the explanation which was already on its way, Walpole threw caution to the winds and wrote to the *marquise* with his final, flattering conclusions. He was so sure of not being mistaken that his only concern was for the best way of expressing his gratitude.

WALPOLE TO MADAME DU DEFFAND   *{Tuesday 19 June}*

I am quite convinced that it was Madame la duchesse de Choiseul who was so kind as to give me the charming present about which I have told you so much. There is no way of answering the letter properly; it would require her wit or yours. Add to that the difficulty of expressing myself in a foreign language; in fact it is all desperate. I have no less difficulty when I think of sending her some trifle; it should be nothing too recherché, that would always be an imitation, and a clumsy, inappropriate imitation; neither should it be too costly, that would be an impertinence on my part and nothing could be less gallant. In fact it should be something which could only be found in this country; unfortunately our products are neither rare nor gallant; if my beautiful castle weighed two ounces less, I could well send her that, and it is certainly something she would not have seen elsewhere.

The letter of explanation had left Paris on Thursday 19 June and, according to Madame du Deffand's calculations, it should have reached London on Monday the 23rd; she could then have expected a reply from

Walpole on Friday the 27th. Such precise calculations denote her perfect knowledge of a swift and efficient system whereby it took only four days for a letter to go from Paris to London. In fact Walpole wrote a letter on the 24th to which Madame du Deffand replied on the 28th. Meanwhile on around the 28th, Walpole received a package containing, besides a letter from Madame de Choiseul and one from Monsieur de Guerchy, another letter from the *marquise* dated 23–24 June with further comments on the chain of misunderstanding which had developed—an intense but not unusual exchange of letters between the two correspondents. But rarely had the post brought Walpole such unwelcome news as that which reached him between 23 and 28 June.

The situation was suddenly turned totally upside down. Walpole had been disturbed and excited by the exquisite attention and homage of Madame de Choiseul for which the flower of the French aristocracy vied. She was the wife of Louis XV's great minister and diplomatist, and her attentions made Walpole the object of admiration and envy in two capitals. The whole thing had been turned into a most terrible mockery. The obsession of a thoughtless old woman who tyrannised him with unsolicited attentions had exposed him to the mockery of those he saw as bearing witness to his worldly success! His "fatuity" was talked of (Monsieur de Guerchy in his report/letter to Madame de Choiseul on 11 June), and the *marquise* herself advised him to present his excuses to one of the most important women in France for whom he professed a very special admiration! Not only had Walpole fallen into a trap, but he had shown himself to be ingenuous, vain and unprepared: "Why, with such suspicions and a desire to see clearly, did you not reply to Madame de Sévigné, asking me to forward the letter? That would have been an ingenious ploy,"[99] Madame du Deffand retorted, and with her greater worldly wisdom, she advised him on how to remedy the matter.

Three months of preparation, all her psychological know-how, her agitation, her great social prestige, all rebounded against the *marquise* and caused a reaction in Walpole which reminded Lewis of "a screaming child 'going' limp or rigid in the throes of a temper-tantrum."[100]

All we know of Walpole's letter of 24 June to Madame du Deffand is what he wrote about it to Lady Hervey: "I still shudder when I think of it and I have scolded Madame du Deffand black and blue."[101] The *marquise*'s reply leaves the matter in no doubt.

MADAME DU DEFFAND TO WALPOLE   *Paris, Saturday 28 June 1766*

Ah! my dear Tutor, you are troubled in your mind. I know you well, I am in despair, but be persuaded that you are wrong; when you wrote to Madame de Choiseul, there could not have been a shadow of ridicule. You must have been led to believe that the joke was hers; you can see from her letter which I sent you; I advise you to write to her in the same vein as my reply, and, I repeat, do not concern yourself. I would despair were I to have occasioned you the least sorrow; they no longer speak about it here, and I can assure you that I never speak about you.

With regard to your letters, with the exception of half of one (the one in which you described receiving the box) which I had Madame de Jonzac and Madame de Forcalquier read, no one in the world has known, nor will know the slightest thing about them. I find it very sad that a token of attention and friendship which it pleased me to give you might cause some change in your way of thinking and acting with me. I would be very sensible to such a misfortune which I could neither have foreseen nor feared.

Madame du Deffand behaved foolishly and was guilty of a serious psychological misjudgement, but she knew Walpole's tastes better than anyone else: "When in 1774, Walpole described Strawberry Hill, he devoted more space to the snuffbox and the letter than to all the other treasures of the house, including Cardinal Wolsey's hat. He published the letter in full and announced *sans peur et sans reproche*: 'This box with the letter in it from Madame de Sévigné in the Elysian Fields to Mister Walpole, was sent to him by Madame du Deffand.'"[102]

When the storm had died down, the *marquise* lent herself patiently to wiping out all trace of it whilst systematically repeating the mistakes that gave rise to it. She suffered the restraint of prudence and lived in obedience as if it were an act of love and declared her indifference with the casualness of a woman who knows she is not believed. The *marquise*'s main objective was Walpole's return, an event to which, for fear of annoying her correspondent, she usually referred only incidentally and with discretion whilst describing the Parisian scene.

At the beginning of September Walpole suffered a serious attack of gout. Madame du Deffand's childishness gave way to maternal anxiety.

Walpole's condition turned out to be serious and everything contributed to increasing the *marquise*'s panic: distance, difficulties of communication and a typically nationalistic mistrust of foreign treatment.

MADAME DU DEFFAND TO WALPOLE *Paris, Thursday 11 September 1766*

Your letter which should have been delivered on Tuesday, only reached me today. It confirms and increases all my anxiety; I told you in my last letters what alarmed me and since you hate repetition, I will restrict myself to repeating only that I consent to whatever privations—to not seeing you again, to not receiving letters from you—but I must have news of you, not just once a week but twice by the post, and then by any means which may present itself; four lines will suffice; in English or in French, as you wish, but I must have your news. It is a favour which you cannot refuse me and which is absolutely necessary to me. If I am alive, it is not my fault, nature ordained it. I do not however wish you to be responsible for my vivacity, and although our characters are alike in many ways, I concur that you are a great deal calmer than I . . .

This Sunday

. . . I supped with the Président who grows weaker every day. It is a very sad outlook and one which with my other anxieties makes my life hateful. I no longer dare to speak to you about what affects me; how is it possible for there to be even the appearance of anything ridiculous in what I say and what I think? How can you fear to share what does not exist? What can give you such an idea, such a thought? What then is friendship? I thought that it was not to be blushed at; to conclude I no longer understand anything about it. Is indifference alone honest, then? So let us keep to it, but allow me to desire and demand news of your health; beyond that I ask nothing of you . . .

MADAME DU DEFFAND TO WALPOLE *Paris, 21 September 1766*

I see that my anxieties were only too well founded. I did not however believe you to be so ill as you have been; your doctors are worse than ours. You must have been poisoned, my Tutor, I am sure of it; the hot drugs they made you take, the wine which they prescribed against all reason and all good sense, were all designed to kill you. You will have seen from my letters how against it I was. But which day, then, were you so sick? The last letter you wrote to me was on the 25th, you complain of some pains, of weariness and weakness; you were at Strawberry Hill and you finished your letter the next day in London. Since then you have written to Mesdames d'Aiguillon, de Forcalquier and to the Président on the 8th. You tell them that you have been ill, but that you are much better. The letter I have received today is dated the 16th and you have been at death's door. How can you expect me not to be horribly anxious, especially knowing you to be in such a prodigiously weak state. I ask you as a favour to send me your news by every post, to have whosoever you like write to me in whatever language you choose, I do not mind which. I am having Wiart learn English; his teacher will come on alternate days, or every day if I wish; you see how that should put you at your ease. What is more, I will be satisfied with four lines, that is to say, the details of your condition; I dispense you from all the rest and even beg you to refrain from anything which might tire you. You believe your pupil to be mad, but you are quite mistaken . . .

MADAME DU DEFFAND TO WALPOLE   *Paris, 24 September 1766*

I believe you to be very ill and the account you gave me of your condition causes me great anxiety, and so much so that you would be lacking in friendship were you not to send me news twice a week, as I begged you to do in my last letter . . . Do you know what I would like? I would like to be an old man rather than an old woman; I would go, I swear, to Bath to keep you company and to care for you: I am quite convinced, I cannot even doubt it, that you do not at all deserve what I think about you; but what is to be done? It is neither your fault nor mine; we should spare each other; I spare you from reproach and you spare me from reprimands . . .

Anxiety made the *marquise* unusually bossy and busy: she demanded news, made Wiart learn English and planned to send him to England. She could not bear the waiting, the immobility and her powerlessness, all of which made her forget Walpole's demands and to try rudely to impose her own. Wiart, who was quite used to the perpetual tension between Madame du Deffand and Walpole, could not tolerate his mistress's anguish and momentarily abandoned the role of a silent, devoted ghost. His proud, deferential style and elegantly blackmailing tone go to show how much of the *marquise* he had absorbed; a brief reference to friendship appears to explain, in case it were questioned, the legitimacy of his requests.

WIART TO WALPOLE   *Paris, Wednesday 24 September 1766*

Monsieur, I dare most humbly to beg you to be so kind as to order your servants to post twice a week a bulletin of your state of health; I cannot tell you how anxious Madame is. I take the liberty of asking you this without her knowledge because I know that she is resolved not to write to you in order not to put you in the position of replying which would tire you greatly in your present weak condition. But, Monsieur, I beg of your favour to have a short bulletin in English sent twice a week. I have at present an English master who gives me lessons every day and who will translate what you are so good as to send: do not give yourself the trouble, Monsieur, of writing yourself.

I cannot express how anxious Madame is about your condition: every minute she tells me that I must leave for England; that I could perhaps be of some service to you and for her, a strength. I would be very happy, Monsieur, could I hope to be of any use to you; I would not delay leaving for a moment: I can assure you of my truth and sincerity.

I am able to tell you, Monsieur, that if true friends exist, you can boast of having found a rare example of one in Madame. Allay her anxiety as soon as possible: if, like me, you could see the condition she is in, you would pity her; it prevents her from sleeping and agitates her a good deal.

I am studying the English language with great application so as to be able to translate your letters, but I foresee that I will not be able to do that for four or five months: but, Monsieur, I repeat, do not take the trouble to write yourself; one of your servants can write the bulletin in English and my English master who is always here when the postman brings the letters, will translate them at once.

I beg you a thousand pardons, Monsieur, for taking this liberty; but I thought it was my duty to inform you of Madame's anxiety over your health; it gives me the opportunity, Monsieur, to thank you for the kindness you have deigned to show me. I beg you to be persuaded of my attachment and my respect.

Walpole was not moved by Madame du Deffand's growing anxiety; gout no doubt increased his irritability but her insistence annoyed him and her uncontrolled plans worried him. To him her behaviour seemed indiscreet and overbearing rather than devoted and affectionate. So, as soon as he was strong enough (a letter from Saint-Joseph brought about another access of fever), he sent his friend another memorable lecture. On 28 September the *marquise* replied: "There is so much shame in being ridiculed that it is stupefying. I cannot find a word to say to you. I am floored, crushed," but two days later, reassured about Walpole's improving health and with a certain immunity to his outbursts, she pleaded her cause in a long letter imbued with affection and good-humoured commonsense.

MADAME DU DEFFAND TO WALPOLE

This Tuesday, 30 September 1766 at four o'clock
in the morning, written by my own hand before the
arrival of the letter which I expect by today's post

No, no, you will not abandon me; if I had made mistakes, you would forgive them, and I have only made one except in thought; for I defy you to reproach me with any by word or action. "You have written me," you will say, "'Portuguese letters,' elegies like Madame de La Suze; I had forbidden you friendship and you dare to have friendship for me and to declare it; I am ill and your head is turned immediately; you exceed yourself to the point of wishing to have news of me twice a week; true, you would be satisfied with simple bulletins in English, and before receiving my reply on this matter, you have the face, the boldness, the indecency of thinking to send Wiart to London as your representative. Mercy me! what would have become of me? I would have been the hero of a novel or a character in a comedy, and who would be the heroine?"

Have you finished, my Tutor? Listen to me in my turn. If, as you say, you are ridiculed, or even thought ridiculous, you have only yourself to blame; it was the fuss you made about Madame de

Sévigné's confounded letter which drew attention to us; it may have made your compatriots envious when they thought it came from Madame de Choiseul. When it was known to come only from me, your enemies were triumphant, they will have exaggerated my passion for you and will have made all the jokes they could to ridicule your misunderstanding; so in fact, albeit quite innocently, I was the occasion of a small chagrin. Here the letter would have been ignored if it were not for Milord Holderness who brought news of it before you wrote; not one here has made the slightest criticism although I suspect Madame la duchesse d'Aiguillon of having joked about it to Milady Hervey. She has been jealous of me for a long time; in the first place it was because of Madame de Flamarens, today it is because of you. I may be wrong, but you can judge the matter for yourself by paying attention to Milady's conversation.

I wanted to send you Wiart; this plan would not have been at all extraordinary under the circumstances in which I would have carried it out, I would have had the same thought for my poor late friend, Formont, if he had been ill in Rouen and if there were no one to bring me his news; that is your greatest grievance. Ah! there is another which according to me is much worse, that is the tedium of my letters; you find them insipid, involved like our most irksome novels; perhaps you are right and on that point I will admit my guilt. I can speak of friendship for too long, too often and at too great length, but, my Tutor, mine is but a poor intelligence; I do not have several ideas in my head, one alone fills it. I think I write very badly, and would reply to anyone who told me the opposite and wished to praise me: "You know nothing about it, you have not read de Sévigné's letters, Voltaire's or my Tutor's." For instance the one dated the 22nd, in which you treat me with Sarmatian ferocity, is wonderfully written.

To return to our affairs; the case has been reported, be judge and litigant and I promise to carry out your sentence: describe exactly the behaviour you require of me; you can have no control over my thoughts because I am not responsible for them, but as for the rest, you will be the absolute master.

I pray to your saint and beg her to appease your anger; she will tell you that she has had feelings as criminal as mine, for all that she was no less honest; she will return you to your senses and make you see as clearly as day that a woman of seventy years who has shown no sign of madness or dementia is not to be suspected of ridiculous sentiments and is not unworthy of respect and friendship. But let us say no more, my dear Tutor, and forget the past; let us just talk nonsense, and abandon for ever love, friendship and intrigue; let us not love each other but always take an interest in each other without ever betraying your principles; I wish to follow and respect them always without understanding them; you will be happy, my Tutor, rest assured and you will make me perfectly happy if you cause me no anxiety over your health and if you cease to be so angry with me that you call me "Madame"; the word freezes all my senses; let me always be your "little one"; no title has ever suited anyone better for I am, in fact, very small.

Do not shudder when you think about your return to Paris, remember that I have caused you no embarrassment here and that I have received gratefully and with pleasure the attention you have paid me, but I demanded none of it. We have been mocked, you say, but here everything is mocked, and instantly forgotten. I would not like to deceive you, my Tutor, and I can truthfully affirm that I have done nothing to displease you and that since I have been concerned with you, I have become more discreet, more reasonable because I have become indifferent to everything; most particularly yesterday evening I was exceedingly gentle and patient whereas before I would have been bitter and angry because I was being contradicted in bad faith. Is that not a child's tale? And do you refuse to call me "my little one"!

It remains for me to make another small observation to prevail upon you to be a little gentler and more indulgent: my misfortune, my great age, and now I can add, my infirmity; if it was within your power to help me to bear my condition and assuage its bitterness, would you refuse? Would perhaps the first malicious and jealous gossip be able to turn you against me? No, no, my Tutor, I know you well, you are a little mad but you have an excellent heart, which although incapable of friendship is worth more than all those which profess it: scold me as much as you wish; despite envy, I will always be your pupil.

I wrote all that with my own hand, without too much hope of its being legible; Wiart deciphered it wonderfully and so easily that I was tempted to send you my rough copy; but I did not want to give you that trouble.

I await your first letter with impatience to know your news; but in trepidation, expecting many insults, I have gladly anticipated them and I warn you that I will not reply to them.

This Wednesday, 1 October before the arrival
of the postman, and consequently not in answer
to your letter if he brings me one and which
I cannot yet have received

You are right, you are right, in fact you are all reason; I am no longer oppressed but I am truly converted. A shaft of light struck me as it did St Paul; he was swept off his horse and my chimeras have been swept away. I do not know what their nature was, nor what language they made me use; but I confess that they must have seemed ridiculous to you, and the effect they had on you no longer shocks me today. For a long time now, when thinking of your return here, I felt that your presence might embarrass me. I said to myself: "Oh! my God, why?" and I found that it was your reprimands which my nonsense had attracted that would shame me. Burn any of my letters (if you still have them) which might contain a trace of all that twaddle; I am your friend, I have never had any thoughts or feelings beyond that and I do not understand how I descended to the use of language which I have always avoided and denounced and which you have every reason to detest. There then is a new baptism and now we will both be more at our ease.

This Wednesday after the arrival of
the postman

Oh my God, how happy I am! You are well, that is all I wanted; you will see from what I wrote this morning and yesterday whether I am vexed with you. It remains only for me to say one thing: in this country they do not think it possible to be the lover of a woman of seventy without being paid; but they believe you can be her friend, and I can tell you that they will find nothing ridiculous in your being mine. I cannot guarantee that no jokes will be made, but to pay attention would be to honour our nation too highly. I do not know where all your fears can come from and you ought to talk to me with the same trust with which I talk to you. I have an idea that some bad jest on the part of Madame la duchesse d'Aiguillon to Milady Hervey which has troubled you; I have not given the least cause for it. I have long known about her jealousy, but she is not at all dangerous. I have only allowed myself to speak of you with friendship and concern to Mesdames de Jonzac and de Forcalquier who both love you very much and are without jealousy.

Throughout October and for most of November the two correspondents remained on cordial, almost serene terms. On 30 October in one of those sudden outbursts of happiness which are not uncommon in gloomy people, the *marquise* threw herself into the writing of a long and overwhelming parody of their relationship. Walpole, for his part, wrote her an "enchanting" letter which "disturbed " her and made her feel as if she were "drunk." In this unusually relaxed climate Madame du Deffand attempted a "portrait" of her friend, a eulogy which must have greatly flattered his self-respect. Compared to some of Madame du Deffand's masterpieces, her profile of Walpole may be disappointing; it has none of the *marquise*'s customary freedom and dazzling ability to capture the essence of character. But despite its panegyrical nature, its reticence and artificial rhetoric, according to Lewis, "Her 'Portrait' of Walpole is the most valuable passage ever written upon him."[103]

PORTRAIT OF MR WALPOLE BY
MADAME LA MARQUISE DU DEFFAND WRITTEN IN THE
MONTH OF NOVEMBER 1766[104]

No, no, I cannot do your portrait, no one knows you less well than I; you seem to me to be at once what I would like you to be, at once what I fear you may be, and perhaps never what you are.

I know well that you have a great deal of intelligence; intelligence of every kind, of every sort, everyone knows that as well as I do, and you must know it better than anyone.

It is your character that needs be depicted, and this is why I cannot be a good judge; indifference is required, or at least impartiality; however I can say that you are a very upright man, that you have principles, that you are courageous, that you pride yourself on steadfastness, that when you have made a decision, for good or ill, nothing can make you change, which means that your steadfastness resembles stubbornness. You have a good heart and your friendship is solid, but neither gentle nor easy; a fear of weakness makes you hard, you are on your guard against all sensibility; you cannot refuse essential favours to your friends, you sacrifice your own interests to them, but you refuse them the smallest service. Good and human towards all that surrounds you, towards everything which is indifferent to you, you take little trouble to please your friends or to satisfy them over trifles.

You have a most agreeable disposition although not always an easy one. All your manners are noble, easy and natural; your desire to please leads to no affectation; the knowledge you have of the world and your experience have given you a great contempt for all men and have taught you to live with them; you know that all they profess is false, in return you give them respect and politeness in all things; those who are not concerned to be loved are pleased with you.

I do not know if you have many feelings; if you have, you fight against them; to you they appear to be a weakness, you only allow those which have an air of virtue; you are a philosopher; you have no vanity although you have a great deal of self-respect; but you are not blinded by self-respect, it causes you to exaggerate your failings rather than to hide them; you value yourself only because you are, so to speak, obliged to when you compare yourself to others. You have discernment, and refined tact, discerning taste, excellent style; you would have been part of the best company in the world in centuries gone by, as you are in this one and would be in those to come. Your character comes a good deal from your nation, but, as for your conduct, it suits all countries equally.

You have one unpardonable weakness to which you sacrifice your feelings and to which your behaviour is subject; this is the fear of ridicule: it makes you dependent on the opinion of fools and your friends are not protected from the impressions that fools wish to give you of them. You are easily troubled in the mind. It is an inconvenience of which you are aware and which you correct by sticking firmly to your decisions; your resistance to changing them is sometimes carried too far, and over things that are not worth it.

Your inclinations are noble and generous, you do good for the pleasure of doing it, without ostentation and without claiming gratitude; in fact your soul is beautiful and good.

ADDITION TO THE PORTRAIT, 30 NOVEMBER 1766[105]

Only truth and simplicity please you; you despise subtlety and hate metaphysics; great arguments tire you and you do not much like aphorism, considering it to be of little use; your philosophy informs you that it is better to be distracted from your passions than to fight them. You seek to distance yourself from them by amusement; you mock everything and, O new Democritus, for you the world is no more than a performance whose actors you boo; your taste and talent lie in irony, you excel in this genre which requires considerable wit, charm and delicacy. You are naturally very gay, but you were born with great sensibility and this sensibility often mars your gaiety. To remedy this inconvenience you seek extraordinary ways of occupying and amusing yourself. You build irregular castles, you raise monuments to a brigand king,[106] you affect great patience, etc. etc. Finally you devote yourself to oddities, this seems a little like madness, but arises from your reason.

I can say nothing about your horror of friendship, it is apparently based on a great sorrow caused by friendship, but as you only speak vaguely about the matter, one might be led to believe that this is a mania you have, or perhaps a system which you wish to establish with as little basis as any other system, and which will never succeed despite your eloquence, since you do not act according to your precepts.

You have friends, you are entirely devoted to them, their interests are yours, and neither all your lectures nor all your arguments against friendship will persuade people that you are not the man most capable of it in the world.

Serenity in Madame du Deffand's correspondence with Walpole could only be fleeting. Perhaps the *marquise* really was impossible to please, but Walpole was frightened of complying with her and so stiffened every time he suspected his tolerance of being taken for acceptance. Like a hundred-headed hydra, Madame du Deffand's voracious emotions were always lying in wait; however bloody the battle, Walpole could never claim a decisive victory.

The correspondence developed a rigid structure, incorporating two clear and precisely defined roles, with on the one hand a continuously repeated pattern of hopes raised only to be permanently disappointed, and on the other a constant state of alarm and a need of defence against an unbearable and unreasonable threat.

Walpole reacted violently to the ever-mounting siege; a letter written on 28 November and described by the *marquise* as "shameful" may be the cruellest he ever wrote her.

MADAME DU DEFFAND TO WALPOLE

12–13 December 1766 in reply to that
of 4 December

... You take care to point out to me that your style has quite changed. Oh! I noticed that long ago! Oh! In your last two letters it exceeds itself and I do not understand how you allowed yourself to write such outrageous things to a woman of my age and who (I think I can say without vanity) deserves some consideration, and whose friendship neither dishonours nor makes ridiculous those on whom it is bestowed, and whose enemies even do not speak of her with scorn; and it's from you that she would receive her greatest humiliation if she were so unfortunate as to have the feelings which you suppose; in that case would it not be for you to pity her and attempt to cure her? But, thank God! she has no need. Yes, I admit it (I have not the intelligence to disguise the truth), you are of all men, the one whose mind most pleased me, and consequently in whom I most believed. I also believed you to have an excellent character, and because of this idea and the signs of friendship which you gave me, I gave myself unreservedly to you; I told you all my thoughts, I regarded you as my strength; the certainty of having a friend made me happy despite all my misfortunes, I allowed myself some warmth of expression, some complaints and some reproaches; when I felt disposed to sadness, I sought consolation by writing to you. I made a mistake; your respect and your liking for me have vanished. I beg you to be inwardly convinced that I have neither the intention, nor the plan, nor even the desire to bring them back to life, I could no longer count on them. Do not think that I am laying traps for you, in all my life I will not forget the way in which you have treated me, and my trust is lost for ever ...

MADAME DU DEFFAND TO WALPOLE　　　　*This Sunday, 4 January 1767*

Ah! Cease to wear yourself out with imprecations against friendship. Why remind me endlessly of everything you have said and written which could discourage my having any friendship for you? What does it matter to you what I think when you are free to think as you like? It is, you say, fear of making me unhappy; on my behalf you take a precaution in the style of Gribouille who threw himself in the water for fear of the rain. But why always repeat the same thing? How useless it is, how superfluous! Remember three[107] words which you wrote me in one of your last letters; they made quite the impression you could have wished on me, and perhaps an even greater one, since I do not imagine that you wished to harm either my repose or my health. I assure you that I will never forget those three words. You ought to notice that I behave accordingly and if my letters in future seem tiresome, it will not be from the same kind of tedium.

MADAME DU DEFFAND TO WALPOLE   *This Friday, 16 January 1767*

. . . Oh! no, I have not left you, that good or bad event will never happen to you. I await your letters with the impatience I would if they were to bring me great pleasure, and for more than two months I find in them only bitterness and aridity; but, no matter, I am always very glad to receive them; you are not at all obliged to write them. I would prefer them to cost you nothing and not to owe so much gratitude . . .

This Saturday, the 17th

. . . Look, my Tutor, I would not in the least like to abuse your kindness to me, and oblige you to come to Paris if that did not suit you to any degree, but I cannot tell you how glad I would be if you came. My only fear, and what I say is true, is that I may die before that time. I do not speak to you about my health at all because of my horror of inciting pity, but, in fact, you would do a good deed in all sorts of ways were you to come here. I take the liberty of telling you how much I desire it, do not scold me, I beseech you, no longer distress your pupil and retract the three villainous words which you wrote her; I would prefer to hear: "I hate you" . . .

Although two months of "bitterness or aridity" failed to make Madame du Deffand yield, they did at least placate her correspondent. The peace—or rather the truce—was sanctioned by a portrait of Madame du Deffand in verse sent by Walpole to his friend. The gesture, ostensibly an exchange of compliments, indicated how Walpole wanted the relationship to be: an idealised friendship with a literary slant designed to bring them equal glory.

A comparison of the two portraits may reveal a marked divergence not only of temperament and sensibility, but of culture and national style. Despite her obvious concern for diplomacy and desire to please, Madame du Deffand outlines an unmistakable character whose failings are more revealing and more alive than his virtues. Her psychological insight and extraordinary ease of style are the triumph of French civilisation. Walpole's sculptured portrait is more like a tablet in the Gothic style that might adorn a corner of Strawberry Hill. A traditional Anglo-Saxon symbolism, which is both solemn and somewhat intimidating, dispels any idle of worldliness: the *marquise*'s wit, intelligence and humour are unrecognisable when stripped of their elegant trappings and couched in the crude stuff of allegory. Madame du Deffand's portrait of Walpole captures a real person with all his contradictions, all the more loved for that. Walpole's tedious lines solemnly depict an heraldic shield with which to adorn his own family tree.

PORTRAIT OF THE MARQUISE
DU DEFFAND   1766

Where do Wit and Memory dwell,
Where is Fantasy's preferr'd retreat?
Where does Judgement hold her court,
Decree the laws of Gaiety and Games?
And reason—not that Lady
Who adopts the name of Sage,
And, unworthy of the title that she claims,
Calls herself Philosophy—
But Reason to whom I refer
The Slave of Truth and Passion's Queen
Who doubts but does not now dictate: aims at excellence,
And to Presumption leaves the rest;
By whom does that triumphant beauty dwell?
By Rousseau? No, by Voltaire neither.
Nor yet where eloquence's blast
Veils the sense that she should ornament,

Blinds the passions she should excite,
Making them accomplice to imposture.
You who know, say where Patience
Bears her irreparable loss;
And deprived of her most precious object,
Smiles about the little that remains?
Say at last where irresistibly runs
The richest river known to friendship?
Which neither ripples o'er the banks of Love
Nor bathes the feet of haughty Pride;
But winding twixt divided banks
Impartial slides through rival armies:
And, like Holy Charity equally divides
Her flood between Gaul and Albion?
Together all these virtues live:
The convent of Saint Joseph is their home:
Their sanctuary du Deffand's mind—
Censor, be still! She is old and blind.[108]

MADAME DU DEFFAND TO WALPOLE   *This Thursday, 22 January 1767*

. . . Now for my portrait; it is the most charming in all the world; but
what most pleases me about it, is: Censor, be still etc., that causes me
to flatter myself that you believe what comes before. But, my Tutor,
that is not how I would like to be depicted by you; I would like to
hear harsh truths; that is to say that you should not spare me any of
my faults, as you would not have done in moments of anger. Is there
not by chance one? If so, please tell me; rest assured that I will not be
vexed. I would not count on you, if I were not persuaded that you see
me as I am, which is perfectly imperfect. I am convinced that you
would like me less if I were free from fault; I judge by the grandmama;
I would like her far more if, with all her virtues, she had some
weaknesses; she has perfected herself too much; all the qualities one
acquires do not equal first impulses. But as for you, my poor Tutor,
you rend my heart when you expand on your hatred of the human
race. How is it possible for you to have had so much cause for
complaint? Have you encountered monsters, hyenas, crocodiles? For
myself, I have met, and I still meet, only fools, idiots, liars, the envious

and sometimes the treacherous; ah well! that did not discourage me, and my persistent belief that it was not impossible to find an honest man, caused me to find one. Do not take it upon yourself to ask who he is; it is a secret which I will tell neither to you nor to anyone; I can see that you believe you can guess at it; if that is so, I wash my hands of the matter, it is not my fault . . .

This Sunday the 25th

. . . Ah! I have been thinking deeply for several days and I have pronounced myself guilty in the case against you. I approve of your behaviour towards me on every point; you have suspected me of folly of which I am not guilty, but suspecting it, you have behaved with all possible wisdom, friendship and truth, besides you can trust that my feelings for you are equal to those which you have for me, except for my respect which is greater and must be greater since you do not owe me as much as I owe you. Can there be no more of this trial, my Tutor? You will no longer fear me in any way, you will cause me no more sorrow? . . .

"Trial," "fear," "sorrow," these became the words of a correspondence which, bereft of the misunderstanding which continually gave rise to them, might well have been unable to continue. Nevertheless, these three words have left a mark; the attitudes of the two correspondents remained essentially unchanged with on the one side demands, and on the other rejection, but Madame du Deffand's attitude altered slightly so that she became more reasonable, not so much by conviction as by necessity. Her desire to conquer was changed into tactical resistance; she never gave up Walpole, but resigned herself to not having him. Fatalism and bitterness brought about the change and after a brief period of illusion, the *marquise*'s pessimism was re-awakened.

MADAME DU DEFFAND TO WALPOLE   *Paris, this 4 April 1767*

Surely, some sorcerer, or perhaps your bad angel benumbs you or troubles your intelligence when you receive my letters; every word and every syllable must have pleased you because of the degree of your friendship; and supposing you to have none, there is nothing to displease you or for you to find intolerable. But it is destiny: I can never have any pleasure unless it be counterbalanced by great pain. Resignation can go no further; I submit myself without a murmur, without complaint to whatever you decide, to whatever suits you. I would like to be able to send you my soul instead of a letter. Then you would see if my feelings are ridiculous and if I think I am right to demand nothing, what opinions I have of you, whether I am romantic, whether or not I value myself justly, whether you can fear your own ingratitude, finally, whether there is another creature in the universe capable of an attachment like mine. Since I can only express myself in words and since all my words shock or wound you, I wisely and very necessarily decide to say no more. I will only tell you that I am very pleased by your repeated promise to come and see me. You owe this act of kindness to your virtues; only they demand it, not I; all my desires end with spending a few days with you before an eternal separation. I cannot believe that separation is far away, which is why any delay terrifies me. I often tell myself that should I reach my end before seeing you again, I will not suffer in the other world; but this idea wounds me so long as I am in this one. Tell me again that this is some "Scudéry"![109] I do not know how you understand it; I only know the friendship one feels; and I can only speak of what I feel. I do not think that you should have made any sacrifice for me, nor that you should have loved me in preference to all else. Ah! my God! That idea is a thousand leagues away. Nothing seems more extraordinary to me than the favours which you are so kind as to do me. Only my honesty can have deserved your affection: suffer it then, for what it is, and bear with patience what you call the outpourings, the effusions etc. . . .

MADAME DU DEFFAND TO WALPOLE   *This Saturday, 23 May 1767*

You want me to hope to live ninety years? Ah! Good God, what an accursed hope! Do you not know that I detest life and despair at having lived so long and that I can find no consolation for being born? I was not made for this world; I do not know if there is any other; if there is, whatever it is, I fear it. It is impossible to be at peace with others or with oneself; one displeases everyone: some who fear they are not respected or loved enough, others for the opposite reason. One needs to develop feelings to suit everyone, or at least to

pretend to them, and I am not capable of that. Simplicity and naturalness are extolled, yet those who have them are hated; one knows all
that and yet, despite it, one fears death, and why does one fear it? Not
only because of uncertainty of the hereafter, but because of a great
repugnance for destruction, which reason cannot overcome. Ah! reason, reason! What is reason! What power has she? When does she
speak? When can she be heard? What good does she do? Does she
conquer the passions? It is not so; and if she prevented the soul's
expansion she would be a hundred times more harmful to our happiness than our passions could ever be; so one would live to experience
nothingness, and nothingness (which I greatly value) is only good
because it cannot be experienced. Here are some fourpenny metaphysics, I humbly beg your pardon; you have a right to tell me: "Be
content to tire yourself, abstain from tiring others." Oh! you are right.
Let us change the conversation.

MADAME DU DEFFAND TO WALPOLE   *Paris, this Sunday, 26 July*

In all the fifteen months and more of our correspondence, there is no
sensation, no impression, no situation that you have not made me
feel, which you have not made me experience. I often wish to write a
history of it, or at least a novel, for that is what you would perhaps
like to call it, but today I think it would be more dignified for me and
much less tiresome for you, to throw our memoirs in the fire and
throw our caps over the windmill, and to offer each other, when we
meet again, the flowering of a new acquaintanceship . . .

In letter after letter patience and impatience march hand in hand in a
bold, paradoxical symmetry. But quarrelling, humiliation and resignation never destroy Madame du Deffand's hope that her friend will
return. Perhaps the illusion was essential to her fantasy. Or had she an
awareness of inevitability. However it may have been, after sixteen
months of an exhausting, cruel correspondence and much procrastina-
tion and without any apparent motive other than to see her, Walpole
announced his return to Paris. Madame du Deffand's happiness was
complete. None of the misunderstandings and insults or words too
rashly spoken had taken root; they melted away like snow in the sun.

The *marquise* prepared herself for a new meeting, to give and to receive "the flowering of a new acquaintanceship."

MADAME DU DEFFAND TO WALPOLE   *Paris, Sunday 9 August 1767*

Ah! Do not accuse me of lacking faith, I have complete faith in you, and, if you are not the most sincere man in all the world, I am the person most devoid of discernment. It is the only aspect of your character which I perfectly know; I am far from knowing the other with such certainty, I find so many contradictions in you which I cannot explain to myself; considerable examination on my part and considerable trust on yours will dissipate these shadows: we will both gain a great deal and we will be imperturbable when we see ourselves revealed; you will not have very much more to learn about me, you will see only that that which you called folly was not so, that I am further removed than anyone from romantic ideas, and that my friendship for you has all the gravity and solidity suitable to my age and our condition; but we must put off discussing this matter until we meet again.

You plan then, to leave on the 17th; I confess that I do not have too much hope, Monsieur, your brother's state of health[110] seems most precarious and that is a reason to alter your plans about which I would have nothing to say; but, if in fact you come, believe that I will realise the price of such a favour; your heart must be truly grateful and very tender for you to make so considerable an effort as to leave all that concerns you, all that pleases you and all that interests you, to transplant yourself to a country which is, for you, worse than a desert, and where you will find only me whom you esteem worthy of you. I am so perfectly sensible to the excessiveness of such a favour that I should have the gratitude to free you from your word, to relieve you of your promise, in a word to give up the pleasure of seeing you again, but, I confess, that is impossible for me; I would that my age, my condition, my health and propriety might allow me to go and see you, then I would certainly spare you the trouble of coming to see me; but as that is impossible I accept with perfect gratitude the proof of friendship which you give me in coming to spend several weeks with me. You want, you say, to be incognito for two days. Ah! my

God, two days, as many as you would like, nothing can give me more pleasure . . .

MADAME DU DEFFAND TO WALPOLE   *Sunday {23 August} at seven o'clock in the morning*

At last, at last, there is no longer any sea to divide us; I can hope to see you from today; I would certainly have been alone if it were not for your changed plans; but as I expected you to leave on the 17th and to arrive on Thursday, the 20th, I had not cancelled my Sunday but had taken care to have only your special acquaintances, except for Madame de Vallière who had agreed to come fifteen days earlier, and I had invited Mademoiselle Clairon; so she will be here at 7 o'clock today; the spectators will be Mesdames de Villeroy, d'Aiguillon, de Chabrillan, de La Vallière, de Forcalquier, de Montigny. The men, de Sault and Pont-de-Veyle, the Président and Madame de Jonzac who will not stay to supper.

Yesterday, I sent to ask Madame Simonetti to send word as soon as you arrive; if you wish to come to me, as I hope you will, you shall have my carriage at once; but if, as I fear, you wish to stay in, I will send you for supper, some rice, a chicken, some fresh eggs, in a word whatever suits you.

I hope that tomorrow you will dine and sup with me tête-à-tête; we will have a lot to say. I am overwhelmed with joy but, at the same time I have a terrible fear; expect to find me quite up and down.

Except for this accursed company which I have so foolishly assembled, and which, as I have told you, is due to arrive at seven o'clock, you would have found me on alighting from your chaise; that would have greatly displeased you, but I would not have cared.

Have courage, my Tutor, if you are not wearied to death, come and sup with me, or at least come and spend a moment with me. Ah well! What am I saying, you will not arrive today; I have calculated the times of the *post-chaise* and, if you slept at Arras, you will have forty-one leagues to go. Finally, if you arrive and you do not wish to see me today, allow me at least to have news of you before I retire. Let me know what you want for your dinner tomorrow, and the time.

You will find in your room all your charming "Julienne"[111] gems, and a miserable breakfast service and a little bowl and a small milk jug for your daily use and also for mine when I have the idea of going to take tea with you.

Oh! I cannot convince myself that a man of your importance, who holds the reins of a great State in his hands, and consequently those of Europe, should determine to leave everything in order to come and see an old Sibyl. Oh! How ridiculous; such a decision is to have no shame, I confess, however, that I am very glad.

This time Madame du Deffand was not disappointed. On the evening of the 23rd, with only an hour's delay, Walpole appeared in the Saint-Joseph salon. He noted briefly and precisely in his diary: "23 August, arrived at Paris a quarter before seven. At eight to Madame du Deffand. Found the Clairon acting Agrippina and Phedra. Not tall, but I liked her acting more than I expected. Supped there with her, and the Duchesses de Villeroy, d'Aiguillon, and de La Vallière, Mesdames de Forcalquier, Plessis-Châtillon and young Chabrillan, and Messieurs de Saulx, Pont-de-Veyle and Grave."[112]

Madame du Deffand would have liked their first meeting to have taken place in private, but perhaps the need to control herself and to welcome Walpole with no more than the affectionate solicitude due to an old *habitué* after a long absence, may have helped her to overcome the first violent emotion. As for Walpole, it would be hard to imagine a welcome more suited to his tastes. The "accursed company" which Madame du Deffand would willingly have sacrificed, was for him a source of real delight. His adoration of the nobility and his passion for the theatre must have been fully satisfied by this small aristocratic élite gathered around Diderot's symbol of "the most perfect recitation."[113] Since 1766, Clairon had officially given up the theatre and agreed to perform only occasionally in private houses. The great actress who was a friend of Voltaire and the *philosophes,* was probably introduced to Saint-Joseph by Pont-de-Veyle with whom she had had a relationship. But those who cared to listen to such great interpretations of Racine, lived as if they themselves were eternally on the stage. Many of them even gained immortality for their relentless frivolity, because of one repartee, one aphorism or one gesture. For instance the beautiful duchesse de La Vallière, who on her arrival at court caused the duc de Gèvres to exclaim: "We have a queen!" and who replied to an old man who had long loved her without daring to declare himself, "My God, why did you not tell me? You would have had me like the others."[114] And then Madame de Forcalquier who, outraged by a slap in the face from her husband, went into his study to slap his face in return and said, "Here you are, Monsieur, here is your slap, I can do nothing with it."[115] Walpole was lucky enough to hear for himself a few memorable witticisms such as he dreamed made history, as for instance when Madame de Plessis-Chatillon exclaimed on hearing her husband sing the praises of his first wife: "I can assure you, Monsieur, that no one regrets her more than I."[116] And when Madame du Deffand asked Mademoiselle Clairon, "What is Garrick like in person?" she replied, "Like he wishes, Madame!"[117]

A period of intense happiness had begun for Madame du Deffand: Walpole had returned to France for her alone and he devoted almost all his time to her. He stayed in Paris from 23 August until 8 October and throughout these forty-eight days, which he recorded punctiliously in his diary, there are only two, 1 and 8 September on which there is no mention of the *marquise*. The two friends nearly always supped together at Saint-Joseph or at the Président's house, or less frequently at Madame de Forcalquier's, the Prince de Beauvau's or with Madame de Choiseul. He occasionally visited Madame Geoffrin where he once met d'Alembert, and once Julie de Lespinasse, and exceptionally ventured into other circles, but he had been adopted by Madame du Deffand's circle and there received, in homage to her, very special treatment of which he was extremely sensible.

Walpole's presence which in the more dramatic letters was referred to as a supreme act of compassion towards a poor, infirm old woman at death's door, in fact had an extremely enlivening effect. The *marquise* was driven by a feverish energy which belied both her infirmity and her age. She accompanied her friend to the theatre, to the Foire Saint-Ovide, and walked with him along the boulevards. Insomnia and excitement made her put off going to bed and thus being separated from Walpole, until the last possible moment. "Madame du Deffand came home and sat with me till 2,"[118] Walpole notes in his diary on 21 September. Madame du Deffand's aim was no longer "to kill time"[119] but to live it with intensity; it was no longer so much a question of entertaining herself, as Walpole. In a letter written to Montagu in 1769 on his next visit to Paris, Walpole perfectly illustrates Madame du Deffand's frantic happiness, the "herculean weakness" with which she devoted herself to his amusement.

"My dear old friend was charmed with your mention of her, and made me vow to return you a thousand compliments. She cannot conceive why you will not step hither. Feeling in herself no difference between the spirits of twenty-three and seventy-three, she thinks there is no impediment to doing whatever one will, but the want of eyesight. If she had that, I am persuaded no consideration would prevent her making me a visit at Strawberry Hill. She makes songs, sings them, remembers all that ever were made; and having lived from the most agreeable to the most reasoning age, has all that was amiable in the last, all that is sensible in this, without the vanity of the former, or the pedant impertinence of the latter. I have heard her dispute with all sorts of people on all sorts of subjects, and never knew her in the wrong. She humbles the learned, sets right their disciples, and finds conversation for everybody. Affectionate as Madame de Sévigné, she has none of her prejudices, but a more universal taste; and with the most delicate frame, her spirits hurry her through a life of fatigue that would kill me if I was to continue here. If we return by one in the morning from suppers in the country, she proposes walking to the boulevard or the Foire St Ovide because it is too early to go to bed. I had great difficulty last night to persuade her, though she was not well, not to sit up till between two and three for the comet, for which purpose she had appointed an astronomer to bring his telescopes to the Président Hénault's, as she thought it would amuse me. In short, her goodness to me is so excessive, that I feel unashamed at producing my withered person in a round of diversions, which I have quitted at home. I tell a story; I do feel ashamed and sigh to be in my quiet castle and cottage; but it costs me many a pang, when I reflect that I shall probably never have resolution enough to take another journey to see this best and sincerest of friends, who loves me as much as my mother did! But it is idle to look forward—what is next year—a bubble that may burst for her or me before even the flying year can hurry to the end of its almanac!"[120]

Madame du Deffand took Walpole on pilgrimages to the scenes of her youth such as Sceaux. Walpole was impressed by the *marquise*'s tales and vividly struck by visiting the kingdom which fifteen years later still retained traces of the terrible *duchess*'s tyranny: "I myself saw an instance of the Duchess du Maine's *princely* disposition at Sceaux whither Madame du Deffand carried me many years after her Serene Highness's death. In a closet at Sceaux painted in grotesque by Clermont, she had obliged several of her favourite courtiers to be drawn with faces of monkeys, the rest of their persons as human figures. In one panel I remember was Madame de Staal and Monsidur de Malézieu playing at tric-trac[121]—but the Princess herself (who in reality was extremely crooked) and her daughter were represented as beautiful as Venus and one of the Graces. Insolent superiority could not play the tyrant with more insensibility; nor female vanity exact more mortifying homage."[122]

Adulated, spoilt, entertained and, above all, rid of the fear of his correspondence being intercepted, Walpole, who was also reassured by the temporary nature of the situation, again acknowledged his pleasure in being loved as much as his mother had loved him. He once more enjoyed his tête-à-tête with the *marquise*; together with a few friendly witnesses he indulged in childish behaviour which under any other circumstances would have made him shudder. "Scene of my asking Madame du Deffand in marriage of Madame de Choiseul," he wrote in his diary on 19 September 1767.[123]

So Madame du Deffand's dream, wonderfully re-created, lived for a new, brief season which came to an end at four o'clock in the afternoon of 8 October when Walpole left Paris for England.

MADAME DU DEFFAND TO WALPOLE   *Paris, Friday 9 October 1767*
                                       at ten o'clock in the morning

What cowardliness, what weakness and what ridiculousness I allowed you to perceive! I had quite promised myself the opposite; but, but . . . , Forget all that, forgive me for it, my Tutor, and think no more of your little one than that she is reasonable, obedient, and above all grateful; that her respect, yes, I say respect, her fear, her filial fear, her tender but serious attachment will be all her life's happiness until her last moment. What do age and blindness matter? What does it matter where one lives? What does it matter to be surrounded by nothing which is not foolish or extravagant? When the soul is fully occupied, only the object which occupies it is lacking; and when that object responds to what one feels for him, there is nothing more to be desired . . .

Following fast upon the pain of separation, the *marquise*'s dream that Walpole's visit might mean an improvement in their relationship, faded for ever, as is evident in a later passage from the same letter, written after the arrival of one from Walpole. The *marquise* is confronted by a well-worn path and the only novelty is that nothing will persuade her to tread it with resignation and humility.

Saturday the 10th at one o'clock
in the afternoon

Here is the letter from Chantilly which I expected yesterday, and which evidently found the package closed when it was brought to the post. I will begin by thanking you, and by assuring you that I am very glad of it; I would be quite tempted to send you a quotation from "my brother" Quinault,[124] but you would scold me, and I will allow myself nothing more to vex you, and never, never will I write you a word which might force you to cause me sadness by your replies. I prefer to stifle all my thoughts rather than to allow you to glimpse one which might tire or weary you, or displease you. What I think about you has become so much part of my existence that so long as I live it will be quite impossible for me to entertain any other idea; but as for you, my Tutor, who have six or seven things in your head and for whom every day of the week differs, one from the other, your style must vary more than mine; whatever you write to me will be equally agreeable. Allow yourself to tell me whatever passes through your mind; do not think about me when you write, tell me only about yourself, do not concern yourself with my happiness; have no etiquette with me; allow yourself to express yourself naturally, but above all, never have the intention of changing anything in the way I think about you; you would work at it uselessly; in wishing to succeed you would destroy my happiness.

Do you know what madness came to my mind? Give your letters the sound of your voice, your accent, then I would be as happy once a week as I am every day when you are here. Oh! now, you will say, the little one is wandering; *hé, point au tout au contr-aire,*[125] and to prove it, let us talk of something else.

Unexpressed as they were, even suffocated—albeit not always so—Madame du Deffand's thoughts continued to dog Walpole. Is someone who becomes, despite himself, the "essence" of another's life, not bound to feel involved and blackmailed? Are Madame du Deffand's good resolutions not admission in themselves of the danger of compromising behaviour? Is it not a declaration of love to forbid oneself to talk of love? Madame du Deffand's letters continued to present a permanent threat to Walpole; they did not even need to become explicit to provoke an immediate reaction. The correspondence subsequently resumed its usual pattern, outlined by Lewis, just as it did after Walpole's subsequent visits in 1769, 1771 and 1775. An internal dynamism unconnected with reality and the outside world, caused stormy quarrels and moments of good cheer to alternate with the regularity of clockwork.

Year after year Madame du Deffand forced herself to the best of her ability to satisfy her correspondent and preserve him from the tedium of her feelings by filling her letters with "the proper names" that Walpole "love[d]"[126] and with the "nothings" which he so often "mourned."[127] The *marquise* could become a scrupulous chronicler of events around her, but she was unable to disguise her own indifference. Her egocentricity automatically protected her entirely from any element of surprise at her surroundings. She was as indifferent to the marquis de Sade's first exploit as she was to Louis XV's daughter's decision to become a Carmelite nun. The absence of any form of value-judgement allowed her to recount both these events with the scientific objectivity of one observing the symptoms of a single disease, the folly of mankind.

MADAME DU DEFFAND TO WALPOLE   *Paris, this 12 April 1768*
                                                       on Easter Tuesday

. . . A certain comte de Sade[128] nephew of the *abbé,* author of *Pétrarque* met a tall, shapely woman of thirty who begged him for alms; he asked her a great many questions and showed interest in her, offered to take her out of her misery and to make her concierge of a small house he has near Paris. This woman accepted; he told her to come and find him on the following morning; she went; he first led her into all the rooms in the house, all the corners and all the nooks, then he led her into the attic; there he shut himself in with her and ordered her to take all her clothes off; she resisted his suggestion, threw herself at his feet, told him that she was an honest woman; he showed her a pistol which he took from his pocket and told her to obey which she immediately did; then he tied up her hands and beat her cruelly. When she was covered in blood, he took a jar of ointment from his pocket, dressed her wounds and left her; I do not know if he gave her anything to eat or drink; but he did not see her again until the next morning. He examined her wounds and saw that the ointment had had the effect he expected; then he took out a pocket-knife and slashed her body; he then took the same ointment, covered the wounds with it and went away. This woman in her despair, struggled in such a way that she broke her ties and threw herself out of the window overlooking the road. It is not thought that she hurt herself in falling; crowds flocked round her; the lieutenant of police was informed of the matter; Monsieur de Sade has been arrested; he is, so they say, in the Château de Saumur. No one knows what the outcome of this affair will be, or whether this imprisonment will be all his punishment which it may well be as he belongs to an important and well-considered family; it is said that the motive for this execrable deed was to test the ointment . . .

MADAME DU DEFFAND TO WALPOLE

Paris, this Saturday, 14 April 1770

. . . Today's great event is Madame Louise's[129] retreat. Eighteen years ago she wanted to become a nun; ten years ago she decided to become a Carmelite; only the King and the Archbishop[130] were in her confidence, and they opposed her plans. Apparently, after she had made them consent, she decided on the day with them; it was to be the Wednesday of Holy Week. On the eve of that day the King told Monsieur de Croismare, the equerry, to go and take orders from Madame Louise and that all her orders were to be obeyed. She asked for a carriage at seven o'clock the following morning, with no body-guards and no pages; she ordered Madame de Guistelle,[131] one of her ladies, to be dressed and in attendance at seven o'clock. She said nothing to her sisters who had not the slightest suspicion of her resolve. On the Wednesday, she stepped into her carriage at precisely seven o'clock, changed horses at Sèvres, and said: "To Saint-Denis." On arriving at Saint-Denis, she said, "To the Carmelites." With the door open she embraced Madame de Guistelle: "Adieu, Madame," she said, "We will never see each other again." She gave her a letter for the King and for one of her sisters; she had brought neither a shift, nor a nightcap. She was to take the white veil on arrival. On

Thursday they brought her some clothes from which she took only two shifts and an under-bodice; she called herself Sister Thérèse-Augustine. That is how she signs the second letter she wrote to the King with the permission of "our reverend mother." She begs him to be so kind as to pay twelve thousand francs for her dowry. It is twice the usual dowry, but it is what the more ill-favoured pay, who are more delicate and may require certain comforts; she also asks him to continue paying her annuity until she takes her vows so that she is able to remunerate in some way those men and women who have served her. Do you not pity that? We are a strange kind! When neither passion nor fortune makes us unhappy, we make ourselves unhappy with chimeras. That is all you will have from me today; I need a little while to re-establish the calm in my soul: I am overjoyed to be on good terms with you, and it will certainly not be my fault if in future I am on bad terms.

This Easter Day

. . . The King had known of Madame Louise's plans for only two months; she had allowed all her clothes for the marriage festivities[132] to be made; she has not taken the white veil, but will do so in six months' time. The event did not cause a great sensation; people shrug their shoulders, pity weakness of spirit, and talk of other things.

You have fine weather in your countryside; I congratulate you.

XI

Old Age

HENCEFORTH MADAME DU DEFFAND inevitably gives the impression of having outlived herself. Her letters convey more and more the feeling of an ended life, a resigned existence without expectation, desire or hope. The life of her imagination, monopolised by Walpole, is paralysed by rejection and distance, and her practical, everyday life made sterile by indifference. This slow, majestic agony lasted for thirteen years with the obsessive repetition of the same emotional game and the same worldly functions now devoid of their former meaning. The *marquise* left a self-portrait written during these last years, dictated in about 1774 when she was seventy-eight years old. Her long decline had become a way of life which could be described objectively, with no apparent emotion:

"M[adame du Deffand] is thought to be more intelligent than she is, she is praised, she is feared, she deserves neither the one nor the other, her intelligence is as her appearance was, and as her birth and fortune are, neither extraordinary, nor distinguished; she had no education to speak of and has acquired nothing except by experience; this experience came late and was the fruit of many misfortunes.

"I would say of her character that justice and truth are natural to her and that they are the virtues which she most values.

"Her constitution is weak, all her qualities bear witness to this.

"Born without talent, incapable of great application, she is very susceptible to ennui, and, not finding any resources within herself, she seeks them in her surroundings and this search is often unsuccessful.

This same weakness means that the impressions she receives, although very vivid, are rarely profound; those that she makes are similar; she is capable of pleasing but inspires little emotion.

"She is wrongly suspected of jealousy, she is never jealous of worth nor of preferences given to those who deserve them, but she has little patience with quackery or false pretentions which seek to impose themselves. She is always tempted to tear off the masks she encounters, and that, as I have said, is what makes others fear her and praise her."[1]

A comparison of this self-portrait with the one written in 1728 gives an idea of a profoundly altered person. The essential characteristics — sincerity, naturalness, justness and the worm of ennui — remain the same but are less marked and less defined. Caught in the twilight, the outline of the picture has become blurred; it has a transitory, fleeting air. Madame du Deffand feels that way about herself: "I seek my soul and find only the recollection of it."[2] This was certainly not what inspired the continual flux of visitors who came to admire her at Saint-Joseph.

The *marquise*'s outward appearance was miraculously unmarked by unhappiness, age, infirmity and an unhealthy life. Mademoiselle d'Aïssé, Voltaire and Hénault inform us incidentally that Madame du Deffand was very attractive in her youth. (The virtuoso psychology so typical of eighteenth-century France was accompanied by an almost total disregard for physical appearance.) Neither years nor sickness had destroyed all "traces of beauty,"[3] and Miss Berry's description being based on Walpole's observation must be credited: "Her eyes were closed, but her face was in no way altered; her features had all retained their regularity, and were of a great finesse and great beauty. A freshness and delicacy which she preserved till an advanced age emanated from her person . . . She could not bear to be pitied for her infirmity and did her very best to have it forgotten, by always turning towards the person to whom she was talking, or towards the object she was discussing. She was as careful as she was clever in avoiding the embarrassed manners of the blind."[4]

Although she disguised it — even in her letters the verb "to see" recurs constantly — her blindness created an aura around her, whilst pride and indifference caused her to assume a mask of Olympian detachment. Talleyrand, who met Madame du Deffand in 1772 when he was eighteen and she was seventy-six, was both moved and misled by her apparent serenity.

"It would be impossible to imagine a countenance which exuded more goodness than Madame du Deffand's. In her person as well as in her dress she presented a perfect example of respectable beauty... Blindness, far from disfiguring her as one might think, lent to the gentle calm of her appearance, an expression close to bliss."[5]

Madame du Deffand's letters to Walpole show how deceptive her appearance could be; in her letters to the man who was the object of all her affection, there is no sign of "gentle calm," but rather of anguish, nor any sign of "bliss" but rather of estrangement from her everyday life and her life-long friends.

20 October 1766

... Last evening I was admiring the numerous gathering assembled at my house; both men and women seemed like clockwork machines who came and went and talked and laughed without thinking, without reflection and without feeling; each one acted his part out of habit: Madame la duchesse d'Aiguillon was dying of laughter, Madame Forcalquier despised everything, Madame de La Vallière prattled about everything. The parts played by the men were no better, and I was sunk in the blackest of thought; I imagined I had spent my life in illusions; that I had dug for myself every abyss into which I had fallen; that all my judgements had been false and fearful, and always too sudden, and that in the end I had never known anyone perfectly; and that I had not been known either, and that perhaps I did not know myself...

*Monday { 16 November 1767} at
seven o'clock in the evening*

... Twelve people came yesterday, and I admired the different kinds and nuances of folly: we were all perfectly foolish, but each in his own way; they all left me at one o'clock and they all left me without regret...

22 May 1768

... My God, my God! How few bearable people there are! And there are no agreeable ones. The more prudent I become, the more I observe; for the less one talks, the more one reflects. I find everyone detestable: one [Mme de Forcalquier] is an honest person, but she is stupid, muddled, dull, and full of nonsense which she mistakes for thought; another [Mme de Jonzac] is reasonable; but she is cold, mediocre; everything she does or says is contrived; another [Mme d'Aubeterre] chatters like a magpie, her accents are those of an opera girl; another [the duchesse d'Aiguillon] talks as though she were inspired, hardly ever knows what she is saying; her only conclusion is that she has a great mind, is learned, brilliant etc. That is a picture of a circle. There are many more who could be described and who are far worse, for at least there is not too much falseness, jealousy or ill-will in these ...

On this unchanging scene where the same actors forever play the same parts, only the mood changes. Within the company, friendships are made and broken, there are moments of indulgence or intolerance, of goodwill and sarcasm. The permanently ridiculed *Idole* is occasionally recognised objectively; the generally tolerated Madame de Forcalquier manages to provoke a quarrel which causes a stir;[6] Madame de Mirepoix and Madame d'Aiguillon, who were both blamed for their acceptance of Madame du Barry, are defended against excessive attack.

This everyday tapestry, endured and despised as it was, was nevertheless indispensible to the *marquise* for whom anything was preferable to solitude. "I have, you say, a critical mind, and you have a proud one: that may be, and I believe it, but I am weary and you amuse yourself; you find resources within yourself; I find only nothingness, and it is as bad to find nothingness within oneself as it would be fortunate to have remained in nothingness. So I am obliged to try to pull myself out of it; I attach myself to what I can, from thence comes all the disdain and the everyday discontent, and a disgust for life which may serve some purpose; it allows me to bear patiently the decrepitude of age, and diminishes vitality and my sensibility to everything."[7]

Seen as a negative necessity, social life excluded any expression of affection since, "friendship and enmity have the same aspect in this world."[8] The price of such immunity guaranteed by indifference, was solitude: "Indifference to those around one, like their indifference to one, makes for great solitude."[9] The *marquise* never felt the "loneliness of high society" more than she did now.[10]

But it is questionable whether the last part of Madame du Deffand's life can be seen as an entirely negative, detached and nonsensical existence. This is the reality which undoubtedly emerges from her letters to Walpole, but the reality is permanently emphasised as a supreme homage to him and as a form of emotional blackmail.

Dazzled as she was by her encounter with "a man of stone or of snow,"[11] Madame du Deffand destroyed the world around her. If only she were allowed to love him and be accepted by him, her life would be different. But the rich social activity and the forest of acquaintances surrounding the barrenness and the inner desert which the *marquise* permanently analysed and denounced, must have made some mark. Madame du Deffand used her acquaintances as the chronically sick use drugs which have no real effect whilst giving an illusion of momentary relief; she used them constantly, and was frightened of ever being without them, but the methodical way in which she replenished her store may have produced far greater results than she was prepared to recognise.

This uninterrupted attempt at distraction had of necessity to take others into account, and it required a method and a discipline quite alien to a condition of total depression. Every afternoon, day after day, year after year, Madame du Deffand installed herself in her drawing-room where she received varying numbers of visitors whose comings and goings she observed with a careful attention sharpened by blindness. She concerned herself with entertaining them, she followed and controlled their conversation, she was up to date with all the news and topics of discussion necessary to enrich it; later with a few of her afternoon guests or others, a "small" or "large committee" would go through the ritual of supper according to a more or less fixed schedule either in her house or elsewhere. Sometimes when there were too many people, or when she was tired, the *marquise* did not leave her *tonneau* and someone would come and keep her company and eat with her. When the guests left the table conversation would start again, games would be played and the numbers would swell as new arrivals came from other suppers bringing the latest news, and then the evening stretched on until late into the night. Madame de Deffand hung on to her guests so as to delay for as long as possible the moment of retiring and facing insomnia. Fortunately she was not the only one; Madame de Luxembourg also liked to stay up late and, according to Mercier, "several women in Paris only get up towards evening and retire at the approach of dawn; a woman *bel esprit* usually adopts this practice and comes to be known as a lamp."[12]

This way of life required a rich network of acquaintanceship to which newcomers were constantly being added. Madame du Deffand filled her solitude with a series of ornaments which served her in turn according to circumstances, but which she knew how to manipulate and fuse into a rich apparatus of grand ceremony.

The oldest and most usual adornments to her salon consisted of the ageing Président and Pont-de-Veyle, the maréchales de Luxembourg and de Mirepoix, Messieurs de La Vallière, de Forcalquier and d'Aiguillon, the Princes de Beauvau whom she had come to know in about 1755. In more recent times, the *marquise* introduced among the new *habitués* her nephew, the Archbishop of Toulouse. A warmer and more intimate little circle was created by those who gathered round Madame de Choiseul, l'abbé Barthélemy, Monsieur Thiers—known as the *petit-oncle*—and a few others. This group was sometimes overrun by the rich and colourful crowd who invaded the Chief Minister's house. Then there was the strangers' (or foreigners') gallery consisting mostly of diplomats and which was constantly changing. In 1771 the *marquise*'s friend and correspondent, Count Scheffer, reappeared in Paris. As Gustavus III's chief minister, he now held the reins of Sweden in his hands. Then there was the Neapolitan ambassador, Caracciolo, who was guilty of dividing his time between Julie de Lespinasse's salon and Saint-Joseph. There were the ambassadors of Sweden, Denmark, Gleichen and Creutz, there was the huge English community which besides the ambassadors included Hume, Fox, Gibbon and Burke, the old friends Selwyn and Craufurd and innumerable visitors sent by Walpole. Finally, there was the vast but select network created by the comings and goings of high society, by the first pilgrimages of new generations, the fleeting appearance of passing celebrities, like Franklin (the envoy to Versailles from the British–American colonies), great aristocrats, princes, and foreign kings visiting Paris.

Lescure maintains that Walpole's appearance and his monopolisation of Madame du Deffand provoked a decline or at least an alteration in the character of the famous *salon*.[13]

But it must not be forgotten that Madame du Deffand's heart was not all that had changed. Louis XV was about to end a long reign of apathy and cynicism with a final explosion of degradation. The death of Madame de Pompadour, the advent of Madame du Barry, the fall and exile of Choiseul, the disgrace of many great aristocrats loyal to the chief minister, beginning with the Prince de Beauvau, a succession of discreditable ministers and the dissolution of parliament were all final stages in the slow irreversible process of decline which involved the whole of society and the whole ruling class to which Madame du Deffand's friends belonged.

With the accession of Louis XVI power passed into the hands of new men like Turgot and Necker whose intellectual training had taken place far from the old aristocratic élite, and whose social centres were the houses of Julie de Lespinasse, baron d'Holbach and the Neckers. When, in 1774, Turgot was made comptroller general of finance, he chose many of his colleagues from Julie's entourage. She had been a friend for many years. He nominated Suard and Condorcet "historians of the currency." He took the abbé Morellet with him and put him in charge of his correspondence. Julie de Lespinasse triumphed and on 24 July 1774 Madame du Deffand commented on it sarcastically to Walpole: "The post has been given to Monsieur Turgot whom I used to see every day fourteen or fifteen years ago but with whom Lespinasse caused me to quarrel, as she did with all the encyclopaedists ... We will be governed by philosophers."

The cultural scene too had completely changed; men of letters were becoming more and more like journalists or polemicists, and from 1772 when Duclos died and d'Alembert was elected as permanent secretary, the *Académie* found itself besieged by illuminists. Besides, with a few exceptions, the *marquise* no longer frequented writers. Past disappointments only accentuated her attitude of aristocratic detachment and her feeling of belonging to a higher social cast. The words of her friend, Madame de Choiseul, might have been the *marquise*'s own: "I love letters and honour those who profess them, but I wish only to meet them in their books and I like only to see them in paint" (7 August 1768).

In this changing world the Saint-Joseph *salon* was by now a legendary institution, which no longer needed to represent anything other than itself; Madame du Deffand seemed like an extraordinary monument from the past whom the younger generation, like that improbable "ninny,"[14] the Prince de Ligne, Lauzun and Talleyrand hurried to admire before it was too late.

Could inertia and despair alone mastermind for so long such a perfect, relentless mechanism involving thousands of hours of conversation and a huge cast of people? And could such despair establish priorities, make introductions, seduce and conquer high society? Could the curiosity and ambition combined with indifference which had sustained Madame du Deffand for so long have now finally abandoned her? The chronicle of her daily existence partly belies the cry of icy despair running through her letters to Walpole. Perhaps the artificial existence which she adopted with such splendid tenacity, in some way became objective reality, life itself?"

Away from Walpole, Madame du Deffand never ceased to hope for that miracle of perfect friendship which she had realised in her youth with Madame de Flamarens and then with Formont. She could never renounce a need, the fulfilment of which was made impossible by her mistrust. Besides, her suspicions had been justified by Hénault's, Julie's and d'Alembert's betrayals. Thus her quest for friendship which, to judge from their language and behaviour, seems to have ended with Madame de Choiseul, was compromised from the start.

Thirty years younger than Madame du Deffand, Louise-Honorine Crozat du Châtel, niece of the extremely rich financier, Crozat, was married in 1750 at the age of fifteen to Etienne-François, comte de Stainville, later duc de Choiseul. Her immense bourgeois fortune breathed new life into his dissipated aristocratic inheritance. As soon as she was married, the young bride accompanied her ambassador husband to Rome and then Vienna. When, in 1758, he became foreign minister, they returned to France where, between Paris and Versailles, they lived a life dependent on his duties and rank. Madame du Deffand had been closely connected with her parents and so had known Madame de Choiseul since she was a child, but the friendship which flowered in about 1760 grew gradually closer in subsequent years. It can hardly be coincidence that it began at the time of the break with Mademoiselle de Lespinasse. The *marquise* was experiencing one of the darkest moments of her life, suddenly alone at the end of an association lasting ten years—her weak, obliging, but mediocre new companion, Mademoiselle Sanadon was hardly a substitute for Julie. The *salon* had been decimated by schism and Madame du Deffand, who was wounded by d'Alembert's betrayal, was more than ever disposed to make new friends.

What did the old sibyl, now nearly seventy and the young, thirty-year-old *duchesse* have in common beyond social convention and a distant connection? (Madame du Deffand's maternal grandmother had married, as his second wife, the duc de Choiseul's father.) What induced Madame de Choiseul to address her much older friend in a somewhat sickly way as "granddaughter" and to be called in return "grandmama"?

Madame du Deffand's vanity must have been flattered by the attention of the wife of one of the most powerful men in France, and more to the point, the perfect grace of this *"Vénus en abrégé,"*[15] this tiny, delicate "Queen of allegory"[16] conformed exactly to her conception of aristocracy. For her part, Madame de Choiseul was looking for personal friends and intellectual stimulation to alleviate the stultifying emptiness of public life.

Their different lives did not prevent the two women from having many things in common. Both had an unhappy past: "I had nothing from youth, but the happy illusion which was so early and so inhumanely snatched from me,"[17] the *duchesse* confided in her friend. And Madame du Deffand was no less bitter about the past than about the present. Madame de Choiseul had also experienced the pangs of unrequited love. She was married almost as a child to fulfil a promise extracted from her on the deathbed of her elder sister, the duchesse de Gontaut and mistress of the duc de Choiseul who, in her turn, wanted to at least assure Choiseul's fortune. Thereafter she passionately loved a husband who met her feelings with courteous indifference.

Choiseul had all the egoism and charm of a great aristocrat. He was intelligent, fascinating and witty, he accumulated success along his way without apparently seeking it. Life for him was a game in which one competes out of sporting instinct, careful only of one's own amusement and honour. His code was the code of the great French aristocracy which saw itself as in service to the kingdom but was unwilling to bow even to the monarch, *primus inter pares*. Such aristocrats despised their own money and that of others, they never hesitated to ruin themselves or to run into debt in order to display the magnificence due to their rank; they respected and claimed to consider their wives only in order

to safeguard the honour of their name. But Madame de Choiseul's real
place in her husband's life is described with brutal frankness in a letter
to Voltaire.

"I passionately love my pleasure, I am rich, I have a very beautiful
and very comfortable house in Paris; my wife is very intelligent; most
extraordinarily she does not cuckold me; my family and the society I
keep are infinitely agreeable to me . . . It has been said that I have some
passable mistresses, myself, I find them delicious."[18] Her intelligence did
not prevent Madame de Choiseul from the pain of being unloved; timid,
childless, deprived of domestic authority by her sister-in-law, Madame
de Gramont, for whom Choiseul nurtured an almost incestuous affection, the young *duchesse* was reduced to venerating her husband and to
cherishing the idea that one day she would be loved in return. The
comparison with Madame du Deffand is obvious. Both women were
determined to pursue their passion and whereas friendship was a consolation, partly a substitute for these passions, it also helped to keep
them alive. By confiding their sorrows and illusions in each other, both
friends brought their feelings into the open, thus giving them an element
of reality. The objects of both passions were absent—the improbable
Walpole far away, Choiseul simply uninterested.

In resisting Walpole's maltreatment, Madame du Deffand had recourse to Madame de Choiseul's feminine complicity to flatter his proverbial vanity. For her part, Madame de Choiseul, determined in the
hope of attracting her husband's attention, confided her pathetic fears:
"Tell me, my dear granddaughter, did the grandpapa come to see you
on Wednesday after having seen me into my carriage? Did he speak of
me? What did he say and in what tone? It seems to me that he is
beginning to be no longer ashamed of me, and it is already something
not to wound the self-respect of those by whom one wishes to be
loved!"[19] Ever waiting for the love she would never gain, Madame de
Choiseul lived the exemplary life of an official wife. Always self-effacing
as a private individual, she was uncompromising where her reputation
and public person were concerned. Her honour was a reflection of her
husband's honour and was the strongest link, indeed the only indisput-
able link between her and him.

Although there are comparisons to be made between the emotional
lives of the two women, they confronted life with radically different
attitudes. Madame du Deffand gave way without resistance to her
changing moods and black despair: "I am subject to chance . . . I do not

hold the reins of my soul in my own hands."[20] She analysed her existential malaise with lucidity and commented on it ruthlessly, with ferocious self-loathing: "I am never pleased with myself ... I hate myself to death."[21] Madame de Choiseul on the other hand displayed exemplary self-discipline. In contrast to Madame du Deffand's existential pessimism, her attitude was an ethical one: "To be just in order to be good, to be discreet in order to be happy."[22] Her formula for happiness was more of a recipe for not suffering, and consisted of activity, concern for others, the will to develop the mind and the heart. The advice she gave her friend may have seemed simple but it came from her tireless quest for serenity: "Live each day as it comes, take time as it comes, use every moment."[23] Mauzi judges her advice to be banal; to him Madame de Choiseul appears to avoid: "all philosophy, even all thought,"[24] when she says: "Without knowing how or why, I am happy, very happy ... where happiness is concerned one must ask neither why nor how."[25] The *duchesse* seems intentionally to avoid thoughts which might lead to a depressing conclusion. The elementary rules which she tried in vain to inculcate in Madame du Deffand were born of years of suffering from the "sad experience which withers the heart"[26] and which despite everything occasionally returned to torment her.

The problem of happiness was strictly tied to the emotions and was the main subject of thought for both friends, and the pivot of all their correspondence. They both recognised an absolute necessity for happiness, but confronted each other from different angles. Madame du Deffand imbued emotions with an absolute and magical quality whilst seeing herself as excluded from it. Humiliated, her passionate nature could produce only suffering: "In the end, there is only misfortune for those who, having been born with sensibilities, encounter only indifference."[27] Her gruelling egocentricity could not protect her from feeling deprived, hence the terrible sentence: "I am out of place with happy people."[28] But Madame de Choiseul celebrated the emotions with religious devotion. Unlike the *marquise,* she was not led by disappointed love to avoid all emotions, but rather to affirm their positive side: "I thank you for loving me; in my heart only the pleasure of loving prevails over the pleasure of being loved."[29] Friendship, charity and *pietas* all assiduously practised, contributed to her cult. At moments when she felt no other emotion, even fear could help: "When I am at Versailles, I often go riding only in order to make me afraid."[30]

But such intense activity was not enough to remove all shadow of suspicion from Madame de Choiseul: were all the lucky recipients of her affections still not enough to replace the real, unobtainable object of her passion? Madame du Deffand sensed an element of voluntarism and artificial perfectionism: "I am more happy with the grandmama than I can express; but in the same way as the devout are happy with their patrons in heaven,"[31] she wrote to Craufurd, and, with subtle innuendo to Madame de Choiseul: "It seems incomprehensible that with so much sensibility one can submit so absolutely and so completely to reason."[32]

Madame de Choiseul's availability was a result of her personal freedom. Nothing was really indispensible to her serenity. Madame du Deffand was in a quite different position—tormented by ennui: "What prevents me from being happy is an ennui which resembles a tapeworm and which eats everything that could bring me joy."[33] She was unable to accept herself and needed others, but her egoism and mistrust turned all social intercourse into a numbing, sterile distraction which prevented any real affection from developing.

Madame de Choiseul's assiduous attention for nearly twenty years never really reassured the older friend. Two different forms of therapy competed unsuccessfully to heal the old wound. Madame de Choiseul chose the path of constructive resignation, "perhaps misfortune's school is the best of all."[34] Madame du Deffand entrenched herself behind an immutable awareness of her own despair and this unalterable difference hovers over their whole correspondence, preventing any real discussion. The reasonable control of her emotions whereby Madame de Choiseul expressed her resignation did nothing to appease the *marquise*'s absolute anxiety. So from the very beginning of their friendship Madame du Deffand demanded unreasonable promises which she knew were impossible: "You only say what you want to say."[35] "You *know* that you love me but you do not *feel* it."[36] And Madame de Choiseul continued patiently to offer reassurances which she knew were unconvincing: "I love you because I love you,"[37] "I love you and want you from pure personality."[38]

In the end Madame du Deffand's mistrust was more convincing than Madame de Choiseul's patient reasoning. The old *marquise*'s gloomy egocentricity may seem monstrous, but its absolute tragic authenticity gave it weight. Madame de Choiseul's refined altruism certainly reveals a strong and noble nature, but it also reveals a respect for propriety and shows how, as she herself has reasoned,[39] she sacrificed the most genuine and personal aspects of her nature to the *nécessité de plaire* demanded by society.

So, from the beginning of the 1760s Madame de Choiseul's friendship became an ever more constant point of reference and a great strength for Madame du Deffand. Inspired by compassion and wishing to do her best, the *duchesse* devoted herself to the best of her ability to her friend. She was often separated from the *marquise* by official duties at Versailles, Compiègne and Fontainebleu and extended visits to her estate at Chanteloup, but even then she never forgot her and kept her entertained with long letters—which reveal a warm desire to distract and to cheer.

MADAME DE CHOISEUL TO MADAME DU DEFFAND

Versailles, December 1761

Spare me, my dear child, from the people of Versailles. I have, as you say quite rightly, been here for five months; it seems longer to me. Why do you not speak to me about the Président? I have not seen him for a thousand years, he has abandoned me completely; I would be very glad of an opportunity to upbraid him; besides why do you need so many people? You may fear to be alone with me, but I do not fear to be alone with you. The more people you have, the more distracted I will be from the pleasure of seeing you; at present I am being distracted from the pleasure of writing to you, and made to despair. I have just dragged myself from my bed to have some curling finished which was begun yesterday; four heavy hands weigh down my poor head. But that is not the worst, I can hear the curling iron and the curling papers echoing in my ears. It is too hot ... What ornament will Madame wear today? ... This suits such a dress ... arrange the bonnet then, Angélique; prepare the hoop petticoat Marriane—you understand that it is the great Tintin who gives orders like this. She has tremendous trouble cleaning my watch with an old glove; she shows me how black the back of it always is. That is not all. A soldier expounds on the expulsion of the Jesuits; two doctors are talking about war, I think, or are attacking each other perhaps; an archbishop shows me an architectural decoration; one wants to attract my glance, the other to occupy my mind, they all want my attention. You alone are of interest to my heart. They are calling me from the other room: "Madame, it is three quarters after the hour; the King is about to pass on his way to mass ... come along, quick, quick! My bonnet, my coif, my muff, my fan, my book: no one must be offended. My chair, my chairmen; let us go!" I have just returned from mass, a woman who is one of my friends comes in almost as soon as I do. She wants me to continue: "I will do nothing about it, Madame; I will not be my own enemy to the point of depriving myself of the pleasure of seeing and hearing you ..." She has left at last; let me continue with my letter; but they have come to tell me that the courier is about to leave for Paris: "He asks if Madame has any orders for him—Ah! of course! I am writing to my dear child. Let him wait." A young Irish woman comes to beg a favour which I will not be able to obtain for her. A manufacturer from Tours comes to thank me for something which I did not procure for him. Someone else comes to present his brother to me, but I will not see him; only Mademoiselle Fel does not come.

I can hear the drum; the chairs in my ante-chamber are overturned: the Swiss officers are rushing into the courtyard.

The steward comes to ask me if I want dinner served. He warns me that the drawing-room is full of people, that Monsieur has returned and is asking for dinner. Well then, I must close. This is an exact picture of everything I felt yesterday and today while writing to you, and most of it all at once; imagine how weary I am of the world; imagine too how much I must love you to be able to think of you, and how your poor grandmama's patience is tried, how harrassed she is, and how importuned! Pity her, love her and you will console her for everything.

Sometimes the abbé Barthélemy, an exceptional secretary, was entrusted with the task of writing. His pleasant manner, his biting wit, his fight for peace and his literary *divertissements* like *La Canteloupée ou la guerre des puces contre Mme la duchesse de Choiseul* make him quite unlike the typical figure of an eighteenth-century *chevalier-servant* abbé. Jean-Jacques Barthélemy was a man of great learning, the leading numismatist of his day and the author of *Voyage du jeune Anarcharsis en Grèce* (1787). On the eve of the Revolution, he offered this most loving and serious picture of the Greek world to a France where it was fashionable to look back on antiquity.

In 1754, Monsieur de Stainville, before he became duc de Choiseul, took Barthélemy with him to the embassy in Rome and gave him the job of finding antique medallions for the *cabinet des médailles du Roi,* thus enabling him to live for three years in the heart of classical antiquity. From that date the *abbé* or, as Madame de Choiseul called him, the *grand abbé*'s life became closely linked with the lives of his protectors. Not only did Barthélemy feel devotion and gratitude, but he had a deep and delicate attachment to the *duchesse* which closely resembled love. He lived contentedly beside her, devoted himself to her, knew her painful secret, worried himself over her poor health, spent much of his time with her and was her greatest support. Such devotion was not devoid of sacrifices which may have passed unnoticed by the *duchesse* who was totally absorbed in her own passion. In a moment of dejection, however, the *abbé* confided his secret to Madame du Deffand: "At bottom I am not lovable and was not suited to living in the world ... I knew the grandpapa and the grandmama by chance. The feelings I have devoted to them have altered my career. You know how much their goodness has touched me, but you do not know that in sacrificing my time, my obscurity, my peace of mind and above all the reputation I might have had in my work, I made the greatest possible sacrifices; they sometimes come to my mind and then I suffer cruelly."[40]

Barthélemy often makes an appearance as a third voice in the twenty-year correspondence between Madame du Deffand and Madame de Choiseul.

L'ABBÉ BARTHÉLEMY TO MADAME DU DEFFAND

Chanteloup, 28 June 1768

... You should see Monsieur le chevalier de Listenay today. He will tell you what kind of life we lead here, and how many times we have spoken of you, if however, he were able to count them, but he will not tell you how delighted we were to have him here and how grieved we were to lose him. Your grandmama now has only the little uncle with her, who will stay until the end of our visit. Do you know that she finished *Pamela*[41] three days ago? Four volumes in duodecimo were a great undertaking and yet it only took her two months to finish. She is quite well but she has not grown any fatter. I am very glad that there is to be no gathering at Compiègne, she will be less tired. You are wearied by the news from Paris; would it be any different if I told you that the other day we trapped a big wolf, that the big bull is very fierce and the little one is very funny, that the sheep have been sheared, that their wool is very delicate, that your grandmama this year had some larger and livelier lambs which are nearly as pretty as she, and that the other day she asked for a backgammon table[42] to be put on a very green piece of grass, that she then had her hundred and thirty sheep brought with all the children from the château who gave them bread and salt, that it was the most beautiful day in the world, that today is the most unpleasant; that she has been having a boudoir built for three years and that during this time some colonnades have been built, some courtyards, some stables, some ponds and some fountains but that the boudoir is not finished, that she had counted on enjoying it before she left, but that the glass panes which were expected from Paris and which need to be fitted into the windows, are too big or too narrow and have been made for other windows, and that in order to use them these other windows, which are, perhaps in the Franche-Comté or the Languedoc, must be sent for, that the little uncle reads novels all day which amuse him at the time but that he forgets, according to him, instantly; that I register them in a library catalogue which I also began three years ago and which is no more advanced than the boudoir; that last evening we read the great Corneille's inaugural speech at the *Académie Française* which amused us greatly; finally that amongst all these details, I find that the time passes as quickly at Chanteloup as it does with you. Your grandmama still loves you tenderly and will be delighted to see you; the same is true of the little uncle and myself. The grandmama has asked me to add that she may not write again before she leaves because she has a great deal of business to attend to with Monsieur de Mondomaine, the equerry, Monsieur de Perceval, the head huntsman, Monsieur Bibol, the steward, Monsieur Teillier the concierge, Chauvin, the farmer, Nicolas, the gardener, Claude, the cowman, Robin the shepherd, Madame Grisemine the turkey keeper, etc. What a lot of nonsense, Madame, but I am telling you everything I know.

Receive, I beg you, renewed assurance of my respect and of my unlimited attachment.

P.S. I said in my letter that the grandmama is left with only the little uncle for company; I forgot to tell you that I, too, am here.

The storm which had been brewing over Choiseul's head since the death of Madame de Pompadour and the arrival of Madame du Barry broke in December 1770. It was a storm which the *duc* had done nothing to avoid and which, encouraged by the arrogance of his sister, the duchesse de Gramont, he had even fomented with a public display of all but aristocratic disdain for the new favourite. On Christmas eve he received a *lettre de cachet* demanding his resignation as Secretary of State and his exile within twenty-four hours to his estate at Chanteloup. So great was Choiseul's prestige—he had more or less ruled France for twelve years—and his reaction to the King's will so dignified, that he transformed his exile into a personal triumph, a challenge to the King. Madame de Choiseul was perfectly happy: the moment had come to show that she could live up to her role as a wife and she deluded herself that exile would restore her husband's attention to her now that he was no longer distracted by public responsibilities, social life and his innumerable love affairs. She had barely arrived at Chanteloup when she confided pathetically in Madame du Deffand: "I want to become young again, and, if I can, pretty! I will at least try to make the grandpapa believe that I am both!"[43] For the *marquise* the Choiseul's exile was a matter of extreme gravity which deprived her of the protection and prestige of powerful friends, and above all of the *duchesse*'s affectionate attentions.

MADAME DE CHOISEUL TO MADAME DU DEFFAND
Chanteloup, 26 December 1770

How are you, my dear granddaughter? What a state I left you in! You grieved me yesterday, today you make me uneasy. You believed me to be insensible to the point of fierceness. Ah! How little you know the heart which you rend! Vanity prevented me from giving way to my sensibility, the object of which might have caused a misunderstanding. Vanity can strengthen courage, but fortunately can do nothing to combat the sentiment which you certainly made me feel! The *abbé* must have given you news of us. The grandpapa is marvellously well. The journey which was a great event and a powerful diversion, did me good. I had just lost a friend,[44] and a friend who loved me so much! That was the real misfortune. But is it not good to preserve one's honour and to gain peace and tranquility of mind? I cannot grieve, even out of modesty. I am with what I most love in the place which most pleases me. You will come here too, my dear granddaughter; I hope and wish you will. But wait for the good season. Meanwhile think of me and love me always as I love you.

The grandpapa embraces you. Send a thousand sweet messages to the prince for me.

MADAME DU DEFFAND TO MADAME DE CHOISEUL

Thursday, 27 December 1770

What can I say to you, dear grandmama? You witnessed my grief. I never cease thinking of you. If I could be consoled, I would be by seeing that everyone is dispirited, and by hearing you and your husband spoken of in terms which please me. I supped yesterday at the "little Saint's"[45] with Madame d'Enville and the poor *abbé*. You will hear from him at what point he is with Madame de la Vallière. I hope that he will soon go and join you. My only desire at present, dear grandmama, is to hear news of you and of the grandpapa. Do not forget your granddaughter.

From January 1771 Madame du Deffand's friendship with Madame de Choiseul was dominated by distance, and her correspondence with Walpole and her exiled friend became inextricably intertwined. The pain of separation and the hope of return ran through letters to both, but the difference of tone was enormous.

Like waves beating endlessly against the same rock, uselessly returning to the assault, the letters to Walpole obsessively repeated the same request which was always refused; an awareness of this merciless refusal gave rise to both mortification and humility. The correspondence with Madame de Choiseul, on the other hand, arose from a far less violent and less fundamental feeling but was freely nurtured on the regularity and concern that might be given to a tender plant. So Madame du Deffand's letters to her absent friend reflect all the emotion and sensibility and tenderness forbidden by Walpole. Her feelings flourished on a barren earth of mistrust.

Paradoxically the best period of Madame du Deffand's relationship with the duchesse de Choiseul was during the years of exile. Regret and distance made sublime a friendship no longer exposed to the perpetual poison of suspicion, jealousy and possessiveness. The *marquise* could delude herself that only a practical obstacle stood between her and the comforts of a pure affection.

At the height of the friendship, and at Madame du Choiseul's warmest request, Madame du Deffand, after much understandable hesitation, decided to spend a few weeks at Chanteloup. This was despite her seventy-four years, her blindness, the long journey and her fear that in revenge Madame du Barry might deprive her of the King's annuity. Walpole was only told about the journey as a *fait accompli.* In the preceding months he had made no secret of his violent opposition to the plan: "What madness to want to go to Chanteloup to rid you of your ennui! It is absolute folly the way you speak of ennui, you sound like a sixteen-year-old girl who despairs lest she is not allowed to amuse herself as much as she wishes. What do you seek? You see a lot of people and do you not yet know that everyone is not perfect? That there are fools, tedious people and traitors? You complain just as if you had made your first discovery of falseness, or of frivolity. Give yourself over to reason, take the world as it is, do not expect to recreate it to your taste and do not behave like the prince in the *Contes persans* who ran around the world looking for a princess who resembled a certain portrait he had seen in his father's treasury and who turned out to have been Solomon's mistress. You will not find Solomon's mistress at Chanteloup."[46]

What was the point of such a lesson in realism to an old, sick person whose illusions provided a respite for her paralysing pessimism? Was Walpole jealous of the absolute hold he had over Madame du Deffand? And did she consequently behave with circumspection? The *marquise* seemed to want to hide precisely from Walpole the fact that Madame de Choiseul might represent something more than a fond and concerned acquaintance and a friendship ruled by propriety, and that her desire for the absolute extended even to the little *duchesse.* In her letters to Strawberry Hill the *marquise* often tempered her praise for Madame de Choiseul with reserve and even criticised the *duchesse*'s very perfection: "It is a pity she is an angel, I would have preferred her to be a woman, but she has only virtues, no weaknesses, not one fault."[47]

The *marquise* was probably making no sacrifice to Walpole's vanity since she was quite sincere in belittling with him whatever did not immediately concern their relationship. Her friendship with Madame de

Choiseul represented her most successful attempt at creating an emotional life to fill, at least in part, the great void left by Walpole. When evoked by the ritual of letter-writing, Walpole painfully absorbed the *marquise*'s whole attention, causing her to re-experience her emotional defeat and re-awakening her basic pessimism. The fragments of serenity so painfully garnered from her daily life were shattered by the weight of her insecurity, by fear of betrayal and by her demand for the absolute.

This time, however, Walpole's negative attitude did not succeed in frustrating Madame du Deffand's plans. The Choiseuls' disgrace, and their separation from the *marquise* had created exceptional emotional tension, and she was not prepared to give up the journey. On arriving at Chanteloup, she became terrified of the consequences of a breach of trust and tried to make amends with an ingratiating letter.

MADAME DU DEFFAND TO WALPOLE   *Wednesday 20 May 1772*

Guess from where I am writing to you; from somewhere where you have never seen me, where I had never been and where I was never to go, where I was not at all expected, where I find myself very well, where I have been admirably and especially welcomed; can you guess? Ah! yes; it is quite difficult. It is Chanteloup. Ah, yes, it is true, you like details so I will spare you none.

I have been feeling much better for three weeks; but I had no intention of such an undertaking. I had written to the grandmama, as I had to you, that I was too old, that I could not support a tiring journey, that I could cause only embarrassment, that everyone would ridicule me, that they would all say: "Can one flatter oneself that one is wanted at her age? Ought she not to see that the pressing invitations sent her are due only to politeness and a kind of gratitude owed her? Will she not feel out of place among people she does not know and whose attentions paid her out of respect to their hosts will be a burden to them, so that they will repay themselves by seeking the ridiculous which they will have no difficulty in finding?" That is what I thought, what I said to myself, and what made me write several times to you, saying that I would not leave home. This is what changed my mind.

On Sunday, the 10th of this month, Madame de Mirepoix came to take tea with me. We were alone together when an hour or two later the Bishop of Arras[48] was announced. "Ah, so you are in Paris, Monseigneur. And since when?" "Since last evening, Madame la marquise." "Will you stay here long?" "As long as you command." "How so?" "I have come to propose that we carry out our old plan." "Ah! I have abandoned it!" "Why so?" Then I explained all the above reasons. "Oh, my God! What madness! You are very well, so your health is no obstacle; you will be strong enough to support the journey. You will sleep three nights, four nights, five nights if need be, on the way. If you find it uncomfortable you will not continue the journey: I will take you home. We will have two carriages, mine which is very big will be for your two women, your valet and mine and for all your packages. We will only stay as long as it suits you. Far from harming you, I am convinced that this journey will do you good; besides, as for your other fears, they are ridiculous, ask Madame la maréchale." Far from dissuading me, the maréchale pressed me to agree to these proposals. Finally I allowed myself to be persuaded and we decided to leave at the end of the week and resolved to speak of it to no one. I did not even want to confide the secret to the abbé Barthélemy who was in Paris and who was to leave the next day. The *maréchale* did not agree with this because she said that he must take care to ensure that on my arrival I should find lodgings to suit me, which he could do without it being noticed; all that having been decided, the company arrived. The *abbé* came to bid me farewell, I made him go into my study to tell him the surprising news; he was completely amazed and his first reactions (which rarely deceive) were of the greatest joy. I made him swear that he would not announce my arrival and would keep the surprise for the grandpapa and the grandmama. I was not to find Madame de Gramont. She was about to leave to visit the Bishop of Orléans and Monsieur de la Borde. Only Madame de Brionne, Mademoiselle de Lorraine, Messieurs de Castellane, de Boufflers, de Besenval and a few Swiss were there with Mesdames de Luxembourg and de Lauzan who were on the point of departure and whom I might easily meet on the road.

All these circumstances combined with the good weather suited me perfectly; so I made up my mind and was greatly impatient to leave. I said nothing to my servants all day; on the next day, Monday, I told them that they must prepare their parcels and mine and that I would leave on Thursday, or Friday at the latest. They were very surprised and did not put much faith in the plan; I told them it was a secret; it was well kept that day. After dinner I saw Pont-de-Veyle to whom I said nothing; likewise Mademoiselle Sanadon. On Tuesday there was the same silence. In the evening I went to supper at the Carrousel; I thought it only honourable to inform Madame de La Vallière. I wrote a little note which I gave her and which informed her of all my arrangements. She read it, threw it in the fire and said nothing. On Wednesday, seeking the workmen attending to my berlin and all the bags and portmanteaus we were taking, the servants in the courtyard guessed the great secret. Mademoiselle Sanadon and Pont-de-Veyle reproached me. I told them that I had wanted to avoid discussion, contradictions and criticism and that I did not yet want to speak about it to everyone, that I was leaving on Friday and that the next day, Thursday, I would inform the people of my acquaintance, which I did in fact to all those who called. I wrote to Mesdames de Jonzac, de Beauvau, de Boufflers, d'Aiguillon, to the Archbishop of Toulouse etc. I supped on the same day with Madame de La Vallière: I bid her farewell out loud, as I did to all those present.

Thursday, 21st at ten o'clock
in the morning

I will continue my tale. On Friday I was feeling very well, I was full of courage; I awaited Monseigneur the bishop until three o'clock (the hour fixed for our departure). He arrived, we settled ourselves in my berlin, and our servants in his, and there we were on our way. We reached Etampes at eight o'clock, I was quite tired. I ate a very bad supper, I retired immediately, I slept quite badly. We left on Saturday at eleven o'clock; on the way we had some quite good conversation and a reading of several articles from the *Encyclopédie*[49] by Voltaire, and we arrived at Orléans between six and seven o'clock; I was more tired than on the previous evening and wanted nothing more urgently than to retire ... After two good hours of sleep, I awoke between eight and nine and supped again, I slept badly for the rest of the night, I rose between ten and eleven o'clock ...

I leave Orléans at one o'clock, I reach Blois towards eight o'clock; I alight at the bishop's palace where I was well lodged, I slept very well; we leave there at two o'clock and arrive at Chanteloup at six o'clock. I find in the courtyard the grandmama, Madame de Luxembourg and the *grand abbé*. The carriage is halted, the door is opened, the bishop is made to descend and the grandmama gets in in his place and throws herself into my arms. We stifle each other with kisses and caresses, she finds me as beautiful as the day with the best face in the world, there are cries of joy, natural delight, very true, very sincere . . .

I must, however, add that I am pleased with everyone; that in order to please the grandmama, I am fêted and caressed; but that does not prevent me from being amazed at finding myself so far from home . . . This letter will leave on Monday the 24th, you will receive it on Monday the 29th [sic]. I beseech you not to let your reply be too severe, do not condemn my journey. I did as you dictated last year; I left in the fine season; my visit will be short; I will have shown a mark of affection; the more my age excused me, the more pleasure the effort I have made will cause. I will not be inconvenienced by it and I will have the satisfaction of having expressed my friendship. In fact do not poison a deed which I believed to be honest and which can only cause me happiness, if you do not disapprove of it . . .

For four weeks Madame du Deffand was happy. All Chanteloup gathered around a *tonneau* which was identical to the one at Saint-Joseph and which the *duchesse* had had made in the event of a visit — another had been installed in the *marquise*'s apartment. Spoilt, fêted, looked after, the old sibyl did not regret her sanctuary, but allowed herself to be carried away by the atmosphere so that she seemed really to attach herself to the life of the little community. Perhaps she looked back on the far off years at Sceaux and reflected how profound the difference in life style was. Despite the truly princely magnificence of the house, the crowds of guests, the hours beguiled only by idleness and amusement, the climate at Chanteloup was far, far removed from that at Sceaux. The natural world, although still misinterpreted, was no longer merely a subject for literature: the scent from the fields flooded into the house through the wide open windows and the baa-ing of the *duchesse*'s hundred and ten beribboned sheep was heard, together with the lowing of the *duc*'s famous Swiss cows. Tyranny had been replaced by philanthropy — Ferney was not far away — and by the cult of friendship to which the Choiseuls had erected a temple in the park, which is all that now remains of the château. Watteau and Arcadian poetry had made way for Greuze and Gessner's idylls, their bourgeois element diluted by the Choiseuls' aristocratic taste. It was a Utopia not unlike that which Marie-Antoinette, dressed as a shepherdess, would try to create a few years later in the park at the Petit-Trianon, with her rustic hamlet, her Louisiana windmill and her dairy full of especially designed Sèvres china.

When after an absence of about six weeks Madame du Deffand returned to Paris, she found a letter from Walpole awaiting her. He had reacted to the news of his friend's impulse with an icy letter, the only one sent her during her visit to Chanteloup. In retaliation he left her without news which had the desired effect of making the *marquise* return early to Paris. Madame du Deffand might then have reasonably supposed that the scores were equal and the matter forgotten.

But Walpole merely awaited her return to Saint-Joseph to give vent to his contempt: at Chanteloup there would have been embarrassing witnesses to the vendetta which would have been appeased by the *duchesse*'s intervention. To the anger of a bully faced by an act of insubordination was added Walpole's old, reawakened fear that his letters might be intercepted and read by the *Cabinet noir*. He had been warned in a letter written without the *marquise*'s knowledge by Mademoiselle Sanadon so telling him of her mistress's journey and how his last letter had reached Saint-Joseph already opened.

In the six years of their relationship, Madame du Deffand had experienced Walpole's primitive aggression on many occasions, and appears to have entirely given up any sense of her own autonomy or pride. "You have taken me where you wanted,"[51] we hear her state with bitter detachment sixteen months before this new conflict. But the injustice of Walpole's accusations, his poisonous attack combined with the sudden change from the warm, cotton-wool intimacy of Chanteloup to such brutal pointless treatment caused her to reply with an unexpected flourish of pride.

MADAME DU DEFFAND TO WALPOLE   *Paris, Tuesday 23 June 1772*

Your pen is of iron dipped in gall. Good God! What a letter! None could be more biting, drier, or more churlish: I have been thoroughly rewarded for my impatience to receive it! I hoped for a little indulgence for a mistake which concerned me alone and could never reflect on you. You fear only the ridicule which I might bring to you; have I ever done or said anything of that kind for which you can reproach me? Never, no never do I speak your name first. When people speak to me of you or when you are spoken of in front of me I cut short the conversation or if possible I take no part in it. So I have done you no wrong. I did not keep my word to you, I went to Chanteloup, I told you all the reasons which might excuse me, it would be tiring and tedious to repeat them, I am, however, going to add one more: I thought I need not literally keep the promise you demanded of me, and I thought your only intention in demanding it was to spare me the inconvenience of the journey and that if the outcome was happy as I foresaw it would be (in ways which I have explained to you), you would easily forgive me for breaking my word, and you promised me that in your letter before last. I arrived at five o'clock yesterday evening, feeling wonderfully well, not tired by my journey, overjoyed to be home, delighted by my visit to Chanteloup and hoping to find news of you and that your letter would make my pleasure complete. Ah! my God, how surprised I was! It produced quite the opposite effect. All my happiness was destroyed, one moment did more harm than five weeks had done good . . .

Wednesday 24th

. . . I was about to close my letter, but I cannot make up my mind to let it go without speaking naturally. You make me too unhappy. Is that your intention? You say that you are greatly obliged to me: for what, if not for my friendship? Do you recognise it by refusing to send me your news? If you have ever experienced disquiet, you must know that it is an unbearable ill; I beg you as a favour, and as a final entreaty, not to condemn me to it. I do not know what cause I have given you for complaint (except my journey). I have a mind which is even more easily troubled than yours. Do not put me in a position of doing anything which might displease you . . .

MADAME DU DEFFAND TO WALPOLE   *Paris, 28 June 1772*

You try my patience to the limit, Monsieur, I can no longer bear it. Is it because you believe that since my journey to Chanteloup our letters are more punctiliously opened that you write me such strange ones?

I am not at all troubled by what may be thought of mine; you are the only person in the world who can give them such a ridiculous interpretation. I have absolutely no fear, Monsieur, that all the offices where they will have been read and all the extracts which will have been passed around can persuade anyone that I am mad or extravagant; but I would soon be so were I to continue to wish to maintain such a correspondence.

I agree very willingly to ending all communication. It could only be agreeable to me so long as it was based on respect and friendship. From the moment that it is proved to me that you believe my feelings to be other, it would be shameful for me to continue to write to you and to expose myself to receiving such outrageous replies. I leave you to your regrets, it would be hard for you to have none after having so basely treated someone who, more than anyone else in the world, deserved your respect and esteem and, dare I say it, a little gratitude . . .

Madame du Deffand kept to her decision not to write for nearly two months; it was the longest break in all her relationship with Walpole; but on 30 August, terrified of the void which yawned ahead of her, she gave in and resignedly took up the yoke again.

Walpole's appearance in Madame du Deffand's life relegated Voltaire to a secondary position, without really interrupting their correspondence. The *marquise*'s admiration for Voltaire had never been unqualified and their friendship had never been founded on trust or affection, nor on the certainty of mutual loyalty. From 1765 — the year of the fatal meeting — their relationship was further hampered by the vague mistrust which Walpole's cult imposed on anything not strictly connected to it.

Voltaire was continuously betrayed by Madame du Deffand: with Madame de Choiseul the *marquise* commented on his ambitions and political passions with aristocratic detachment; his greatness as a writer, his judgement, his tastes, his attitudes were continually sacrificed to Walpole's vanity. But in 1777, when the correspondence with Ferney had worn itself out and Madame du Deffand was to write to her English friend: "I had nothing to say to him, nor he to me, it was a drudgery from which I have spared myself," she was — as she sometimes did in her mercilessness — telling only half the truth.

Madame du Deffand and Voltaire did not write to each other so much for what they had to say as from a desire to do so. They used each other for practical purposes which, however, did nothing to diminish their relationship, but rather consolidated their mutual respect. As we have seen, Voltaire used Madame du Deffand to keep in touch with the great aristocratic élite with whom he would otherwise have lost touch—for instance the Luxembourgs who were warned against him because of their protegé, Rousseau, the King's personal friend, Madame de Mirepoix, and so forth. And until 1770 the *marquise* was also a precious intermediary with the Choiseuls. Voltaire needed the political and economic aid of the government to support the small community of persecuted people who had gathered at Ferney and whose products, such as silk stockings and clocks, were advertised by the duchesse de Choiseul's use of them. Such delicate intervention could only be entrusted to special people for whom it was an indirect proof of esteem, intelligence and trust.

For her part, the *marquise*'s main objective in writing to Voltaire was to receive his replies. What she had to tell him was entirely subordinate to the expectation of what she would receive in exchange. His replies amused her, gave her prestige and provided her with a valuable topic of conversation for her daily task as a hostess. They were the finest trophy she could offer to Walpole's vanity.

But it would be wrong to put too much stress on the practical reasons for the correspondence. All the *marquise*'s correspondence arose, above all, either from the need to be reflected in another or from her incapacity for self-sufficiency. Just as Madame du Deffand wanted to be swathed in Voltaire's prestige, and he needed to draw strength from her network of acquaintances, so she needed to write to Walpole to give meaning to her life and Walpole needed those letters to experience French society vicariously. Earlier, d'Alembert wrote to Madame du Deffand in order to use her as a sounding board for his intellectual monologue whilst she replied so as to reflect her intelligence in that of her protégé.

The *marquise*'s correspondence with Voltaire was kept alive by a variety of elements which must inevitably have been destined to weaken with time as the couple grew old and their profound differences of opinion became more and more marked making any real dialectic impossible. The perennial game of vanity, hypocrisy and banter may be both amusing and aggravating but the letters retain a sense of instinctive,

MADAME DU DEFFAND AND HER WORLD

sincere and deep sympathy and genuine affinity. Voltaire, knowing the strength of the attachment, seems to have wanted to explain it in terms of his own essential interests: "What I have always loved in you, Madame, among several other qualities, is that you are not a mountebank. You are honest in your likes and in your dislikes, in your opinions and in your doubts. You love truth, capture it who can. I have sought it all my life without ever being able to encounter it. I have only glimpsed a few rays which were mistaken for her."[52]

These likes, opinions and dislikes were by now almost invariably in contradiction with Voltaire's own, but he continued to be just as full of admiration for the intelligence which produced them as he had been in years gone by. And despite her many reserves, her chronic mistrust, the permanent obstacle constituted by the *philosophes* and the abstract nature of a relationship between two people who had not met for ten years, Madame du Deffand continued to feel an affinity for Voltaire and to share the same cultural background, language, spirit and tone.

Once their correspondence took off, however laboriously and despite all the diplomacy and manipulation, the *marquise* expressed herself with a freedom of thought found nowhere else in her letters. In writing to Walpole her preoccupation with pleasing and obliging her "tutor" demanded continuous self-control, and a denial of her own nature. In her letters to Madame de Choiseul, the exercise of sensibility led to elegant mannerism. In her letters to Voltaire her reflections on life and death, happiness and pain, sense and the world's folly, were meant neither to move nor to persuade but had the essential dryness of one speaking freely to someone capable of listening and understanding. So the correspondence with Voltaire provides absolutely the best example of Madame du Deffand's style. Only there is the *marquise* perfectly true to her own intelligence: there is no trace of the suffering, trembling "pupil" nor of the "granddaughter" in need of consolation and spoiling; there are only her fierce materialism, her pessimism, her courage and her regal impatience.

MADAME DU DEFFAND TO VOLTAIRE   *Paris, 14 January 1766*

I have neither your erudition nor your intelligence, but for all that my opinions are none the less in agreement with yours. To tell the truth, it does not seem to me to be of the greatest importance that everyone should think alike. It would be a great advantage if all those who govern, from kings to the least village bailiff, had only the soundest morality for principle and system, that alone can make men happy and tolerant. But do the people know about morality? By the people I mean the greatest number of men. The court is as full of them as the towns and fields are. If you take away such people's prejudice, what would be left them? It is their strength in misfortune (and it is in that way that I would like to resemble them); it is what bridles their behaviour and acts as a brake, and it must be what makes them wish not to be enlightened; but then could they be enlightened? Anyone who, having reached the age of reason, is not shocked by all the absurdity and cannot glimpse the truth, will never allow himself to be instructed or convinced. What is faith? It is a firm belief in what one does not understand. This gift from heaven must be left with those to whom it has been granted. That is in general what I think; if I were to converse with you, I flatter myself that you would not think that I preferred mountebanks to good doctors. I would always be delighted to receive instructions and receipts from you; give me some to counteract ennui, that is what I need. The search for truth is your universal medicine; it is mine too, but not in the same way as it is for you; you believe you have found it but I believe that it is not to be found. You wish to make it clear that you are convinced of certain opinions that were held before Moses and which he did not have or at least did not hand on. Did the fact that peoples held that opinion make it any clearer or more probable? What does it matter if it is right? If it were, would that be a consolation? I greatly doubt it. It would not be one at least for those who believe that there is only one misfortune, that of being born . . .

VOLTAIRE TO MADAME DU DEFFAND   *19 February 1766*

You write in your last letter that we were both quite agreed about what is not; I set myself to seek what is. It is a terrible task, but curiosity is the sickness of the human spirit. At least I had the consolation of seeing that all the fabricators of systems knew no more than I did, but they all gave themselves importance which is not what I want: I frankly admit my ignorance.

Besides, however empty my research, I find it has a great advantage.

The study of those things which are so much above us makes the affairs of this world so small in our eyes, and when one has the pleasure of losing oneself in immensity, one hardly worries about what happens in the streets of Paris.

Study has one good thing in that it allows us to live at peace with ourselves, delivering us from the burden of idleness and preventing us from running out of our houses to go and say and listen to trifles from one end of the town to another. Thus surrounded by eighty-four leagues of mountains and snow, besieged by a very harsh winter, with my eyes refusing to work, I have spent all my time in meditation.

Do you also not meditate, Madame? Do a hundred ideas about the world's eternity, about matter, thought, space and the infinite not sometimes come also to you? I am tempted to believe that one thinks of all that when one has no more passions, and that we are all like Matthieu Garo who tries to discover why pumpkins do not grow on the tops of trees[53] . . .

MADAME DU DEFFAND TO VOLTAIRE   *Paris, 28 February 1766*

Your letters, and especially the last one, cause me to make a reflection. So you believe that there are truths which you do not know but which it is important to know? So you think that it is not enough to know what is not, because you seek to know what is? You apparently believe that to be possible, but do you think it necessary? That is what I beseech you to tell me. I had thought until now that our understanding was limited by the capability, faculty and breadth of our senses; I know that our senses are subject to illusion, but what other guide can we have? Tell me quite clearly what leanings or what motive leads you to the research which occupies you? Is it simple curiosity and how can this sentiment alone protect you from all the objects that surround you? However puerile they may be in themselves, it is only natural that they should affect us more than vague ideas which are chaos or even nothingness for us. For myself, Monsieur, I admit that I have only one fixed idea, one feeling, one sorrow, one misfortune, it is the pain of having been born; there is no part to be played on the world's theatre to which I do not prefer nothingness, and, what will appear to be of no consequence to you, is that when I have the final proof of having to return to it, my horror of death will be none the less. Explain me to myself, enlighten me, tell me the truths which you discover; teach me how to bear life or how to face its end without repugnance. Your ideas are always clear and just; I wish only to discourse with you; but despite the opinion which I have of your understanding, I will be greatly beguiled if you can satisfy the questions I put to you . . .

In the spring of 1770 the philosophers' party decided to erect a statue to Voltaire. The gesture was deeply significant. It was a solemn celebration of a great national genius who had lived for twenty years in exile and so was not devoid of obvious polemical implications against the government. It was an act of homage to the charismatic leader of the enlightenment who had, however, often displayed a careless individualism and a desire to stand alone, forgetting his colleagues along the way.

Naturally none of these implications escaped Madame du Deffand who could not however avoid the courtesy of commenting on the event to her correspondent: "the compliment is not, as one might think, a way of absorbing the shock of two ideologues meeting, it has a strategic value . . . For a compliment to be successful, the recipient must be taken by surprise so that he can neither evade it, nor parry it."[54]

MADAME DU DEFFAND TO VOLTAIRE   *Paris, 8 May 1770*

. . . Here the talk is only of your statue; the century honours itself by paying you such homage; you should be flattered; but, however, never forget, my dear contemporary, that you belong to Louis XIV's century. You are the most perfect and the most singular of the seven marvels it produced; I wanted to make you Saint Michael's counterpart with all the mistakes and fanaticism wiped out, but so many attributes would need to be gathered together for all those which describe you to be included! If you do not see my name on the list of subscribers, believe me that it is out of humility; it would be too vain to name oneself among the men of letters and the fine minds. I treat you as the divinity which is satisfied with being adored in spirit and in truth . . .

Six years were not enough to allay d'Alembert's bitterness towards Madame du Deffand. It could have been merely persecuted suspicion which prompted him to write to Voltaire on 2 July, or perhaps it was simply another good opportunity to try by his usual telltale means to break up the old friendship which filled him with such jealousy. "... I know, my dear *maître,* that you have had a letter from Paris which attempts to poison your pleasure, and to say that this monument is not being erected to the author of the *Henriade, Zaïre* etc., but to the destroyer of religion. Do not believe such calumny and in order to prove to you and to the whole of France how atrocious it is, the titles of your principal works can easily be engraved on the statue; rest assured that Madame du Deffand who wrote that enormity is far less your friend than we are, that she reads and applauds the works of Fréron and admiringly quotes from them the malice about you. I have witnessed that more than once. So do not believe the wicked things she writes to you."

Madame du Deffand seems to have written nothing about the statue apart from the elegant and elusive praise of 8 May. Voltaire, however, took d'Alembert's information into consideration and was evidently alarmed by the possibility of the *marquise* exercising a negative influence over the Choiseuls or the court and so frankly explained the delicacy of the situation.

VOLTAIRE TO MADAME DU DEFFAND   *12 July 1770*

I have opened my heart to you more than once, Madame, but it is now broken in two and I send you both halves in this letter. Envy and slander are two immortal nymphs. These young ladies have spread it about that certain philosophers whom you dislike thought to erect a statue to me as their representative; that it was not literature which they wanted to encourage but they wanted to use my name and my face to build a monument to freedom of thought. This idea, which has something amusing about it, could harm me in the eyes of the King. I am even assured that you thought like me and that you mentioned it to a woman friend. Poor philosophy is somewhat persecuted. You know that the large collection of the *Encyclopédie* is a prisoner of the State in the Bastille[55] with Saint Billard and Saint Grisel; this augurs very ill.

At the moment I am in a position of having the greatest need of the King's kindness. I do not know if you are aware that I have gathered here a hundred emigrants from Geneva, that I am building them houses and that I am establishing a watch manufactory; and if the King does not grant us the privileges we must have, I run the risk of being entirely ruined, especially after the distinctions with which M. l'abbé Terray has honoured me.[56]

So it is most expedient that the King should not be told jokingly at supper: the encyclopaedists are having their patriarch sculpted. This jest, which might be too well received, would put me in very bad favour. I could offer my protection in Siberia or Kamchatka; but in France I am in need of a number of people's protection and even the King's. So my marble statue must needs not crush me . . .

Did Madame du Deffand understand the precise nature of his appeal and the reasons which gave rise to it? It is hard to tell from the vagueness of her elegant, gently ironical reply.

Fear nothing, Monsieur, neither for yourself, nor for your statue; you are both sheltered from any kind of damage. Time may harm the statue; but as for you, who can harm you? Your glory will grow continuously if that were possible; banish all panic and fear; we are no longer in the century of witticisms and it would have been difficult in any century to say anything against you. The jests of fools are not much to be dreaded. I would like it to be as easy for you to obtain privileges for your emigrants as it is for you to overthrow those who envy you.

Occasionally the correspondence lapsed for several weeks and then Madame du Deffand was ready to abandon her old friend for fear of him abandoning her. "I no longer hear Voltaire spoken of. I do not mind very much," she wrote to the abbé Barthélemy on 27 September 117, and, four days later to Madame de Choiseul: "He does not reply to my last letter," and she commented ironically on Voltaire's admiration for Catherine the Great, "She will have displeased him. I console myself." But Voltaire only had to remember her for the dialogue to start again with its usual mixture of truth and falsehood.

MADAME DU DEFFAND TO VOLTAIRE   *Paris, 12 October 1772*

No letter was ever better timed than your last. I was suffering from the greatest anxiety; the rumour was rife here that you were extremely ill. This anxiety gave way to another; having no news of you, I feared that my last letter had vexed you. But all is well, thank God; your health, your friendship, two things which are very necessary to my peace of mind and my happiness.

I do not know, my dear Voltaire, how you envisage death; I would look at life in the same way if I could. In truth I do not know which of the two deserves to be preferred; I fear one and I hate the other. Ah! if one had a true friend one would not be in such a state of indecision; but it is the philosopher's stone; one ruins oneself searching for it: instead of universal cures one finds nothing but poison. You are a thousand thousand times happier than I. My *Quinze-Vingts*[57] condition is not my greatest misfortune: I console myself at seeing nothing, but I grieve at what I hear and at what I do not hear. Taste, like commonsense, has been lost. This may seem like old woman's talk; but no, in truth, my soul has not grown old. I am as touched by the good and the agreeable as I was in my youth; that is true. So do not repeat again that you do not know if this or that one of your works will please me: I have told you a thousand thousand times, and I will say it today for the last time that I can read only your work. So send me everything that you write. I do not know if I like Horace,[58] but I know that I like you in whatever guise you may come, or whatever subject you may treat. Why do I not have *Les lois de Minos*?[59] There are some extracts around which give me great pleasure.

Make fun of those who envy you, their anger does you no harm and you know how to make them turn it back on themselves; you have already killed three or four of them.

Come here, my dear Voltaire; how glad I would be to embrace you! But, my God! Why are there no Elysian fields? Why have we lost that chimera? Farewell.

VOLTAIRE TO MADAME DU DEFFAND   *23 October 1772*

I boast, Madame that my hearing is as hard as yours, and that my heart is even harder; for I assure you that I have not understood one word of almost all the works in prose or verse which have been sent me for the last ten years. Most of them have put me into a great rage. I have been exasperated that the century has fallen from such a height. I no longer recognise France in any genre except finance.

In the tragedy *Les lois de Minos* I wanted to write verse as it was written about a hundred years ago. I wanted you to judge it. I must at least procure this little amusement for you. You will tell the reader to stop when tedium overtakes you: with such a precaution you will run no risks. My idea is that you should beg Lekain to sup with you in a very small gathering of very good company. By a small gathering of good company I mean four or five people at most who like verse, who have something to say, and who are not at all Allobrogical.

I also insist that your guests love the King of Sweden and even the King of Poland a little. I want them to be convinced that men have been sacrificed to God, from Iphigenia to the Chevalier de La Barre.

Besides that, I want your guests, both men and women, to be a little indulgent since folly exists and there is no longer a way of making any amends.

I further demand that the thing should be a secret and that your friends should at least have the pleasure of a little mystery, if mystery is a pleasure.

In case you accept all the conditions, I enclose a little note for Lekain in my letter. Read the note or rather have someone read it you, then have it sealed.

I will not speak to you at all this time about the *Epître à Horace*. What I am suggesting seems far more agreeable. This *Epître à Horace* is not finished: besides it is very uneven and would require a much deeper secret than the supper for the *Lois de Minos*.

I admit, Madame, that I would prefer to read you this Cretan tragedy than have it read by another; but I have made a vow not to go to Paris so long as I am suspected of having failed your grandmama.[60] I am still very ulcerated and my wound will never close. Do not be vexed if I remain constant in all my feelings.

VOLTAIRE TO HENRI-LOUIS LEKAIN   *Ferney, 23 October*

... You will receive a letter from a lady, it is not a lucky opportunity; but I ask you of your favour to kindly oblige her, to enjoin her to secrecy, and to keep it ...

The concern with which Voltaire welcomed his friend's request no doubt depended on his desire to circulate his new tragedy and to sound it out on a small qualified public such as might gather in the Saint-Joseph *salon*. In 1769 Voltaire had turned to Madame du Deffand in the hope that she would champion his tragedy about tolerance, *Les Guèbres,* and help him to obtain permission for it to be performed. Voltaire's request was also a kindness to a sufferer from eternal ennui, to guarantee her a few hours of distraction.

MADAME DU DEFFAND TO VOLTAIRE   *Paris, 18 November 1772*

I have grasped everything, my dear Voltaire, and I owe you infinite gratitude. I doubt that the dead are as pleased with you as the living. Horace will blush (if the shades can blush) to know that he has been outdone, and Minos to see himself so well assessed and at being forced to admit that he ought to suffer the punishment to which he condemns people far less guilty than himself. Astérie is very interesting. The king portrays Gustav III excellently; it is a great eulogy. Without doubt, I like this Gustav; I had the good fortune to know him when he was here. I can assure you that he is as agreeable in society as he is great and respectable at the head of the public thing. He is the hero you should celebrate and depict, there would be no shade in the painting.

I took real pleasure in thinking of the allusions which you had in mind when writing your play. In truth, my dear Voltaire, you are only thirty years old. If you know to whom it is thanks that you do not grow old, you confirm the proverb: "*Oignez vilain*" etc. etc.[61]

I was very pleased with Lekain, he read beautifully; but I am not at all pleased with the casting, I would like him to play the King; he says that that is not possible; I do not understand rank within the theatre; yet there is enough of that kind of thing at court and in the town.

Wherefore do you not wish to see all this for yourself? Stop writing then, if you are trying to convince us that it is your age which prevents you from coming. You are forty years younger than I, and I went to Chanteloup this year. When the soul is as young as yours is, the body feels it; you have no positive disability.

I would be delighted to embrace you, to discourse with you and to find you in agreement with what I think about bad taste, and the bad tone which rules everything which is done, everything which is said and everything which is written. Give me your news; send me all you produce; they are arms you send me to defend a good cause.

Farewell, love me a little always, and I will always love you infinitely.

The reading of *Les lois de Minos* took place on 16 November. Before even writing her complimentary thank you letter to Voltaire, Madame du Deffand hurried to put Walpole in the picture: "Last evening I had quite a gathering for supper; Lekain, at Voltaire's behest, came to read *Les lois de Minos*. Ah! it was quite confirmed that the efforts of old age can only be impotent; the time for creation has passed, it is too late to think of adding to a reputation, and if it is not to be diminished, it is better not talked about. I will be most surprised if this play has the least success although it does contain some fine verse" (17th November 1772).

Not only was the opinion expressed to Walpole diametrically opposed to what the *marquise* wrote the following day to Voltaire, but the theme of the triumph of genius over age on which she based her praise was the opposite of what she really thought about the distressing nature of senile decadence in a great writer.

The harshness of this judgment expressed to Walpole can be partly explained by Walpole's antipathy for Voltaire, with which the *marquise* never hesitated to comply, sometimes praising Walpole and comparing him more or less explicitly and to his advantage with Voltaire. The hypocrisy of her letter to Ferney should not so much shock as impress by its elegance and the worldly way in which Madame du Deffand gets herself out of a corner. What is really striking is the divergence of interests and values which has developed between Louis XIV's two contemporaries: *Les lois de Minos* is the third last of Voltaire's tragedies, and, in literary terms, one of the most indifferent. Inspired by a strict aesthetic criteria, and with the critical precision that Sainte-Beuve was later to recognise, the *marquise* spotted the artistic weakness of a mannered work in a style which belonged for ever to the past, by a writer who had outlived his prime. But what she failed to notice was the enormous vitality and open-mindedness with which, for purely political ends, a writer of nearly eighty used a literary form of which he had been master. *Les lois de Minos* represents an act of faith in natural law, in its final triumph over the monstrous obscurantism of religion and tradition.

This profession of faith is all the more passionate by reason of recent historical events which might rather seem to shatter the great polemicist's dreams. "Fate had frustrated the hopes nourished by Voltaire in the years before the conflict between Russia and Turkey. To apply natural law to Poland, would be to create a task riddled with difficulties. Prejudice and self-interest had prevailed. Yet the battle enjoined by Voltaire was just, the road he described was the only possible one. He wanted to say so again in his last play [sic] *Les lois de Minos*. Gustav III's recent experience had confirmed him in his beliefs, that King had succeeded in Sweden where Stanislas Poniatowski had failed in Poland."[62]

Here once more are two truths, two contrasting ways of being true to oneself. Until the end Madame du Deffand never betrayed her own vigorous rules of taste, nor Voltaire his political vocation. For the *marquise*, Gustav III was the elegant, agreeable, young hereditary prince, enamoured of French culture who came and paid homage to her at Saint-Joseph,[63] and for whom she agreed to sing a song she had composed, the *Philosophes*.[64] For Voltaire, Gustav III was a sovereign who abolished torture, who introduced civil liberties and who fought against feudal privilege—leading to his assassination at a masked ball in 1792.

During her last ten years, Madame du Deffand was obliged to alter some of the habits which had been intrinsically part of her existence; death began to create voids and finally to interrupt relationships, or rather ancient rituals.

On 24 November 1770 the Président Hénault died. The *marquise* had anguished over his slow decline, more especially from the fear of having to suffer a similar fate. But in the end, the period of mourning became an occasion of distraction for her. Everyone hurried to offer their condolences which she received with the utmost dignity. To the chevalier de l'Isle she spoke of "her grief" at "the loss of the oldest of her friends" (29 October 1770); with Voltaire she engaged in a real defence of the Président. After a first letter of condolence and on learning that Hénault's will did not mention the *marquise* (there was a bequest to Julie among others), Voltaire immediately changed his tone and gave vent to his indignation in some extempore verse:

> *Je chante la palinodie,*
> *Sage du Deffand, je renie*
> *Votre président et le mien*

A tout le monde il voulait plaire
Mais ce charlatan n'aimait rien,
De plus il disait son bréviaire.[65]

The *marquise* reacted loyally and firmly.

MADAME DU DEFFAND TO VOLTAIRE   *28 December 1770*

I am not at all pleased by the ill that you speak of our old friend. I admit that he was weak, but he had a very agreeable mind, and the best tone in the world: he made his will at a time when he was greatly captivated by a girl I had here and who became my enemy...

As usual, Madame du Deffand confided her negative version of the truth to Walpole, thus exalting the unique nature of her relationship to him.

MADAME DU DEFFAND TO WALPOLE   *Paris, Sunday 25 November 1770*

... The Président died yesterday at seven o'clock in the morning; I judged him to be breathing his last on Wednesday; he was neither suffering nor conscious that day nor afterwards; never has an end been more peaceful. He passed away. Madame de Jonzac's sorrow seems extreme, mine is more moderate. I had so much proof of his lack of friendship, that I feel I have lost only an acquaintance; however, as the acquaintanceship was very old and everyone believed us to be intimate (except for a few who know some of the things which I have to complain about), I am receiving condolences from every side. It is only up to me to believe that I am loved; but I have renounced the pomp and vanity of this world and you have made me a perfect proselyte; I have all your scepticism about friendship, although I have difficulty in extending it to the grandmama...

In 1774 it was Pont-de-Veyle's turn; his legendary egoism and self-sufficiency had exempted him from the *marquise*'s demands. Available, but elusive, he never provoked the chain of possession and mistrust which paralysed Madame du Deffand's emotional life. So the *marquise*'s regrets were heartfelt and sincere; there was no reserve or bitterness to temper the loss of her old friend.

MADAME DU DEFFAND TO WALPOLE   *Paris, Sunday 4 September 1774*

... I learned this morning on waking, of the death of my poor friend; I had left him yesterday at eight o'clock in the evening; I found him very unwell, but I thought that he would last for a few more days; for four or five he had been more or less unable to speak, but his mind was all there. I have suffered a very great loss; fifty-five years of acquaintanceship which had turned to intimate friendship are irreplaceable. What are the ties one forms at my age? But it is useless to complain, one must learn to bear all the situations in which one finds oneself, and say to oneself that one could be even more unhappy ...

Death did not only strike her friends. In 1776, aged only forty-four and consumed by tuberculosis, passion and opium, Julie died. On 22 May the *marquise* commented briefly on the event to Walpole: "mademoiselle de Lespinasse died this night, two hours after midnight; it would have meant something to me once, today it is nothing at all." A few weeks later Madame du Deffand returned to the subject to comment on the "perfectly ridiculous holographic will" left by Julie.

A will may be an individual's last social act and the ultimate expression of the deceased's relationship to society with its bequests of varying sizes, and an often long and detailed list of personal mementoes to be distributed among friends. Such a document relating to eighteenth-century France must therefore be of primary interest. Even so, Julie's last wishes are particularly fascinating because on her death-bed she reassumed the name of her family who had rejected her. The *marquise* did not know that this would provide her with the most unhoped for revenge. When d'Alembert, who was Julie's executor, was sorting through her papers, he discovered a far crueller and more final betrayal than any he had suffered at the hands of the *marquise*. The woman he loved and by whom he believed himself to be loved, had spent the last ten years of their life together passionately in love with another man. Like one of her favourite author, Rousseau's, heroines, Julie died of love, but not for d'Alembert. Luckily for him, the *philosophe* only discovered half the truth; for besides the young Spanish aristocrat, José y Gonzaga, marques di Mora, who died of tuberculosis, Julie also loved with a passion that hastened her end a mutual friend, Jacques-Antoine-Hyppolyte de Guibert, an ambitious young officer with literary pretentions. In the light of this discovery, d'Alembert viewed Julie's behaviour over the last years in a different light: his friend's coldness, her impatience and her nerves were not caused by the unbalanced emotions of a delicate and sensitive nature but by a relationship which excluded him from her affections. The discovery of betrayal did nothing to alleviate d'Alembert's despair at the loss of a friend. When, in attempting to console him, Marmontel reminded him of Julie's faults, d'Alembert, prostrated by grief, could only reply, "Yes, she had changed but I have not."[66]

If Madame du Deffand could have read the harrowing accusation and declaration of love, *Aux mânes de Mademoiselle de Lespinasse,* in which d'Alembert, addressing the deceased, recalled the story of their relationship, perhaps she would have found in it a catharsis for her own terrible bitterness. "The only moment in which I could have bared my stricken anxious soul to you, was at that fatal instant when a few hours before dying you asked for heart-rending forgiveness, the last sign of your love, the dear cruel memory of which will always remain at the bottom of my heart. But you no longer had the strength either to speak to me, or to listen; like Phaedra I had to abstain from tears that would have troubled your last moments, and I lost irredeemably the moment in my life which would have been the most precious; the moment in which I could tell you again how dear you were to me."[67]

With the death of the prince de Conti[68] the doors were finally closed on the famous "four looking-glass *salon*" at the Temple, one of the most celebrated of all the Parisian social institutions. For a moment Madame du Deffand was tempted to be moved by Madame du Boufflers's genuine sorrow. She softened on reading a "well-written and moving" letter from the *Idole,* but only for an instant: "But I remembered her behaviour with the late *demoiselle* [de Lespinasse] and my heart hardened. Oh! You are right; one must be made of stone and ice, and above all never esteem anyone enough to trust them."[69]

When Madame de Geoffrin was struck down by apoplexy in September 1776, the *marquise* remarked that the idle would regret her just as they did Julie, "until such times as some other appear who are ridiculous enough to be worthy of succeeding them."[70]

Death was gradually drawing its net around Madame du Deffand: in her letters to Walpole and Voltaire she both evoked and feared it, in her daily life she underplayed it and minimised it. However, true to her ideals of propriety, she decided to be officially reconciled with her religion which, in any case, her scepticism had never prompted her to deny. She had reached the third stage common to women of her generation: after debauchery and the establishment of a worldly position, a return to religious practice was only suitable.

So Madame de Luxembourg redressed the sins of the past with charitable works: "She went walking almost every day, for her it was an opportunity to exercise charity, for, so as not to be caught unawares, she had had the idea of filling the knob of her walking-stick with coins. In this way she could benefit in two ways from her walk, from bodily exercise and from the satisfaction of doing good."[71] Religious zeal, however, was not enough to make this "arbiter of elegance" forget the superior religion of *bon ton* or the terrible bad taste of devotional texts.[72]

Madame de Talmont was the mistress of Edward, the Pretender and last of the Stuarts who also lived in an apartment at Saint-Joseph. Madame du Deffand often spoke of her in her letters to Walpole and has left a dazzling portrait of her; she describes her fine example with a certain respect.

MADAME DU DEFFAND TO WALPOLE　　　　　　　*29 December 1773*

. . . On the eve of her death she had gathered round her bed doctors, her confessor and her steward; she said to the doctors: "Gentlemen, you have done your duty by instilling in me a great terror": and to her steward: "You are here at the request of my servants who wish me to make a will; you are all playing your parts very well; but admit too that I am not playing mine badly." Then she confessed, took communion, added a codicil to her will which had been made long before . . . It is said that she had made a blue and silver dress to be buried in, and that she had her hair arranged in a very beautiful embroidered cornet. The archbishop did not approve of this luxury, he had the dress and cornet sold for alms . . .

Madame du Deffand's attitude to religion and death were, on the other hand, caricatured by La Harpe. Attached to Mademoiselle de Lespinasse's circle and a part-time chronicler, the author of *Correspondence littéraire* wrote a stylised sketch which included not a trace of benevolence. But, like all caricatures, it is bound to contain some truth and reflect the spirit of the times.

"It was apparently in order to love something that she wanted on several occasions to become religious; but she was never able to complete the task. The first time she threw herself into reform and wrote about various things she was going to give up: 'Where rouge or the *Président* are concerned, I will not do them the honour of abandoning them.' That was the Président Hénault. Madame du Deffand's different attempts to embrace religion did not succeed. She had her maid read the epistles of Saint Paul to her because she had already lost her sight; and impatient at not understanding the apostle's style as easily as she would have understood a novel, she shouted out from time to time, 'But, Mademoiselle, do you understand anything of all that?' It seems that it was her fate to love nothing either in this world or the next. As a last resort, she had taken the abbé Lenfant to instruct her: he is an ex-Jesuit and a preacher of some worth and reputation. She began to loathe him by the end of six months, so much so that when the *curé* from Saint-Sulpice came to see her during her last illness, she spoke these very words: 'Monsieur le Curé, you will be very pleased with me; but grant me three favours: no questions, no reasons, no sermons.'"[73]

Like the duchesse de Talmont, Madame du Deffand was playing her part, that of a brilliant, superficial, heartless woman; a part which guaranteed her no pity, protected her solitude, and hid her passionate soul and her fear of death from others and herself if possible.

Madame de Genlis, who also went to live at Saint-Joseph, leaves in her *Mémoires*—"which can only mystify"[74]—an accurate account of her visits to the *marquise*. "Her heart had grown old; philosophy had withered her and her mind had not matured," she wrote in patronising tones of bigoted superiority. But Madame de Genlis recorded several details which prove the *marquise*'s loyalty to her society image: "she conversed agreeably; quite unlike the idea that I had of her, she never displayed any pretension to wit ... This laziness of mind and this unconcern gave her in conversation a pleasing air of gentleness. She did not argue; she was so little attached to the opinion she was pronouncing that she only ever supported it in a distracted kind of way. It was almost impossible to contradict her; either she did not listen or she appeared to give in, and she quickly spoke of other matters ... She had a mortal fear of serious conversations; she rebuffed them dryly; to please her it was necessary to entertain her with trifles."[75]

But in her letters to Walpole and Voltaire, with her social mask removed, Madame du Deffand did not avoid meditating with anguish on death.

MADAME DU DEFFAND TO WALPOLE   1 April 1769

. . . Tell me why, detesting life, I dread death? Nothing points to everything not finishing with me; on the contrary, I am aware of it from the deterioration of my mind, as well as of my body. Nothing which is said for or against makes any impression on me. I listen only to myself, and I find only doubt and darkness. "Believe," they say, "it is the surest way," but how can one believe what one does not understand . . . If it were enough not to deny at the right moment, but that is not enough. How can one decide between a beginning and an eternity, between the full and the empty? None of my senses can answer me; and what can one learn without them? Yet, if I do not believe what is to be believed, I am threatened with being a thousand thousand times more unhappy after my death than I am during my life. What is to be decided, and is it possible to decide? . . .

It has been remarked[76] that the inevitable alternative between two absolutes which emerges here—"a beginning and an eternity," "the full and the empty"—and the need to take up a position recall the Pascalian *pari* and *vous êtes embarqé*. "But the thought remains doubtful and advances towards no conclusion. Madame du Deffand—and this is where she differs radically from Pascal—remains trapped within the dilemma of *divertissement* . . . She is not interested in the substance of religion but only in its outward wrapping, that is to say in what it has in common with *divertissement*. She misses the routine of regular devotion and the whole appearance of movement and occupation which would have delivered her from the need to think."[77]

Permanently attempting to escape from herself, Madame du Deffand did not seek knowledge; her scepticism over religion was not, as it was for Voltaire, the triumph of reason over superstition, so much as the rout of a kindly illusion. She wanted religion for reasons quite opposed to those for which the *philosophes* fought it, as a drug which stupefies both the intelligence and the heart.

In September 1775 Walpole came to see Madame du Deffand for the last time. The *marquise* wrote to reassure him: "You will be totally free in all your thoughts, words and actions; you will not find in me one wish, one desire that might contradict your thoughts and your wishes."[78]

To judge from the letter sent back to England by her visitor, Madame du Deffand cannot have failed in her task, and once again she must have rallied all her strenth to fête him.

HORACE WALPOLE TO H.S. CONWAY   *Paris, 6 October 1775*

... Madame du Deffand has been so ill, that the day she was seized I thought she would not live till night. Her Herculean weakness, which could not resist strawberries and cream after supper, has surmounted all the ups and downs which followed her excess; but her impatience to go everywhere and do everything has been attended with a kind of relapse, and another kind of giddiness: so that I am not quite easy about her, as they allow her to take no nourishment to resore herself, and she will die of inanition, if she does not live upon it. She cannot lift her head from the pillow without *étourdissements*; and yet her spirits gallop faster than anybody's, and so do her repartees. She has a great supper tonight for the Duc de Choiseul, and was in such a passion yesterday with her cook about it, and that put Tonton into such a rage, that *nos dames de Saint-Joseph* thought the devil or the philosophers were flying away with their convent! As I have scarce quitted her, I can have nothing to tell you. If she gets well, as I trust, I shall set out on the 12th; but I cannot leave her in any danger—though I shall run many myself, if I stay longer. I have kept such bad hours with this *malade,* that I have had alarms of gout; and bad weather, worse inns, and a voyage in winter, will ill suit me" ...

Walpole's hopes for Madame du Deffand's physical condition were evidently fully realised because on 12 October he set out on his return to England. Before getting into his carriage he was handed the following note by one of the *marquise*'s servants: "Adieu. This is a very sad word; remember that you leave here the person by whom you are most loved and whose happiness and unhappiness consists in what you feel for her. Send me news of yourself as soon as possible.

"I am well, I have slept a little, my night is not yet over; I will be very careful with my diet, and I will take care of myself since you take an interest."

Madame du Deffand was never to see Walpole again. In 1778 France was once more at war with England—this was a war outside Europe, for the American colonies—but apart from a few delays due to the post going via Ostend instead of Calais, the correspondence between the two friends was not interrupted. Nevertheless the likelihood of another trip to France for Walpole became highly improbable.

The *marquise*'s attitude to Walpole had, however, altered. She had resigned herself to defeat, and acceptance had brought a new kind of melancholy serenity. Perhaps, as Lescure suggests, the *marquise* had accepted what Sainte-Beuve described as her "out of season" maternity, or perhaps she no longer had the energy to struggle. Madame du Deffand herself used a beautiful metaphor to describe her new state of mind.

Sunday, 3 March 1776

. . . I thought the other day that I was a garden and you were the gardener; that seeing the approach of winter, you had pulled up all the flowers which were not in season although there were still a few which had not quite faded, like some little violets and daisies, etc., that you had only left a particular flower (which perhaps you do not have) and which has no scent and no colour and is known as "everlasting" because it never fades. This is the emblem of my soul from whence comes a great privation of thoughts and imagination but where there remains a great constancy of esteem and attachment . . .

With the acceptance of the reality of Walpole's character, Madame du Deffand could recognise outbursts and his acts of kindness for what they were and appreciate, whenever the occasion arose, his marks of affection rather than noticing only his rebuffs. And Walpole's attentions to Madame du Deffand were not negligible. There were four long journeys which he undertook entirely in order to go and see her, despite his delicate health, his gout and the fact that he was a creature of habit who shut himself away increasingly at Strawberry Hill. Besides he sent her and her friends endless generous little gifts: sets of china, boxes of tea, materials and fans. Or he paid his respects in a way which for him was very significant, by for instance dedicating to her the sumptuous edition of Hamilton's *Mémoires du comte de Gramont* which was printed in 1772 in the small press at Strawberry Hill. Madame du Deffand's name is not mentioned, but the dedication speaks for itself:

To Madame XXX

The publisher dedicates this edition, as a monument to his friendship, his admiration and his respect, to you whose charms, wit and taste echo in the present century, the century of Louis XIV and the charms of the author of these *Mémoires.*"

Yet Walpole's only action which was for Madame du Deffand an absolute proof of his affection took place in 1770. In that year the pension granted to the *marquise* in 1763 by the Queen was in danger of being reduced by the restrictions of the new *contrôleur général,* the abbé Terray. When Walpole was consulted by his friend on the strategy she should take to avoid these restrictions, he reacted with an outburst of indignant chivalry: "Do not deign to take one step, if you have not already done so, to replace your three thousand livres. Have enough friendship for me to accept them from me. I wish the sum were not of so little importance to me as it is, but I swear that it will cause me to cut back in nothing—not even my amusements. Would you take it from the hands of the great and refuse it from me? You know me well; make this sacrifice to my pride which will be delighted to have prevented you from having to stoop to begging. Your note hurts me![79] What! You! You reduced to reporting your misfortunes! Grant me, I beseech you, the favour which I ask on bended knee and rejoice in the satisfaction of saying to yourself, I have a friend who will never allow me to throw myself at the feet of the great. My little one, I insist! ... Allow me to taste the purest of joys by relieving you of your discomfort, and let this joy be a deep secret between us both."[80]

Lescure was probably right in claiming this to be "the only real joy, the only ray of sunshine which she owed to her friendship with Walpole."[81]

The *marquise* refused the offer—the loss was made good by investment in an annuity and conversion of stock—but she was overwhelmed with emotion and gratitude: "If I had not lost the gift of tears, [your letters] would make me shed a great many. They give me a delicious, if sad, sensation. Ah! my friend, why did I not know you earlier? How different my life would have been!" (24 February 1770).

In January 1771 Madame du Deffand asked Walpole for permission to leave him her papers: "I want your consent before beginning anything. I want to entrust all my manuscripts to you; I am determined in not wanting them to be in any hands other than yours. There is certainly nothing precious about them and if you do not accept them I will throw them all in the fire without any regret."[82]

The marquise must certainly have known that her offer would have appealed to Walpole as a passionate collector. But the proposition was not aimed solely at pleasing him. It had a symbolic meaning for her. Madame du Deffand was not being honest in minimising the value of her manuscripts, in particular her portraits and letters to Voltaire. Despite her constant dismissal of their "intrinsic value,"[83] in her last years, Madame du Deffand revealed a certain awareness of the quality of some of her writing. In tidying her papers and re-reading her correspondence—especially with Voltaire[84]—she realised that her letters were worthy of being compared with his. It must have been an important discovery for someone who had been faithful throughout her life to the one religion of taste. She faced it now, on the threshold of death, unprepared and with incredulity. Perhaps, for a fleeting moment, she glimpsed immortality, and decided to consign her destiny to Walpole. Thus the literary fortunes of one of the finest examples of pure French style were entrusted to an Englishman whose name was indissolubly linked to the Gothic Revival, a cultural phenomenon diametrically opposed to the classicism of the Grand Siècle.

Having obtained Walpole's consent, Madame du Deffand drew up her will on Wednesday 13 February.[85] Four days later she recounted the event to Walpole with worldly charm and in a cheerful, joking manner which defied the solemnity of the act and the fear of death: "I was forgetting to tell you that on Wednesday last, Ash Wednesday, I made use of your "I consent."[86] It was quite a comical scene; I was with two gentlemen who were the actors and Pont-de-Veyle was there as spectator. The scene which should naturally have been a serious one, was very gay; the two gentlemen are characters out of comedy. They were very embarrassed at having to name the seat on which I was sitting. It was not, they said, a chair, or an armchair, or a couch, or a wing chair, or a *duchesse*; a *tonneau* or a *ravaudeuse* would have been too surprising for them; they would not have wanted to use such words; in the end they wrote 'armchair.' I am truly satisfied by the conclusion of this affair."

Madame du Deffand's horizons were shrinking and her main objective was to avoid being alone at all costs. Mademoiselle de Sanadon, the silly, timorous, boring "Sanadona" as Walpole called her, had become her "support"[87] since "habit had made her a necessity."[88] Although she summarised her feelings for her family magnificently in claiming: "I have no relation with whom I would like to be acquainted,"[89] the *marquise* did not give up hope of support from them. After going blind and after the break with Julie, Madame du Deffand had turned to her sister, Madame d'Aulan, who spent a short time at Saint-Joseph but who subsequently died prematurely. Now, terrified by the threat of deafness and other possible infirmities, she arranged for her sister's son, the young d'Aulan who was "neither engaging nor charming but very bearable"[90] to be installed with his wife in an independent apartment at Saint-Joseph. The move took place at the end of 1778. It was not a matter of sentiment but an entirely practical arrangement: "I organize myself as best I can to support these sad, tedious last days."[91] The faithful Wiart, his wife and a small household of servants assured her of material comfort. In the last two years, Pétry, a reader from the Invalides replaced Colmant who died in 1778 to help during the hours when the others slept.

With the practical problems solved, there remained the irresistible demands of society life; although "everything that happens in my life, happens in my head,"[92] and although company brought her no affection and no surprises, it was the one thing to which the *marquise* could turn: "I notice very markedly that little by little I am losing all my faculties of mind; memory, application, the power of expression, everything fails me when I need it. I do not want to be loved; I know that I am not loved, and I know it on my own; I do not expect others to have feelings for me which I do not have for them; what prevents my happiness is ennui which like a tapeworm consumes everything that could make me happy."[93] Yet, despite this and precisely because of this: "I have never had so great a need of society and never has society seemed less agreeable. It is my fault, you will tell me; you will prove that my faults and not the faults of others make me unhappy. I need only alter myself, you will say; it is that which is impossible. If I could become religious, nothing would make me happier. I would certainly not be discouraged by false modesty ... Today I hold to nothing, I have only my intrinsic worth, and that is to be reduced to less than nothing."[94]

The *marquise* need not have feared solitude. The numerous gaps which had been created, "Since I lost my friends it has become almost impossible for me to make others; I must be satisfied with having acquaintances"[95]—and the fear of being "out of place"[96] in society made her plan always to sup at home with whatever company had gathered. But she did not have to resort to this contingency plan. She, like Fontenelle before her, gave the impression of being "like a masterpiece of art, worked with care and delicacy which one must take care not to destroy as they are no longer made that way."[97] Her two suppers—now on Wednesdays and Fridays—continued to attract numerous guests and the *marquise* continued to be revered. No distinguished foreigner came to Paris—from Gibbon to Franklin—without paying her a visit. New acquaintances were added to the old. The Neckers' friendship with the *marquise* was based on habit and respect; it was in their house in 1777 that she was presented to the Emperor Joseph II who was on his way through Paris. "When I entered the room, he came up to me and said to Monsieur Necker: 'Present me.' I curtseyed deeply; I was led to my chair: the Emperor wanting to talk to me but not knowing what to say, saw that I had a bag of ribbons, and said: 'Are you knotting?' 'I can do nothing else.' 'It does not prevent you from thinking.' 'No. Above all today when you give me so much cause for thought.'"[98]

On 10 February 1778 Voltaire returned to Paris. The following day he gave Wiart, who had come to enquire after him on behalf of the *marquise,* a note to take back to her. The style of the note is worthy of the golden age of their correspondence which had been gradually waning.

VOLTAIRE TO MADAME DU DEFFAND   *Paris, 11 February {1778}*

I have arrived dead and want to be resuscitated only in order to throw myself at the knees of Madame du Deffand.

Voltaire had returned to the capital to attend a performance of his play *Irène*[99] which was being performed by "what remained of the

Comédie"[100]—the great Lekain had recently died. The arrival of the eighty-four-year-old writer, a bag of bones dressed in most unusual garb, released an explosion of uncontainable joy among the Parisians. "He was in such singular dress, wrapped in a great fur cloak, with a woollen wig on his head and on top of that a red, fur-lined bonnet, that the small children who, at this carnival time mistook him for a Jack-Pudding, ran behind him shouting."[101] "He received ineffable honours; every kind of honour was bestowed upon him. In the street he was followed by the people calling him 'The Calas man.' Only the court remained unenthusiastic."[102] Two days after his arrival, on 14 February, the *marquise* accompanied by Monsieur de Beauvau, went to see the patriarch.[103] The meeting was bound to be moving and despite her usual realism the *marquise* had to admit to her pleasure and recognise that her vanity had been satisfied: "He showed the greatest friendship and the greatest joy at seeing me once more; it was reciprocal. He expects to leave again in Lent, I do not think he will be able to; he has a pain in the bladder and hemorrhoids, yesterday they were saying that he has colic; his extreme liveliness sustains him but wears him out; I would not be surprised were he soon to die."[104]

The "cult"[105] devoted to him by the whole of Paris, the apotheosis of the triumph brought about by the first performance of *Irène,* coming as it did after a series of exhausting rehearsals, the work, the emotion and sickness which kept him in bed causing fears for his life, all prevented him from paying his respects to the *marquise.* Madame du Deffand was ready to disown him when on 11 April he appeared in person at Saint-Joseph.

MADAME DU DEFFAND TO WALPOLE   *12 April 1778*

... At last I had a visit from Voltaire yesterday; I put him at his ease by not reproaching him in any way; he stayed an hour and was infinitely agreeable ... He is eighty-four years old, and to tell the truth, I believe him to be almost immortal; he rejoices in all his senses, not even one of them is impaired: he is a singular creature indeed, and in truth, a very superior one. If he sees me often, I will be very glad; if he leaves me there, I will do without him, I no longer allow myself any desires or any plans ...

The *marquise* was right to arm herself against possible disappointment:

this was to be Voltaire's only visit. "Killed by an excess of opium taken to dull the pain of his strangury" and "by an excess of fame which was too much for the old machine"[106] Voltaire died in Paris without seeing his old friend again. The philosopher's body, disguised as a traveller, was loaded on to a wagon in order to slip unseen out of Paris which only a few weeks earlier had welcomed him with such delirium, but which now refused him burial. Meanwhile the *marquise* dismissed her contemporary without emotion in a brief, indifferent announcement to Walpole: "Indeed I was forgetting an important event, which is that Voltaire is dead."[107]

With her usual masterful tactics, Madame du Deffand protected herself from the anguish of death by the projection of "non life," and from the risk of feeling by denial.

Not even Madame de Choiseul could escape a clean sweep. From December 1776, when the *duchesse* returned from exile, her relationship with Madame du Deffand had gradually been growing colder. The excitement imposed by forced separation was over and Parisian life made so many demands on the *duchesse* that the *marquise* began to feel herself overshadowed and excluded from the *duchesse*'s affection. Once again possessiveness and mistrust made her choose surrender. Paradoxically Madame du Deffand blamed both Madame de Choiseul and Walpole for a detachment and an insensitivity to suffering which she could not achieve. "I see the grandmama once a week. Do you remember that I used to write to her: that she knew she loved me, but that she did not feel it? She is the same in everything: everything for her is principle, rule or habit; nature never shows through. You have suppressed yourself as much as possible and I believe that nothing is in effect necessary to you today."[108]

Now the Choiseul's departure for long visits to Chanteloup no longer caused her "great regret,"[109] their company was for the *marquise* only an agreeable "distraction"[110] and when the *duchesse* wrote her an affectionate letter, she found it necessary to remark: "I do not believe that she feels all she says, but kind words are always agreeable if only for their sound."[111] Thirteen years after the *marquise*'s death, in discussing "the depth of her feelings of ennui," Madame de Choiseul would say of her: "Poor woman . . . , I still pity her."[112]

Once again the illusion of a perfect friendship dissolved when confronted with reality; perhaps with Walpole, the dream persisted precisely because, until the very end, it never ran the risk of becoming reality.

To deny feelings so as not to suffer, to repudiate friends so as to avoid "the humiliation which comes from abandonment,"[113] and to disguise solitude at all costs was not enough to procure peace of mind for a soul "which is as active as if I were only thirty," but which, imprisoned in an eighty-year-old body "can make no use of this activity." Perhaps the *marquise* was "less unhappy by virtue of the little liking" people had for her "than because of her indifference to everything."[114] Walpole was never the subject of this indifference; the *marquise* could go on asking herself whether to know him had been fortunate or unfortunate, but he remained until the very end as the essential purpose of a life which could have been different.

MADAME DU DEFFAND TO WALPOLE   *22 August 1780*

I receive your letter of the 13th and 14th. I wrote to you in my last that I was not well; it is even worse today. I have no fever, at least they think not, but I am excessively weak and faint; my voice has gone, I cannot stand, I cannot allow myself to move at all, my heart oppresses me; I have no difficulty in believing that this condition presages an early end. I do not have the strength to be frightened, and as I will not see you again in my life, I have nothing to regret. My present circumstances mean that I am very isolated; my acquaintances are all dispersed. Your cousin[115] is deeply involved in his lawsuit, I have not seen him for eight days.

Can you imagine that he knows how I am? Oh! it is quite simple, he is not concerned, and I am far from holding it against him; today his entire fortune and that of his adored son are in danger.

Amuse yourself, my friend, as much as you can; do not grieve for my condition; we were almost lost to one another; we were never to meet again; you will miss me because one is glad to know that one is loved.

Perhaps Wiart in future will send you my news; it is hard for me to dictate.

P.S. Wiart did not want such a sad letter to be sent; but he had to concede: he admits, no doubt, that Madame is very weak, but not as ill as she thinks: a great deal depends on the vapours and she sees everything in black. M. Bouvard has just prescribed two ounces of cassia, she took half of it this evening, she will take the other half tomorrow morning; she has just eaten a good plate of soup and a little biscuit, she is stronger than she was earlier; she was in a bad condition when she wrote.

Wiart will take care to put a bulletin in the post every day until her health has returned to normal.

That was Madame du Deffand's last letter to Walpole. Aware of her approaching end, the *marquise* symbolically cut the thread which tied her to the man in whom she had found her *raison d'être*, and prepared to die as she had lived, alone, surrounded by people. From the short entries in the diary she began in 1779 it is possible to reconstruct roughly her last twenty days.

Wednesday, 23 [August 1780]. Supped at home. Received a letter from Monsieur de Beauvau, dated 23rd. Monsieur Necker's visit.

Thursday 24. Supped at home with Madame Oels. The abbé de Vaumal arrived and read a speech.

Friday 25. Supped at home with Monsieur and Madame de Beauvau, Mme de Gramont, etc. Visit from Monsieur Necker whom I did not receive.

Saturday 26. Supped at home.

Sunday 27. Supped at home with Mesdames de Luxembourg, de Gramont, de Cambis, etc. Visit from Monsieur le Curé, Monsieur de Toulouse, the abbé Barthélemy. Departure of Monsieur de Beauvau for Le Val, and Madame de Mirepoix for Roissy. Took on a nurse.

Monday 28. Supped at home.

Tuesday 29. Supped at home with Mesdames de Luxembourg, de Lauzun, de Gramont, de Cambis and de Mirepoix . . .

Wednesday 30. Supped at home with Madame de Luxembourg etc. Madame de Cambis has been to Le Val and has returned with a migraine. She left to go to bed. Mademoiselle Sanadon and Monsieur de Beaune have come back from Praslin. Monsieur Necker spent the evening with me. Monsieur Mouchard took me this afternoon to see the notary and I added a codicil.

Thursday 31. Supped at home with Mesdames de Gramont, de Luxembourg, de Cambis, Monsieurs de Toulouse, Walpole, de Beaune etc.

September. Friday 1st. Supped at home with Mesdames de Mirepoix, de Luxembourg, de Gramont, de Cambis, de Boisgelin, de Boufflers. Fourteen people. Visit from Monsieur and Madame Necker.

Saturday 2. Supped at home with Madame de Luxembourg, the duchesse de Boufflers and Madame de Cambis etc. Received a letter from Spa from the comtesse de Boufflers, dated 28 August.

Sunday 3. Supped at home with Mesdames de Luxembourg, de Cambis etc. Received a letter from Avignon. The abbé de Choisy's journey.

Monday 4. Supped at home. Received a letter from Mr Walpole, dated 20 August.

Tuesday 5. Supped at home with Mesdames de Luxembourg, de Lauzun de Gramont; Monsieurs de Toulouse, Necker etc. Thirteen people.

Wednesday 6. Supped at home with Mesdames de Luxembourg, de Lauzun. Nine people. Madame de Necker whom I could not receive called. Letters from Chanteloup and from Mr Walpole dated 28 August. Two cornets and two *bagnolettes.*

Thursday 7. Supped at home.

Friday 8. Supped at home.

Saturday 9. Supped at home with the usual people. Monsieur de Beaune has gone to Fitzjames.

Sunday 10. Supped at home with the usual people. Monsieur de Choiseul arrived. The Briennes left for Brienne after supper. Monsieur de Toulouse is back.[116]

Until the very end the diary keeps up the appearance of a scanty social gazette. Supper which the *marquise* once described as "one of mankind's four chief businesses; I have forgotten the other three," remained the central point of her day.

The guests depended on the *marquise*'s state of health; she had only to feel a little better for there to be a gathering of thirteen or fourteen people. Then gradually lulled by the buzz of guests, Madame du Deffand would sink into a deep lethargy. She was no longer tormented by her thoughts; now at last she was enveloped by a pure state of existence: "to fall asleep in universal connivance with beings without conscience,"[117] the elms and beeches[118] whose simple vegetable existence she had often envied. She died peacefully on 23 September 1780.

A month later Wiart was to write to Walpole:

WIART TO WALPOLE   *Paris, 22 October 1780*

You ask me, Monsieur, for details of your worthy friend's sickness and death. If you still have the last letter she wrote to you, re-read it, you will see that it bids you an eternal farewell, and this letter is, I believe, dated 18 August:[119] She did not yet have a fever then, but it is clear that she felt her end approaching since she told you that you would nave no more news of her except from me. I cannot describe the pain I felt at having that letter dictated to me; I could never re-read it all through to her after I had written it, sobs choked my words. She said to me: "Do you love me then?" This scene was sadder for me than a real tragedy because one knows the latter to be only fiction; but I could see only too well that in the other she was speaking the truth and this truth pierced my soul. Her death was in the course of nature, she had no illness and at least she suffered no pain: when I heard her groan, I asked her if she had a pain somewhere, she always answered no. She was in a complete lethargy for the last eight days of her life; she was no longer conscious; she had the most peaceful death, although she had long been sick.

She was very far, Monsieur, from desiring honours after her death; in her will she requested the simplest funeral. Her orders were carried out; she also asked to be buried in her parish, in the church of Saint-Sulpice, and it is there that she rests. The parish would not have allowed her to be particularly honoured after her death; those gentlemen were not very pleased. But her *curé* saw her every day and had begun to hear her confession; but it was not finished because her mind wandered and she could not receive the sacraments; but Monsieur le curé behaved wonderfully; he did not think her end to be so near. I will keep Tonton[120] until Mr Thomas Walpole's departure. I take great care of him; he is very gentle and bites no one; he was only naughty with his mistress. I remember very well, Monsieur, that she begged you to take care of him after her.

Bibliographical Notice

BENNETT: Peter R. Bennett, *Lettres inédites de Madame du Deffand à sa famille*, in "Revue d'Histoire Littéraire de la France," nos. 3–4, 1968, pp. 533–557.

BESTERMAN: *Voltaire's Correspondence*, edited by Theodore Besterman, Institut et Musée Voltaire, "Les Délices," Geneva, 1953–1965.

Hervé: Georges Hervé, *Les correspondantes de Maupertuis. Dix lettres inédites de Madame du Deffand*, in "Revue de Paris," XVIII, V, 1911, pp. 751–778.

HUNTING SMITH: Warren Hunting Smith, *Letters to and from Madame du Deffand and Julie de Lespinasse*, New Haven and London, 1938.

LESCURE: *Correspondance complète de la Marquise du Deffand avec ses amis le Président Hénault, Montesquieu, d'Alembert, Voltaire, Horace Walpole, classée dans l'ordre chronologique et sans suppressions, augmentée des lettres inédites au Chevalier de l'Isle, précédée d'une histoire de sa vie, de son salon, de ses amis, suivie de ses oeuvres diverses et éclairée de nombreuses notes par M. de Lescure. Ouvrage orné des deux portraits través par Adrien Nargeot et de plusieurs facsimile*, 2 vols., Paris, 1865; reprinted Geneva, 1971.

LEWIS: *Horace Walpole's Correspondence with Madame du Deffand and Wiart*, edited by W.S. Lewis and Warren Hunting Smith, New Haven and London, 1939 (1), 1962 (2). (The correspondence between Walpole and Madame du Deffand, with separate numbering from I to VI, forms volumes 3 to 8 of Horace Walpole's *Correspondence*, also edited by W.S. Lewis and W. Hunting Smith, 39 vols., New Haven and London, 1937–74.)

MASSON: *Oeuvres complètes de Montesquieu*, publiées sous la direction de M. André Masson, Paris, 1950–1955, vol. III.

PROSCHWITZ: *Lettres inédites de Madame du Deffand, du président Hénault et du comte de Bulkeley au baron Carl Frederik Scheffer (1751–1756)*, edited by Gunnar von Proschwitz; offprint from "Studies on Voltaire and The Eighteenth Century," X, 1959, pp. 267–412.

SAINTE-AULAIRE: *Correspondance complète de Madame du Deffand avec la duchesse de Choiseul, l'abbé Barthélemy et M. Craufurt, publiée avec une introduction par M. le M' de Sainte-Aulaire*, Paris, 1866.

Ségur: Pierre-Marie-Maurice-Henri de Ségur, *Esquisses et Récits. Madame du Deffand et sa famille. L'éducation féminine au XVIIIe siècle*, Paris, 1908.

GRIMM: *Correspondance littéraire, philosophique et critique, adressée à un souverain d'Allemagne, depuis 1753 jusqu'en 1769, par le baron de Grimm et par Diderot. Première partie*, tome I–VI, Paris, 1813; *Correspondance littéraire [. . .] depuis 1770 jusqu'en 1782 [. . .]. Seconde partie*, tome I–V, Paris, 1812; *Correspondance littéraire [. . .] pendant une partie des années 1775–1776, et pendant les années de 1782 à 1790 inclusivement . . .]. Troisième et dernière partie*, tome I–V, Paris, 1813.

SAINT-SIMON: Louis de Rouvroy duc de Saint-Simon, *Mémoires*, Bibliothèque de la Pléiade, Paris, 1959–1961.

N.B. The following works and editions were used throughout this book: Lescure for the general correspondence of Madame du Deffand; Besterman for Voltaire's correspondence; Lewis for Horace Walpole's correspondence; Sainte-Aulaire for the correspondence with Madame de Choiseul, l'abbe Barthélemy and Craufurd (using Lescure for the letters between Madame du Deffand and Madame de Choiseul that are not published by Sainte-Aulaire); Hunting Smith for the correspondence concerning Julie de Lespinasse.

Biographical Notes

AIGUILLON, Anne-Charlotte de Crussol de Florensac (1700–1772), duchesse d': married in 1718 Armand-Louis Vignerot du Plessis-Richelieu, comte d'Agénois, later duc d'Aiguillon, mother of Emmanuel-Armand, enemy of Choiseul and one of Louis XV's ministers. See ch. IV pp. 86–87. Madame du Deffand often refers to her in her correspondence as the "*grosse duchesse*" or as the "*Grossissima.*"

AIGUILLON, Armand-Louis Vignerot du Plessies-Richelieu (1683–1750), duc d': member of the *Académie des Sciences* from 1744.

AÏSSÉ, Mademoiselle (*c.* 1693–1733): in 1698 the French Ambassador to Constantinople, comte Charles de Ferriol, bought a Circassian child in the slave market of that city and entrusted her to the care of his sister-in-law Marie-Angélique de Ferriol, Madame de Tencin's sister. The little Aïssé (gallicisation of Haydée) was brought up with Madame de Ferriol's two sons, Pont-de-Veyle and d'Argental, and given an excellent education. Admired for her charm and beauty, Aïssé fell in love with Blaise-Marie d'Aydie, became his mistress and secretly bore him a daughter, but she feared that by agreeing to marry him she would compromise his career and reputation. Thus she never married but neither did she renounce her love. When, under the influence of a Genevan friend, Madame Calandrini, Aïssé was converted to true Catholicism, the conflict between love and morality became impossible. Forced to leave Aydie and to abandon for ever any hope of recognising her child, Aïssé, who was probably already threatened by tuberculosis, let herself die in 1733: she was supported to the end by her lover. Madame du Deffand took her own confessor, père Boursault, to the deathbed so that Aïssé might be finally reconciled to the religion for which she had chosen to die. The *Lettres de Mademoiselle Aïssé* to Madame Calandrini are an intimate diary of the young Circassian's conversion. Sainte-Beuve dedicated a famous essay to Aïssé (*Mademoiselle Aïssé, Portraits littéraires*).

ALBON, Camille-Alexis, Éléonor-Marie (1724–1789) comte d': son of Claude, comte de Saint-Marcel and of Julie-Claude-Hilaire d'Albon, Julie de Lespinasse's half-brother. He married Marie-Jacqueline Ollivier in 1750 and had five children.

ALEMBERT, Jean-Báptiste Le Rond, d': born in Paris on 16 November 1717 and abandoned by his mother, Madame de Tencin, on the steps of Saint-Jean-le-Rond, the baptistry for Notre Dame, and hence named Jean-Baptiste Le Rond. He was entrusted to the care of Madame Rousseau, a glazier's wife, in the rue Michel-le-Comte, and brought up by her as her son. His father, Louis Camus, chevalier Destouches, a career soldier who became a field-marshal and, in 1720, director-general of the school of artillery, provided for his education and left him an annuity of 1200 *livres*. He went to study as a gentleman at the *collège des Quatre Nations*, took the name of d'Alembert and having acquired an excellent education in the humanities, gained his diploma in 1735. Having completed his studies in law he became a lawyer, but then decided to devote himself to the mathematical sciences. After some communication with the *Académie des Sciences* (he first became attached to the astronomy section in 1741, then became associate geometer in 1746 and *pensionnaire* in 1756), d'Alembert published the fundamental *Traité de dynamique* in 1743. In 1744 he published the first draft of the *Traité de l'equilibre des fluides*; in 1747 his first *Recherches sur les cordes vibrantes,* and finally, in 1749, the book "which would be enough to make him immortal" (J. Bertrand), *Recherches sur la précession des équinoxes* in which the mathematical theory of the phenomenon was presented for the first time. In 1750 Diderot invited him to collaborate in the practical and theoretical production of the *Encyclopédie* with the job of writing the preface. The *Discours préliminaire* appeared on 1 July 1751 and is considered a masterpiece. In 1752 the *Eléments de Musique théorique et pratique suivant les principes de M. Rameau, éclaircis, développés et simplifiés* appeared. The *Essai sur la société des gens de lettres et des grands,* which was destined to provoke much quarrelling, was published in France in 1753, and in the same year in Prussia, the *Mélanges de littérature et de philosophie.* The third volume of the *Encyclopédie* also appeared that year, with a polemical preface by d'Alembert in reply to the criticism provoked by his *Discours* and to accusations of irreligion. In 1752 Frederick II of Prussia—to whom d'Alembert had dedicated the second edition of his *Recherches sur la cause générales des vents* (1747)—invited him to succeed Maupertius as president of the Berlin Academy. The *philosophe* refused. Despite d'Alembert's refusal, Frederick II granted the *philosophe* a pension of 1200 *livres*: D'Alembert died in 1783.

ARGENS, Jean-Baptiste de Boyer (1704–1771), *Marquis* d': author of a great number of *Mémoires* on historical subjects and of *Lettres (juives, chinoises, cabalistiques).* On coming to the throne, Frederick II summoned him to

Prussia and made him his chamberlain and director of the *Belles Lettres* section of the Berlin Academy.

ARGENSON, Marc-Pierre de Voyer de Paulmy (1696–1764), comte d': son of Marc-René, Louis XIV's famous lieutenant of police and keeper of the Seals under the Regency, and was himself lieutenant-general of police in 1720 and 1722, Chancellor to the duc d'Orléans, director of the *Librairie*, Minister and Secretary of State for War from 1743–1757 when he was involved in the disgrace of the keeper of the seals, Michault, and exiled to his property at Ormes. A friend of Voltaire.

ARGENSON, René-Louis de Voyer de Paulmy (1694–1757), marquis d': nick-named "*d'Argenson la bête*" to distinguish him from his younger brother, the above. Foreign Minister from 1744–1747; he dedicated the last nine years of his life to social reform and philanthropy. A friend of the *philosophes*.

ARGENTAL, Charles-Augustin de Ferriol (1700–1788), comte d': Pont-de-Veyle's brother and nephew of Madame de Tencin, at least part of whose novels are attributed to him. He was a magistrate and then the Duke of Parma's representative at Versailles. D'Argental is known particularly for his great friendship with Voltaire whom he knew at school. Madame du Châtelet was also extremely fond of him.

AUBETERRE, Marie-Françoise Bouchard d'Esparbez de Lussan (1720–1772), marquise d': cousin and wife of Henri-Joseph Bouchard d'Esparbez de Lussan (1714–1788), marquis d'Aubeterre, sister of the marquis de Jonzac and Hénault's niece. She lived on the floor above the Président, in rue Saint-Honoré and presided over her uncle's social gatherings. She had neither the charm nor the qualities of her sister-in-law, Madame de Jonzac. Madame du Deffand did not like her.

AULAN, Anne de Vichy (1706–1769), marquise d': Madame du Deffand's younger sister; married in August 1724 Jean-François de Suarez, Marquis d'Aulan and went to live in his château near Avignon. Madame d'Aulan was widowed in 1764 and she allowed her sister to persuade her to come and live with her in Paris in a small independent apartment in the Saint-Joseph convent. In 1769 Madame d'Aulan returned to Avignon where she died the same year. Madame du Deffand always maintained her relationship with her far away sister even—as with all the other members of her family—to the point of keeping up a flourishing correspondence, now preserved in the departmental archives of the Drôme. Little is known of the sisters' cohabi-tation; but Madame du Deffand's remark on hearing of Madame d'Aulan's death hardly implies a strong bond between them: "She was a good woman, but for whom one could have no feeling." (To Walpole, 15–16 April 1769.)

AULAN, Denis-François-Marie-Jean de Suarez (1729–1790), marquis d': son of Madame du Deffand's sister and married to Anne-Suzanne Arouard de

Beignon, he was called upon to help his aunt during her last years. He was her executor. Walpole recounted his horrible death at the outbreak of the Revolution to Miss Berry: "... Monsieur d'Aulan, a worthy man, and nephew of my dear friend Madame du Deffand, has been taken out of his bed, to which he was confined by the gout, at Avignon, and hanged by the mob!" (2 July 1790.)

AUTREY, Marie-Thérèse (1698–1753), comtesse d': daughter of Fleuriau d'Armenonville, married in 1717 Henri de Fabry de Moncault, comte d'Autrey who died in 1730.

AYDIE, Blaise-Marie d' (1692–1761): a native of Perigord and nephew on his mother's side of the marquis de Sainte-Aulaire, a non-professed Knight of the Order of Saint John of Jerusalem. He was introduced into Parisian society under the Regent by his cousin, the comte de Rions, the lover and secret husband of Madame de Berry, and was about to join the ranks of the libertines when he met and fell in love with Madamoiselle Aïssé. When she died, he retired to his country property and devoted himself to the education of the child born of the relationship.

AVERNE, N. de Brégis, wife of Fernand d'Averne, she replaced Madame de Parabère as the Regent's official mistress in 1721. The event was celebrated on two memorable occasions by the maréchale d'Estrées at her property, Bagatelle, and by the Regent himself at Saint-Cloud. The Regent dismissed Madame d'Averne in November 1722.

BARTHÉLEMY, Jean-Jacques (1716–1795), abbé: after seven years in a seminary he renounced the ecclesiastical condition whilst retaining the habit, and still being addressed as "abbé." In 1747 he was made a member of the Académie des Inscriptions and in 1753 keeper of the King's medals. As a protégé of the Choiseuls, Barthélemy asked permission to follow them into exile to Chanteloup where he stayed for four years. See Chapter XI, pp. 350–52.

BATH, William Pulteney (1682–1764), Earl of: heir to a great fortune, he entered Parliament as a Whig, but his political career consisted in a long struggle against Robert Walpole with whom he almost immediately quarrelled.

BEAUVAU-CRAON, Charles-Juste (1720–1793), prince de Beauvau: "one of the men at court with the most nobility and dignity" (Grimm, 1770–1782, May 1771, I, p. 495), he joined the army at eighteen, was Governor of Lunéville, fought under Broglie in Germany, commanded the army in the Languedoc where he distinguished himself for religious reasons by his humanity towards Protestant prisoners. As Choiseul's friend and relation, Beauvau expressed his solidarity with the exiled minister in a provocative fashion.

BEAUVAU, Marie-Sylvie de Rohan-Chabot (1729–1807), princesse de: married firstly Jean-Baptiste-Louis de Clermont d'Amboise, marquis de Renel, and, secondly, in 1764, Charles-Juste de Beauvau-Craon, prince de Beauvau. The princesse de Beauvau exercised enormous power over her husband.

BERNOUILLI, Jean (1667–1748): belonged to a scientific family of Belgian origin, resident in Basle. According to Leibniz, Jean and his brother Jacques were responsible for the rapid spread throughout Europe of infinitesimal calculus. His works contained a great many discoveries including the first attempt at interpreting logarithms by imaginary numbers.

BERNSTORFF, Johan Hartvig Ernst (1712–1772): German by birth, the King of Denmark's special envoy in France from 1744 to 1750. When recalled to Denmark and nominated Foreign Minister, Bernstorff distinguished himself by his intelligent policies designed to safeguard the country from Swedish ambition by favouring relations with Russia. "The Danish oracle" as Frederick II called him, was profoundly francophile and always longed for Paris where he had achieved notable personal and diplomatic success.

BERRY, Marie-Françoise-Élisabeth de Bourbon-Orléans (1695–1719), duchesse de: daughter of Philippe II d'Orléans and of Mademoiselle de Blois, legitimised bastard daughter of Louis XIV and Madame de Montespan, married in 1710 Charles, duc de Berry son of the *Grand Dauphin* and of Marie-Anne-Christine of Bavaria, Louis XIV's grandson who soon left her a widow. When her father, over whom she exercised absolute power, became Regent, Madame de Berry moved to the Luxembourg Palace, acquired her own personal guard and ladies-in-waiting and "on more than one occasion usurped the rank of Queen" (Saint-Simon, VI, p. 365). Amongst other accusations levelled at the *duchesse* was that of incest with her father in whose orgies she never failed to participate. She fell madly in love with the lieutenant of her guard, the comte de Rions who subjected her to public humiliation and tremendous oppression. She died at the age of only twenty-four, half mad, drunk and pregnant for the second time by Rions who appears to have married her in secret.

BERRY, Mary (1763–1852): Miss Berry and her sister, Agnes, were born of a romantic union. Their father was disinherited for marrying a penniless woman, and, as a widower, brought up his daughters on his own. In 1788, after a nomadic existence, the Berrys came to Twickenham where they met Walpole. Walpole was dazzled by his young neighbours' charm, beauty and intelligence so that their company soon became indispensable to him. In 1791 the Berrys moved into Clivendon, a house belonging to Walpole where Kitty Clive had lived. There were rumours that Walpole was prey to a senile passion, that Mary Berry had designs on his fortune and that he meant to marry her. There was no substance to these insinuations. Miss Berry helped him with filial affection until his death and dedicated herself completely to

him, even renouncing an old plan to marry. Just as Madame du Deffand
wanted to leave her correspondence to the man she loved, so Walpole
entrusted the *marquise*'s letters to Miss Berry. It was not a bad choice. Despite
a certain moralism, an obvious partiality for Walpole and a total lack of
philological scruples, the first edition of the *Letters of the Marquise Du Deffand
to the Hon. Horace Walpole [. . .], from the Year 1766 to the Year 1780. To which
are added Letters of Mme du Deffand to Voltaire from the Year 1759 to the Year
1775. Published from the Originals at Strawberry Hill* edited by Miss Berry
appeared in London in 1810 and marked not only the beginnings of the
marquise's posthumous fame, but made good use of Miss Berry's close
knowledge of Walpole's life.

BESENVAL, Pierre-Joseph-Victor (1721–1794), baron de: Swiss by birth, joined
the Swiss Guards in the service of France at an early age, and remained in
the French army until the Revolution, having reached the rank of lieutenant-
general. Besenval was a brilliant soldier who distinguished himself on many
occasions: he fought in the Seven Years War at Minden and contributed to
the success of Kloster-Camp. In 1762 he became inspector general of the
Swiss and the Grisons. He was a friend of Choiseul's and remained loyal to
him throughout the disgrace. His *Mémoires* are without any literary merit,
but rich with political intrigue and gossip about the aristocratic world in
which Besenval lived.

BOISMONT, Nicolas de Thyrel de (1715–1786): ordained priest in 1743 and
gained a considerable reputation as a preacher on coming to Paris from the
provinces. Boismont was asked to preach at the funerals of the Dauphin
(1766) of Louis XV and of his wife, Maria Teresa of Austria. His election to
the *Académie* in 1755 gave rise to general indignation among the literati.

BOISSY, Louis de (1694–1758): playwright and society figure. He entered the
Académie in 1754. According to d'Argenson and Collé, Boissy was elected
thanks to Madame de Luxembourg's intrigue. She had persuaded Madame
de La Vallière to take him as a lover.

BOLINGBROKE, Henry Saint-John (1678–1751), Viscount: statesman and philosopher who settled in France for the first time on the death of Queen Anne
in 1714, when the Whigs blamed him for the unfavourable conditions of the
Treaty of Utrecht. In the tranquility of his beautiful country property in the
Orléanais, La Source, where he lived with Madame de Villette whom he
married in 1720, Bolingbroke wrote *Reflexions upon Exile* and the famous
letter of apologetics to Windham. La Source became a centre of hospitality
and a meeting place for, among others, the Tencins, the Ferriols, Voltaire,
Madame du Deffand, Mademoiselle Aïssé. Bolingbroke returned to England
in 1723 but was soon obliged to go back into exile and returned to France
where he remained from 1736–1744. His *Letters on the Study and Use of History*
appeared posthumously in 1752 in both England and France.

BOUFFLERS, Marie-Anne-Philippine-Thérèse de Montmorency (d. 1797) duchesse de: married 1747 Charles-Joseph duc de Boufflers (1731–1751) son of the maréchale de Luxembourg from her first marriage.

BOUFFLERS, Marie-Charlotte-Hippolyte de Camps de Saujon (1725–1800) comtesse de: married 1746 Edouard, comte and later marquis de Boufflers-Rouverel (d. 1763); mistress of the prince de Conti, known as *l'Idole du Temple* by Madame du Deffand. See Ch. IV, pp. 83–85.

BOUFFLERS, Stanislas-Jean de (1737–1815): son of Marie-Françoise-Catherine de Beauvau-Craon and of Louis-François de Boufflers, Knight of Malta, he was an officer and a field-marshal, Governor of Senegal (1785) and finally deputy at the States General. In 1786 the chevalier de Boufflers was elected to the *Académie Française* with a lightweight baggage of verse and prose to his name.

BOUGAINVILLE, Jean-Pierre de (1722–1763): brother of the famous navigator, prolific writer and historian, became a member and later secretary to the *Académie des Inscriptions* from 1749–1755. As a protégé of the Queen's, Bougainville tried three times to become a member of the *Académie Française* and succeeded in 1754. His popularity at court among the *devots* made the encyclopaedists dislike him intensely.

BOURBON, Louis-Henri de (1692–1740): son of Louis III de Condé et d'Enghien and of Mademoiselle de Nantes, legitimised daughter of Louis XIV and Madame de Montespan, known as Monsieur le Duc, he was nominated chief minister of Louis XV's government after Philippe d'Orléans' death in 1723. Monsieur le Duc was completely dominated by his mistress, Madame de Prie, who had a disastrous influence over his policies. Louis-Henri de Bourbon changed the Regent's foreign policy suddenly by breaking the engagement between the young King and Philip V of Spain's daughter, in favour of marriage to Maria Leszczynska in 1725. Then, basking in the new Queen's gratitude, the Duc and Madame de Prie tried to remove the influential Cardinal de Fleury, but Louis XV was very fond of his old preceptor and Monsieur le Duc was forced to resign whilst Madame de Prie was exiled to Normandy where she died soon afterwards under mysterious circumstances.

BOUZOLS, Laure-Anne Fitzjames (c. 1710–1766): wife of Joachim-Louis de Montaigu, marquis de Bouzols.

BRANCAS-VILLARS, Élisabeth-Charlotte-Candide de: wife of Louis, marquis de Brancas-Céreste, lieutenant general in 1710, envoy extraordinary to Spain, grandee of Spain in 1730, governor of Nantes, maréchal de France in 1741.

BRIONNE, Louise-Julie-Constance de Rohan-Montauban (1734–1815), comtesse de: wife of Charles-Louis de Lorraine, comte de Brionne, died in 1761. "Madame de Brionne inspired strong feelings in the duc [de Choiseul], who spent considerable sums of money on her. Madame de Choiseul did not know her and only met her for the first time in exile." (C. Maugras, op. cit., II, pp. 126–7.) Even on this occasion, the duchesse with all her willpower and dedication to her husband, hid her real feelings and welcomed Madame de Brionne with open arms on 29 September 1771.

BROGLIE, Charles-Guillaume (*c.* 1669–1751), marquis de: brilliant career soldier. Thanks to the duc d'Orléans he was made lieutenant-general of the Infantry in 1719. He brought about a series of important reforms within the army. Intelligent and a libertine.

BROGLIE, Victor-François (1718–1804), duc de: he distinguished himself in the Seven Years War but fell from favour after the defeat of Willingshausen in 1762 which resulted from lack of agreement among the French generals. Broglie was extremely popular and everyone thought his exile unjust. In 1771 Broglie was made Governor of the *Trois Évêchés* and in 1778, of Alsace. Besides his correspondence with Prince Xavier de Saxe, some of his oratory, letters and military orders have been published.

BULKELEY, Francis (1686–1756), comte de: born in London of Irish parents, he joined the French army, took part in many campaigns, was made field-marshal in 1734 and in 1738 lieutenant-general in which capacity he took command in Bavaria, on the Rhine, in Flanders and elsewhere. He retired from the army in 1748.

BUSSY, born Mademoiselle de Messey, married in 1765 the marquis Charles de Bussy, cousin of the Caramans, friend of Beauvau, the Choiseuls and the Luxembourgs.

CANAYE, Étienne de (1694–1782): descended from a family of magistrates, he joined the *Oratoire* in 1716 and left it twelve years later. Although he had no qualifications, he was elected to the *Académie de Inscriptions* in 1728 and was a friend of d'Alembert's and Foncemagne's.

CARACCIOLO, Domenico (1715–1789): he arrived in Paris as the King of Naples' ambassador at the end of 1771 and remained there until 1781 when he was recalled to Italy and made viceroy of Sicily. Caracciolo allied himself to the *philosophes* and participated in the economic debate initiated by the physiocrats. He was an *habitué* of Saint-Joseph but made the mistake of also being a fervent admirer of Mademoiselle de Lespinasse.

CARAMAN, Victor-Maurice de Riquet (1727–1807) comte de: married in 1750 Marie-Anne-Gabrielle-Josèphe-Françoise-Xavière de Alsace-Hénin. Madame du Deffand began to see them a certain amount at the time of her friendship with Walpole who had pronounced a favourable verdict on them. Considerably younger than the *marquise,* the Caramans paid her great attention.

CASTELLANE, Jean-Baptiste de (d. 1790), marquis d'Esparron et de La Garde: faithful friend of Choiseul's.

Castelmoron, Cécile-Geneviève Fontanieu, Marquise de: married in 1715 Charles-Gabriel de Belsunce, marquis de Castelmoron, died 3 November 1761. Her friendship with Hénault must have dated from about 1721; see Ch. II, pp. 32–33.

Caylus, Anne-Claude-Philippe de Tubières de Grimoard de Pestel de Lévis (1692–1765), comte de: brilliant officer, man of the world, writer of verse, comedies and stories, he was among those most passionately in favour of returning to the study and imitation of antiquity. Member of the *Académie des Beaux-Arts* (1731) and of the *Académie des Inscriptions et Belles Lettres* (1742), he introduced reforms designed to restore Le Brun's academic doctrine.

Cellamare, Antonio del Giudice (1657–1733), duque de Giovinazzo and principe: he was Spanish ambassador to Versailles at the time of Louis XIV's death in 1715 when Philippe d'Orléans became Regent. Influenced by courtiers from the Sun King's court and encouraged by Philip V of Spain's old jealousy of the Regent, Cellamare outlined a plan for Philip V to claim the throne of France which he had renounced on becoming King of Spain. But the Regent was aware of the plot from the start and was ready to confront it. Many people were arrested; some condemned to death, the *duc* and *duchesse* du Maine and the marquis de Pompadour were exiled and war was declared in Madrid. The weakness of the plot was obvious but it gave the French government the opportunity of putting an end to Spanish claims on France.

Céreste, Bufile-Hyacinthe-Toussaint de Brancas de Forcalquier (1697–1754), comte de: younger brother of Louis, marquis de Brancas (1672–1750) and uncle on their father's side of Monsieur de Forcalquier, Monsieur de Brancas and Madame de Rochefort.

Chabot, Lady Mary Apolonia Scolastica Stafford-Howard (1721–1769), comtesse de: wife of Guy-Auguste de Rohan-Chabot, comte de Chabot.

Chabrillan, Innocente-Aglaé Vignerot du Plessis-Richelieu d'Aiguillon (1747–1776): wife of Joseph-Dominique Guigues de Moreton, marquis de Chabrillan.

Chastellux, François-Jean (1734–1788), chevalier and later marquis de: career soldier (he reached the rank of field-marshal), was concerned with literature, economics and music, and took part in Mesmer's experiments on magnetism. He was one of the first people to be vaccinated against smallpox. He was linked to the *philosophes* and his most important work was *De la félicité publique, ou considérations sur le sort des hommes dans les différentes époques de l'histoire* (1772).

Chaulnes, Anne-Josèphe de: daughter of Joseph Bonnier de la Mosson, treasurer of the Languedoc, married in 1734 the duc Michel-Ferdinand d'Albert d'Ailly, duc de Pecquigny and later de Chaulnes (1714–1769), she died in 1787. See Ch. II, pp. 21–23.

CHOISEUL, Louise-Honorine Crozat du Châtel (1735–1801) duchesse de: married Etienne-François in 1750.

CHOISEUL-STAINVILLE, Etienne-François de (1719–1785), comte de Stainville, later duc de Choiseul. After embarking on a brilliant military career and thanks to Madame de Pompadour's support, he became a diplomat. Ambassador to Rome (1754–1757) and to Vienna (1757), he returned to France as Secretary of State for Foreign Affairs (1758–1761). Choiseul strengthened the alliance between France and Austria with the third Treaty of Vienna (1758); in 1761 he signed the "Family Compact," was replaced by his cousin, César-Gabriel de Choiseul, duc de Praslin as foreign minister and became Minister for War (1761–1770) and for the Navy (1761–1766). In 1766 Choiseul returned to the Ministry of Foreign Affairs whilst remaining in charge of War. From 1758 until his exile in 1770, Choiseul was the arbiter of French politics with all the authority of a prime minister.

CLAIRON, Mademoiselle: stage name of Claire-Josèphe-Hippolyte Leris, known as Hippolyte Leris de la Tude (1723–1803): joined the *Comédie-Française* in 1743 and left it out of disgust with the public in 1765 and because she was offended by an action taken against her for refusing to act with Dubois who was accused of perjury. The French theatre owes much to her fundamental innovations, like the change from the traditional declamatory style to a more natural way of speaking, the abandonment of the pannier and gala wig. As an *habitué* of Madame Geoffrin's salon and a friend of Diderot and Voltaire, she made no secret of her allegiance to the *philosophes'* ideas.

CLERMONT, Louis de Bourbon-Condé (1709–1771), son of Louis II de Bourbon-Condé and of Mademoiselle de Nantes, comte de: great-grandson of the Grand Condé, he received the tonsure at the age of nine; Clermont was a general, a courtier and masonic Grand Master. Although his only attempt at literature was to have collaborated with Collé in a short comedy, *Barbarin ou le fourbe puni,* he decided to join the *Académie Française* in 1754. When the *prince-abbé* realised that as the most recently elected member, he was destined to take the last seat, he protested and because Duclos stood up to him, never attended the sittings.

CLERMONT, Marie Anne de Bourbon-Condé (1697–1741) known as Mademoiselle de: sister of the above and of Monsieur le Duc. Mademoiselle de Clermont lived at Chantilly and then at Versailles.

CLIVE, Kitty, name by which Catherine Raftor (1711–1785) is known. Of Irish origin she married and was subsequently separated from the lawyer George Clive and was possibly the most famous comic actress of her day. She was engaged by Garrick to play at Drury Lane from 1746–69, and lived with her brother not far away in a house at Twickenham. When Walpole settled at

Strawberry Hill he made great friends with the actress who was six years older than he and offered her a small house on his estate.

CONDORCET, Marie-Jean-Antoine-Nicolas Caritat (1743–1794), marquis de: distinguished himself from youth by his aptitude for geometry and, aged only twenty-six, was elected to the *Académie des Sciences* of which he was soon to become Secretary in perpetuity. He was a student of d'Alembert's and aligned himself with the *philosophes*. He later played a great part during the Revolution. Friend and confidant of Julie de Lespinasse with whom he maintained a lengthy correspondence.

CONTI, Louis-François de Bourbon (1717–1776), comte de La Marche, later in 1727, prince de: after a short but brilliant military career which ended with his resignation in 1746, Conti was Louis XV's private political adviser from 1747 for ten years. The King had absolute faith in him. But in 1757, a combination of pressure from Madame de Pompadour, who hated him, and his own independent judgement and free thinking brought about his downfall. Conti retired to the Temple as Grand Prior of the Order of Malta in France (a position he acquired in 1749). Well known for his atheism, Conti never disguised his sympathy for the *philosophes* and adopted an irreverent attitude, taking on the defence of the *parlament* in 1770. In 1731 he married Mademoiselle de Chartres, the Regent's seventh daughter who died five years later.

CONWAY, Henry Seymour (1721–1795): Walpole's oldest friend and first cousin, for whom he felt the greatest affection and admiration. Walpole took a close interest in Conway's political and military career. In 1744 Conway fell in love with Caroline FitzRoy, but he was not rich enough to aspire to her hand. Walpole offered him half his fortune and reluctantly accepted his cousin's refusal. Famed as a soldier for his courage and sang-froid, Conway was less successful in politics. From 1765–68 he was Secretary of State and Leader of the House of Commons in a predominantly Whig administration.

CRAUFURD, John (d. 1814) son of Patrick of Drumsoy Auchinames in Scotland. Member of parliament, like his father (for Old Sarum 1768 and Renfrew 1774). Friend of C.J. Fox and Boswell, known by Madame du Deffand as "*le petit Craufurd*" and by his English friends as "Fish" Craufurd. Craufurd spent a long time in Paris in 1765. When Walpole came to Paris he probably met the young Scotsman for the first time at Saint-Joseph and took an instant liking to him. Their friendship must have developed later in England. Madame du Deffand met him a few months before she met Walpole and her interest in him, her enthusiasm for him and her possessiveness show how ready she was to centre her thoughts and imagination round a new exclusive object of interest. As soon as Craufurd left for England on 27 January 1766, the *marquise* began to write to him in a tone which naturally terrified

Craufurd: "I want, you say, my friends to be lovers, even passionate ones. Ah! my God! What thoughts! What ideas! How can I have given rise to them?" On 8 March 1766 she tried to reassure him.

CREUTZ, Gustaf Philip (1731–1785), Swedish ambassador to Paris (1766–83). Friend of the *philosophes* and an *habitué* of Madame Geoffrin's *salon*. He was warmly praised by Marmontel.

DENIS, Marie-Louise Mignot (1712–1790): daughter of Voltaire's older sister Marie-Catherine Arouet and Pierre-François Mignot, "*correcteur*" at the *Cours des comptes,* married in 1738 a young officer, Nicolas-Charles Denis and settled in Landau. Widowed at thirty-two, Madame Denis returned to Paris in 1744 and settled in the rue du Bouloi where she entertained a cheerful, lively group of friends. Her relationship with her uncle dates from that time and ended only, despite its ups and downs, with Voltaire's death.Voltaire's most passionate letters to his niece go back precisely to 1745.

DEVREUX, Louise-Catherine, Madame du Deffand's maid and wife of Nicolas Brulart, also a servant of Madame du Deffand's. Madame Devreux entered the *marquise*'s service in 1737 and stayed with her until 1775.On her death the *marquise* left her an annuity of 1000 *livres.*

DREUILLET, Élisabeth Thomas de Monlaur, born at Toulouse in 1656 and died at Sceaux in 1730. She married in 1664 Jacques de Dreuillet, *président aux requêtes at the Parlement de Toulouse* in 1654. Madame Dreuillet held a literary *salon* of some importance in Toulouse, at which, among other things, her own poetry was read. In 1706 and 1710 she was awarded a prize for her eclogue of the Jeux Floraux. As a widow she moved to Paris and was introduced to literary circles there and at Sceaux by her fellow Toulousains, Campristron and Dumas d'Ayguebère. Her *Nouveaux contes de fées allégoriques* appeared in 1735.

DU CHÂTEL, Louis-François Crozat (died in 1750), marquis: son of Antoine Crozat, "the richest man in France," married Marie-Thérèse-Catherine Gouffier. The title was granted on the acquisition of a property in Brittany. As a career soldier he distinguished himself in several campaigns: Spain, the Rhine, Flanders and Italy. He was made lieutenant-general in 1744 and awarded the grand cross of Saint Louis in 1747. He had two daughters: Antoinette-Eustachie, duchesse de Gontaut and Louise-Honorine, duchesse de Choiseul-Stainville. See Ch. IV, pp. 88–89.

DU CHÂTELET, Gabrielle-Émilie Le Tonnelier de Breteuil, marquise: born in Paris on 17 December 1706, daughter of Louis XIV's reader Louis-Nicolas by his second marriage to Anne Gabrielle de Froulay. As a small child Émilie showed a liking for learning; she translated the *Aeneid* and began to study mathematics and physics with a country neighbour. She learned to play music and to sing. Her passionate, impetuous temperament expressed itself particularly in her love-life. The marriage she contracted at the age of 18 with a career soldier, the mild marquis Florent-Claude du Châtelet by whom she had three children, was as far as Émilie was concerned no obstacle to her various unscrupulous affairs. When Madame du Châtelet met Voltaire in 1733 she had already attempted suicide over a disappointment of the heart and had an affair with the most famous libertine of the time, the maréchal de Richelieu with whom she remained friends. A passionate and complicated relationship developed between the *belle Émilie* and Voltaire who was twelve years her senior and on the crest of a wave as a playwright—*Zaïre* had proved a triumph at the *Comédie-Française* the year before. Madame du Châtelet took Voltaire to her country house at Cirey which he restored at his own expense, and there she strove to keep him as long as possible. Any initial embarrassment vis-à-vis Monsieur du Châtelet was soon overcome. The *marquis* was throughout submissive and conciliatory with regard to his wife whom he admired and whose superiority he recognised. In 1734 the scandal of the *Lettres philosophiques* obliged Voltaire to flee to Lorraine; in 1736 he took refuge in Holland for fear of the consequences of the satire *Le Mondain* which was circulating in Paris. In 1740 when the lovers were busy in Belgium with a lawsuit over a Châtelet inheritance, Voltaire accepted Frederick II's invitation to go to Prussia. On his return Madame du Châtelet rejoiced, but in June 1743, Voltaire, flattered by the Philosopher King's insistence, returned to Prussia and Germany for a visit which lasted more than six months and which nearly drove Émilie mad. In 1744 the lovers returned to Cirey where they lived peacefully for several years. Just when they no longer seemed threatened by outside events—Voltaire was protected by Madame de Pompadour and on excellent terms with the powers that be—the relationship between the lovers began to show signs of strain. In 1746 Voltaire became the lover of his recently widowed niece, Madame Denis, and Madame du Châtelet recognised that their passion had died. But she could not do without passion and when in 1748 she was invited to King Stanislas's court at Lunéville, she fell hopelessly in love with Saint-Lambert, a young and brilliant officer with literary ambitions whom she met there. The affair was short, but dramatic. Madame du Châtelet died of puerperal fever a week after giving birth to Saint-Lambert's daughter at Lunéville on 10 September 1749. After an initial bout of jealousy, Voltaire had accepted his friend's new relationship. His despair at her death and Monsieur du Châtelet's sorrow were far greater than the last lover's tepid, embarrassed displeasure. The intensity of her love-life never affected Madame du Châtelet's passion for science. She was an ardent Newtonian and had studied under two eminent members of the *Académie des Sciences,* Maupertius and Clairaut, and, while in Belgium, under the German, Samuel Koenig who had taught her about Leibniz. In 1740 she published *Les Institutions de physique*. With Voltaire she competed in the 1737 *Académie des Sciences* contest with a *Dissertation sur la nature et la propagation du feu*. Just before her death she completed the French translation of Newton's *Philosophiae naturalis principia mathematica*, which Voltaire had published posthumously in 1759.

DUCLOS, Charles-Pinot (1704–1772), among friends he met at the Café Procope or the Café Gradot were Piron, Voisenon, Crébillon *fils*, Collé and Caylus. Duclos also enjoyed the friendship and support of many powerful patrons: thanks to Maurepas he became a Member of the *Académie des Inscriptions* (1738) and thanks to the Brancas and to Madame de Pompadour, he was elected after many setbacks to the *Académie Française* in 1747. In 1755 he became secretary in perpetuity to the *Académie* and strove to remove it from outside influences, making it more and more a literary court. He altered the competitions, transformed the award for eloquence and instituted eulogies of great men, but above all fought for the *philosophes*. He wrote two short novels and an *Histoire de Louis XI* which earned him the position of historiographer to the King. Duclos is interesting today as a writer of memoirs. The *Considérations sur les moeurs de ce siècle* (1751), the *Mémoires pour servir à l'histoire des moeurs du XVIIIe siècle* (1751) and the *Mémoires secrets sur le règne de Louis XIV, la Régence et le règne de Louis XV* (1791) are invaluable sources of eighteenth-century study.

DUPIN, Louise-Marie-Madeleine de Fontaine (1707–1799): wife of Charles Dupin, rich farmer-general, the Dupins lived in the *hôtel* Lambert and had a *salon* frequented by the best society; Madame Dupin patronised writers and entrusted the education of her son to Jean-Jacques Rousseau which caused him to write a *Mémoire presenté à Monsieur Dupin sur l'éducation de Monsieur son fils*. She was a friend of Madame de Forcalquier and cordially disliked by Madame du Deffand.

DU PLESSIS-CHÂTILLON, Catherine-Pauline Colbert de Torcy (1699–1773), married in 1788 Louis du Plessis, marquis du Plessis-Châtillon.

DU RESNEL, Jean-François du Bellay (1692–1761), ex-Oratorian, member of the *Académie des Inscriptions* (1733) and of the *Académie Française* (1742), collaborator and later editor of the *"Journal des Savants."* A prolific writer l'abbé du Resnel translated Alexander Pope's *Essay on Criticism, Essay on Man*, and his *Principles on Morals and Taste*.

ELLIOT, Sir Gilbert, third baronet (1722–1777), statesman, philosopher and poet. Several times a Scottish member of Parliament, a friend of Hume with whom he collaborated in drafting the *Dialogues of Natural Religion*. Elliot and his wife, Agnes Dalrymple, were frequent visitors to Paris and were good acquaintances of Madame du Deffand's with whom they exchanged courtesies. Walpole met Elliot during his visit to Paris in 1765–6.

ESTRÉES, Lucie-Félicité de Noailles d'Ayen (1683–1745), maréchale d': married in 1698 the comte Victor-Marie d'Estrées, later *duc* and *maréchal de France*.

FARGIS, Jean-Louis de Rieu (*c.* 1681–1742), comte de: son of Bernard de Rieu, the King's Secretary, and of Marguerite Habert de Montimort. Fargis was Chamberlain under the Regent and captain-lieutenant of the queen's cavalry. He was Madame du Deffand's lover and rejoiced in the reputation of a perfect roué.

FEL, Marie (1713–1794), famous soprano. She made her debut at the *Opéra* in 1734 and became known as the greatest interpreter of Rameau; she also took part in the *concert spirituel* and sang at court. Grimm had a violent passion for Mademoiselle Fel, but she preferred the painter, Maurice Quentin de La Tour with whom she lived, and whose famous pastel portrait of her hangs in the Louvre.

FERRIOL, Marie-Angélique Guérin de Tencin, sister of the cardinal and of Madame de Tencin, she married Augustin de Ferriol (1653–1736), comte de Pont-de-Veyle by whom she had two sons, Antoine de Ferriol, comte de Pont-de-Veyle (Madame du Deffand's friend) and Charles-Augustin de Ferriol, comte d'Argental. She was a friend of Voltaire's and mistress of, among others, Vauban, Torcy and Bolingbroke. She welcomed Mademoiselle Aïssé to her home and brought her up with her sons.

FLAMARENS, Anne-Agnès de Beauvau (1699–1742), marquise de: married in 1717 Agésilas-Joseph de Grossolles, the only woman for whom Madame du Deffand seems to have had an unreserved, straightforward friendship. Madame de Flamarens probably died before the *marquise* had time to involve her in the web of mistrust and jealousy from which none of her friends was spared. But all accounts agree in describing her as a woman with no failings. Hénault has left a long and admiring portrait of her (Lewis, VI, pp. 97–100) and he dwells at length on her charms in his *Mémoires*.

FONTENELLE, Bernard Le Bovier de (1657–1757), nephew of the great Corneille, born in Rouen and destined for the law which he abandoned almost immediately to devote himself to literature. He moved to Paris and from 1677 collaborated in the "Mercure Galant" and began to consolidate his position as a poet and playwright. The failure of his tragedy *Aspar* in 1680 drove him to leave Paris and return to Rouen. During the next ten years in his native city, Fontenelle wrote his most important works, including the celebrated *Entretiens sur la pluralité des mondes* (1686) and *Doutes sur les causes occasionnelles* in which he criticised Malebranche's doctrines. In 1687, with the *Histoire des Oracles* and *Digression sur les anciens et les modernes,* Fontenelle entered the famous *querelle,* siding with the modernists. In 1691, on becoming a member of the *Académie Française* he returned permanently to Paris. In 1697 he was elected to the *Académie des Sciences* and two years later was made

Secretary in perpetuity. For another fifty years Fontenelle led an intensely active life as a populariser of science, philosopher, writer, poet, prolific playwright, man of the world and elegant ornament of the most exclusive *salons* on which he imposed his own inimitable style. He reigned at the Court of Sceaux as he did in the houses of Mesdames de Lambert, de Tencin and Geoffrin.

FORCALQUIER, Louis-Bufile de Brancas (1710–1753), comte de: son of Louis, marquis de Brancas. See Ch. IV, p. 87.

FORCALQUIER, Marie-Françoise-Renée de Carbonnel de Canisy (1725–1796), marquise de: married firstly in 1737 Antoine-François de Pardaillan de Gondrin, marquis d'Antin, was widowed and in 1742 married Louis-Bufile de Brancas, comte de Forcalquier. See Ch. IV, pp. 87–88.

FORMONT, Jean-Baptiste-Nicolas (1694–1758), born at Rouen and married in 1727 Françoise-Élisabeth-Louise Deschamps, daughter of a local writer. Formont's meeting with Voltaire who went to Rouen in 1723 to discuss the publication of the *Henriade* with the bookseller, Abraham Viret, was a turning point in his life. Under Voltaire's influence he went to Paris where he eventually spent several months a year and formed a close friendship with Madame du Deffand. But from 1738 Formont returned more permanently to Rouen to look after his patrimony; when he visited the capital he stayed in a small independent apartment which Madame du Deffand had at her disposition in Saint-Joseph. Formont published nothing, but in 1860 C. de Robillard de Beaurepaire discovered in the possession of Formont's heirs a collection of 90 large pages of manuscript which constituted his literary output.

FRÉRON, Élie-Catherine (1718–1776), brought up by the Jesuits and collaborated with the abbé Desfontaines, from 1749 he edited the *Lettres sur quelques écrits de ce temps,* the title of which was altered in 1754 to *L'Année littéraire* (1754–1775) and consisted of a pamphlet every ten days. Voltaire found Fréron guilty of catholicism, monarchism, patriotism and above all journalism and called him in turn an "animal," a "viper," a "thief," a "villain," a "scoundrel," a "drunk," and a "good-for-nothing." There was a marked division between the literati and the *philosophes* who both valued their independence and dignity and determined to conquer the *Académie,* and the subculture of salaried journalists. For instance, not one of Paris's big daily papers sided with enlightenment.

FROULAY, Louis-Gabriel de (1694–1766), Bailiff of the Order of Malta and twice admiral of that Order's fleet. In 1741 Ambassador for the Order of Malta to Paris. An intimate friend of the chevalier d'Aydie who was also a member of the Knights of Saint John of Jerusalem, and mentioned in Voltaire's letters.

GARASSE, François (1585–1631), Jesuit and polemicist, whose violence and intolerance were proverbial. Author of numerous works directed against the libertines.

GAUSSIN, Jeanne-Catherine Gaussem (1711–1767), known as Gaussin. Actress at the *Comédie-Française,* of which she became a full member in 1731. She reached the peak of her career between 1731 and 1743 with an uninterrupted series of triumphs.

GENEST, Charles-Claude (1639–1719) had had many varied professions before coming to Sceaux and offering his services as court poet and *chevalier-servant.* Employed in Colbert's ministry, professor at London, Secretary to the duc de Nevers, preceptor to Mademoiselle de Blois at Versailles, abbé d'Ahun in 1704 and member of the *Académie Française.*

GENLIS, Stéphanie-Félicité du Crest de Saint-Aubin, marquise de Sillery (1746–1830), comtesse de: prolific writer. She came to the Palais-Royal as part of the household of the duc de Chartres whose children she educated, among them the future king, Louis-Philippe. The *comtesse* saw herself as the standard-bearer for the moral and social values of the *ancien régime* and, in the *Dictionnaire critique et raisonné des étiquettes de la cour et des usages du monde,* she listed the old rules with a zeal which leaves some doubt as to her competence. Madame de Genlis, convinced that she was gifted with a philosophical turn of mind, hated the *philosophes,* which is perhaps why Madame du Deffand whom she met as an old lady, did not dislike her.

GEOFFRIN, Marie-Thérèse Rodet (1699–1777). Daughter of one of the Dauphine's servants, she lost both parents and was married at fourteen to François Geoffrin, a prosperous bourgeois of nearly fifty who had amassed a considerable fortune in administrating the glassworks, *Compagnie de Saint-Gobain* of which he had become a shareholder. If, as Segur points out, she had not met Madame de Tencin in about 1730, this beautiful virtuous and intelligent young woman would probably have been content merely to supervise her domestic affairs and the education of her only daughter, Marie-Thérèse (the future marquise de La Ferté-Imbault, writer of informative *Mémoires*). Madame Geoffrin became an *habituée* of the ex-canoness's *salon* and began to open the doors of her rich, comfortable, bourgeois home in rue Saint-Honoré to artists and writers. Monsieur Geoffrin's resistance was in vain and after a period of disagreement, he resigned himself to presiding in silence at his wife's receptions. In 1749 both Monsieur Geoffrin and Madame de Tencin died and Madame Geoffrin, now fifty years old, inherited the *habitués* of the latter's *salon* (see above Ch. IV, p. 64). Madame Geoffrin received on two fixed days: at dinner on Mondays she welcomed artists like Vanloo, Vernet, Boucher, La Tour, Vien, Lagrenée, Soufflot, Cochin, Lemoine, art lovers and patrons of art. Wednesday dinners, on the other hand, were reserved for writers like Mairan, Marivaux, Marmontel, Morellet, d'Alembert, Saint-Lambert, Helvétius, Grimm, d'Holbach and for foreigners living in Paris like Galiani, Caracciolo, Hume, etc., or for distinguished visitors passing through. Otherwise Madame Geoffrin organised intimate suppers for distinguished members of the aristocracy. The *salon* in rue Saint-Honoré stood halfway between Fontenelle's light-hearted scepticism and the encyclopaedists' driving philosophy. The authority with which Madame Geoffrin circumnavigated compromising subjects of discussion was proverbial. She was as discreet in her own private opinions as she was in tacitly controlling the free-thinkers. This conformist lady was determined to maintain her own serenity at all costs and her protégés had to avoid being sent to the Bastille, as Marmontel had cause to note when his *Belisaire* was published, but she was capable of great, impartial and courageous generosity. It was Madame Geoffrin who saved the *Encyclopédie* when half way through publication in 1759 it was condemned for the second time and the undertaking seemed definitively doomed. A sum of no less than a hundred thousand écus paid in secret by her, allowed the printer to continue and Diderot, who was no friend of hers, to carry the enterprise to its conclusion. Madame Geoffrin's rough but secretive generosity was a great characteristic of hers: she helped painters by buying their works and commissioning others, and writers with subsidies and pensions. One of her chief beneficiaries was Julie de Lespinasse who, when she left Madame du Deffand, found in Madame Geoffrin who had long been a friend of d'Alembert's a constant support. Madame Geoffrin gave her an annuity of three thousand livres and admitted her—a single woman—to her famous suppers. Madame du Deffand and Madame Geoffrin, who could not have been less alike in temperament and style, disliked each other cordially. Founded at about the same time, the two women's *salons* opposed each other for about thirty-five years, symbolic of two profoundly different realities: one represented the ascendant, enlightened bourgeoisie, eager for cultural recognition; the other, the entrenchment of an exclusive aristocracy whose only imperative was the safe-guarding of its own language and style. The wife of the former employee of Saint-Gobain was acknowledged in high places, she had a continuous correspondence with Catherine of Russia whom she tried to influence politically and she had the filial devotion of Stanislas Augustus Poniatowski, the young King of Poland whom she had known as a boy in Paris. The forty years of her *salon* were only interrupted once when she went to Poland in 1766 to see the new King, a visit which represented the culmination of her life as a hostess.

GLEICHEN, Carl Heinrich (1733–1807), Danish envoy extraordinary to France. Madame du Deffand liked Gleichen, whom she nicknamed "Trufaldin" very much, and did not disguise her displeasure when he was recalled to Denmark.

GRAMONT, Béatrix de Choiseul-Stainville (1730–1794), duchesse de: sister of
the duc de Choiseul, married in 1759 the duc Antoine-Antonin de Gramont
from whom she separated after a few months. She went to live with her
brother over whom she exercised enormous influence. Brilliant and authoritative, she entirely usurped her sister-in-law's domestic and social position.
The affection between brother and sister was such as to give rise to suspicions of incest. Madame de Gramont, who was both courageous and inordi-
nately proud, was partly responsible for her brother's disgrace, having
incited him to defy the King by despising Madame du Barry. At the outbreak
of the Revolution she refused to leave France and fearlessly faced the
guillotine.

GRANDVAL, François-Charles Racot de (1710–1784) belonged to a theatrical
dynasty of actors and playwrights. He made his debut at the *Comédie-Française*
in 1729 and stayed there until 1768.

GRIMM, Melchior (1723–1807), German by birth and education, he was fascinated by French culture and came to Paris, where he finally settled as
secretary to the young Count Friesen. He was friendly with the encyclopaedists and became a personality in his own right in Parisian society. In 1753 he
became the principle editor, along with Diderot, of the abbé Raynal's hand-
written review, *Correspondance littéraire,* which produced monthly accounts of
Parisian events for foreign princes and kings, from Frederick II and Catherine of Russia to Gustav III of Sweden and Stanislas Augustus of Poland. The
Correspondance was produced without interruption until 1790.

GUERCHY, Claude-Louis-François de Regnier (1715–1767), comte de: French
ambassador to London and friend of Walpole. Madame du Deffand was
distantly related to his wife, Gabrielle-Lydie d'Harcourt, and met him on 12
August 1766.

GUIBERT, Jacques-Antoine-Hyppolyte (1743–1790), comte de: brilliant officer
with literary aspirations, he had a great success with his *Essai général de
tactique* which was first published anonymously in 1770, but subsequent
writings did not fulfil his early promise. He gained immortality, however, by
inspiring a legendary passion in Julie de Lespinasse and preserving her love
letters which were published by his wife in 1809 and hailed by Sainte-Beuve
as *"la nouvelle Héloïse en action"* (Sainte-Beuve, *Lettres de Mademoiselle de
Lespinasse, Causeries du Lundi,* cit., II, p. 130).

HARENC, Madame: wife of the banker, Harenc de Presle of rue Santier who
owned a famous collection of paintings. Marmontel often refers to her in his
Mémoires.

HELVÉTIUS, Claude-Adrien (1715–1771). Extremely rich farmer-general and
chief patron of the encyclopaedists. In 1758 Helvétius published *De l'Esprit*
which was condemned by the Sorbonne, the *parlement* and the Pope and
burnt by the public executioner, making him famous throughout Europe.

HÉNAULT, Charles-Jean-François (1685–1770): 1706 *Conseiller au parlement* and in 1707 laureate at the *Académie Française* for his discourse, *Il ne peut y avoir de vrai boneur pour les hommes que dans la pratique des vertus chrétiennes*; the following year he won the first prize at the *Académie des Jeux Floraux* in a competition entitled: *L'incertitude de l'avenir est un bien qui n'est pas assez connu*. In 1710 he became *Président de la première Chambres des Enquêtes*. Meanwhile he had been made *sous-lieutenant des chasses* and charged with the administration of Corbeil; in this capacity he came to know the maréchal de Villeroy, the duc de Bourgogne and the duc de Berry and to build up an important social network of acquaintances. With reference only to his theatrical work, a mediocre tragedy, *Cornélie Vestale* (1713) gave him the entrée to the *Comédie-Française*; in 1715 he produced another, not much better, *Marius à Cirthe*. In later years he consolidated his reputation more successfully in comedy, with *La Petite Maison*, *Le jaloux de lui-même* and *Le reveil d'Epiménide*, but his most interesting play was the historical drama *François II* (1745). In 1770 Hénault produced an edition of his own theatrical works. In 1723 he became a member of the *Académie Française* and in 1731 gave up the position of *président au parlement* and became honorary Président. At Montesquieu's death, Hénault became known in society as the Président. His *Mémoires* were published posthumously in 1855. See in particular Ch. I, pp. 16–19.

HERVEY, Lady, Mary Lepell (1706–1768) married in 1720 Lord Hervey, eldest son of the 1st Earl of Bristol: she was beautiful, fascinating and attractive and was part of the social and literary circle which surrounded the Prince of Wales, later George II, and which included Pope, John Gay, Lord Chesterfield and the future Lady Suffolk. Lady Hervey was widowed in 1732 after which time she travelled frequently to France and became a great friend of Madame Geoffrin with whom she had a lengthy correspondence. Her friendship for Madame du Deffand's rival and the affectionate trust which Walpole placed in her were enough to incur the *marquise*'s dislike.

HOLBACH, Paul-Henri Thiry (1723–1789), baron de: of German origin and the possessor of a great fortune resulting from his ability as a financier and farmer-general. "The baron was one of the most cultivated men of his time, he had a vast and excellent library, a rich collection of drawings by the best masters. To these advantages were added great courtesy ... The baron Holbach had two regular dinners a week, on Sundays and on Thursdays. ... It was there then that the freest conversation was to be heard, the most animated and the most instructive ever: when I say 'free,' I mean in matters of philosophy, religion and government for free joking in the other sense was forbidden" (*Memoires de Morellet* op. cit. pp. 132–3). Among those who for twenty years from 1750 made up Holbach's coterie were Diderot, Grimm, Marmontel, Raynal, Saint-Lambert, Suard, Chastellux, Morellet, Helvétius, and Galiani.

JÉLYOTTE, Pierre (1711–1782) born at Lasseube in the Basses-Pyrénées, he first studied music in Toulouse. He moved to Paris in 1733 and began working at the *Opéra.* in 1734 he became one of the Queen's musicians for her concerts. On 23rd August 1735 he triumphed in the double role of Valère and Don Carlos in Rameau's *Les Indes Galantes.* From then onwards, and coincidentally with Tribou's retirement, Jélyotte, supported by constant public enthusiasm, became the number one at the *Opéra.* He was musically very gifted and became the King's *instrumentiste* and first cellist in Madame de Pompadour's orchestra in her *petits appartements.* He retired from the *Opéra* in 1755 and from his court appointments in 1765 but continued to be seen in certain grand Parisian houses, most particularly the prince de Conti's. He was Madame de La Vallière's lover.

JOLY DE FLEURY, Jean-Omer (1700–1755), abbot and author of numerous meditational, religious works. Confirmed enemy of the *philosophes.*

JONZAC, Élisabeth-Pauline-Gabrielle Colbert (d. 1786), marquise de: married in 1736 François-Pierre-Charles Bouchard d'Esparbez de Lussan, marquis de Jonzac and Hénault's nephew. The Président was very fond of his nephew's wife who repaid his support and affection with filial devotion. In the last seven years of Hénault's life, Madame de Jonzac helped him ceaselessly, ran his houshold and acted as his hostess.

KOENIG, Samuel (1712–1757), German mathematician, friend of Voltaire and Madame du Châtelet, member of the Berlin Academy, he initiated a violent polemic against Maupertius whom he accused of having stolen one of Leibniz's discoveries.

LA CHAUSSÉE, Pierre-Claude Nivelle de (1692–1754) rich, hedonistic bourgeois, ruined by Law: from the age of forty he devoted himself to writing for the theatre and became a member of the *Académie Française* in 1736. A writer of little talent, he has however been credited with the invention of the *comédie larmoyante,* which heralded bourgeois drama and had an enormous success equal to that of the novel.

LA CROIX, Charles-Eugène-Gabriel de Castries (1727–1801), marquis de: *Commandant de gendarmerie* (1770) and later Minister for the Navy, a friend of the Aiguillons, the Beauvaus, the Brancas etc. Mentioned sympathetically more than once in Madame du Deffand's letters to Walpole.

LA FARE, Philippe-Charles (1687–1752), marquis de: captain-general of the duc d'Orléans' guard in 1712 and lieutenant-general of the Languedoc in 1718, maréchal de France in 1746. La Fare was noted among the Regent's roués for his greed.

LA FERTÉ-IMBAULT, Marie-Thérèse Geoffrin (1715–1791), *marquise* de: married in 1731 Philippe-Charles d'Estampes, marquis de La Ferté-Imbault. Only daughter of Madame Geoffrin, beautiful, good and devout, as a widow she held a *salon* in competition with her mother's and hostile to the encyclo-paedists. In the last years of her life, when Madame Geoffrin fell ill, the *marquise* looked after her, keeping her away from the *philosophes*. Her as yet unpublished *Mémoires* are a valuable source of information about the cultural life of the time.

LA HARPE, Jean-François (1739–1803); orphaned in early childhood, he was raised by the Sisters of Charity and succeeded brilliantly in his studies, thanks to a grant for his education, and took to a literary career. By the mid-1760s he had already produced *Héroïdes* (1759), *Poésies fugitives* (1762) and several tragedies. Many more were to follow. Before revealing his real talent as a critic with his *Cours de littérature ancienne et moderne* held with great success at the Lycée between 1786 and 1798, La Harpe was known for his aggression and for the polemic verve with which he made enemies. He wrote for the *Mercure* from 1774 to 1789 and enjoyed a *Correspondance littéraire* with a Russian grand-duke, a very useful document for understanding the literary life of the time.

LAMBERT, Anne-Thérèse de Marguenat de Courcelles (1647–1733), marquise de: her magistrate father died young and she learned her love of literature from her mother's second husband, the famous Bachaumont, author of *Voyage*. At nineteen she married the marquis de Lambert, a brilliant officer and future Governor of Luxemburg, a happy marriage made more so by the birth of two children. As a widow she devoted herself seriously and with great ability to running the estates and educating her children. She wrote for the *Avis d'une mère à son fils* and *Avis d'une mère à sa fille*, both strongly influenced by Fenelon's *Télémaque* and which appeared respectively in 1726 and 1728. She also wrote *Réflexions nouvelles sur les femmes* (1727) and essays: *La Vieillesse* (1732) and *Traité de l'amitié* (1732). In about 1710, aged sixty, she opened the doors of her beautiful *salon* decorated by Robert de Cotte in the *hôtel* de Nevers. Madame de Lambert's *salon*, founded as it was during the court's greyest moment, became the first meeting place for aristocrats and intellectuals and it gradually developed a character quite opposed to cynicism and licence of the Regency and to Sceaux's *galères du bel esprit*. Sainte-Aulaire took refuge there. The *marquise* received on two days. On Tuesdays there was a dinner at about one in the afternoon, followed by literary and philosophical discussions whilst politics and religion were strictly banned. Writers read their latest works aloud and those present were invited to speak or write down what they thought. The Tuesday gatherings were usually presided over by Fontenelle and attended, among others, by the marquis de Sainte-Aulaire, the *marquise*'s daughter's father-in-law and, according to Hénault, her secret husband; by the celebrated playwright, La Motte, and by Marivaux who depicted both Madame de Miran and Madame de Lambert in *La vie de Marianne*. Then there were Hénault, the erudite academician Dortous de Mairan, the Greek scholar and mathematician abbé Terrasson, and the transvestite abbé de Choisy whom Madame de Lambert persuaded to write his *Mémoires*: the lawyer and translator of Pliny, Monsieur de Sacy, père Buffier, the abbés de Chaulieu and de Bragelonne, Mongault, Trublet, Fraguier, the Boivin brothers, the marquis d'Argenson. There were playwrights like Campistron, Danchet and Rameau, painters like Watteau, Rigaud and Nattier. The women included Madame de Staal Delaunay, Madame Dacier who translated Homer and sided passionately with the Ancients in the famous *querelle* but whom Madame de Lambert succeeded in reconciling with the modernists, Madame Drouillet who had won the Jeux Floraux, Madame de Caylus, and Madame de la Force. The tone of the *hôtel* de Nevers reflected its mistress, it was elegant, respectful of *bienséances,* thoughtful, cultured and moralising. It was an honour to be accepted there, and certain rules had to be respected. In reacting to the intellectual decadance of the court aristocracy, Madame de Lambert did not simply align herself with outdated form or with the whims pilloried by Molière in *Les Femme Savantes.* The *marquise* expressed her intellectual independence and moral freedom not only in her writing, but more than once in her life. Indifferent to scandal, she immediately supported *Les Lettres Persanes* and was responsible for the happy outcome of Montesquieu's bitterly opposed election in 1727. Madame de Lambert was the first high-born woman to receive actors like Adrienne Lecouvreur and Baron. This was as an implicit protest against the barbarous political and religious discrimination they endured—they were not, for instance, allowed to be buried in consecrated ground.

La Noue, Jean-Baptiste Sauvé (1710–1761), known as dramatic author and actor, a member of the *Académie Française.*

Lassay, Léon de Medaillon de Lesparre (1678–1750), *comte,* later marquis de, lieutenant-colonel of Enghien's regiment in 1710, brigadier in 1719.

La Tour, Maurice Quentin de (1704–1788), famous portraitist who specialised in pastels. Between 1740 and 1760 at the time of his greatest success, La Tour numbered some of the greatest names in France among his clients, including the King, the Dauphin and Madame de Pompadour.

Lauzun, Amélie de Boufflers (1751–1795), duchesse de: daughter of Charles-Joseph duc de Boufflers and Marie-Anne-Philippine-Thérèse de Montmorency, and granddaughter of the maréchale de Luxembourg. Although universally praised for her beauty and charm Amélie did not distract her husband for one moment from his brilliant career as a libertine. In fact Mademoiselle de Boufflers married the duc de Lauzun at fifteen and the marriage was unhappy from the start. The *duchesse* often appears in Madame du Deffand's letters as the protégée of her aunt-in-law, Madame de Choiseul. The *marquise* did not appear to like the young woman very much and referred to her as *la petite femme*. Amélie was guillotined in 1794.

LAUZUN, Armand-Louis de Gontaut (1747–1793), comte and, from 1766, duc de Brion: the son of Madame de Choiseul's sister, he married at nineteen Amélie de Boufflers, nephew of Madame de Luxembourg. He was attractive, unscrupulous, ambitious, a squanderer of fortunes and seems to be an exemplary heir to the aristocratic-libertine tradition whose most distinguished representative was the maréchal de Richelieu. Lauzun took part in the American War of Independence, was a deputy in the States General, and in 1792 general in charge of the Rhine Army; after having led the military campaign in the Vendée, he resigned, was arrested and condemned to the guillotine.

LA VALLIÈRE, Anne-Julie-Françoise de Crussol (1713–1793), duchesse de: married in 1732 Louis-César de la Baume le Blanc, duc de La Vallière (1708–1780), grandson of Louis XIV's famous mistress, and famous for his vast collection of books, his numerous lovers and his prodigality. She was beautiful and a dedicated libertine.

LAW, John of Lauriston: Scotsman famed for his banking and financial talents, he was able to put his theories to the test in France. In 1716 the Regent gave him permission to found a private bank, the *Banque générale*. The Regent contributed to the bank's success by ordering the payment of taxes in notes. In 1717, Law founded the *Compagnie d'Occident* which, as a result of privileges, developed into the *Compagnie des Indes* with a rapid increase in the value of its shares. In 1718 the *Banque générale* became the *Banque Royale* and the Regent introduced measures to prevent the circulation of specie. Law was then charged with printing more money and with collecting indirect taxes, so that he in fact entirely controlled the Regent's financial policy, initiating fiscal reform and the conversion of public debt, transforming the State's creditors into company shareholders. The paper money was soon devalued, giving rise to rapid inflation. At the end of 1720, the *Banque Royale* collapsed and Law had to leave France and return to England where he wrote *Mémoire justificatif* (1723).

LEKAIN, Henri-Louis Caïn or Kaïn (1728–1778) known as Lekain: joined the *Comédie* in 1750, having performed at Sceaux and in the prince de Conti's little theatre. He made his debut as Tito in Voltaire's *Brutus* which caused a great stir and divided the public and the critics: Lekain was devoid of physical attraction, he was ugly with a weak voice but immediately conquered his audience by the pathos of his performance. He particularly shone in Voltaire's plays whose main performer he was in the 1760s.

LE MONNIER, Pierre-Charles (1715–1799): astronomer and friend of Madame du Deffand.

LENNOX, Lady George formerly Louisa Kerr (1739–1830): wife of Lord

George Henry Lennox (1737–1805). In 1765 Lennox came to Paris as Secretary to the British embassy where his brother, Charles Lennox, third Duke of Richmond was Ambassador Extraordinary and Plenipotentiary. The Lennoxes, of great aristocratic lineage, were friends of Walpole.

LIGNE, Charles-Joseph (1735–1814), Prince de: Born in Brussels of an old noble family from the Low Countries; he joined the army at an early age which soon led to a brilliant military career. He never took part in any war against France and in old age was made a field-marshal. Between his military duties, Ligne undertook diplomatic assignments and was a great social success in various European courts. Both Maria Theresa and Catherine of Russia treated him informally; he was a friend of Joseph II and Frederick of Prussia and devoted to Marie-Antoinette, welcomed in the most exclusive Parisian *salons* and on terms with the most famous, from Voltaire and Rousseau to Casanova. Ligne left 36 volumes of *Mélanges militaires, Littéraires et sentimentales* (1794–1811).

LISTENOIS, Charles-Roger de Bauffremont (1713–1795), chevalier de: "A really good man, easy of conversation, well informed, knowing everyone and liked by all, a good acquisition" (Madame du Deffand to Walpole, 30 April 1768).

LORRAINE, Anne-Charlotte de (1755–1786), daughter of Madame de Brionne, future abbess of Remiremont. In September 1771 she accompanied her mother to visit the Choiseuls at Chanteloup; the abbé Barthélemy praised her to Madame du Deffand.

LUXEMBOURG, Madeleine-Angélique de Neufville (1707–1787), maréchale and duchesse de: married in 1721 Joseph-Marie, duc de Boufflers and secondly in 1750 Charles-François-Frederic de Montmorency-Luxembourg, duc de Luxembourg, maréchal de France. See Ch. IV, pp. 76–80.

LUYNES, Marie Brûlart (1684–1763), duchesse de: daughter of Nicolas II Brûlart and of his second wife Marie Bouthillier who, widowed in her turn, married César-Auguste, duc de Choiseul. Marie Brûlart was Madame du Deffand's mother's sister. Left childless on the death at Malplaquet of her husband, the marquis de Charost, she married in 1732 Charles-Philippe d'Albert duc de Luynes. Madame de Luynes dedicated herself to society and gained an important position at Versailles. On 14 October 1735 she replaced Madame de Boufflers as lady-in-waiting to the Queen. Having won Maria Leszczynska's trust, Madame de Luynes busied herself with the fortunes of her old friend Hénault. Having been presented to the Queen, Hénault became an ever more assiduous courtier at Versailles. The *duchesse* was always very concerned for her niece, and she obtained for her an annuity of 6000 livres from the Queen.

MACDONALD, Sir James (*c.* 1742–1766). MacDonald, who died young in

Frascati, spent a few months in Paris after the 1763 peace, where he was much liked.

MÂCON, Henri-Constance de Lort de Sérignan de Valras (1690–1763) Bishop of: visited Madame du Deffand and Champrond and was her host for several months (1752–3) in the episcopal see at Mâcon.

MAINE, Anne-Louise-Bénédicte d'Enghien (1676–1753): formerly Mademoiselle de Charolais, later duchesse du: eighth daughter of Anne of Bavaria, Princess Palatine and Henri-Jules de Bourbon, prince de Condé, extremely vivacious and authoritarian, she married in 1692 Louis-Auguste de Bourbon (1670–1736), duc du Maine, legitimised son of Louis XIV and Madame de Montespan. The marriage was part of the Sun King's policy of uniting the princes of the blood with his bastards. In the same year Louis XIV passed a law giving royal bastards a rank between the princes of the blood and the peers of France. From 1700 she lived mostly at the Château de Sceaux, a few kilometres outside Paris.

MALÉZIEU, Nicolas de (1650–1727): man of letters and mathematician, member of the *Académie des Sciences* and of the *Académie Française*. Mathematics tutor to the duc de Bourgogne (*Nouveau traité de la Sphère, 1679, Éléments de géométrie de M. le duc de Bourgogne, 1715*), and also preceptor to the duc du Maine. With the *duc*'s marriage, Malézieu acquired a new and very demanding pupil, and "he devoted himself to the last and minutest details of the entertainment and spectacles with which the *duchesse* attempted to adorn her court at Sceaux" (A. Jullien, op. cit., p. 3). Much of his literary output, his poetry, novellas, comedies, have been collected in *Divertissements de Sceaux,* 1712, 1715, in the *Pièces échappées du feu,* 1717 which includes a one act play, *Polichinelle demandant une place à l'Académie*. His theatrical works include *La Tarantole,* a masque, 1705, *Les importuns de Châtenay,* 1706, *Pyrgopolénice, Capitaine d'Ephèse,* 1708. Posthumously, in 1749, there appeared *Les Amours de Ragonde,* a musical comedy in three acts, after a text by Destouches.

MARMONTEL, Jean-François (1723–1799): of humble origins, he arrived in Paris from the provinces in search of literary fame and attached himself to Voltaire and the encyclopaedists. His philosophical novel, *Belisaire,* condemned by the Sorbonne which made him famous throughout Europe. Poet, playwright, story-teller, Marmontel was an extremely popular author who enjoyed a certain authority in the intellectual world. In 1783 he succeeded d'Alembert as Secretary in perpetuity at the *Académie Française*. His best work was his *Mémoires d'un père pour servir à l'instruction de ses enfants*.

MARMONTEL, Jean-Paris de (1690–1766): guardian of the royal treasury.

MASSILLON, Jean-Baptiste (1663–1742): born at Hyères, in Provence, he studied at Marseilles and in 1681, against the wishes of his lawyer father and inspired by a true vocation, he joined the order of *Oratoriens* at Aix and was ordained to the priesthood in Vienna in 1692. In 1698 he began his great career of preaching, first during Lent at Montpellier and the following year in Paris, in the church of the *Oratoire* in rue Saint-Honoré. In 1717 he was made Bishop of Clermont and a year later elected to the *Académie Française.* He settled in his diocese and gave up preaching in favour of pastoral work in which he distinguished himself by his zeal and piety. His sincere religiosity did not protect him from criticism. He was involved in anti-Jansenist polemic and much blamed for having been partly responsible for the consecration as archbishop of the Regent's unscrupulous minister, Dubois.

MAUPERTIUS, Pierre-Louis, Moreau de (1698–1759), distinguished geometer, member of the *Académie des Sciences* 1723, passionate propagator of Newton's theories in France and Madame du Châtelet's friend and teacher. In 1744 he moved to Prussia where Frederick II made him president of the Berlin Academy. The last years of his life were embittered by a quarrel with Voltaire who pilloried him in *Diatribe du docteur Akakia* and in *Micromégas.* Before leaving France Maupertius had been one of Madame du Deffand's circle and a close friend of the *marquise.*

MAUREPAS, Jean-Frédéric Phélypeaux (1701–1781), comte de Maurepas and de Pontchartrain: Minister for the Navy from 1738, exiled in 1749 for an epigram mocking Madame de Pompadour, a minister again under Louis XVI in 1774.

MAUREPAS, Marie-Jeanne Phélypeaux de la Vrillière (1704–1793), comtesse de: married in 1718 Jean-Frédéric Phélypeaux, the comte de Céreste was her *chevalier-servant* (Madame du Deffand to Walpole, 16 November 1772).

MENOU, Joseph de (1695–1766), Jesuit, Superior of the Missionaries at Nancy, confessor and friend of King Stanislas Leszczynski at his court at Lunéville, in Lorraine. He is said to have collaborated in Stanislas's work, *L'Incrédulité combattue par le simple bons sens* in which he tried to demonstrate that deist reasoning was a contradiction in itself: but it was Menou who sent a copy to Voltaire in the King's name. Voltaire despised Menou and accused him in his *Mémoires* of having tried to persuade Madame du Châtelet to be Stanislas's mistress.

MIREPOIX, Anne-Marguerite-Gabrielle de Beauvau-Craon (1707–1791), maréchale and duchesse de: married in 1721 Jacques-Henri de Lorraine, prince de Lixin, and secondly in 1739, Pierre-Louis de Lévis de Lomagne, duc de Mirepoix, maréchale de France. See Ch. IV, pp. 80–83.

MODENA, Charlotte-Aglaé d'Orléans (1700–1761), formerly Mademoiselle de Vallois, then duchesse de: daughter of the Regent and Mademoiselle de Blois, she married Francesco Maria d'Este, Duke of Modena.

MONCRIF, François-Augustin Paradis de (1687–1770), son of a procurator and of a Scotswoman of the Moncrif clan, whose name he took. Poet, musician, actor, secretary to the comte d'Argenson, to the prince-abbé de Clermont and the duc d'Orléans and reader to Maria Leszczynska to whose service he devoted his talents as a wit and entertainer. His humorous *Histoire des chats* was very successful but made him the butt of endless jokes.

MONTAGU, George (*c.* 1713–1780). A member of the aristocratic Montagu family and friend of Walpole's from Eton days, he spent most of his time in the country, reading, hunting and playing cards. He was one of Walpole's earliest correspondents; their letters cover a period of twenty-five years, and are a chronicle of English society of the time.

MONTESQUIEU, Charles-Louis de Secondat (1689–1755), baron de La Brède et de Montesquieu: he seems to have had an admiration and deep affection for Madame du Deffand whose *salon* he frequented assiduously when in Paris. Only five letters from Montesquieu survive from their correspondence (1751–54), but their tone is remarkable. "You say you are blind! Do you not see that in the past you and I were two rebellious spirits condemned to the shadows? We should be consoled by the fact that those who see clearly are not, for that, more enlightened" (13 September 1754. Masson p. 1515), he wrote to the *marquise*. Montesquieu's sight was also very bad.

MONTIGNY. Jean-Charles-Philibert Trudaine de (1733–1777), *Intendant général* of finances in 1769. The Montignys were one of the most powerful families in France and open to new ideas. Madame du Deffand was on very cordial terms with Montigny and his wife and was grateful to him for his attention and favours. Montigny was in touch with the encyclopaedists and a friend of Hume's. His two sons also distinguished themselves by their enlightened ideas and patronage of the arts, they welcomed the Revolution as the end of secular injustice and were both guillotined the day after their great friend Chénier.

MORELLET, André (1727–1819), laureate of the Sorbonne and *abbé*; in 1752 he joined the group of *philosophes* who met at Madame Geoffrin's and the baron d'Holbach's houses, and bravely aligned himself with them at the time of the Palissot scandal. Morellet participated actively in the philosophical, economic and institutional discussions of the enlightenment period, more as a conversationalist than by his many writings. See particularly his *Mémoires sur le XVIIIᵉ Siècle et sur la Révolution.*

NECKER, Jacques (1732–1804), married in 1765 Suzanne Curchod (1739–1794), daughter of a Protestant pastor, and together they founded a *salon.* They received on Fridays and welcomed the enlightenment élite. Within a few years their *salon* was established as a major institution. With Marmontel and Morellet's help, d'Alembert, Diderot, Malsherbes, Buffon, Saint-Lambert, Galiani etc. were all numbered among Madame Necker's guests. Despite her beauty and intelligence, she never quite acquired the charm and social ease of the French *salonnières.* Madame du Deffand began to visit the Neckers in 1774, the year after the Swiss banker published his famous *Essai sur la législation et le commerce des grains.* A year later he became Minister of Finance. An extremely cordial relationship developed between the Neckers and the old *marquise.*

NIVERNAIS, Louis-Jules-Barbon Mancini Mazzarini (1716–1798), duc de: Spanish grandee, ambassador to Rome, Berlin and London, minister with Necker in 1789, Nivernais was a man of many talents—as a poet, playwright, scholar and writer of fables. He took part in performances in the *petits appartements* at Versailles. The *duc* was an old friend of Hénault's and on good terms with Walpole whose *Essay on the Art of Modern Gardens* he translated in 1785, but he was not an *habitué* of Saint-Joseph. Nivernais was the lover of Madame de Rochefort with whom Madame du Deffand had quarrelled.

ORLÉANS, Philippe d' (1674–1723), duc de Chartres and later, from 1701, d'Orléans: the son of Louis XIV's brother, Philippe d'Orléans, known as Monsieur, and founder of the Bourbon-Orléans line. The duc de Chartres was indebted to his preceptor, the abbé Dubois, for his passionate interest in politics, his sympathy for English liberalism and his considerable culture, but also for hedonism and dissipation. The young *duc* set out on a brilliant military career which was thwarted by family jealousy so that he seemed destined to a life of idleness and pleasure. But on Louis XIV's death in 1715 his luck changed, in clear preference to Louis XIV's bastard son, the duc du Maine, the duc d'Orléans became Regent on behalf of the five-year-old king. In the first years of the Regency he took a liberal stand in accordance with his education. Then from 1718, he turned back to a form of absolutism, whilst maintaining a mild and tolerant attitude, except in serious cases like the Cellamare conspiracy. He was well able to tackle the crisis provoked in those years by Alberoni's politics in Spain and neither did he fail to back initiatives which might, like Law's, have failed, but which were inspired by courageous experimentalism. The Regency was typified by the Court's return to worldliness, by a strong anti-religious bias, by frenzied love of luxury and pleasure and by contempt for traditional standards of behaviour. When Louis XV came of age in 1723, Philippe d'Orléans became chief minister, and maintained his policy of liberalised absolutism whilst favouring an agreement with the Spanish Bourbons involving the engagement of the French King and Philip V's daughter, but he died suddenly, three months later, on 2 December 1723.

OSSORY, John Fitzpatrick (1745–1818), second Earl of Upper Ossory. Walpole met him in Paris in 1765 and their friendship continued in England. Madame du Deffand shared Walpole's liking for Ossory.

Palissot, Charles de Montenoy (1730–1814) tried in vain with his comedies and tragedies to take the theatre by storm, but later specialised in satire and caused tremendous scandal by violently attacking his enemies, either in person or for their ideas. The *philosophes* above all paid the price of Palissot's popularity. Writers hated Palissot and kept him at a distance.

Parabère, Marie-Madeleine de la Vieuville (1693–1755), comtesse de: widowed in 1716 after five years of marriage to César-Alexandre de Beaudéan, comte de Parabère. She was one of the Regent's official mistresses, but did not limit herself to the duc d'Orléans.

Phalaris, Marie-Thérèse Blonel d'Haraucourt (1697–1782), wife of Pierre-François Gorges d'Entraigues, duc de Phalaris "a very sweet adventuress who married another adventurer" (Saint-Simon, VII, p. 379).

Pompignan, Jean-Georges Lefranc de (1715–1790): younger brother of Jean-Jacques, doctor at the Sorbonne, Bishop of Le Puy (1742) and later archbishop of Vienne. Preacher and apologist.

Pompignan, Jean-Jacques Lefranc de (1709–1784): after a short but brilliant career as a magistrate, he devoted himself to literature, wrote tragedies and poetry and translated from Greek and Latin. Among other things he translated the Georgics. When elected to the *Académie Française* in 1760, he took the opportunity of his inaugural speech to attack the *philosophes*.

Pont-de-Veyle, Antoine de Ferriol (1697–1774), comte de: he soon gave up his career as a magistrate, to devote himself entirely to the theatre, literature and society. His father acquired the position of King's reader for him, a prestigious sinecure given that Louis XV was known to read nothing. Thanks to his friendship with the comte de Maurepas, he was *Intendant général* of the Navy from 1740–9. With his brother d'Argental and Thiériot, Pont-de-Veyle formed what Voltaire called his "triumvirate" whose approval he sought before having his works printed. Pont-de-Veyle had a large theatrical library and he wrote several plays; he was also said to be co-author, if not author, of some of the novels by his maternal aunt, Madame de Tencin. See Ch. IV, pp. 75–76.

Prades, Jean-Martin de (1720–1782): he caused a sensation with his doctoral thesis at the Sorbonne in 1715, in which he drew a parallel between Christ's miracles and those of Aesculapius. The thesis was condemned by the *parlement* as was his piece entitled *Certitude* in the *Encyclopédie*. Prades had to leave France; he took refuge first in Holland and then Germany where, on Voltaire's recommendation he became a reader to the King of Prussia. In reply to the Bishop of Auxerre who had attacked his thesis with an *Instruction Pastoral*, he produced in 1752 *l'Apologie de Monsieur l'abbé de Prades* with an appendix by Diderot entitled *Suite de l'apologie de M. l'abbé de Prades ou réponse à l'instruction pastorale de M. l'évêque d'Auxerre*.

PRÉVILLE, Pierre-Louis Dubus or Du Bus (1721–1799): he joined the *Comédie-Française* in 1753 after a long apprenticeship in the provinces, and immediately established himself by his versatility and intelligence, as a great comic actor. In 1775 he created the part of Beaumarchais's Figaro in the *Barbier de Séville.*

PRIE, Agnès Berthelot de Pleneuf (1698–1727), marquise de: daughter of a rich financier, married in 1713 the marquis Louis de Prie, French ambassador in Turin. On returning to France in 1719, Madame de Prie dedicated herself to intrigue and debauchery and became Louis-Henri de Bourbon's mistress. Dragged down by his disgrace, she was exiled to her property at Courbépine in Normandy where she died a mysterious and tragic death.

QUESNAY, François (1694–1774): doctor and surgeon, he quarrelled with the famous Silva about the practise of bleeding and by his numerous writings, contributed to the development of surgery. Under Madame de Pompadour's protection Quesnay went in 1748 to live at Versailles and four years later was made head physician to the King. Meanwhile his interests were changing from medicine and surgery to economics and in the presence of Diderot, d'Alembert, Helvétius, Buffon, Turgot, etc., he developed his physiocratic theory in his mezzanine at Versailles.

RICHELIEU, Louis-François-Armand Vignerot du Plessis (1696–1788), duc de: great-great-nephew through the female line of the Cardinal, he was held at his baptism by Louis XIV. He lived under three kings, was imprisoned three times in the Bastille, had three wives, was a general, an ambassador, governor, first gentleman of the King's bedchamber, but could never achieve his greatest ambition which was to become a minister like his ancestor. Disappoint by politics, Richelieu devoted himself instead to his other great ambition—to be unequalled in the art of seduction. The legend of his debauchery began when he was only a boy. Richelieu may in fact have been the inspiration for Lovelace in Richardson's *Clarissa Harlowe*, Beaumarchais's Cherubino, Sélim in Diderot's *Bijoux indiscrets* and Valmont in Laclos's *Liaisons dangéreuses*. Although the *duc* treasured the documents concerning his public activities and his love affairs throughout his life, he only wrote, in old age, some 150 pages about his military and diplomatic life (*Mémoires authentiques du Maréchal de Richelieu (1725–1757) publiés d'après le manuscrit original pour la Société de l'Histoire de France par A. de Boislisle,* Paris, 1919).

ROBECQ, Anne-Maurice de Montmorency-Luxembourg, married Anne-Louis-Alexandre de Montmorency, prince de Robecq. Mistress of the duc de Choiseul, before dying of tuberculosis in 1760, she promoted a campaign against the *philosophes.*

ROCHEFORT, Marie-Thérèse de Brancas (1716–1782), married firstly in 1735, Jean-Anne-Vincent de Larlan de Kercadio, comte de Rochefort and, secondly in 1782, Louis-Jules Barbon Mancini-Mazzarini, duc de Nivernais. See Ch. IV, p. 87.

SABRAN, Madeleine-Louise-Charlotte de Foix-Rabat (1693–1768), comtesse de: wife of Jean-Honoré de Sabran and one of the most fascinating women of her time.

SADE, Jacques-François-Paul-Alphonse de (1705–1778), younger brother of Jean-Baptiste-François-Joseph (1701–1767) comte de Sade (father of the marquis de Sade). Vicar General of the Archbishopric of Toulouse, later Bishop of Narbonne. Learned, a translator of Petrarch (*Oeuvres choisies de François Pétrarque*, Amsterdam, 1764) and author of a study of Troubador poetry (*Remarques sur les premiers poètes français et les trobadours*), and of *Mémoires sur sa vie*.

SAINTE-AULAIRE, François-Joseph de Beaupoil (1643–1742), marquis de: like the more famous Fontenelle, Sainte-Aulaire was fairly typical of the cultural climate at the turn of the seventeenth century. His poetry writing followed inevitably from his brilliant career as a man of the world. Despite Boileau's violent opposition, he became a member of the *Académie Française* in 1706, and became director three times. Besides being an *habitué* of Sceaux, Sainte-Aulaire was a frequent and assiduous visitor to Madame du Lambert's *salon*, and was genuinely devoted to her. It is likely that the old poet and the *marquise* who were already linked by the marriage of her daughter to his son, may have been secretly married themselves.

SAINT-MARC, Jean-Paul-André de Razins (1728–1818), marquis de: descended from a family of Venetian origin and related to Montesquieu, served in the *gardes françaises* from 1744–62. Poet of variable talent, he wrote among other things, a poem in honour of Voltaire which was read in the *Théâtre Français* at the famous celebration of Voltaire in 1778.

SANADON, Mademoiselle, niece of père Noël-Étienne Sanadon (1676–1733), author of much poetry in Latin. In 1767 Mademoiselle Sanadon settled in a small independent apartment at Saint-Joseph as a companion to the *marquise* in place of Julie de Lespinasse.

SARRAZIN, Pierre-Claude born into a well-to-do bourgeois family in 1686 at Nuits Bourgogne. He joined the duc de Gesvres's company at Château Saint-Ouen and from there moved to the *Comédie-Française* where he made his debut in 1729. For thirty years he played leading parts, excelling in tragedy. Voltaire's *Brutus* was one of his greatest successes.

SAULX, Charles-Henri de Saulx-Tavannes (1697–1768), marquis de.

SCHEFFER, Carl Frederik (1715–1786), count, Swedish ambassador to France from 1744 to 1751, he was made a senator on his return to Sweden and later, in 1756, nominated by the Swedish Diet to replace Tissin as preceptor and adviser to the future Gustav III. He was an able diplomat, a great francophile and defender of Swedish liberties.

SÉGUR, Philippe-Angélique de Froissy (1700–1785), comtesse de, having married Henri-François, comte de Ségur in 1718.

SELWYN, George Augustus (1719–1791), educated at Eton and Oxford, he became a member of Parliament in 1744 but had no taste for politics and accepted a series of honorary sinecures. He was famous for his wit and liked to play cards, hunt, travel and be talked about for his many eccentricities which included his passion for public executions. Selwyn felt at home in Paris and knew Madame du Deffand with whom he corresponded. It was he who gave Walpole a letter of introduction to the *marquise.*

SHUVALOV, Ivan Ivanovic (1727–1797). "Favorite of Elisabeth of Russia" (Lewis I, p. 130, note 40), introduced to the best Parisian society, and a friend of Madame du Deffand. After fourteen years abroad he returned to Russia in 1778. "He enjoyed the greatest favour, the empress made him her chamberlain. The first day she made him take tea with her, she said to him: 'I want you to be at ease with me, as you were with Mme du Deffand'" (to Walpole, 20 September 1778).

SIGORGNE, Pierre (1719–1809): a graduate of the Sorbonne where he distinguished himself as an apostle of Newton's, the abbé Sigorgne went on to teach philosophy at the Collège du Plessis. His *Institutions newtoniennes* (1747) were very successful and were translated into five languages. He refused to denounce a pupil—Jacques Turgot—who had written and circulated a pamphlet said to be dangerous, and was tried and sent to the Bastille in 1749. After a few months in prison, the *abbé* was exiled from Paris and in 1752, just as Madame du Deffand was there, he settled in Mâcon. His acquaintanceship with the *marquise,* however, seems to date from before this time.

SILHOUETTE, Étienne de (1709–1767), *controleur général des Finances.*

STAAL, Marguerite-Jeanne Cordier Delaunay de (1684–1750), daughter of an expatriate painter, living in England, she took her mother's surname, Delaunay and changed her name to Rose. Despite having received an excellent education in a convent in Rouen, necessity obliged mademoiselle Delaunay to enter the duchesse du Maine's service as a simple maid. After a humiliating apprenticeship as a secretary and companion, she accidentally revealed her literary talent and was promoted. In 1718 Mademoiselle Delaunay was arrested as an accomplice to the duc and duchesse du Maine in the Cellamare conspiracy, and was sent to the Bastille for eighteen months which, she claims, was the happiest period of her life. On leaving prison in 1720 she returned to her former employment. Her position as a dependent remained unchanged even when in 1735 she married the Baron de Staal. Besides her wonderful *Mémoires* published posthumously in 1758, Madame de Staal left an interesting correspondence and two comedies, *L'engouement* and *La mode,* written for the ephemeral theatre at Sceaux, but destined to survive among the most interesting plays of the Regency.

SUARD, Jean-Baptiste (1734–1817): he came to Paris from the provinces as a poor young man, he was helped by Madame Geoffrin and later, thanks to the duc de Choiseul's support, he succeeded in becoming editor of the "Gazette de France" and thus began a brilliant career as a journalist. Suard became a welcome member of the *philosophes'* circle, and a friend of Julie de Lespinasse, thanks to whose influence he was elected to the *Académie* in 1772. But the maréchal de Richelieu, as the King's spokesman, expressed disapproval at the election which was subsequently nullified, of a man too closely associated with the encyclopaedists. Nevertheless Suard became an academician two years later. With his wife, the famous printer, Panckoucke's daughter, Suard held a lively *salon* frequented by writers and encyclopaedists. Madame Suard has left some *Essais de Mémoires sur M. Suard.*

SUFFOLK, Henrietta Hobart (*c.* 1681–1767), Lady: married firstly Charles Howard (later 9th Earl of Suffolk) and after she was widowed, married secondly in 1737, George Berkeley. For seven years, from 1728–35, Lady Suffolk was George II's official mistress and although much loved by the King, she tried in vain to influence him politically in opposition to the Prime Minister, Robert Walpole. After she retired from court and was widowed for the second time, Lady Suffolk settled in her villa, Marble Hill, at Twickenham, so that when Horace Walpole bought Strawberry Hill, they became neighbours, and Lady Suffolk grew very fond of her ex-rival's son. Walpole was never tired of listening to tales of the old court which complemented what his father told him. Such material formed the basis of the *Reminiscences* written during the last years of his life.

TAAFFE, John (*c.* 1715–1773), third son of Stephen and brother of Theobald and certainly more respectable than the latter. Although addicted to gambling, he was honest. He had cultural interests and seems to have been much appreciated in the *salons,* especially Madame du Deffand's. When, at the outbreak of the Seven Years War, John left Paris, Madame du Deffand started to correspond with him. She never lost touch completely.

TAAFFE, Theobald (*c.* 1705), son of Stephen, a Dublin landowner. Theobald was an unscrupulous adventurer who converted to Protestantism in order to be able to carry a sword and fight a duel, both of which things were forbidden to Irish Catholics. He was imprisoned in Paris in 1751 for having cheated and robbed a money-lender, and four years later he caused the death of an English aristocrat whom he had robbed of all his worldly goods. In 1758 Theobald was sent to the Bastille for suspicious behaviour, but immediately released by order of the duc de Choiseul who may have wanted to use him as a spy. No more was heard of him after 1777.

TALMONT, Marie-Louise Jablonowska (1701–1773), princesse de: married in 1730 Antoine-Charles-Frédéric de la Trémoïlle, prince de Talmont. "The princess of Talmont, not so great a lady, nor an historic personage, made a figure, however in her time in the court of Louis Quinze. She was born in Poland, and related to his Queen Mary Leszczynska, with whom she came into France where she married a prince out of the house of Bouillon who left her a widow ... Her last lover had been the Young Pretender whose picture she wore in a bracelet, on the other side of which was one of Jesus Christ" (Horace Walpole, Lewis, vi, pp. 57–8).

TENCIN, Claudine-Alexandrine Guérin de (1682–1749): she and her brother were made of the stuff of great adventurers and they contributed greatly to the scandalous happenings of the Regency. Born to a magistrate's family of the provincial nobility, they were both destined for the Church. But in 1715, probably because of her unsuitable behaviour, Claudine-Alexandrine was released from her vows, made "canoness of I know not where, a place she never visited" (Saint-Simon, vi, p. 426), and moved to Paris. Two years later she abandoned a male child in a churchyard. This child was later to take the name of d'Alembert. But Madame de Tencin continued to be connected to the Church, albeit in a profane fashion. After being the Regent's mistress, she became the mistress of the Chief Minister, the Cardinal Dubois, and soon concerned herself with her brother's ecclesiastical career and joined passionately in the anti-Jansenist polemic. The ex-canoness was made rich by Law but was unharmed when his system collapsed. One of her lovers, Monsieur de la Fresnaye, committed suicide in her house after having accused her of robbing him. But Madame de Tencin was not merely an intriguer. She was an intelligent woman, loved and respected by the most famous men of letters of the day, starting with Fontenelle. She was a regular visitor to the marquise de Lambert's *salon* and when the *marquise* died in 1733 she inherited her most distinguished *habitués*. She wrote many enormously popular novels, the most famous of which was the *Mémoires du Comte de Comminges*. Pierre de Tencin was also involved in intrigue and took full advantage of his sister. In 1721 he went to Rome with the Cardinal de Rohan who had him nominated responsible for French affairs at the Vatican. In 1724 Tencin was made an archbishop and he returned to France where he distinguished himself in the struggle against Jansenism and became a leader of the extremists loyal to papal policies. In 1727 Tencin presided over the commission which deposed Soanen, the Jansenist bishop of Senez. The incident provoked a violent resurgence of the polemic caused fourteen years earlier by the papal bull *Unigenitus,* condemning Jansenism. In 1739 he was made a cardinal and was shortly afterwards entrusted with the diocese of Lyons. Tencin reached the peak of his political career in 1742 when the all powerful Cardinal de Fleury made him a minister, and for a moment he deluded himself that he might become Chief Minister. Fleury died and, without his patron, Tencin lost all credit at court. He retired to Lyons where he found Madame du Deffand in the spring of 1753, and died there in 1758.

TERRASSON, Jean (1670–1750): a figure of great importance in the cultural life of the first half of the eighteenth century. A member of the *Académie des Sciences* (1707) and of the *Académie Française* (1732), he studied ancient philosophy and was one of the most intransigent supporters of the superiority of the moderns over the ancients in the famous *querelle* and a keen proponent of the nationalist ideal.

TERRAY, Joseph-Marie (1715–1778), an ex-magistrate who had turned his back on the *parlement* and sided with the court. On Maupoeu's suggestion he was made *contrôleur général* of finance on 23 December 1769. In trying to contain the state deficit of more than 76 millions, the abbé Terray applied a system bringing immediate and certain results, favouring a kind of disguised state bankruptcy and imposing a tax per capita on every Frenchman as well as a cut in pensions and annuities from the crown. He was succeeded by Turgot.

THIERS, Louis-Antoine Crozat (*c.* 1699–1770), baron de: son of the great financier and brother of Monsieur du Châtel, he married in 1726 Marie-Louise-Augustine de Laval-Montmorency with whom he had no children. The *baron* was very attached to his niece, Madame de Choiseul, who called him the *petit-oncle* and with whom he spent most of his time.

TOULOUSE, Étienne-Charles Loménie de Brienne (1727–1794), archbishop of: Madame du Deffand's nephew, his paternal grandmother was the *marquise*'s mother's half-sister—he was a frequent visitor to the Saint-Joseph *salon* and to the Choiseuls, the Luxembourgs and Madame de Boufflers.

TRÉGUIER, Joseph-Dominique de Cheylus (1719–1797), Bishop of: well known to Madame du Deffand, the duchesse d'Aiguillon, Madame de Forcalquier and Madame de Rochefort.

TRONCHIN, Théodore (1709–1781): famous Genevan doctor, he came to fame by vaccinating the duc d'Orléans' children against smallpox. The duc invited him to settle indefinitely in France (1765), where despite the hostility and jealousy of the medical profession, he made his fortune and came to be known by the *philosophes* as the perfect incarnation of a humane, disinterested and passionate doctor.

TURGOT, Anne-Robert-Jacques, baron d'Aulne (1727–1781). Collaborator in the *Encyclopédie,* he was made *intendant* of Limoges in 1761 and so was able successfully to apply physiocratic theories in the Limousin. On 24 August 1774, Turgot replaced the abbé Terray as head of finance, but his bold reform programme ran counter to the interests of financiers and the privileged, so he was disgraced and obliged on 12 May 1766 to resign. As a very close friend of Mademoiselle de Lespinasse's, Turgot was naturally disliked by Madame du Deffand.

VAUBAN, Anne-Josèphe de la Queuille de Châteaugay (*c.* 1713–1776), comtesse de: married Jacques-Philippe-Sébastien le Prestre.

VAUBRUN, Nicolas-Guillaume de Bautru (1662–1746), abbé de, exiled in Anjou from 1700–10.

VICHY, Gaspard-Nicolas de (1699–1781), comte de Champrond: Madame du Deffand's eldest brother, he married in 1739 Marie-Camille-Diane d'Albon de Saint-Marcel (1714–1773). He joined the army at the age of twenty and fought in the campaigns in Spain, on the Rhine, in Italy and Bohemia and reached the rank of field-marshal. In 1752 when Madame du Deffand stayed at Champrond, Vichy had been out of the army for ten years and spent his time looking after his property.

VICHY, Nicolas-Marie de (d. 1783): Madame du Deffand's brother who, as was usual for second sons of aristocratic families in the *ancien régime*, went into the Church. The abbé de Champrond moved to Paris where he became treasurer of the Sainte-Chapelle. Madame du Deffand lived with him from 1740 to 1747 in the chapter house next to the Sainte-Chapelle and frequently visited his country house at Montrouge just outside Paris.

VILLARS, Amable-Gabrielle de Noailles (1706–1771), duchesse de: she married in 1721, Honoré-Armand, duc de Villars and was lady-in-waiting to the Queen in 1725 and *dame d'Atour* to the Dauphine in 1742.

VILLARS, Honoré-Armand (1702–1770), marquis and later duc de: son of the famous *maréchal,* brigadier in 1734 and member of the *Académie Française.*

VILLEROY, Jeanne-Louise-Constance d'Aumont (1731–1816), duchesse de: wife of Gabriel-Louis-François de Neufville. Her house was a centre for brilliant social gatherings frequented by the greatest aristocrats. The most refined theatrical performances were to be seen there and Mademoiselle Clairon was often invited to perform.

WALPOLE, Horace (1717–1797), fourth son of Sir Robert Walpole and Catherine Shorter, he was educated at Eton and King's College, Cambridge. Between 1739 and 1741 he did the Grand Tour with Thomas Gray in France and Italy and between 1741 and 1767 he was Member of Parliament for Callington, Castle Rising and Lynn. In 1747 he bought Strawberry Hill and in 1757 set up a press there and printed in that year Thomas Gray's *Odes.* The following year he printed *A Catalogue of the Royal and Noble Authors of England, with Lists of their Works.* He also printed there (1762–80) his *Anecdotes of Painting in England* and in 1765 his *Catalogue of Engravers in England.* In 1765, as soon as he had finished *The Castle of Otranto,* he went to Paris for the second time and on this occasion met Madame du Deffand. In 1768 he retired definitively from politics and published a five act tragedy, *The Mysterious Mother* and his *Historical Doubts on the Life and Reign of King Richard the Third.* In 1769 he came into contact with Thomas Chatterton and began the unfortunate correspondence which ended in Chatterton's suicide. The scandal brought him much criticism. In 1774 Walpole printed *A Description of the Villa of Mr Horace Walpole*; in 1787–8 he came to know Mary and Agnes Berry who were—especially Mary—his greatest interest during his last years. One of his last literary works is dedicated to the sisters: *Reminiscences, written in 1788, for the Amusement of Miss Mary and Miss Agnes Berry.* In 1791, on the death of his nephew, he inherited the title of 4th Earl of Orford. He died in Berkeley Square and was buried in the family tomb at Houghton.

WALPOLE, Thomas (1727–1803): son of Horace Walpole's uncle, Horatio, Lord Walpole of Wolterton; a banker, he came to Paris in 1768 and stayed for some time. Thomas Walpole had to return to Paris in 1779 for a court case of extreme importance to him. He had agreed to a mortgage against the estate of a trader living in Grenada in the Caribbean, to guarantee an enormous sum of money he had lent him, but the trader was bankrupted and meanwhile the island—an English possession—was occupied by the French. So Walpole was obliged to return to France to fight the legal battle in Paris.

WIART, Jean-François: he entered Madame du Deffand's service before 1752 and remained with her until her death. He was a devoted secretary. The first letter known to be written by Wiart is one written by Madame du Deffand to her sister, Madame d'Aulan, on 18 March 1752 (Ségur, p. 81).

Notes

I. YOUTH

1. *Portrait de Mme la M[arquise] du D[effand] fair par elle-meme en 1728,* Lewis, VI, pp. 48–9.

2. Lewis sets the date of Marie de Vichy's birth at 25 September 1696, a year earlier than the traditional date. "The year of her birth has usually been given as 1697, on the authority of [Miss] B[erry]'s 'Life' prefixed to D[effand]'s letters, 1810. . . . D[effand] to H.W. 30 Oct. 1766 says that she is 70. Her letter of 4 June 1768 says that she is 71, that of 13 February 1769 gives her age as 72; that of 13 Oct. 1769 gives it as 73. Her letter of 29 Jan. 1770 encloses her petition to the King about her pension, stating her age as 73. H.W.'s letters at the time of her death (23 Sept. 1780) usually speak of her as 84 (see H.W. to Lady Ossory 23 and 27 Sept. 1780, and to Mann 7 Oct. 1780) but as she died only two days before her birthday, this is an excusable exaggeration. . . . Her death notice in the *Gazette de France,* 29 Sept. 1780, says that she was aged 84 (*Rep. de la Gazette* iii 108). The proximity of her approaching birthday may explain these discrepancies also. There is no doubt that D. herself believed that she was born in 1696." Lewis, v, p. 368, note 23.

3. Madame du Deffand to Madame de Choiseul, 14 February 1770.

4. Or perhaps in the other family estate at Auxerre.

5. Madame du Deffand to Madame de Choiseul, 22 July 1771.

6. "This very ancient noble house is mentioned as early as 1065 and takes its name from the town of Vichy which it ceded to the Bourbons in 1344. It produced a crusader in 1248, a Grand Master of the Order of the Temple in 1250 and numerous comtes de Brioule who were canons.

(*Grand Armorial de France*, VI, R. de Warren, Paris, 1975, p. 448.) In the fourteenth century Robert de Vichy married his first wife, Alix de Pont-gibaud, thus founding the Vichy-Champrond branch. In December 1644, under Gaspard de Vichy, the first of that name, the lordship of Champrond was raised to the rank of a county.

7. Gérard Doscot, *Madame du Deffand ou le monde où l'on s'ennuie*, Lausanne–Paris, 1967, p. 24.

8. From a description of the château in 1735, Pierre-Marie de Ségur, *Julie de Lespinasse. Les années de jeunesse*, "Revue des Deux Mondes," 1 April 1905, p. 533.

9. Peter R. Bennett. *Étude lexicologique du vocabulaire de Madame du Deffand dans sa Corréspondance*, doct. thesis, Paris, 1966, p. 8.

10. "The abbess at the time was Madame de Villemont, a pleasant woman of great intelligence and captivating charm who managed, despite the grills and bolts, to lead a very worldly existence." Lucien Perey, *Le Président Hénault et Madame du Deffand*, Paris, 1893, pp. 29–30.

11. Grimm (1753–1769), June 1756, II, pp. 45–7.

12. Edmond and Jules de Goncourt, *La femme au dix-huitième siècle*, Paris, 1896, p. 19.

13. Ibid.

14. Madame du Deffand to Walpole, 11 December 1767.

15. Madame du Deffand to Voltaire, 16 May 1764.

16. Madame du Deffand to Walpole, 6 September 1778.

17. "But what I would like would be to be devout, to have faith, not so as to remove mountains, nor to cross the sea with dry feet, but to go from my *tonneau* to my gallery [which gave on to the convent chapel] and to fill my day with practices which by a new twist of the imagination would be worth at least as much as all my present occupations. I would read sermons instead of novels, the Bible instead of fables, the lives of the saints instead of history and such reading would tire me less or no more than all the reading I do at present." (Madame du Deffand to Walpole, 15 November 1772.)

18. Madame du Deffand to Madam d'Aulan, 10 February 1755: Bennett, op. cit., p. 549.

19. Chamfort, *Caractères et Anecdotes* in *Oeuvres complètes de Chamfort*, II, Paris, 1808, p. 162.

20. Although renowned for their traditional loyalty to the Second House of Burgundy, the du Deffands' genealogy was established only at the end of the fifteenth century; they were however known in the preceding century among the nobility of the Nivernais. At the beginning of the sixteenth century, they divided into two branches, the cadet branch being again

divided at the end of the same century. Louis, who advanced the family fortunes and even went to court, belonged to the new cadet branch. In 1647 he married Madeleine Brûlart. Louis was made King's Lieutenant General in the Orléanais. His son, Jean-Baptiste, became Lieuténant-général of the King's *Armées* and Governor of Neuf-Brisac. He died in 1728, having married firstly Charlotte Amelot de Bienville with whom he had Jean-Baptiste-Jacques, b. 1688. Jean-Baptiste-Jacques also followed a military career: in 1705 he had command of a regiment of dragoons, he was made brigadier in 1713 and was later to inherit from his father the lieutenancy in the Orléanais, the lieutenancy of the King's *Armées* and the governorship of Neuf-Brisac. In 1718 Jean-Baptiste-Jacques married his second cousin, Mademoiselle de Vichy: the bride's maternal grandfather, Nicholas Brûlart, and Charlotte Brûlart, the bridegroom's maternal grandmother were brother and sister. Cf. *Dictionnaire de la noblesse contenant,* etc. by de la Chenaye-Desbois & Badier, 3rd ed., Paris, chez Schlesinger frères, 1863–76.

21. Lescure, I, p. xv.

22. Chamfort, *Maximes et Pensées,* in *Oeuvres,* II, p. 90.

23. *Mémoires, correspondance et ouvrages inédits de Diderot,* I, Paris, 1841, cited in Goncourt, *La femme au dix-huitième siècle,* p. 26.

24. Madame du Deffand to Madame de Choiseul, 2 April 1773.

25. A passage from one of Madame du Deffand's letters (28 October 1724) eloquently describes life in the Château de La Lande: "We are in a place far from the post where we only receive letters once a week and to which we can reply only eight days later. We hear no news and our life is perfectly tedious." (Ségur, pp. 42–3)

26. Chamfort, *Caractères et Anecdotes,* in *Oeuvres,* II, p. 277.

27. The *marquise*'s legal separation occurred on 21 January 1721.

28. Walpole to T. Gray, 25 January 1766.

29. This was the name given to Phillippe d'Orléans's companions in debauchery. The etymology is uncertain, but Lescure suggests the implication that they were fit to be tied to the wheel. [*Les Maîtresses du Régent. Etude d'histoire et de moeurs sur le commencement du XVIIIe siècle,* par M. de Lescure, Paris, 1860, p. 209.]

30. Charles-Pinot Duclos, *Mémoires secrets sur le règne de Louis XIV, la Régence et le règne de Louis XV* (1791) in *Oeuvres complètes,* Paris, 1820–1821, VI, p. 210.

31. *Nouveaux mémoires du maréchal duc de Richelieu 1696–1788, rédigés sur les documents authentiques, en partie inédits, par M. de Lescure,* Paris, 1869, pp. 39–45.

32. *Vie privée du maréchal de Richelieu, contenant ses amours et intrigues et tout ce*

qui a rapport aux divers rôles qu'a joués cet homme célèbre, pendant plus de 80 ans, Paris, 1791, t. III, pp. 244–5.

33. *Journal et mémoires de Mathieu Marais, avocat au Parlement de Paris sur la régence et le règne de Louis XV (1715–1737)*, M. de Lescure, Paris, 1864, ii, p. 181.

34. Untranslatable play on words. Literally: "he had robbed /flown so much as to have lost a wing."

35. M. Marais, op. cit. (8 September 1722), II, pp. 347–8.

36. L. de Rochefort, *Souvenirs et mélanges*, Paris, 1826, I, p. 463, in André Monglond, *Le Préromantisme français*, Paris, 1966, I, p. 28.

37. Antoine Houdar de La Motte's five act tragedy in verse is considered to be the first example of sentimental drama.

38. Pierre-Édouard Lemontey, *Histoire de la régence et de la minorité de Louis XV jusqu'au ministère du cardinal de Fleury*, Paris, 1832, II, p. 261. A *lettre de cachet* was a despatch under the King's Seal, usually containing an order of imprisonment or exile.

39. "[. . .] although it was well known at the time of his death that it was not a slow poison, but rather a very violent and fast-acting one" (*Journal et Mémoires du marquis d'Argenson*, Paris, 1859–1867, I, p. 62).

40. Gaspard-Nicolas de Vichy.

41. Marie Bouthillier de Chavigny, widow of Président Brûlart, married for the second time César-Augusta, duc de Choiseul. Lepire was an estate belonging to the *duchesse*.

42. See below, Ch. v.

43. Ségur, pp. 44–6.

44. Bennett, p. 538.

45. Ibid., pp. 537–8.

46. According to Lewis the bequest amounted to 92,588 livres. We know, however, from a letter to Madame d'Aulan of 24 September 1728, that Madame du Deffand was disappointed by her inheritance from her Choiseul grandmother.

47. Fargis.

48. *Lettres portugaises (de Marianne Alcoforado) avec les réponses. Lettres de Mademoiselle Aïssé, suivies de celles de Montesquieu et de Madame du Deffand au chevalier d'Aydie*, Eugène Asse, Paris, 1873 (Slatkine Reprints, Geneva, 1970) letter XVI, pp. 283–6.

49. M. Marais, op. cit. (24 June 1721), II, p. 165.

50. *Mémoires et Journal inédit du marquis d'Argenson, ministre des Affaires étrangères sous Louis XV, publiés et annotés par le Mis. d'Argenson*, Paris, 1857–1858, v, pp. 91–2.

51. The *Mémoires du Président Hénault* were published by his great-nephew, the baron de Vigan, in 1855.
52. Lucie-Félicité de Noailles d'Ayen (1683–1745) duchesse d'Estrées, known for her excessive amorous adventures.
53. *Nouvel abrégé* appeared successively in 1746, 1749, 1752, 1756 and 1765, edited by the author.
54. Grimm (1753–1769) July 1754, I, p. 199.
55. Lewis, VI, pp. 75–7.
56. H. Walpole, *Portrait de Madame la Marquise du Deffand,* Lewis, VI, 59.

II. FRIENDSHIP WITHOUT ROMANCE

1. To this day the three thermal springs are called la Royale, la Reinette and la Cardinale in memory of this visit.
2. Voltaire to H.-L. Lekain, 25 April 1770.
3. Alfred Franklin, *La Civilité, l'étiquette, la mode, le bon ton du XIIIᵉ au XIXᵉ siècle,* Paris, 1908, I, pp. 222–3.
4. E. and J. de Goncourt, *La duchesse de Chaulnes,* in *Portraits intimes . . . ,* I, pp. 101–13.
5. Madame du Deffand to Hénault, 9 July 1742.
6. Ibid.
7. Gabriel Sénac de Meilhan, *Portraits et caractères des personnages distingués de la fin du XVIII siècle . . . ,* Paris, 1813, p. 9.
8. On the death of her husband the duchesse de Chaulnes started proceedings against her son, over inheritance. The support of Monsieur Giac, the *maître de requêtes* won her case, but he was subsequently obliged to retire from the magistrature. Madame de Chaulnes married Monsieur Giac on 30 November 1773.
9. Lescure, I, p. LXVI.
10. G. Sénac de Meilhan, *Portraits et caractères de personnages distingués de la fin du XVIIIᵉ siècle . . . ,* Paris, 1813, p. 10.
11. Chamfort, *Caractères et Anecdotes,* in *Oeuvres,* II, p. 203.
12. "They were especially efficacious against sterility." (A. Franklin, *La vie privée d'autrefois,* Paris, 1891, IX, *Les médicaments,* p. 176.)
13. Ségur, p. 53.
14. "Monsieur du Deffand [La Lande] died on 24th [June 1750], on St. John's Day, in Paris at four o'clock in the morning; he was sixty-two years old and was lieutenant-general in the King's armies." (*Mémoires du duc de Luynes sur la Cour de Louis XV (1735–1758),* Paris, 1860–1865, X, p. 286.)
15. Montesquieu to Madame du Deffand, 15 July [1751]; Mason, p. 1383.

16. Five-act comedy in verse by Charles Dufresny (1648–1724), produced posthumously with great success in June 1731.
17. For Madame du Maine's famous remark, see below, ch. III.
18. Tragedy by Voltaire, 1730.
19. Elisabeth-Charlotte, Candide de Brancas-Villars.
20. The Comtesse de Rochefort.
21. Possibly Louis-Bufile de Brancas, comte de Forcalquier (1710–1753) or Louis de Brancas, duc de Villars-Brancas (1715–1793), or Louis-Paul de Brancas, *marquis,* later duc de Céreste (1718–1802).
22. This event must have takn place during Walpole's visit to Paris in 1769. Hénault died in 1770.
23. *Walpole's Anecdote of the Président Hénault,* Lewis, VI, p. 77.
24. *Mémoires du Président Hénault,* new edition completed, corrected and annotated by François Rousseau, Paris, 1911, p. 169.
25. "She felt my joy, shared my sorrow, she was my refuge from ennui and chagrin; she soothed my pain during the bitter illnesses I suffered: without her I would be alone in the world. I never knew a more reasonable soul, a firmer mind or sounder judgment . . ., devoid of envy, jealousy and pretention, she lived only for others." (*Mémoires du Président Hénault,* pp. 168–9).
26. "Madame du Deffand still tyrannised her old lover, the Président Hénault, who being of a naturally timid nature, had remained a slave to fear long after ceasing to be a slave to love." (*Mémoires de Marmontel, publiés avec préface, notes et tables, par Maurice Tourneux,* Paris, 1891, II, p. 231).
27. *Portrait de Madame la Marquise du Deffand par M. le Président Hénault,* Lewis, VI, pp. 52–3.

III. SCEAUX

1. *Portrait of Madame la Duchesse du Maine by Madame la M. du Deffand,* Lewis, VI, p. 113.
2. Saint-Simon, IV, pp. 460–1 (October 1714).
3. Claude Perrault built the château in 1673. The duc du Maine bought it from Colbert's son, the marquis de Seignelay, in 1699.
4. C.-P. Duclos, cited by Marguerite Glotz and Madeleine Maire, *Salons du XVIIIe siècle,* Paris, 1945, pp. 64–5.
5. Mademoiselle de Nantes, bastard daughter of Louis XIV and Madame de Montespan married in 1686 the duchesse du Maine's brother, Monsieur le Duc. Cf. Adolphe Jullien, *Les Grands Nuits de Sceaux. Le théâtre de la duchesse du Maine,* Paris, 1876, p. 14.

6. An ambition which was unleashed on 2 August 1714 when the *parlement de Paris* registered the act whereby Louis XIV allowed his bastards to succeed to the throne.

7. Madame de Staal Delaunay, *Mémoires*, in *Oeuvres*, Paris, 1821, I, pp. 109–10.

8. Jean Starobinski, *L'Invention de la liberté (1700–1789)*, Geneva, 1965, p. 85.

9. Especially Anet (cf. below, note 46), and Sorel (cf. below, note 44), and Clagny "a house near Versailles ... beautifully built for Madame de Montespan, which [Louis XIV] had given to Monsieur du Maine" (Saint-Simon, II, p. 528).

10. Saint-Simon, III, p. 456 (1710).

11. Madame de Staal Delaunay, *Mémoires*, in *Oeuvres*, I, pp. 110–11.

12. Cf. A. Maurel, *La Duchesse du Maine, reine de Sceaux*, Paris, 1923, p. 78.

13. This picture, although probably painted some years earlier, was presented for admission to the Académie Royale de Peinture et de Sculpture on 28 August 1717 and labeled on that occasion *Pèlerinage à l'Isle de Cythère*; the name was changed by the same hand to *Fête galante*. It comes after the *Isle de Cythère* and before the *Embarquement*, both in Berlin. Cf. Giovanni Macchia, "Il mito teatrale di Watteau," in *I fantasmi dell'Opera*, Milan, 1971, pp. 22–4.

14. *Watteau*, E. C. Montagni, "Classici dell'arte Rizzoli," Milan, 1968, p. 114.

15. According to Fourcaud (1904) the painting was inspired by Dancourt's play, *Les Trous Cousines*, G. Macchia (op. cit., pp. 27–8) but it is more likely to be linked to *La Venitienne, comédie-ballet*, 1705, by Houdar de la Motte, with music by de la Barre.

16. G. Macchia, op. cit., p. 19.

17. J. Starobinski, op. cit., p. 85.

18. Torquato Tasso, *L'Aminta*, act II, SCENE I. The *Ordre de la mouche à Miel* was instituted on 11 June 1703.

19. *Mémoires du Président Hénault*, p. 133.

20. M. Glotz and M. Marie, op. cit., p. 65.

21. *Mémoires du Président Hénault*, p. 133.

22. *Mémoires et Journal inédit du marquis d'Argenson*, V, p. 85.

23. *Mémoires du Président Hénault*, p. 135.

24. Boileau, *Oeuvres complètes*, Bibliothèque de la Pléiade, Paris, 1966, p. 831.

25. "In vain you preach without cessation, / That I might go and make confession / Shepherdess I've searched within / There is nothing on my conscience / I beseach you make me sin / That I may then do holy penance."

26. "If I succumbed to your exigence / Prevented you would surely be / From

sinning as you'd like with me / More than from the act of penance."
Gustave Desnoiresterres, *Les Cours galantes,* Paris, 1864, IV, pp. 210–11.

27. Madame de Staal Delaunay, *Mémoires,* in *Oeuvres,* I, pp. 314–15.

28. *Mémoires du Président Hénault,* p. 129.

29. Bennett, p. 540.

30. Ibid.

31. Robert Mauzi, *L'idée du bonheur dans la littérature et la pensée françaises au XVIIIe siècle,* Paris, 1964, p. 111.

32. Ségur, p. 61.

33. The duc du Maine died on 13 May 1736.

34. Madame de Staal Delaunay, *Mémoires,* in *Oeuvres,* I, p. 338.

35. Bennett, pp. 541–2.

36. Voltaire to Madame du Deffand, ? May 1732.

37. Hervé, p. 771.

38. *Portrait de Madame la Duchesse du Maine par Madame la M. du Deffand,* Lewis, VI, p. 113.

39. Madame de Staal Delaunay, *Mémoires,* in *Oeuvres,* I, p. 109.

40. Ibid., p. 85.

41. In 1735 Madame du Maine married her to a widower, the baron de Staal, a captain in the duc du Maine's Swiss Guard. The marriage formally altered Madame de Staal's status: from a lady's maid, she became a "lady of the *princesse*'s household" and was allowed to sit at the table and ride in a carriage with her mistress. But the old dependency was unchanged since as Madame de Staal wrote in her *Mémoires* (I, p. 335) "unlike baptism, the sacrament of matrimony does not remove original sin."

42. Sainte-Beuve, *Mme de Staal Delaunay, Portraits littéraires,* in *Oeuvres,* Bibliothèque de la Pléiade, Paris, 1960, II, p. 899.

43. Grimm (August 1755), I, p. 428.

44. A league from the château d'Anet (see below, note 46) of which it was a dependency, Sorel was, according to Madame de Staal, "one of the most enchanting places on earth."

45. Sainte-Beuve, *Mme de Staal Delaunay, Portraits littéraires,* p. 906.

46. Anet is one of the most curious monuments in France. It was rebuilt in 1552 by Philibert Delorme for Diane de Poitiers who lived there; in the eighteenth century it passed to the Vendômes and then to the Condés and in 1718 to the duchesse du Maine.

47. *Le Comte de Boursouffle.*

48. The doctor in question is a character in Molière's three-act comedy, *Monsieur de Pourceaugnac,* 1669, who instead of diagnosing Pourceaugnac's madness prescribed enema after enema.

49. Game of chance not unlike "lotto" in which each player drew a number

from a bag. If the number corresponded to the square on the board on which the player had placed his money, the banker paid him 64 times his stake.

50. Voltaire read his *Oedipe* at Sceaux in 1717.

51. Gustave Desnoiresterres, *Voltaire et la société française au XVIII siècle*, Paris, 1871–1876, III, p. 138.

52. See above, p. 40.

53. Madame de Staal to the marquis de Silly, cited in Sainte-Beauve, *Madame de Staal Delaunay, Portraits littéraires*, p. 906.

54. Madame du Châtelet, *Discours sur le bonheur, Edition critique et commentée par Robert Mauzi*, Paris, 1961, p. 4.

55. *Portrait de Madame la Marquise du Châtelet*, Lewis, VI, p. 116.

56. Madame Geoffrin to Montesquieu, 16 August 1748; Masson, p. 1126.

57. A. Jullien, op. cit., p. 52.

58. R. Mauzi, Introduction to *Discours sur le bonheur* by Madame du Châtelet, p. LXXIII.

59. Here lies one who lost her life / doubly delivered / of a philosophical treatise / and an unfortunate child / which of the two carried her off? / On this fatal event / what opinion should we have? / Saint Lambert blames the book / Voltaire says it was the child." Grimm (1755–1769), February 1769, VI, p. 297.

60. The Luxembourg's magnificent country residence stood in the small town of Montmorency to the north of Paris. Madame d'Epinay's house, the *Ermitage* where J.-J. Rousseau lived between 1756 and 1762 was not far away, on the edge of the Forest of Montmorency.

61. Henriette Verneuil, natural daughter of Louis-Henri de Bourbon-Condé and of Madame de Nesle, married Jean, comte de La Guiche in 1740 and gave birth to her second child on 24 September 1747.

62. "I have Sainte-Aulaire's room / without having his charm, / Perhaps at ninety / I will have the heart of his shepherdess. / One must expect everything from time, / And above all from the desire to please." Lescure, I, p. 94, n.7.

63. Madame du Châtelet.

64. "Let us submit: resistance is in vain, / One must indeed sacrifice oneself for the pleasures of Anet. / There are only a hundred of you, gentlemen, in these parts: You will keep the secret." A. Jullien, op. cit, p. 55.

65. *Mémoires du Président Hénault*, p. 131.

66. A. Jullien, op. cit., p. 55.

67. *Portrait de Madame la Duchesse du Maine par Madame la M. du Deffand*, Lewis, VI, p. 113.

68. Madame de Staal to Monsieur d'Héricourt, 18 February 1749, in *Oeuvres*, II, p. 426.
69. Ibid., I, p. 341.
70. Montesquieu to Madame Dupré de Saint-Maur, 6 November 1750; Masson, p. 1339.

IV. MADAME DU DEFFAND'S "*SALON*"

1. "O respectable Tuesday! Imposing Tuesday, Tuesday to be more dreaded by me than all the other days of the week, Tuesday which has so often served for the Fontenelles, the La Mottes and the Mairans to triumph [...]" (Madame du Maine to Madame de Lambert, cited in A. Maurel, op. cit., p. 175). Madame du Maine's request to be admitted on Tuesdays was not granted; the duchesse herself "renounced her claim out of two-fold respect, for honour and for independence of spirit." (*Oeuvres morales de la marquise de Lambert, précédées d'une étude critique par M. de Lescure...*, Paris, 1883, p. XVIII.)
2. Jean le Rond d'Alembert, *Eloge de Saint-Aulaire* [sic], in *Oeuvres de d'Alembert*, 1821–22, III, p. 295.
3. C.-P. Duclos, *Considérations sur les moeurs de ce siècle* [listed 1751] in *Oeuvres complètes*, I, pp. 135–6.
4. Ibid., p. 15.
5. Chrétien-Guillaume Lamoignon de Malesherbes, *Discours prononcés dans l'Académie française, le jeudi XVI février M.DCC.LXXV à la reception de M. de Lamoignon de Malesherbes*, Paris, 1775, p. 5.
6. "Paris seems to be recognized as the one city in the world where the spirit of conversation and the taste for it are most widespread; and what may be called home-sickness, that indefinable longing for the homeland which is independent even of friends left behind, applies particularly to this pleasure in conversing which the French find nowhere else. Volney tells of some French émigrés who, during the Revolution, wanted to establish a colony and reclaim some land in America; but every so often they abandoned what they were doing to go, they said, and "converse in the city"; the city in question was New Orleans, six hundred miles from where they lived. In France all social classes feel the need for conversation: the spoken word is not as elsewhere, a means of communicating one's ideas, feelings, business, but it is an instrument which it is enjoyable to play and which raises the spirits as music does with some people, and strong liquor with others. The kind of well-being caused by animated conversation depends not precisely on the subject of that conversation,

neither the ideas nor the knowledge which may be developed from it are
the principle interest; it has to do with a certain way people react to each
other, of taking reciprocal pleasure, of speaking as quickly as one thinks,
of appreciating oneself in the moment, of being applauded without having
to work, of manifesting one's wit in all the nuances of accent, of gesture,
of look, and finally in producing at will like a kind of electricity producing
sparks, relieving some of an excess of vivacity and awakening others from
a painful apathy." (Anne-Louise-Germaine Necker, baronne de Staël-
Holstein, *De l'Allemagne*, Paris, Garnier, pp. 58–9).

7. *De la Conversation*, in *Éloges de Madame Geoffrin, contemporaine de Madame
du Deffand par M. Morellet, Thomas et d'Alembert; suivis de Lettres de Madame
Geoffrin et à Madame Geoffrin et d'un Essai sur la conversation, etc. etc., par M.
Morellet...*, Paris, 1812, p. 162.

8. *Trois Mois à la Cour de Frédéric. Lettres inédites de d'Alembert, publiées et
annotées par Gaston Maugras*, Paris, 1886, p. 140.

9. Jacques Delille, *La Conversation*, poem published in 1802.

10. François-Augustin Paradis de Moncrif, *Essai sur la nécessité et sur les moyens
de plaire*, Paris, 1738, p. 67.

11. 1. Lack of attention. 2. Interrupting and speaking more than one at a time.
3. Excessive eagerness to display wit. 4. Egoism. 5. Despotism or a desire
to dominate. 6. Pedantry. 7. Lack of continuity in conversation. 8. A taste
for jokes. 9. *Esprit de contradiction*. 10. Quarrelling. 11. Private conversation
replacing general conversation (Morellet, op. cit., pp. 169–70).

12. Ibid., p. 225.

13. Voltaire, *Lettre à Monsieur Lefèvre sur les inconvénients attachés à la littérature*,
1732, in *Oeuvres complètes*, de Kehl, 1785–1789, vol. 64. [vol. IV, *Mélanges
littéraires*], p. 20.

14. E. et J. Goncourt, *La femme au dix-huitième siècle*, p. 375.

15. Ibid., pp. 400–401.

16. *Mémoires de Marmontel*, II, p. 83.

17. "Great French cooking, however, did not assert itself until later [under]
the Regency with the Regent's active good taste. Or later still, in 1746,
when Menon's *la Cuisinière bourgeoise* finally appeared [...] We have
known how to eat delicately, claims a Parisian in 1782, for only half a
century" (Fernand Braudel, *Civilisation matérielle, Économie et Capitalism,
XVe–XVIIIe siècle*, Paris, 1967, p. 158.

18. Louis-Sébastien Mercier, *Tableau de Paris* [1st ed. 1781], Paris, 1906, I,
p. 63.

19. Count Scheffer to Madame du Deffand, 1 November 1753. See below, ch.
VII, p. 141.

20. Jean-Claude Bonnet, *Le réseau culinaire dans l'Encyclopédie*, "Annales," XXXI,
1976, p. 897.

21. Jean-Paul Aron, *Le Mangeur du XIXe siècle*, Paris, 1976, p. 229.
22. E. et J. de Goncourt, *La femme au dix-huitième siècle*, p. 83.
23. A popular pastime in good society at the time, "knotting," according to Littré, consisted of "making with the help of a little shuttle and a silk or cotton thread, a row of tight little knots." "Knotting," Rousseau writes in his *Confessions* (*Oeuvres complètes*, I, p. 202), "is to do nothing and as much attention is needed to amuse a woman who is 'knotting" as one whose arms are folded."
24. Walpole to Lady Suffolk, 20 November, 1765.
25. The new postal service, independent of the national system, was organized by Monsieur de Chamousset in imitation of the one in London. It began working on 9 June 1766. Paris was divided into nine areas each with its own office. Each office served the streets in its own area and the office in the Place de l'Étoile co-ordinated between the others. Letters were initially delivered three times a day.
26. *Mémoires de Marmontel*, I, pp. 233–4.
27. Ibid., II, p. 82.
28. The *Président* attended either Madame de Lambert's society gatherings or her literary ones ["I belonged to both schools: I dogmatized in the morning and sang in the evening." (*Mémoires du Président Hénault*, p. 120.)]
29. Madame du Deffand to Maupertuis, 26 December 1749; Hervé, p. 777.
30. "[The Renget] detested the roués who were only half drunk, and coquettes who were women of affairs. Madame du Deffand and Madame de Tencin were not concerned with a prince who immediately discovered them to be too intelligent to be satisfied with being loved." (*Nouveaux Mémoires du maréchal duc de Richelieu*, II, p. 20.)
31. M. Glotz and M. Maire, op. cit., p. 89.
32. *Mémoires du Président Hénault*, p. 129.
33. Ségur, pp. 66–7.
34. "The house and community of the *Filles de la Providence*, better known as the *Filles de Saint-Joseph* were established in this street (10-12 rue Saint-Dominique) on 16 June 1641. The object of the community was to take in poor orphans of ten years old, to give them a Christian education and training, so that at the age of twenty they could find employment, marry, or become nuns. By 1645 the convent housed 686 orphans for whom there was an embroidery workshop which remained fashionable until 1750." (*Dictionnaire Historique des rues de Paris par Jacques Hillairet*, Paris, Edition de Minuit.)
35. Ségur, p. 73.
36. From 1667 the only legal currency in France was the livre which divided into 20 sous. A sou was divisible into 12 deniers. Its relationship to the

franc — the old French gold coin — varied continuously according to circumstances. Between 1700 and 1726 the value of currency against money on account changed 85 times. At the end of this time the livre had dropped from 1,655 francs to 1,022.

37. The *marquise* was a careful organizer who managed to ensure a certain comfort for herself. Lewis (op. cit., I, p. XXVIII, note 2) gives us a detailed account of her patrimony: the act of separation gave her 50,000 livres invested in *aides et gabelles* with an income of 1,250 livres per annum. In 1723 Madame d'Averne obtained two pensions for her with a total income of 6,750 livres (reduced to 4,950 in 1726). In 1728 her grandmother, Madame de Choiseul left her 92,588 livres (with, according to Mademoiselle Aïssé, an income of 4,000 livres per annum) which was probably re-invested in the annual annuity of 4,600 livres (an investment taken care of by Hénault in 1741), and 3,000 livres (in the Hôtel de Ville, 1750). On the death of her husband in 1750, she recuperated her dowry of 4,000 livres a year. In 1764 her aunt, Madame de Luynes left her a legacy which produced 6,500 livres per annum plus a further 1,000 livres from the conversion of part of the monies into a fixed annual income. At the same time, the Queen gave her a pension of 1,000 livres a year. Her total income in 1769 was around 38,000 livres. This was reduced to 35,000 in 1770, but was soon increased by fixed income investments, many of which, after her death, went to her servants.

38. "I can certify that the reputation is deserved for the richness and marvellous splendour of tone, the beauty of the material and the brocade in perfect taste." (Ségur, p. 66.)

39. P.-P. des Alleurs to Madame du Deffand, 17 April 1749.

40. Ségur, p. 75.

41. Ibid., p. 76

42. Hervé, p. 773.

43. Lewis, VI, pp. 5–47.

44. In 1750 Madame du Deffand decided to buy a carriage and horses (Madame du Deffand to Madame d'Aulan, 3 May 1750; Bennett, p. 547.

45. Lewis. VI, p. 12.

46. Armchairs in the style of Louis XV or Louis XVI with a curved back.

47. The bedroom in Charles-Nicolas Cochin's engraving is usually thought to be the one in the Saint-Joseph apartment. But the engraving pre-dates the *marquise*'s move to the rue Saint-Dominique as can be seen from her letter to Maupertius of 18 April 1746 in which she mentions Cochin's work, and sends him some lines of verse which reveal her love of animals. This passion was to develop over the years along with her indifference to mankind.

48. Henry Gabriel Ibels, *Le costume et le meuble,* in *La vie parisienne au XVIIIe siècle,* Paris, 1914, p. 93.

49. The *Académie royal de Musique,* known as the *Opéra,* the *Comédie française* and the *Comédie italienne* were the three Parisian theatres subsidized by the Crown. From the time of the Regency until the end of Louis XV's reign, performances began at 5 o'clock in the afternoon. Under Louis XVI, they took place between six and nine in the evening.

50. Raymond Picard, *De Racine au Parthénon,* Paris, 1977, p. 198.

51. See above, ch. III, pp. 39–40.

52. *Portrait de Madame la M. D[u] D[effand] par elle-même, fait en 1774,* Lewis, VI, p. 61.

53. The Président's house in rue Saint-Honoré was large and sumptuous with richly furnished rooms and overlooking a beautiful French garden. Hénault's favorite room was the library. The Président received guests frequently and lavishly. The suppers of Legrange, his famous cook, were at least as well known as Hénault's historical works.

54. In 1743, at the request of the Queen's *superintendante,* Mademoiselle de Clermont, Hénault wrote a little theatrical composition the *Réveil d'Epiménide* designed as an ending to a fête in honor of Maria Leszczynska. It was much appreciated and a year later Hénault was presented to the Queen by Madame de Luynes. From 1746 Hénault became part of Maria Leszczynska's small circle of friends and in 1753, on the death of Samuel Bernard's son, Rieux, he became *Surintendant des Finances, des Domaines et des Affaires* of the Queen's household. In July 1757 he was given right of entry to the King's Chamber.

55. Paradis de Moncrif, op. cit., pp. 1–2.

56. Madame de Choiseul to Madame du Deffand, no date; Sainte-Aulaire, I, p. 4.

57. See above, p. 59.

58. C.-P. Duclos, *Considérations sur les moeurs,* in *Oeuvres complètes,* I, pp. 98–9.

59. Lewis, VI, pp. 92–4.

60. *Mémoires de Marmontel,* II, pp. 97–8.

61. Grimm (1753–1769), November 1754, I, p. 241.

62. "Ah! That unimaginable Pont-de-Veyle! He has just put on a performance at M. le duc d'Orléans: the scene which you know with the charlatan . . . he distributed at least two hundred boxes with a couplet for everyone; he is younger than when you saw him for the first time; he mocks everything and loves nothing." (Hénault to Madame du Deffand, 5 April 1753.)

63. "At the *Comédie-française* they are to perform a prose comedy in three acts, called *Les Soupirs,* by Monsieur de Pont-de-Veyle, Monsieur d'Argental's brother. I tell you this in secret." (*Journal de l'Inspecteur d'Hémery, 1750–*

1769, Paris [Bibliothèque Nationale, nouv. acq. fr. 10781–10783], 23 February 1753, p. 108.)

64. *Correspondance littéraire adressée à S.A.I. Mgr le grand duc, aujourd'hui empereur de Russia, et à M. le comte André Schowalow . . . depuis 1774 jusqu'à 1789, par Jean-François La Harpe . . . ,* Paris, 1801–1807, III, pp. 145–6.

65. Stendhal, *De l'Amour* in *Oevres complètes,* Paris, Del Litto, 1963, III, pp. 145–6.

66. "Madame du Deffand's raillery, the '*bon ton*' of the French is like eunuchs mocking those who catch syphillis." (Ibid., p. 150.)

67. Madame du Deffand to Walpole, 5 July 1767.

68. *Esquisse du portrait de M. de Pont-de-Veyle par Madame la Marquise du Deffand, 1774,* Lewis, VI, p. 82.

69. Hénault to Madame du Deffand, 5 April 1753.

70. *Mémoires du Président Hénault,* p. 191.

71. Paradis de Moncrif, op. cit., p. 16.

72. When Boufflers appeared at court / one thought to see Love's mother: / everyone sought to please her / and everyone had her in his turn . . ."; *Mémoires du Baron de Besenval. Collé, La Vérité dans le vin, ou les désagréments de la galanterie, comédie,* "Bibliothèque des Mémoires relatifs à l'histoire de France pendant le XVIIIe siècle," Paris, 1846.

73. Ibid., p. 51.

74. Ibid., p. 53.

75. Ibid., pp. 52–3.

76. Ibid., pp. 56–7.

77. *Nouveaux mémoires du maréchal duc de Richelieu,* II, p. 312.

78. Ibid., p. 312.

79. *Souvenirs et Portraits 1780–1789, par M. le duc de Lévis, nouvelle édition augmentée par la censure de Buonaparte,* Paris, 1815, p. 54.

80. J.-J. Rousseau, *Confessions,* in *Oeuvres complètes,* I, p. 519.

81. Madame du Deffand to Walpole, 20 May 1775.

82. Lewis, VI, pp. 83–4.

83. *Nouveaux mémoires du maréchal duc de Richelieu,* II, p. 312.

84. Duc de Lévis, op. cit., p. 62.

85. *Mémoires du Président Hénault,* p. 229.

86. Duc de Lévis, op. cit., pp. 62–3.

87. Lewis, VI, pp. 78–9.

88. *Journal et mémoires du marquis d'Argenson,* II, p. 93.

89. See above, ch. III, note 49.

90. *Journal et mémoire du marquis d'Argenson,* II, p. 92. Madame du Deffand also had this experience. "[gambling] oh! the wicked passion! I had it for three months; it removed me from everything else, I thought about nothing, I

loved lotto; I developed a horror of it and cured myself of this madness."
(To J. Craufurd, 13 February 1767.)

91. S. Mercier, op. cit., II, p. 77.

92. London, 1787, IV, pp. 277–8, cited in Gustave Desnoiresterres, *Voltaire et la société française au XVIIIᵉ siècle*, III, p. 135.

93. Madame du Deffand to Walpole, 21 February 1771.

94. Lewis, VI, pp. 84–7.

95. Sainte-Beuve, *La Comtesse de Boufflers, Nouveaux Lundis*, Paris, 1897, IV, pp. 178–9.

96. Ibid., p. 179.

97. Ibid., p. 212.

98. Ernest Campbell Mossner, *The Life of David Hume*, Oxford, 1970, p. 474.

99. Franco Venturi, *Settecento riformatore. La prima crisi dell'Antico Regime*, Turin, 1979, III, p. 334.

100. Cf. *Lettres de Gustave III à la comtesse de Boufflers et de la comtesse au Roi, de 1771 à 1791, publiées avec une introduction et des notes par M. Aurélien Vivie . . .* Bordeaux, 1900.

101. Exhibited in the 1777 Salon and entitled *le Thé à l'anglaise dans le salon des Quatre Glaces au Temple, avec toute la Cour du prince de Conti, écoutant le jeune Mozart*, this picture was painted between May and July 1766 on Mozart's second visit to Paris. He was returning with his mother and sister from a tour in England and was ten years old at the time.

102. Tea was imported into Europe in about the second half of the seventeenth century where it was especially successful on the English and Dutch markets. Towards the second half of the eighteenth century, elegant French people, inspired by Anglomania, took to drinking tea. For a long time it was believed to be like coffee, a dangerous drug. Madame de Mirepoix's tic, whereby she continually shook her head was blamed on "the use of tea of which she drank several cups a day, a habit she had picked up in England where her husband had been ambassador." (Duc de Lévis, op. cit, p. 61.)

103. "Le chevalier de Laurency, M. de Trudaine, Mademoiselle Bagarotti, Madame de Viervelle, Mademoiselle de Boufflers, the prince de Henin, the two comtesses d'Egmont, the comtes de Chabot and de Jarnac, the bailli de Chabrillan and the famous mathematician Dortous de Mairan" (Arthur Pougin, *Un tenor de l'Opéra au XVIIIᵉ siècle, Pierre Jélyotte, et les chanteurs de son temps*, Paris, 1905, pp. 221–2.

104. The comte de Bulkeley to Count Scheffer, 4 January 1753, in Proschwitz, p. 303.

105. Duc de Lévis, op. cit., p. 262.

106. *Portrait de Madame la Duchesse d'Aiguillon par Mme D[u] D[effand]*, Lewis, VI, p. 81.

107. *Dictionnaire de Biographie Française.*
108. No one was allowed to sit at court in the presence of the King and Queen. Only duchesses could have a stool in the Queen's apartments or when they ate with the King. Princes of the blood and pregnant women also were allowed to sit in the King and Queen's presence, because, according to Brantôme "You only sit on the floor in front of the Queen" (cf. Alfred Franklin, *La Civilité, l'étiquette . . .* I, p. 101).
109. *Epître d'Héloise à Abélard* by Pope, Geneva, 1758 and *Carthon* by Ossian Macpherson, London, 1762.
110. The *Lettres philosophiques* appeared in 1734 and was immediately attacked by the authorities. The publisher was put in the Bastille, the book condemned by the *parlement* and author obliged to take refuge in Lorraine. Madame d'Aiguillon intervened with the princesse de Conti on Voltaire's behalf and he sent her in gratitude en edition of the *Histoire de Charles XII* and the *Heniade* inscribed: "For you Henry IV would have left d'Estrées / And Charles XII would have known love."
111. Robert Shackleton, Montesquieu, Oxford, 1963, p. 180.
112. Jannette Geffriaud Rosso, *Montesquieu et la feminité*, Pisa, 1977, p. 92.
113. "She was a woman of great intelligence, very well informed and quite infatuated with modern philosophy, which is to say materialism and atheism." (*Mémoires secrets pour servir à l'histoire de la république des lettres en France depuis 1762 jusqu'à nos jours, ou Journal d'un observateur . . . par feu M. de Bachaumont . . . (continué par Pidansat de Mairobert et Mouffle d'Angerville,* London, 1777–1789, VI, p. 150.)
114. "At the time we performed plays written by ourselves. Monsieur du Châtel presented *Zoïde,* a comedy based on a novel with quite an unusual subject. A man falls in love with his Turkish slave, and in the end marries her. Monsieur de Forcalquier presented *l'Homme du bel air.* I presented *Le Jaloux de lui-même* and *La Petite Maison.* It was great entertainment. Our main actors were Madame de Rochefort, d'Ussé, Pont-de-Veyle, Forcalquier, the late Madame de Luxembourg [Marie-Sophie-Emilie-Honorate Colbert de Seigneley, the maréchal de Luxembourg's first wife] and Madame du Deffand." (*Mémoires du Président Hénault,* p. 189.) Edouard de Berthélemy (*Le Théâtre des Porcherons, une soirée chez la marquise du Deffand,* "Artiste," August 1868) has described one of these performances which took place on 1 March 1741. "*La Petite Maison* was performed first, a three-act comedy by the président Hénault. Then *Zoïde ou la Grecque moderne,* a three-act comedy by M. du Châtel. Then there was dancing and finally came *l'Apothéose de Pont-de-Veyle* by an unknown author" (p. 227). In 1742 the company broke up and the Mirepoix formed a rival troupe. Madame du Deffand gave up acting altogether.

115. Montesquieu to Duclos, 15 August 1748, cited in R. Shackleton, op. cit., p. 181.

116. *Mémoires du Président Hénault,* p. 191.

117. *Portrait de Monsieur le comte de Forcalquier par Madame la Marquise du Deffand,* Lescure, II, p. 744.

118. *Mémoires du duc de Luynes* (21 July 1742), IV, p. 193.

119. Madame du Deffand to Walpole, 8 March 1767.

120. *Mémoires du Président Hénault,* p. 190. "Madame de Rochefort deserves the love and respect of all honorable people. . . . The charm of her person has spread to her spirit; she has made friends of all her acquaintances. I do not know if she has any faults." (Ibid.)

121. Walpole to T. Gray, 25 January 1766.

122. Ibid. In 1782 Madame de Rochefort married Louis-Jules-Barbon Mancini-Mazzarini, duc de Nivernais, thus regularizing their long-standing relationship.

123. Ibid.

124. E. and J. de Goncourt, *La femme au dix-huitième siècle,* p. 240.

125. *Mémoires du Président Hénault,* p. 238.

126. Ibid.

127. *Portrait de Monsieur du Châtel, fait par lui-même,* Lewis, VI, p. 103.

128. High Society spent four or five hours, two or three times a week visiting. "After considerable hesitation you leave your name at about twenty doors; you appear for a quarter of an hour in half a dozen houses; it is necessary to be seen in the *salon,* to greet the company, and to sit from time to time in an empty chair and seriously to believe it possible to cultivate the acquaintanceship of a hundred and sixty or eighty people. In Paris this coming and going characterizes a man of the world." (S. Mercier, II, p. 80.)

129. Monsieur du Châtel to Madame du Deffand (*c.* 1742); Lescure, I, p. 81.

130. Madame de Choiseul to Madame du Deffand, 25 June 1767.

131. "The natural method of acting advocated by Diderot resulted excellently in Agrippine being acted in the style of a fishwife." (Madame du Deffand to Voltaire, 24 March 1760.)

132. "It is true," Walpole notes at this point in the text, "Madame du Deffand adored Madame de Flamarens's spirit and virtue and spoke about them with enthusiasm many years after her death." (Lewis, VI, p. 51, note 2.)

133. *Portrait de Madame la Marquise du Deffand par Monsieur de Forcalquier,* Lewis, VI, pp. 51–2.

134. Chamfort, *Maximes et Pensées,* in *Oeuvres complètes,* II, p. 46.

135. C.-P. Duclos, *Considérations sur les moeurs,* in *Oeuvres complètes,* I, p. 118.

136. F. Venturi, *Cronologia e geografia dell'Illuminismo,* in *Interpretazioni dell'Illuminismo,* Bologna, 1979, pp. 116–17.
137. *Journal de l'Inspecteur d'Hémery,* pp. 117–18.
138. "When Madame de Tencin discovered that D'Alembert, who was still very young, was a star at Geometry, she summoned him, caressed him a great deal and revealed the mystery of his birth. 'What are you telling me, Madame?' he cried. Ah! you are but a stepmother, the glazier's wife is my mother.'" (*Notice historique sur d'Alembert* in *Oeuvres philosophiques, historiques, littéraires* by d'Alembert, Paris, 1805, I, p. xx). But Madame de Tencin's claims are controversial. Madame Suard leaves quite a different version. "She asked him if he had really said that he recognized only his adoptive mother. . . . D'Alembert shook his head sadly. 'I would never have refused the affection of a mother who recognized me as her son.'" (J. Christopher Herold, *Love in Five Temperaments,* New York, 1961.)
139. D'Alembert, *Portrait de l'auteur fait par lui-même* (1760) in *Oeuvres,* I, p. XLV.
140. Ibid.
141. Ibid.
142. Madame du Deffand to Maupertuis, 18 April 1746, Hervé, p. 765.
143. D'Alembert, *Portrait de l'auteur fait par lui-même,* p. XLIV.
144. Chamfort, *Caractères et Anecdotes,* in *Oeuvres complètes,* II, p. 128.
145. *Portrait de Monsieur d'Alembert part Madame du Deffand,* Lewis, VI, pp. 94–5.
146. Il marchese Caracciolo to d'Alembert, Paris, 1 May 1781, in *Mélanges publiés pour la Société des Bibliophiles Français,* VI, Paris, 1828 (Slatkine Reprints, Geneva, 1970), p. 4.
147. Count Scheffer to Madame du Deffand, 15 December 1752.
148. Count Scheffer to Madame du Deffand, 4 January 1754.

V. ILLNESS

1. See ch. I, p. 16.
2. *Mémoires inédits de Mme la comtesse de Genlis, sur le dix-huitième siècle et la Révolution Française, depuis 1756 jusqu'à nos jours,* III, Paris, 1825, pp. 115–16.
3. R. Mauzi, *Les maladies de l'âme au XVIII siècle,* in "Revue des Sciences humaines," October–December 1960, p. 462.
4. *Traité élémentaire de morale et de bonheur* (1784), cit. in Mauzi, ibid., pp. 459–60, note 1.
5. Ibid., p. 461, note 1.
6. Madame du Deffand to Walpole, 17 March 1776.
7. Madame du Deffand to Walpole, May 1771.

8. Wilhelm Klerks, *Madame du Deffand. Essais sur l'ennui,* Leiden, 1961, pp. 15–16.
9. Madame du Deffand to Madame de Choiseul, 17 August 1772.
10. R. Manzi, *Les Maladies de l'âme . . . ,* p. 463.
11. Madame du Deffand to Walpole, 17–19 December 1770.
12. W. Klerks, op. cit., p. 31.
13. Madame du Deffand to Madame de Choiseul, 2 January 1773.
14. Madame du Deffand to Walpole, 3 May 1767.
15. Madame du Deffand to J. Craufurd, 12 February 1774.
16. Madame du Deffand to Walpole, 15 June 1777.
17. W. Klerks, op. cit., p. 29.
18. Madame du Deffand to Walpole, 22 November 1773.
19. W. Klerks, op. cit., p. 20.
20. Madame du Deffand to Walpole, 3 November 1773.
21. Madame du Deffand to Voltaire, 29 May 1764.
22. Madame du Deffand to Walpole, 23–24 August 1777.
23. Cited in Lionel Duisit, *Madame du Deffand epistolière,* Geneva, 1963, p. 53.
24. Ibid., pp. 52–3.
25. R. Mauzi, *Les maladies de l'âme . . . ,* p. 464.
26. Madame du Deffand to Walpole, 15 February 1771.
27. Cited in *Un magistrat homme de lettres au XVIII siècle: le Président Hénault, 1685–1770, sa vie, ses oeuvres, d'après des documents inédits par Henri Lion,* Paris, 1903, p. 136, note 1.
28. *Portrait de Madame la Marquise du Deffand par Monsieur de Forcalquier,* cf. Ch. IV, p. 91.
29. Madame du Deffand to Walpole, 11 June 1769.
30. Louis-François de Crozat du Châtel died in 1750.
31. *Portrait de Madame la Marquise du Deffand par Monsieur du Châtel,* Lewis, VI, p. 50.
32. R. Mauzi, *Les maladies de l'âme . . . ,* p. 461.
33. *Nouveau dictionnaire universel et raisonné de médicine, du chirurgie et de l'art vétérinaire,* Paris, 1772, vol. VI.
34. The theory of the vapors developed from Galeno's opinions on the fermentation of urine, can be attributed to Jean Fernel (1497–1558), professor at the Paris School of Medicine and author of *Universa medicina* (1567). The metaphoric, euphemistic use of the term 'vapors' was introduced by Joseph Raulin in the second half of the eighteenth century. Then the 'vapors' were defined as typically affecting women. "The vapors have become fashonable with society women; Hunauld in *Dissertation sur les vapeurs* (1756) and Vaudermonde in *Essai sur la manière de perfectionner l'espèce humaine* (1756) both find that women express a certain pleasure at

being affected. Thus Hunauld establishes what he calls "fashionable" vapors which, he pertinently remarks, "have as much to do with the mysteries of the heart as with the disposition of the humors." The above quotation and preceding information comes from: Paul Hoffmann, *La femme dans la pensée des Lumières,* Paris, 1977, pp. 177–98.

35. Madame du Deffand to Walpole, 21 February 1772.
36. Madame du Deffand to Walpole, 21–22 February 1772.
37. Madame du Deffand to Madame de Choiseul, 13 July 1766.
38. Nicolas-Antoine Pétry (*c.* 1734–1812), ex-soldier accepted at Les Invalides in 1765 who came to read aloud to the *marquise* early in the morning before the servants were up.
39. Madame du Deffand to Walpole, 4 April 1780.
40. Madame du Deffand to Count Scheffer, 2 May 1753; Proschwitz, pp. 320–1.
41. J.-L. Saladin to Madame du Deffand, 6 July 1751.
42. Montesquieu to Madame du Deffand, La Brède, 12 October [1755]. "You say, Madame, that nothing is happy, from an angel to an oyster: you must make distinctions. Seraphs are not happy, they are too sublime. They are like Voltaire and Maupertiue, and I am certain that they are doing themselves harm up there; but you cannot doubt that cherubims are very happy. The oyster is not as unhappy as we. It does not notice when it is swallowed; as for us we are told that we will be swallowed and we are made to touch and to see that we will be digested for ever. I could speak to you who are greedy about those creatures which have three stomachs: it would be devilish unlucky if one of the three were not good. I return to the oyster: it is unhappy when some long sickness makes it into a pearl: that is precisely the happiness brought about by ambition. One is no happier as a green oyster; it is not only an ugly color, but has a badly constructed body," Masson, pp. 1473–6.

VI. THE RETURN TO CHAMPROND

1. Ségur, p. 84.
2. Drawing reproduced in Antoine Fargeton, *Une famille du XVIII siècle à la ville et aux champs. Mesdames du Deffand et de Lespinasse nées Vichy.* Les Cahiers du Bourbonnais, 1975.
3. P.-M. Ségur, *Julie de lespinase. Les années de jeunesse,* p. 533.
4. Letter from the comtesse de Vichy, 1 January 1768, ibid., p. 524.
5. Cited in Claude Ferval [pseud. Marguerite Aimery de Pierrebourg], *Madame du Deffand. L'esprit et l'amour au XVIII siècle,* Paris, 1933, p. 119.

6. Madame du Deffand to Walpole, 9 March 1777.

7. Proschwitz, pp. 287–8.

8. Ibid., p. 295.

9. *Eloge d'Eliza,* in *Lettres de Mademoiselle de Lespinasse, precédées d'une notice de Sainte-Beuve et suivies des autres écrits (Portrait de M. le marquis de Condorcet, Suite du Voyage Sentimental) de l'auteur, et des principaux documents (Eloge d'Eliza, par M. de Guibert, Portrait de Mademoiselle de Lespinasse, Aux Mânes de Mademoiselle de Lespinasse, Sur la tombe de Mademoiselle de Lespinasse, par d'Alembert) qui le concernent,* Paris, 1893, pp. 404–5.

10. The marriage took place in 1739.

11. J. de Lespinasse to M.-J.-A. Condorcet, 19 October 1773. *Lettres inédites de Mademoiselle de Lespinasse, à Condorcet, à d'Alembert, à Guibert, au Cte de Crillon, publiées, avec des lettres de ses amis, des documents nouveaux et une étude par M. Charles Henry,* Paris, 1887, p. 109.

12. *Journal d'Abel de Vichy* (23 July 1769), cited in P.-M. Ségur, *Julie de Lespinasse. Les années de jeunesse,* p. 526.

13. Ibid., p. 536.

14. Ségur, pp. 99–100.

15. J.-A.-H. Guibert, *Eloge d'Eliza,* p. 406.

16. Ségur, p. 89.

17. Proschwitz, p. 298.

18. Madame du Deffand to Mademoiselle de Lespinasse, 3 February 1753.

19. F. Venturi, *Le Origini dell'Enciclopedia,* Florence, 1946, pp. 61–2.

20. Ibid., pp. 32–3.

21. Ibid., p. 62.

22. Ibid., p. 63.

23. The Ministry of War: Hénault's great friend, Marc-Pierre de Voyer de Paulmy, comte d'Argenson, was minister from 1743.

24. D'Alembert, *Essai sur la société des gens de lettres et des grands, sur la réputation, sur les mécènes, et sur les récompenses littéraires,* in *Oeuvres,* IV, p. 339.

25. Ibid., p. 355.

26. Postal charges were paid by the recipient. See above: ch. IV, note 25.

27. "Of a soldier who knows ill how to embellish the truth," Racine, *Brittannicus,* Act I, Scene II.

28. "La Tour painted the portrait of d'Alembert and all his friends vied to write verses on it . . . to understand [these] verses you must know that d'Alembert is almost impotent." (*Journal de l'Inspecteur d'Hémery,* p. 129.)

29. Voltaire to Madame du Deffand, 12 September 1760.

30. In 1750 Voltaire accepted Frederick II's repeated invitation to move to Prussia. The beginning of the visit was glorious, but as time went by the relationship between the two men grew steadily worse. Voltaire insisted

on seeing Frederick as a philosopher and man of letters to be treated as an equal and forgot only too often that he was dealing with a king. A tense situation developed which was aggravated by the inevitable gossip of a small court like Potsdam. "The King gives me his dirty linen to wash," Voltaire murmured on receving the King's manuscripts to be corrected. The inevitable break came when Voltaire, in *Diatribe au Docteur Akakia,* libelled Maupertius, Frederick's protégé and the President of the Berlin Academy, who was involved in a lively quarrel with the German scientist, S. Koenig. The pamphlet which was seen as a direct insult to the King, was confiscated and burned on the public square. Voltaire returned his Chamberlain's cross and key to Frederick accompanied by the following verse: "I received them tenderly / I return them with sorrow / Like a lover burning with jealousy returns her portrait to his mistress." Voltaire left Prussia, not without difficulty or incident, at the beginning of 1753.

31. See above, p. 86.
32. An old commune outside the domain of the *Fermiers Généraux,* and parish since 1342. The Manor of Vaugirard which declined in importance in the eighteenth century stood on what is now the site of nos: 355–371 rue de Vaugirard. Jean de Rohan, Field Marshal and comte de Sommery lived there in 1720. In 1860 Vaugirard became part of the *banlieu* of Paris. From d'Alembert's reply (14 April 1753) it seems that the *marquise* was referring to herself, but the reference is obscure. "The abbé de Canaye does not think that you look at all like the *greffier* de Vaugirard."
33. The Cardinal de Tencin.
34. D'Alembert. The cardinal was Madame de Tencin's brother.
35. According to Barbier, "It was a brochure entitled *Thérèse philosophe* which told the story of the Jesuit father Girard, and the *demoiselle* La Cadière at Aix-en-Provence, which caused such a stir. This book, which is charming and very well written, contains some very powerful and dangerous discussions about natural religion." (*Journal de Barbier,* IV, p. 378.) In reality, *Thérèse philosophe,* by Jean-Baptiste de Boyer, marquis d'Argens, published in 1748, was "a pornographic fiction" (Mario Praz, *La Carne, la Morte e il Diavolo,* Florence, 1948). Hence Madame du Deffand's desire to conceal her reading of it.
36. In a letter addressed to Berryer, the Lieutenant-General of Police on 10 August 1749, Diderot did not hesitate to use his acquaintanceship with the *marquise* as a guarantee of respectability.
37. "Your Diderot is a really extraordinary man," wrote Catherine of Russia to Madame Geoffrin. "I do not escape from conversation with him without having my thighs beaten black and blue. I was obliged to place a table between him and myself, so as to sheler myself and my limbs from his

gesticulations." (*Le Royaume de la rue Saint-Honoré. Madame Geoffrin et sa fille,* by Peirre-Marie de Ségur, Paris, 1897, pp. 315–16.)

38. Proschwitz, pp. 309–10.
39. *Le Méchant,* comedy by Jean-Baptiste-Louis Gresset (1709–1777).

VII. PARIS AGAIN

1. Proschwitz, pp. 336–7.
2. Ibid., p. 356.
3. Reference to the *Entretiens sur la pluralité des mondes* by Fontenelle in which the author turns to a *marquise* as interlocutor.
4. The two articles were written by the chevalier de Jancourt, who ended the one called "Démocratie" by noting: "There you practically have an excerpt from *L'Esprit des lois.*"
5. Masson, pp. 1479–80.
6. Proschwitz, p. 360.
7. Letter of 16 July 1754; ibid., p. 372.
8. Louis-Gabriel de Froulay.
9. Ironical reference to Madame de Chaulnes.
10. Montesquieu to Madame du Deffand, 13 September [1754]; Masson, pp. 1515–16.
11. Marc-Pierre de Voyer de Paulmy comte d'Argenson.
12. Jean-Frédéric Phélypeaux, comte de Maurepas.
13. Madame de Tencin.
14. *Mémoires et Journal inédit du marquis d'Argenson,* I, p. 164.
15. Lucien Brunel, *Les philosophes et l'Académie française au dix-huitième siècle,* Paris, 1884, p. 19.
16. Voltaire, *Lettre à M. Lefèvre sur les inconvénients attachés à la littérature,* p. 23.
17. D'Alembert to Madame du Deffand, 11 December 1753.
18. D'Alembert to Madame du Deffand, end October *c.* 1753.
19. P.-P. des Alleurs to Madame du Deffand, 17 April 1749.
20. D'Alembert, *Essai sur la société des gens de lettres,* etc. in *Oeuvres,* IV, p. 369.
21. Ibid., p. 372.
22. L. Brunel, op. cit., p. 39.
23. D'Alembert to Madame du Deffand, 11 October 1753.
24. Montesquieu to d'Alembert, 16 November 1753; Masson, p. 1480.
25. Property of Bénigne-Jérôme de Trousset d'Héricourt who was raised to the rank of *marquis* in 1749.
26. Grimm (1753–1769) July 1753, I, p. 35.
27. B.-M. d'Aydie to Madame du Deffand, 29 December 1753.

28. Collé, cited in Lescure, I, p. LXV.
29. *Mémoires du duc de Luynes,* XIII, pp. 393–4.
30. J.-B.-N. Formont to Madame du Deffand, 4 December [1754].
31. J.-B.-N. Formont to Madame du Deffand, 29 December [1754].
32. Ibid.
33. F. Venturi, *Le Origini dell'Enciclopedia,* p. 80.
34. Camille d'Albon's financial position was not apparently brilliant. His father was still alive and his mother's fortune had been partly dissipated.
35. Camille d'Albon.
36. Probably the Cardinal de Tencin.
37. Hunting Smith, p. 27.
38. Madame de Luynes to Madame du Deffand, 5 April 1754.
39. Madame du Deffand to Madame de Luynes, 8 April 1754.
40. Mademoiselle de Lespinasse to Monsieur de Guibert, 1775, letter XCVIII, in *Lettres de Mlle de Lespinasse,* p. 231.

VIII. MADAME DU DEFFAND AND JULIE
DE LESPINASSE AT SAINT-JOSEPH

1. *Les noeuds* for instance (see ch. IV, note 23) or, later, *parfilage.* This activity which, according to the Goncourts, was common around 1770, consisted in "undoing thread after thread of gold or silver cloth and separating the gold from the silver" (Littré) in order to sell or use it again. Society women sought out old epaulettes and military uniforms and every kind of ribbon, even from the servants' uniforms, so long as it contained silver or gold. Money-making was secondary to the pleasure of the pastime itself, although Madame de Genlis pointed out that "a clever *parfileuse* earned a hundred *louis* a year from her strange employment." (Op. cit., III, p. 174.) So that there was always something to undo, things soon began to be made in various shapes out of suitable material for *parfilage.* Madame du Deffand gave Madame de Luxembourg a New Year's present of a little hood to unthread, accompanied by some lines by Saint-Lambert. The *duchesse* in return gave the *marquise* a miniature Tonton (name of the *marquise*'s dog) for the same purpose. (La Harpe, *Correspondance littéraire,* II, pp. 197–8.) Madame de Genlis boasts that she ended the fashion with a violent attack against it in her "lettres sur l'education," *Adèle et Théodore* (1785).
2. "Madame du Deffand," writes Lescure, "whose tact had acquired all the certainty and all the delicacy of the sense she had lost, usually touched and felt the faces of newcomers, and she claimed by this manual inspection

of their physiognomy, to be able to gain some idea of their character, and even of their mind." (I, p. CCX.)

3. J.-A.-H. Guibert, *Eloge d'Eliza*, p. 405.

4. Mademoiselle de Lespinasse to Condorcet, 7 September 1774, in *Lettres inédites de Mademoiselle de Lespinasse*, p. 127.

5. Sainte-Beuve, *Mémoires de Madame de Staal Delaunay*, p. 897.

6. Mademoiselle de Lespinasse to Monsieur de Guibert, 23 September 1774, letter LIII, in *Lettres de Mademoiselle de Lespinasse*, p. 131.

7. Cited in P.-M. Ségur, *Julie de Lespinasse. Les années de la jeunesse*, p. 547.

8. J.-F. La Harpe, *Correspondance littéraire*, I, p. 385.

9. J.-A.-H. Guibert, *Eloge d'Eliza*, p. 408.

10. Ibid., p. 407.

11. P.-M. Ségur, "Julie de Lespinasse. Le couvent de Saint-Joseph," *Revue des Deux Mondes*, 15 April 1905, p. 873.

12. Ibid.

13. D'Alembert, *Portrait de Mademoiselle de Lespinasse* (1771) in *Oeuvres*, III, p. 727.

14. Ibid., p. 722.

15. B.-M. d'Aydie to Madame du Deffand, 27 June 1755.

16. *Mémoires du Président Hénault*, p. 131.

17. B.-M. d'Aydie to Madame du Deffand, 27 June 1755.

18. Madame du Deffand to Mademoiselle de Lespinasse, 13 February 1754.

19. D'Alembert, *Aux Mânes de Mademoiselle de Lespinasse* (1776) in *Oeuvres*, III, p. 733.

20. D'Alembert, *Portrait de Mademoiselle de Lespinasse*, in *Oeuvres*, III, p. 721.

21. *Portrait de d'Alembert par lui-même* [1760] in *Oeuvres*, I, p. 12.

22. Mademoiselle Rousseau was the subject of a semi-serious quarrel between d'Alembert and Madame du Deffand, as his letter to her of 21 October 1753 shows. See above, ch. VII, pp. 144–45.

23. *Journal de l'Inspecteur d'Hémery*, p. 129.

24. *Mémoires de Marmontel*, II, pp. 231–4.

25. Expression of Julie's, quoted by P.-M. Ségur, "Julie de Lespinasse. Les amis de passage. La vie intime," *Revue des Deux Mondes*, 1 July 1905, p. 79.

26. In Giovanni Macchia, *Galiani e la "Necessité de plaire,"* Accademia Nazionale dei Lincei, anno CCCLXXII, Quaderno, 211, Rome, 1975, p. 73.

27. *Mémoires du duc de Luynes*, XIV, p. 7.

28. Madame du Deffand to Walpole, 6 May 1772.

29. In the eighteenth century, opium, which could easily be acquired from a druggist, was measured by the same unit as pharmaceutical products, precious metals and grain, which equalled 0.053 gr. (Bruno Kisch, *Scales and Weights. An Historical Outline*, New Haven and London, 1965, p. 251.)

Opium was used for a great variety of purposes. The *Dictionnaire ou Traité universel des drogues simples* by Nicolas Lemery (Rotterdam, 1727, p. 392) says opium is "indicated to thicken the humors, to provoke sleep, alleviate pain, combat dyssentry, vomitting, haemorrages, hiccoughs, to provoke sweating as well as for illnesses of the eyes and teeth. The dose varies from half a grain to two grains." Forty years later, the *Nouveau dictionnaire universel et raisonné de médecine, de chirurgie et de l'art vétérinaire* (Paris, 1772) repeats the same indications but stresses the calming effects of opium on the nervous system. "Besides its properties as a soporific, opium has the effect of alleviating pain, provoking sweating, relaxing the fibres, moderating the ardor of the blood, diminishing tension and irritation of a nervous origin" (vol. v, p. 64). Despite the generally recognized uses of opium for medicinal purposes in the eighteenth century, the drug was still seen to have exotic and worrying characteristics. Opium was used not only as a cure for suffering, but for purposes of suicide. It is doubtful that Julie really intended to take her own life, but if La Harpe is right about the 60 grains of opium, the suspicion remains.

30. J.-F. La Harpe, *Correspondance littéraire . . .* , I, p. 385.

31. *Souvenirs inédits de Madame de la Ferté-Imbault,* in P.-M. Ségur, *Julie de Lespinasse. Le couvent de Saint-Joseph,* p. 876.

32. Ibid., p. 877.

33. This comedy by Palissot was performed for the first time and to great acclaim on 2 May 1760 at the *Théâtre français.* It took its inspiration from Molière's *Femmes savantes* and Saint-Evremont's *Académistes,* and violently attacked the new philosophical ideas and various representatives of the philosophical movement. Palissot was not attacking the *philosophes* for the first time; in 1755 he had ridiculed Rousseau in *Le Cercle, ou les originaux*; in 1757 he attacked Diderot in *Petites lettres sur les grand philosophes.* The encyclopaedists were all violently indignant, but they did not manage to obtain the censor's intervention. The play which was protected from on high continued to be performed.

34. D'Alembert to Voltaire, 6 May 1760.

35. Voltaire to d'Alembert, 2 May 1760.

36. D'Alembert to Voltaire, 26 May 1760.

37. Voltaire to d'Alembert, 20 June 1760.

38. Voltaire to d'Alembert, 31 May 1760.

39. D'Alembert to Voltaire, 11 June 1760.

40. P.-M. Ségur, *Julie de Lespinasse. Le couvent de Saint-Joseph,* p. 889.

41. D'Alembert to Voltaire, 18 October 1760.

42. Mademoiselle de Lespinasse to Madame du Deffand, 2 and 4 July 1761.

43. *Mémoires* of the abbé Morellet, cited in P.-M. Ségur, *Julie de Lespinasse. Le couvent de Saint-Joseph,* p. 892.

44. D'Alembert to Frederick II, 7 March 1763, in *Trois Mois à la Cour de Frédéric*, pp. 12–13.

45. Cited in P.-M. Ségur, *Julie de Lespinasse, Le couvent de Saint-Joseph*, p. 892.

46. D'Alembert to Mademoiselle de Lespinasse, Potsdam, 18 August 1763, in *Trois Mois à la Cour de Frédéric*, p. 82.

47. From Sans-Souci, 22 June 1763; ibid., p. 26.

48. Tragedy by Racine.

49. The house she shared with her brother, Nicolas-Marie, abbé de Champrond, treasurer of the Sainte-Chapelle.

50. Letter, the whole of which has never apepared. Extracts have been published by P.-M. Ségur and C. Maugras, Bibliothèque Nationale, Paris, *Fonds français, Catalogue général des manuscrits français, 15230, Recueil de differents morceaux en prose et en vers du XVIII siècle*, vol. III, pp. 204–7.

51. Contract signed by the *marquise* on 7 December 1754 which came into effect on 1 January 1755. The apartment comprised "a large room on the first floor, two other rooms for the servants and a dining-room." (Ségur, p. 74.)

52. *Correspondance littéraire, philosophique et critique de Grimm et de Diderot depuis 1753 jusqu'en 1790*, Paris, 1830, IX [May 1776], p. 79.

53. Ibid.

54. J.-F. La Harpe, *Correspondance littéraire*, I, p. 386.

55. J.-A.-H. Guibert, *Eloge d'Eliza*, p. 411.

56. *Mémoires inédits de Madame de la Ferté-Imbault*, cited in P.-M. Ségur, *Julie de Lespinasse. Les amis de passage. La vie intime*, p. 71.

57. Walpole to H. S. Conway, 28 September 1774.

58. Madame du Deffand to Madame de Choiseul, 3 December 1777.

59. Cited in P.-M. Ségur, "Julie de Lespinasse. Le salon de Rue Saint-Dominique," *Revue des Deux Mondes*, 15 June 1905, p. 872.

60. F. Galiani to B. Tanucci, 13 March 1769. *Opere di Ferdinando Galiani*, F. Diaz and L. Guerci, Milan–Naples, 1975, pp. 977–8.

61. Ibid., p. 977, note 1.

62. J.-F. La Harpe, *Correspondance littéraire*, I, p. 388.

63. D'Alembert, *Portrait de Mademoiselle de Lespinasse*, in *Oeuvres*, III, p. 725.

64. Lewis, VI, pp. 66–70.

IX. FRIENDSHIP WITH VOLTAIRE

1. J.-J. Rousseau, *Les Confessions*, in *Oeuvres complètes*, pp. 555–6.

2. In a letter of 13 July 1768, Voltaire wrote to Madame du Deffand, "I have been attached to you for forty-five years."

3. He who sees and he who hears you / soon forgets his philosophy / And every sage with Madame du Deffand / Would like to spend his life as a madman.

4. See above, ch. III, p. 47.

5. See above, ch. IV, note 110.

6. *Alzire ou les Américains,* tragedy by Voltaire, performed for the first time in Paris on 27 January 1736. Grandval, see below, was one of the actors.

7. "One truth is clear, 'Whatever IS, is RIGHT,'" the last line of Epistle I in Alexander Pope's *Essay on Man.*

8. Voltaire was convinced that Pope had taken his ideas from Shaftesbury's *Characteristics* (1721).

9. Pope expressed this concept somewhat differently: "true self-love and social are the same," *An Essay on Man,* IV, p. 396.

10. Sainte-Aulaire, *Notice sur Madame du Deffand,* I, p. XVIII.

11. "Here you are in the happy land / Of beautiful and fine spirits / Of recurrent trifles / Of good and bad writing / On Fridays you hear / the long and touching clamor / with which le Maure enchants Paris. / Suppers with chosen people / Of your days threaded with laughter / end the charming hours. / But what is surely worth / more than a new play / and than the greatest supper / you live with du Deffand. / The rest is but amusement / True happiness lies with her." Catherine-Nicole le Maure (1704–1786) was a famous soprano at the *Opéra.*

12. In Italian in the text.

13. "She is tested by enigmas."

14. Madame du Deffand is replying to a letter from Voltaire of 27 December [1758] in which he told her that he had learned of Formont's death.

15. Formont.

16. "Oh divine friendship! Perfect felicity etc." *Epître de la modération en tout, dan l'étude, dans l'ambition dans les plaisirs.* Written in January 1738. The fourth and last of the *Discours en vers sur l'homme,* printed 1739.

17. *"Pour moi, vous le savez, descendu d'Ismael, / Je ne sers ni Baal, ni le dieu d'Israel,"* Racine, *Athalie,* Act II, sc. III.

18. In his letter of 27 December [1758], Voltaire wrote to her: "The King of Prussia sometimes tells me that I am much happier than he, and he is really quite right."

19. Free from ambition, from care and slavery, / enlightened spectator of the world's folly / he took care not to be an actor, / and was as happy as he was wise. / He shunned the empty name of author / He scorned to live in the Temple of memory, / But he will live in your heart. / That is doubtless glory enough for him."

20. Voltaire's reference is to the *Cabinet noir,* the secret agency whereby the

government controlled suspect correspondence. It came into being under Louis XIV, but, under Louis XV, it developed into an established and efficient organization. There were four employees who worked under the supervision of the director of postal services. The *Cabinet noir*'s methods became well known and foreign diplomats living in France took various precautions. The existence of the *Cabinet noir,* which was universally known, presented a real threat to the private lives of French citizens. This censorship, which was seen as a disgraceful example of the corruption and amorality of the *Bien Aimé*'s reign, was attacked by Turgot who was unable to abolish it, but who managed to establish that intercepted letters could not be used as legal proof.

21. Reference to *Le Neveu de Rameau* by Diderot.

22. Sainte-Beuve, *Lettres de la Marquise du Deffand, Causeries du Lundi,* Paris, Garnier, I, p. 413.

23. Madame du Deffand to Voltaire, 20 December 1769.

24. Madame du Deffand to Voltaire, 18 July 1764.

25. Madame du Deffand to Walpole, 15 December 1768.

26. Madame du Deffand to Walpole, 8 October 1779.

27. Madame du Deffand to J. Crauford, 3 June 1766.

28. Sainte-Beuve, *Lettres de la Marquise du Deffand, Causeries du Lundi,* p. 416.

29. Madame du Deffand to Voltaire, 8 May 1770.

30. Voltaire to Madame du Deffand, 6 September 1769.

31. Lionel Duisit, "Madame du Deffand et Voltaire: Le Mythe du progrès et la decadence du goût," *French Review,* January 1963, vol. XXXVI, n. 3, p. 291.

32. Madame du Deffand to Walpole, 27 October 1766.

33. Furio Diaz, *Filosofia e politica nel Settecento francese,* Turin, 1962, pp. 161–2.

34. "Trousers without a pocket." *Culottes* in the eighteenth century were trousers which ended below the knee.

35. An overcoat without pleats.

36. Silhouettes and profiles which were made very popular by Carmontelle. The connection between these drawings and the *contrôleur générale* derives from his fiscal policy which hit tax-payers so hard that they acquired an elegant slimness.

37. These edicts aimed to collect money by instituting 72,000 bonds on the *fermes générales* of 1000 francs each.

38. The *contrôleur général,* Silhouette.

39. Jacques-Auguste de Thou, *Histoire universelle,* vol. XVI, London, 1734.

40. Gabriel Daniel, *Histoire de France depuis l'établissement de la monarchie française dans les Gaules,* Paris, 1696–1713.

41. Madame du Deffand may refer here particularly to the *Histoire de France,* Paris, 1755–7, by the Jesuit, Henri Griffet.

42. The duc de Broglie succeeded the maréchal Contades as commander of the French army engaged in war against Prussia.

43. Hénault.

44. Henry Fielding's novel was translated into French by La Place in 1750 under the title, *Histoire de Tom Jones.*

45. *Roland furieux,* translated by J.-B. de Mirabaud, The Hague, 1741.

46. *La Pucelle d'Orléans* by Voltaire, Paris, 1755. Copies of various canti of the poem had been circulating in Paris since 1735. The *Pucelle* was condemned by the Roman Curia and put on the index on 20 January 1757, and so banned in France, but it continued to be printed abroad. The reference here is probably to the London or Geneva edition of 1757 or to one of the two London editions of 1758.

47. Hénault.

48. King of the Francs and Duke of Burgundy, died in 936.

49. Eudes, King of Aquitaine, died *c.* 736, or Eudes, King of the Francs, died in 898.

50. Zell, a city on the Mosel and Wolfenbüttel in the duchy of Brunswick, ruled over by Frederick II's brother-in-law, Prince Ferdinand, were probably two centers of peasant enrollment in the Prussian army.

51. *The Tale of the Tub* by Jonathan Swift was translated as *Le conte du tonneau,* The Hague, 1721.

52. The *Anti-Lucrèce,* a philosophical poem in nine canti by Cardinal Melchior de Polignac, published posthumously in 1745 by the abbé de Rothelin.

53. Lucrèce, *De la nature des choses,* new translation by J.-P. Des Coutures, Paris, 1685.

54. Voltaire never carried out his plan.

55. *De Rerum Natura,* III, v. 607. Voltaire's quotation refers to the edition *De l'origine et de la nature de toutes choses,* Amsterdam, 1742. The passage which Voltaire asks Madame du Deffand to read is Lucretius's argument against immortality of the soul.

56. Voltaire, *Histoire d'un bon bramin,* 1761.

57. See above, note 37.

58. *Mémoires de Monsieur de Voltaire écrits par lui-même,* Geneva, 1784.

59. Ibid.

60. Ibid.

61. Voltaire to Madame du Deffand, 25 April [1760].

62. F. Diaz, op. cit, p. 146.

63. The explanation of this expression used elsewhere by Madame du Deffand is in a letter she wrote to Walpole (22 September 1776): "The Praslins have not dropped their airs *à la Prasline,* an expression of Madame de

Luxembourg's indicating this kind of pretention and nonsense." The Praslins were great aristocrats and well known to Madame du Deffand.

64. Opinion expressed by Pococurante, *Candide,* ch. xxv. *Candide ou l'optimisme. Traduit de l'allemand de M. le docteur Ralph* [Geneva], 1759.

65. *Pamela* was translated into French in 1742, *The History of Clarissa Harlowe* in 1751–2, and *The History of Sir Charles Grandison* in 1753. It was not long before Madame du Deffand discovered that *Clarissa,* like everything else, bored her to death.

66. On 13 September 1759 on the plains of Abraham in Canada, the English army commanded by Wolf, beat the French, commanded by Montcalm. Both generals were killed. On 18 October Quebec fell to the English.

67. Perhaps Madame du Deffand is referring to the afflictions of Job.

68. See above, p. 209.

69. The correspondence between Voltaire and Frederick II was interrupted after Voltaire fled from Berlin and was arrested at Frankfurt, but it was revived on a bittersweet note in 1757. From 1765 the earlier continuity was re-established.

70. The Jesuits were expelled from Portugal in 1759.

71. Frederick II.

72. In 1758 the English fleet attacked French ships and ports and captured and burned many merchant vessels. The coast of Brittany and Normandy was sacked around the Bay of Saint-Malo: Cancale and Saint-Servan in June, Cherbourg in August and Saint-Briac in September. Cancale and Saint-Servan belonged to the maritime department of Ille-et-Vilaine, so called after the confluence of the Ille and the Vilaine at Rennes, some ten kilometres from the coast. Voltaire comments sarcastically on the enemy offensive advancing inland.

73. See above, note 7.

74. A *billet de confession* was a certificate given to an individual by a priest who had heard his confession in compliance with the precept of confessing and taking communion once a year. This was indispensible in many circumstances of political and civil live.

75. Voltaire refers ironically to one of Silhouette's economic plans, to melt down precious metals including dining-room silver.

76. Voltaire's mistake for Benedict XIV.

77. The Ferney property.

78. F. Diaz, op. cit., p. 142.

79. *Mémoires de Monsieur de Voltaire.*

80. Cited in L. Brunel, op. cit., p. 79.

81. Voltaire to Duclos, 20 June 1760.

82. On this date d'Alembert wrote to Voltaire that he had received the pamphlet.

83. Cited in L. Brunel, op. cit., p. 80.

84. *Les Quand* is the first of a long series of satires with which Voltaire and the abbé Morellet bombarded Pompignan.

85. D'Alembert to Voltaire, 6 May 1760.

86. Voltaire to d'Alembert, 21 May 1760.

87. See above, ch. IV, pp. 77–78.

88. *Préface de la comédie des "Philosophes" ou la vision de Charles Palissot,* Paris, 1760.

89. Voltaire to d'Alembert, 31 May 1760.

90. Voltaire to d'Alembert, 26 May 1760.

91. D'Alembert to Voltaire, 31 May 1760.

92. F. Diaz, op. cit., pp. 192–3.

93. *Le Pauvre diable, ouvrage en vers aisés de feu M. Vadé, mis en lumière par Catherine Vadé, sa cousine, dedié à maître Abraham**** (Chaumeix), Paris, 1758 [sic]. Antedated. The satire was written in 1760.

94. *Petit poème en vers alexandrins, composé à Paris au mois de mai 1760, par M. Ivan Alethof, secrétaire de l'ambassade russe,* n.d. [1760].

95. *La Vanité, par un frère de la doctrine chrétienne,* n.d. [1760].

96. L. Brunel, op. cit., p. 86.

97. Madame du Deffand to Voltaire, 16 April 1760.

98. The exact title of the pamphlet, which was in fact by Voltaire, was *Relation de la maladie, de la confession, de la mort et de l'apparition du Jésuite Berthier,* n.d. [Geneva, 1759].

99. Madame du Deffand to Voltaire, 16 April 1760.

100. Voltaire to C.-A. Ferriol, comte d'Argental, 6 July [1760].

101. Jean-Gilles du Coëtlosquet who had left his diocese in 1758.

102. *Tancrède* a five-act tragedy in verse by Voltaire, performed on 3 September 1760.

103. *Zulime,* a five-act tragedy by Voltaire, Geneva, 1761.

104. *Histoire de l'empire de Russie sous Pierre le Grand,* vol. I [Geneva], 1759, vol. II [Geneva], 1763.

105. *Dictionnaire philosophique portatif ou la Raison par alphabet,* Geneva, 1764.

106. A *lettre de change* was a bill of exchange whereby a banker or tradesman could draw a sum of money from a correspondent at the demand of a third person who had made the amount available himself or through other people. "Bills of exchange circulate like currency in commerce." (F. Braudel, *Civilisation matérielle, economie et capitalisme, XV–XVIII siècle. Le temps du monde,* Paris, 1979, pp. 205–206.)

107. *Ecclesiastes,* I, 2. According to Besterman, Voltaire had meant the Old

Testament, but since the same expression is used for a quotation from the Gospels, he may have meant God.

108. Reference to the *Batracomyomachia,* a pseudo-Homeric burlesque poem.

109. See above, note 75. Voltaire wrote, "nos vaisseaux et notre vaisselle" with an intended play on words which is hard to translate into English.

110. In 1757 the comte d'Argenson fell into disgrace and left the Ministry of War to be exiled to *Les Ormes,* his estate near Saumur, where Hénault visited him every year. Voltaire's letter is obviously that of 20 June.

111. La Fontaine, *Fables,* IV, xi: *La grenouille et le rat.*

112. Voltaire's reference is to a passage from Dupré de Saint-Maur's harangue addressed to the two Pompignan brothers.

113. Jean-George Lefranc de Pompignan.

114. "Be assured too that she [Madame du Deffand] leads the partisans of the play [by Palissot], that she protects and greatly appreciates Fréron's writings, that she finds the *Ecossaise* a very bad play and greatly applauds a very bad criticism of it, said to be by Fréron." (D'Alembert to Voltaire, 1 June [1760].)

115. Voltaire refers to a passage from the *Mémoire présenté au roi, par M. de Pompignan, le 11 Mai 1760* (Paris, 1760).

116. See above, ch. VIII, p. 172.

117. *Acts of the Apostles,* V, 1–12.

118. "Lettres de M. de *** a M. Fréron sur le mot 'Encyclopédie' du Dictionnaire qui porte ce nom," *L'année littéraire,* Paris, 1760, III, pp. 245–66.

119. Formont.

120. The *"soeur du pot"* was Madame d'Aiguillon but the allusion is obscure.

121. Reference to Pompignan's discourse. See above, note 116.

122. Alenxandrine Lullin, née Fatio, to whom Voltaire dedicated the quatrain: "Our grandfathers saw you were beautiful" on her hundredth birthday. Born in 1659, she died in 1762.

123. Ferdinand, duke of Brunswick, brother-in-law and ally of Frederick II of Prussia.

124. Between August and November 1759, the English inflicted irreparable losses on the French fleet, thus gaining definitive maritime supremacy.

125. The distinguished astronomer, Charles-Marie de la Condamine (1701–1774) had travelled widely in Africa, Peru and Europe. Already a member of the *Académie des Sciences,* he was admitted to the *Académie française* in 1761.

126. *Le Café ou l'Ecossaise, comédie par Monsieur Hume, traduite en français,* London [Geneva], 1760. The play, which was really by Voltaire, was a satire on Fréron who was depicted as a hack and a scoundrel and called Frelon

[hornet]; at the last moment "Frelon" was changed to "Wasp." The first performance took place on 26 July 1760.

127. Play on words unclear in English based on the double meaning of *feuille*: "leaf" and "leaflet."

128. *Tancrède* was performed on 3 and 13 September and 4 October.

129. "I could not bend my knee to Aman, / nor pay him respect which is owed only to you," adapted from Racine, *Esther,* act III, scene V.

130. *Tancrède,* act V, scene V.

131. Freeport. A character in the *Ecossaise.*

132. Letter of 15 August 1760.

133. David Hume, *The History of Great Britain under the House of Stuart,* Edinburgh [1754–1757], trans. 1760 by Prevost as *Histoire de la maison de Stuart sur le trône d'Angleterre* (London [Paris]).

134. Jacques-Philippe de Choiseul, comte de Stainville.

135. A term used in backgammon.

136. At the Battle of Kloster-Camp, on the night of 15–16 October 1760, the English failed in their objective, but inflicted greater losses than they suffered.

137. On 9 and 10 October a Russian and an Austrian contingent advanced to Berlin and occupied it for three days. Frederick II's position seemed badly compromised between 1759 and 1760.

138. Frederick II.

139. Gabriel Malagrida (1689–1761), the Italian Jesuit who in 1758 made an attempt on the King of Portugal's life. The Roman Curia did not authorize a trial by the Portuguese government, but the Jesuits were expelled from Portugal and Malagrida was tried by the Inquisition as a heretic and on 20 September 1761 condemned to be burned at the stake.

140. Voltaire had written the part of Aménaïde, the heroine of *Tancrède,* especially for Mademoiselle Clairon, and the great actress "surpassed herself" (D'Alembert to Voltaire, 27 September 1760). But Mademoiselle Clairon had a tendency to manipulate the play by inserting passages, skipping others and changing the scenery to enhance her performance. "The poet got his revenge by refusing to accept the peculiar stage direction that the actress had requested for the third act, the one showing [Aménaïde's] torture. She had asked Voltaire to build a scaffold in the theater, to put in executioner's assistants, and in short to represent the entire apparatus of an execution.... Voltaire, frightened by the realism of this theatrical approach, rejected the actress's request outright" (Jean-Jacques Olivier, *Voltaire et les Comédiens interprètes de son théâtre,* Paris, 1900, pp. 134–5.).

141. The Parisian Square, now the Place de l'Hôtel de Ville, where criminal executions were held.

142. *Histoire de Charles XII, roi de Suède, par M. de V****, Basle, 1731, 2 vols. Madame du Deffand probably refers to the Geneva edition of 1760 which was enhanced by the *Anecdotes sur le tsar Pierre le Grand* and numerous additions concerning the *Histoire de Charles XII.*

143. "Apart from him, all men are equal." *Sir John Chardin's Travels in Persia,* 1927, p. 10. Madame du Deffand was to quote the same line to Walpole in her letters of 21 April 1766 and 9 August 1767.

144. "Hark, I lose my two eyes; you have lost yours / O wise Du Deffand is it a great loss? / At least we will never see again / The fools who cover the earth / And then everything is blind in the human sojourn / We only feel our way on this round machine / We are blindfold in the town, at court / Plutus, fortune and love / Are three who, born blind, rule the world. / If we are deprived of one of our five senses / We possess four others, and it is an advantage / Which nature leaves to few of her friends / When they reach our age. We have seen Popes and Kings die / We live and think and still have our soul / Epicurus and his followers used to claim / That this sixth sense was a heavenly gift / Which was worth the others all together / But when our soul has perfect enlightenment / Perhaps it would be even better / If we had kept our eyes / Even if we had to wear glasses."

145. François-Augustin Paradis de Moncrif, *Essai sur la nécessité et sur les moyens de plaire,* Paris, 1738.

146. Voltaire, *Ce qui plaît aux dames,* l. 427. Published in 1763 and reissued the following year in the *Contes de Guillaume Vadé* [Geneva], 1764.

147. *Pucelle,* I, Voltaire's note to line 206: "The good Denis is actually not Denis, the supposed areopagite, but a bishop of Paris. The abbé Hildouin was the first to write that this bishop, having been beheaded, carried his head in his arms from Paris all the way to the abbey that bears his name. Later, they erected crosses in all the places where the saint had stopped on his way. When the cardinal of Polignac told the marquise du Deffand this story, adding that Denis had had difficulty carrying the head only up until the first station, the latter answered: 'I don't doubt it, since everyone knows that the first steps are the hardest.'"

148. The legendary Big-Footed Bertha, wife of Pépin the Short, mother of Charlemagne, and certainly less bigoted than Marie Leszczynska.

149. The duc de Choiseul. As minister, the duc enjoyed free postage and a private correspondence that was not subject to outside controls.

150. *L'Education d'une jeune fille* (no place or date of publication), a story by Voltaire published in the *Contes de Guillaume Vadé,* op. cit.

151. *Macare et Thélème. Allégori par M. de Voltaire,* n.d., reprinted in *Contes de Guillaume Vadé.*

152. *Les Trois Manières,* printed in 1764 in *Contes de Guillaume Vadé.*

153. Character in *Trois Manières*. Madame du Deffand must have been lent the story.

154. Madame de Pompadour died on 15 April of that year.

155. Destroyed during the Revolution, the royal château at Choisy "was said to be one of the most beautiful in the environs of Paris. Louis XV had a particular predilection for that residence, and had it embellished by the best architects, sculptors and painters." (Charles Oudiette, *Dictionnaire topographique des environs de Paris*, op. cit., p. 167.)

156. Madame du Deffand feared the repercussions that Madame de Pompadour's death might have on her protégé, the duc de Choiseul.

157. The letter of 27 January.

158. That is God, cf. above, note 120. *The Gospel according to St. John*, III, 8.

159. Formont to Madame du Deffand, 12 July 1754.

160. Norman L. Torrey, *The Spirit of Voltaire*, New York, 1930, p. 170.

161. W. Clerks, op. cit., p. 92.

162. The break with Mademoiselle de Lespinasse.

163. La Fontaine, *Fables*, I, xvi: *La mort et le bûcheron*.

164. *Théâtre de Pierre Corneille avec des commentaires* [Geneva], 12 vols.

165. *The Gospel according to Saint Mark*, XIV, 21.

166. Seneca, *Epistulae*, CI, 2.

167. Misquotation from La Fontaine, *La mort et le bûcheron*, op. cit.: "It is better to suffer than to die, / This is the motto of mankind."

168. "She was not, but was very interested in Monsieur de Choiseul," Walpole noted in the margin of this letter.

169. Madame de Mirepoix was an intimate of Madame de Pompadour's and a frequent visitor to the *petits appartements*.

170. The Jesuits.

171. Hénault.

172. Voltaire, "encorneillé" (to d'Argental, 26 November 1760) by the poet Le Brun, had, toward the end of 1760 welcomed to his house Marie Corneille, a young relation of Pierre and Thomas Corneille, and daughter of Jean-François. When Voltaire then learned that the *Académie Française* was planning to publish a collection of French authors, he asked to take care of Corneille and that the income from the edition produced by subscription be paid to Jean-François and his daughter. The first volume did not appear until the spring of 1764 and the edition raised no less than 52,000 *livres* which were divided between the editor and the poet's niece. Voltaire had himself underwritten the publication of the first 100 copies.

173. "*De toutes choses non mest demuré que l'honn et la vie qui est sayne*," François I wrote to his mother after the Battle of Pavia (23 December 1525), cited in Besterman, vol. xxxiv, letter 7230, note 1, p. 194.

174. Léopold-Charles de Choiseul-Stainville, archbishop of Alby, brother of the duc de Choiseul.

175. Madame de Mirepoix, Madame de Gramont—Choiseul's sister—and Honorée de Joyeuse, wife of Augustin-Vincent, marquis d'Ecquevilly, were part of the small circle who enjoyed the King's friendship and confidence and who were allowed to be part of his private life.

176. Voltaire later made various alterations to the copy of this letter in our possession. Besterman thinks that these alterations lend a general rather than a personal tone to the opinions expressed in it and that they introduce a deistic element.

177. This passage is annotated in Voltaire's own hand: "The author was threatened with becoming entirely blind."

178. On 12 December 1764 Bertin was replaced by Clément-Charles-François de Laverdy.

179. Not La Rochefoucauld, but La Bruyère, *Les Caractères*, "De la cour," VII, p. 1.

180. "Changes for the better all the ills to which the heavens have submitted me. Without you every man is alone." Does not seem like Ovid.

181. Bernis succeeded Choiseul.

182. In a note to the copy of the letter kept by Madame du Deffand, Wiart wrote, "the substitution did not take place." The parish priest was Jean du Lau d'Allemans, vicar of Saint-Suplice (1748–1777).

183. Madame de Luxembourg had lost her husband Charles-François-Frédéric, duc de Luxembourg, maréchal de France.

184. Jean Croiset, *Retraite spirituelle pour un jour chaque mois,* Lyon, 1694.

185. Pascal, *Pensées,* ed. L. Brunschvieg, Paris, 1904, n. 199, vol. II, p. 124.

186. Hénault to Voltaire, 28 December 1765.

187. A line from Racine: *Britannicus,* act II, scene II.

188. A letter from Walpole addressed to Jean-Jacques Rousseau and signed "your good friend Frederick" (of Prussia). The letter was reproduced in full in the *Correspondance* of Grimm in January 1766 (Grimm, 1753–1769, V, pp. 125–6). See below, p. 259.

189. Lytton Strachey, *Literary Essays,* London, 1948, p. 259.

X. THE ROMANCE: HORACE WALPOLE

1. E. Campbell Mossner, op. cit., p. 511.

2. Ibid., p. 513.

3. Ibid.

4. Thomas Gray to Ashton, 21 April 1739, in *Gray, Walpole, West and Ashton,*

London, 1915, I, p. 206, cited in R. W. Ketton-Cremer, *Horace Walpole,* London, 1964, p. 52.

5. E. Campbell Mossner, op. cit., p. 445.

6. Walpole to Lady Suffolk, 20 September 1765.

7. *Paris Journals,* Lewis, v, p. 261.

8. Walpole to H. S. Conway, 2 October 1765.

9. Walpole to Lady Hervey, 21 November 1765.

10. "Although I form one body, I am but one idea; / The more my beauty ages, the more decided she is: / To find me one must not know from whence I come, / I owe everything to her, who reduces everything to nothing." The answer is nobility.

11. Pierre-Marie de Ségur, *Le Royaume de la rue Saint-Honoré. Madame Geoffrin et sa fille,* p. 74.

12. Walpole to G. Selwyn, 2 December 1765.

13. Walpole to H. S. Conway, 12 January 1766.

14. Walpole to T. Gray, 25 January 1766.

15. Thomas Babington Macaulay, *Critical and Historical Essays,* London, 1946, I, pp. 331–2.

16. Since the 1740s, Walpole had cherished an ambition to become the century's great chronicler. Within a few years he definitely decided on an epistolary form. His correspondence with H. Mann dating from the time of his journey to Italy was a determining factor. In 1748 Walpole asked for the return of the letters he had written to the English consul in Florence up to that date and began to annotate and correct them. From that time he conceived of a project which would be a vast edifice of which Mann's letters would be the cornerstone. "As Walpole's life advances, one realises ever more clearly, with what intelligence and skill he selected his principal correspondents." (R. W. Ketton-Kremer, op. cit., pp. 117–8.) Besides Mann, there were G. Montagu for social anecdotes, T. Gray for literature, W. Cole for antiquarianism and so forth. When, for some reason, one of his correspondents disappeared, Walpole quickly found another.

17. In May 1747 Walpole had, as he himself wrote, bought a seventeenth-century "little rural jewel" on the Hampton Road at Twickenham, with five acres of land by the Thames. "In 1796 the property was increased to 46 acres, and the house, renamed Strawberry Hill was transformed into the most famous Gothic house in England, for 20,720 pounds sterling." (Michael Snodin, *Horace Walpole, Builder and Designer* in *Horace Walpole and Strawberry Hill,* published by the London Borough of Richmond upon Thames, Libraries Department, 1980, p. 9.) The plan for the Gothic development of Strawberry Hill was only initiated in 1751 with the

"Committee on Taste" which included Walpole, John Chute, the dilettante architect, and Richard Bentley, an outstandingly inventive draftsman. The building of Strawberry Hill took place in three stages which reveal a Gothic crescendo: the first was completed in 1753, the second begun in 1758, and the third and last stage in which Walpole turned to professional architects like Robert Adam, in 1771.

As Kenneth Clark writes: "but when the exquisite, cultivated Walpole took up Gothic, society began to feel that there might be something in it." (*The Gothic Revival*, London, 1762.)

18. R. W. Ketton-Cremer, op. cit., p. 44.
19. Lytton Strachey, op. cit., pp. 267–8.
20. See above, p. 263.
21. *Memoirs of Miss Laetitia-Matilda Hawkins*, cited in R. W. Ketton-Cremer, op. cit., p. 300.
22. Walpole to H. S. Conway, 28 October 1765.
23. T. B. Macaulay, op. cit., pp. 343–4.
24. Ibid., p. 343.
25. See above, pp. 265–66.
26. C. Ferval, *Madame du Deffand*, op. cit., pp. 214–5.
27. Ibid., p. 215.
28. F. Galiani, op. cit., pp. 977–8.
29. Madame du Deffand to Madame de Choiseul, 26 May 1765; Lescure, I, p. 323.
30. Walpole's *Eulogy of an Old Venus* cannot be seen merely as a brilliant literary paradox.
31. Madame du Deffand to Walpole, 30 October–1 November 1766.
32. Walpole to G. Selwyn, 3 April 1766.
33. Hénault.
34. Madame de Jonzac.
35. *Lettre d'Emilie à Jean-Jacques Rousseau* with which Walpole continued the quarrel provoked by his first letter to Rousseau written in Frederick II's name. The letter, partly on Madame du Deffand's advice, was never published.
36. "Madame de Valentinois hated the English," note by Walpole.
37. At that time Madame du Deffand had a regular Sunday supper which Walpole took to never missing.
38. "Dilige et quod vis fac," Saint Augustine, *Epistolam Joannis ad Parthos*, ch. IV, *Tractatus* VII, in J. P. Migne, *Patrologia*, Paris, 1835, XXXV, p. 2033.
39. "Madame du Deffand, thanks to a very simple little machine, wrote very well and managed without a secretary: her handwriting was large but

very legible." (*Mémoires inédits de Madame la comtesse de Genlis* . . . , Paris, 1825, III, p. 113.)

40. Thanks to Madame de Luynes, Madame du Deffand had acquired a pension from the Queen but without any guarantee of its being for life. Hence the *marquise*'s concern with Maria Leszczynska's illness. The Queen died in 1768.
41. David Hume.
42. Walpole to Madame du Deffand, 10 October 1766.
43. Lewis, I, P. XXXII.
44. Ibid.
45. Ibid., p. XXXVI.
46. Walpole to W. Cole, 9 March 1765.
47. *The Mysterious Mother,* 1768.
48. Madame de Sévigné.
49. In the eighteenth century the letters of Abelard and Eloise enjoyed a great popularity due to the fashion for epistolary novels.
50. Louise Duchâtel de Charmoisy (m. 1645), 'Philothée' in *L'Introduction à la vie dévote* by Saint François de Sales (1567–1622). This was the saint's most famous work based on letters written under instruction by him between 1607 and 1608 for Madame de Charmoisy.
51. Victor-François, duc de Broglie, maréchal de France (1718–1804); Charles-François, comte de Broglie (1719–1781); Charles de Broglie, Bishop of Noyon (1733–1777).
52. Charles-Maurice de Broglie, abbé de Mont-Saint-Michel, died in Paris 21 April 1766.
53. Country property of the *ducs* d'Aiguillon, not far from Versailles.
54. "Apart from him all men were equal." See above, ch. IX, note 153.
55. See above, note 35.
56. Letter from Jean-Jacques Rousseau to the "Saint James's Chronicle," April 1766, published in No. 796 of 10 April 1766.
57. The Dauphin's children.
58. Marie-Josèphe de Saxe (1731–1767), wife of the Dauphin, Louis, son of Louis XV, died 1765.
59. Affectionate name by which Walpole addressed Madame du Deffand.
60. Madame du Deffand to Walpole, 8 July 1772.
61. Madame du Deffand to Walpole, 27 January 1771.
62. R. Mauzi, *Lés maladies de l'âme,* . . . p. 466.
63. Madame du Deffand to Walpole, 8 March 1778.
64. L. Duisit, *Madame du Deffand épistolière,* p. 71.
65. The duchesse de Choiseul.
66. Madame d'Aubeterre.

67. "In King Guillemot's time" was an expression meaning "long ago."
68. Madame de Luxembourg.
69. Madame de Boufflers.
70. Walpole never lived at Saint-Joseph during his visits to Paris.
71. Walpole's dogs and cats. Animals were not least among the interests which drew the correspondents to one another.
72. Karl Wilhelm Ferdinand (1735–1806), later Prince of Brunswick; "yours" because he was married to George III of England's sister.
73. Madame du Deffand's dog.
74. Madame de Boufflers.
75. The mountebank was Jean-Jacques who had written to Madame de Boufflers on 5 April 1766.
76. Rousseau was staying with Richard Davenport at Wootton in Derbyshire; Lewis points out that the mansion was neither "magnificent" or "near London," nor, for that matter, was Davenport a "Milord."
77. The Residence in the rue de l'Université of the Duke of Richmond, British Ambassador to Paris.
78. Place du Carrousel, near the Tuileries where Madame de La Vallière lived.
79. The Bishop of Noyon.
80. *Extrait d'une lettre de Saragosse du 8 avril 1766* (Lewis, VI, pp. 119–21) which the *marquise* enclosed in a letter to Walpole and which described serious incidents that had taken place during a popular uprising in Saragossa.
81. R. W. Ketton-Cremer, op. cit., p. 223.
82. Ibid., p. 243.
83. On 10 May the *marquise* had sent Walpole a letter full of good intentions in which her apparent compliance amounted to an explicit declaration of love.
84. Hénault.
85. Madame de Jonzac.
86. Reference to a popular song quoted by Molière in the *Misanthrope,* act I, scene II. Walpole makes a play on the probable etymology of *gué* (an exclamation of happiness) and *gai* meaning happy.
87. Henriette de Coligny (1618–1673) poetess who married secondly the comte de la Suze.
88. *Lettres d'amour d'une religieuse portugaise, écrites au Chevalier de C..., officier français en Portugal,* first published 1699. Oroondate is the lover of Statira, Alexander the Great's widow in *Cassandre* by Gautier de Costes de la Calprenède (1614–1663).
89. *Portrait de Madame du Deffand par Mademoiselle de Lespinasse.* Cf. above, chapter VIII, p. 184.
90. *Mémoires du Président Hénault,* p. 130.

91. See above, note 86.
92. L. Duisit, *Madame du Deffand épistolière,* p. 61.
93. Ibid., p. 63.
94. Reference to the poetry written by Ovid in exile.
95. *Mémoires du Président Hénault,* p. 130.
96. Madame du Deffand to Walpole, 21 April 1766.
97. Madame du Deffand to Walpole, 9 July 1766.
98. On 12 April Walpole had been "to see the collection of M. Doumenil in rue Desmarais" where among some 420 portraits, the writer saw an enamel of Madame de Sévigné by Petitot. (*Paris Journals,* p. 313).
99. Madame du Deffand to Walpole, 17 June 1766.
100. Lewis, I, p. xxxiv.
101. Walpole to Lady Hervey, 28 June 1766.
102. *Horace Walpole's Letter from Madame de Sévigné,* by W. S. Lewis, privately printed, Farmington, Conn., 1933, pp. 20–1.
103. Lewis, I, p. xxxiv.
104. Lewis, VI, pp. 71–3. Madame du Deffand probably sent a copy of her portrait to Walpole with her letter of 30 November 1766.
105. Date added by Walpole.
106. King Theodore. Note by Walpole.
107. Probably the words "je suis refroidi" contained in Walpole's letter of 28 November 1766.
108. Lewis, VI, pp. 55–6.
109. Madeleine de Scudéry (1607–1701), one of the greatest exponents of "precious" taste, author of successful novels.
110. Sir Edward Walpole had been seriously ill.
111. A painting and a few objects acquired at the famous Parisian collector, Julienne's, sale.
112. *Paris Journals,* p. 316.
113. D. Diderot, *Paradoxe sur le comédien* in *Oeuvres,* Bibliothèque de la Pléiade, Paris, 1969, p. 1007.
114. Lescure, I, p. LXXV.
115. E. & J. de Goncourt, *La femme au dix-huitième siècle,* p. 66.
116. *Paris Journals,* p. 1, *Anecdotes 1769–1771,* p. 370.
117. Ibid., p. 337, 4 August 1774.
118. Ibid., p. 321. 21 September 1767.
119. "I like very much what you say, that you have only followed your campaigns to kill time, and that you have never felt so strongly that it deserved to be killed. So let it be, let us kill it; but I know it well, it will come back to enrage us." Montesquieu to Madame du Deffand, 15 July 1751; Masson, p. 1384.

120. Walpole to G. Montagu, 7 September 1769.

121. Backgammon.

122. *Portrait de Madame la Marquise du Deffand,* Lewis, VI, p. 57.

123. *Paris Journals,* p. 321.

124. Philippe Quinault (1635–1688), poet and librettist, despised by Boileau for his "preciousness" and his coquettish mannerism.

125. The words in italics are divided to indicate how Walpole pronounced them when speaking French.

126. Madame du Deffand to Walpole, 18 December 1776.

127. Madame du Deffand to Walpole, 9 June 1776.

128. This letter and the next one, dated 13 April but not quoted here, was one of three contemporary versions of Donatien-Alphonse-François de Sade's second encounter with the law. In 1763 the *marquis* had already been imprisoned for fifteen days in Vincennes, for excesses committed in a brothel. On 3 April 1768 in the Place des Victoires, Rose Keller, the thirty-seven-year-old German widow of a pastry cook begged Sade for alms. The *marquis* made an excuse to take her to his country house at Arcueil where he shut her in a room and made her undress. When Keller later managed to escape and tell her story, she accepted 2400 livres in damages plus seven gold louis for the violence done to her. A few days later Sade was interned by the King's order. The *Chambre criminelle de la Tournelle* (the criminal department of the *parlement* de Paris) started proceedings against him and, in their turn, ordered his arrest on 19 April. This order could clearly not be carried out as the *marquis* was already in prison. However, the *Chambre* went ahead with the proceedings, having declared Sade absent, and again ordered his arrest on 11 May and again declared him absent. Since the Paris tribunal must have known that the *marquis* had been arrested by the King's men, the *Chambre* probably persisted with proceedings against Sade because of a notorious rivalry between its president, Maupeou, and another powerful member of the *parlement,* the Président de Montreuil, and with the intention of giving maximum publicity to the scandal. But on 10 June, the *Chambre* had to take account of the "letters of immunity" which Sade could produce, and interrupt the proceedings. The royal proceedings, begun with the April imprisonment, took their course. Sade was not freed until 16 November with the obligation of retiring to his property at La Coste.

129. Louise-Marie (1737–1787), youngest daughter of Louis XV who entered the Carmelite convent at Saint-Denis on 11 April 1770.

130. Christophe de Beaumont du Repaire, Archbishop of Paris.

131. Louise-Elisabeth de Melun (b. 1738) married the prince de Guistelle in 1758. In 1768 she entered the service of the *Maison des Mesdames de France.*

132. The marriage of the Dauphin—the future Louis XVI—to Marie-Antoinette.

XI: OLD AGE

1. Lewis, VI, p. 61.
2. Madame du Deffand to Walpole, 21 February 1772.
3. Lady Mary Coke, *Journal,* 6 September 1767, in Lewis, vol. 31, p. 134.
4. Preface to the *Lettres de la Marquise du Deffand à Horace Walpole,* ed. by Mrs. Paget Toynbee, London 1912, I, pp. XLVIII–XLIX.
5. *Révélations de la vie du Prince de Talleyrand,* 1805, p. 264 and p. XLVIII, note 5.
6. Madame du Deffand to Walpole, 7–11 March 1770.
7. Madame du Deffand to Walpole, 26 June 1768.
8. Madame du Deffand to Walpole, 27 July 1773.
9. Madame du Deffand to Walpole, 19 January 1771.
10. Ibid.
11. Madame du Deffand to Walpole, 3–6 February 1767.
12. S. Mercier, op. cit., I, p. 62.
13. Lescure, I, p. CLXXXVI.
14. Madame du Deffand to Walpole, 3 August 1767.
15. Voltaire to Madame du Deffand, 19 January 1771.
16. Walpole to Lady Hervey, 11 January 1766.
17. Madame de Choiseul to Madame du Deffand, [?] 1765 (Lescure, I, p. 324).
18. Monsieur de Choiseul to Voltaire, 22 April [1760].
19. Madame de Choiseul to Madame du Deffand, 13 May 1770.
20. Madame du Deffand to Madame de Choiseul, 28 December 1766.
21. Madame du Deffand to Madame de Choiseul, 7 September 1772.
22. Madame de Choiseul to Madame du Deffand, 23 [?] 1766.
23. Ibid.
24. R. Mauzi, *L'Idée du bonheur au XVIII siècle,* p. 36.
25. Madame de Choiseul to Madame du Deffand, 5 June 1775.
26. Madame de Choiseul to Madame du Deffand, n.d. (Sainte-Aulaire, I, p. 2).
27. Madame du Deffand to Madame de Choiseul, 14 April 1773.
28. Madame du Deffand to Madame de Choiseul, 1 November 1772.
29. Madame de Choiseul to Madame du Deffand, 22 March 1764.
30. Madame de Choiseul to Madame du Deffand, 23 May 1767.
31. Madame du Deffand to J. Craufurd, 13 February 1767.
32. Madame du Deffand to Madame de Choiseul, 27 April 1772.
33. Madame du Deffand to Walpole, 17 March 1776.

34. Madame de Choiseul to Madame du Deffand, 25 July 1766.
35. Madame du Deffand to Madame de Choiseul, 24 February 1773.
36. Madame du Deffand to Walpole, 3 May 1767.
37. Madame de Choiseul to Madame du Deffand, 3 February 1771.
38. Madame de Choiseul to Madame du Deffand, 9 August 1771.
39. See above, ch. IV, p. 73.
40. J.-J. Barthélemy to Madame du Deffand, 18 February 1771 (Sainte-Aulaire, I, p. 346).
41. See above, ch. IX, note 65.
42. See above, ch. X, note 121.
43. Madame de Choiseul to Madame du Deffand, 12 January 1771.
44. Monsieur de Thiers, the *duchesse*'s father's brother, nicknamed the *petit-oncle.*
45. The Comtesse de Choiseul-Betz.
46. Walpole to Madame du Deffand, 10 April 1772.
47. Madame du Deffand to Walpole, 20–22 May 1772.
48. Louis-François-Marc-Hilaire, Bishop of Arras.
49. In 1770 the *Questions sur l'Encyclopédie* began to appear, in which Voltaire published items not included in the *Dictionnaire philosophique portatif* (1764), or reprinted articles which, altered to a certain extent, had already appeared. Publication of the *Questions* ceased in 1772.
50. Mademoiselle de Sanadon had taken it upon herself to warn Walpole of Madame du Deffand's journey in a letter that has been lost. In her next letter of 3 June 1772, she appeared terrified lest the *marquise* learn of her informing. Madame du Deffand's attitude toward her dependants does not seem to have altered as a result of the episode with Julie. "... you can imagine if she had the slightest inkling of the letter which I had the honor of writing to you about her journey, with what mistrust she would treat me in future. She would continually suspect me of actions designed to harm her and this would make our cohabitation terrible."
51. Madame du Deffand to Walpole, 9 January 1771.
52. Voltaire to Madame du Deffand, 18 May 1772.
53. La Fontaine, *Fables,* IX, iv: *Le gland et la citrouille.*
54. L. Duisit, *Madame du Deffand épistolière,* p. 54.
55. "When, in January 1766, the bookseller, Le Breton, circulated in Paris the last ten volumes of the great *Dictionnaire* which had finished being printed in the preceding August by Samuel Faulche and falsely claiming publication in Neufchâtel, distribution to subscribers took place without too much difficulty. Measures taken with some delay by the government consisted of an order from Saint-Florentin, the minister of the *"Maison du roi"* to subscribers to return copies received, and Le Breton's imprisonment in

the Bastille for eight days from 23 to 30 April 1766." (F. Diaz, op. cit., p. 288.) As for "Saint Billard and Saint Grisel," Voltaire refers to Billard de Monceau and to the abbé Joseph Grisel imprisoned in the Bastille: the former for bankruptcy, the latter for corruption.

56. Joseph-Marie de Terray, *contrôleur général* from 1770, enemy of the physiocrats and accused of having been one of the organizers of the *pacte de Famine.*

57. See above, ch. IX, pp. 238–39.

58. Madame du Deffand refers to the *Epître à Horace,* n.d. which appeared at the end of October 1772.

59. *Les lois de Minos ou Astérie,* five-act tragedy written between 17 December 1771 and 12 January 1772. Although the *Comédie-Française* began rehearsals in September 1772, the play was never performed, but was published, unknown to Voltaire, in 1773 by Valade at Geneva.

60. Voltaire had expressed sincere grief at Choiseul's disgrace and had given him his unqualified support. But when the *duc*'s old enemy, the chancelier Maupeou had the *Parlement de Paris* dissolved by a *lit de justice* on rebellious members of the *parlement,* Voltaire rejoiced to see the assassins expelled.

61. *"Oigneẑ vilain, il vous poindra, poigneẑ vilain, il vous oindra":* "Caress the villain and he will beat you, beat the villain and he will caress you."

62. F. Venturi, *Settecento riformatore,* in *La prima crisi dell'Antico Regime (1768–1776),* III, p. 184.

63. Madame du Deffand to Walpole, 15 February 1771.

64. Madame du Deffand to Walpole, 10 March 1771.

65. "I sing the recantation / Wise du Deffand, I deny / Your Président and mine / He wanted to place the whole world / But that charlatan loved nothing / Furthermore he read his breviary." Voltaire to Madame du Deffand, 16 December 1770.

66. Quoted by Jean Lacouture in *Julie de Lespinasse. Mourir d'amour,* Paris, 1980, p. 299.

67. D'Alembert, *Aux mânes de Julie de Lespinasse,* in *Oeuvres,* Paris, 1821–1822, III, p. 730.

68. 2 August 1776.

69. Madame du Deffand to Walpole, 9–10 December 1776.

70. Madame du Deffand to Walpole, 7 September 1776.

71. Duc de Lévis, op. cit., p. 56.

72. E. M. Cioran, *L'écartèlement,* Paris, 1970, p. 26.

73. J.-F. La Harpe, *Correspondance littéraire,* III, pp. 146–8.

74. Sainte-Beuve, *Mémoires de Madame de Genlis, Premiers Lundis,* Bibliothèque de la Pléiade, Paris, 1956, p. 97.

75. Madame de Genlis, op. cit., III, pp. 111–15.

76. L. Duisit, *Madame du Deffand épistolière,* p. 12.

77. Ibid., pp. 112–13.

78. Madame du Deffand to Walpole, 5 August 1775.

79. The reminder (of which Madame du Deffand had sent Walpole a copy in her letter of 29 January 1770) by which the King's attention was drawn to the fact that the *contrôleur général,* the abbé Terray had halved the pension granted the *marquise* by the Queen in 1763.

80. Walpole to Madame du Deffand, 9 February 1770.

81. Lescure, I, p. CXCVIII.

82. Madame du Deffand to Walpole, 2 January 1771.

83. Madame du Deffand to Walpole, 6 September 1778.

84. Madame du Deffand to Walpole, 22 July 1778 and 23 August 1778.

85. This was not, however, the *marquise*'s final will. On 24 January 1780, she drew up another to which a codicil was added on 30 August, a few weeks before her death. Cf. Lewis, VI, pp. 5–10.

86. Walpole had accepted the inheritance of all the *marquise*'s manuscripts and wrote on 1 November 1780 to Lady Ossory: "She has left me all her MSS—a compact between us—in one word I had at her earnest request consented to accept them, on condition she should leave me nothing else—She had indeed intended to leave me her little all, but I declared I would never set foot in Paris again (this was ten years ago) if she did not engage to retract that designation. To satisfy her, I at last agreed to accept her papers, and one thin gold box with the portrait of her dog [. . .] ; and I have ordered her own servant, who read all letters to her, to pick out all the letters of living persons, and restore them to the several writers, without my seeing them."

87. Madame du Deffand to Walpole, 7 September 1776.

88. Madame du Deffand to Walpole, 2 August 1778.

89. Madame du Deffand to Walpole, 10 August 1777.

90. Madame du Deffand to Walpole, 1 February 1778.

91. Madame du Deffand to Walpole, 20 December 1778.

92. Madame du Deffand to Walpole, 19 November 1777.

93. Madame du Deffand to Walpole, 20 April 1777.

94. Madame du Deffand to Walpole, 6 September 1778.

95. Madame du Deffand to Walpole, 20 April 1777.

96. Madame du Deffand to Walpole, 6 August 1779.

97. See above, ch. III, p. 39.

98. Madame du Deffand to Walpole, 18 May 1777.

99. *Irène,* Voltaire's last tragedy, was performed for the first time on 16 March 1778 at the *Comédie Française.* It had been begun in 1776 and sent to

d'Argental on 15 December 1776. During the sixth performance a bust of Voltaire was crowned on the stage.

100. Madame du Deffand to Walpole, [? February 1778].

101. *Mémoires secrets,* . . . XI, p. 97.

102. Madame du Deffand to Walpole, 12 April 1778.

103. Voltaire was the guest of the Marquise de Villette in rue de Beaune.

104. Madame du Deffand to Walpole, ? February 1778.

105. Madame du Deffand to Walpole, 8 March 1778.

106. Madame du Deffand to Walpole, 31 May 1778.

107. Ibid.

108. Madame du Deffand to Walpole, 8 February 1778.

109. Madame du Deffand to Walpole, 31 March 1777.

110. Madame du Deffand to Walpole, 20 December 1778.

111. Madame du Deffand to Walpole, 21 September 1777.

112. Sainte-Aulaire, I, p. VII.

113. Madame du Deffand to Walpole, 18 April 1779.

114. Ibid.

115. Thomas Walpole.

116. *Journal de Madame du Deffand,* Lewis, V, pp. 460–1.

117. R. Mauzi, *Les Maladies de l'âme,* . . . p. 466.

118. Madame du Deffand to Madame de Choiseul, 27 September 1771.

119. Dated 22 August.

120. Madame du Deffand's last dog, which was taken to England. Tonton became part of Walpole's daily life as described by Pinkerton, and survived his mistress for a further nine years.

ABOUT THE AUTHOR

BENEDETTA CRAVERI, granddaughter of the noted philosopher Benedetto Croce, is a professor of French literature at
the University of Tuscia, Viterbo, and a frequent contributor
to the *New York Review of Books* and *La Repubblica.* Her other
works include the Italian edition of André Chénier's *Poésies,*
the letters of *Mademoiselle Aïssé,* and *La vie privée du Maréchal
de Richelieu.*

ABOUT THE BOOK

Designed by Ann Chalmers and set in Fournier type with
Cochin display by Brevis Press, Bethany, Connecticut.
Printed in the United States of America by Book Press, North
Brattleboro, Vermont.